W9-BPO-440

Central Australia

Charles Rawlings-Way, Meg Worby
Lindsay Brown, Paul Harding

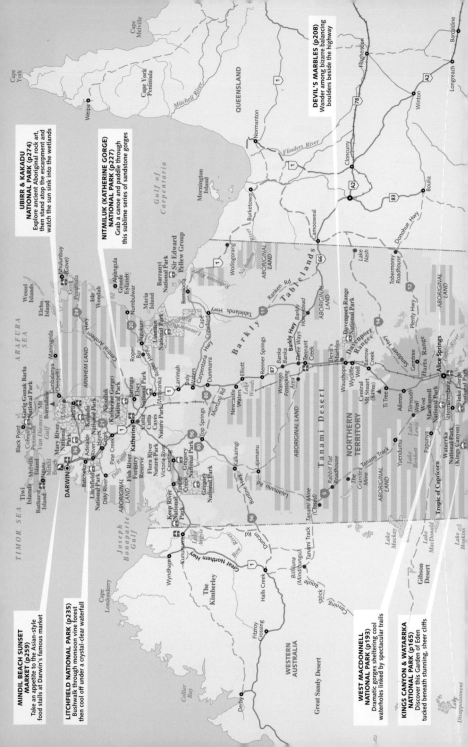

MINDIL BEACH SUNSET MARKET (p259)
Take an appetite to the Asian-style food stalls at Darwin's famous market

LITCHFIELD NATIONAL PARK (p235)
Bushwalk through monsoon vine forest then cool off under a crystal-clear waterfall

UBIRR & KAKADU NATIONAL PARK (p274)
Explore ancient Aboriginal rock art, then stand atop the escarpment and watch the sun sink into the wetlands

NITMILUK (KATHERINE GORGE) NATIONAL PARK (p227)
Grab a canoe and paddle through this sublime series of sandstone gorges

DEVIL'S MARBLES (p208)
Wander among bizarre balancing boulders beside the highway

WEST MACDONNELL NATIONAL PARK (p193)
Dramatic gorges sheltering cool waterholes linked by spectacular trails

KINGS CANYON & WATARRKA NATIONAL PARK (p165)
Discover this Garden of Eden tucked beneath stunning, sheer cliffs

ULURU-KATA TJUTA NATIONAL PARK (p147)
Don't miss a sunset-illuminated Rock or a walk into Kata Tjuta's Walpa Gorge

COOBER PEDY (p140)
A postapocalyptic cave-land in the middle of the desert: there's nowhere on Earth quite like Coober Pedy

WILPENA POUND (p125)
The highlight of the Flinders Ranges is this astonishing natural basin, encircled by jagged peaks and ridges

ADELAIDE HILLS (p66)
Spend a few days getting lost in the vineyards, valleys and villages in the hills behind Adelaide

ADELAIDE (p46)
Cultured yet decadent, established yet emerging: Adelaide is Australia's best middle-sized city

McLAREN VALE WINE REGION (p74)
Forget the Barossa, McLaren Vale is the new kid (or rather, vintner) on the block

ROBE (p96)
Historic Robe makes a great weekend getaway, with pubs, cafes, restaurants and surf beaches

KANGAROO ISLAND (p83)
Flush with wild life and fine things to eat and drink, wild KI is quintessentially South Australian

COORONG NATIONAL PARK (p94)
Indigenous heritage, pelicans, beaches, dunes and lagoons: the Coorong is utterly mesmerising

LEGEND

Primary
Secondary
Tertiary
Unsealed

Visitors wishing to travel on Aboriginal land must obtain a permit before entering.

Crocodiles inhabit rivers, billabongs & estuaries in tropical areas; swimming is not recommended.

0   150 km
0   80 miles

ELEVATION

1500m
1000m
500m
200m
0

On the Road

CHARLES RAWLINGS-WAY
Coordinating Author
Cultured South Australia has a refreshing dearth of tacky 'big' tourist attractions (banana, pineapple, koala etc). But this one crept in under the radar: 'Larry' the big lobster in Kingston SE. And, I suppose, as far as accurate supersizings of Australian beasts go, Larry is fairly authentic! (My baby daughter seemed suitably impressed.)

PAUL HARDING If there's one thing the locals in the Top End love, it's fishing. Especially barramundi fishing. There were missed opportunities at Mary River, Kakadu and even the legendary Daly River, but I wasn't about to miss out. On a billabong near Litchfield I was able to spend an afternoon casting a lure. It might not be for the purists, but we pulled in a dozen decent-sized barra (releasing all but one each). Now I know what all the fuss is about!

MEG WORBY Coordinating Author
We thought we might see brumbies under the searing outback sun of the Flinders Ranges…but all we saw were wedge-tailed eagles soaring on their 2m wingspans past the crags of 600 million-year-old Wilpena Pound, a herd of six emus running past, and a muscular red roo. I was happy with that.

LINDSAY BROWN Refuelling stops are a welcome break on any journey up or down the Track, but it's not bush tucker that replenishes the traveller. Roadhouses fuel the 4WDs and road trains on diesel, iced coffee, beer and burgers – skewered towers of artery-hardening ingredients assembled under the phrase 'one with the lot'.

For author biographies, see p316.

Central Australia Highlights

Here at Lonely Planet, we reckon we know central Australia better than anyone. We're Australians ourselves, of course, and we've been criss-crossing the Red Centre's highways and byways for over 30 years, poking our noses into every nook and cranny in the search for great travel content. Here, our authors share a few of their top central Australian spots, and we also asked our travellers – you – about your favourites: everything from Kangaroo Island, McLaren Vale and Coober Pedy in South Australia to Kings Canyon, Kakadu and Darwin's Mindil Beach Sunset Market in the Northern Territory. Did we miss your own secret highlight? Share it with our community of travellers at www.lonelyplanet.com/australia.

WIBOWO RUSLI

1 KATA TJUTA, NORTHERN TERRITORY

Not as famous as Uluru (Ayers Rock) but within sight is Kata Tjuta (the Olgas; p156), a series of huge mounds – exploring them on foot makes for a gorgeous hike. Keep to the marked trails: this is another spot that's sacred to local Aborigines, so you're not permitted to climb these boulders.

jk_luedtke33, Traveller

DAVID WA

2 OODNADATTA TRACK, SOUTH AUSTRALIA

Why travel a straight, boring highway? Take the Oodnadatta Track (p145) through the centre. Visit Marree and learn about the history of the *Ghan*, view Lake Eyre, bathe in the artesian springs and have a coldie at the William Creek Hotel at William Creek (population six; pictured above).

jubehead, Traveller

GRANT DIXO

3 KATHERINE GORGE, NORTHERN TERRITORY

Sunlight dances on the water – there's barely a sound but for the mostly unseen birdlife and the slosh of the paddle slipping through the water. The river widens and narrows between the steep sandstone gorge walls, and sandy beaches beg you to stop for a break. As a tour boat chugs past, you realise there's no better way to see Katherine Gorge (p227) than from this little yellow canoe.

Paul Harding, Lonely Planet Author

YELLOW WATER WETLANDS, NORTHERN TERRITORY

The jewel of Kakadu National Park is Yellow Water wetlands (p280). Picture the setting: a huge, red sun kisses the tops of pandanus and melaleucas as water birds glide lazily across the scene, reflected perfectly in the glassy, smooth water. Occasionally the head of a patrolling croc pops into view. The beauty and tranquillity of this place is simply surreal.

Gary William Topic, Traveller, Australia

4

RICHARD I'ANSON

LEFT: RICHARD I'ANSON / RIGHT: JOHN BANAGAN

5 **UBIRR, NORTHERN TERRITORY**

Experience the beauty and serenity of a sunset at Ubirr (p274) in Kakadu National Park. On your way to view the sunset, check out the awesome Aboriginal rock art here. A magnificent experience!

kikepa, Traveller

ULURU SUNSET, NORTHERN TERRITORY

The hopefuls arrived in all manner of vehicles, from battered old Holdens to luxurious 4WDs. Camera tripods were extended, chairs unfolded, and wine uncorked as the overcast sky shadowed the scraped, pitted surface of Uluru (p154). It wasn't looking promising. Only when the sun dipped to the horizon, when all hope seemed gone, did the full intensity of the sun hit the face of the rock unimpeded. It was worth the wait. Against a leaden sky the rock glowed, seemingly from within, spectacularly red.

Lindsay Brown, Lonely Planet Author

6

LINDSAY BROW

WINE REGIONS, SOUTH AUSTRALIA

Many of Australia's best drops flow within an hour of Adelaide: McLaren Vale (p74) and the Barossa Valley (p107) for Cabernets and world-class Shiraz, and the Adelaide Hills (p66) for supple Chardonnay. Stay in a B&B for some warm hospitality and an authentic outback feel.

marlonkobacker, Traveller

8

MICHAEL COYNE

7

BETHUNE CARMICHA

PALM VALLEY, NORTHERN TERRITORY

For something different visit Palm Valley (p169) in Finke Gorge National Park. The valley is set along a beautiful, million-year-old river and there are unique red cabbage palms.

Nicole Bosland, Traveller, Australia

ANDREW MARSHALL & LEANNE WALKER

9 WILPENA POUND, SOUTH AUSTRALIA

In the heart of the Flinders Ranges is Wilpena Pound (p125), known to the local Adnyamathanha people as Ikara. The camp ground is unusually shady, the facilities are attractive and there are walks to suit both overachievers and the terminally lazy.

Meg Worby, Lonely Planet Author

ANDREW MARSHALL & LEANNE WALKER

10 LELIYN, NORTHERN TERRITORY

Within Nitmiluk (Katherine Gorge) National Park, but not in the main touristy part, is Leliyn (Edith Falls; p231). There is a lovely shaded camp ground here and a huge swimming hole with a waterfall and freshwater crocs (but they don't stop you enjoying a dip).

Juliet Mackenzie, Traveller, Australia

11 TIWI ISLANDS' FOOTBALL GRAND FINAL, NORTHERN TERRITORY

A cyclone couldn't stop the March football grand final on the Tiwi Islands (p261). Bathurst Island hosts a winning combination of community footy and a huge art show. Join the planeloads of folk flying in from Darwin for the day, watch the game and browse the Tiwi art produced during the wet season.

jackstar, Traveller

12 KANGAROO ISLAND, SOUTH AUSTRALIA

Yes it's an adventure! Kangaroo Island (p83) has everything that's Australian and great in one package: see roos, fairy penguins, koalas; walk among endangered fur seals or through deserts, rugged bush and along magnificent beaches – all in the most wonderful natural environment that has not been spoiled by overdevelopment. A piece of heaven on earth.

harmonybree, Traveller

MINDIL BEACH SUNSET MARKET, NORTHERN TERRITORY

Every Thursday night in the dry season (May to October), Mindil Beach Sunset Market (p259) sets up on the reserve immediately behind Darwin's Mindil Beach. The market includes an exotic range of food stalls. Take your pick of the many culinary delights, then sit on the sand with a couple of cold ones and watch the sunset.

tdpsmith, Traveller

HOLGER LEUE

13

MT GAMBIER & THE COONAWARRA, SOUTH AUSTRALIA

Visit Mt Gambier (p99) with its Blue Lake. The colour of the lake (in an extinct volcano) is *reeaalllly* blue! Make a pit stop in the Coonawarra Wine Region (p102) for some great reds on your way to the scenic Great Ocean Road (p102).

Mollymc, Traveller

RICHARD I'ANSON

14

15

HOLGER LEUE

THE GHAN, SOUTH AUSTRALIA & NORTHERN TERRITORY

You may be sleeping in a seat, but a train ride on the *Ghan* (p303) from Adelaide to Darwin is worth it for the spectacular views. Wake up to sunrise over the outback with kangaroos hopping alongside the train – literally. Not cheap, but an amazing way to see the country.

JenniferWren, Traveller

ADELAIDE FRINGE, SOUTH AUSTRALIA

Now held annually, the Adelaide Fringe (p54) really is the people's festival. Everyone is welcome to perform, there's a parade and street party, the tickets are priced within most people's budgets and there's plenty of comedy. Arts to the people – the Fringe rocks Adelaide!

mariesulda, Traveller

16

PORT ADELAIDE, SOUTH AUSTRALIA

Old working-class Port Adelaide (p65) has long been deemed inferior by Adelaide society, but there's a revival afoot. And with at least nine heritage pubs to choose from, it's a great place for a beer!

Charles Rawlings-Way, Lonely Planet Author

17

18 ## KINGS CANYON, NORTHERN TERRITORY

Between the more famous Alice Springs and Uluru is the isolated Kings Canyon (p165), a beautiful, 300-million-year-old sandstone chasm. Complete the rim walk with lovely views of the Watarrka National Park, or take the easier creek walk and rest in the Garden of Eden.

Chelsea Steinohrt, Traveller, Australia

Contents

Regional Map Contents

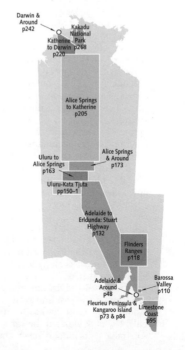

Darwin & Around p242

Kakadu National Park p268

Katherine to Darwin p220

Alice Springs to Katherine p205

Alice Springs & Around p173

Uluru to Alice Springs p163

Uluru-Kata Tjuta pp150–1

Adelaide to Erldunda: Stuart Highway p132

Flinders Ranges p118

Adelaide & Around p48

Barossa Valley p110

Fleurieu Peninsula & Kangaroo Island p73 & p84

Limestone Coast p95

Destination Central Australia: Adelaide to Darwin

On a continent where a 'road trip' can be anything from a drive to the shop to a summer holiday, this epic heartland journey is the big daddy of them all: 3000km of iconic landscapes, from the wild Southern Ocean, through South Australia's wine-growing valleys, past Uluru (Ayers Rock) in the central desert, and into the tropical north. Locals call it 'going up the guts'.

Start your big drive along the Limestone Coast, past the dunes and lakes of the sea-salty Coorong National Park. Further north, the Fleurieu Peninsula is a decadent weekender for Adelaidians, with expansive (often private) beaches, the magical McLaren Vale wine region, and Kangaroo Island's wildlife, forests and seafood just offshore. Adelaide itself remains a cultural high-water mark – a chilled-out city of 1.5 million people with world-class festivals, sensational restaurants and a hedonistic arts scene. Further north, the Barossa and Clare valleys are self-assured viticultural success stories.

Wheeling into the Flinders Ranges, wheat fields give way to arid cattle stations beneath russet and purple peaks and crags. North of here, you run headlong into the desert. As the dead-flat Stuart Hwy beats out across the red sand and scrub, you'll be forgiven for feeling sunstruck and a little parched! Eccentric outback towns such as Woomera and Coober Pedy emerge from the heat haze as welcome oases.

Of course, you can't visit central Australia without seeing Uluru and Kata Tjuta (the Olgas): big country, big desert, and some mighty big rocks. As the sun cuts into the horizon every night, 50 buses carrying as many nationalities pull up to watch Uluru glow with deep, bloodlike intensity: red, orange and burnt umber. The air out here is charged with desert ions; the night sky is milky with stars: camping out in a swag is an unmissable experience.

Back on the highway, Alice Springs and Katherine have rough-hewn, outback appeal. As you approach the tropical Top End, the foliage becomes taller, then denser and more lush, lusty clouds appear and the air gains a sweetness and humidity. Darwin is a city on the rise. It has the youngest population of any Australian capital, a billion-dollar redevelopment of Darwin Harbour underway, and high-rise apartment blocks emerging as fast as tenants can sign up. Spotlit in Baz Luhrmann's film *Australia*, this is also a city with a turbulent history, bombed beyond recognition in WWII, then flattened again by Cyclone Tracy in 1974. Beyond the city, don't miss a detour to gorgeous Kakadu National Park, with its crocodiles, ancient Aboriginal rock art and crystal-bright waterholes.

Pull up a barstool in a country pub anywhere north-to-south and it won't take much to get the locals talking: the plight of the dwindling Murray River in South Australia and the federal government's 'intervention' into Northern Territory Indigenous communities are red-hot issues. Towns along the lower Murray are in an economic sleeper hold, while there are almost as many social workers as tourists occupying beds in Alice Springs. Out here, X-rayed under the southern sun, the nation's social conscience and environmental policies receive the toughest of scrutiny.

So forget the east and west coasts – if you want a definitive encapsulation of all Australia has to offer, central Oz is it! Crank up Midnight Oil's *Diesel & Dust* on the car stereo and hit the wide, open road: this is Australia at its most diverse, challenging and potent.

FAST FACTS

Population: SA 1,584,500; NT 217,600

Area: SA 984,400 sq km; NT 1.35 million sq km

Unemployment rate: SA 5.4%; NT 3.8%

Median age: SA 38.8 (Australia's oldest); NT 30.9 (Australia's youngest)

Indigenous percentage of population: SA 1.7%; NT 31.6%

Median house price: Adelaide $412,000; Darwin $480,000

Koalas on Kangaroo Island: 18 in 1925; 27,000 in 2001; 16,000 in 2008

Percentage of Australian wine produced in SA: 50%

Air rescues from Uluru per year: 3 to 4

Central Australia's fly population: six trillion (and then some…)

Getting Started

The only thing better than actually going on your trip is planning for it. Unfolding maps, dog-earring guidebooks, surfing the internet, reading up on history and dreaming of chance encounters – it's all part of the drill.

Australia is generally an easy, hassle-free country to explore. Central Australia is no exception, but it can cough up a few tricky situations by virtue of its size and remoteness. Travellers to South Australia (SA) will be met by a proficient tourism operation, primed to cater for every traveller's budget and whim: hurl yourself into arts and festivals in Adelaide, laze around on white sandy beaches, wobble through wine regions, and explore the natural landscape and its creatures. The Northern Territory (NT) offers up some of Australia's essential national parks – Uluru-Kata Tjuta, Kakadu and Litchfield – plus a hell of a lot of simmering, parched desert. If you're planning on bushwalking or outback driving here, you'll need to be better prepared than if you're sticking to the Stuart Hwy or taking a tour.

The following tips should get you primed.

WHEN TO GO

Any time is a good time to be *somewhere* in central Australia. Across SA and the NT there are remarkably diverse climates – you'll always find somewhere that's sunny and warm.

Southern SA has a Mediterranean climate – hot, dry summers and cool winters. Spring and autumn afford the greatest flexibility for travellers, when you can see the sights and dodge the hot and cold weather. In summer (December to February) South Australians beat the heat by migrating to the coast. Further north, the hot, dry desert grips the landscape. Daily summer maximums of 40°C or more are par for the course in the outback – too hot to do anything much except slump under an air-conditioner with a cold beer. SA winters are chilly in the south, but the outback beckons with mild days and clear skies. It's cold at night here, which kills off pesky flies. Late winter (August) and spring (September to November) bring out SA's magnificent wildflowers, blooming from the coastal heath up through the mallee, the Flinders Ranges and into the outback.

See Climate (p288) in the Directory for more information.

ITINERARIES

If you're not into aimless wandering, try the following itineraries on for size:

- **Adelaide to Darwin** – The classic central Australian dash: up the Stuart Hwy via Coober Pedy, Uluru-Kata Tjuta, Alice Springs and Katherine. It's 3500km one-way; takes two weeks.

- **SA Wine Regions** – Circle Adelaide through McLaren Vale, the Adelaide Hills, Barossa Valley and Clare Valley. It's a 500km loop; takes one week.

- **Darwin, Kakadu and Litchfield** – The essential Top End experience. It's a 1300km loop; takes two to three weeks.

- **The Red Centre** – Really explore the 'dead heart': Alice Springs, Uluru-Kata Tjuta, Kings Canyon, Finke Gorge and the MacDonnell Ranges. It's 1000km (plus 3000km return to Alice from Adelaide or Darwin, driving or on the *Ghan* train); takes three weeks.

- **Cruising the Coast** – Roam SA's fringes from the Limestone Coast to Kangaroo Island, the Fleurieu Peninsula, Adelaide and the Yorke and Eyre Peninsulas. It's 1700km one-way; takes three to four weeks.

One thing to heed in SA is school holidays, when familes hit the road – highways are cluttered, accommodation books out, prices soar and things get hectic, particularly during Christmas and Easter. The main holiday period is from mid-December to late January, with fortnight holidays also occurring early to mid-April, late June to mid-July, and late September to mid-October.

Southern NT has the same desert weather as northern SA – summers hot enough to fry eggs on your car roof, and mild-mannered autumns and springs. Spring can, however, be marred by plagues of flies if there's been recent rain, but rain also kicks the outback wildflowers into gear. Winter days remain warm, but temperatures plummet after dark – overnight temperatures below 0°C aren't uncommon around Alice Springs and Uluru. Rug up if you're camping!

In the tropical north there are two distinct seasons: the Wet and the Dry. The best time to visit weather-wise is the dry season between May and October – days are rain-free and warm, outback roads are open, swimming holes at Litchfield, Kakadu and Katherine are accessible and the northern beaches are free of stingers (box jellyfish).

The wet season (November to April) in the Top End is steamy and tropical with momentous downpours on most afternoons. The obvious disadvantages – apart from the rain and humidity – are that unsealed roads become impassable, you can't swim in the sea (stingers!) or waterholes (crocodiles!), and some attractions and camping grounds shut up shop. But it's not all bad during the Wet – everything is green and lush, electrical storms ravish the sky, there are no tourists crowding up the joint and you can fish with the locals for barramundi.

The best of the NT festivals kick off between June and September – accommodation prices are higher during this period, and camping grounds and sights can get crowded. School holidays add more bodies to the mix (late June to mid-July, and late September to early October).

COSTS & MONEY

Holidays in central Australia are economical for international visitors, with reasonably priced accommodation, and affordable food and everyday costs.

In Adelaide, Darwin and Alice Springs, costs for most goods and services are comparable to the rest of Australia, but it's when you start getting into more remote areas that travel here becomes more expensive – especially for fuel and accommodation. Long distances mean that fuel will be a major expense. While the price per litre in Australian cities is normally less than half of what you'd pay in Europe (or half as much again compared to the USA), in remote areas you can expect to pay a fair bit more than this. For many travellers, fuel costs are offset by camping and self-catering. In most towns there are backpacker hostels with dorm beds for $24 to $30, or private doubles for around $60 to $100. Motel rooms range from $80 to $140 a double, while urban hotel rooms cost anywhere from $120 and up. Resorts such as Yulara (at Uluru) charge premium prices for accommodation.

How much you should budget for depends on what kind of traveller you are, and how you'll be occupying yourself. At the low-cost end, if you camp or stay in hostels, cook your own meals, avoid heavy nights out in the pub and catch buses everywhere, you could probably eke out an ascetic existence on $70 per day. For a budget that realistically enables you to enjoy life, set aside $100 per day. Midrange travel – seeing the sights, having a few drinks, staying in decent places and enjoying food a few rungs up from muesli bars and rice will cost you at least $150 per person per day (twin share). With $200 a day or more you can start to travel in style. Adding shopping,

HOW MUCH?

Cup of decent coffee
$3 to $4

Stubbie holder $6 to $10

Ticket to an AFL football
match in Adelaide $25

Didgeridoo $150 to $400

See also the Lonely
Planet Index, inside the
front cover.

DON'T LEAVE HOME WITHOUT...

- Sunscreen, sunglasses and a broad-rim hat to keep you UV-protected (see p313)
- Superstrength insect repellent to fend off flies and mosquitoes (see p313)
- A compass and good maps if you're bushwalking or headed for the outback
- A satellite phone, global positioning system (GPS) unit, emergency position-indicating radio beacon (EPIRB) and/or high-frequency (HF) radio if you're really going bush (see p309)
- Extra water – the central Australian desert heat can hit you for six (see p313)
- A belly primed to try some bush tucker, Shiraz and Coopers beer
- Heavy-duty travel insurance in case of an outback mishap (see p292)
- A swag or sleeping bag – for camping out under the stars
- A swimsuit and a towel – for beaches, billabongs and hotel pools
- The willingness to call everyone 'mate', whether you know them (or like them) or not

---

entertainment, long-haul transport and car hire to these estimates will further stress your wallet.

Outside the essential expenses, remember there are lots of free things you can do in central Australia. Bushwalking, swimming, wildlife-spotting, bush camping, beaches and parks can all be had for nothing more than the time and effort it takes to get there. Families with young kids will find that the ankle-biters get free (or heartily discounted) entry to most attractions and some transport and tours. For more info on travelling with children, see p287.

TRAVELLING RESPONSIBLY

Since our inception in 1973, Lonely Planet has encouraged our readers to tread lightly, travel responsibly and enjoy the magic that independent travel affords. International travel is growing at a jaw-dropping rate, and we still firmly believe in the benefits it can bring – but, as always, we encourage you to consider the impact your visit will have on both the global environment and the local economies, cultures and ecosystems.

There are myriad ways to minimise the impact of your central Australian experience. Here are 10 quick ideas to get you thinking:

- Do your homework on tour companies: do they employ locals and put money back into local communities? What size groups do they take on the road? Are they sensitive to Indigenous land rights and interactions?
- Don't feed native wildlife or encroach on habitats – if an animal knows you're there, you're too close.
- Always ask if it's OK to photograph Indigenous sites or people, and exercise cultural awareness. For example, Uluru's traditional owners don't like visitors climbing the rock (see A Question of Climbing, p155).
- Want to take home an authentic didgeridoo or dot painting? Make your purchase direct from an Indigenous community or artist, or if you're buying from a dealer, ask to see a certificate of authenticity and/or artist's biographical information.
- Hungry? Consider supporting local businesses by buy your food supplies from local, family-run stores rather than chain supermarkets.
- Thirsty? Try quality, local microbrews, or SA-owned Coopers.
- Use a tough, refillable canteen rather then buying a new plastic water bottle every time you're dry.
- In pancake-flat Adelaide, hire a bike rather than car to get around, or take a bus, tram, train or the free city-loop bus.

- Don't swim in waterholes if you're caked in sunscreen – oil slicks are unsightly and environmentally damaging.
- Sleeping out in the desert is a remarkable experience; see p284 for tips on responsible bush camping.

To help you choose eco-accredited and sustainable accommodation, tour, activity, eating and drinking operators, see our GreenDex on p329. See also p299 in the Transport chapter for info on climate change and travel.

Online, the following websites offer plenty of sustainable travel information:

Ecotourism Australia (www.ecotourism.org.au) National site listing eco-accredited tourism operators.

Leave No Trace (www.lnt.org.au) Nonprofit organisation promoting responsible outdoor travel.

Lonely Planet (www.lonelyplanet.com/responsibletravel) Lonely Planet's online compilation of smart, sustainable travel info.

South Australian Tourism Commission (www.southaustralia.com) Click on 'Experiences' then 'Nature' for info on SA ecotourism and conservation.

Sustainable Living Choices (www.sustainableliving.sa.gov.au) SA government site with info on getting around, carbon emissions, publications and links to ecological footprint calculators.

TRAVEL LITERATURE

Holing up with some travel lit or regionally biased fiction and projecting yourself into your future holiday is the perfect way to fuel your wanderlust. Swing by your local bookshop and browse around for any of the following tomes.

In *All Things Bright and Beautiful: Murder in the City of Light* (2004), Susan Mitchell explores Adelaide's notoriously snooty social structures and how the Snowtown murders, dubbed the 'body-in-the-barrel murders', could have occurred in this civilised and cultured city. Are there repressed evils lurking beneath the piety and fortitude upon which Adelaide was built?

In *The Dog Fence* (2004) James Woodford tracks life, people and dingoes along the 5400km fence that stretches from Surfers Paradise in Queensland to the Great Australian Bight near the Western Australian border and cuts through the Great Victorian Desert, Coober Pedy, Moon Plain and the road to Oodnadatta.

We of the Never Never (1908) by Jeannie Gunn is an autobiographical account of her 1902 experiences at Elsey Station, 480km south of Darwin in the NT (Darwin was still called Palmerston in those days). The book was made into a film in 1982.

Burke's Soldier (2003) by Alan Atwood is a great historical novel set in central Australia, telling the story of the Burke and Wills expedition (and more) through the eyes of John King, the sole survivor of the ill-fated cross-country attempt.

Dollar Dreaming – Inside the Aboriginal Art World (2008) by Benjamin Genocchio is an exposé of the booming Aboriginal art industry; from humble beginnings to a controversial and complex present where a masterpiece can sell for hundreds of thousands of dollars while its creator can die in poverty.

Flinders Ranges Dreaming (1988) by Dorothy Tunbridge is a collection of 50 *stories* of the Dreaming from the Adnyamathanha people of the northern Flinders Ranges in SA. Dreaming *stories* are like a map of the environment, showing where resources are located and the laws relating to them.

Journey in Time: the 50,000 Year Story of the Australian Aboriginal Rock Art of Arnhem Land (1993) by George Chaloupka is the best reference on

'Dreaming *stories* are like a map of the environment, showing where resources are located and the laws relating to them'

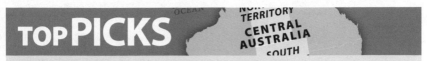

TOP PICKS

MUST-SEE MOVIES

Trundle down to your local DVD store and check out some classic SA Film Corporation–produced flicks, or films that showcase the NT in all its desert/tropical splendour.

1 *Storm Boy* (1976) Director: Henri Safran

2 *Breaker Morant* (1980) Director: Bruce Beresford

3 *Gallipoli* (1981) Director: Peter Weir

4 *Crocodile Dundee I & II* (1986 & 1988) Director: Peter Faiman/John Cornell

5 *Evil Angels* (*A Cry in the Dark*; 1988) Director: Fred Schepisi

6 *The Adventures of Priscilla, Queen of the Desert* (1993) Director: Stephan Elliott

7 *Yolngu Boy* (2000) Director: Stephen Johnson

8 *Australian Rules* (2002) Director: Paul Goldman

9 *Wolf Creek* (2005) Director: Greg McLean

10 *Ten Canoes* (2006) Directors: Rolf de Heer and Peter Djigirr

FAB FESTIVALS

If there's one thing South Australians know how to do, it's run a good festival: Adelaide boasts some of Australia's classiest arts and cultural events. Not to be outdone, SA's wine regions also know how to party. Conversely, the NT proudly claims some of the weirdest festivals in Australia. See also p290.

1 Adelaide Fringe (Adelaide; p54) February–March

2 WOMADelaide (Adelaide; p54) March

3 Adelaide Festival of Arts (Adelaide; p54) March in even-numbered years

4 Barossa Vintage Festival (Barossa Valley; p109) April in odd-numbered years

5 Barunga Festival (Katherine; p224) June

6 Sea & Vines Festival (McLaren Vale; p75) June

7 Beer Can Regatta (Darwin; p251) July

8 Camel Cup (Alice Springs; p184) July

9 Darwin Festival (Darwin; p251) August

10 Henley-on-Todd Regatta (Alice Springs; p184) September

Arnhem Land rock art. An awesome coffee-table book (you got a coffee table handy?) and still widely available.

Ash Rain (2002) by Adelaide Hills writer Corrie Hosking won the 2002 Adelaide Festival award for best unpublished manuscript. Set on the Eyre Peninsula and in the Adelaide Hills (and incongruously, Edinburgh), it's a complex family tale exploring the ties between adults and children, with potent descriptions of the SA landscape.

Knitting (2006) by Anne Bartlett is set in Adelaide – an unravelling story of two dissimilar women who stop to assist a stranger. Their friendship blossoms over a shared love of knitting, as they help each other deal with profound loss.

101 Adventures That Got Me Absolutely Nowhere (2000) and *The 'Minor Successes' of a Bloke That Never Really Had Any Luck* (2008) by Phil O'Brien are full of entertainingly offbeat outback yarns. Phil is no literary genius, but he's experienced more than most in a lifetime of outback wandering.

INTERNET RESOURCES

Useful websites are listed throughout this book. A few general sites:

Adelaide Review (www.adelaidereview.com.au) Adelaide's fortnightly cultural publication with listings on what's happening in and around town.

Australia Bureau of Meteorology (www.bom.gov.au) The latest weather reports, warnings and forecasts.

Department for Environment & Heritage (www.environment.sa.gov.au/parks) Government site detailing SA's parks and conservation areas.

Department of Natural Resources, Environment, the Arts & Sport (www.nt.gov.au /nreta/parks) Government site with info on the NT's national parks.

South Australian Tourism Commission (www.southaustralia.com) Official SA tourism site with vast amounts of information on accommodation, activities, events, tours and transport.

Travel NT (www.travelnt.com) A comprehensive travel guide produced by Tourism NT. See also www.tourismtopend.com.au.

History

ABORIGINAL SETTLEMENT

Human contact with Australia began around 60,000 years ago, when Aboriginal people journeyed across the straits from what is now Indonesia and Papua New Guinea – the beginning of the world's longest continuous cultural history.

Within a few thousand years, Aboriginal people populated much of Australia. In South Australia (SA), the earliest known Aboriginal relics are rock carvings near Olary, dated at 43,000 years – these are 16,000 years older than Europe's Neanderthal carvings. In Kakadu National Park in the Northern Territory (NT), the oldest rock-art sites date back 20,000 years, while further east in Arnhem Land, evidence suggests that rock art was being produced as far back as 60,000 years ago. Other clues can be found throughout the region in middens, campsites and rock quarries where stone tools were made. Central Australia was occupied about 24,000 years ago.

Aboriginal peoples traded goods, items of spiritual significance, songs and dances across central Australia and beyond, using routes that followed the paths of ancestors from the Dreaming, the complex system of country, culture and beliefs that defines Indigenous spirituality. An intimate understanding of plant ecology and animal behaviour ensured that food shortages were rare. Even central Australia's hostile deserts were occupied year-round, thanks to scattered permanent wells. Firestick farming was practised in forested areas to the south and north of the deserts, involving the burning of undergrowth and dead grass to encourage new growth, attract game and reduce the threat of bushfires (see Aboriginal Land Management, p42).

The Australian Museum's Indigenous Australia website (www.dreamtime.net.au) is chock full of historic and cultural information, plus Dreaming *stories*, an Indigenous glossary and insights into Aboriginal spiritual values.

EARLY CONTACT

The Chinese eunuch Admiral Cheng Ho (Zheng He) may have been the first non-Aboriginal visitor to northern Australia. He reached Timor in the 15th century, and some suggest he also made it to Australia. In 1879, a small, carved figure of the Chinese god Shao Lao was found lodged in the roots of a banyan tree in Darwin. That's the clincher, the pro-Zheng camp says: the carving apparently dates from the Ming dynasty (1368–1644).

There's evidence to suggest that the Portuguese were the first Europeans to sight Australia's northern coast, sometime during the 16th century, followed promptly by the Dutch. Famed Dutch navigator Abel Tasman charted the north coast, from Cape York to the Kimberley in Western Australia, in 1664.

Other 17th-century visitors to the north were Macassan traders from the island of Celebes (today's Sulawesi in Indonesia), who came for trepang (sea cucumber). The Macassans set up seasonal camps for three months at a time, gathering and curing trepang and trading dugout canoes, metal

For a timely and deeply moving account of early Indigenous history in SA and the NT, grab the DVD of the TV series *First Australians* (2008), or a copy of the accompanying book, edited by Rachel Perkins and Marcia Langton.

TIMELINE

60,000 BC	AD 1627	1836
Experts say that Aboriginal people settled in Australia around this time. The oldest rock-art sites in the NT date from 50,000 years ago; those in SA date from 43,000 years.	Dutch captain Francois Thijssen, aboard the *Gulden Zeepaard,* is the first European to spy the coast of SA. The French follow in the 1700s, the British in the 1800s.	The Province of South Australia is proclaimed. The first official settlement at Kingscote on Kangaroo Island is soon replaced by Adelaide, on the advice of Colonel William Light.

LAND RIGHTS IN CENTRAL AUSTRALIA

Britain colonised Australia on the legal principle of terra nullius, meaning the country was unoccupied. Early colonists could therefore take land from Aboriginal peoples without signing treaties or providing compensation. This principle remained legally potent until the landmark Mabo High Court decision in 1992, which voided the presumption of terra nullius and officially recognised native title as a traditional connection to or occupation of the land.

Preceding the Mabo decision, in 1966 the South Australian government made the first move of any Australian state to give Aboriginal peoples title to their land. The Aboriginal Lands Trust was created, vesting title to the missions and reserves still operating in South Australia. These lands are leased back to their Aboriginal occupants, who have repeated rights of renewal. The South Australian parliament then passed two pieces of legislation, the *Prohibition of Discrimination Act* and the *Aboriginal Affairs Act,* giving South Australian Aboriginal peoples the right to run their own communities.

In 1981 the *Pitjantjatjara Land Rights Act* came into effect, granting freehold title over a vast area of northwest SA to the Anangu-Pitjantjatjara. A further 76,000 sq km, occupied by the federal government as part of the Maralinga project, was returned to its traditional owners in 1984. Land held under Aboriginal freehold title cannot be sold or resumed (taken back into public ownership), and no development of any kind can take place without the permission of traditional owners.

A more convoluted land-rights path has been navigated in the Northern Territory. In 1962 a bark petition was presented to the federal government by the Yolngu peoples of Yirrakala, in northeast Arnhem Land, demanding the government recognise Aboriginal peoples' occupation and ownership of Australia since time immemorial. The petition was ignored, so the Yolngu peoples took the matter to court – and lost.

But the wheels had begun to turn, and under increasing pressure the federal government passed the *Aboriginal Land Rights (Northern Territory) Act* in 1976, establishing three Aboriginal land councils empowered to claim land on behalf of traditional owners.

Under the Act, the only claimable land is crown land outside town boundaries that no one else owns or leases – usually semidesert or desert. So when the Anangu, Uluru's traditional owners, claimed ownership of Uluru and Kata Tjuta, their claim was overruled because the land was within a national park. It was only by amending two Acts of Parliament that Uluru-Kata Tjuta National Park was handed back to its traditional owners on the condition that it was immediately leased back to the federal government as a national park.

Around half of the NT has been claimed, or is under claim. The native-title process is tedious and can take years to complete, often without success. Many claims are opposed by state and territory governments, and claimants are required to prove they have continuous connection to the land and are responsible for sacred sites under Aboriginal law. If a claim is successful, Aboriginal peoples have the right to negotiate with mining interests and ultimately accept or reject exploration and mining proposals. This right is often opposed by Australia's mining lobby, despite traditional Aboriginal owners in the Northern Territory rejecting only about a third of such proposals outright.

1862	**1869**	**1894**
John McDouall Stuart makes the first south–north crossing of the continent from SA into the NT, the highlight of his many epic explorations.	After three other NT colonies all fail to take hold, Palmerston (renamed Darwin in 1911) is established by George Goyder, South Australia's Surveyor-General.	South Australian women are the first in the British Empire permitted to vote, and the first in the world eligible to stand for Parliament.

items, food, tobacco and glass objects with local Aboriginal people. There were many interracial relationships, with some Aboriginal people journeying to Celebes to live.

Down south, the Dutch ship *Gulden Zeepaard* made the first European sighting of the SA coast in 1627. The French ships *Recherche* and *L'Esperance* followed in 1792, while the first British explorer on the scene was Lieutenant James Grant in 1800. In 1802, Englishman Matthew Flinders charted Fowlers Bay, Spencer and St Vincent Gulfs and Kangaroo Island on his ship the *Investigator*.

EUROPEAN COLONISATION

In 1829, Captain Charles Sturt headed inland from Sydney and fell into the Murray River, floating downstream to Lake Alexandrina (in today's SA). His glowing reports inspired the National Colonisation Society to propose a utopian, self-supporting South Australian colony founded on planned immigration with land sales, rather than convict-based grants. The British Parliament then passed the *South Australian Colonisation Act* in 1834, making SA the only Australian colony established entirely by free colonists (a distinction most South Australians are happy to highlight).

The first official settlement was established in 1836 at Kingscote on Kangaroo Island, before colonial surveyor-general Colonel William Light chose Adelaide as the site for the capital. The first governor, Captain John Hindmarsh, landed at present-day Glenelg on 28 December 1836, and proclaimed the Province of South Australia.

In the NT, early European attempts at settlement – on Melville Island in 1824, Raffles Bay in 1829 and the Cobourg Peninsula in 1838 – all failed in the face of indigenous resistance, disease and climate, until the settlement of Palmerston (renamed Darwin in 1911) was established in 1869.

Conflict marked the arrival of European cattle farmers across central Australia. The Arrernte (*uh*-rahn-da) people defended their lands and spiritual heritage, spearing cattle for food as farmers had destroyed many of their traditional hunting grounds. In return, those waterholes not already ruined by cattle were poisoned, and reprisal raids saw many massacres. German Lutheran missionaries at Hermannsburg Mission on the Finke River tried to convert the Arrernte to Christianity, a process also fraught with conflict.

IMMIGRATION & SECOND-WAVE EXPLORATIONS

The first immigrants to SA were poor, young English, Scots and Irish. About 12,000 landed in the first four years of settlement, followed by 800 German farmers and artisans – mainly Lutherans fleeing religious persecution – who arrived between 1838 and 1841. Around 5400 more Germans arrived by 1850 and many more followed during the next decade. They settled mainly

The History Trust of South Australia website (www.history.sa.gov.au) is a rich resource, with links to the Migration Museum, the National Motor Museum and SA's Maritime Museum.

Colonel William Light, celebrated planner of Adelaide, died from tuberculosis in 1839, aged 54. Dogged by criticism and character slurs, he passed away before his vision for the city could fully be appreciated.

1901	1942	1974
With the federation of the disparate Australian colonies, South Australia becomes a state of the Commonwealth of Australia.	Darwin is bombed by the Japanese during WWII – 243 people lose their lives in 64 raids. A mass exodus cripples the Top End economy.	Cyclone Tracy tears through Darwin on Christmas Eve, demolishing 70% of the city's buildings and killing 65 people. Much of the city was rebuilt (more strongly) within four years.

DINNER ON KI

British explorer Matthew Flinders bumped into Kangaroo Island on 2 March 1802. His crew of hungry sailors stormed ashore in search of sustenance – their eyes boggled at the thousands of kangaroos bouncing around on the beach. Flinders described the inevitable feeding frenzy in his journal: 'The whole ship's company was employed this afternoon in the skinning and cleaning of kangaroos. After four months' privation they stewed half a hundredweight of heads, forequarters and tails down into soup for dinner... In gratitude for so seasonable a supply, I named this south land "Kangaroo Island".' Of course, you can still get roo on the menu today: it's local, sustainable and delicious.

Adelaide's King William St is 40m wide – the broadest Australian capital-city thoroughfare. It was once famed for its mud; picking up a stray hat would likely reveal someone underneath (and possibly a horse below them!).

in the Adelaide Hills and the Barossa Valley, where the soil and sunshine were ideal for wine-growing – their vineyards formed the beginning of the SA wine industry. Thousands of Cornish people then came to SA following the discovery of copper in the 1840s.

In the NT, the discovery of gold and copper south of Darwin attracted miners, and settlers with cattle moved into the NT from SA and northern Queensland. In 1877 the first Lutheran mission was established at Hermannsburg; Catholic and Methodist missions followed elsewhere.

Successive waves of immigration fuelled the search for new arable land. Between 1839 and 1841, Edward John Eyre made the first traverse of the Flinders Ranges in SA. In 1839, Charles Bonney drove the first herd of cattle from Melbourne to Adelaide via Mt Gambier, opening up southeastern SA.

Five years later, Charles Sturt set off from Adelaide with a whaleboat to find the mythical central Australian inland sea, but after 18 months of hardship he abandoned it in a waterless red expanse of stones and sandhills. If nothing else, he had discovered the Simpson Desert.

In 1844 Prussian scientist Ludwig Leichhardt set off from Queensland to blaze an overland route into the NT. The party reached the Gulf of Carpentaria and headed northwest. Leichhardt was afforded hero status for his efforts, but his route was too difficult for regular use and no promising grazing areas were discovered.

Rock Star: The Story of Reg Sprigg – An Outback Legend by Kristen Weidenbach (2008) unearths the life and times of legendary South Australian Reg Sprigg, who pioneered mineral exploration across the state.

John McDouall Stuart made several epic forays into central Australia between 1858 and 1862. His successful crossing of the continent from south to north led to SA taking governmental control of the NT in 1863 (it was previously part of New South Wales). The Stuart Hwy, from Port Augusta in SA to Darwin, is named in his honour.

WHEAT, SHEEP, COPPER & GOLD

By 1865 SA was growing half of Australia's wheat. Overcropping in the Adelaide Hills and Fleurieu Peninsula led to more land being opened up in the Mid-North and Flinders Ranges. A 'wheat boom' ensued. Enthusiastic

1978	1980	1995
The NT is granted legislative self-government, but remains under the constitutional auspices of the federal government (and does to this day).	A dingo kills infant Azaria Chamberlain at Uluru, and her mother Lindy is jailed for murder (later exonerated). Nothing exonerates Meryl Streep for her Australian accent in the movie, *Evil Angels* (aka *A Cry in the Dark*).	After 10 noisy years, Adelaide hosts the Australian Formula One Grand Prix for the last time. Bon Jovi closes the show with some raucous, pyrotechnic cock rock.

trumpeting of 'a rich golden harvest' extending into the NT continued until drought struck in the mid-1880s.

Sheep farmers also helped to open up SA, but a tendency to overestimate carrying capacity led to gross overstocking, and with no pasture kept in reserve, the 1880s drought ruined many. The SA breeders survived by developing a strain of merino sheep better suited to semiarid conditions.

By the 1870s, SA had replaced Cornwall as the British Empire's leading copper producer, making many South Australians wealthy and leaving a legacy of fine public buildings in mining towns such as Burra, and around Adelaide.

The NT was opened up with the discovery of gold at Yam Creek, 160km south of Darwin. The find fired up local prospectors, and it wasn't long before other discoveries at Pine Creek, south of Darwin, sparked a minor rush. The SA government built a railway line in 1883 from Darwin to Pine Creek, but the gold rush was soon over. Subsequent government-backed NT projects like sugar, tobacco and coffee plantations, peanut farming, pearling and crocodile- and snakeskin trading either failed completely or provided only minimal returns.

A bottle of 1951 Penfolds Grange – the legendary South Australian Shiraz – recently sold for just over AU$50,000 (approximately the average Australian yearly salary).

FINDING FEDERATION

When its Parliament sprang up in 1856, SA began with the most democratic constitution of any Australian colony. Prior to that it was governed by representatives from the SA Board of Commissioners and the British Government.

Fighting off recession, transport and communications systems grew rigorously in SA. By 1890 railways connected Adelaide with Melbourne, Oodnadatta in the outback, and Cockburn on SA's border with NSW. There were also 3200km of sealed roads and 100-plus steamboats trading on the Murray River. The SA Parliament established Australia's first juvenile court in 1890, and granted free education in 1891. In 1894 SA became the first Australian colony to recognise women's right to vote in parliamentary elections, and the first place in the world to allow women to stand for Parliament.

With Federation – the amalgamation of disparate colonies into the states of the Commonwealth of Australia – in 1901, SA experienced slow but steady growth. The Overland Telegraph Line between Adelaide and Darwin had been completed in 1872, linking central Australia to the world telegraph network, but South Australian speculators and investors in the NT were getting cold feet. Soon after Federation the South Australian government threw in the towel, offering control of the ugly NT duckling back to the federal government.

In 1872, Adelaide became the first Australian capital to be connected by telegraph with London, slashing communication times from six months to seven hours.

TWENTIETH-CENTURY TRIALS

After Federation, manufacturing and heavy engineering became increasingly important in SA. The Port Pirie smelter was enlarged during WWI, and was soon producing 10% of the world's lead, as well as silver and zinc.

1998	1998	2000
The NT returns a negative result in a referendum on whether it should become a state rather than federally administered territory. The result surprises many.	Ross Fargher stubs his toe on the world's oldest vertebrate fossil on his Flinders Ranges property in SA. At 560 million years old, it beats the previous oldest find by 30 million years.	Mandatory sentencing laws and zero-tolerance policing in the NT increase the jailing of Aboriginal people for trivial offences, causing national outrage. The laws are repealed in 2001.

WWI was a time of division in SA. Before 1914 the state had many German placenames, but in a fit of anti-German zeal these were either anglicised or replaced. Hahndorf was changed to 'Ambleside' (before reverting to Hahndorf in 1935). Other names were reinstated during 1936's centennial celebrations, when the German settlers' huge contribution to SA's development was officially recognised.

The early 1920s brought prosperity across Australia, before a four-year drought led into the Great Depression. All states suffered during this period, but SA fared worst of all: in 1931 more than 70,000 people out of a population of 575,000 were dependent on welfare.

Industrial development in SA quickened during WWII – water-pipeline construction, ship building and coal mining all took off – but people in the NT had more pressing issues to contend with. At 9.57am on 19 February 1942, nearly 200 Japanese aircraft bombed Darwin's harbour and the RAAF base at Larrakeyah. Darwin was attacked 64 times during the war and 243 people lost their lives; it was the only place in Australia to suffer prolonged attacks. In March 1942 the entire NT north of Alice Springs was placed under military control and by December there were 32,000 troops stationed in the Top End.

> The Northern Territory Library has an online exhibition of photographs, reports, journals and articles on the bombing of Darwin in WWII. Go to www.ntl.nt.gov.au/online_resources/australias_northern_territory_wwii.

After WWII, the Australian government launched an ambitious scheme to attract immigrants. Thousands of people from Britain, Greece, Italy, Serbia, Croatia, the Netherlands, Poland, Turkey, Malta and Lebanon took up the offer of government-assisted passage. The immigration boom fuelled growth in SA, which shifted from a rural economy to a predominantly industrial one. In the NT, the urban areas of Darwin and Alice Springs also grew, but a shortage of federal funds meant there was little development, and the postwar rebuilding of Darwin proceeded at a snail's pace.

The 1960s and '70s were difficult times in SA – economic and population growth were stagnating, and overseas competition heightened a deepening industrial recession. Socially, however, SA premier Don Dunstan's progressive Labor government was kicking goals, passing an act prohibiting racial discrimination (the first in Australia), and creating the South Australian Film Corporation (1972) and State Opera of South Australia (1976).

The NT was also ailing economically, and the good citizens of Darwin were soon brought to their knees once more. On Christmas Eve 1974, Cyclone Tracy ripped through the city, killing 65 people and destroying more than 70% of Darwin's buildings.

> In the aftermath of Cyclone Tracy in 1974, an exodus saw Darwin's population fall from 45,000 to just 11,000. These days it's bounced back to a cosmopolitan 120,000.

From the late '70s into the 1990s, mining dug a tunnel to economic recovery. In SA, huge deposits of uranium, copper, silver and gold were found at Roxby Downs, plus oil and gas in the Cooper Basin. In the NT, copper and gold were unearthed at Tennant Creek, and oil and gas bubbled up in the Amadeus basin. Bauxite was found at Gove, manganese at Groote Eylandt, and uranium at Batchelor and (more controversially) Kakadu.

2001	2004	2007
The federal government incarcerates asylum seekers at the Baxter Detention Centre in SA's outback. Some Adelaidians display signs 'Asylum seekers welcome here' in their windows; others go to jail for protesting. Many more remain silent.	After a 70-year wait, the *Ghan* passenger train runs from Adelaide to Darwin, finally linking the Top End with the southern states.	Ignominious South Australian terrorism supporter David Hicks is freed from the United States' Guantánamo Bay detention centre and serves out his time in Adelaide's Yatala Prison.

WHAT LIES BENEATH

In 2005, making way for the billion-dollar Darwin City Waterfront development, Darwin Harbour was dredged for unexploded Japanese bombs. The harbour was peppered with 60kg bombs during WWII, sinking eight ships and damaging many more. Some estimates placed 160 unexploded bombs lying latent at the bottom of the harbour.

With the developers wringing nervous hands, scans detected 230 metal chunks in the mud. Disposal experts were called in, but turned up little more than a brass fuse, a Chinese jug and some remnants of the sunken ship MV *Neptuna*. No bombs, but we suggest you don't go poking around in the sludge…

CENTRAL AUSTRALIA TODAY

These days, mining continues to drive the economies of SA and the NT (and Australia's as a nation), but tourism is the big success story in central Australia. SA has an extremely well-oiled governing tourist body extolling the virtues of the state's diverse regions. In the NT, the tourist magnets of Uluru and Kakadu each receive over half a million visitors per year. At the end of WWII the population of Alice Springs (Uluru's main access point) was around 1000; today it's around 28,000 – a direct result of selling the central Australian outback as 'the real-deal Aussie experience'. The rise in environmental awareness and ecotourism has also boosted the popularity of Kakadu.

The most contentious contemporary issue in the NT remains the 2007 *Northern Territory National Emergency Response*, aka 'The Intervention'. The federal government introduced this package of law enforcement, welfare and land tenancy changes in response to a damning report looking into Aboriginal child abuse. The Intervention has been heavily criticised for a lack of Indigenous consultation, and for taking backward steps in Aboriginal land rights and social self-determination.

Down south, the plight of the Murray River is the talk of SA. Irrigators, environmentalists, state and federal governments have been butting heads over what to do about the ever-dwindling river flow. Flood the lower lakes with seawater? Force upstream irrigators to cut quotas? A new dam at Wellington? Pray for rain? With every month of inaction, the river gets drier and drier…

In the cities, Adelaide retains its lofty position at (or maybe just a bit below) Australia's cultural high-water mark, with a barrage of quality festivals dappling the calendar. This is a city of substance, grace and poise. Shedding its redneck skin (well, mostly), contemporary Darwin is vibrant, multicultural and increasingly urbane. A 1998 referendum on granting constitutional statehood to the NT returned a (surprisingly) negative result. Although legislative self-governance was granted to the NT in 1978, the federal government retains arms-length control. Is Darwin the teenage city that will never quite leave home?

In 1996, the Northern Territory government became the first in the world to legalise voluntary euthanasia. Although the legislation was soon overturned by the federal government, by then three people had voluntarily died.

In 2005 the NT government released declassified files that detailed masses of UFO sightings across the Top End over the previous 30 years, including unexplained sightings by air-force pilots.

2007	**2007**	**2009**
Causing general public outrage, the NT government introduces speed limits of 130km/h on the Stuart, Victoria, Arnhem and Barkly Hwys.	The federal government's 'Intervention' policy in NT Indigenous communities is controversially received in both black and white communities.	Seven time Tour de France winner Lance Armstrong joins the peloton for the Tour Down Under, in SA.

Indigenous Cultures & Identities Dr Irene Watson

ABOUT THE AUTHOR

'I am a Tanganekald and Meintangk woman. My knowledge in law, Aboriginal culture and history is in the essence of this material, as is the knowledge I have gained from Aboriginal Elders, my mother, uncles and aunties.' For more biographical information, see p317.

Aboriginal societies are diverse. We are not one large homogeneous group but hundreds of different sovereign First Nation peoples.

There are many common stereotypes of Aboriginal peoples. One is that we are all the same and conform to the idealised image of the naked Aborigine standing with spear in hand watching the sun set. This is a picture that quickly dissolved into the reality of the 21st century. We are as different as the landscapes of coast, desert, rainforest and mountains. The land is different and so are we, the first peoples of the land.

Another misconception is that our cultures are static. We, like the people of other nations, live in the modern world and we embrace both traditional and contemporary lifestyles.

TRADITIONAL & NONTRADITIONAL

Many Aboriginal people still live in communities where their families and clan members retain the connections to a common Dreaming ancestral being. Spirituality and the land are central to our Aboriginal identity.

However, most Aboriginal families have experienced the government policy of removing young 'mixed-blood' children to place them in non-Aboriginal families or institutions, a group commonly known as the stolen generations. This practice has impacted on the wellbeing of communities and has eroded traditional Aboriginal society, especially as the policy was directed at the heart of our culture, the family.

The policy of forced removal of Aboriginal children from their families has created a separation and a difference in culture among Aboriginal peoples. The negative impact of these policies is revealed when Aboriginal identity and culture are constructed as having two categories: traditional and nontraditional.

WE ARE ALL REAL ABORIGINES

A more positive view of Aboriginal identity is one in which there are no categories or divisions, for we are all traditional as we are all of an Aboriginal culture and tradition. The maintenance of tradition holds greater meaning than the idea of being a 'full-blooded Aboriginal' or 'traditional Aboriginal', living in a remote region of Australia.

The construction and identification of 'traditional Aboriginal' has also led to the creation of other categories: 'nontraditional' Aborigines, 'rural' Aborigines, and 'urban' Aborigines. It is often assumed that these other categories are 'of a lesser quality' or are not authentic; that these people are not 'real Aborigines'. But we are all 'real' and though we identify with a diverse range of lifestyles, skin colours, cultures and languages, we are all equally Aboriginal. We are the descendants of the original ancestors of this place of creation, now known as Australia.

KINSHIP WITH FAMILY, ANCESTORS & LAND

Studies of the Aboriginal peoples of Australia frequently make the comment that our kinship and social systems are among the most complicated in the world. That may be so.

The difficulty in understanding how our kinship system works is perhaps because of our special relationship to our country, our kin and our ancestral spirits of the Dreaming. We believe we are related to all things in the natural world. These relationships were formed in the Dreaming, our time of creation.

FAMILY

The core of Aboriginal society is the extended family and our relationships to kin and clan members, whether it is in a remote region or a big city. The family clan groups are also connected to a larger collective, which shares a common language, land, culture, history, tradition and customs, sometimes called a nation.

The clan group shares Dreaming ancestors, whose spirits are alive in the land. Our relationships to family and country identify who we are as Aboriginal people. These relationships are spiritual and are recorded in Dreaming stories and songs.

DREAMING ANCESTORS

The Aboriginal relationship to a spirit ancestor is more commonly known as a totem. The idea of a totem is a simple explanation for the very complex and spiritual relationship that Aboriginal people have with their country, the ancestors and the Dreaming.

These beings are our spiritual guides, and one may take the form of a bird, animal or natural feature. Our spirit guide is our connection to both country and the Dreaming and it is our teacher, who teaches us much about our relationship with all things in the natural world.

LAND

In walking over the land in the steps of the creative ancestors, we are affirming our relationship to the Dreaming. When we return to our sacred places we fulfil our cultural obligations to the ancestors by taking care of the country and protecting the spirit places of our ancestors through ceremony.

Our traditional identity comes from the land, and an important Aboriginal tradition is to introduce ourselves in relation to the country of the grandmothers and grandfathers. We will talk to the spirit ancestors to tell them where we come from, and who our people, kin and family are. It is one of our ways.

Our relationship to country determines how we speak to one another; who speaks about our culture, country and our laws; and how we speak about them. These protocols are important to the identity of who is traditional to the country.

For more information on relationships with the land, see p40.

'relationships to family and country identify who we are as Aboriginal people'

CEREMONIES

Ceremonies are an integration of song, dance, art and mime. They are a time when the best dancers and singers become the ancestral beings and they reenact the activities of the ancestors. Ceremonies regenerate Aboriginal communities and are reminders of our roots and the expected behaviour that has been set down in law by the ancestors.

The ceremonies are Aboriginal law in action, involving the serious business of maintaining the law. Ceremonies serve many purposes. They provide a forum for the settling of disputes which may arise over land, marriages, hunting and gathering rights and a whole range of community conflicts. They are a process of teaching cultural knowledge and the spirituality of the ancestors to the next generations. There are also community forums where information about the best times to hunt and gather are discussed. They may also remind the community of taboos and the correct marriages for their families and children.

The spiritual significance of ceremonies is in their focus on the land. A ceremony is a collective act of the people in honouring and celebrating the ancestors and the Dreaming. At these times we are given the opportunity to reaffirm our connection to the Dreaming and to maintain and protect the spirit places of our ancestors. Ceremonies are also a celebration for the renewal of life, and the changing of seasons.

ABORIGINAL CULTURES TODAY

Colonisation and dispossession from our traditional lands has impacted upon the traditional culture of Aboriginal societies across Australia, damaging some groups more than others. Some Aboriginal peoples living in remote regions have been able to retain their traditional lands, and land-related aspects of their traditional culture. This is often because of their remoteness and the fact that no one has yet wanted their lands for development or exploration.

'languages are spoken, kinship obligations are met, traditional customs are observed'

However, traditional culture is not only being maintained in remote, northern Aboriginal communities. In the southern areas – including the more settled and densely populated cities and rural towns – languages are spoken, kinship obligations are met, traditional customs are observed and Aboriginal people are caring for their country. It is here that culture and tradition takes on a more contemporary form, where Aboriginal culture coexists with the changed environment.

Aboriginal peoples, like other cultures, embrace different walks of life: from academic professions in big city universities to teaching the law in traditional communities, from nursing in a modern hospital to gathering bush medicines in a remote community.

While our population comprises a very small minority group (2% of the whole population), we have survived as culturally distinct peoples against the brutal colonisation of our territories. In our struggle to survive assimilation, many of our people have retained connections to our culture and are still living on the lands of our ancestors. We have retained many of our traditional customs and many of our ancient ceremonies are being revived throughout Australia.

Aboriginal culture moves in the cycles of the past, present and future: 'always was, always will be'. We are culturally diverse. We are living both a traditional life and a modern one; maintaining traditional cultural beliefs in the middle of populated cities as well as by remote billabongs in the Northern Territory.

Indigenous Visual Arts Brenda L Croft

Visual imagery is a fundamental part of Indigenous life, a connection between past and present, between the supernatural and the earthly, between people and the land. The early forms of Indigenous artistic expression were rock carvings (petroglyphs), body painting and ground designs, and the earliest engraved designs known to exist date back at least 40,000 years.

While it has always been an integral part of Indigenous culture, Indigenous art, with some notable exceptions, was either largely ignored by non-Indigenous people or simply viewed in an ethnographic, *'primitif* arts' context, with most examples of Indigenous material culture placed in natural-history museums, as opposed to fine-art museums. There were exceptions to this, such as the first acquisition of a work of Aboriginal art by a fine-art museum in 1939, when the Art Gallery of South Australia bought a watercolour by Western Arrernte artist Albert Namatjira. In the 1950s works collected during Charles Mountford's 1948 American-Australian Scientific Expedition to Arnhem Land were distributed to major state galleries.

The efforts of people such as acclaimed artist and curator Tony Tuckson were also instrumental. A great admirer of Aboriginal art, Tuckson undertook trips to Arnhem Land and Melville Island in the Northern Territory (NT), acquiring works for the (then) National Art Gallery of New South Wales collection from 1950 onwards. Others, such as Frank Norton, director of the Art Gallery of Western Australia (1958–75), followed suit, with collecting trips to the Kimberley in northwestern Australia, Arnhem Land and the Tiwi Islands.

Then, in 1971 an event took place that challenged non-Indigenous perceptions of Indigenous art. At Papunya, northwest of Alice Springs, a group of senior men from the community, led by Kaapa Mbitjana Tjampitjinpa (from the Anmatyerre/Arrernte people; 1925-89), along with Long Jack Phillipus Tjakamarra (Pintupi/Luritja/Warlpiri) and Billy Stockman Tjapaltjarri (Anmatyerre), all elders of the community and employed as groundsmen at the Papunya school, were encouraged to paint a mural on one of the school's external walls by art teacher Geoffrey Bardon, who was instrumental in the genesis of Papunya Tula Artists. Shortly after work commenced, other members of the community became enthused by the project and joined in creating the mural *Honey Ant Dreaming*. Government regulations later saw the mural destroyed, but its effect on the community was profound. Images of spiritual significance had taken on a permanent and very public form. Notwithstanding the debate the mural caused at Papunya, other members of the community expressed a desire to paint. Initially the paintings were executed on smallish boards, but within a short time canvases were used.

From this fractured beginning in a remote Aboriginal community began the commencement of the contemporary Indigenous art movement. That it developed in Papunya is not without irony, since Papunya was established in 1960 under the auspices of the Australian government's cultural assimilation policy – a policy designed in combination with others, such as the forced removal of Indigenous children from their families, to undermine Indigenous culture. *Honey Ant Dreaming* and the creative and cultural energy this painting unleashed helped to strengthen Indigenous culture and contributed to the abandonment of assimilation as the foundation stone of non-Indigenous social policy.

ABOUT THE AUTHOR

Brenda L Croft was born in Perth, and now lives in Adelaide, where she is a lecturer at the University of South Australia. As an artist, Ms Croft has exhibited her work nationally and internationally. For more biographical information, see p317.

ROCK ART OF ARNHEM LAND & KAKADU

Arnhem Land, in the Top End of the NT, is an area of abundant artistic and cultural heritage. Recent finds suggest that rock paintings were being produced as long as 60,000 years ago, and some of the rock art galleries in the huge sandstone Arnhem Land plateau are at least 18,000 years old.

The rock art of Arnhem Land depicts ancestral stories for the many language groups and clans of the region, with stylised designs, often hatched and *rarrk* (cross-hatched), of Ancestral Beings, spirits, totems, and exchanges with the Macassans – Indonesian mariners from Sulawesi who regularly visited the north coast for at least three centuries until their visits were banned by government regulations in 1906.

The paintings contained in the Arnhem Land rock-art sites constitute one of the world's most significant and fascinating rock-art collections. They provide a record of changing environments and lifestyles over the millennia.

In some places they are concentrated in large galleries, with paintings from more recent eras sometimes superimposed over older paintings. Some sites are kept secret – not only to protect them from damage, but also because they are private or sacred to the Aboriginal owners. Some are believed to be inhabited by malevolent beings, who must not be approached by those who are ignorant of the Indigenous customs of the region. However, two of the finest sites have been opened up to visitors, with access roads, walkways and explanatory signs. These are Ubirr (p274) and Nourlangie (p278) in Kakadu National Park, although the irony is that the original custodians no longer paint at these sites.

'Some of the animals depicted have long been extinct on mainland Australia'

The rock paintings show how the main styles succeeded each other over time. The earliest hand prints were followed by a 'naturalistic' style, with large outlines of people or animals filled in with colour. Some of the animals depicted, such as the thylacine (Tasmanian tiger), have long been extinct on mainland Australia.

After the naturalistic style came the 'dynamic', in which motion was often depicted (a dotted line, for example, to show a spear's path through the air). In this era the first Ancestral Beings appeared, with human bodies and animal heads.

The next style mainly showed simple human silhouettes, and was followed by the curious 'yam figures', in which people and animals were drawn in the shape of yams. Other painting styles, including the 'X-ray' style, which displays the internal organs and bone structure of animals, also appeared around this time.

By about 1000 years ago many of the salt marshes had turned into freshwater swamps and billabongs. The birds and plants that provided new food sources in this landscape appeared in the art of this time.

From around 400 years ago, Indigenous artists also depicted the human newcomers to the region – Macassan traders and, more recently, Europeans – and the things they brought, or their modes of transport such as ships and horses.

PAINTING
Western Desert Painting

Following the developments at Papunya and with the growing importance of art as both an economic and a cultural activity, an association was formed to help the artists sell their work. Papunya Tula Artists Pty Ltd in Alice Springs is the longest-running Aboriginal-owned and -directed gallery in the country. Although very few galleries in central Australia are owned and directed by Indigenous people, there are numerous art centres governed by Aboriginal people and these centres are instrumental in protecting the rights and interests of the artists they represent. Desart is the advocacy agency for central Australian art centres and Ku Arts was established in South Australia to cover the Anangu Pitjantjatjara Yankunytjatjara (APY) Lands.

Painting in central Australia has flourished to such a degree that it is now a major source of income for many communities. It has also been an important educational tool for children, through which they can learn different aspects of religious and ceremonial knowledge. In the past decade or so women have played a much greater role in the visual-arts movement, with some of the most innovative work being created by women artists.

Western Desert painting, also known as 'dot' painting, evolved from 'ground paintings', which formed the centrepiece of ceremonial dances and songs. These were made from pulped plant material, and the designs were made on the ground using dots of this mush. Dots were also used in other ways: to outline objects in rock paintings, to highlight geographical features or vegetation, and in body painting, using the pulped material, ochres and feathers.

'they can be read in many ways, including as aerial and underground geographical maps'

While these paintings may look abstract, they depict Ancestral Tjukurrpa/Jukurrpa (Dreaming) stories, and can be read in many ways, including as aerial and underground geographical maps, though not always literally. Many paintings feature the tracks of birds, animals and humans, often identifying the Ancestral Beings. Subjects may be depicted by the imprint they leave in the sand – a simple arc depicts a person (as that is the print left by someone sitting), a coolamon (wooden carrying dish) is shown by an oval shape, a digging stick by a single line, a campfire by a circle. Men or women are identified by the objects associated with them – digging sticks and coolamons for women, spears and boomerangs for men. Concentric circles usually depict Dreaming sites, or places where ancestors paused in their journeys.

While these symbols are widely used, their meaning in each individual painting is known only by the artist and the people closely associated with him or her – either by clan or by the Tjukurrpa/Jukurrpa – since different clans apply different interpretations to each painting. In this way sacred stories can be publicly portrayed, as the deeper meaning is not revealed to uninitiated viewers. Many recent works are far more coded in their imagery with few or no figurative symbols.

Bark Painting

Bark painting is an integral part of the cultural heritage of Arnhem Land's Indigenous people. It's difficult to establish when bark was first used, partly because it is perishable, so very old pieces don't exist and none were created in the format that we know today. The paintings were never intended to be permanent records but were painted on the bark shelters in much the same way as the art on rock galleries. Non-Indigenous explorers travelling through the region in the early 19th century observed the practice of painting the inside walls of bark shelters, and later in the 19th century and early in the 20th century the trade in examples of bark paintings brought them to the notice of museums around the world.

The bark used is from the stringybark tree (*Eucalyptus tetradonta*), and it is taken off the tree in the wet season when it is moist and supple. The rough outer layers are removed and the bark is dried by placing it over a fire and then under weights on the ground to keep it flat. In a couple of weeks the bark is dry and ready for use.

The pigments used in bark paintings are red and yellow (ochres), white (kaolin) and black (charcoal) with different tones achieved through the mixing of these natural pigments. The colours are gathered from special ceremonial sites by the traditional custodians, and they were customarily traded with other clans. An incredible range of colours can be mixed from the four pigments available and many artists are identified by their choice of a particular tone. These natural pigments give the paintings their superb soft and earthy finish. Binding agents such as egg yolks (from native birds), wax and plant resins were added to the pigments. Recently some of these materials have been replaced by synthetic agents such as wood glue. Similarly, the brushes used in the past were obtained from the bush materials at hand – twigs, leaf fibres, feathers, human hair and the like. Artists today sometimes choose commercial brushes but many continue to use traditional materials.

'natural pigments give the paintings their superb soft and earthy finish'

One of the main features of Arnhem Land bark paintings is the use of *rarrk* designs. These designs identify the particular clans, and are based on body paintings handed down through generations. More recently, artists are recognised by their specific stylistic signature. The paintings can also be broadly categorised by their regional styles. In the region's west the tendency is towards naturalistic and figurative images and plain backgrounds, although many renowned artists from Western and Central Arnhem Land cover the entire surface of the bark or carving in intricate linework. To the east, the use of geometric, abstract designs is more common.

The art reflects themes from ancestral times that vary by region. In eastern and central Arnhem Land the most prominent Ancestral Beings are the Djan'kawu Sisters, who travelled the land with their elaborate dillybags (string carry bags) and digging sticks (for making waterholes), and the Wagilag Sisters, who are associated with snakes and waterholes and creation of the clans of the regions. In Western Arnhem Land, the significant being (according to some clans) is Yingarna, the Rainbow Serpent, as is one of her offspring, Ngalyod. Other groups paint Nawura as the principal Ancestral Being – he travelled through the rocky landscape creating sacred sites and giving people the attributes of culture.

The Mimi spirits are another feature of Western Arnhem Land art, on both bark and rock. These mischievous spirits are attributed with having taught the Indigenous people of the region many things, including hunting, food-gathering and painting skills. More recently, many of the most senior artists have become renowned for their highly innovative depictions of these ancestral stories; they include John Mawurndjul (Kunwinjku) from Maningrida and Philip Gudthaykudthay (Liyagulawumirr) from Ramingining.

CONTEMPORARY PAINTING
Utopia

This community northeast of Alice Springs came into existence in 1977 when the Anmatyerre and Alyawarre people reestablished their community on traditional homelands taken from them to create what had been Utopia Station for 50 years. The service centre for the Utopia community is Arlparra. Initially, batik was produced following, as in other communities, the influence of the women batik artists of Ernabella. Batik was introduced by art coordinator Jenny Green in the early 1980s. In the late 1980s, members of the community started to paint on canvases with acrylics, largely abandoning batik. While some men in the community paint, Utopia is best known for the work produced by its women artists, especially Emily Kam Kngwarreye (Anmatyerre; c 1910–96), and others such as Ada Bird Petyarre (Anmatyerre), Kathleen Petyarre (Anmatyerre/Eastern Alyawarre), Gloria Tamerre Petyarre (Anmatyerre), Angelina Ngal/Pwerl.

Of this group of extremely talented artists, Emily Kam Kngwarreye holds a special place. Her life as an artist commenced only when she was in her late 70s, first with batik and then in the late 1980s with acrylic paints. Thematically, Kngwarreye's paintings are closely connected to

KUNWINJKU PAINTING *Reverend Nganjmirra, with the assistance of Denise Lawungkurr Goodfellow*

I am of the Djalama clan of the Kunwinjku (freshwater people of northwest Arnhem Land). We call ourselves Bininj (the people). Painting has always been very important to Bininj. Old men like my *mowa* (father) and my *mowa's mowa* (grandfather) painted on rocks to teach their children and grandchildren about their country and the animals, like kangaroos and snakes. They were guided in what to paint by the land's ancient spirits, which grew from generations of Bininj living and dying there. Some *stories* were good, showing people gathering food; others were bad, showing people as food for crocodiles! Bininj also paint on tree bark for initiation ceremonies. Balanda (white people) who came to Gunbalanya were interested in the painting, and together Bininj and Balanda decided we should paint for exhibitions down south.

The bark is cut from *manborrogorr* (Darwin stringybark), at Gunumeleng (the time of the first storms) to Bangerreng (the end of the wet season). At this time the bark is easily removed because the sap is flowing. Otherwise, it sticks really hard to the tree and can't be removed. The bark is now called *dolobo*. While wet, it is laid flat and weighed down with stones until it dries. This takes about a month, depending on how much sun there is. Then it is sanded. The traditional way is to use the leaves of *manlarr* (sandpaper fig). Cross-sticks are made from young *manbohdogorr* saplings to keep the bark from twisting. The cross-sticks are tied together with *kunyarl* (bush string) made from *manbornde* (banyan tree).

Our paints come from special white and yellow clay found in fresh water. Red, brown and orange come from rocks, which are on the top of hills or near creeks. It is hard to find good rocks. These rocks are ground on a hard stone and water is added to make the colour bright. Gum is taken from *manmolak* (billygoat/Kakadu plum tree) and mixed in to make the finished paint. Big brushes made from the bark of *manborrogorr* are used to paint the background. The stems of *manyilk* (sedge) are split and chewed to make small brushes for *rarrk* (cross-hatching) – the fine lines are drawn at angles to each other and used to fill in the figure. The *rarrk* is different for each clan. Even the thickness of the line depends on your *moiety* (skin classification). People belonging to the Duwa *moiety* paint thick lines, while Yirridja people paint thin ones. If a Yirridja artist wants to paint thick lines, he must ask a Duwa person either for permission, or to do it for him. This person can be a father or their father's brothers or sisters (children and mothers share one *moiety*; fathers have the other). If the artist wants to paint another's Dreaming, then again he must ask permission. For instance, if a man with Water Python Dreaming wanted to paint Crocodile Dreaming, then he would have to ask permission of a person who had that Dreaming. When there is a ceremony, men paint Dreaming animals on their bodies. Red is mainly worn by men who want to scare people; white and yellow are worn by older, wiser men who are highly respected.

both her people's relationship with the land and her totem, the Yam and Emu Woman ancestral stories. This is evident throughout, though her paintings, with their beautiful use of textured colour, are simultaneously reminiscent of expressionist paintings of the non-Indigenous art world (not that she was aware of such terms). Another startling feature of her work was the number of stylistic changes made over her painting life of a mere decade. Kngwarreye was selected as one of three Indigenous women artists officially representing Australia in the 1997 Venice Biennale. In 2008 she was honoured with a retrospective in Japan. The National Gallery of Australia in Canberra, the Art Gallery of New South Wales in Sydney and the National Gallery of Victoria in Melbourne hold particularly fine examples of Kngwarreye's paintings.

Ngukurr

Since the late 1980s the artists of Ngukurr, a settlement near Roper Bar in southeastern Arnhem Land (NT), have been producing works using acrylic paints on canvas. People from a number of language groups live at Ngukurr. This is reflected stylistically in the art emerging from this community, as can be seen in paintings by Ginger Riley Munduwalawala (a Mara elder, c 1937–2002), Willie Gububi/Gudapi (Mara; 1916–96), Amy Johnson, Gertie Huddleston (Nameratjara), Angelina George, Dinah Garadji and Barney Ellaga. Although Ancestral Beings feature very prominently, there are many other subjects depicted including bush tucker, seasonal cycles, the cattle industry and mission life. The works of these artists are recognised by their use of vibrant palettes, and differ markedly from the bark painting and associated art of their contemporaries in other regions of Arnhem Land.

Metropolitan & Rural Artists

The output and creativity of work being produced in the desert regions, Arnhem Land, Far North Queensland and Kimberley regions has sometimes resulted in the work of Indigenous artists based in metropolitan and rural regions, especially in the southern states, being somewhat overshadowed. However, this has changed markedly in the past decade with many artists achieving national and international renown, and representation in major public galleries and museums in Australia and overseas.

Subject matter covers myriad issues, including land, dispossession, dislocation, oppression, recollection, the stolen generations, assimilation, effects of Christianity, revival of cultural practices such as weaving, cloak-making and shellwork, survival, satire, reclamation of identity and cultural pride, and political injustices and international influences of the past 200-plus years. Through the use of every form of media, access to the internet, a sophisticated approach, and the capacity to engage with and challenge non-Indigenous stereotypes, the work of Indigenous artists reflects the strength, unity and diversity of contemporary Indigenous culture.

ARTEFACTS & CRAFTS

Objects traditionally made for practical or ceremonial uses, such as weapons and musical instruments, often featured intricate and symbolic decoration. In recent years many communities have also developed nontraditional craft forms that have created employment and income, such as weavings and objects, and the growing tourist trade has seen demand and production increase steadily.

Didgeridoo (Yidaki)

The most widespread craft objects seen for sale these days are didgeridoos. There has been a phenomenal boom in their popularity and they can be found in outlets around the country, although not always made by an Indigenous artisan.

Originally they were (and still are in many communities) used as ceremonial musical instruments by Indigenous people, the Yolngu in Arnhem Land (where they are known as *yidaki*). The traditional instrument was made from particular eucalypt branches that had been hollowed out by termites, and sometimes from bamboo, a plant that was introduced by the Macassans. The tubes are often fitted with a wax mouthpiece made from sugarbag (native honeybee wax) and decorated with traditional designs.

Although they may look pretty, many didgeridoos made these days bear little relation to traditional ones: they may be made from the wrong or inferior wood, have been hollowed out using mechanical or other means, have poor sound quality, and may have never had an Indigenous person anywhere near them, since many have been manufactured overseas or by visiting backpackers. However, those made by Indigenous people, particularly musicians, have a magnificent sound and have been used in traditional and contemporary performances, including especially commissioned operas.

'The traditional instrument was made from particular eucalypt branches hollowed out by termites'

PANDANUS WEAVING *Esther Managku, with the assistance of Denise Lawungkurr Goodfellow*

First you go into the bush to get that *manbelk* (pandanus). The best ones have long, long leaves. They can't have (insect) holes in them. They high up, so you get hook stick (inverted fork of a branch) and you bring those leaves down, wrap them in your hand and then pull them out of the tree. Then those leaves are broken (split in sections with the thumb) and the little prickles are taken off. Then you boil him with colour.

There are many colours and they come from many plants. Yellow is from the root of two trees – *mandjundum* (*Pogonobolus reticulatum*) and *mangukmayin* (cheesefruit; *Morinda citrifolia*). You dig him up with crowbar and digging stick. Sometimes those roots go straight down. Hard work that one. We put that colour in a billy can with the pandanus. First of all we make him yellow, that pandanus. And after that if we take the ashes from where you make your fire, you can make him turn to red. I tell you straight (I tell you the truth)! To make green I put dry pandanus in the fire. Then I take those ashes and put them in the billy can and make him little bit green (pale green) in colour. Other colours come from grass roots. *Wirdilwirdil* (*Haemodorum coccineum*) is that small grass. *Wirndilk* is a bigger grass (*Haemodorum*). I wash those roots, take the skin off with a knife, then smash the roots with a stone and put it in the billy can. But this one I don't put ashes. It turn to pink, light purple, dark purple. If I have lots I can cook it in a drum. February is purple time. We call that time *gudjewg* (wet season). But March/April is good too. That time we call *banggereng*. Those *gundalk* (grasses) start getting seed then.

Each billy can and each colour separate together (colours are made in separate containers). Then you hang that pandanus out to dry. I leave it there in the hot sun. Then you thread him (put a pandanus strand through the eye of a large needle). Then you hold that bunch of pandanus – make him straight. You stitch (blanket stitch) and then you pull them stitches tight. I make him bend (fold the sewn pandanus over). I make a hole here tight. Then go (stitch) in same hole. I learned this weaving from my teacher when I was in the school. Her country was at Gunbalanya (northwest Arnhem Land). She the same skin colour as me. I don't know the number how old I was when I learn, maybe six year old; that's the time I been start, maybe even seven or eight. That's a long time to make baskets – more than 60 years. My mother she didn't know how to make this type of basket, only *gundjabarrk* (shoulder bag), *djerret* (string bag), *balabala* (floor mat), *walabi* (net for catching fish) and *mandjabo* (big net for catching fish). They use that medicine tree – *mangolk*, and also *manbudbud, manwonge* and *manbonde* – all got string.

When we make big mats we sit on them, on the floor. Miriam my *dada* (little sister) she can make them, but she got bad eye now. I now want to teach my other *dada*, Lawungkurr… If I feel good I can make basket with handle, or without. Tablemats too. I can make two baskets in one sun. I start morning time. By afternoon I finished.

Fibre Art & Weaving

Articles made from fibres are a major art form among women, although in some regions men also made woven objects as ceremonial and hunting tools. String or twine was traditionally made from bark, grass, leaves, roots and other materials, hand-spun and dyed with natural pigments, then woven to make dilly bags, baskets, garments, fishing nets and other items. Strands or fibres from the leaves of the pandanus palm (and other fibrous palms or grasses) were also woven to make dillybags and mats. While all these objects have utilitarian purposes, many also have ritual uses and were often painted with natural pigments. Exquisite contemporary fibre works are sold by many art centres and represented in numerous public galleries and museums. Likewise, artists are highly innovative in creating woven sculptures.

The Outback Environment
Dave Fuller & Kylie Strelan

THE LAND

SA's low and unreliable rainfall has resulted in water from the Murray River being piped over long distances to ensure the survival of many communities, including Adelaide. More than 50% of South Australians depend entirely on the Murray for their water supply, and this figure can rise to 90% in drought years.

Parts of the Australian outback are among the world's oldest land surfaces. Australia's last great mountain-building events took place over 300 million years ago, and it's hard to believe that Uluru was once part of a mountain range that would have rivalled the Andes in height. Erosion and the relentless cycle of drought and flood have leached the nutrients away from Australia's ancient soils and prevented the creation of new soils, resulting in the vast sandy plains of the Australian outback.

The Stuart Hwy passes through some of the lowest, flattest and driest parts of Australia, but there are numerous ranges and individual mountains scattered through the outback. At 1531m, Mt Zeil is not remarkable by world standards, but it is the highest mountain west of the Great Dividing Range. The rocky ranges of the outback provide important refuges for a diverse collection of plants and animals, and are significant in the ancient song lines and *stories* (accounts of the Dreaming which link into the law) of the traditional Aboriginal custodians of these areas.

In the outback you will drive past huge salt or clay pans that rarely fill with water. These may be dry for decades, but when there is an abundance of rain they become important arid wetland systems: they hold water long after the surrounding landscape has dried out and are crucial to the survival of many plants and animals, especially those that require inundation during their life cycles.

While spectacular geological formations are characteristics of the south and central deserts, it is the extensive river systems and wetlands that herald your arrival in the Top End. The sandstone escarpment and plateau of western Arnhem Land is a magnificent sight, but the life-sustaining floodplains at its base are just as impressive.

THE LAND & INDIGENOUS PEOPLES Dr Irene Watson

ABOUT THE AUTHORS

Dave Fuller has worked for the past 18 years as a parks and wildlife ranger, and Kylie Strelan is an editor with an environmental consultancy. The author of 'the Land & Indigenous Peoples' section, Dr Irene Watson, works at the University of South Australia. For more biographical information, see p317.

The earth is our sacred relative; it is a relationship that is based on nurturing, caring and sharing. From birth we learn of the sacredness of all living things. Every aspect of the natural world is honoured and respected, and we learn to tread lightly on the earth.

The spirit of creation is in all things, for all life forms are related. The philosophy of respect for all living things is an idea central to Aboriginal spirituality and is an idea that nurtured and kept the land in a pristine state prior to colonisation.

The Spirit in the Land

The land is sacred because the essence of our spirituality lies in the earth; our spirit guides are resting in the mountains, in the rocks and in the rivers, and they are everywhere in the land. The land is sacred because it carries the footsteps of our spirit ancestors as they walked every part of it, laying tracks and spiritual songs across the country. The ancestors lie sleeping deep in the earth and we are responsible for the care of their places of rest, for their creative powers are alive and influence all things still in the natural world.

If these spirits are disturbed, so too are the natural order and cycles of life. Where sacred sites are destroyed we believe the ancestors are disturbed and will no longer protect or provide for the people. As a result of damaged or destroyed sacred sites, natural disasters and sickness may occur and afflict communities who have not fulfilled their cultural obligations as custodians. By neglecting our spiritual and cultural obligations we bring disharmony to the country and the community.

The Relationship to the Land

The idea of the land being terra nullius, or a vast empty space across which we range sporadically, is a myth. We know the land intimately: every rock and every river has a name and is remembered in the Dreaming, as it is still remembered today.

To own the land as a piece of real estate, as a 'property', is an idea remote to Aboriginal people. Our relationship to the land is considerably more complex. The land cannot be treated as a consumable, which can be traded or sold. We believe the land cannot be sold.

We have always lived as a part of the natural world, and we take from the environment only what is needed to sustain life; we nurture the land as we do ourselves, for we are one.

The land is both nurturer and teacher from which all life forms grow; all life is inseparably linked. The Aboriginal relationship to the land carries with it both obligations and rights. The relationship to land is at once one of traditional owner and of custodian. It is a relationship that is difficult to explain in a foreign language, because the term 'owner' has different meanings across cultures. Ownership is not viewed in relation to ownership of material goods, but is more accurately viewed as in possession of other values: knowledge, culture and law business, a relationship, a problem, a dispute, a ceremony.

The idea of Aboriginal ownership is not exclusive, and it does not define the owned object as a commodity. Instead, that which is owned is defined as the concern of a limited group of people who stand in a particular relationship to the owner, and whose various responsibilities depend on that relationship.

Managers & Bosses

There are both managers and bosses for country, and each party has a different responsibility or right. The manager is the custodian and the boss is the owner. Naming the parties a manager or a boss is simply a way of discerning between custodian and owner, although in reality these two roles are not always strictly separate and are often merged to become one.

Some of these responsibilities are made known to the members of an Aboriginal community through songs and ceremonies. For example, there may be a particular obligation not to kill the females of a certain animal, in order to preserve the species.

When traditional custodians and/or owners approach their country they will talk to the spirit ancestor of the place. They will tell them who they are and also who they may have brought with them to the place. When food is taken from the land, thanks are given to the ancestors. Nothing is assumed or taken for granted, not even the next meal. We are always seeking permission from the spirit world for our actions.

The Devil's Marbles (known as Karlu Karlu in the local Aboriginal languages) is an important Aboriginal Dreaming site. For fascinating stories from women of the area go to www.clc.org.au /OurLand/land_management/reports/report 2-karlu-karlu.asp.

Bushfires and Bushtucker and *The Flaming Desert*, both books written by renowned central Australian botanist-ecologist Peter Latz, are well worth a read. Find them in Alice Springs bookshops.

Lake Eyre has filled only three times in the last century. When filled, it takes up an area of about 9500 sq km and resembles a giant aviary.

WHY WOULD YOU WANT TO LIVE IN THE DESERT?

'This is home. I love the colours – the blue sky, red sand, red rocks – and the big, open spaces. And when it does rain, and you smell that rain on the wind in the desert, that's something special.'
Andrew Schubert, senior ranger at Finke Gorge National Park, has lived in central Australia for the last 20 years.

ABORIGINAL LAND MANAGEMENT *Barry Hunter*

For more than 50,000 years Aboriginal and Torres Strait Islander peoples have occupied the full range of environments within Australia. Indigenous people have successfully utilised and renewed the country, using an accumulated intimate knowledge of the land, and have implemented innovative management regimes with traditional customs to keep the country healthy and productive.

Through this long-term use and occupation, Indigenous people developed an intimate understanding of the environment including the flora and fauna, and the environmental conditions. This knowledge was crucial for long-term survival in a land that can be harsh and uninviting at the best of times. The land has always nurtured and provided for Indigenous people, through meats like kangaroo and emu or vegetables like yams and sweet potatoes. However, the land means a great deal more than that – it also provides spiritual strength. Through *story* places (where special Dreaming events occurred) and Dreaming tracks throughout the landscape, our attachment to land provides us with our identity – where we come from as Aboriginal people, who we are, where our land is, our languages and our social structure.

The land is all important. However, with invasion many Aboriginal people were denied access to their land – they were killed, dispersed or taken away to Aboriginal missions. This has had a variety of effects on Aboriginal people, including separation from family, loss of identity and the myriad social problems that accompany these things, such as alcohol abuse and unemployment.

Nevertheless, Aboriginal occupation and day-to-day use have been, and in many places continue to be, significant factors in maintaining the landscape. Firestick farming (burning off) is a well-documented technique Aboriginal people used to renew and manage the land. In most areas burning off the country with fire was, and in some areas continues to be, an annual occurrence. In the north of Australia it is carried out at the beginning of the cool Dry season. Firestick farming serves two main purposes. One is to decrease the chance of a bushfire by reducing the vegetation build-up after a wet season. This vegetation could be fuel for a major fire. Secondly, fire is used to clear the country and encourage new growth. This new growth attracts wildlife such as kangaroos and other species, which are drawn to nibble on the soft, new shoots sprouting after the fire.

Although much of the special knowledge of the environment has been lost due to the various impacts upon traditional culture, a great deal still exists. Aboriginal people's special attachment to land is tied to their social, cultural and economic wellbeing. Understanding this attachment can provide a good insight into the way Aboriginal people used and continue to use the land, and their aspirations for looking after their 'country'. Many Aboriginal and Torres Strait Islander people want to play a role in managing their country. Since invasion, Australia has lost a large percentage of its native vegetation and many native species are in danger of extinction. For Australia to maintain its unique environmental credentials, it needs Aboriginal people and their knowledge to play a role in environmental management.

Barry Hunter is an Indigenous Land Management Facilitator for the Balkanu Cape York Development Corporation in Queensland. For more biographical information, see p318.

The boundaries between different Aboriginal clans or nations are sometimes marked. These boundaries are not straight lines but may be determined by the footsteps and tracks of the ancestors, by bends in the creek or the river, the rain shadow, trees or rocks. Some regions were shared between different Aboriginal peoples and some were restricted, with strict rules for obtaining permission to travel across the country.

For guaranteed wildlife sightings, visit the Alice Springs Desert Park (p175) or the Territory Wildlife Park near Darwin (p239).

WILDLIFE

The timing of your visit to central Australia will determine the variety and types of wildlife you are likely to see. In January, a flooded wetland in the north will be teeming with wildlife, whereas a searing hot January day in the desert may leave you wondering if anything lives there at all apart from flies and ants.

WORKING TOGETHER – JOINT MANAGEMENT OF NATIONAL PARKS *Greg Peckham*

Four national parks in South Australia and 32 in the Northern Territory are managed jointly by traditional owners and state, territory or federal governments. Partnerships have been born out of the recognition of the traditional owners and their ties to country, bringing both parties together to manage land for conservation.

'I spent 10 years working at Nitmiluk and I reckon we led the way with the joint management model that was developed there. Joint management offers traineeships for the young fellas, economic opportunities for the broader Jawoyn community, and the chance for Jawoyn to get out on their land. I loved being a ranger at Nitmiluk because every day I got to work on my own country. Now, I'm enjoying learning about other people's country up here in the wetlands.'

Greg Peckham, ranger, Wildman River Ranger Station, (Proposed) Mary River National Park

---

Animals

BIRDS

The rivers and wetlands of both South Australia (SA) and the Northern Territory (NT) are home to an incredible variety of birds, as well as playing host to migratory birds from other parts of Australia and the world. Away from water, birdwatchers will need to put in more time and effort, as the birds of the dry desert regions are generally more secretive than many of their coastal cousins. Early morning and late afternoon are the best times for birdwatching. Some species are rarely seen, while others hang around in flocks so large that you can't possibly miss them. Australia is in fact the perfect place for lazy birdwatchers because many of our birds are noisy and easily identifiable, such as pink cockatoos, red-tailed black cockatoos, sulphur-crested cockatoos, galahs, kookaburras, parrots and corellas. Australia's majestic wedge-tailed eagles are a common sight along the Stuart Hwy and you will often hear a whistling kite before you see it.

Field Guide to Australian Birds by Michael Morcombe is a well-designed field guide, with beautiful colour illustrations and just the right amount of detail.

REPTILES

Despite their abundance in Australia, most reptiles are difficult to observe because many of them are inactive during hot summer days and hibernate during winter. Snakes tend to move around more between October and April, and you may spot a large, active daytime predator such as a perentie or a sand goanna. In southern and central Australia, following an ant trail in the red desert sand may lead you to a small thorny devil taking lunch. In the tropical woodlands of the north, the larger frill-necked lizards spend most of their days in trees eating insects and termites. When a 'frilly' is frightened or defending its territory, its defensive strategy is to open its mouth, widen its impressive frill and hiss. This menacing show is all bluff and a frilly will generally run very fast on its two hind legs in the opposite direction when the show is over. In June and July, when many other reptile species are hibernating, Australia's best-known reptiles – the freshwater and estuarine crocodiles – can be seen warming themselves on the banks of Top End rivers.

If you stay overnight in Alice Springs, a visit to Simpsons Gap just before dark is your best bet for seeing black-footed rock wallabies in their natural environment.

MAMMALS

Most of Australia's mammals are small, secretive and nocturnal, so you're unlikely to see them in the wild. Of the larger mammals, you may see the occasional dingo but are more likely to see mobs of Australia's unique marsupial macropods, either bounding away from you, grazing quietly with ears twitching or resting in the shade of a tree. In southern and central Australia, the most common macropod species is the red kangaroo, the world's largest marsupial. Males are a reddish brown colour and can grow to 2m, while females are smaller with blue grey colouring. Yellow-footed rock wallabies are making a comeback in the Flinders Ranges, thanks in part to a feral-animal eradication program. In the north, the most common macropod species is the agile wallaby, which grows to about 1m and has a distinct white line from the tip of its nose to its eye.

FERAL ANIMALS

The introduction of animals from other countries in the last 200 years has contributed significantly to the fragmentation of ecosystems in Australia. Introduced species include foxes, rabbits, cats, pigs, goats, donkeys, horses, camels, starlings, sparrows, cane toads, mosquitofish and carp. They each bring a unique suite of problems as they carve out a niche for themselves in their new environment – some as predators of native animals, others as competitors for the limited resources of food, water and shelter.

> Join a community 'toad muster' to help keep the cane toad count down. To learn more about how cane toads affect biodiversity, and how you can help, go to www .frogwatch.com.au.

Plants

There is a high diversity of vegetation between Adelaide and Darwin and the regions in between, reflecting the diversity in climate and rainfall. Much of the Top End receives an annual rainfall of around 1600mm, while the desert regions of SA receive less than 150mm (median) of annual rainfall.

Commonly known as wattles in Australia, acacia species generally dominate the woodlands that occupy large areas of the arid zone, with mulga varieties having by far the largest representation. Mulga has varying forms, from a multibranched shrub of 1m to an erect tree of 7m. Once used by Aboriginal people to make spear throwers and long, narrow shields, the wood is very hard and is used for turning, craftwork and fence posts. Gidgee is another acacia that covers large areas of central Australia.

> A visit to the 200-hectare Australian Arid Lands Botanic Garden (p137), on the Stuart Hwy in Port Augusta, is a great way to see a range of different arid-zone plants in one place. Check out the website at www .australian-aridlands -botanic-garden.org.

Some of the deserts of southern and central Australia are surprisingly well vegetated, usually with tough, dry chenopod shrublands (such as saltbush) and spinifex-dominated hummock grasslands. After heavy rains, seeds that have been lying dormant are triggered into life and the desert is then blanketed in wildflowers. The brightly coloured poached-egg daisy is one of the most abundant and conspicuous wildflowers.

You'll see a wide variety of eucalypt species, from multistemmed mallee to giant, shade-giving coolibahs. The bright green leaves and glossy white bark of the ghost gum are a common sight in tropical northern Australia, but it's around Alice Springs that they've achieved most of their fame, largely through the work of artists such as Albert Namatjira. The impressive river red gums lining the creeks of the Flinders Ranges and the dry

---

SIX EASY WAYS TO AVOID HARMING WILDLIFE

- Take your rubbish with you so critters don't choke on it.
- Have small campfires to leave more habitat for wildlife.
- Don't poo near waterways.
- Don't drive off-road.
- Drive during daylight hours.
- Don't feed wildlife.

JOEY FACTORIES

A kangaroo's breeding cycle will be suspended during periods of severe drought. In a good year, however, a doe may have an unweaned joey on foot, one suckling from inside the pouch and a dormant embryo in the uterus. The embryo is prevented from developing by the suckling of the joey in the pouch, but it's ready for birth within a day of that joey's departure. Each of the offspring feeds only from one teat and each teat supplies a different mix of nutrients depending on the age of the young.

---

riverbeds of central Australia offer refuge to a variety of wildlife, such as bats, birds, small mammals, lizards and insects. One of the dominant Top End eucalypts is the Darwin woollybutt, a tall tree that produces large clusters of bright orange flowers (usually from May to August). Whether flowering or not, it is easily recognisable by the 'stocking' of rough, dark-coloured bark on its lower trunk, which is in stark contrast to the smooth, white upper trunk and branches.

WEEDS

Plant invasion can destroy wildlife habitats and make pastoral and cropping land unusable – the cost in environmental and economic terms is incalculable.

In northern Australia, weeds such as para grass, mimosa and salvinia have invaded floodplains and choked out native vegetation, while gamba grass has devastated large areas of native woodlands. In the sandy riverbeds of central and Southern Australia, buffel grass is threatening entire ecosystems. Add fire to the mix and you have a recipe for disaster for native vegetation, as weeds such as buffel and gamba are highly flammable and recover quickly after being burnt; they are thus able to regenerate faster than the native plants in the area.

Established in the 1800s, Goyder's Line (see p120) marks the 250mm rainfall isobar as the recommended northern limit for cropping in SA. With the increase in temperature and reduction in rainfall, there have been suggestions that the line should shift as far south as the Clare Valley.

Adelaide & Around

Sophisticated, cultured, neat-casual – this is the self-image Adelaide projects, a nod to the days of free colonisation without the 'penal colony' taint. Adelaidians may remind you of their convict-free status, but the city's stuffy, affluent origins did more to inhibit development than promote it. Bogged in the old-school doldrums and painfully short on charisma, this was a pious, introspective place. As Paul Kelly sang in 'Adelaide': 'Find me a bar or a girl or guitar where do you go on a Saturday night?/…And the streets are so wide everybody's inside/Sitting in the same chairs they were sitting in last year'.

But these days – thanks in part to progressive premier Don Dunstan, who started to shake things up in the '70s – things are much improved. Multicultural flavours infuse Adelaide's restaurants, there are pumping pub, arts and live-music scenes, and the city's festival calendar has vanquished dull Saturday nights. And, of course, there's the local wine. Residents flush at the prospect of a punchy McLaren Vale Shiraz or summer-scented Clare Riesling.

That said, a subtle conservatism remains. 'What school did you go to?' is a common salvo from those unsure of your place in the social hierarchy, while countercultural urges bubble up through Adelaide's countless sex shops, kung-fu dojos and canyon-sized bottle shops.

Just down the tram tracks is beachy Glenelg – Adelaide with its guard down and boardshorts up – and Port Adelaide, a historic enclave fast becoming South Australia's version of Fremantle. Inland, Adelaide's plains rise to the Adelaide Hills, just minutes up the freeway. The Hills' gorgeous valley folds, old-fangled towns and cool-climate vineyards are all close at hand.

HIGHLIGHTS

- Sniffing out the ripest cheese, fullest fruit and strongest coffee at Adelaide's world-class **Central Market** (p51)
- Dining out – feasting or snacking – on Rundle St in Adelaide's **East End** (p58)
- Exploring the historic streets and museums in **Port Adelaide** (p65)
- Diving headlong into musical frenzy at **WOMADelaide** (p54)
- Wobbling between cool-climate vineyards in the **Adelaide Hills Wine Region** (p69)
- Catching a gig at the **Grace Emily** (p59), the rockin' heart of Adelaide's ubercool West End

★ Port Adelaide

Grace Emily Hotel ★ ★ WOMADelaide
★ East End
★ Central Market

Adelaide Hills ★ Wine Region

■ TELEPHONE CODE: ☎ 08   ■ www.adelaidecitycouncil.com   ■ www.visitadelaidehills.com.au

ADELAIDE

pop 1,158,300

HISTORY

There have been a lot of jokes about Adelaide over the years – 'Adelaide is well laid out because it's been dead so long', and the nickname 'the Delayed' (Adelaide's time zone is 30 minutes behind Sydney and Melbourne) spring to mind – but this rock-solid city has weathered the jibes with grace. Indeed, the city *is* well laid out – no other Australian capital had such a complete, functional town plan as its basis. Most cities developed randomly and sporadically; even Canberra failed to adhere fully to Walter Burley Griffin's grand urban plans. Against this trend, Adelaide has remained true to its design: a pure, orderly grid that has informed both its growth and social consciousness.

But the choice of Adelaide's location wasn't clear-cut: Colonel William Light, assigned the task of establishing the South Australian capital, had to argue with Governor Hindmarsh and the South Australian Commissioners in London who wanted a coastal city built at Port Lincoln or Encounter Bay, and before that at Kingscote on Kangaroo Island. Much squabbling transpired but Light eventually won through, seeing that Adelaide's fertile plains, river and rain-catching hills and were firm footings on which to build the capital. So said the Colonel:

> The reasons that led me to fix Adelaide where it is I do not expect to be generally understood or calmly judged of at present. My enemies, however, by disputing their validity in every particular, have done me the good service of fixing the whole of the responsibility upon me. I am perfectly willing to bear it; and I leave it to posterity, and not to them, to decide whether I am entitled to praise or to blame.

We vote praise!

ORIENTATION

Adelaide's city grid is bordered by North, East, South and West Tces. King William St bisects the city north–south; most cross-streets change names here. Victoria Sq, the city's geographical centre, has bus stops and the Glenelg tram terminus. Franklin St, west of Victoria Sq, has the regional bus station.

Heading north, King William St crosses the River Torrens then rises into elevated North Adelaide. In the East End, Rundle St is Adelaide's social epicentre, dotted with restaurants, bookshops, retro-chic boutiques and independent cinemas. Heading west Rundle St becomes Rundle Mall, the main shopping strip, then Hindley St in the West End, with its grungy ramble of bars, clubs and strip joints.

Maps

The free maps from the South Australian Visitor & Travel Centre (p50) are fine for navigating your way around central Adelaide.

For more detailed maps:

Map Shop (Map p48; ☎ 8231 2033; www.mapshop .net.au; 6-10 Peel St; ☻ 9am-5.30pm Mon-Fri, to 12.30pm Sat) Maps, charts and guides for walking, hiking and touring, plus GPS sales and advice.

Royal Automobile Association of South Australia (RAA; Map p48; ☎ 8202 4600; www.raa.net; 55 Hindmarsh Sq; ☻ 8.30am-5pm Mon-Fri, 9am-noon Sat) RAA, Hema and Westprint maps.

INFORMATION

Bookshops

ABC Shop (Map p48; ☎ 8410 0567; www.shop.abc .net.au; level 2, Myer Centre, Rundle Mall; ☻ 9am-5.30pm Mon-Fri, to 5pm Sat)

Adelaide Booksellers (Map p48; ☎ 8410 0216; www.adelaidebooksellers.com.au; 1st fl, 6a Rundle Mall; ☻ 9.30am-5.30pm Mon-Fri, 10am-4pm Sat) Quality secondhand books.

Dymocks Booksellers (Map p48; ☎ 8223 5380; 135 Rundle Mall; ☻ 9am-6pm Mon-Thu, to 9pm Fri, to 5.30pm Sat, 11am-5pm Sun) Mainstream books & mags.

Imprints Booksellers (Map p48; ☎ 8231 4454; www.imprints.com.au; 107 Hindley St; ☻ 9am-6pm Mon, Tue & Sat, to 9pm Wed-Fri, 11am-6pm Sun) Jazz, floorboards, Persian rugs and the best books in print.

Mary Martin Bookshop (Map p48; ☎ 8359 3525; www.marymartin.com.au; 249 Rundle St; ☻ 10am-late) Adelaide's oldest bookshop (since 1945).

Emergency

Ambulance (☎ 000 emergency, 13 29 62 non-emergency; www.saambulance.com.au)

Fire (☎ 000 emergency, 8204 3600 nonemergency; www.samfs.sa.gov.au)

Lifeline (☎ 13 11 14; www.lifeline.org.au; ☻ 24hr) Crisis counselling.

Police (Map p48; ☎ 000 emergency, 8303 0525 non-emergency; www.sapolice.sa.gov.au; 26 Hindley St)

RAA Emergency Roadside Assistance (☎ 13 11 11; www.raa.net)

CENTRAL ADELAIDE

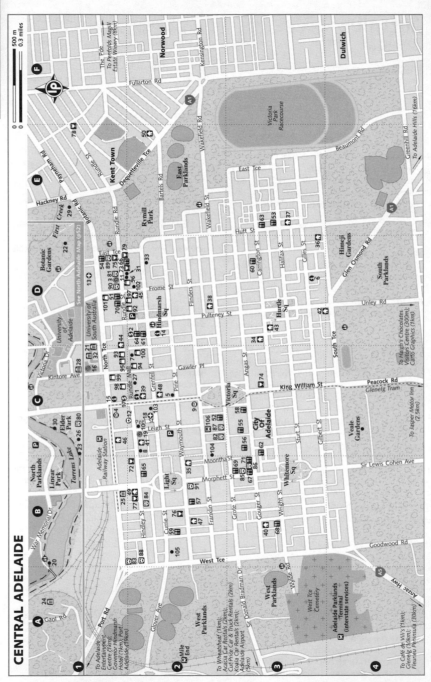

Internet Access

Arena Internet Café (Map p48; ☎ 8223 3481; upstairs, 264 Rundle St; ⏰ 11am-midnight Mon-Thu, 10am-late Fri-Sun)

State Library of South Australia (Map p48; ☎ 8207 7250; www.slsa.sa.gov.au; 1st fl, cnr North Tce & Kintore Ave; ⏰ 10am-8pm Mon-Wed & Fri, to 6pm Thu & Fri, to 5pm Sat & Sun) Free access; book ahead.

Wireless Café (Map p48; ☎ 8212 1266; 53 Hindley St; ⏰ 7am-8pm Mon-Fri, 9am-8pm Sat & Sun, later Dec-Feb)

Medical Services

Corner Chemist (Map p48; ☎ 8231 2460; cnr Pirie & King William Sts; ⏰ 7.45am-5.30pm Mon-Fri)

Emergency Dental Service (☎ 8378 7939 Mon-Fri, 8272 8111 Sat, Sun & after hr) Provides contact details for dentists.

Royal Adelaide Hospital (Map p48; ☎ 8222 4000; www.rah.sa.gov.au; 275 North Tce; ⏰ 24hr) Emergencies department (not for blisters!) and STD clinic.

Traveller's Medical & Vaccination Centre (Map p48; ☎ 1300 658 844, 8212 7522; www.traveldoctor .com.au; 27 Gilbert Pl; ⏰ 9am-5pm Mon-Fri, to 7pm Wed, to 1pm Sat)

Women's & Children's Hospital (Map p52; ☎ 8161 7000; www.cywhs.sa.gov.au; 72 King William Rd, North Adelaide; ⏰ 24hr) Emergency and sexual-assault services.

Money

Banks and ATMs prevail throughout the CBD, particularly around Rundle Mall.

American Express (Map p48; ☎ 1300 139 060; Shop 32, Citi-Centre Arcade, Rundle Mall; ✆ 9am-5pm Mon-Fri, to noon Sat) Foreign currency exchange.

Travelex (Map p48; ☎ 8231 6977; www.travelex.au; Shop 4, Rundle Mall; ✆ 9am-5.30pm Mon-Fri, to 5pm Sat) Foreign-currency exchange.

Post

Australia Post Shop (Map p48; ☎ 13 13 18; www.auspost.com.au; Station Arcade, 136 North Tce; ✆ 9am-5pm Mon-Fri)

Main Post Office (Map p48; ☎ 13 13 18; www.auspost.com.au; 141 King William St; ✆ 8am-5pm Mon-Fri) Poste Restante; have mail addressed to you c/o Poste Restante, Adelaide 5001.

Tourist Information

Adelaide Visitor Information Kiosk (Map p48; ☎ 8203 7611; Rundle Mall; ✆ 10am-5pm Mon-Thu, to 8pm Fri, to 3pm Sat & Sun) Adelaide-specific information and free city-centre walking tours at 9.30am Monday to Friday.

South Australian Visitor & Travel Centre (Map p48; ☎ 1300 655 276; www.southaustralia.com; 18 King William St; ✆ 8.30am-5pm Mon-Fri, 9am-2pm Sat & Sun) Abundantly stocked with leaflets and publications on Adelaide and SA. Superpatient staff and a BASS ticket-selling outlet, too.

Women's Information Service (Map p48; ☎ 1800 188 158, 8303 0590; www.wis.sa.gov.au; Station Arcade, 136 North Tce; ✆ 8.30am-5.30pm Mon-Fri; 🖳) Information and counselling services.

SIGHTS

Most of Adelaide's big-ticket sights are within walking distance of the city centre, with many strung along North Tce. It's also de rigueur to make a day trip out to beachside Glenelg (p63), historic Port Adelaide (p65), or the nearby Adelaide Hills (p66), Barossa Valley (p107) or McLaren Vale (p74) regions.

The **Adelaide Attractions Pass** (☎ 1300 661 711, 9906 2711; www.adelaideattractionspass.com; adult/child $79/59) can be an economical way of seeing the sights; choose six of the 15 wildlife parks, museums and tours available.

Art Galleries

Spend a few hushed hours in the vaulted, parquet-floored **Art Gallery of South Australia** (Map p48; ☎ 8207 7000; www.artgallery.sa.gov.au; North Tce; admission free; ✆ 10am-5pm), which represents the big names in Australian art. Permanent exhibitions include Australian, modern Australian, contemporary Aboriginal, Asian, Islamic and European art (there are 20 bronze Rodins!). Temporary exhibitions occupy the basement. Free audio tours of the Australian collection are insightful, as are the free guided tours (11am and 2pm daily). There's also a bookshop and **Art Gallery Restaurant** (mains $29; ✆ lunch; 😮) to distract you.

For an insight into Adelaide's **public artworks** (including the infamous *Mall's Balls*), pick up a walking-tour map from the visitor centre.

Adelaide's private gallery scene swings between snooty, la-di-dah openings peopled by turtle-necked doyens, and rootsy garage exhibitions in the city's West End. Two West End favourites:

Experimental Art Foundation (Map p48; ☎ 8211 7505; www.eaf.asn.au; Lion Arts Centre, cnr Morphett St & North Tce; admission free; ✆ 11am-5pm Tue-Fri, 2-5pm Sat) A focus on innovation, with a bookshop specialising in film, architecture, culture and design.

Jam Factory Craft & Design Centre (Map p48; ☎ 8410 0727; www.jamfactory.com.au; 19 Morphett St; admission free; ✆ 10am-5pm Mon-Sat, 1-5pm Sun) Quality contemporary local arts and crafts, plus a hell-hot glass-blowing studio (watch from the balcony above).

Museums

The **South Australian Museum** (Map p48; ☎ 8207 7368; www.samuseum.sa.gov.au; North Tce; admission free; ✆ 10am-5pm) digs into Australia's natural history, with special exhibits on whales, Antarctic explorer Sir Douglas Mawson and an Aboriginal Cultures Gallery, displaying artefacts of the Ngarrindjeri people of the Coorong and lower Murray. Free tours are conducted at 11am Monday to Friday; 2pm and 3pm Saturday and Sunday (don't miss the giant squid!). There's a cool cafe (mains $10 to $17; open for lunch) here too.

The engaging **Migration Museum** (Map p48; ☎ 8207 7580; www.history.sa.gov.au; 82 Kintore Ave; admission by donation; ✆ 10am-5pm Mon-Fri, 1-5pm Sat & Sun) tells the social history of the many migrants who have made SA their home. The museum has info on 100-plus nationalities in its database, along with some poignant personal stories.

Only decommissioned in 1988, the **HM Adelaide Gaol Historic Site** (Map p48; ☎ 8231 4062; www.adelaidegaol.org.au; Gaol Rd, Thebarton; admission adult/concession/child $8.50/7/6.50; ✆ 11am-3.30pm Mon-Fri, 1.30am-3.30pm Sun) has a grim vibe, but displays of homemade bongs, weapons and escape devices are amazing. Commentary tapes for self-

ADELAIDE IN...

Two Days

If you're here at Festival, WOMADelaide or Fringe time, lap it up. Otherwise, kick-start your day at the **Central Market** (below) then wander through the **Botanic Gardens** (below), finishing up at the **National Wine Centre** (below). After a few bohemian beers at the **Exeter** (p59), have a ritzy dinner on **Rundle St** (p58). Next day, visit the **South Australian Museum** (opposite) and the **Bradman Collection Museum** (p52). Check out **Tandanya National Aboriginal Cultural Institute** (p53) before riding the tram to **Glenelg** (p63) for an evening swim and fish-and-chips on the sand.

Four Days

Follow the two-day itinerary – perhaps slotting in the **Art Gallery of South Australia** (opposite) and **Jam Factory Craft & Design Centre** (opposite) – then pack a picnic basket of Central Market produce and day-trip out to the nearby **Adelaide Hills** (p66), **McLaren Vale** (p75) or **Barossa Valley** (p111) wine regions. Next day, truck out to the museums and historic centre of **Port Adelaide** (p65), then catch a band at the **Grace Emily** (p59) back in the city and dinner on **Gouger St** (p57).

guided tours; guided tours at 11am, noon and 1pm Sunday. Ghost tours by appointment.

See also the Bradman museum (p52).

Markets

Satisfy both obvious and obscure culinary cravings at the 250-odd stalls in Adelaide's superb **Central Market** (Map p48; ☎ 8203 7203; www.adelaidecentral market.com.au; btwn Grote & Gouger Sts; ☽ 7am-5.30pm Tue, 9am-5.30pm Thu, 7am-9pm Fri, to 3pm Sat). A gluten-free snag from the Gourmet Sausage Shop; a sliver of English stilton from the Smelly Cheese Shop; a tub of blueberry yoghurt from the Yoghurt Shop – you name it, it's all here. Good luck making it out without eating anything (see p57). For market tour details, see p54.

In the East End, don't miss Sunday's **Rundle St Market** (Map p48; ☎ 8203 7203; www.cityofadelaide .com.au; Rundle St; ☽ 11am-4pm Sun), with food stalls, fashion, buskers, jewellery, arts and crafts.

Wine, Beer & Chocolate

Check out the self-guided, interactive 'Wine Discovery Journey' exhibition, paired with tastings of Australian wines, at the very sexy **National Wine Centre of Australia** (Map p48; ☎ 8303 3355; www.wineaustralia.com.au; cnr Botanic & Hackney Rds; exhibition free, tastings $8-16; ☽ 10am-5pm). You'll get an insight into the issues winemakers contend with, and even have your own virtual vintage rated. A heady range of wine appreciation courses (from $55) is also available, and there's a cool cafe here, too.

The 100-year-old **Penfolds Magill Estate Winery** (off Map p48; ☎ 8301 5569; www.penfolds.com .au; 78 Penfolds Rd, Magill; tastings free, mains $42-45; ☽ tastings 10am-5pm daily, lunch Fri, dinner Tue-Sun) is home to

Australia's best-known wine – the legendary Grange. Taste the product at the cellar door, dine at the slick, glass-fronted restaurant, take the 'Heritage Tour' ($15), or steel your wallet for the 'Great Grange Tour' ($150).

You can't possibly come to Adelaide without entertaining thoughts of touring the **Coopers Brewery** (off Map p52; ☎ 8440 1800; www .coopers.com.au; 461 South Rd, Regency Park; 1½hr tour per person $20; ☽ tours 1pm Tue-Fri). Tours take you through the brewhouse, bottling hall and history museum, where you can get stuck into samples of stouts, ales and lagers. Bookings required; minimum age 18. The brewery is in the northern suburbs: grab a cab, or walk 1km from Islington train station.

If you've got a chocolate problem, get guilty at the iconic **Haigh's Chocolates Visitors Centre** (off Map p48; ☎ 8372 7070; www.haighschocolates.com; 154 Greenhill Rd, Parkside; admission free; ☽ 8.30am-5.30pm Mon-Fri, 9am-5pm Sat). Free factory tours (with samples if you're good) take you through the chocolate life-cycle from cacao nut to hand-dipped truffle. Tours run at 11am, 1pm and 2pm Monday to Saturday; bookings essential.

Gardens & Parklands

Meander, jog or chew through your trashy airport novel in the city-fringe **Botanic Gardens** (Map p48; ☎ 8222 9311; www.botanicgardens.sa.gov .au; North Tce; admission free; ☽ 7am-sunset Mon-Fri, 9am-sunset Sat & Sun). Highlights include a restored 1877 palm house, the new waterlily pavilion (housing the gigantic *Victoria amazonica*) and the fabulous steel-and-glass arc of the **Bicentennial Conservatory** (admission adult/child/family $4.50/2.50/9.50; ☽ 10am-5pm), which recreates a tropical rainforest. Free 1½-hour guided walks depart the garden cafe at 10.30am daily.

The city and ritzy North Adelaide are surrounded by a broad band of **parklands**. Colonel William Light, Adelaide's planner, came up with the concept, which has been both a blessing and a curse for the city. Pros: heaps of green space, clean air and sports grounds for the kids. Cons: bone-dry in summer, perverts loitering and a sense that the city is cut off from its suburbs. Convinced he was right, the **statue of Colonel William Light** (Map p52) overlooks the gleaming city office towers from Montefiore Hill.

Adelaide Zoo

Around 1400 exotic and native mammals, birds and reptiles roar, growl and screech at Adelaide's **zoo** (Map p52; ☎ 8267 3255; www.adelaide zoo.com.au; Frome Rd; admission adult/concession/child/family $20/12/16/60; ⏲ 9.30am-5pm). There are free walking tours half hourly, feeding sessions and a children's zoo, but the major drawcard (until the pandas arrive in late 2009 –

pandemonium!) is the Southeast Asian rainforest exhibit.

You can take a river cruise to the zoo from the Festival Centre on **Pop-eye** (Map p48; ☎ 8295 4747; cruises adult/child $10/5; ⏲ hourly 11am-3pm Mon-Fri, every 20min 10.30am-5pm Sat & Sun). Weekends only in winter.

Adelaide Oval

Hailed as the world's prettiest **cricket ground** (Map p52; ☎ 8300 3800; www.cricketsa.com.au; King William Rd, North Adelaide) the Adelaide Oval hosts interstate and international cricket matches, plus South Australian National Football League (SANFL) Aussie Rules matches in winter. A bronze statue of 'The Don' (Sir Donald Bradman) cracks a cover drive out the front. When there's no game you can take a two-hour **tour** (adult/student $10/5; ⏲ 10am Mon-Fri), departing the Phil Ridings Gates on War Memorial Dr.

At the **Bradman Collection Museum** (admission free; ⏲ 9.30am-4.30pm Mon-Fri, gates open-4.30pm match days) devotees of the Don can pore over personal items of the cricketing legend. Call or check the website for tour details.

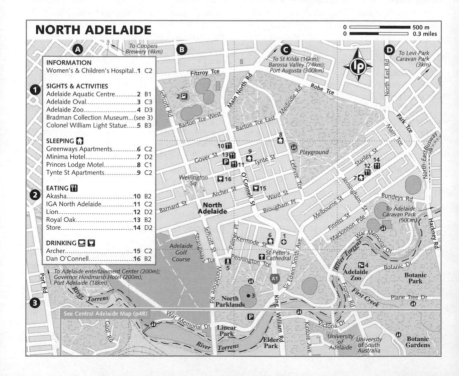

NORTH ADELAIDE

0 — 500 m
0 — 0.3 miles

INFORMATION
Women's & Children's Hospital..**1** C2

SIGHTS & ACTIVITIES
Adelaide Aquatic Centre............**2** B1
Adelaide Oval............................**3** C3
Adelaide Zoo.............................**4** D3
Bradman Collection Museum....(see 3)
Colonel William Light Statue.....**5** B3

SLEEPING
Greenways Apartments..............**6** C2
Minima Hotel..............................**7** D2
Princes Lodge Motel...................**8** C1
Tynte St Apartments...................**9** C2

EATING
Akasha......................................**10** B2
IGA North Adelaide...................**11** C2
Lion...**12** D2
Royal Oak.................................**13** B2
Store...**14** D2

DRINKING
Archer.......................................**15** C2
Dan O'Connell...........................**16** B2

ABORIGINAL AUSTRALIA: TANDANYA NATIONAL ABORIGINAL CULTURAL INSTITUTE

Tandanya (Map p48; ☎ 8224 3200; www.tandanya.com.au; 253 Grenfell St; admission adult/concession/family $5/4/12; ☼ 10am-5pm) offers an insight into the culture of the local Kaurna people, whose territory extends south to Cape Jervis and north to Port Wakefield. Inside are interactive displays on living with the land, galleries, gifts and a cafe. There are didgeridoo or Torres Strait Islander dance performances at noon from Tuesday to Sunday, plus Indigenous short film and documentary screenings in the theatre.

ACTIVITIES
Cycling & Walking

Adelaide is pancake flat – perfect for cycling and walking (if it's not too hot!). You can take your bike on trams during off-peak periods and trains any time, but not buses.

There are free guided walks in the Botanic Gardens (p51), plus self-guided city walks detailed in brochures from the South Australian Visitor & Travel Centre (p50). The riverside **Linear Park** (Map p48) is a 40km walking/cycling path running from Glenelg to the foot of the Adelaide Hills, mainly along the River Torrens. Another popular hiking trail is the **Waterfall Gully Track** (Map p67; 1½ hours return) up to Mt Lofty summit and back, departing the end of Waterfall Gully Rd.

Mountain bikers should check out the **Eagle Mountain Bike Park** (Map p67; ☎ 8416 6677; www.bikesa.asn.au; admission free; ☼ dawn-dusk) in the Adelaide Hills; phone for directions. If you're feeling hyperactive, wheel off along the **Mawson Trail** (www.southaustraliantrails.com), from Adelaide to Blinman in the Flinders Ranges. **Ecotrek** (☎ 8346 4155; www.ecotrek.com.au) runs one-day cycling tours of the Adelaide Hills ($207).

Useful organisations:

Bicycle SA (Map p48; ☎ 8168 9999; www.bikesa.asn.au; 111 Franklin St; ☼ 9am-5pm) Free city bikes (see p62), cycling maps and info, plus details on the Mawson Trail from Adelaide to the Flinders Ranges.

Bikeabout (☎ 0413-525 733; www.bikeabout.com.au) Cycling day trips to the Barossa Valley and coast ($75).

Linear Park Hire (Map p48; ☎ 0400-596 065; Elder Park; bikes per day $20; ☼ 9am-5pm) Bike hire.

Trails SA (www.southaustraliantrails.com) SA cycling and hiking trail info. Download their *40 Great South Australian Short Walks* brochure.

Water Activities

Adelaide gets *reeeeally* hot in summer. For details on Adelaide's beaches, see p63. The closest swimming pool to the city is the **Adelaide Aquatic Centre** (Map p52; ☎ 8344 4411; Jeffcott Rd, North Adelaide; casual swim adult/concession/child $6.50/5.60/5; ☼ 5am-10pm Mon-Sat, 7am-8pm Sun), with swimming and diving pools, gym, sauna, spa and other facilities.

Maybe if you squint…no, it still doesn't look like Venice…but cruising the River Torrens on the **Adelaide Gondola** (Map p48; ☎ 8358 1800; www.adelaidegondola.com.au; 4 people per 40min $100) may still float your boat. You can even order a bottle of wine!

See also Pop-eye (opposite) and Captain Jolley's Paddle Boats (below).

For the low-down on local scuba-diving, skin-diving and kiteboarding, see p63.

ADELAIDE FOR CHILDREN

The free monthly paper **Adelaide's Child** (www.adelaideschild.com.au), available at cafes and libraries, is largely advertorial but contains comprehensive events listings. *Adelaide for Kids: A Guide for Parents*, by James Muecke, has comprehensive details and is available at bookshops.

There are few kids who won't love the **tram ride** from the city down to Glenelg (kids under five ride for free!). You may have trouble getting them off the tram – the lure of a high-speed dash across the bay with **Hel-a-va Jet Boats** (p63) might help. If it's a scorcher, consider a splash in the shallows at **Glenelg Beach**. You can hire the requisite water toys from **Beach Hire** (p63), and finish up with some fish-and-chips on the lawns.

During school holidays, the **South Australian Museum** (p50), **State Library of South Australia** (p49), **Art Gallery of South Australia** (p50), **Adelaide Zoo** (opposite) and **Botanic Gardens** (p51) run inspired kid- and family-oriented programs with accessible and interactive general displays.

Along North Tce every Sunday, Adelaide City Council runs **Sunday Fundays** (☎ 8207 7575; www.adelaidecitycouncil.com; ☼ 2-4pm Sun), featuring giant games, juggling workshops, clowns and musical entertainment. Not far away, **Captain Jolley's Paddle Boats** (Map p48; ☎ 8223 5863; Jolley's La; hire per 30min $12; ☼ 10am-5pm Sat, Sun & school holidays) make a splash on the River Torrens.

Live out the kids' (and perhaps your own) *Charlie and the Chocolate Factory* dreams on a tour at **Haigh's Chocolates Visitors Centre** (p51). Not the best for young diets, perhaps, but the chocolates sure are Wonka-worthy.

In Port Adelaide, check out the **Kids' Port Walk** (p66), **Maritime Museum** (p66) and **Seahorse Farm** (p66).

If you've got a few spare hours and a car, traipse north to **St Kilda** (p66). The **adventure playground** here is the best you'll ever see, and there's a **mangrove boardwalk**.

Dial-An-Angel (☎ 8267 3700; www.dialanangel .com.au) provides nannies and babysitters.

TOURS

You can circle around the main Adelaide sights on the free city buses (p62), or on the **Adelaide Explorer** (☎ 8293 2966), a jump-on–jump-off tram-bus. Two-day tickets cover the city and coast (adult/child $30/10), or city only ($25/10); there are three departures daily. For details on boat cruises, see Adelaide Zoo (p52), Port Adelaide (p66) and Glenelg (p63).

Beyond the city a plethora of day tours covers the Adelaide Hills (p68), Fleurieu Peninsula (p75) and Barossa Valley (p108). Note that one-day trips to the Flinders Ranges and Kangaroo Island are very rushed and not recommended.

Adelaide-focused operators:

Adelaide Sightseeing (☎ 1300 769 762, 8231 4144; www.adelaidesightseeing.com.au) Runs a city-highlights tour ($55) incl North Tce, Glenelg, Haigh's Chocolates and the Adelaide Oval (among other sights). Barossa Valley, Clare Valley & Fleurieu Peninsula tours also available.

Adelaide's Top Food & Wine Tours (☎ 8263 0265; www.topfoodandwinetours.com.au) Uncovers SA's gastronomic soul with dawn ($48) and morning ($35) tours of the buzzing Central Market where stallholders introduce their varied produce. Dawn tours include breakfast. McLaren Vale and Clare Valley tours also available.

Bookabee Tours (☎ 8235 9954, 0408-209 593; www.bookabee.com.au) Indigenous-run Adelaide tours focusing on bush foods in the Botanic Gardens ($42, two hours) or Tandanya National Aboriginal Cultural Institute and the South Australian Museum ($42, two hours) or Cleland Wildlife Park (half-day from $80), plus half-/full-day city tours ($138/180). A great insight into Kaurna culture. Longer outback tours also available (see p131).

Enjoy Adelaide (☎ 8332 1401; www.enjoyadelaide .com.au) Runs a half-day city-highlights tour ($40) with diversions to Mt Lofty Summit and Hahndorf. Barossa Valley and Fleurieu Peninsula tours also available.

Gray Line (☎ 1300 858 687; www.grayline.com.au) Old-school city coach tours, with extensions to the Adelaide Hills and Glenelg, plus river-cruise and wildlife-park options. Barossa Valley tours, too.

Premier Stateliner (☎ 8415 5566; www.premier stateliner.com.au) Runs a 'City Sights & Seaside' tour ($55), plus Barossa Valley and Adelaide Hills day trips.

FESTIVALS & EVENTS

As local licence plates attest, SA is the 'Festival State'. A continuous stream of high-calibre international and local events lures artists and audiences from around the world, particularly for the Adelaide Festival of Arts, WOMADelaide and the Adelaide Fringe.

JANUARY
Tour Down Under (www.tourdownunder.com.au) The world's best cyclists sweating in their lycra: six races through SA towns, with the grand finale in Adelaide.

MARCH
Adelaide Festival of Arts (www.adelaidefestival.com .au) Culture vultures absorb international and Australian dance, drama, opera and theatre performances in even-numbered years.

Adelaide Fringe (www.adelaidefringe.com.au) An annual independent arts festival, second only to Edinburgh Fringe.

Clipsal 500 (www.clipsal500.com.au) Revheads flail their mullets as Adelaide's streets become a four-day Holden versus Ford racing track.

WOMADelaide (www.womadelaide.com.au) One of the world's best live-music events with more than 300 musicians and performers from around the globe.

JUNE
Adelaide Cabaret Festival (www.adelaidecabaret festival.com) The only one of its kind in the country.

JULY
Adelaide's Festival of Ideas (www.adelaidefestival ofideas.com.au) The glorious, the good and the innovative descend on Adelaide for a biennial talkfest (odd-numbered years).

AUGUST
South Australian Living Artists Festival (www .salafestival.com) Progressive exhibitions and displays across town.

SEPTEMBER
City to Bay (www.city-bay.org.au) Annual 12km fun run from the city to Glenelg; much sweat and cardiac duress.

Royal Adelaide Show (www.adelaideshowground.com.au) Agricultural and horticultural displays and show bags. Mooo...

SANFL Grand Final (www.sanfl.com.au) Zenith of the local Aussie Rules season. Can anyone beat Central Districts?

OCTOBER
Classic Adelaide Rally (www.classicadelaide.com.au) Full of lovingly maintained machines.

NOVEMBER
Christmas Pageant (www.cupageant.com.au) An Adelaide institution for 70-plus years – floats, bands and marching troupes occupy city streets for a day.

Feast Festival (www.feast.org.au) Three-week gay and lesbian festival with a carnival, theatre, dialogue and dance.

DECEMBER
Adelaide Guitar Festival (www.adelaidefestivalcentre.com.au) Annual axe fest with a whole lot of rock, classical, country, blues and flamenco.

Bay Sports Festival (www.baysportsfestival.com.au) Sports fest in Glenelg, featuring beach volleyball, an aquathon and surf carnival.

SLEEPING
Most of Adelaide's budget accommodation is in the city centre, but in a town this easy to navigate, staying outside the CBD is viable. For peace and quiet, consider leafy North Adelaide; for beachside accommodation, see Glenelg (p64). 'Motel Alley' is along Glen Osmond Rd, the main southeast city access road. See www.bandbfsa.com.au for B&B listings.

Adelaide's top-end hotels usually offer weekend package deals, when room prices are cheaper than midweek. Holiday apartments generally offer competitive weekly and monthly rates. Book accommodation ahead during December and January, and expect price spikes during school holidays.

Budget
HOSTELS
Backpack Oz (Map p48; ☎ 8223 3551; www.backpackoz.com.au; cnr Wakefield & Pulteney Sts; dm/s/d from $22/50/60; ✖ ▣) It doesn't look like much externally, but this converted pub (the old Orient Hotel) strikes the right balance between party and placid. There are spacious dorms, a guesthouse over the road (great for couples), and guests can still get a coldie and shoot some pool in the bar. Communal area; free dinner on Wednesday. Linen provided.

our pick My Place (Map p48; ☎ 8221 5299; www.adelaidehostel.com.au; 257 Waymouth St; dm incl breakfast $24, d incl breakfast & TV $64; ▣) The antithesis of the big formal operations, My Place has a welcoming, personal vibe and is just a stumble from the Grace Emily, arguably Adelaide's best pub! There's a cosy TV room, barbecue terrace above the street, beach bus in summer, and regular pizza and pub nights – great for solo travellers. Free bike hire, too.

Adelaide Backpackers Inn (Map p48; ☎ 1800 247 725, 8223 6635; www.adelaidebackpackersinn.net.au; 112 Carrington St; dm/tw incl breakfast $24/48; ✖ ▣) A relaxed and surprisingly clean place (inside an old pub), with the emphasis on 'free' (pickups, breakfast, videos, linen, storage etc).

Hostel 109 (Map p48; ☎ 1800 099 318, 8223 1771; www.hostel109.com; 109 Carrington St; dm/s/tw/d $25/50/58/65; ✖ ▣) A small, well-managed hostel in a quiet corner of town, with a couple of little balconies over the street and a cosy kitchen-communal area. Spotlessly clean and superfriendly, with lockers, travel info, good security and gas cooking. The only negative: rooms open onto light wells rather than the outside world.

Adelaide Travellers Inn (Map p48; ☎ 8224 0753; www.adelaidebackpackers.com.au; 220 Hutt St; dm $25, d with/without bathroom $75/60, f $100–125; ✖) Steps away from the Hutt St eateries, this shabby-but-sociable joint has a maze of dorms and old-time motel units out the back. Rates include linen and light breakfast. Beery balcony above the street.

Blue Galah Backpackers Hostel (Map p48; ☎ 8231 9295; www.bluegalah.com.au; Level 1, 62 King William St; dm/tw from $26/70; ✖ ▣) A friendly, 140-bed hostel with an enormous balcony above King Willie St (perfect for the Oz boutique beers from the bar) and an environmental bent. Rooms have good security and excellent mattresses, but some are sans windows and a little squishy.

Adelaide Central YHA (Map p48; ☎ 8414 3010; www.yha.com.au; 135 Waymouth St; dm/d/f from $28/80/110; ✖ ▣) The YHA isn't known for its gregariousness, but you'll get plenty of sleep in the spacious and comfortable rooms here. This is a seriously schmick hostel with great security, roomy kitchen and lounge area and immaculate bathrooms. A real step up from the average backpackers around town.

MOTELS
City Central Motel (Map p48; ☎ 8231 4049; www.arta.com.au/ccentral.html; 23 Hindley St; s/d/tw $70/75/80; ✖) Small but clean, secure and comfortable

ADELAIDE & AROUND

motel-style rooms poised above the Hindley St melee. Have a few beers on the balcony and watch the crowds pass onwards to oblivion. Discounted multistorey parking across the street.

CAMPING

Levi Park Caravan Park (off Map p52; ☎ 8344 2209; www .levipark.com.au; 69 Lansdowne Tce, Walkerville; unpowered/powered sites $27/31, cabins & ste $86-120; ⊠) Another Torrens-side park, 5km from town and loaded with facilities, including tennis courts and a massive oval. Suites are in restored Vale House, purportedly Adelaide's oldest residence!

Adelaide Caravan Park (off Map p52; ☎ 8363 1566; www.adelaidecaravanpark.com.au; 46 Richmond St, Hackney; powered sites $30, cabins/units from $85/113; ⊠) An orderly park on the River Torrens, just 2km northeast of the city centre. Clean and well run, but not much grass.

Adelaide Shores Caravan Resort (off Map p64; ☎ 8356 7654; www.adelaideshores.com.au; 1 Military Rd, West Beach; powered sites from $31, on-site vans/cabins from $61/85; ⊠ ▣ ☎) Hunkered-down behind the West Beach dunes with a walking-cycling track extending to Glenelg (3.4km) in one direction and Henley Beach (3.5km) in the other, this is a choice spot in summer. There are lush sites, glistening amenities and passing dolphins.

Midrange
HOTELS & MOTELS

Jasper Motor Inn (off Map p48; ☎ 8271 0377; www .jaspermotorinn.com.au; 17 Jasper St, Hyde Park; d $88-118; ⊠ ▣) Just beyond the city (3.5km), Jasper is off King William Rd in upper-crust Hyde Park. It's a low-slung '70s number without much style, but on a superquiet street – far preferable to the traffic rumble of Glen Osmond Rd's 'Motel Alley'. Great value.

Princes Lodge Motel (Map p52; ☎ 8267 5566; www .princeslodge.com.au; 73 Lefevre Tce, North Adelaide; s/d/f incl breakfast from $65/95/160; ⊠) In a grand 1913 house overlooking the parklands, this friendly (but achingly uncool) lodging has high ceilings and a certain faded grandeur. Close to the chichi North Adelaide restaurants and walking distance of the city.

City Parklands Motel (Map p48; ☎ 8223 1444; www .citypark.com.au; 471 Pulteney St; d with/without bathroom from $120/99, tr/f from $130/150; ⊠) Immaculate bathrooms, leather lounges, winsome French prints and an easy walk to the Hutt St restaurants. Free parking, bike hire, DVDs and wi-fi, too.

Minima Hotel (Map p52; ☎ 1800 779 954, 8334 7766; www.majestichotels.com.au; 146 Melbourne St, North Adelaide; d from $100; ⊠ ▣) A spaceship has landed in ye olde North Adelaide! Minima is so new the paint has barely dried, so you'll be assured of a clean, quality night's stay. Small but superstylish rooms in a winning Melbourne St location; check-in at 9 Jerningham St.

Mercure Grosvenor Hotel (Map p48; ☎ 8407 8888; www.mercuregrosvenorhotel.com.au; 125 North Tce; d $120-270; ⊠ ▣) This place was built in 1918, but there's not much old-world vibe left inside – slick modern rooms and friendly staff compensate. Kids under 16 stay free.

Royal Coach Motor Inn (Map p48; ☎ 8362 5676; www.royalcoach.com.au; 24 Dequetteville Tce, Kent Town; d from $145, extra adult/child $15/10; ⊠ ☎) Three-storey brick motel monster just beyond the parklands at the eastern end of town, with good facilities and late-'90s decor. There's a restaurant downstairs, but Rundle St is just a 10-minute walk away.

APARTMENTS & COTTAGES

Greenways Apartments (Map p52; ☎ 8267 5903; www .greenwaysapartments.com; 41-45 King William Rd, North Adelaide; 1-/2-/3-bedroom apt $95/125/175; ⊠) These 1938 apartments ain't flash (floral tiles and rude '70s laminates), but if you have a pathological hatred of 21st-century open-plan 'lifestyles', then Greenways is for you! And where else can you stay in clean, perfectly operational apartments so close to town at these rates? A must for cricket fans; the Adelaide Oval is a lofted cover-drive away – book early for test matches.

BreakFree Director's Studios (Map p48; ☎ 8213 2500; www.breakfree.com.au; 259 Gouger St; d/studio from $120/145; ⊠) Unfussy but not the slickest, these corporate hotel rooms and studios (with kitchenettes) on the west side of town are a safe business bet. Close the deal, then close your eyes.

Tynte Street Apartments (Map p52; ☎ 1800 779 919, 8334 7783; www.majestichotels.com.au; 82 Tynte St, North Adelaide; d from $150, extra adult/child $20/6; ⊠) Comfortable, redbrick, self-contained studio apartments on a tree-lined street near the O'Connell St cafes, sleeping three. Check-in is 1km away at 9 Jerningham St.

Quest on King William (Map p48; ☎ 8217 5000; www .questonkingwilliam.com.au; 82 King William St; studio/1-/2-bedroom apt from $150/165/220; ⊠ ▣) These immaculate downtown apartments (72 of them over eight levels) are central – perfect for business bods. All have kitchenettes and DVD players. On-site laundry; family units sleep five.

Top End

HOTELS

Hotel Richmond (Map p48; ☎ 8223 4044; www.hotel richmond.com.au; 128 Rundle Mall; d from $160; ☒ ▣) This opulent hotel in a grand 1920s building in the middle of Rundle Mall has mod-minimalist rooms with king-sized beds, marble bathrooms and American oak and Italian furnishings. Oh, and that hotel rarity – opening windows. Rates include breakfast, movies, papers and gym passes. Great value!

Majestic Roof Garden Hotel (Map p48; ☎ 8100 4400; www.majestichotels.com.au; 55 Frome St; d from $199, extra person $30; ☒ ▣) Everything looks new in this place – a speck of dirt would feel lonely. Book a room facing Frome St for a balcony and the best views, or take a bottle of wine up to the rooftop garden to watch the sunset.

Adelaide Old Terraces (Map p48; ☎ 8364 5437; www.adelaideoldterraces.com.au; 26 Blackburn Street; d $200, extra person $35; ☒) Actually it's just one old terrace house near Hutt St, but it's a good 'un: gorgeously furnished, heritage-listed, four bedrooms, two bathrooms and plenty of living space – perfect for a group of friends. Continental breakfast provisions included; two-night minimum.

Rockford Adelaide (Map p48; ☎ 1800 888 241; 8211 8255; www.rockfordhotels.com.au; 164 Hindley St; d from $209; ☒ ▣ ☒) Deep in the dark heart of Hindley St, the Rockford is a bastion of style and moderation. Rooms have a boutique vibe, with warm, natural tones as smooth as chocolate. Expect bathrobes and complimentary champagne.

EATING

Eating out in Adelaide is a divine pleasure, with reasonable prices, multicultural offerings and high standards.

Foodies flock to Gouger St (pronounced googer) for Chinatown, the food-filled corridors of Central Market, and eclectic international eateries (from Argentine to Vietnamese and everywhere in between). Rundle St in the East End is the place for all-day alfresco cafes and people-watching; nearby Hutt St has some quality food rooms. Artsy-alternative Hindley St – Adelaide's dirty little secret – has a smattering of good eateries and some great pubs (in fact, you can get a decent pub meals all over Adelaide; see www.beerandburger.info for reviews). Across the river in North Adelaide, Melbourne and O'Connell Sts have a healthy spread of bistros, providores and pubs.

Gouger St, Chinatown & Central Market

Central Market (Map p48; ☎ 8203 7203; btwn Grote & Gouger Sts; ☽ 7am-5.30pm Tue, 9am-5.30pm Thu, 7am-9pm Fri, to 3pm Sat; ▼) This place is an exercise in sensory bombardment: a barrage of smells, colours and yelling stallholders selling fresh vegetables, breads, cheeses, seafood and gourmet produce. Cafes, hectic food courts and a supermarket, too.

Lucia's Pizza & Spaghetti Bar (Map p48; ☎ 8251 2303; 2 Western Mall, Central Market; meals $8-10; ☽ breakfast & lunch Tue & Thu-Sat, dinner Fri; ☒) This little slice of Italy has been around since Lucia was a lot younger. All her pasta, sauces and pizzas are authentically homemade – perfection any time of day. If you like what you're eating, you can buy fresh pasta next door at Lucia's Pasta.

Ying Chow (Map p48; ☎ 8211 7998; 114 Gouger St; mains $10-17; ☽ dinner daily, lunch Fri; ☒ ▼) This fluorolit, utilitarian eatery is a culinary gem, serving cuisine styled from the Guangzhou region such as crispy salt-and-pepper squid and steamed duck with salty sauce. It gets packed with queues out the door, but it's well worth the wait.

Ding Hao (Map p48; ☎ 8231 6683; 26 Gouger St; mains $10-17; ☽ 11am-3pm & 5pm-late) Ding Hao is *the* place for yum cha. Even if you book a table, you might find yourself waiting outside as reluctant-to-leave diners spin lazy Susans full of prawn dumplings, shredded duck, pork buns and (eek...) chicken feet.

Mesa Lunga (Map p48; ☎ 8410 7617; cnr Gouger & Morphett Sts; tapas $6-14, mains $19-24; ☽ lunch Wed-Fri & Sun, dinner Tue-Sun, all-day tapas & pizza Fri & Sun; ☒ ▼) In a fishbowl corner room with an amazing dark-wood wine wall, sassy Mesa Lunga serves tapas and quality pizzas. Order some *queso manchego* – aged sheep cheese with *membrillo* (quince) – and anchovies stuffed with Manzanillo olives, washed down with some sparkling sangria. Magic.

Thali Room (Map p48; ☎ 8212 2411; 270-276 Morphett St; thalis $21; ☽ dinner Tue-Sun) Tacked onto the more upmarket British India restaurant, the moody Thali Room offers a selection of eight thalis (curry platters), all served with dhal, mango chutney, rice and naan. Try the Goan (hot beef) or the Malabar (prawns in mild coconut).

Gaucho's (Map p48; ☎ 8331 2299; 91 Gouger St; mains $35-80; ☽ lunch Mon-Fri, dinner daily; ☒) Low on iron? Book a seat at this Argentinean meat house and order the 300g full-blood Wagyu steak, grain-fed for 500 days and air-dried for 14. Eighty dollars well spent!

Àuge (Map p48; ☎ 8410 9332; 22 Grote St; mains from $36, 2/3 courses $59/78; ☒ lunch Tue-Fri, dinner Tue-Sat; ☒) 'To continually strive to be at one's peak' is the motto here, and palate-peaking cuisine is what to expect. Try the seared medium-rare pigeon breast with soft parmesan polenta, cured pork-cheek pancetta and confit pigeon legs. WOW! (Àuge rhymes with 'R-J', in case you want to name-drop).

Self-caterers head to **Coles** (Map p48; ☎ 8231 6683; Central Market Arcade, cnr King William & Gouger Sts; ☒ midnight-9pm Mon-Fri, to 5pm Sat, 11am-5pm Sun).

East End

Vego & Lovin' It (Map p48; ☎ 8223 7411; 1st fl, 240 Rundle St; meals $5-10; ☒ lunch Mon-Fri; ☒ V) Get your weekly vitamin dose disguised in a scrumptious veggie burger, wrap or focaccia at this artsy upstairs kitchen. Dreadlocked urban renegades order 'extra alfalfa but no hummus'.

Biga (Map p48; ☎ 8232 8880; cnr Halifax & Hutt Sts; mains $6-18; ☒ breakfast & lunch daily, dinner Wed-Sat; ☒ V) A cool cafe popular with Adelaide's weekend cycling set, who exhaustedly sprawl across the outdoor tables. Head-kicking coffee and creative breakfasts – try the *uova e pancetta* (baked free-range eggs wrapped in pancetta and roasted mushrooms and fat toast).

Amalfi Pizzeria Ristorante (Map p48; ☎ 8223 1948; 29 Frome St; mains $13-25; ☒ lunch Mon-Fri, dinner Mon-Sat; ☒) What a classic! Authentic pizza and pasta with bentwood chairs, terrazzo floors, red-and-white checked tablecloths, potent coffee and imagined Mafioso mutterings in the back room.

Lemongrass Thai Bistro (Map p48; ☎ 8223 6627; 289 Rundle St; mains $14-22; ☒ lunch Mon-Fri, dinner daily; ☒ V) Cheap, breezy Thai joint right in the Rundle St mix. Mango and coconut chicken, red curry beef, clattering chairs and chilli chatter.

our pick **Jasmin Indian Restaurant** (Map p48; ☎ 8223 7837; basement, 31 Hindmarsh Sq; mains $24-26; ☒ lunch Thu & Fri, dinner Tue-Sat; ☒ V) Magical North Indian curries and consummately professional staff (they might remember your name from when you ate here in 1997). There's nothing too surprising about the menu, but it's done to absolute perfection. Bookings essential.

Farina Kitchen & Bar (Map p48; ☎ 8227 1007; basement, 39 Hindmarsh Sq; mains $25-33; ☒ lunch Mon-Fri, dinner Mon-Sat; ☒) Wander downstairs into this contemporary Italian restaurant, decked out with white-yellow-black Miró-meets-

Rorschach graphics and industrial light globes. Sip a cocktail at the bar while the effortlessly hip staff checks if your table's ready.

Enoteca (Map p48; ☎ 8359 2255; 262 Carrington St; mains $27-37; ☒ lunch Wed-Fri, dinner Wed-Sat; ☒ V) In a timber-floored glass box dangling off the side of the Italian Chamber of Commerce, Enoteca plates up superb modern Italian. The gnocchi with Spencer Gulf prawns, shredded pork belly, roast tomato, white beans and truffles is heaven sent. Classy, classy, classy.

Botanic Café (Map p48; ☎ 8224 0925; 4 East Tce; mains $27-41; ☒ lunch & dinner; ☒) Order from a seasonal menu of quality SA produce in this linen-crisp, modern Italian eatery opposite the Botanic Gardens. Offerings might include goats-cheese tartlets with pear chutney, or pappardelle with braised lamb shank and thyme *ragù*. The tasting menu (two courses and a glass of wine for $25) is a steal.

See also Good Life (p65) and Penfolds Magill Estate Winery (p51). For self-catering try **Woolworths** (Map p48; ☎ 8232 0787; 86 Rundle Mall; ☒ 7am-9pm Mon-Sat, 11am-5pm Sun).

West End

Café de Vili's (off Map p48; ☎ 8234 2042; 2-14 Manchester St, Mile End; mains $5-15; ☒ 24hr; ☒) Vili's pies are a South Australian institution. Next to their factory just west of the West End is an all-night cafe serving the equally iconic 'pie floaters' (a meat pie floating in pea soup, topped with mashed potato, sauce and gravy – outstanding!).

Jerusalem Sheshkabab House (Map p48; ☎ 8212 6185; 131 Hindley St; mains $10-15; ☒ lunch Tue-Sat, dinner Tue-Sun; ☒ V) A skinny Hindley St room that's been here for ever, serving magnificent Middle Eastern and Lebanese delights: felafels, hummus, tabouleh, tahini and (of course) shish kebabs. The plastic furniture and draped tent material are appropriately tacky.

For a bang-up West End pub meal:

Edinburgh Castle (Map p48; ☎ 8231 1435; 223 Currie St; mains $10; ☒ lunch & dinner; ☒) Supercheap $10 menu (the students love it) featuring bangers-and-mash, burgers, veggie lasagne and beer-battered whiting.

Prince Albert (Map p48; ☎ 8212 7912; 254 Wright St; mains $12-25; ☒ lunch & dinner; ☒) Cheap pub grub that looms large: steaks, rissoles, hanging-off-the-plate schnitzels and inexplicably popular lambs brains.

Cumberland Arms (Map p48; ☎ 8231 3578; 205 Waymouth St; mains $14-21; ☒ lunch & dinner; ☒) Ignore the pokies for excellent rump steaks, warm chicken salads and 'Cumby' burgers. Cheap schnitzels Monday and Tuesday; cheap steaks Wednesday.

North Adelaide

Store (Map p52; ☎ 8361 6999; 157 Melbourne St; breakfast $8-17, mains $10-28; ☽ breakfast, lunch & dinner; ☒ Ⓥ) A much-needed slice of bohemia amid the North Adelaide affluence, Store is a casual corner eatery with a built-in deli, serving great coffee, pastas, risottos and gourmet mains such as crispy chicken breast on mascarpone mash with grilled asparagus, prosciutto and sage butter.

Royal Oak (Map p52; ☎ 8267 2488; 123 O'Connell St; mains $16-23; ☽ breakfast Sat & Sun, lunch Wed-Sun, dinner daily; ☒) Winning pub-grub at this enduring pub boozer: steak sangers, veggie lasagne, lamb-shank pie, king-prawn salad and blueberry pancakes. Quirky retro vibe; live jazz/indie-rock Tuesday, Wednesday and Sunday.

Akasha (Map p52; ☎ 8267 5000; 8/157 O'Connell St; mains $16-33; ☽ breakfast Fri & Sat, lunch & dinner Tue-Sat; ☒ Ⓥ) Modern Greek fills a niche on upper O'Connell St at Akasha, a classy glass-fronted restaurant serving meze and hefty platters. Ouzo, ascending bouzouki music and knowledgeable staff. The $36 lunch for two is top value.

Lion (Map p52; ☎ 8367 0222; 161 Melbourne St; mains $30-34; ☽ lunch Sun-Fri, dinner Mon-Sat; ☒) Ooh-la-la! Off to one side of this popular, upmarket boozer (all big screens, beer terraces and business types) is a sassy restaurant with a cool retro interior and romantic vibes. Hot off the menu are luscious Coorong Angus steaks, market fish and corn-fed chicken breasts, served with a professionalism far exceeding the average pub.

Self-caterers can swing into **IGA North Adelaide** (Map p52; ☎ 8223 3114; 113 O'Connell St; ☽ 8am-10pm).

DRINKING

For a true Adelaide experience, head for the bar and order a schooner of Coopers, the local brew, or a glass of SA's impressive wine. Rundle St has a few iconic pubs, while along Hindley St in the West End, grunge and sleaze collide with student energy and groovy bars. Most bars are closed on Mondays.

PINT OF COOPERS PALE THANKS!

Things can get confusing at the bar in Adelaide. Aside from 200ml (7oz) 'butchers' – the choice of old men in dim, sticky-carpet pubs – there are three main beer sizes: 285ml (10oz) 'schooners' (pots or middies elsewhere in Australia), 425ml (15oz) 'pints' (schooners elsewhere), and 568ml (20oz) 'imperial pints' (traditional English pints). Now go forth and order with confidence!

---

ourpick Grace Emily (Map p48; ☎ 8231 5500; 232 Waymouth St) Duking it out with the Exeter for 'Adelaide's Best Pub' bragging rights (it pains us to separate the two) the 'Gracie' has live music most nights, featuring up-and-coming Australian acts. Inside it's all kooky '50s-meets-voodoo decor, open fires and great beers. Cult cinema Tuesday nights. Look for the UFO on the roof.

Exeter (Map p48; ☎ 8223 2623; 246 Rundle St) The best pub in the East End, this legendary city boozer attracts a mix of postwork, punk and uni drinkers, shaking the day off their backs. Pull up a stool or a table in the grungy beer garden and settle in for the evening. Music most nights; curry nights Wednesday and Thursday.

Universal Wine Bar (Map p48; ☎ 8232 5000; 285 Rundle St) A hip crowd clocks in to this stalwart bar to select from 200-plus South Australian and international wines, and a menu (mains $22 to $36) packed with SA produce. 'The scene is very Italian', says the barman.

Crown & Sceptre (Map p48; ☎ 8212 4159; 308 King William St) An urbane boozer drawing all comers, from legal eagles on adjournment from trial to ditch diggers in their boots. Ambient tunes, DJs most nights, sidewalk tables, a cool little beer garden and better-than-average pub food (mains $15 to $28).

Supermild (Map p48; ☎ 8212 8077; 182 Hindley St) A downsized basement bar that stays and stays while other West End bars come and go. Hip staff, retro-lounge interior, funky tunes – arguably the best bar in town (if you can get in!).

Other eclectic spots:

Wheatsheaf (off Map p48; ☎ 8443 4546; 39 George St, Thebarton) A hidden gem under the flight path in industrial Thebarton, with an artsy crowd of students, jazz musos, lesbians, punks and rockers. Tidy beer garden; live music Friday to Monday.

Apothecary 1878 (Map p48; ☎ 8212 9099; 118 Hindley St) Classy coffee and wine at this gorgeous chemist-turned-bar. Medicine cabinets, bentwood chairs and Parisian marble-topped tables.

Distill (Map p48; ☎ 8227 0825; 286 Rundle St) Super-sassy Rundle St bar with a tight dress code (to the nines) and a kickin' organic cocktail list. Sustainable snacks (sourced within 100 miles) are creatively paired with wines: Limestone Coast cloth cheddar with juicy 'wet dog Shiraz'; organic basil pesto with 'herbaceous, grassy Riesling'.

Belgian Beer Café (Map p48; ☎ 8359 2233; 27-29 Ebenezer Pl, off Rundle St) Shiny brass, sexy staff, much presluicing of glasses and somewhere upwards of 26 imported Belgian superbrews (we lost count…).

Tap Inn (Map p48; ☎ 8362 2116; 76 Rundle St, Kent Town) A huge pub doubling as a shrine to golf, with an indoor driving range and rooftop putting green.

In North Adelaide, worthy drinking dens include the Royal Oak (p59), Lion (p59) and the following:

Dan O'Connell (Map p52; ☎ 8267 4034; 165 Tynte St, North Adelaide) An Irish pub without a whiff of kitsch Celtic cash-in! Just great Guinness, open fires, acoustic music and a house-sized pepper tree in the beer garden (161 years old and counting).

Archer (Map p52; ☎ 8361 9300; 47 O'Connell St, North Adelaide) A cool place for SA wines and microbrews, with a jovial big-screen front bar, snooker room, music room (weekend DJs), and fireside lounge with chesterfields. Classy pub food, too (mains $15 to $25).

ENTERTAINMENT

Artsy Adelaide has a phenomenal cultural life that stacks up favourably with much larger cities. The free monthly *Adelaide Review* (www.adelaidereview.com) features theatre and gallery listings, and on Thursday and Saturday the *Advertiser* (www.theadvertiser .news.com.au) newspaper lists events, cinema programmes and gallery details. The *Adelaide Theatre Guide* (www.theatreguide .com.au) lists booking details, venues and reviews for comedy, drama, musicals and other performance arts.

Big-ticket events can be booked through **Ticketek** (☎ 13 28 49; www.ticketek.com.au), **Moshtix** (☎ 1300 428 849; www.moshtix.com.au), or **BASS** (☎ 13 12 46; www.bass.sa.com.au), which has outlets at the South Australian Visitor & Travel Centre (p50), and the riverside **Adelaide Festival Centre** (Map p48; ☎ 8216 8600; www.adelaidefestivalcentre.com .au). The hub of performing arts in SA, the crystalline white Festival Centre opened in June 1973, four proud months before the Sydney Opera House! The **State Theatre Company** (www .statetheatrecompany.com.au) is based here.

Other entertainment venues:
Adelaide Entertainment Centre (off Map p48; ☎ 8288 2222; www.theaec.net; cnr Port Rd & Adam St, Hindmarsh) Everyone from the Wiggles to Stevie Wonder.
Her Majesty's Theatre (Map p48; ☎ 8212 8600; 58 Grote St)
Lion Theatre (Map p48; ☎ 8231 7760; Lion Arts Centre, cnr North Tce & Morphett St)

Live Music

With serious musical pedigree (from Cold Chisel to the Superjesus and the Audreys),

Adelaide knows how to kick out the jams! The free street-press papers *Rip It Up* (www.ripitup .com.au) and *db* (www.dbmagazine.com.au) – available from record shops, pubs and cafes – have band and DJ listings and reviews. Cover charges vary with acts. Online resources:
Adelaide Symphony Orchestra (www.aso.com.au) Listings for the estimable ASO.
Jazz Adelaide (www.jazz.adelaide.onau.net) Finger-snappin' za-bah-dee-dah.
South Australian Music Online (www.musicsa.com.au) All-genre listings.

OUR PICK Governor Hindmarsh Hotel (off Map p48; ☎ 8340 0744; www.thegov.com.au; 59 Port Rd, Hindmarsh) Ground Zero for live music in Adelaide, 'the Gov' hosts some legendary local and international acts. The odd Irish band fiddles around in the bar, while the main venue features rock, folk, jazz, blues, salsa, reggae and dance. A huge place with an inexplicably personal vibe.

Jive (Map p48; ☎ 8211 6683; www.jivevenue.com; 181 Hindley St) In a converted theatre, Jive caters to an offbeat crowd of student types who like their tunes funky and left field. A sunken dance floor = great views from the bar!

HQ Complex (Map p48; ☎ 7221 1245; www.hq complex.com.au; 7 West Tce) Primarily a dance venue, HQ is big and powered-up enough to entice touring rock powerhouses such as the Living End and Shihad.

Fowlers Live (Map p48; ☎ 8212 0255; www .fowlerslive.com.au; 68 North Tce) Inside the former Fowler Flour Factory, this 500-capacity venue is a temple of hard rock, metal and sweaty mayhem.

Pubs around town with regular live gigs (everything from DJs to indie-rock and acoustic duos) include the following:
Grace Emily (p59) West End alt-rock, country and acoustic.
Wheatsheaf (p59) Eclectic offerings in the semi-industrial Thebarton wastelands.
Crown & Sceptre (p59) Grooves, beats and funky stuff from resident selectors.
Royal Oak (p59) Lounge and jazz spicing up North Adelaide.
Exeter (p59) The East End's rockin' soul: indie bands, electronica and acoustic.

Cinemas

Check the *Advertiser* for what's screening around town. Tickets generally cost around adult/concession/child $15/11/9 (cheaper on 'tight-arse' Tuesdays).

GAY & LESBIAN VENUES

For the local gay and lesbian low-down, grab a copy of *Blaze* (www.blaze.e-p.net.au), available around the city: reviews, community news and G&L-friendly venues, accommodation, restaurants and classifieds.

Popular venues include **Mars Bar** (see below) Adelaide's best G&L club with awesome sonics and drag shows on weekends; **Sugar** (Map p48; ☎ 8223 6160; www.sugarclub.com.au; 1st fl, 274 Rundle St), which has a gay disco party every Wednesday night; and the **Metropolitan Hotel** (Map p48; ☎ 8231 5471; 46 Grote St), which hosts the hirsute **Bear Men of Adelaide** (www.bmofa.org.au) every Friday night.

If you're in town in November, check out the **Feast Festival** (www.feast.org.au), a three-week G&L fest with a whole slew of events, including the Adelaide Pride March.

Palace Nova Eastend Cinemas (Map p48; ☎ 8232 3434; 250 & 251 Rundle St; adult/concession) Facing-off across Rundle St, both cinemas feature new-release art-house, foreign-language and independent films as well as some mainstream flicks.

Mercury Cinema (Map p48; ☎ 8410 1934; www.mercurycinema.org.au; Lion Arts Centre, 13 Morphett St) The Mercury screens art-house releases, and is home to the Adelaide Cinémathèque (classic, cult and experimental flicks).

Moonlight Cinema (Map p48; ☎ 1300 551 908; www.moonlight.com.au; Botanic Gardens; ☉ mid-Dec–mid-Feb) In summer, pack a picnic and mosquito repellent, and spread out on the lawn to watch old and new classics under the stars.

Nightclubs

The scene is ever changing, though the West End and Light Sq are safe bets for club activity. Online check out www.pubscene.com.au or *Onion* (www.onion.com.au) for the 'word from the street'. Cover charge can be anything from free to $15, depending on the night; most clubs are closed Monday to Wednesday.

Lotus Lounge (Map p48; ☎ 8231 0312; 268 Morphett St) We like the signage here – a very minimal fluoro martini glass with a flashing olive. Inside it's a glam lounge with cocktails, quality beers and Adelaide dolls cuttin' the rug. Expect queues around the corner on Saturday nights.

Zhivago (Map p48; ☎ 8212 0569; 155 Waymouth St, Light Sq) The pick of the Light Sq clubs (there are quite a few of 'em – some are a bit moron-prone), Zhivago's DJs pump out everything from reggae and dub to quality house. Popular with the 18-to-25 dawn patrol.

Mojo West (Map p48; ☎ 8231 9290; www.mojowest.net; 258 Hindley St) One of the more relaxed clubs around town (dress code and atmosphere), Mojo West has freaky blue light emanating from under the pool-table cushions and quasi-Easter Island graffiti art – it certainly looks the part! Thursday Uni nights attract pretty young things to the lights.

HQ Complex (Map p48; ☎ 7221 1245; www.hqcomplex.com.au; 7 West Tce) Adelaide's biggest club occupies the bad old Heaven complex, filling five rooms with shimmering sound and light. Night-time is the right time on Saturdays – the biggest (and trashiest) club night in town.

Mars Bar (Map p48; ☎ 8231 9639; www.themarsbar.com.au; 120 Gouger St) The linchpin of Adelaide's nocturnal G&L scene, always-busy Mars Bar features glitzy decor, flashy clientele and over-the-top drag shows.

See also Sugar (above).

Sport

As most Australian cities do, Adelaide hangs its hat on the successes of its sporting teams. In the **Australian Football League** (AFL; www.afl.com.au), the Adelaide Crows and Port Adelaide have sporadic success. Suburban Adelaide teams compete in the **South Australian National Football League** (SANFL; www.sanfl.com.au). The football season runs from March to September.

In the **National Basketball League** (NBL; www.nbl.com.au), the Adelaide 36ers have been a force for decades. In soccer's **A League** (www.a-league.com.au), Adelaide United are always competitive. Under the auspices of **Cricket SA** (www.cricketsa.com.au), the Redbacks play one-day and multiday state matches at the Adelaide Oval (p52).

SHOPPING

Shops and department stores (including Myer, David Jones, Harris Scarfe et al) line Rundle Mall. The beautiful old arcades running between the mall and Grenfell St retain their original splendour, and house eclectic little shops. Rundle St and the surrounding lanes are home to boutique and retro clothing shops.

Tacky souvenir and opal shops are clustered around Rundle Mall and King William

St corner. For something a little classier, try **Tandanya National Aboriginal Cultural Institute** (p53), or local arts and crafts at the **Jam Factory Craft & Design Centre** (p50) or **T'Arts** (Map p48; ☎ 8232 0265; 10g Gays Arcade, Adelaide Arcade, Rundle Mall).

The catch-cry at **Urban Cow Studio** (Map p48; ☎ 8232 6126; 11 Frome St) is 'Handmade in Adelaide' – a brilliant assortment of paintings, jewellery, glassware, ceramics and textiles, plus a gallery upstairs.

A international success story, the gorgeous cosmetics from SA's own **Jurlique** (Map p48; ☎ 8410 7180; www.jurlique.com.au; 22-38 Rundle Mall Plaza, Rundle Mall) are pricey but worth every cent. Another SA smash hit is **RM Williams** (Map p48; ☎ 8232 3611; 6 Gawler Pl) selling boots handmade from single pieces of leather.

For new and secondhand CDs and vinyl, swing into the excellent **Big Star** (Map p48; ☎ 8232 1484; 197 Rundle St). Not far away is **Midwest Trader** (Map p48; ☎ 8223 6606; Shops 1 & 2, Ebenezer Pl), which stocks a toothy range of punk, rock, skate and rockabilly gear.

Outdoor shops convene around Rundle St:
Annapurna (Map p48; ☎ 8223 4633; www.annapurna .com.au; 210 Rundle St)
Mountain Designs (Map p48; ☎ 8232 1351; www .mountaindesigns.com; 187 Rundle St)
Paddy Pallin (Map p48; ☎ 8232 3155; www.paddy pallin.com.au; 228 Rundle St)

GETTING THERE & AROUND

International, interstate and regional flights service **Adelaide Airport** (off Map p48; ☎ 8308 9211; www.aal.com.au), 7km west of the city centre. The usual car-rental suspects all have desks here.

Interstate trains grind into the recently tarted-up **Adelaide Parklands Terminal** (Map p48; ☎ 13 21 47; www.gsr.com.au; Railway Tce, Keswick), 1km southwest of the city centre.

Adelaide's new **Central Bus Station** (Map p48; ☎ 8221 5080; www.bussa.com.au; 85 Franklin St) has ticket counters for all major interstate and statewide services, and left-luggage lockers. For details on travelling to/from Adelaide see the Transport chapter (p298).

To/from the Airport & Train Station

Skylink (☎ 8413 6196; www.skylinkadelaide.com; adult/child one-way $8/3) runs around 20 shuttles between 5.50am and 9.15pm to/from Adelaide Airport via Adelaide Parklands Terminal (adult/child one-way $5/3). Bookings are essential for all city pick-up locations other than the Central Bus Station.

Adelaide Metro's **JetBus** (☎ 1800 182 160, 8210 1000; www.adelaidemetro.com.au) runs several routes linking the suburbs, city and airport, starting around 5am and running until 11.30pm. Standard fares apply.

Many hostels will pick you up and drop you off if you're staying with them. Taxis charge around $20 between the airport and city centre.

Bicycle

With a valid photo ID you can borrow a bike for the day (for free!) from **Bicycle SA** (Map p48; ☎ 8168 9999; www.bikesa.asn.au; 111 Franklin St; ☺ 9am-5pm). Keep your bike overnight for a $25 charge. Helmet and lock provided.

Car & Motorcycle

Check the local *Yellow Pages* for Adelaide car-rental companies, including the major internationals. See p306 for campervan-hire details. Note that some companies don't allow vehicles to be taken to Kangaroo Island. Expect to pay around $45 per day (less for longer rentals) for car hire with the cheaper companies, such as the following:
Acacia Car Rentals (off Map p48; ☎ 8234 0911; www .acaciacarrentals.com.au; 91 Sir Donald Bradman Dr, Hilton) Cheap rentals for travel within a 100km radius.
Access Rent-a-Car (Map p48; ☎ 1800 812 580, 8359 3200; www.accessrentacar.com; 60 Frome St)
Cut Price Car & Truck Rentals (off Map p48; ☎ 8443 7788; www.cutprice.com.au; cnr Sir Donald Bradman Dr & South Rd, Mile End) Rental of 4WDs available.
Koala Car Rentals (off Map p48; ☎ 8352 7299; www .koalarentals.com.au; 41 Sir Donald Bradman Dr, Mile End)

Public Transport

The **Adelaide Metro InfoCentre** (Map p48; ☎ 1800 182 160, 8210 1000; www.adelaidemetro.com.au; cnr King William & Currie Sts; ☺ 8am-6pm Mon-Fri, 9am-5pm Sat, 11am-4pm Sun) provides timetables and sells tickets for the integrated city bus, train and Glenelg tram network. Tickets can also be purchased on board, at staffed train stations, and in delis and newsagents. There are day-trip ($8), and two-hour peak ($4.20) and off-peak ($2.60) tickets. Train tickets can be purchased from vending machines on board trains, or at staffed train stations. The peak travel time is before 9am and after 3pm. Kids under five ride free!

BUS
Adelaide's clean and reliable suburban buses are the best way to get around town.

Most services start around 6am and run until midnight.

The free **City Loop** bus runs clockwise and anticlockwise around the CBD fringe from Adelaide Railway Station on North Tce, passing the Central Market en route. It runs every 15 minutes on weekdays from 8am to 6.15pm (plus every 30 minutes from 6.15pm to 9.15pm on Fridays), and every 30 minutes on Saturday between 8.15am and 5.45pm, and on Sunday between 10.15am and 5.45pm.

The free **Bee Line** bus runs a loop from Victoria Sq, up King William St and past the Adelaide Railway Station on North Tce. It leaves Victoria Sq every five to 10 minutes on weekdays from 7.40am to 6pm (9.20pm Friday), every 15 minutes on Saturday from 8.27am to 5.35pm, and every 15 minutes on Sunday from 10am to 5.30pm.

Saturday night/Sunday morning **After Midnight** buses run select standard routes (including to Glenelg and the Adelaide Hills), but have an 'N' preceding the route number on their displays. Buses run generally from midnight to 5am; standard ticket prices apply.

TRAIN
Adelaide's hokey old diesel trains depart from Adelaide Railway Station on North Tce, plying five suburban routes (Belair, Gawler, Grange, Noarlunga and Outer Harbour). Trains generally run between 6am and midnight (some services start at 4.30am).

TRAM
State-of-the-art trams rumble between Moseley Sq in Glenelg, through Victoria Sq in the city and along North Tce, approximately every 15 minutes from 6am to midnight daily. Standard ticket prices apply, except for the section between North Tce and South Tce which is free!

Taxi
There are licensed taxi ranks all over town.
Adelaide Independent Taxis (☎ 13 22 11, wheelchair users 1300 360 940)
Suburban Taxis (☎ 13 10 08)
Yellow Cabs (☎ 13 22 27)

AROUND ADELAIDE

Adelaide's beaches (www.coastaladelaide .com.au) – stretching from nudie Maslin

Beach in the south through laid-back Glenelg to Henley Beach and Semaphore in the north – are excellent for swimming and sunsets, but are lousy for surfing. Inland from Semaphore on the Port River, Port Adelaide is a booming 'burb midway through gentrifying its historic centre.

GLENELG
Fifteen minutes' drive from the city, palindromic Glenelg, or 'the Bay' – the site of SA's colonial landing – is Adelaide at its most chilled out and eccentric. Glenelg beach faces west, and as the sun sinks into the sea, the pubs and bars burgeon with surfies, backpackers and sun-damaged, leopard print–clad sexagenarians; while families stroll the promenade, ploughing into mountainous ice-cream cones. The tram rumbles in from the city, past the Jetty Rd shopping strip to the alfresco cafes around Moseley Sq.

Information
Glenelg Visitor Information Centre (☎ 8294 5833; www.glenelgsa.com.au; Moseley Sq; ☖ 9.30am-5pm Mon-Fri, to 3pm Sat, 10am-2pm Sun; ☐) Behind the Town Hall; internet access available.
Bettanet Internet Café (☎ 8294 8977; 142 Jetty Rd; per 15min/1hr $2/5; ☖ 9.30am-5.30pm Mon-Fri, to 5pm Sat) Internet access.

Sights & Activities
The **Bay Discovery Centre** (☎ 8179 9504; www .baydiscovery.com.au; Town Hall, Moseley Sq; admission free; ☖ 10am-5pm) depicts the social history of Glenelg from colonisation to today, and addresses the plight of the local Kaurna people, who lost both their land and voice. Don't miss the rusty relics dredged up from the original pier, and the spooky old sideshow machines.

Near the visitors centre, **Beach Hire** (☎ 8294 1477; Moseley Sq; ☖ sunny days Sep-Apr) hires out wave skis (per hour $14), bodyboards ($5) and bikes ($12), plus deckchairs, umbrellas and cricket sets.

Hel-a-va Jet Boats (☎ 8376 8288; www.helava .com.au; Marina Pier; 20min rides adult/concession/child $70/60/50; ☖ from 10am) takes thrillseekers on high-speed jet-boat rides (how long since you had breakfast?), and five-hour Port River cruises (adult/concession/child $190/180/169).
Temptation Sailing (☎ 0412-811 838; www.dolphinboat .com.au; Holdfast Shores Marina; 3½hr dolphin watch/swim $58/98; ☖ 8am) runs eco-accredited catamaran cruises to watch or swim with dolphins.

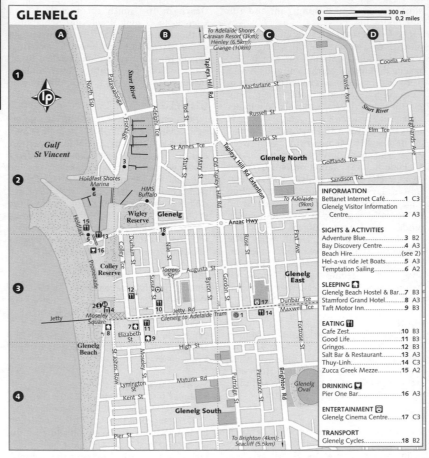

GLENELG

INFORMATION
Bettanet Internet Café...........**1** C3
Glenelg Visitor Information
Centre............................**2** A3

SIGHTS & ACTIVITIES
Adventure Blue.....................**3** B2
Bay Discovery Centre.............**4** A3
Beach Hire........................(see 2)
Hel-a-va ride Jet Boats..........**5** A3
Temptation Sailing...............**6** A2

SLEEPING 🛏
Glenelg Beach Hostel & Bar....**7** B3
Stamford Grand Hotel...........**8** A3
Taft Motor Inn....................**9** B3

EATING 🍴
Cafe Zest..........................**10** B3
Good Life..........................**11** B3
Gringos............................**12** B3
Salt Bar & Restaurant...........**13** A3
Thuy-Linh..........................**14** B3
Zucca Greek Mezze...............**15** A2

DRINKING 🍷
Pier One Bar.......................**16** A3

ENTERTAINMENT 🎭
Glenelg Cinema Centre.........**17** C3

TRANSPORT
Glenelg Cycles.....................**18** B2

Adventure Blue (☎ 8294 7744; www.adventureblue
.com.au; Patawalonga Frontage, Glenelg North; ⊙ 8.30am-
5.30pm Mon-Fri, 8am-5pm Sat & Sun) hires snorkelling gear ($25 per day), and offers one-day
Discover Scuba courses ($250) and two-hour
kiteboarding lessons at West Beach ($199
including transport).

There are some great **beaches** extending
north and south of Glenelg. Spend a day exploring hip **Henley** and low-key **Grange** to the
north; bubbly **Brighton** and relaxed **Seacliff** to
the south.

Sleeping

Glenelg Beach Hostel & Bar (☎ 8376 0007; www
.glenelgbeachhostel.com.au; 1-7 Moseley St; dm from $27, d/f
from $60/80; 🖥) A couple of streets back from

the beach, this beaut old terrace (1879) is
Adelaide's budget golden child. Fan-cooled
rooms maintain period details and are bunk-
free. There's cold Coopers in the basement
bar, open fireplaces, lofty ceilings, girls-only
dorms and a courtyard garden. Book *waaay*
in advance in summer.

Taft Motor Inn (☎ 1800 060 905; 8376 1233; www.taft
motorinn.com.au; 18 Moseley St; motel d from $115, 1-/2-bedroom
apt from $145/155; 🅿 🖥) Revamped motel rooms
and apartments with lashings of timber and
taupe. Some rooms have kitchenettes; there's a
barbecue and kidney-shaped pool on-site.

Stamford Grand Hotel (☎ 8376 1222; www.stamford
.com.au; Moseley Sq; d city/ocean views from $180/220; 🅿 🖥)
The first Glenelg edifice to scrape the sky with
any real authority, this plush, pink-hued hotel

overlooks Gulf St Vincent. Dinner, bed and breakfast packages are decent value.

For nearby camping, see p56.

Self-contained beachside apartment rentals from one to five bedrooms:

Glenelg Holiday & Corporate Letting (☎ 8376 1934; www.glenelgholiday.com.au; 1-bedroom apt from $135; 🕵)
Glenelg Letting Agency (☎ 8376 0933; www.baybeachfront.com.au; 1-bedroom apt per week from $1204; 🕵)

Eating & Drinking

our pick **Cafe Zest** (☎ 8295 3599; 2A Sussex St; meals $5-16; 🕑 breakfast & lunch; 🕵 Ⓥ) This cafe-gallery fills a tiny crack between buildings, but its laid-back vibe and brilliant breakfasts more than compensate for any shortcomings in size. Baguettes and bagels are crammed with creative combos, or banish your hangover with some 'hells eggs': two potted eggs with tomato, capsicum and rosemary salsa, topped with grilled cheese and Tabasco sauce. Great coffee, arty staff and vegetarian specials, too.

Thuy-Linh (☎ 8295 5746; 168C Jetty Rd; mains $11-19; 🕑 lunch Tue-Sat, dinner Tue-Sun; 🕵) Astonishingly unpretentious Vietnamese/Chinese eatery at the city end of Jetty Rd, with attentive service and a swath of fresh seafood, meat and noodle delights. Bring some mates and spin the lazy Susan (banquets $20 per person).

Good Life (☎ 8376 5900; 1st fl, cnr Jetty Rd & Moseley St; pizzas $13-37; 🕑 lunch Tue-Fri & Sun, dinner daily; 🕵 Ⓥ) At this brilliant organic pizzeria above the Jetty Rd tramscape, thin crusts are stacked with tasty toppings like free-range roast duck, Spencer Gulf 'monster' prawns and spicy Angaston salami. *Ahhh*, life is good… Also at 170 Hutt St in the city (Map p48; ☎ 8223 2618).

Gringos (☎ 8295 3524; Shop 1, Colley Tce; mains $16-24; 🕑 lunch & dinner; 🕵) Crack a cold Corona and chilli-up in the sun at this casual, good-time Mexican cantina opposite Moseley Sq, or take your bulging burrito down to the beach. Dangling sombreros and margaritas by the jug.

Zucca Greek Mezze (☎ 8376 8222; Shop 5, Marina Pier, Holdfast Shores; meze $17-19, mains $28-43; 🕑 lunch & dinner) Spartan linen, marina views, super service and a contemporary menu of meze plates – you'd be doing well to find anything this classy on Santorini. The saganaki is sheer teeth-squeaking joy.

Salt Bar & Restaurant (☎ 8376 6887; Holdfast Shores; mains $20-36; 🕑 lunch & dinner; 🕵) Sassy Salt pulls the punters to dine (upper-crust oysters, fish and steak) or just for drinks from the island

bar. Live DJs and duos Thursday to Saturday; jazz on Sunday afternoon.

Pier One Bar (☎ 8350 8188; 18 Holdfast Promenade) A cavernous sports bar with voyeuristic beach views and fold-back windows for when the sea breeze drops. As many screens as staff (a lot of each), and raucous Sunday sessions.

Entertainment

Glenelg Cinema Centre (☎ 8294 3366; www.wallis.com.au; 119 Jetty Rd; adult/concession/child $11.50/11/8.50; 🕑 11am-midnight) Mainstream films in an old, art deco theatre, plus movie-and-meal deals with local restaurants.

Getting There & Around

The scenically suburban **tram** (☎ 8212 1000; www.adelaidemetro.com.au) ride between Victoria Sq in the city and Glenelg is the easiest way to get to the Bay. Trams leave every 15 minutes or so from 6am to midnight, arriving at Moseley Sq 35 minutes later. There are day-trip ($8), and two-hour peak ($4.20) and off-peak ($2.60) tickets. Or take bus 135, 167, 168, 190 or 264 from the city down Anzac Hwy to Glenelg.

You can hire mountain bikes from **Glenelg Cycles** (☎ 8294 4741; www.glenelgcycles.com.au; 754 Anzac Hwy; bikes per day $30; 🕑 9am-5.30pm Mon-Fri, 9am-4pm Sat).

PORT ADELAIDE

Bogged in boganity for decades, Port Adelaide – 19km northwest of the city, and known as *Yerti Bulti* to the Kaurna people – is in the midst of gentrification, morphing its warehouses into art spaces and museums, and its brawl-houses pubs into boutique beer emporia. Things are on the up! The Port Adelaide footy team has been kicking goals too, winning the AFL premiership in 2004 and making the Grand Final in 2007 (just don't mention the score…).

The megahelpful **Port Adelaide Visitor Information Centre** (☎ 1800 629 888, 8405 6560; www.portenf.sa.gov.au; 66 Commercial Rd; 🕑 9am-5pm) is in the middle of the heritage area.

Sights & Activities

The visitors centre books guided **Port Walks** (gold-coin donation; 🕑 2pm Thu & Sun) around the heritage area, and **Kaurna Cultural Heritage Walks** (free; 🕑 10.30am 1st Sun of the month), unearthing the Port's indigenous heritage with an Aboriginal guide. The visitors centre also stocks brochures on local self-guided tours, including the following:
Walking the Port A ramble around the Port's history-rich heritage zone, via 38 key sights.

DETOUR: ST KILDA

No, no, not the St Kilda in Melbourne. And not the one in Scotland. This **St Kilda** (off Map p52) is 20 minutes north of Port Adelaide on the soupy seashore – a strange little enclave with a weird sense of abandonment to it. There's not much here except a pub, a few shacks and a marina, but it's worth the drive (bring a good map) for the swashbuckling **St Kilda Adventure Playground** (☎ 8406 8222; www.salisbury.sa.gov.au; admission free; ☼ dawn-dusk), with giant slides, a maze, castle and shipwreck); and the **St Kilda Mangrove Trail & Interpretive Centre** (☎ 8406 8222; www .salisbury.sa.gov.au; adult/concession/child $7/6/4; ☼ 10am-4pm), featuring a 45-minute boardwalk loop through remnant mangrove swamp, all a-twitter with birdlife.

Dolphin Trail Shore-based driving tour of bottlenose-dolphin viewing points along the Port River.

Kids' Port Walk A backpack stuffed with maps, activity sheets, a magnifying glass and stickers for kids over eight.

Heritage Pub Trail Detailed walking tour (or pub crawl, if you're thirsty) of nine classic Port Adelaide's booze barns.

Ships' Graveyards If you've got wheels, scoot between five watery sites of maritime misery.

The sea-salty **Maritime Museum** (☎ 8207 6255; www.history.sa.gov.au; 126 Lipson St; admission adult/concession/child/family $8.50/6.50/3.50/22; ☼ 10am-5pm daily, lighthouse 10am-2pm Sun-Fri) is the oldest of its kind in Australia. Highlights include the iconic Port Adelaide Lighthouse, busty figureheads made everywhere from Londonderry to Québec, shipwreck and explorer displays and a computer register of early migrants.

Trainspotters rejoice! The **National Railway Museum** (☎ 8341 1690; www.natrailmuseum.org.au; Lipson St Sth; admission adult/concession/child/family $12/9/5/29; ☼ 10am-5pm) has a hefty collection of railway memorabilia. The **South Australian Aviation Museum** (☎ 8240 1230; www.saam.org.au; Lipson St; adult/concession/child/family $8/5/4/16; ☼ 10.30am-4.30pm) has a similarly impressive collection of old planes.

Kids adore the **Seahorse Farm** (☎ 8447 7824; www.seahorses.com; adult/concession/child/family $8.50/8/7.50/26; ☼ 11am-4pm), with an educational DVD and walls of aquariums full of the squiggly little critters.

Cruises departing Port Adelaide Wharf to ogle the local bottlenose dolphins are run by **Port Princess Dolphin Cruises** (☎ 8447 2366; www .portprincess.com.au) and **Dolphin Explorer Cruises** (☎ 8447 2366; www.dolphinexplorer.com.au), both offering 90-minute, two-hour and lunch cruises from $4 per person. Alternatively, **Blue Water Sea Kayaking** (☎ 8295 8812; www .adventure-kayak.com.au) runs a range of guided and self-guided kayak tours around the Port River estuary from $50 per adult.

If you're here on a Sunday, the **Fisherman's Wharf Market** (☎ 8341 2040; ☼ 9am-5pm Sun) has antiques, bric-a-brac and crappy collectables.

Sleeping & Eating

For sleeping options you'll be better off in Glenelg (p64) or back in the city (p55).

In a converted warehouse opposite the Maritime Museum, **Lipson Café** (☎ 8341 0880; 117A Lipson St; breakfast $4-12, lunch $8-15; ☼ breakfast & lunch; Ⓥ) keeps the arts community fed and caffeinated with great food (big breakfasts, chunky sandwiches from the breadboard, salads and noodles) and peppy coffee.

Getting There & Around

West-bound buses 150 and 153 will get you here from North Tce, or take the train.

The visitors centre has a limited number of free bikes.

ADELAIDE HILLS

When the Adelaide plains are desert-hot in summer, the Adelaide Hills (technically the Mt Lofty Ranges) are always a few degrees cooler, with crisp air, woodland shade and a labyrinth of cool valleys. Fleeing the sweaty city, early colonists built stately summer houses around Stirling and Aldgate. German settlers escaping religious persecution also arrived, infusing towns such as Hahndorf and Lobethal with European values and architecture.

The Hills make a brilliant day trip from Adelaide – hop from town to town (all with pub), passing carts of fresh produce for sale, stone cottages, olive groves and vineyards along the way. The Hills are especially beautiful in autumn, with fiery red deciduous leaves and rows of hillside vines aglow at sunset.

Activities here include visiting wildlife sanctuaries and bushwalking: the region is criss-crossed by hundreds of kilometres of tracks, including the Heysen Trail. And the Hills are alive with the sound of clinking wine glasses: pick up the *Adelaide Hills Wine Region Cellar Door Guide* and *Fabulous Adelaide Hills Food Trails* brochures from visitors centres and go exploring. For a more structured, self-drive picnic experience, see www.cheeseandwine trails.com.au/adelaidehills.html.

Getting There & Around
BUS
Adelaide Metro (☎ 1800 182 160, 8212 1000; www .adelaidemetro.com.au) runs several buses between the city and most Hills towns. The 864 and

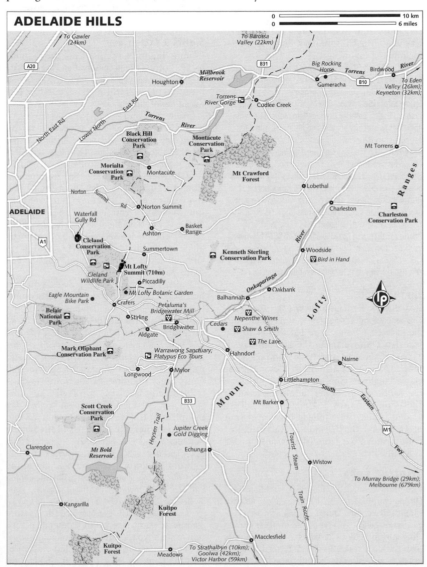

ADELAIDE HILLS

0   10 km
0   6 miles

To Gawler (24km)

To Barossa Valley (22km)

A20

B31

Big Rocking Horse   *Torrens*   Birdwood   *River*

Millbrook Reservoir

Houghton

Gumeracha   B10   To Eden Valley (26km); Keyneton (32km)

Torrens River Gorge

Cudlee Creek

North East Rd

Lower North East Rd

Torrens   *River*

Black Hill Conservation Park

Montacute Conservation Park

Mt Torrens

Morialta Conservation Park

Montacute

Mt Crawford Forest

Lobethal

Ranges

Norton   Summit Rd

Norton Summit

Charleston

Charleston Conservation Park

ADELAIDE

A1

Waterfall Gully Rd

Ashton

Basket Range

River

Woodside

Cleland Conservation Park

Summertown

Kenneth Sterling Conservation Park

Bird in Hand

Mt Lofty Summit (710m)

Cleland Wildlife Park

Piccadilly

Mt Lofty Botanic Garden

Onkaparinga

Oakbank

Lofty

Eagle Mountain Bike Park

Crafers

Petaluma's Bridgewater Mill

Balhannah

Belair National Park

Stirling

Bridgewater

Cedars

Nepenthe Wines

Shaw & Smith

Aldgate

The Lane

Mark Oliphant Conservation Park

Warrawong Sanctuary; Platypus Eco Tours

Hahndorf

Nairne

Longwood

Mylor

Littlehampton

South

Mount

Mt Barker

Eastern

Scott Creek Conservation Park

B33

M1

Fwy

Clarendon

Mt Bold Reservoir

Heysen Trail

Jupiter Creek Gold Digging

Echunga

Tourist Steam

Wistow

To Murray Bridge (29km); Melbourne (679km)

Kangarilla

Kuitpo Forest

Train Route

Macclesfield

Kuitpo Forest

Meadows

To Strathalbyn (10km); Goolwa (42km); Victor Harbor (59km)

864F buses are useful, departing Currie St in the city and stopping at Crafers, Stirling, Bridgewater and Hahndorf en route to Mt Barker. The 864 also services Aldgate. The 823 runs from Crafers to Mt Lofty Summit and Cleland Wildlife Park; the 830F runs from the city to Oakbank, Woodside and Lobethal.

TOURS

Day tours from Adelaide are a package-sized way to see the Hills in quick time. Operators include the following:

Bikeabout (☎ 0413-525 733; www.bikeabout.com.au) Cycling day tours ($75 including bikes, helmets and lunch) through the Hills. Minimum six people.

Enjoy Adelaide (☎ 8332 1401; www.enjoyadelaide .com.au) Runs a half-day city-highlights tour ($40) with diversions to Mt Lofty Summit and Hahndorf, and a full-day combined Hahndorf and Barossa Valley tour ($60).

Gray Line (☎ 1300 858 687; www.grayline.com.au) Comprehensive 'Best of Adelaide' tours include the Hills and Hahndorf ($186), Hills/Barossa day tours ($117) with loads of stops, plus dedicated Cleland Wildlife Park tours ($55).

Premier Stateliner (☎ 8415 5566; www.premierstate liner.com.au) Half-day tours to the Hills ($55), taking in Stirling, Mt Lofty Summit, Hahndorf and Cleland Wildlife Park.

Prime Mini Tours (☎ 1300 667 650, 8556 6117; www .primeminitours.com) Day tour to Hahndorf and Victor Harbor ($60 including Mt Lofty Summit); tour of wineries from the Hills to McLaren Vale ($102 including tastings and lunch).

TRAIN

SteamRanger Heritage Railway (☎ 1300 655 991, 8263 5621; www.steamranger.org.au) runs steam and diesel tourist trains from Mt Barker to the Fleurieu Peninsula. On the last Sunday in May and the first and third Sundays from June to November, trundle to Victor Harbor via Strathalbyn, Goolwa and Port Elliot on the *Southern Encounter* (adult/concession/child/family return $64/55/35/155). Every second Sunday from June to November (not in October), the *Highlander* (adult/child/family return $26/16/68) runs only as far as Strathalbyn.

STIRLING AREA

The photogenic little villages of establishment **Stirling** (population 2870), one-horse **Aldgate** (3350), drive-thru **Crafers** (1950) and market-garden **Piccadilly** (530) are famed for their bedazzling autumn colours, thanks to the deciduous trees the early residents saw fit to seed. There's not a great deal to do 'round these here parts, but there are some excellent cafes, restaurants and atmospheric (read: pricey) places to stay.

Information

Matilda Bookshop (☎ 8339 3931; 8 Mt Barker Rd, Stirling; ⊗ 9.30am-5.30pm Mon-Fri, 9am-5pm Sat, 11am-5pm Sun) Outstanding village bookshop, with an especially good range of kids' books.

Mt Lofty Summit Visitor Information Centre (see below).

Sights & Activities

Clambering up the slopes from the foothills to Mt Lofty, **Cleland Conservation Park** (☎ 8339 2444; www.environment.sa.gov.au/parks) has steep bushwalking trails through tall eucalypt forest and cool gullies.

Inside the Conservation Park, the fab **Cleland Wildlife Park** (☎ 8339 2444; www.clelandwildlifepark.sa.gov .au; Mt Lofty Summit Rd; admission adult/concession/child $14/11.50/8.50; ⊗ 9.30am-5pm, last entry 4.30pm) lets you interact with all kinds of Australian beasts. There are keeper talks, feeding sessions throughout the day, nocturnal tours (bookings required), and you can have your mugshot taken with a koala ($15, 2pm to 4pm). The **Cleland Café** (meals $3-16; breakfast & lunch) serves light lunches and snacks. To get here by bus from the city, take bus 864 or 864F from Grenfell St to Crafers for connecting bus 823 to the park.

From Cleland Wildlife Park you can bushwalk (2km) or drive up to **Mt Lofty Summit** (a surprising 710m), which has eye-popping views across Adelaide and Gulf St Vincent. **Mt Lofty Summit Visitor Information Centre** (☎ 8370 1054; www.mtloftysummit.com; Mt Lofty Summit Rd; ⊗ 9am-5pm) has oodles of info on local attractions and walking tracks, including the steep Waterfall Gully Track (8km return, 2½ hours) and Mt Lofty Botanic Gardens Loop Trail (7km loop, two hours). The video of the Ash Wednesday bushfires of 16 February 1983 is harrowing. If you're hungry, the snazzy **Mt Lofty Summit Restaurant** (lunch $10-18, dinner $27-33; breakfast & lunch daily, dinner Wed-Sun; ✉) is in the same building.

From Mt Lofty, truck south 1.5km to the cool-climate slopes of **Mt Lofty Botanic Garden** (☎ 8222 9311; www.botanicgardens.sa.gov.au; gates on Mawson Dr & Lampert Rd; admission free, parking $2; ⊗ 8.30am-4pm Mon-Fri, 10am-5pm Sat & Sun). Nature trails wind past a lake, exotic temperate plants, native stringybark forest and bodacious rhododendron blooms. Free guided walks depart the Lampert Rd car park at 10.30am on

TOP FIVE ADELAIDE HILLS WINERIES

With night mists and reasonable rainfall, the Adelaide Hills' mid-altitude slopes sustain one of SA's cooler climates – perfect for producing some complex and truly top-notch white wines, especially Chardonnays and Sauvignon Blancs. There are 20-plus wineries here, but these are our favourite five:

- **Bird in Hand** (☎ 8389 9488; www.birdinhand.com.au; cnr Bird in Hand & Pfeiffer Rds, Woodside; 11am-5pm Mon-Fri, 10am-5pm Sat & Sun) Brilliant sparking red, Shiraz, Merlot and blends, plus an olive oil distillery. Worth at least two in the bush.

- **The Lane** (☎ 8388 1250; www.thelane.com.au; Ravenswood La, Hahndorf; mains $27-35; 10am-4pm Mon-Thu, to 5pm Fri-Sun) Wow! What a cool building, and what a setting! Camera-conducive views and contemporary varietals (Viognier, Pinot Grigio, Pinot Gris), plus an outstanding restaurant. Hard to beat.

- **Nepenthe Wines** (☎ 8388 4439; www.nepenthe.com.au; Jones Rd, Balhannah; 10am-4pm) Homer described nepenthe as a potion to ease grief and banish sorrow from the mind. Accordingly, Nepenthe Wines bring great happiness, especially the Semillon, Chardonnay and (surprisingly) Cabernet Sauvignon.

- **Petaluma's Bridgewater Mill** (☎ 8339 9200; www.bridgewatermill.com.au; Mt Barker Rd, Bridgewater; 2/3 courses $68/87; 10am-5pm, lunch Thu-Mon;) In a restored 200-year-old flour mill, this is one of SA's premier winery restaurants. Book for a tasting followed by lunch. Exquisite Chardonnay, Riesling and Sauvignon Blanc.

- **Shaw & Smith** (☎ 8398 0500; www.shawandsmith.com; Jones Rd, Balhannah; 11am-4pm Sat & Sun) Picture-perfect Mt Lofty Ranges views almost steal the show at this mod winery, run by two cousins. Outstanding Chardonnays and Sauvignon Blancs, holding hands with grand Shiraz.

Thursdays from September to October, and 2pm on Sundays from March to May.

Stirling Markets (☎ 8339 3378; brycarm@bigpond.net.au; Druids Ave, Stirling; admission free; 10am-4pm) happen on the fourth Sunday of the month (the third in December). Much plantlife, busking and Hills knick-knackery.

Sleeping & Eating

Mount Lofty Railway Station (☎ 8339 7400; www.mlrs.com.au; 2 Sturt Valley Rd, Stirling; d/f from $95/110) With four bedrooms, five bathrooms, two lounges, a kitchen and kitchenette, this disused, heritage-listed train station is affordable and versatile. You can book the whole thing, or divide it into two self-contained apartments. The catch: the train line is *not* disused (10 trains every 24 hours – bring earplugs). Two-night minimum.

Mt Lofty House (☎ 8339 6777; www.mtloftyhouse.com.au; 74 Summit Rd, Crafers; d incl breakfast from $180;) Proprietarily poised above Mt Lofty Botanic Garden (*awesome* views!) this 1850s baronial mansion has lavish heritage rooms and garden suites, plus an upmarket restaurant (also with killer views). The perfect dirty weekender!

Aldgate Creek Cottage B&B (☎ 8339 1987; www.aldgatecreekbnb.com; 3 Rugby Rd, Aldgate; d from $210;) A romantic, two-storey cottage-for-two in a grove of vegetation above Aldgate Creek, just across the road from the improving Aldgate Pump Hotel. Bonuses include flat-screen TV in the bedroom, a spa and a family of resident ducks.

our pick Organic Market & Café (☎ 8339 4835; 5 Druids Ave, Stirling; meals $6-12; breakfast & lunch;) Rejecting Stirling's pompous tendencies, hirsute Hill-types flock to this vibrant, hippie café. It's the busiest spot in town – and rightly so; the food's delicious and everything's made with love. Gorge on bruschetta, plump savoury muffins, great coffee and wicked Portuguese custard tarts.

Stirling Hotel (☎ 8339 2345; 52 Mt Barker Rd, Stirling; bistro $14-26, restaurant $26-36; lunch & dinner;) The owners spent so much tarting up this gorgeous old dame, it's a wonder they can pay the staff. A runaway success, the free-flowing bistro (classy pub grub) and romantic restaurant (upmarket regional cuisine) are always packed.

Jimmies (☎ 8339 1534; 6 Main St, Crafers; mains $17-20; breakfast Sun, lunch Sat, dinner Tue-Sun;) Always-busy pizza joint (kid friendly) serving great gourmet pizzas. Enjoy a delicious disc with pumpkin, Danish fetta, rocket and *za'atar* (Middle Eastern spices) at the outdoor tables.

See also Petaluma's Bridgewater Mill (above) in neaarby Bridgewater.

MYLOR

pop 740

The going concern in leafy Mylor is **Warrawong Sanctuary** (☎ 8370 9197; www.warrawong.com; Stock Rd, Mylor; admission free before 4pm, adult/child/family $5/3/13 4pm-9pm; ☺ 9am-9pm), 3km from town – a feral-free private wildlife sanctuary with a cafe and accommodation. Take a self-guided walk, check out a wildlife show (adult/child/family $5/3/13; 11am and 2pm daily), or book a 1½-hour guided dusk walk (adult/child/family $25/16/65). Accommodation is in en suite ecotents, each sleeping up to eight. B&B costs adult/child/family $75/45/195; packages including bed, show, walk, dinner and breakfast are also available (adult/child/family $120/70/350). The windows in the **cafe** (lunch $6-14, dinner $9-20; ☺ lunch & dinner) look onto a fern grove full of squawking ducks, parrots and lorikeets.

Never seen a platypus? **Platypus Eco Tours** (☎ 8370 8628; www.platypusecotours.com.au; Lot 14, Williams Rd, Mylor; tours adult/child $40/20; ☺ dusk) runs small-group ecotours – you're guaranteed to see more than just the disappearing splash of a tail! Other critters here include bandicoots, wallabies, kangaroos and koalas. Tours at sunset year-round; call for bookings and times.

HAHNDORF

pop 1700

Like the Rocks in Sydney and Richmond near Hobart, Hahndorf is a 'ye olde worlde' colonial enclave that trades ruthlessly on its history. The town has become a kitsch parody of itself with very little actual 'life', just busloads of tourists picking over the bones of former glories.

That said, Hahndorf is undeniably pretty, with Teutonic sandstone architecture, European trees, and flowers overflowing from half wine barrels. And it *is* interesting: Australia's oldest surviving German settlement (1839), founded by 50 Lutheran families fleeing religious persecution in Prussia. Hahndorf was placed under martial law during WWI; its Lutheran school was boarded up and its name changed to 'Ambleside' (changed back to Hahndorf in 1935).

Information

The **Adelaide Hills Visitor Information Centre** (☎ 1800 353 323; 8388 1185; www.visitadelaidehills.com.au; 41 Main St; ☺ 9am-5pm Mon-Fri, 10am-4pm Sat & Sun) has the usual barrage of brochures, books, accommodation, and has internet access.

Sights & Activities

The 1857 **Hahndorf Academy & Heritage Museum** (☎ 8388 7250; www.hahndorfacademy.org.au; 68 Main St; Academy free, museum by donation; ☺ 10am-5pm) houses an art gallery with rotating exhibitions and several original sketches by Sir Hans Heysen, the famed landscape artist and Hahndorf homeboy. The museum depicts the lives of early German settlers, with pious church pews, dour dresses, horse-drawn buggies and a collection of bizarrely carved pipes.

You'll see more than 300 of Sir Hans' original doodles on a tour through his studio and house, the **Cedars** (☎ 8388 7277; fax 8388 1845; Heysen Rd; tours $8; ☺ tours 11am, 1pm & 3pm Sep-May, 11am & 2pm Jun-Aug, Tue-Sun), 2km northwest of town.

Pick your own strawberries between November and May from the famous **Beerenberg Strawberry Farm** (☎ 8388 7272; www.beerenberg.com.au; Mount Barker Rd; strawberries from $9/kg; ☺ 9am-5pm, last entry 4.15pm), also big-noted for its plethora of jams, chutneys and sauces.

Sleeping & Eating

Stables Inn (☎ 8388 7988; www.stablesinncafemotel.web syte.com.au; 74 Main St; d with/without spa $120/100, f $160, extra person $22; ☒) The most affordable beds within cooee are in this converted 1860s stable, with small but comfy bottle-green motel rooms. The family-sized house out the back sleeps eight.

Manna (☎ 1800 882 682, 8388 1000; www.themanna .com.au; 25 & 35a Main St; d/tw/f from $130/140/160; ☒ ☐) Behind the Hahndorf Inn you'll find this refurbished, exposed-brick motel complex with an indoor pool (formerly the Hahndorf Inn Motor Lodge), and brand-spankin'-new upmarket suites.

Chocolate @ No 5 (☎ 8388 1835; 5 Main St; items $2-8; ☺ breakfast & lunch Thu-Mon; ☒ V) Everyone knows why you're here, so don't feel embarrassed. Just plough into the homemade choc desserts and delicious 'milk, dark or white' hot chocolates.

Udder Delights (☎ 8388 1588; www.udderdelights .com.au; 91A Main St; breakfast $6-10, mains $12-32; ☺ breakfast & lunch; ☒ V) The shining light of Hahndorf's food scene, this udderly delightful cheese cellar–café serves salads, tarts, pies, soups, cakes, generous cheese platters and the best coffee this side of Stirling. There's also a self-contained, Spanish-style studio apartment here (double $200, including breakfast).

For slatherings of sauerkraut, wurst, pretzels, strudel and clinking beer steins, try Hahndorf's pubs:

German Arms Hotel (☎ 8388 7013; 69 Main St; mains $12-30; ☺ lunch & dinner; ⊠) Packed on weekends (with 18-to-25-year-olds, oddly enough), the bratwursts and schnitzels here are legendary.

Hahndorf Inn (☎ 8388 1000; 35 Main St; mains $14-30; ☺ breakfast, lunch & dinner; ⊠) Heart-clogging cheese kranskys, Vienna sausages, sauerkraut and apple strudels; a friendly buzz and no pokies.

See also the Lane (p69).

OAKBANK
pop 450

Strung-out Oakbank lives for the annual **Oakbank Easter Racing Carnival** (www.oakbankracing club.com.au), said to be the greatest picnic race meeting in the world. It's a two-day festival of equine splendour, risqué dresses and 18-year-olds who can't hold their liquor.

Adelaide Hills Country Cottages (☎ 8388 4193; www.ahcc.com.au; Oakwood Rd, Oakbank; d incl breakfast from $220; ⊠) On 200 acres 2km north of Oakbank, these five retreats (three traditional, two contemporary) have racked up a wall-ful of awards. Open fires, breakfast provisions, spas and wi-fi. Two-night minimum.

WOODSIDE
pop 1830

Agricultural Woodside has a few enticements for galloping gourmands.

Melba's Chocolate & Confectionery Factory (☎ 8389 7868; www.melbaschocolates.com; 22 Henry St, Woodside; admission & tastings free; ☺ 9am-4.30pm) Watch choc-coated sultanas tumbling in huge cement mixers and stock up on rocky road, scorched almonds and appallingly realistic chocolate cow pats.

Woodside Cheese Wrights (☎ 8389 7877; www.woodsidecheesewrights.com.au; 7 Henry St, Woodside; admission & tastings free; ☺ 10am-4pm) A passionate but unpretentious Woodside gem producing classic, artisan and experimental cheeses (soft styles a speciality) from locally grazing sheep and cows.

Woodside Providore (☎ 8389 9510; 69 Main Rd, Woodside; mains $10-23; ☺ breakfast & lunch; ⊠ Ⓥ) An understated, organic Hills hit, with super coffee, salads, soups, gourmet pizzas, local wines and international offerings such as osso bucco and Sri Lankan curries.

LOBETHAL
pop 1660

In the 'Valley of Praise', Lobethal was established by Lutheran Pastor Fritzsche and his followers in 1842. The church opened for business in 1843. Like Hahndorf, Lobethal was renamed during WWI – 'Tweedale' was the unfortunate choice. The main street has the usual complement of soporific pubs and hardware stores, but the town really hits its straps during December's **Lights of Lobethal** (www.lights oflobethal.com.au) festival – a blaze of Christmas lights brings sightseers from the city.

While you're in town, check out the local arts and crafts at the **Heart of the Hills Market** (☎ 8389 5615; www.marketsatheart.com; 1 Adelaide-Lobethal Rd; admission free; ☺ 10am-4pm Fri-Sun) then repair to the streetside terrace of the **Lobethal Bierhaus** (☎ 8389 5570; www.bierhaus.com.au; 3A Main St; ☺ noon-10pm Fri & Sat, to 6pm Sun) for some serious microbrewed concoctions. The Red Truck Porter will put hairs on your chest.

The modest **Lobethal Bakery** (☎ 8389 6318; 80 Main St; items $2-7; breakfast & lunch Mon-Sat; ⊠ Ⓥ) is a Hills institution, spawning franchises in other towns. Germanic biscuits, cakes, pies and takeaway soup-in-a-cup.

The **Mawson Trail** (p287) tracks through here.

GUMERACHA & BIRDWOOD

A scenic drive from Adelaide to Birdwood leads through the **Torrens River Gorge** and **Gumeracha** (population 400), a hardy hillside town with a pub at the bottom (making it hard to roll home). The main lure here is the 18.3m-high **Big Rocking Horse** (admission $2), which doesn't actually rock, but is unusually tasteful as far as Australia's 'big' tourist attractions go. It's part of the **Toy Factory** (☎ 8389 1085; www.thetoyfactory.com .au; Main Adelaide Rd, Gumeracha; ☺ 9am-5pm), which turns out quality handmade wooden toys (oh, and Big Rocking Horse stubbie holders).

National Trust–classified buildings line the slumbering main drag of **Birdwood** (population 1130), which began as a wide-awake gold-mining and agricultural centre in the 1850s. Behind the town's impressive old flour mill (1852) are immaculate vintage and classic cars and motorcycles at the **National Motor Museum** (☎ 8568 4000; Shannon St; www.history.sa.gov.au; adult/concession/child/family $9/7/4/24; ☺ 9am-5pm). The museum marks the finishing line for September's **Bay to Birdwood** (www.baytobirdwood.com.au) – a convoy of classic cars chugging up from the city.

Fleurieu Peninsula & Kangaroo Island

Tracking down through Adelaide's southern suburbs, a string of white-sand beaches rims the coastline of the Fleurieu Peninsula (pronounced 'floo-ree-o'). The suburbs soon fray away to the bountiful vineyards of McLaren Vale, turning out show-stopping Shiraz. A vigorous foodie culture has grown up alongside the grapes – make sure there's plenty of room in your stomach as well as your car boot!

Further east, the rugged Encounter Coast is awash with surf beaches, soporific sea-salt towns, passing whales and early white history: explorers Flinders and Baudin 'encountered' each other here in 1802, racing each other around the shore naming geographic features in both French and English. The southern Fleurieu is much less developed, and makes a low-key agricultural escape. The epic Heysen Trail jags through here, meandering from Cape Jervis north through the Adelaide Hills and beyond.

From Cape Jervis, car ferries chug across the swells of the Backstairs Passage to Kangaroo Island. Long devoid of tourist trappings, the island these days is a booming destination for fans of wilderness and wildlife (not to mention wine and seafood). Southern Ocean Lodge, a new luxury retreat for the exquisitely rich, has propelled 'KI' onto the international stage. The island markets itself as 'unspoiled' – visit now while it still is.

HIGHLIGHTS

- Quaffing Shiraz and hitting the gourmet trail around **McLaren Vale** (p74) and **Willunga** (p76)
- Catching the rattly horse-drawn tram out to **Granite Island** (p78) in Victor Harbor
- Seeking leafy sea dragons on a dive at **Rapid Bay** (p78) or the scuttled **HMAS Hobart** (p77)
- Cruising the coast on the **Encounter Bikeway** (p79) between Goolwa and Victor Harbor
- Adoring the residents of KI's **Seal Bay Conservation Park** (p90)
- Peering at the waddling **little penguins** at Penneshaw on KI (p86)
- Remarking over the **Remarkable Rocks** (p92) in wild, western Flinders Chase National Park

■ TELEPHONE CODE: ☎ 08   ■ www.fleurieupeninsula.com.au   ■ www.tourkangarooisland.com.au

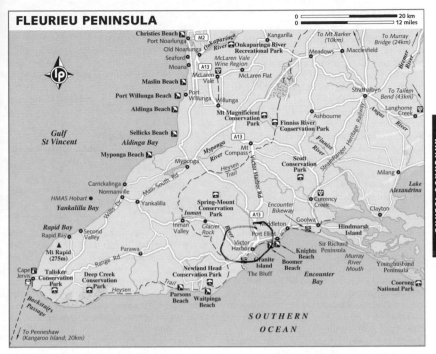

FLEURIEU PENINSULA & KANGAROO ISLAND

FLEURIEU PENINSULA

Patterned with vineyards, olive groves and almond plantations, the Fleurieu Peninsula is Adelaide's weekend (and often midweek) playground, with straw-coloured hills running down to the sea. McLaren Vale is a booming wine region, producing gutsy reds (salubrious Shiraz) to rival those from the Barossa Valley (actually, we think McLaren Vale wins hands-down).

Further afield, the Encounter Coast is a curious mix of surf beaches and historic towns with either plenty to offer or limited appeal.

Getting There & Around

Premier Stateliner (☎ 8415 5555; www.premierstateliner.com.au) runs up to four buses daily from Adelaide to McLaren Vale ($8, one hour), Willunga ($9, 1¼ hours), Victor Harbor ($19, 1¾ hours), Port Elliot ($19, two hours) and Goolwa ($19, 2¼ hours).

Regular **Adelaide Metro** (☎ 1800 182 160, 08-8210 1000; www.adelaidemetro.com.au) suburban trains run between Adelaide and Noarlunga. From here, **Southlink** (☎ 08-8186 2888; www.southlink.com.au) buses 751 and 753 run to McLaren Vale and Willunga. Regular Adelaide Metro ticket prices apply.

Sealink (☎ 13 13 01; www.sealink.com.au) operates vehicular ferries to Kangaroo Island from Cape Jervis on the southern end of the Fleurieu Peninsula (see p85). The company also operates a morning and afternoon bus service between Cape Jervis and Adelaide's Central Bus Station (adult/child $20/10, 2¼ hours), stopping in towns en route. Coaches also connect Cape Jervis with Goolwa and Victor Harbor ($20/10, 40 minutes).

The **SteamRanger Heritage Railway** (☎ 1300 655 991, 08-8263 5621; www.steamranger.org.au) operates tourist trains from Mt Barker in the Adelaide Hills down into the Fleurieu Peninsula (see p80 for details).

Bicycle hire is available in McLaren Vale (p75) and Victor Harbor (p80). For details on Fleurieu Peninsula tours departing from Adelaide, see p54.

STRATHALBYN
pop 3220

Just south of the Adelaide Hills (Strath, the locals insist, is more McLaren Vale than Mt Barker), Strathalbyn was established in 1839 by Scottish immigrants. Many of the old streetscapes and buildings have been preserved, and while there's a weary aimlessness to the place, it does makes a good place to stop for a bed or bite. The town's many cappuccino joints, bakeries and antique stores fill with antique connoisseurs on weekends.

Strathalbyn visitors centre (☎ 8536 3212; www .visitalexandrina.com; 20 South Tce; ✆ 9am-5pm Mon-Fri, 10am-4pm Sat & Sun), in the train station, has an attached gallery and racks of info on Strathalbyn, including walking-tour maps with detailed heritage information.

Manicured gardens flank the **Angas River** as it flows through town, overlooked by the turreted **St Andrew's Church** (1848). History buffs can bone up on the town's Celtic heritage at the National Trust–run, 1858 **Old Police Station & Courthouse Museum** (☎ 8536 8053; www.strathmuseum .org.au; cnr South Tce & Rankine St; admission adult/conces-sion/child $5/4/1; ✆ 1.30-4pm Sat & Sun), which in-cludes spooky old cells.

For the bird's-eye perspective, **Adelaide Ballooning** (☎ 1300 730 313; www.adelaideballooning .com.au; Langhorne Creek Rd; flights from $250) will set you aloft and drifting.

Sleeping & Eating
Victoria Hotel (☎ 8536 2202; 16 Albyn Tce; d incl breakfast from $100; ⊠) This renovated country pub opposite the Angas River parkland has comfortable rooms and a deep veranda for lunch, a beer and watching touring bikies rumble past. Beyond the pokies out the back is an enormous bistro (mains $13 to $22, open for lunch & dinner) serving classic pub grub.

Strath Motel (☎ 8536 3311; www.strathmotel .com.au; 4 North Pde; d/tw $130/140; ⊠) Brand-spankin'-new on the outskirts of town, this beaut motel features king-sized beds, flat-screen TVs, slick bathrooms and moody low-volt-age lighting. We wonder how the twiggy steel walkway will hold up in a stiff breeze.

Gasworks B&B (☎ 8536 4291; gasworksstrathalbyn@ bigpond.com.au; 12 South Tce; d from $160, extra person $50; ⊠) Stay in one of the restored stone residences of the old gasworks, with terraced gardens overlooking a sweep of trickling river. Each cottage (chintz-meets–Persian

rug) has a spa and kitchen for cooking up bumper breakfast provisions.

Argus House Patisserie (☎ 0400 522 404; 33 Commercial Rd; meals $7-9; ✆ breakfast & lunch) Run by a Swedish chef (just like on *The Muppets*!), this wholesome little eatery in the old Argus press building plates up pizzas, awesome custard tarts, homemade beef pie and fried Hungarian garlic bread. Wonderful!

Getting There & Away
You can get here via the **SteamRanger Heritage Railway** (see p80), or if you're driving, Strathalbyn is 12 minutes from the wineries at **Langhorne Creek** (see p81).

MCLAREN VALE
pop 2560

Flanked by the wheat-coloured Willunga Scarp, 'The Vale' rivals the Barossa as South Australia's (SA's) most-visited wine region. Just 40 minutes south of Adelaide (if you time your run with the irritating one-way Southern Expressway, which runs south–north in the mornings and north–south in the afternoons, then the other way around on weekends), it's an easy cruise to SA's version of the Mediterranean. Encircled by vines, McLaren Vale itself is the region's service centre – an energetic, utilitarian town that's not much to look at, but has some great eateries.

Information
McLaren Vale & Fleurieu visitors centre (☎ 8323 9944; www.mclarenvale.info; Main Rd, McLaren Vale; ✆ 9am-5pm Mon-Fri, 10am-5pm Sat & Sun), at the northern end of McLaren Vale, can assist with accommoda-tion and Sealink bus and ferry bookings (to Kangaroo Island). There's a cafe here too.

Sights & Activities
Most people come to McLaren Vale to cruise the wineries (see opposite). You could spend days doing nothing else, but there are a few ways to break it up (and sober up) between tastings. For starters, pick up the *McLaren Vale Heritage Trail* brochure from the visitors centre for a self-guided stroll through town.

A South Australian institution, **Medlow Confectionery** (☎ 8323 9105; www.robernmenz.com.au; 203 Main Rd; ✆ 10am-5pm) is the place for a sugar shot: fruit gels, 'fruchocs', choc-coated nuts and chocolates of all persuasions.

A great way to get a feel for the area is to take the **walking & cycling track** along the old railway

TOP FIVE MCLAREN VALE WINERIES

If the Barossa Valley is SA wine's old school, then McLaren Vale is the upstart teenager smoking cigarettes behind the shed and stealing nips from Dad's port bottle. The gorgeous vineyards around here have a Tuscan haze in summer, rippling down to a calm coastline that's similarly Ligurian. This is Shiraz country – solid, punchy and seriously good.

- **Chapel Hill Winery** (☎ 8323 8429; www.chapelhillwine.com.au; cnr Chapel Hill & Chaffeys Rd; ☷ noon-5pm) At the top of the hill is this restored 1865 chapel with vineyard and ocean views. There's brilliant group accommodation (double including breakfast $260; minimum two-night stay) at the four-year-old, stone-and-glass retreat and cooking school.

- **Coriole** (☎ 8323 8305; www.coriole.com; Chaffeys Rd; ☷ 10am-5pm Mon-Fri, 11am-5pm Sat & Sun) Take your regional tasting platter out into the garden of this beautiful cottage cellar door (1860) to share Kalamata olives, homemade breads and Adelaide Hills' Woodside cheeses made loveier by a swill of the Redstone Shiraz or the flagship Chenin Blanc. Aromatic olive oils, sweet vinegars and almonds to take away.

- **D'Arenberg Wines** (☎ 8323 8710; www.darenberg.com.au; Osborn Rd; ☷ 10am-5pm) A favourite spot in the Vale for lunch, 'd'Arry's' relaxes atop a hillside and enjoys fine views. The wine labels are part of the character of this place: Stump Jump Grenache Shiraz, Dead Arm Shiraz, and the Broken Fishplate Sauvignon Blanc are our faves. Book ahead for a fabulous lunch at their restaurant, d'Arry's Veranda.

- **Wirra Wirra Vineyards** (☎ 8323 8414; www.wirrawirra.com; McMurtrie Rd; ☷ 10am-5pm Mon-Sat, 11am-5pm Sun) Fancy a spot of pétanque with your plonk? This friendly barnlike, 1894 cellar door has a grassy picnic area, and there's a roaring fire inside in winter. Sample reasonably priced stickies (dessert wines) and the popular Reserve Shiraz. Whites include the citruslike Scrubby Rise Viognier and an aromatic Riesling.

- **Woodstock Winery & Coterie** (☎ 8383 0156; www.woodstockwine.com.au; Douglas Gully Rd; ☷ 9am-5pm Mon-Fri, noon-5pm Sat & Sun) Their reds are grand but hold out for the stickies and fortified drops. The Coterie does great platters ($30) for lunch, while the surrounding native garden is full of birdlife – a shady option on a hot day.

line from McLaren Vale to Willunga, 6km south. Hire a bike from Blessed Cheese (see p76), or **Oxygen Cycles** (☎ 8323 7345; oxygencycles@gmail.com; 143 Main Rd; bike hire per half-/full day $15/25; ☷ 10am-6pm Tue-Thu, 9am-6pm Fri, 9am to 5pm Sat, 10am-5pm Sun). Helmet, lock and basket (for bottles!) included.

It seems like most of Adelaide gets tizzed up and buses down for the annual **Sea & Vines Festival** (www.seaandvines.com) over the June long weekend. Local wineries cook up seafood, splash wine around and host live bands. The bigger wineries fill with party people – find a lesser-known spot and settle in for the afternoon.

Tours

Expect to pay anything from around $90 to $250 per person for a full-day McLaren Vale tour. For details on other tours departing Adelaide, see p54.

Integrity Tours & Charter (☎ 8382 9755, 0402-120 361) Full-day wine tours $89, including lunch and five wineries. Tours can extend to Victor Harbor.

Life is a Cabernet (☎ 8396 2233; www.lifeisacabernet .com.au) Top-end full-day tours ex-Adelaide, with a gourmet lunch and plenty of tastings.

McLaren Vale Tours (☎ 0414-784 666; www.mclaren valetours.com.au) Invent your own tour (from $70 per person ex–McLaren Vale), or hear some suggestions on lesser-known wineries and lunch spots.

Prime Mini Tours (☎ 1300 667 650; www.prime minitours.com) Full-day McLaren Vale and Adelaide Hills tours ($102), and McLaren Vale cheese and wine tours ($108). Ex-Adelaide, including lunch.

Southern Spirit (☎ 0407-223 361; www.southernlimos .com.au) Limousine and minibus tours through the vines.

Sleeping & Eating

McLaren Vale Lakeside Caravan Park (☎ 8323 9255; www.mclarenvale.net; Field St; unpowered/powered sites $21/25, vans/cabins with bathroom from $50/80; ☷ ☷) A short walk from town, this park by a man-made lake (any water this summer?) is as affordable as McLaren Vale accommodation gets. There's a camp kitchen, pool, spa, tennis court and trashy-book exchange.

McLaren Vale Motel & Apartments (☎ 1800 631 817; 8323 8265; www.mclarenvalemotel.com.au; cnr Main Rd & Caffrey St; s/d/f from $101/116/124; 🖭 🖳) A digestive walk from main-street restaurants, this cheery motel has solid doubles (old fashioned but clean and perfectly adequate), studio apartments and family suites, plus a pool fringed by derelict palms.

Red Poles (☎ 8323 8994; www.redpoles.com.au; McMurtrie Rd; d with/without bathroom $125/115, 🍽 lunch Wed-Sun) Nooked away in a bushy enclave, Red Poles is a great place to stay (and eat!). Try for the rustic-style en suite room – it's bigger than its counterparts. Order up some vegetarian moussaka or saltbush lamb salad (mains $23 to $31, open for lunch Wednesday to Sunday, breakfast Sunday), and check out the local artwork in the gallery while you wait.

Blessed Cheese (☎ 8323 7958; 150 Main Rd; mains $7-18; 🍽 breakfast & lunch; 🖭 Ⓥ) This blessed cafe cranks out great coffee, croissants, wraps, salads, tarts, burgers, cheese platters and murderous cakes. Join their self-guided Cheese & Wine Trail (www.cheeseandwine trails.com.au/mclaren.html; $55) and pick up a mini-esky containing cheeses, crackers, olives and muscatels. Bike hire per day/three hours costs $30/21.

Barn (☎ 8323 8618; 252 Main Rd; tapas $8, mains $19-35; 🍽 lunch & dinner Tue-Sun; 🖭) Retro-mod prints and furniture adorn this 1840s cottage bistro, which quadruples up as a cellar door, art gallery and wine bar. Mains are fishy and meaty, done with contemporary flair, or settle in for some tapas and a glass or two of good local stuff.

Salopian Inn (☎ 8323 8769; cnr Main & McMurtie Rds; mains $32; 🍽 lunch Thu-Tue, dinner Fri & Sat; 🖭) South of town, this vine-covered cottage behind a rosemary hedge has a serious rep. Start with the crumbed lambs brains with roasted cherry tomatoes and lemon, garlic and caper noisette butter, then follow through with the wild rabbit pie with roast veggies. Descend into the cellar for your wine.

See also Top Five McLaren Vale Wineries (p75) for winery-restaurant options.

WILLUNGA
pop 2430

A one-horse town with three pubs (a winning combo!), artsy Willunga took off in 1840 when high-quality slate was discovered nearby and exported across Australia. Today, the pink dollar has helped convert the town's early buildings along sloping High St into gourmet eateries and galleries.

The **Willunga Environment Centre** (☎ /fax 8556 4188; 18 High St; 🕙 10am-3pm Mon-Fri, 9.30am-1.30pm Sat) has basic tourist info and details on local flora and fauna. The town blooms into its own during the **Almond Blossom Festival** (www .willungafestivals.com) in July; if you can't wait that long, the **Willunga Farmers Market** (☎ 8556 4297; www.willungafarmersmarket.com; High St; 🕙 8am-12.30pm Sat) happens every weekend.

The **Kidman Trail** (p287) kicks off here.

Sleeping & Eating

Willunga Hotel (☎ 8556 2135; jhunt@picknowl.com.au; 3-5 High St; s/d $35/60) Straight-up, carpeted pub rooms painted a peachy colour, with clean shared bathrooms and a TV room. Downstairs in the 'Middle Pub' you can get a simple, feed-a-farmer pub meal (mains $16 to $20, open for lunch and dinner) – schnitzels, steaks and pasta.

Willunga House B&B (☎ 8556 2467; www.wil lungahouse.com.au; 1 St Peters Tce; d incl breakfast $190-250; 🖭 🖳) If you're looking for a real treat, this graceful 1850 mansion off the main street is for you: Baltic-pine floorboards, Italian cherry-wood beds, open fires, indigenous art and wireless internet. Breakfast is a feast of organic muesli, fruit salad and poached pears, followed by cooked delights.

Victory (☎ 8556 3083; Main South Rd, Sellicks Beach; mains $10-32; 🍽 lunch & dinner) On the highway just south of Willunga near Sellicks Beach, this rowdy, 1858 pub has awesome views of the silvery gulf and a cheery, laid-back vibe. Factor in inspired pub meals, an impressive cellar and wines by the glass and you're onto a winner. Renovations were afoot when we visited – expect even better views!

ourpick Russell's Pizza (☎ 8556 2571; 13 High St; pizzas from $24; 🍽 dinner Thu-Sat Dec-Feb, Fri & Sat only Mar-Nov; Ⓥ) It may look like a ramshackle chicken coop, but Russell's is the place to be on weekends for sensational wood-fired pizza. No one minds the wait for a meal (which could be hours) – it's all about the atmosphere. It's superpopular, so book way ahead.

Star of Greece (☎ 8557 7420; 1 The Esplanade, Port Willunga; mains $28-37; 🍽 lunch daily, dinner Fri & Sat) In nearby Port Willunga, this eternally busy, clifftop seafood shack has funky decor, a great staff and a sunny outdoor patio. We asked the waiter where the whiting was caught: he looked out across the bay and said, 'See that boat out there?'.

> ### UNDERWATER LOVE
>
> Don your flippers and tanks and check out some Fleurieu marine life – leafy sea dragons, seals, nudibranchs, dolphins and endemic species. Top **diving** sites include Second Valley, Rapid Bay jetty, Cape Jervis and the ex-destroyer HMAS *Hobart*, which was scuttled off Yankalilla Bay in 2002. Pick up a permit from **South Coast Surf** (☎ 8558 2822, fax 8558 2822; 2/79 Main Rd, Normanville; per dive $12; ☺ seasonal). The **Court House Café** (☎ 8558 3532; courthousecafe@optusnet.com.au; 52 Main St, Normanville; s/d $70/80; 💻) has basic diver accommodation in old jail buildings and hires dive gear.
>
> Port Elliot and Middleton have some wicked **surf**, with swells often holding at 3m; other gnarly breaks are Waitpinga Beach and Parsons Beach, 12km southwest of Victor Harbor. The best surfing season is March to June, when the northerlies doth blow. See www.southaustralia .com/fleurieupeninsulasurfing.aspx for info, and www.surfsouthoz.com for surf reports. Learn to surf (from $40 including gear) with **South Coast Surf Academy** (☎ 0414-341 545; www.danosurf .com.au) or **Surf & Sun** (☎ 1800 786 386; www.surfnsun.com.au).

SOUTHERN FLEURIEU

Continuing south from Willunga, the road tracks inland from Sellicks Beach towards rapidly evolving **Yankalilla** (population 550), then hits the coast again at **Normanville** (population 700), a burgeoning town favoured for its 'retirement lifestyles'. The beaches at Normanville and Carrickalinga, just to the north, are the best stretches of sand south of Sellicks Beach. Further south are the small towns of historic Second Valley and fisherfolky **Cape Jervis** (pronounced jar-vis; population 300), the Fleurieu's southernmost tip and departure point for Kangaroo Island ferries.

Yankalilla District visitors centre (☎ 8558 2999; www.yankalilla.sa.gov.au; 104 Main Rd, Yankalilla; ☺ 9am-5pm Mon-Fri, 10am-4pm Sat & Sun) has tips on local sights and books accommodation.

There are two well-maintained caravan parks at Normanville: **Jetty Caravan Park** (☎ 8558 2038; www.jettycaravanparknormanville.com .au; Jetty Rd, Normanville; unpowered/powered sites $21/25, budget d $50, cabins with bathroom from $84; 🐾 💻) is 100m from the beach, with a dune boardwalk and nearby surf club cafe; and **Beachside Caravan Park** (☎ 8558 2458; www.beachside.com.au; Cape Jervis Rd, Normanville; powered sites $24, cabins & villas $78-120; 🐾), over the back of the dunes 2km towards Cape Jervis from Normanville. There's a great camp kitchen here, good security, well-mowed lawns and the odd rabbit bouncing around.

For self-contained cabins and massive counter meals, try the **Normanville Hotel** (☎ 8558 3200, fax 8558 3538; 46 Main Rd, Normanville; d $80; 🐾). There are four neat, faux-wood cabins out the back. The dining room (mains $12 to $25, open for lunch and dinner) is the kind of place you visit on a wintry Tuesday night and find 200 people eating steaks.

New(ish) on the scene in Normanville is the **Jetty Food Store** (☎ 8558 2537; 48a Main Rd, Normanville; meals $10-29; ☺ 10am-6pm Mon-Thu, to 7.30pm Fri, 9am-7.30pm Sat, to 6.30pm Sun), where the motto is 'Coastal food hunted and gathered for you'. Grab a dozen Kangaroo Island oysters, some locally caught fish-and-chips, or a gourmet pizza from Friday to Sunday. Coffee, juices, veggies and cheeses and dips too.

For internet, coffee and cake, try the **Court House Café** (☎ 8558 3532; 52 Main St, Normanville; meals $8-15; ☺ breakfast & lunch; 💻).

There's not much at Cape Jervis, 107km from Adelaide, other than the Kangaroo Island ferry terminal (see p85), and the start (or end) point for the **Heysen Trail** (p287).

There are some rugged walking trails in nearby **Deep Creek Conservation Park** (☎ 8598 0263; www.environment.sa.gov.au/parks/sanpr/deepcreek; admission per car $7.50), with sweeping coastal views, a wicked waterfall, man-size yaccas (*Xanthorrhoea semiplana tateana*), sandy beaches, kangaroos, kookaburras and bush camping areas (per car $15).

Off the road to Deep Creek Conservation Park are the curved roofs of the superb our pick **Ridgetop Retreats** (☎ 8598 4169; www .southernoceanretreats.com.au; d $185), designed by SA architect Max Pritchard: three corrugated iron–clad, self-contained luxury units in the bush, with wood heaters, leather lounges and stainless-steel benchtops. See the website for some less glam accommodation in the same area (doubles from $100).

An unpretentious working sheep farm, **Cape Jervis Station** (☎ 1800 805 288, 8598 0288; www .capejervisstation.com.au; Main Rd, Cape Jervis; unpowered/powered sites $20/25, d/tw from $90/120) has campsites and cottages to suit most budgets. There's lots

---

DETOUR: RAPID BAY

About 15km south of Normanville, follow the signs past bald hills and farmhouse ruins to **Rapid Bay**. In the 1950s this was a boomtown, the local limestone quarry shipping 60,000 tonnes of lime per month from the enormous jetty. Production ceased in 1981; since then Rapid Bay has assumed a Gothic, ghost-town atmosphere. Empty '50s villas and workers' quarters line the streets, and the local shop (closed) has signs advertising soft drinks they don't make any more. Without the shipping, the old jetty has become a popular **fishing** and **diving** site.

Rapid Bay was also the site of Adelaide founder Colonel William Light's first landing in SA in 1836, in his ship the *Rapid*. There's a stone down by the shore with 'WL 1836' carved into it. Also near the foreshore is a basic, exposed **camping ground** (adult/child $5/2.50) backed by Norfolk Island pines.

---

of talk about rain (or the lack thereof) over breakfast (continental/cooked $15/20).

Cape Jervis Tavern (☎ 8598 0276; Main Rd, Cape Jervis; mains $13-20; ☺ lunch & dinner) serves basic pub meals: fish-and-chips, pasta, schnitzels and fish-of-the-day straight from the wharf.

VICTOR HARBOR
pop 10,400

The Fleurieu Peninsula's surf-battered southeast is known as the **Encounter Coast**, the biggest town along which is Victor Harbor. Oddly detached from its rural setting, it's a raggedy, brawling holiday destination, with three huge pubs and circa-1991 decor. In January the grassy foreshore runs rampant with **schoolies** (www.schoolies.org.au/victor-harbor.htm), teenage school-leavers blowing off hormones.

The name 'Encounter Coast' derives from explorers Flinders and Baudin, who bumped into each other here in 1802. There's a memorial to the meeting 4km south of town on the Bluff, below which was Victor Harbor's first whaling station (1837). These days (between June and October) you might spy a southern right whale flouncing happily past, numbers having recovered after whaling ceased in 1864.

Information

Banks, pharmacies and the post office are on Ocean St.

Department for Environment & Heritage (DEH; ☎ 8552 3677; www.environment.sa.gov.au; 41 Victoria St; ☺ 9am-5pm Mon-Fri)

Lewitzka Computer Services (☎ 8552 6269; 2 Coral St; internet access per 10 min/1hr $2/5; ☺ 9am-5pm Mon-Fri)

Royal Automobile Association (☎ 8552 1033; www.raa.com.au; 66 Ocean St; ☺ 8.30am-5.30pm Mon-Fri, 9am-noon Sat)

South Coast District Hospital (☎ 8552 0500; www.encounterhealth.sa.gov.au; Bay Rd; ☺ 24hr) Accident and emergency service.

Victor Harbor visitors centre (☎ 8552 5738; www.tourismvictorharbor.com.au; Causeway; ☺ 9am-5pm) Internet access, and tour and accommodation bookings. Volunteer staff isn't the sharpest harpoon on deck.

Victor Medical Centre (☎ 8552 1444; www.victor medical.com.au; 65 Ocean St; ☺ 8am-6pm Mon-Fri, to noon Sat)

Sights & Activities

Victor Harbor is protected from the angry Southern Ocean by lichen-covered, boulder-strewn **Granite Island**, connected to the mainland by an 1875 causeway. You can ride out there on the 1894 double-decker **Horse-drawn Tram** (return adult/child/family $7/5/20; ☺ trips every 40min 10am-4pm). Buy tickets from Top Choice Travel inside the visitors centre. On the island itself is the 'Kaiki Walk' (1.5km circuit, 40 minutes) and a penguin rookery. **Granite Island Nature Park** (☎ 8552 7555; www.granite island.com.au) runs sunset **penguin tours** (adult/concession/child/family $12.50/11/7.50/36; ☺ nightly) to watch the penguins haul themselves out of the water and waddle along the shore. Bookings essential.

Opposite the causeway, the **Encounter Coast Discovery Centre** (☎ 8552 5388; www.nationaltrustsa.org .au; 2 Flinders Pde; adult/concession/child/family $4/3/2/10; ☺ 1-4pm) has local history displays from pre-European times to around 1900, and includes the musty Old Customs House & Station Master's Residence (1866), set up in its original state.

Victor Harbor is on the migratory path of southern right whales (www.environment .sa.gov.au/coasts/whales). The **South Australian Whale Centre** (☎ 8551 0750; www.sawhalecentre.com; 2 Railway Tce; admission adult/concession/child/family

$8/5.50/4/20; 🕙 9.30am-5pm) has impressive displays on Victor's largest visitors (including a huge stinky skull), and can give you the low-down on where to see them. Downstairs, things get sharky.

The much-wheeled **Encounter Bikeway** (www .tourismvictorharbor.com.au/walks_trails.html) extends 30km from the Bluff in Victor Harbor to Laffin Point, past Goolwa. Distances from Victor Harbor: Port Elliot (8.5km), Middleton (17km), Goolwa (16.5km). The visitors centre stocks maps. For bike hire, see p80.

Top Choice Travel (☎ 1800 088 552, 8552 7000; www .topchoicetravel.com.au; Victor Harbor visitors centre, Causeway; 🕙 9am-5pm) runs **dolphin & seal scenic cruises** (1½hr cruise adult/concession/child/family $48/40/30/125; 🕙 cruises daily), and **whale cruises** (2hr cruise adult/concession/child/ family $60/55/45/175; 🕙 cruises daily).

Surf & Sun Safaris (☎ 1800 786 386; www.surfnsun .com.au) runs two-hour surf lessons ($40) at nearby Middleton, and half-day sea-kayaking adventures ($60) from Victor Harbor to Wright Island.

If you feel like stretching your legs, the visitors centre stocks the *Walks In & Around Victor Harbor* and *Old Port Victor Heritage Walking Trail* brochures.

See also SteamRanger Heritage Railway (p80).

Sleeping

Victor Harbor has the full gamut of holiday accommodation. Book your bed through the visitors centre (opposite), the **Fleurieu Peninsula Booking Office** (☎ 1800 241 033, 8552 3935; www.fpbo .com.au; 66 Ocean St) or **LJ Hooker** (☎ 8552 1944; www .ljh.com.au/victorharbor; 73 Ocean St).

Victor Harbor Holiday & Cabin Park (☎ 8552 1949; www.victorharborholiday.com.au; Bay Rd; unpowered/powered/sites $24/28, vans/cabins from $52/86; 🖳) The friendliest operation in town with tidy

facilities, free barbecues and a rambling grassed area with a few trees to pitch a tent on. Runs rings around Victor's other caravan parks.

Grosvenor Hotel (☎ 8552 1011; www.grosvenorvictor .com.au; 40 Ocean St; dm/s/d/f $30/35/60/80) Passable pub rooms with high ceilings and shared bathrooms; the best ones open onto the balcony above Coral St. Backpacker 'dorms' are actually twin share.

ourpick Anchorage Seafront Hotel (☎ 8552 5970; www.anchorageseafronthotel.com; 21 Flinders Pde; s/d/tr incl breakfast from $40/70/85) This grand, heritage-listed, seafront guesthouse is the pick of the bunch. Immaculately maintained, great-value rooms open off jade-painted corridors with fresh flowers in them. Most rooms face the beach, and some have a balcony (you'd pay through the nose for this in Sydney!). The cheapest rooms share bathrooms. The Ocean Grill cafe-bar downstairs is a winner too (see p80).

Victor City Motel (☎ 8552 2455; www.victorcitymotel .com.au; 51 Ocean St; d from $80; 🐾) A standard, low-slung '70s motel on the main street with clean, affordable rooms and a spiffy new salmon-coloured paint job. The concrete block walls inside are painted grey (why bother?).

Hotel Victor (☎ 8552 1288; www.victorhotels.com.au; cnr The Esplanade & Albert Pl; s/d from $110/120, extra $15 on Sat) There are 30-something motel-standard rooms (all with a bathroom) above this humongous pub, which gets packed to the tops of the pokie machines in summer. Weekend and midweek dinner, B&B packages are pretty good value. Book ahead for rooms overlooking Granite Island.

Eating & Drinking

Beach House Café (☎ 8552 4417; 62 Franklin Rd, Encounter Bay; pizzas $12-19, curries $10-17; 🕙 lunch Sun, dinner daily) Is it Italian-style Indian or the other way around? Make up your mind over a tandoori lamb 'pizza with personality'. The beachside position overlooking Wright Island and the Bluff is spot-on.

Jameelah's Gourmet Café (☎ 0413-585 660; 9/68 Victoria St; mains $13-15; 🕙 lunch Tue-Sat, dinner Tue-Sun; Ⓥ) Not what you'd expect to find in suburban Victor Harbor: an authentically sweaty Lebanese cook nook, serving such delicacies as felafels, *mjuddra* (lentil and rice dish) and *coussseh* (Lebanese zucchini stuffed with rice and mince).

Nino's (☎ 8552 3501; 17 Albert Pl; mains $14-23; 🕙 lunch & dinner; Ⓥ) Nino's cafe has been here

---

HARBOUR OR HARBOR?

Yes, that's correct – unlike every other harbour in Australia, Victor Harbor is spelled without a 'u'. Oddly enough, this glitch crops up in several places around SA, including the Adelaide suburb Outer Harbor. The spelling error allegedly dates back to charts put together by one of South Australia's early (and poorly schooled) Surveyor Generals.

since 1974, but it manages to put a contemporary sheen on downtown VH. Hip young staff and a mod interior set the scene for gourmet pizzas, pasta, salads, risottos and meaty Italian mains. Good coffee too.

Ocean Grill @ Anchorage (☎ 8552 5970; Anchorage Seafront Hotel, 21 Flinders Pde; mains $16-26; ⊗ breakfast, lunch & dinner; ✗) This salty sea-cave, with fishing nets trawling from the ceiling and an old whaling boat for a bar, has a Med-meets–Mod Oz menu with plenty of seafood. There's great coffee, tapas, cakes, Euro beers and a beachside terrace to drink them on. Live acoustic acts Friday nights.

For a cheap pub meal, the following are also recommended:

Crown Hotel (☎ 8552 1022; 2 Ocean St; mains $10-25; ⊗ lunch & dinner; ✗) The biggest boozer in town, with cheap drinks and counter meals. Wednesday is 'Super Schnitz' night (your choice of 10 toppings plus dessert for $11).

Grosvenor Hotel (☎ 8552 1011; 40 Ocean St; mains $12-24; ⊗ lunch & dinner; ✗) A fish-focused bistro (oh, and steaks) with big screens and wailing commercial FM (salt-and-pepper squid and Bryan Adams go surprisingly well together).

Entertainment

Victa Cinemas (☎ 8552 1325; www.victacinema .com.au; Ocean St; tickets adult/concession/child $13/11/9; ⊗ 5pm-late Tue, Wed & Fri-Sun) Cool old art deco cinema screening new-release films daily during school holidays; five days a week at other times.

Getting There & Around

For details on bus services from Adelaide and ferry connections with Kangaroo Island, see p85.

On the last Sunday in May and the first and third Sundays from June to November, **SteamRanger Heritage Railway** (☎ 1300 655 991, 8263 5621; www.steamranger.org.au) operates the *Southern Encounter* (adult/concession/child/family return $64/55/35/155) tourist train from Mt Barker in the Adelaide Hills to Victor Harbor via Strathalbyn, Goolwa and Port Elliot. The *Cockle Train* (adult/child return $26/15) runs along the Encounter Coast between Victor Harbor and Goolwa via Port Elliot every Sunday.

Victor Harbor Cycle & Skate (☎ /fax 8552 1417; 73 Victoria St; ⊗ 9am-5.30pm Mon-Wed & Fri, to 7.30pm Thu, to noon Sat) rents out mountain bikes for $10/45/50 per two hours/day/two days.

Helmets and locks included; baby seats ($5) also available.

For a cab, call the local **Peninsular Taxi Group** (☎ 13 10 08).

PORT ELLIOT & MIDDLETON

About 8km east of Victor Harbor, historic **Port Elliot** (population 3100) is a great little town, set back from **Horseshoe Bay**, an orange-sand arc with surf surging in through granite headlands. Norfolk Island pines reach for the sky, and there are whale-spotting updates posted on the pub wall. **Commodore Point**, at the eastern end of Horseshoe Bay, is a good break for experienced surfers, but there are better ones at nearby **Boomer Beach** and **Knights Beach**, and at the otherwise-missable **Middleton** (population 1340), the next town towards Goolwa.

For surf-gear hire:

Big Surf Australia (☎ 8554 2399, fax 8554 3028; 24 Goolwa Rd, Middleton; ⊗ 9am-5pm) Surfboards/bodyboards/wetsuits per day for $25/15/10.

Southern Surf (☎ 8554 2375; 36 North Tce, Port Elliot; ⊗ 9am-5pm) Surfboards/bodyboards/wetsuits per day for $22/11/11.

Sleeping & Eating

Port Elliot Tourist Park (☎ 8554 2134; www.portelliot caravanpark.com.au; Middleton Rd, Port Elliot; unpowered/powered sites $28/34, cabins/units/cottages from $110/135/160, extra person $9) In an unbeatable position behind the Horseshoe Bay dunes (it can be a touch windy), this grassy, 12-acre park has all the requisite facilities, including a tennis court and all-weather barbecue area. Prices quoted are high season – they're much less scary in winter.

Royal Family Hotel (☎ 8554 2219; www.royalfamily hotel.com; 32 North Tce, Port Elliot; s/d $50/60) It's doubtful that Prince Chuck has ever stayed here, but if he did he'd find surprisingly decent pub rooms with clean shared bathrooms, a TV lounge and balcony over the main street. Downstairs the bistro serves counter meals fit for a king (mains $12 to $24, open for lunch and dinner).

Trafalgar House B&B (☎ 8554 3888; www.trafalgar house.com.au; 25 The Strand, Port Elliot; d incl breakfast from $145, self-contained cottage from $140) At the top of the hill near the whale-spotting cliff, this 1855 cottage is heavy on the floral print and doilies but has 11ft ceilings, a log fire and nostalgia-inducing garden.

Mindacowie B&B (☎ 8554 2112; www.mindacowie .com; 48 Goolwa Rd, Middleton; d incl breakfast $175; ✗ 🖵) It's impossible to miss this 110-year-old, lime-

---

CURRENCY CREEK & LANGHORNE CREEK WINERIES

Once slated as the capital of SA, **Currency Creek**, 10km from Goolwa, is now content with producing award-winning wines. **Currency Creek Winery** (☎ 8555 4069; www.currencycreekwines.com.au; Winery Rd; ☑ 10am-5pm) has a cellar-door, restaurant (mains $20 to $25, open for lunch) and the Black Swamp walking trail (3km), winding past an historic railway bridge.

About 16km east of Strathalbyn on the floodplains between the Angas and Bremer Rivers, **Langhorne Creek** (www.langhornewine.com.au) is one of Australia's oldest wine-growing regions, producing Shiraz, Cabernet Sauvignon and Chardonnay. Just a few of the 20-plus wineries here:

- **Bleasdale Winery** (☎ 8537 3001; www.bleasdale.com.au; Wellington Rd; ☑ 10am-5pm) The district's first winery has a large range, historic cellar and an old red-gum lever press.

- **Cleggett Wines** (☎ 8537 3133; www.cleggettwines.com.au; Strathalbyn Rd; ☑ 10am-6pm) East of the Bremer River, these guys discovered Malian and Shalistin grapes (bronze-pink and golden white mutated Cabernet Sauvignon grapes, respectively).

- **Lake Breeze Wines** (☎ 8537 3017; www.lakebreeze.com.au; Step Rd; ☑ 10am-5pm) This small operation produces some acclaimed reds amid magnificent red gum country by the Bremer River.

---

stone guesthouse as you trundle through Middleton. The best rooms have ocean views, but they're all top notch, with huge en suites, mustard-coloured walls, wireless internet access and gourmet cooked breakfasts.

Cockles on North (☎ 8554 3187; cnr The Strand & Goolwa Rd, Port Elliot; mains $10-15; ☑ breakfast & lunch Thu-Tue; ☒ ⓥ) The new kid on the Port Elliot block is a bright, open-sided foodie haunt with a huge deck overlooking the main street. Expect all-day breakfasts, good coffee, snazzy desserts and mains such as battered barramundi and tasty veggie burgers.

our pick Flying Fish (☎ 8554 3504; 1 The Foreshore, Port Elliot; lunch $21-28, dinner $29-42; ☑ lunch & dinner daily, reduced winter hr) Sit down for lunch and you'll be here all day – the views of Horseshoe Bay are sublime. Otherwise grab some quality takeaway of Coopers-battered flathead and chips and head back to the sand. At night things get a little classier, with à la carte mains or a degustation menu (per person $95, or $130 with wine) focusing on independent SA producers.

GOOLWA
pop 6500

Much more low-key and elegant than kissing-cousin Victor Harbor down the street, Goolwa is an unassuming town where the Murray River empties into the sea. Australia's greatest river has been tragically depleted by climate change and upstream irrigation – Goolwa's jetties and marinas have been left high-and-dry above the shrinking river; a huge banner adorning a local pub says 'We

Need Water Now!'. But beyond the dunes is a fantastic beach with ranks of broken surf rolling in from the ocean, same as it ever was.

Information

The **Goolwa visitors centre** (☎ 8555 3488; www.visit alexandrina.com; The Wharf; ☑ 9am-5pm) has plenty of local info (including accommodation), plus the **Signal Point River Murray Centre** (admission adult/child/family $5.50/3/13.50), an interpretive centre with interactive displays on the life and ecology of the Murray.

Sights & Activities

Goolwa's old-town centre has a few yellow-stone 1850s and heritage buildings, including the 1853 **Goolwa Hotel**, 1857 **Corio Hotel**, and 1859 **Customs House**; pick up a walking-tour brochure from the visitors centre.

Down on the wharf, the **Steam Exchange Brewery** (☎ 8555 3406; www.steamexchange.com.au; The Wharf; ☑ 10am-5pm) is a locally run brewery, turning out manly stouts and ales, such as the Southerly Buster Dark Ale. There's a small fee for tastings; tours by arrangement.

Not far from the brewery, Hindmarsh Island Bridge links Goolwa with **Hindmarsh Island**; see the boxed text on p82 for the spiteful story behind the bridge.

Spirit of the Coorong (☎ 1800 442 203, 8555 2203; www.coorongcruises.com.au; The Wharf) runs eco-cruises on the Murray and into the Coorong National Park, including lunch and guided walks. The 4½-hour Coorong Discovery Cruise (adult/child $74/55)

runs on Monday and Thursday all year, plus Tuesday and Saturday from October to May. The six-hour Coorong Adventure Cruise (adult/child $88/60) runs on Sunday all year, plus Wednesday from October to May. Booking essential.

At **Goolwa Beach** a boardwalk traverses the dunes overlooking barrelling surf. **Barrell Surf & Skate** (☎ 8555 5422; www.barrellsurf.com.au; 10c Cadell St; ☺ 9.30am-5.30pm) has gear hire (longboard/bodyboard/wetsuit $25/10/15).

Not hardcore enough? Throw yourself out of a perfectly good aeroplane with **Skydive the Coast** (☎ 1800 813 557; www.skydivethecoast.com.au). Prices start at $410 for a 2440m tandem jump with a 15-second freefall.

If you'd rather keep your feet (or wheels) on the ground, you can cycle along the coast from Goolwa to Victor Harbor on the **Encounter Bikeway** (see p79; maps from the visitors centre).

Sleeping & Eating

Holiday rentals in and around Goolwa are managed by **LJ Hooker** (☎ 8555 1785; www.ljh.com .au/goolwa; 25 Cadell St) and the **Professionals** (☎ 8555 2122; www.professionalsgoolwa.com.au; 1 Cadell St), both of whom have houses for as little as $70 per night (mostly around $130) and good weekly rates. The best camping option in the area is at Victor Harbor (p79).

Goolwa Central Motel (☎ 8555 1155; www .goolwacentralmotel.com.au; 30 Cadell St; s/d/f from $110/120/160; ✵ ⬜ ⬤) This two-level motel is next to an Irish pub, and has allowed the emerald roguishness to filter through (rooms are called 'Tyrone', 'Fermanagh' etc). Nothing flash, but a solid central option with a tiny pool.

Brooking Cottage B&B (☎ 8555 2387; www.brook ingcottage.com.au; 28a Brooking St; d incl breakfast $170; ✵) A 2½-year-old B&B with all the trimmings, including an outdoor spa, brekkie provisions, a bottle of decent plonk and a cheese platter. The owner used to drive tractors; now he drives the vacuum cleaner. Sleeps six (but no kids).

Boathouse (☎ 8555 0338; www.birksharbour.com .au; 138b Liverpool Rd; 2-night d incl breakfast $500; ✵) When they built this classy, shipshape accommodation, the river was literally on the doorstep. These days it's a little further away, but the atmosphere and design are undiminished. A complimentary bottle of wine will help you ease in. There's a two-night minimum stay.

Hector's (☎ 8555 5885; The Wharf; mains $8-19; ☺ breakfast & lunch Thu-Tue, dinner Jan-Mar; ✵) Under the ugly (in more ways than one) span of the Hindmarsh Island Bridge, eating at Hector's (festooned with fishing rods) is like hanging out in your mate's boathouse. The seafood chowder and spinach-and-fetta pie sweetly complement the local wines.

Café Lime (☎ 8555 5522; 1/11 Goolwa Tce; meals $10-17; ☺ breakfast & lunch; ✵) Pick up heat-and-eat gourmet dinners or a takeaway cone of salt-and-pepper squid with lime-salted fries, or nab a table for beer-battered Coorong mullet (not a description of a haircut at the pub), baguettes, curries, soups and pasta. Espresso perfecto.

Southy's Wood Fired Pizzas (☎ 8555 5055; 1 Cadell St; pizzas $12-17; ☺ dinner Wed-Sun) All the old faves, plus a few good 'gourmet' selections: satay chicken, tandoori lamb and a yiros pizza (chicken, tomato, Spanish onion, hummus and tzatziki).

Corio Hotel (☎ 8555 2011; Railway Tce; mains $12-28; ☺ lunch & dinner) This 1850s hotel is the pick of the town's pubs, serving upmarket(ish) pub grub in a prawn-coloured dining room. The Coorong Angus porterhouse and the mixed

---

ABORIGINAL AUSTRALIA: HINDMARSH ISLAND BRIDGE

First proposed in 1988, construction of the **Hindmarsh Island Bridge** was opposed by Ngarrindjeri women who had concerns about the spiritual and cultural significance of the site. A series of court battles ensued, pitting Aboriginal beliefs against development, and culminating in a Royal Commission (1995) which ruled that the claims of Aboriginal 'secret women's business' were fabricated. Further court appeals were launched, and in August 2001 the Federal Court overturned the Royal Commission, finding the Ngarrindjeri claims to be legitimate. Unfortunately, this vindication came five months after the bridge was officially opened. The decade-long furore was a step backwards for reconciliation, made worse by the media's often-flawed coverage.

grill are meaty monsters (Michael Bublé on the stereo seems rather out-machoed).

Getting There & Around

For bus connections to Goolwa, see p85. For tourist train details between Goolwa, Strathalbyn and Victor Harbor, see p80.

For a taxi, ring **Goolwa Taxi Service** (☎ 8552 8222).

KANGAROO ISLAND

When Adelaide's pubs and events calendar start to exhaust you, take a few days to detox on Kangaroo Island (KI), 13km off the bottom of the Fleurieu Peninsula. The island's isolation has been a boon for its flora and fauna – it's a veritable zoo of seals, birds, dolphins, echidnas and roos. Jagged coastline protects beaches with slow-rolling surf, while the interior sustains native forest and scrub.

Many KI place names are French, attributable to Gallic explorer Nicholas Baudin who surveyed the coast in 1802 and 1803. Baudin's English rival Matthew Flinders named the island in 1802 (see Dining on KI, p26). By this stage the island was uninhabited, but archaeologists think Indigenous peoples lived here as recently as 2000 years ago. Why they deserted KI is a matter of conjecture, though the answer is hinted at in the indigenous name for KI: 'Karta', or 'Land of the Dead'. In the early 1800s an indigenous presence (albeit a tragically displaced one) was re-established on KI when whalers and sealers abducted Aboriginal women from Tasmania and brought them here.

These days the island is low key, rurally paced and underdeveloped, but there's a heck-of-a-lot of land for sale – KI is about to boom! Until that happens, it remains the kind of place where kids ride bikes to school and farmers advertise for wives on noticeboards. There's some brilliant accommodation here, and island produce is just as good (if not the restaurants that serve it). Be sure to try the local seafood, marron (freshwater crayfish), honey, cheese and wine.

Information

The KI visitors centre is in Penneshaw (see p86); the Department for Environment & Heritage is in Kingscote (see p88). There are bank facilities in Kingscote and Penneshaw, and a hospital in Kingscote. Mobile-phone reception on the island is patchy, restricted to Kingscote, Penneshaw, American River, the airport and parts of Emu Bay. There are supermarkets at Penneshaw and Kingscote, and a general store at American River.

Accommodation

KI accommodation is expensive, adding insult to your wallet's injury after the pricey ferry ride across from the mainland. We suspect the locals took one look at the new billionaire's paradise Southern Ocean Lodge (p91) and decided there was some easy money to be made! Self-contained cottages, B&Bs and beach houses proliferate, most charging $150 per night or more per double with a two-night minimum stay. There are some great campsites around the island, though, plus a few midrange motels, but quality caravan parks and hostels are few and far between.

For an atmospheric, remote night's stay, try the historic cottages for rent through the **Department for Environment & Heritage** (☎ 8553 2381; www.environment.sa.gov.au/parks; 37 Dauncey St, Kingscote). These range from a basic stone hut (double $48) and homestead (double $115) at Rocky River, to lightkeepers' cottages at Cape Willoughby, Cape Borda and Cape du Couedic (doubles $150). All have heating and basic cooking facilities. Stays of five nights or more will earn you a free Parks Pass (see p88).

Accommodation booking resources include the Kangaroo Island Gateway visitors centre (p86), Sealink (p85) and **Century 21** (☎ 8553 2688; www.century21.com.au/kangarooisland; 66 Dauncey St, Kingscote).

Activities

ADVENTURE SPORTS

Kangaroo Island Outdoor Action (☎ 8559 4296, 0428-822 260; www.kioutdooraction.com.au; Jetty Rd, Vivonne Bay) rents out sandboards (per four hours $29) and toboggans ($39) to skid down the dunes at Little Sahara, plus single/double kayaks ($39/69). Quad-bike tours are also on offer, exploring 500 bushy acres: daytime nature tours ($79), dusk wildlife-spotting tours ($89) and extreme quad adventures ($229).

Nearby, Vivonne Bay General Store (p91) also rents out sandboards and toboggans at the same rates.

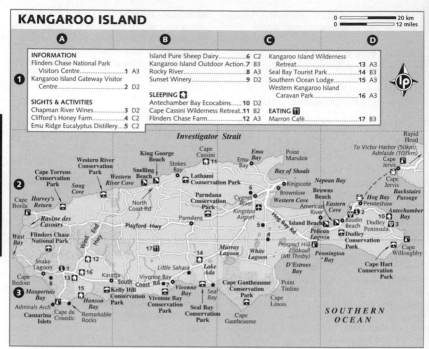

KANGAROO ISLAND

INFORMATION
Flinders Chase National Park
Visitors Centre.........................1 A3
Kangaroo Island Gateway Visitor
Centre...................................2 D2

SIGHTS & ACTIVITIES
Chapman River Wines.................3 D2
Clifford's Honey Farm.................4 C2
Emu Ridge Eucalyptus Distillery....5 C2

Island Pure Sheep Dairy.............6 C2
Kangaroo Island Outdoor Action.7 B3
Rocky River..............................8 A3
Sunset Winery...........................9 D2

SLEEPING
Antechamber Bay Ecocabins......10 D2
Cape Cassini Wilderness Retreat..11 B2
Flinders Chase Farm.................12 A3

Kangaroo Island Wilderness
Retreat.................................13 A3
Seal Bay Tourist Park................14 B3
Southern Ocean Lodge............15 A3
Western Kangaroo Island
Caravan Park........................16 A3

EATING
Marron Café.............................17 B3

BUSHWALKING

There's plenty to see under your own steam on KI. Check out www.tourkangarooisland.com.au/wildlife/walks.aspx for info on day walks from 1km to 18km. For detailed track notes, download the DEH publication *Parks of Kangaroo Island* from the same web address, or pick up a copy from the DEH in Kingscote (p88).

FISHING & CHARTER BOATS

There's plenty of good fishing around the island, including at jetties in Kingscote, Penneshaw, Emu Bay and Vivonne Bay, where you'll reel in garfish, tommy-ruff and squid. The Kingscote jetty also has gummy shark and snook. Rock fishing around the coast can yield trevally and sweep, but watch out for 'king waves', particularly on the south coast.

Salmon, flathead, tommies and whiting are common at surf beaches such as Pennington Bay, the mouth of South West River at Hanson Bay, and West Bay in Flinders Chase National Park. In March and April, most beaches yield good catches of mullet. The best places for King George whiting

are the southern end of D'Estrees Bay, near Point Tinline, and King George Beach, between Snelling Beach and Stokes Bay on the north coast.

Fishing charter tours (half-/full-day from $90/180) run out of Kingscote, Emu Bay, Penneshaw and American River; bait, tackle and refreshments are included and you can keep your catch. Some operators:

Cooinda Fishing Charters (☎ 0439-867 713; www.kidiving.com) Half-day tours from American River. Dive tours also available.

Kangaroo Island Fishing Charters (☎ 8552 7000; www.kifishchart.com.au) Pick-ups at Penneshaw, Emu Bay or Kingscote; accommodation and lunch by arrangement.

Kings Fishing Charters (☎ 8553 7003; www.users.on.net/~thekings) Four-hour charters from American River; accommodation available.

SCUBA DIVING & SNORKELLING

The waters around KI are like an overstocked aquarium, with 230 species of fish, leafy sea dragons and soft and hard corals. There are plenty of shipwrecks too (at least 60), which make interesting, but not spectacular, dive sites. The east- and north-coast waters are sheltered, with visibility usually from 10m to 20m. The east coast has sheer drop-offs, caves and rare black tree corals; along the north coast are shallow rocky reefs, with drop-offs and chasms. Seals, sea lions and dolphins will accompany you on most dives.

Kangaroo Island Diving Safaris (☎ 0427-102 387; www.kidivingsafaris.com) offers boat dives with equipment ($290 per day), boat-based snorkelling ($137 per day), and various multiday packages including accommodation. Scuba gear hire also available ($75).

See also Cooinda Fishing Charters (opposite).

SWIMMING & SURFING
The safest swimming is along the north coast, where the water is warmer and there are fewer rips than down south. The easiest beaches to access are Emu Bay, Stokes Bay, Snelling Beach and Western River Cove.

For surfing, hit the uncrowded swells along the south coast. Pennington Bay has strong, reliable breaks, while Vivonne Bay and Hanson Bay in the southwest also serve up some tasty waves. Beware of rips – Hanson Bay in particular is only for experienced surfers. 'The Sewer' is a 'filthy' break near Point Tinline in D'Estrees Bay. See the *Kangaroo Island Surfing Guide* brochure from the visitors centre for more info.

Tours
See the visitors centre or www.tourkangaroo island.com.au for comprehensive tour listings. Day tours from Adelaide are hectic – stay at least one night on the island if you can! Multiday tours generally include meals and accommodation. A few operators:

Adventure Tours (☎ 1300 654 604; www.adventure tours.com.au) Popular two-day tours ($425) ex-Adelaide with lots of walking and wildlife.

Alkirna Nocturnal Tours (☎ 8553 7464; www .alkirna.com.au) Nightly naturalist-led tours viewing nocturnal critters around American River (adult/child $58/37, two hours).

Exceptional Kangaroo Island (☎ 8553 9119; www .exceptionalkangarooisland.com) Small-group, deluxe 4WD day tours ($348) with either a wildlife or Flinders Chase focus. Tours depart KI.

Groovy Grape (☎ 1800 66 11 77, 8440 1640; www .groovygrape.com.au) Two-/three-day small-group wildlife safaris ($335/435) ex-Adelaide, with sand-boarding, campfires and all the main sights. The three-day tour runs October to May only.

Kangaroo Island Marine Tours (☎ 0427-315 286; www.kimarinetours.com) Water tours from one hour ($55)

to a full day ($275), including swimming with dolphins, visiting seal colonies and access to remote areas of KI.

Sealink (☎ 13 13 01; www.sealink.com.au) The ferry company runs a range of KI highlight day tours ($62 to $131) departing Adelaide or Kingscote. Overnight backpacker tours, self-drive tours and multiday tours also available.

Surf 'n' Sun (☎ 1800 786 386; www.surfnsun.com.au) Two-/three-day 4WD tours ($340/399) ex-Adelaide, with a strong focus on wildlife. Includes surfing lesson (three-day only) and sand-boarding.

Wayward Bus (☎ 1300 653 510; www.waywardbus .com.au) Two-day backpacker tours (from $397) ex-Adelaide, covering all the big-ticket sights.

Getting There & Away
For daily flights (one-way from $77 online) between Adelaide and Kingscote, contact **Regional Express Airlines** (Rex; ☎ 13 17 13; www .regionalexpress.com.au) or **Air South** (☎ 1300 247 768, 8234 4988; www.airsouth.com.au).

Most folks bring their cars across to KI on the ferry between Cape Jervis and Penneshaw. **Sealink** (☎ 13 13 01; www.sealink.com .au) operates at least three vehicular ferries each way daily (one way adult/concession/ child $43/36/24, bicycles/motorcycles/cars $15/30/84, 45 minutes). One driver is included with the vehicle price (cars only, not bikes). Sealink also operates a morning and afternoon bus service between Cape Jervis and Adelaide's Central Bus Station (adult/ child $20/10, 2¼ hours). Coaches also connect Cape Jervis with Goolwa and Victor Harbor ($20/10, 40 minutes).

Getting Around
There's no public transport on the island, so unless you're taking a tour, the only way to get around is to bring or hire some wheels. The

---

IT'S BIGGER THAN IT LOOKS

From the deck on the Backstairs Passage ferry, KI doesn't seem particularly large. But what you're looking at is the pointy eastern end of the Dudley Peninsula – the rest of the island stretches 150km to the west; 55km wide and 307m high. For the geographically minded, that's around twice the size of Luxembourg, or half the size of Crete – a bit smaller than Trinidad, but a bit bigger than Majorca. The 131st-biggest island in the world!

island's main roads are sealed, but the rest are gravel, including those to Cape Willoughby, Cape Borda and the North Coast Rd. Take it slowly, especially at night when roos and wallabies bounce across the headlights. There's petrol at Kingscote, Penneshaw, American River, Parndana, and on the west of the island at Vivonne Bay and Kangaroo Island Wilderness Resort (though this can be intermittent).

TO/FROM THE AIRPORT
Kingscote Airport is 14km from Kingscote; **Airport Shuttle Services** (☎ 0427 887 575) connects the airport with Emu Bay ($17.50), Kingscote ($20), American River ($25) and Penneshaw ($40). Prices are per person, with a minimum of two people; solo travellers pay double (eg Kingscote $40). Bookings essential.

TO/FROM THE FERRY
Once you're on the island, **Sealink** (☎ 13 13 01; www.sealink.com.au) runs a twice-daily shuttle between Penneshaw and American River (adult/child $11/5.50, 30 minutes) and Kingscote ($14/7, one hour). Bookings essential.

CAR HIRE
Not all Adelaide car-rental companies will let you take their cars onto KI; with ferry prices it's often cheaper to hire on the island. **Budget** (☎ 8553 3133; www.budgetki.com) and **Hertz** (☎ 13 30 39, 8553 2390; www.hertz.com.au) supply cars to Penneshaw, Kingscote and Kingscote Airport. Check if they'll let you drive on unsealed roads.

PENNESHAW & DUDLEY PENINSULA
pop 300

Looking across Backstairs Passage to the Fleurieu Peninsula, Penneshaw is the arrival point for ferries from Cape Jervis. The passing tourist trade lends a certain transience to the businesses here, but the pub, hostel and general store remain authentically grounded. As are the resident fairy penguins: you'll hear their clacking safety call (a cross between a quack and a yap) around town at night.

Information
Kangaroo Island Gateway visitors centre (☎ 8553 1185; www.tourkangarooisland.com.au; Howard Dr; ☼ 9am-5pm Mon-Fri, 10am-4pm Sat & Sun) Just outside Penneshaw on the road to Kingscote, this centre is stocked

with brochures and maps. It also books accommodation and sells park entry tickets and passes.
Penneshaw Business Centre (☎ 8553 1020; 99 Middle Tce; ☼ 9am-5pm Mon-Fri, to noon Sat) Acts as a post office, internet cafe and bank agency with cash-withdrawal facilities.

Sights & Activities
To the left of the ferry terminal is **Hog Bay**, where a squat, white dome protects a replica of **Frenchman's Rock**, a 200-year-old piece of graffiti carved by a member of Baudin's expedition. The inscription reads, '*Expedition de decouverte par le commandant Baudin sur le Geographe 1803*'. The original pebble is at the visitors centre.

On the foreshore near the ferry terminal, **Penneshaw Penguin Centre** (☎ 8553 1103; ppenguin centre@bigpond.com.au; tours adult/concession/child/family $10/8.50/8.50/29; ☼ tours 7.30pm & 8.30pm Apr-Oct, 8.30pm & 9.30pm Nov-Mar) provides an unobtrusive view of the little waddlers that nest along the shore. Book ahead.

The **Penneshaw Maritime & Folk Museum** (☎ 8553 1109; www.nationaltrustsa.org.au; 52 Howard Dr; admission adult/concession/child/family $3/2/2/7; ☼ 3-5pm Wed-Sun Sep-May) displays artefacts from local shipwrecks and early settlement, plus endearingly geeky models of Flinders' *Investigator* and Baudin's *Geographe*.

About 28km southeast of town, the **Cape Willoughby Lightstation** (☎ 8553 1191; www.environ ment.sa.gov.au/parks/sanpr/capewilloughby; Cape Willoughby Rd; tours adult/concession/child/family $12/9.50/7.50/33) first shone in 1852 and is now used as a weather station. Tours run at 11.30am, 12.30pm and 2pm, also 3pm and 4pm in holiday periods. There's also basic accommodation here (see p83).

About 24km out towards Kingscote there's a steep staircase heading up **Prospect Hill**, which Flinders used as a lookout while mapping the coast. From the top you can check the swell at **Pennington Bay**, one of KI's best surfing and surf-fishing spots.

See also Chapman River Wines and Dudley Cellar Door & Café (opposite).

Sleeping & Eating
See Accommodation (p83) for details on sleeping at Cape Willoughby Lightstation.

Kangaroo Island YHA (☎ 8553 1344; www.yha .com.au; 33 Middle Tce; dm/d/f from $26/68/103; ☒ ⬜) Occupying an old '60s motel with faux-brick cladding, the island YHA has spacious rooms

KI WINERIES

It's obvious really: KI's clean air, cool wet winters and warm dry summers are perfect for growing grapes! There are more than a dozen vineyards here, many with cellar doors; the *Kangaroo Island Wine* brochure from the visitors centre has listings. Our favourites:

- **Chapman River Wines** (☎ 8553 1371; chapmanriverwines@activ8.net.au; Cape Willoughby Rd, Antechamber Bay; 🕑 11am-4.30pm Thu-Mon, closed Jul & Aug) In a converted aircraft hanger, this eccentric winery does a mean Merlot. The interior is festooned with art and quirky bits of salvage from churches, pubs and homesteads around SA.

- **Sunset Winery** (☎ 8553 1378; www.sunset-wines.com.au; Penneshaw-Kingscote Rd; platters $7-11; 🕑 11am-5pm) Wow, what a view! If you can make it up the steep driveway, Sunset has brilliant Sauvignon Blanc and sparking Shiraz, and serves savoury platters to go with the panorama.

- **Dudley Cellar Door & Café** (☎ 8553 1333; www.dudleywines.com.au; cnr North Tce & Thomas Wilson St, Penneshaw; mains $12-25; 🕑 11am-5pm) A brilliant new outlet for one of the KI's pioneering growers, serving cheese and seafood platters, curries and buckets 'o' prawns – perfect with a bottle of Chardonnay on the outdoor deck! Good sparkling Rosé and Shiraz too.

with en suite bathrooms. There's a small communal kitchen, lounge and laundry, and penguins at the bottom of the garden.

Antechamber Bay Ecocabins (☎ 8553 1557; www.kieco cabins.com; Chapman River East Rd, Antechamber Bay; d from $100, extra adult/child $20/free) Off Cape Willoughby Rd, these two six-bed cabins are run by a couple of IT industry runaways. On 55 acres behind the dunes, the cabins are rudimentary but perfectly comfortable, with roofless showers, self-composting toilets, and solar power and hot water. Kayaks and fishing gear $20 per stay.

Kangaroo Island Seafront Resort (☎ 8553 1028; www.seafront.com.au; 49 North Tce; d $160-220, villas/cottages $190/200; 🔀 🐾) This renovated/extended 1914 guesthouse is the first thing you see when you roll off the ferry. 'Resort' is a bit of a stretch, but there's a range of accommodation from shabby old guesthouse rooms (numbers 14 and 15 have views), to mod suites and self-contained villas and cottages.

Wallaby Beach House (☎ 8362 5293; www.wallaby beachhouse.com.au; Browns Beach; d $180, extra person $25) A secluded, self-contained three-bedroom beach house 13km west of Penneshaw on Browns Beach, with resident penguins to keep you company. Sleeps six.

Saar Beach House (☎ 8370 7119; www.saarbeachhouse .com.au; Island Beach; d from $200, extra person $20; 🔀) Saar Beach House is a self-contained architectural standout atop the dunes along 'Millionaire's Row' at Island Beach, 15km from Penneshaw. Views from the deck are indeed million-dollar! Sleeps 12; good winter rates.

Fish (☎ 8553 1177; 43 North Tce; mains $8-14; 🕑 dinner Sep-Jun) Fish-and-chips like you ain't

never had before – grilled, beer battered or crumbed – plus giant scallops, KI marron and lobster medallions. Free fish-cooking demos at 3.30pm, October to May.

Penneshaw Hotel (☎ 8553 1042; cnr North Tce & Thomas Wilson St; mains $16-23; 🕑 lunch & dinner) Elbow up to the bar with the sea-salty, agrarian Penneshawians and order King George whiting, roo sausages, curries, steaks, schnitzels and KI wines. Renovations were underway when we visited – imminent urbanity!

See also Dudley Cellar Door & Café (above).

AMERICAN RIVER
pop 230

Between Penneshaw and Kingscote, on the way to nowhere in particular, American River squats redundantly by the glassy **Pelican Lagoon**. The town was named after a crew of American sealers who built a trading schooner here in 1804. There's no such industriousness here today, just a daily pelican-feeding frenzy at the pier and wallabies hopping around the streets. The general store is the town's cultural zenith.

From the end of Scenic Dr, a fern-fringed **coastal walk** (2km one way) passes through natural scrub, sugar gums and she-oak en route to some old fish cannery ruins.

Sleeping & Eating
American River Campsite (per car $15) A shady, self-registration campsite by the lagoon, with fire pits, showers and toilets.

Island Coastal Units (☎ 8553 7010; www.kanga rooislandcoastalunits.com.au; Tangara Dr; d from $115, extra person $20) A low row of one- and two-bedroom motel-style units among trees opposite the foreshore, plus four beautiful self-contained cabins with solar hot water, gas cooktops and air-con.

Kangaroo Island Lodge (☎ 8553 7053; www.kilodge .com.au; Scenic Dr; d $155-190; ⚡ ⚖) Up-to-scratch motel suites overlooking either the pool or lagoon (the rammed-earth wing has the best rooms). The restaurant plates-up plenty of local seafood (mains $20 to $30, open for breakfast and dinner).

Matthew Flinders Terraces (☎ 0427-772 646; www .kangaroo-island-au.com/matthewflinders; Bayview Rd; self-contained 2-bed units $125; ⚡) Up a steep slope studded with native trees, these affordable, contemporary rooms have balconies overlooking the currents and shifting colours of Eastern Cove, but are a little short on elbow room.

American River General Store (☎ 8553 7051; Scenic Dr; ⏱ 7.30am-6.30pm) Packed to the northern hemisphere with provisions, bait and tackle, plus there's an amazing hardware 'cupboard', petrol and a bottle shop.

KINGSCOTE
pop 1450

Snoozy seaside Kingscote (pronounced, kings-coat) is the main town on KI, and the hub of island life. The town dates from 1836 when it became the first official colony in SA. The settlement struggled bravely for two years, but the lack of fresh water led most colonists to move to Adelaide. Today it's a photogenic town with swaying Norfolk Island pines, a couple of pubs and some decent eateries.

Information

Department for Environment & Heritage (☎ 8553 2381; www.environment.sa.gov.au/parks; 37 Dauncey St; ⏱ 9am-5pm Mon-Fri) Stocks Island Parks Passes (adult/student/child/family $46.50/36.50/28/126), covering all park and conservation area entry fees, and ranger-guided tours at Seal Bay, Kelly Hill Caves, Cape Borda and Cape Willoughby Lightstations (but not the penguin walks). Passes can also be purchased at most sights. Free passes if you stay five nights in heritage accommodation (see p83).

Kangaroo Island Hospital (☎ 8553 4200; www .kihealth.sa.gov.au; The Esplanade; ⏱ 24hr) Accident and emergency service.

Kangaroo Island Library (☎ 8553 4516; Dauncey St; ⏱ 10am-4.30pm Mon-Fri) Free internet access for travellers; bookings essential.

Kangaroo Island Medical Clinic (☎ 8553 2037; 64 Murray St; ⏱ 9am-4.30pm Mon-Fri, to 11am Sat) General practitioners.

Sights & Activities

The **Kangaroo Island Marine Centre** (☎ 8553 3112; www.kimarinecentre.com.au; Kingscote Wharf; admission adult/concession/child/family $15/13/6/36; ⏱ tours 8.30pm & 9.30pm Nov-Mar, 7.30pm & 8.30pm Apr-Oct) runs one-hour tours of its saltwater aquariums and the local penguin colony. It also runs informative (and comical) **pelican feeding** (Kingscote Wharf; admission $2; ⏱ feeding 5pm) sessions at the adjacent wharf.

Hope Cottage Museum (☎ 8553 2656; Centenary Ave; adult/concession/child $5/3/1; ⏱ 1-4pm daily, Sat only Aug) was built in 1857. It's now a fastidiously maintained National Trust museum decked out in period style, with a reconstructed lighthouse, an amazing old quilt and KI's first piano.

KI's first settlement was at the wind-ravaged **Reeves Point Historic Site** (admission free; ⏱ 24hr), walking distance from town. It's a pretty spot, but there's not much left apart from a cemetery and an 1836 mulberry tree. On the hill above the point is a fabulous **lookout** (also wind ravaged).

Island Beehive (☎ 8553 0080; www.island-beehive .com.au; cnr Playford Hwy & Acacia Dr; tours adult/concession/child/family $4.50/3.50/3/13; ⏱ 9am-5pm) runs factory tours where you can bone up on Ligurian bees and beekeeping, then stock up on byproducts (bee products?), including delicious organic honey and honeycomb ice cream.

Kingscote itself is lousy for swimming; locals usually head 18km northwest to **Emu Bay**, or the **tidal swimming pool** (admission free; ⏱ dawn-dusk) on Chapman Tce.

Sleeping & Eating

Kingscote Nepean Bay Tourist Park (☎ 8553 2394; www.kingscotetouristpark.com.au; Third Ave; unpowered/powered sites from $22/27, vans & cabins $60-130) You'll find the standard gamut of caravan park delights behind the dunes in Brownlow, 3km southwest of Kingscote. You can walk back to Kingscote via a coastal walking trail.

Kangaroo Island Central Hostel (☎ 8553 2787; 0400-197 231; ki_backpackers@bigpond.com; 19 Murray St; dm/d from $22/55) Just a couple of blocks from Kingscote's main strip, this small, innocuous hostel is clean, cheap and has a cosy lounge.

Seaview Motel (☎ 8553 2030; www.seaview.net.au; 51 Chapman Tce; guesthouse s/d $72/82, motel $132/142, extra adult/child $25/15; ⚡) It seems like this place is

---

ALL CREATURES GREAT & SMALL

You bump into a lot more wildlife here (sometimes literally) than on mainland SA. **Kangaroos**, **wallabies**, **bandicoots** and **possums** come out at night, especially in wilderness areas such as Flinders Chase National Park.

Koalas and the **platypus** were introduced to Flinders Chase in the 1920s when it was feared they'd become extinct on the mainland. Ironically, koala numbers have increased to the point where they're at risk of starvation. Debate rages over whether to cull, sterilise or relocate them to the mainland. **Echidnas** mooch around in the undergrowth and are far less obvious.

Offshore, **dolphins** and **southern right whales** are often seen cavorting, and there are colonies of **fairy penguins**, **New Zealand fur seals** and **Australian sea lions** here too.

Of the island's 243 **bird species**, several are rare or endangered. One species – the dwarf emu – has gone the way of the dodo. **Glossy black cockatoos** may soon follow it out the door, due to the widespread destruction of coastal she-oak woodlands (she-oak seeds are their exclusive diet).

On the cold-blooded side of the ledger, **goannas** and **tiger snakes** keep KI suitably scaly.

---

always full – a good sign! Choose from older-style guesthouse rooms with shared facilities, or refurbished '80s motel rooms.

Aurora Ozone Hotel (☎ 1800 083 133, 8553 2011; www.ozonehotel.com; cnr Commercial St & Kingscote Tce; motel d/tr/f from $130/180/202, deluxe d from $193; ✿ ▢ ▣) Opposite the foreshore with killer views, the 100-year-old Ozone pub has standard motel-style rooms and snazzy deluxe suites in a new wing across the street. The eternally busy bistro (mains $17 to $30, open breakfast, lunch and dinner) serves farmer-sized grills and seafood, and you can pickle yourself on KI wines at the bar.

our pick **Kangaroo Island Fresh Seafood** (☎ 8553 0177; 26 Telegraph Rd; meals $6-16; ✿ lunch daily, dinner Tue-Sun) Seriously, this place has the best seafood you're ever likely to taste. A dozen fat oysters go for around a dollar each, then there are all manner of cooked and fresh seafood packs and combos. Superb!

Bella (☎ 8553 0400; 54 Dauncey St; pizzas $12-32, mains $30; ✿ lunch & dinner) Sit inside or sidewalk-alfresco at Bella, a cheery Italian cafe-restaurant–pizza bar. Pizzas run all day (eat-in or takeaway); dinner is à la carte (American River oysters, Spencer Gulf king prawns, local roo and whiting).

PLAYFORD HIGHWAY

The black-snake bitumen Playford Hwy runs east–west across KI, veering away from Birchmore Rd (which turns into South Coast Rd) near Cygnet River, 12km from Kingscote. Here, **Island Pure Sheep Dairy** (☎ 8553 9110; is_pure@bigpond.net.au; Gum Creek Rd, Cygnet River; tours adult/concession/child/family $5.50/4.50/4.50/20; ✿ 1-5pm) is a

family-owned operation where 1500 sheep line up to be milked (from 3pm). Take a tour of the factory, which includes tastings of their yoghurts and cheeses (the haloumi is magic).

Tourist-free **Parndana**, 39km from Kingscote, has a general store, petrol and the **Parndana Wildlife Park** (☎ 8559 6050; www.parndanawildlifepark.com; Playford Hwy; adult/child $9/4; ✿ 9am-5pm), where you can catch up on wildlife (emus, koalas, echidnas and roos) if you've been driving around with your eyes closed.

Travel 15km west of Parndana and turn south down Harriet Rd to reach the much-touted **Marron Café** (☎ 8559 4128; Harriet Rd; mains $20-30; ✿ lunch) where you can check out marron (freshwater crayfish) in breeding tanks, then eat some at the attached cafe. It's a subtle taste, not necessarily enhanced by the heavy sauces issued by the kitchen. Last orders 4pm.

NORTH COAST ROAD

Exquisite beaches (much calmer than those on the south coast), bushland and undulating pastures dapple the North Coast Rd, running from Kingscote along the coast to the Playford Hwy 85km west (the bitumen expires at Emu Bay). There's not a whole lot to do here other than swan around on the beach – sounds good!

Sights & Activities

About 18km from Kingscote, **Emu Bay** is a holiday hamlet with a 5km-long, white-sand beach flanked by dunes – one of KI's best swimming spots. There are no shops or pubs here, but **Emu Bay Lavender** (☎ 8553 5338; ebl04@bigpond.com; admission free; ✿ 10am-4.30pm) sells lavender-infused jams, biscuits, ice cream and shortbread, plus cosmetics and oils. It also does (lavender-free) sandwiches, focaccias and salads ($5 to $10).

Around 36km further west, **Stokes Bay** has a penguin rookery and broad rock pool you access by scrambling through a 20m tunnel in the cliffs at the bay's eastern end (mind your head!). Beware the rip outside the pool.

You won't be able to prevent the word 'Wow!' escaping your lips as you look back over **Snelling Beach** from atop Constitution Hill. Continue 7km west and you'll hit the turn-off to **Western River Cove**, where a small beach is crowded in by sombre basalt cliffs. The ridge-top road in is utterly scenic, but really steep in places – a no-go zone for caravans.

Sleeping & Eating

Western River Cove Campsite (unpowered sites per car $5) This self-registration campsite is a short walk from the beach and a footbridge over the river (so tempting to dangle a line). There's a toilet block and a barbecue hut, but no showers.

Emu Bay Holiday Homes (☎ 8553 5241; www .emubaysuperviews.com.au; 10 Bayview Rd, Emu Bay; d $80-130, extra person $18) Great-value (if a little frilly) cabins and holiday homes amid a large garden set back from the beach (the views are great!). The self-contained cabins (caravan-park cabins with a facelift) sleep four or six; the holiday homes sleep six or 10.

Cape Cassini Wilderness Retreat (☎ 8559 2215; www.capecassini.com.au; off North Coast Rd; d incl breakfast $295) The emphasis is on sustainability and wilderness at this remote retreat, comprising three guest rooms in the owners' rammed-earth-and-stone house. There are two neat en suite doubles and a small twin with separate bathroom: the doubles have sensational views. Call for directions or a pick-up.

Rock Pool Café (☎ 8559 2277; Stokes Bay; mains $13-23; ☺ lunch, closed Jun-Aug) Don't worry about sandy feet at this casual, alfresco joint in Stokes Bay. 'What's the house special?', we asked. 'Whatever I feel like doin'!', said the chef (usually seafood, washed down with local wines and decent espresso). Out the back is a grassy campsite (unpowered sites $10) with rainwater tanks but no showers.

SOUTH COAST ROAD

South Coast Rd turns off the Kingscote-Penneshaw road about 15km from Kingscote, and runs out of steam 105km west in Flinders Chase National Park. The south coast is ex-

posed to the rampaging Southern Ocean – a wild contrast to the sheltered north. Given any sort of blow from the south the shore is awash with booming breakers and great clouds of spray.

Sights & Activities

A detour off Hog Bay or Birchmore Rds will take you to the **Emu Ridge Eucalyptus Distillery** (☎ 8553 8228; www.emuridge.com.au; Willsons Rd, MacGillivary; self-guided tour adult/concession/child/family $4.50/3.50/2.50/14; ☺ 9am-2pm), a self-sufficient operation extracting eucalyptus oil from the KI narrow-leaf mallee. The gallery sells eucalyptus-oil products including chemical-free cosmetics.

It's almost worth swimming the Backstairs Passage for the honey ice cream at nearby **Clifford's Honey Farm** (☎ 8553 8295; fax 8553 8224; Elsegood Rd, Haines; free tastings, self-guided tour adult/child $2/1.50; ☺ 9am-5pm), sourced from a colony of rare Ligurian bees.

A real KI highlight is **Seal Bay Conservation Park** (☎ 8559 4207; www.environment.sa.gov.au/parks /sanpr/sealbay; tours beach adult/concession/child/family $14/11/8.50/38, boardwalk $10/8/6/27; ☺ tours 9am-4.15pm year-round, plus 5.15pm Dec-Feb), where ranger-led guided tours stroll along the beach or boardwalk to a colony of (mostly sleeping) Australian sea lions. Tours depart between 9am and 4.15pm daily (plus 5.15pm during summer). 'Observation, not interaction' is the mentality.

Back on South Coast Rd, the next turn-off south (6km from Seal Bay Rd) leads to **Little Sahara**, a rolling dunescape looming above the surrounding scrub. You can hire sand-boards from Vivonne Bay General Store (opposite) or Kangaroo Island Outdoor Action (p83) for $29 per four hours.

Further west, soporific **Vivonne Bay** has a collection of shacks, a pier and a beautiful sweep of sand. The surf here is OK for beginners, but ask around before taking the plunge – there are some wicked undertows. Vivonne Bay General Store hires out bodyboards and fishing and snorkelling gear. West of town on Jetty Rd, Kangaroo Island Outdoor Action (p83) runs local activities.

Closer to Flinders Chase National Park is **Kelly Hill Conservation Park** (☎ 8559 7231; www.environ ment.sa.gov.au/parks/sanpr/kellyhill; tours adult/concession/child/family $12/9.50/7.50/33; ☺ tours 10.30am, then hourly 11.15am-4.15pm), a series of dry limestone caves 'discovered' in the 1880s by a horse

SOUTHERN OCEAN LODGE

Millionaires, start your engines! The shining star in the SA tourism galaxy is **Southern Ocean Lodge** (☎ 9918 4355; www.southernoceanlodge.com.au; Hanson Bay; d per night $1800-3600; ⌘ ▢ ⌘), billing itself as 'Australia's first true luxury lodge'. Designed by iconic SA architect Max Pritchard (see also Ridgetop Retreats, p77), the lodge is a sexy, low-profile snake tracing the Hanson Bay clifftop, and is an exercise in exclusivity. There's a two-night minium stay: for that you get airport transfers, all meals and drinks and guided tours of KI.

If you want a stickybeak, don't expect to see anything from the road (all you'll find is a steely set of gates and an unreceptive intercom: privacy is what guests are paying for here), but you can catch a sneaky glimpse from Hanson Bay beach.

named Kelly, who fell into them through a hole. Adventure caving tours (adult/concession/child/family $13/24/18/81.50) leave at 2.15pm daily, following on from the standard tour. Minimum age is eight years; bookings essential. The 9km **Hanson Bay Walk** runs from the caves through mallee scrub and past freshwater wetlands.

Sleeping & Eating

Western Kangaroo Island Caravan Park (☎ 8559 7201; www.westernki.com.au; South Coast Rd; unpowered/powered sites $20/25, cabins $110-140; ⌘) A few minutes' drive east of Flinders Chase National Park, this ultrafriendly, farm-based park has shady gums and resident roos. Check out the koala and lagoon walks, and the phone booth inside an old bakery truck. The shop sells groceries, homemade heat-and-eats and (for guests only) beer and wine.

ourpick Flinders Chase Farm (☎ 8559 7223; www.flinderschasefarm.com.au; West End Hwy; dm/cabins $25/60, d & tw with bathroom $100) A farm with charm! A couple of amiable mutts (and maybe a kangaroo) greet you as you check in here, a short drive from Flinders Chase National Park. Accommodation incudes immaculate dorms, a couple of cosy cabins and en suite rooms in a lodge. Outdoors is where it's at: there's a terrific camp kitchen, fire pits and 'tropical' outdoor showers.

Seal Bay Tourist Park (☎ 8559 6115; www.sealbaytouristpark.com.au; South Coast Rd; cabins $105, extra person $20) Opposite the Seal Bay turn-off, these self-contained cedar-coloured cabins sleep up to six. Reception is in an 1873 post office, next to a restaurant/bar (mains $10 to $23) serving pubby lunches. Note that signs still refer to this joint as 'Kaiwarra Food Barn'.

Kangaroo Island Wilderness Retreat (☎ 8559 7275; www.austdreaming.com.au; South Coast Rd; d $150-420; ⌘ ▢) This low-key resort on the Flinders Chase doorstep guarantees guests will see some wildlife: 30 or 40 wallabies graze in the courtyard every evening! Accommodation ranges from basic motel-style rooms to flashy spa suites. There's a restaurant and bar here too, serving breakfast ($12 to $27) and dinner (28 to $34).

Vivonne Bay General Store (☎ 8559 4285; South Coast Rd; meals $6-14; ☖ breakfast & lunch) This chipper little fuel stop–cum–general store–cum–cafe has an exhaustive menu of all-day breakfasts and takeaways. The whiting burger reigns supreme.

FLINDERS CHASE NATIONAL PARK

Occupying the western end of the island, **Flinders Chase National Park** (www.environment.sa.gov.au/parks/sanpr/flinderschasenp; adult/concession/child/family $8/6.50/4.50/21) is one of SA's top national parks. Much of the park is mallee scrub, but there are some beautiful, tall sugar-gum forests, particularly around Rocky River and the Ravine des Casoars, 5km south of Cape Borda. Sadly, around 100,000 acres of bush were burned-out by bushfires in 2007. Many walking tracks and campsites are closed for rehabilitation, but there's still plenty to see and do. Contact the park visitors centre or the Department for Environment & Heritage in Kingscote (p88) for updates on closures.

Flinders Chase National Park visitors centre (☎ 8559 7235; South Coast Rd, Rocky River; ☖ 9am-5pm) supplies info and park maps, and has a cafe and displays on island ecology.

Sights & Activities

Once a farm, **Rocky River** is a rampant hotbed of wildlife, with kangaroos, wallabies and Cape Barren geese competing for your affections. The roos are particularly brazen – they'll bug you for food, but park officers request that you don't feed them. A slew of good walks launches from behind the visitors centre, including one where you might spy a platypus (4.5km return).

From Rocky River a road runs south to a remote 1906 lighthouse atop wild **Cape du Couedic**. A boardwalk weaves down to **Admirals Arch**, a huge archway ground out by heavy seas, and passes a colony of New Zealand fur seals (sweet-smelling they ain't…).

At Kirkpatrick Point, a few kilometres east of Cape du Couedic, are the **Remarkable Rocks**, a cluster of hefty, weather-gouged granite boulders atop a rocky dome that arcs 75m down to the sea.

On the northwestern corner of the island, **Cape Borda** is topped by an 1858 lighthouse, standing tall above the rippling iron surface of the Southern Ocean. There are walks here from 1.5km to 9km, and **lighthouse tours** (☎ 8559 3257; adult/concession/child/family $12/9.50/7.50/33) departing at 11am, 12.30pm and 2pm daily (plus 3.15pm and 4pm during summer holidays).

At nearby **Harvey's Return** a cemetery speaks poignant volumes about the reality of isolation in the early days. From here you can drive to **Ravine des Casoars** (literally 'Ravine of the Cassowaries', referring to the now-extinct

dwarf emus seen here by Baudin's expedition). Check with the visitors centre if the walking trail (6.5km return) down to the coast is open again.

Sleeping & Eating

The 2007 bushfires ravaged many of the park's campsites: the Rocky River, Snake Lagoon and West Bay sites were all closed when we visited, but may have reopened by the time you read this (check with the park visitors centre). The basic campsite at **Harvey's Return** (per car $10) near Cape Borda is still open; book through the DEH in Kingscote (p88).

The Department for Environment & Heritage runs refurbished cottage accommodation at Rocky River (the budget Postmans Hut and family-friendly Mays Homestead), and lightkeepers' cottages at Cape du Couedic and Cape Borda; see p83 for details.

See p91 for sleeping options just outside the national park.

On the food front, the only option here if you're not self-catering is the **cafe** (meals $7-14; �9am-5pm) at the visitors centre, serving burgers, wraps, soup, coffee and wines by the glass.

FLEURIEU PENINSULA & KANGAROO ISLAND

Limestone Coast

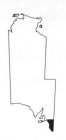

The Limestone Coast is a curiously engaging place. Strung-out southeastern South Australia (SA), it lies between the flat, olive span of the lower Murray River and the Victorian border. On the Princes Hwy you can blow across these flatlands in under a day, no sweat, but around here the delight is in the detail. Detour off the highway and check out the area's lagoons, surf beaches, sequestered bays and omnipresent birdlife. Also on offer are wine regions, photogenic fishing ports and snoozy agricultural towns. And what's *below* the road is even more amazing: a bizarre subterranean landscape of limestone caves, sinkholes and bottomless crater lakes.

In the Coorong National Park, an extensive coastal dune and lagoon system, the Ngarrindjeri Aboriginal community welcomes those curious about the area's ancient natural and cultural heritage. Further south is Robe, a historic lobster port with a slew of top-notch eateries.

Mt Gambier is studded with extinct volcanic vents, crater lakes and sinkholes. There's not much to do above ground here, so get under it! In the Coonawarra, renowned *terra rossa* (red earth) proffers atmospheric wineries making full-blooded reds and surprising whites. Vineyards encircle affable Penola, the spiritual home of Australia's saint-in-waiting, Mary MacKillop.

The World Heritage–listed Naracoorte Caves are astonishing: boneyards full of ancient marsupial fossils, mind-bending stalactites and swarms of bats darkening the dusk sky. More prone to daylight flight, migrating and breeding waterbirds return each year to nearby Bool Lagoon.

So take a relaxing swim, crack a bottle of Coonawarra Cab Sav and settle into a lobster salad – you'll need some energy for spelunking later on.

LIMESTONE COAST

HIGHLIGHTS

- Trundling past pelicans, dunes and lagoons along the **Coorong Scenic Drive** (p94)
- Dangling a lazy line off the 800m-long **Beachport Jetty** (p98)
- Checking to see if Mt Gambier's **Blue Lake** (p99) is blue or grey this time of year
- Clambering around the depths of Mt Gambier's **sinkholes and caves** (p100)
- Agreeing with South Australians when they reluctantly praise Victoria's **Great Ocean Road** (p102)
- Sniffing the good and the very good Cabernet Sauvignon in the **Coonawarra Wine Region** (p103)
- Ogling the Pleistocene beasts at the **Wonambi Fossil Centre** (p106) in Naracoorte Caves National Park

Coorong Scenic Drive ★

Naracoorte Caves National Park ★

Coonawarra Wine Region ★

Beachport Jetty ★

Great Ocean Road

Mt Gambier ★

- TELEPHONE CODE: ☎ 08   - www.thelimestonecoast.com   - www.coonawarra.org

Getting There & Away

AIR

Regional Express (Rex; ☎ 13 17 13; www.regionalexpress.com.au) flies daily between Adelaide and Mt Gambier (one-way from $130).

BUS & TRAIN

Premier Stateliner (☎ 08-8415 5555; www.premierstateliner.com.au) runs two bus routes – coastal and inland – between Adelaide and Mt Gambier ($62, 6¼ hours). From Adelaide along the coast (daily except Saturday), via the Coorong, you can stop at Meningie ($31, two hours), Kingston SE ($49, 3½ hours), Robe ($55, 4½ hours) and Beachport ($58, 5¼ hours). The inland bus runs daily via Bordertown ($47, 3½ hours), Naracoorte ($58, five hours) and Penola ($59, 5½ hours).

V/Line (☎ 1800 817 037, 13 61 96; www.vline.com.au) runs a service between Mt Gambier and Melbourne ($33, seven hours) – you take the bus from Mt Gambier to Ballarat or Warrnambool, where you hop on a train for Melbourne.

PRINCES HIGHWAY

From Murray Bridge the Princes Hwy (B1) follows the coast south through the saltbush of Coorong National Park to Kingston Southeast (Kingston SE), where it veers inland to Millicent and Mt Gambier. If you want to continue along the coast take the B101 from Kingston down through the picturesque fishing ports of Robe and Beachport, before rejoining the B1 at Millicent.

COORONG NATIONAL PARK

The amazing **Coorong** (www.environment.sa.gov.au/parks/sanpr/coorong) is a fecund lagoon landscape curving along the coast for 145km from Lake Alexandrina towards Kingston SE. A complex series of soaks and saltpans, it's separated from the sea by the chunky dunes of the Younghusband Peninsula. More than 200 species of waterbirds live here, including ducks, waders, pelicans, swans and endangered hooded plovers. *Storm Boy*, an endearing film about a young boy's friendship with a pelican (based on the novel by Colin Thiele), was filmed on the Coorong.

The Princes Hwy scuttles through, but you can't see much from the road. Instead,

take the 13km, unsealed **Coorong Scenic Drive**. Signed as Seven Mile Rd, it starts 10km southwest of Meningie off the Narrung Rd, and takes you right into the landscape, with its stinky lagoons, sea mists, fishing shanties, pelicans and wild emus. The road rejoins the Princes Hwy 10km south of Meningie. With a 4WD you can access **Ninety Mile Beach**, a well-known surf-fishing spot. The easiest ocean-access point is 3km off the Princes Hwy at 42 Mile Crossing, 19km south of Salt Creek. From here, it's a 1.3km 4WD or walk to the Southern Ocean.

At the edge of the Coorong on Lake Albert (a large arm of Lake Alexandrina), **Meningie** (population 900) was established as a minor port in 1866. It was a blowy sailboarding spot until climate change and shrinking Murray River flows sent the shoreline receding into the distance. The local pelicans seem unfazed…

Information

The Coorong office of the **Department for Environment & Heritage** (☎ 8575 1200; www.environment.sa.gov.au; 34 Princes Hwy, Meningie; ☽ 9am-5pm Mon-Fri) in Meningie has park maps and access, bushwalking, camping, boating and fishing info.

Tours

Companies running Coorong tours:
Adelaide Sightseeing (☎ 1300 769 762, 8410 2269; www.adelaidesightseeing.com.au; tours adult/child $167/138; ☽ Mon, Wed, Thu & Sun) Runs full-day Coorong tours departing Adelaide, with a cruise on the *Spirit of the Coorong* (see following), a guided walk, picnic lunch and plenty of birdlife.

Ecotrek (☎ 8357 3935; www.ecotrek.com.au; tours from $906) Three-day/two-night canoeing trips on the Coorong, including transport, camping accommodation, meals, wine and a guide.

Spirit of the Coorong (☎ 1800 442 203, 8555 2203; www.coorongcruises.com.au; The Wharf, Goolwa; ☽ Mon, Wed, Thu & Sun) These very popular cruises depart Goolwa (p81) and chug into the Coorong National Park. Take either a 4½-hour (adult/child $74/55) or six-hour (adult/child $88/60) cruise. Adelaide coach connections available; lunch provided.

Sleeping & Eating

There are 11 bush **campsites** (per car $5) in the park, but you need a permit from the Department for Environment & Heritage in Meningie (above), Mt Gambier (p99) or the roadhouse at Salt Creek.

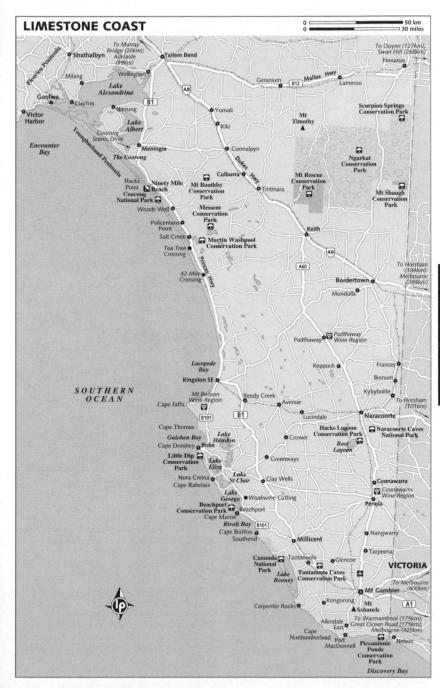

LIMESTONE COAST

0 ——— 50 km
0 ——— 30 miles

LIMESTONE COAST

LIMESTONE COAST

Camp Coorong (☎ 8575 1557; www.ngarrindjeri.net; Princes Hwy, 10km south of Meningie; powered sites/dm/cabins $20/27/70) Run by the Ngarrindjeri Lands and Progress Association, this is the place to learn about the Coorong's Aboriginal history and habitat. Take a guided cultural walk, basket-weaving lesson, museum tour (museum admission per car $5), Coorong tour or session about the Ngarrindjeri's perspective on Australian political history. Call for tour prices, museum hours and to make bookings. The cabins here are modern, well maintained and good value. BYO linen and food.

Coorong Wilderness Lodge (☎ 8575 6001; www.coorongwildernesslodge.com; off the Princes Hwy, 25km south of Meningie; unpowered/powered sites $10/20, dm/d $28/70; 🏊) At Hack Point, this fish-shaped centre is owned by the Ngarrindjeri community. By the time you read this, five amazing new accommodation units should be finished. Until then the ordinary old bunkhouse will have to do, but you can enjoy bush tucker and bush-medicine walks ($10), walking and kayak tours ($20; kayaks per half-/full day $30/50), and bush-tucker meals of Coorong mullet, damper and kangaroo meatballs (meals around $20). Book everything in advance.

Lake Albert Caravan Park (☎ 8575 1411; lacp@lm.net.au; 25 Narrung Rd, Meningie; unpowered/powered sites $20/28, cabins with/without bathroom from $80/55; 🏊) An old park with limited facilities, but a beaut aspect overlooking the (ever-shrinking) lake. Cabins 1, 2 and 3 (with bathroom) have the best views.

Dalton on the Lake (☎ 0428-737 161; admason@lm.net.au; 30 Narrung Rd, Meningie; d from $125; 🏊) Generous in spirit and unfailingly clean, this lakeside B&B goes to great lengths to ensure your stay is comfortable. There'll be fresh bread baking when you arrive, jars of homemade biscuits and bountiful bacon-and-eggs for breakfast. There's a modern self-contained studio off to one side, or a renovated stone cottage – book either, or both.

Cheese Factory (☎ 8575 1914; off Narrung Rd, Meningie; mains $8-21; 🕙 lunch & dinner Tue-Sun) In a converted cheese factory (you might have guessed), this outfit gives Meningie pub a run for its money. Lean on the front bar with the locals, or munch into steaks, lasagne, mixed grills, Coorong mullet or a Coorong burger (with mullet!) in the cavernous dining room. There's a very lo-fi history museum here too (admission $2, open 11am to 5pm).

ABORIGINAL AUSTRALIA: THE COORONG

The name 'Coorong' derives from the Ngarrindjeri Aboriginal word *Karangk*, meaning 'long neck'. In the 1800s the bountiful resources of the Coorong supported a large Ngarrindjeri population. The Ngarrindjeri are still closely connected to the Coorong, and many still live here. Learn more about them at Camp Coorong (left).

ROBE & AROUND
pop 1123

Robe is a cherubic little fishing port that's become a holiday hot spot for Adelaidians and Melburnians alike. The sign saying 'Drain Outlet L' as you roll into town doesn't promise much, but along the main street you'll find quality eateries and boundless accommodation, and there are some magic beaches and lakes around town. Over Christmas and Easter, Robe is packed to the heavens – book *waaay* in advance.

Information
Robe visitors centre (☎ 1300 367 144, 8768 2465; www.robe.com.au; Public Library, Mundy Tce; 🕙 9am-5pm Mon-Fri, 10am-4pm Sat & Sun) has history displays, brochures and free internet access.

Sights & Activities
Heritage-listed buildings dating from the late 1840s to 1870s litter the streets of Robe. The leaflet *Robe Walking Tours* includes the 1863 **Customs House** (🕙 2-4pm Tue & Sun) on Royal Circus, which is now a nautical museum. Ask the visitors centre about access. Nearby is a **memorial** to the 16,500 Chinese diggers who landed at Robe between 1856 and 1858 (see The Long Road to Ballarat, opposite).

Make some time to wander through **Wilsons at Robe** (☎ 8768 2459; www.wilsonsatrobe.com; 5 Victoria St; admission free; 🕙 10.30am-4pm Thu-Sun), an art gallery full of carved stone pelicans, corrugated iron sheep and glass blue wrens – a crafty menagerie!

Little Dip Conservation Park (www.environment.sa.gov.au/parks/sanpr/littledip) runs along the coast for about 13km south of town. It features a variety of habitats including lakes, wetlands and dunes, and some beaut beaches, Aboriginal middens, walks and camping spots ($5 per car). **Bishops Pate**, **Long Gully** and

---

THE LONG WALK TO BALLARAT

Robe set up shop as a fishing port in 1846 – one of SA's earliest settlements. During the 1850s gold rush in Victoria, Robe came into its own when the Victorian government whacked a $10-per-head tax on Chinese gold miners arriving to work the goldfields. Thousands of Chinese miners dodged the tax by landing at Robe, then walking the 400-odd kilometres to Bendigo and Ballarat; 10,000 arrived in 1857 alone. But the flood stalled as quickly as it started when the SA government instituted its own tax on the Chinese. The **Chinamen's Wells** along their route (including one in the Coorong) can still be seen today.

Little Dip are also hot fishing spots. Access is via Nora Creina Rd.

The small town beach has safe swimming, while **Long Beach** (2km from town) is good for surfing, sailboarding and lazy days (safe swimming in some sections – ask at the visitors centre).

Speaking of surf, **Steve's Place** (☎ 8762 8094; 26 Victoria St; ☺ 9am-5pm) rents out beginners' boards (per half-/full day $20/40) and bodyboards ($5/10). Steve's is also the contact for the **Robe Easter Classic**, the longest-running surf contest in SA (since 1968).

In late November, the **Robe Village Fair** (www .robevillagefair.com.au; weekend tickets adult/concession/child $88/44/free) hits town: a weekend food-and-music frenzy with a family bent.

In nearby Kingston SE (www.kingstonsesa .com; population 2230) is one of Australia's 'big' tourist attractions – the lurid but rather well executed **Larry the Lobster**. Kingston SE is a hotbed of crayfishing and hosts the week-long **Lobsterfest** in the second week of January.

To taste some smooth Shiraz, check out the emerging **Mt Benson wine region** (www.mbva .com.au) between Robe and Kingston SE. There are around 20 wineries here, four with cellar doors. **Cape Jaffa Wines** (☎ 8768 5053; www.capejaffa wines.com.au; Limestone Coast Rd; ☺ 10am-5pm) is the pick of the bunch.

Sleeping

Robe has plenty of accommodation, but you'll be lucky to find a bed during peak periods if you haven't booked. Prices jump off the graph during December and January. **Raine & Horne** (☎ 8768 2028; www.rhsa.com.au/robe; 25 Victoria St; ☺ 9am-5pm Mon-Fri, 9.30-11am Sat) books holiday-rental properties from as low as $60 per night in the off-season.

Lakeside Manor Backpackers Lodge (☎ 1800 155 350, 8768 1995; www.lakesidemanorbackpackers.com .au; 22 Main Rd; dm/d $29/77; 🖳) In an 1885 sandstone mansion becalmed in faded grandeur, this place has cavernous dorms and doubles. There's an open fireplace, a library, an orchard and a hallway as long as two cricket pitches (we tested it out with a few leg breaks).

Caledonian Inn (☎ 8768 2029; www.caledonian.net .au; 1 Victoria St; hotel/cottage/villa d from $85/185/310) This historic inn has it all under one roof (actually, several roofs). The half-dozen hotel rooms upstairs share bathroom facilities but are bright and cosy, while the split-level, self-contained units – all rattan and white-painted wood – are sandwiched between the pub and beach. The dead-plush villa sleeps up to eight.

Lake View Motel & Apartments (☎ 8768 2100; www.robelakeviewmotel.com.au; 2 Lakeside Tce; d/apt from $100/195, extra person $15; 🐕) Overlooking Lake Fellmongery (a waterskiing mecca) off the road into town, the enthusiastically managed Lake View is Robe's best motel. The decor is a little 'peachy', but the rooms are roomy and immaculately clean, and the barbecue area pumps during summer.

Robe Cricklewood (☎ 8768 2137; www.cricklewood .com.au; 24 Wollundry Rd; d from $160; 🐕) The catchcry here is 'A first amongst equals' – extract some democracy from this if you can, or just check-in and forget about what the poor people are doing down in the village. It's a country-style villa with cathedral ceilings, exposed beams and a well-balanced mix of cottagelike and modern furnishings and fittings.

For happy campers:

Lakeside Tourist Park (☎ 8768 2193; www.lakeside robe.com.au; 24 Main Rd; unpowered/powered sites from $25/27, cabins & villas $50-150) Right on Lake Fellmongery, this abstractly laid-out park has heritage-listed pine trees, plenty of grass and basic but clean cabins. Bike hire per half-/full day is $20/30.

Discovery Holiday Parks Robe (☎ 8768 2237; www.discoveryholidayparks.com.au; 70 The Esplanade; unpowered/powered sites from $27/29, cabins & chalets $60-180; 🐕 🖳) This humongous value-for-money park is almost beachside. The self-contained cabins and chalets are big and comfortable, plus there's a heated indoor pool, tennis courts, wireless internet, playground, barbecue and crayfish boiler!

Eating

Robe Providore (☎ 8768 2119; 4 Victoria St; breakfast $4-14, lunch $11-17; ☺ breakfast & lunch; Ⓥ) A little bit of 'big city' comes to Robe at this polished-concrete-and-white eatery, serving urbane breakfasts (porridge with fruit compote) and considered lunches (calamari salad on rocket) at communal tables and bench seats. Sketchy winter hours.

Union (☎ 8768 2627; cnr Victoria & Union Sts; breakfast $5-15, lunch $8-17; ☺ breakfast & lunch) Robe's best coffee is at this curiously angled corner cafe with polished glass fragments in the floor and Astroturf on the wall. Unionise your hangover with big breakfasts (banana pancakes with bacon and maple syrup), stir-fries, pastas and risottos.

Vic Street Pizzeria (☎ 8768 2081; 6 Victoria St; mains $9-22; ☺ breakfast, lunch & dinner; Ⓥ) An exciting addition to Robe's foodie scene, Vic Street is a high-energy, all-day cafe, serving gourmet pizzas, good coffee, and an astoundingly good Caesar salad. Mod-Asian interior touches, cool tunes on the stereo and local wines, too.

Gallerie (☎ 8768 2256; 2 Victoria St; lunch $16-24, dinner $20-34; ☺ lunch & dinner) Shiny, clattery Gallerie is the most upmarket eatery in Robe, with lots of polished wood and glass. The fish-of-the-day is always good, as is the chicken Florentine. Contemporary reworkings of Bob Marley classics add an inauthentic tone.

For a decent pub meal:

Robe Hotel (☎ 8768 2077; Mundy Tce; mains $14-32; ☺ lunch & dinner) A salty locals pub serving fresh takings from the adjacent Southern Ocean: crayfish, calamari and Guichen Bay fish-and-chips. The Limestone Coast rib eye or lamb's fry and kidney will give you a shot of iron.

Caledonian Inn (☎ 8768 2029; 1 Victoria St; mains $19-28; ☺ lunch & dinner) First licensed in 1858, the Caledonian has retained its Scottish heritage and has a great atmosphere. There's a beer garden, summer cafe out the back and bar meals aimed towards carnivores and seafood fans.

Entertainment

South Coast Cinema (☎ 8768 2772; www.ausaf.com .au; 37 Victoria St; tickets $10; ☺ shows 7pm Wed, 7.30pm Fri & Sat, 4.30pm Sun) This place has two screens and shows contemporary hits.

BEACHPORT

pop 350

'See and be seen: headlights 24 hours!' say billboards on the way into Beachport. A town that's desperate to be noticed? A plaintive cry for attention? We like it the way it is: low key and beachy, with aquamarine surf, staunch stone buildings and rows of Norfolk Island pines. Take a walk along the jetty, hang out in the old pub, or munch some fish-and-chips on the grassy foreshore. Forget about being seen – your time here will be perfectly anonymous.

Information

Beachport visitors centre (☎ 8735 8029; www.wattle range.sa.gov.au; Millicent Rd; ☺ 9am-5pm Mon-Fri year-round, 10am-4pm Sat & Sun Dec-Feb, 11am-2pm Sat & Sun Mar-Nov) is centrally placed and has internet access.

Sights & Activities

The **Old Wool & Grain Store Museum** (☎ 8735 8313; www.nationaltrustsa.org.au; 5 Railway Tce; adult/concession/child/family $5/4/2/10; ☺ 10am-4pm Mon-Wed, Fri & Sat, to 2pm Sun) is in a National Trust building on the main street. Inside are relics from Beachport's whaling days and rooms decked out in 1870s style. The hours listed here can be a bit hit-and-miss in winter; if it's closed, check the roster in the window or ask at the visitors centre.

There are some great walking tracks in the 710-hectare **Beachport Conservation Park** (www.environment.sa.gov.au/parks/sanpr/beachport), sandwiched between the coast and Lake George 2km north of town. Here you'll find Aboriginal middens, sheltered coves, lagoons and bush camping ($5 per car).

The hypersaline **Pool of Siloam** among dunes on the western outskirts of town is great for swimming. The water is seven times saltier than the ocean.

The 800m-long **Beachport Jetty** provides excellent fishing for local pelicans and fishermen: try your luck for some whiting, school shark, squid and the easy-eating Lake George mullet. Pick up the *Tips on Fishing in and Around Beachport* brochure from the visitors centre. Further south, 200m offshore, **Penguin Island** is a rookery for little penguins. Each summer the parent penguins take their flappy offspring for swimming lessons between the island and the groyne opposite Beachport Caravan Park.

About 12km along the road to Robe, the **Woakwine Cutting** through the Woakwine Range illustrates the lengths (1km, in fact) to which one determined farmer will go to drain a swamp. It took Murray McCourt three years to excavate 276,000 cu metres of mountainside here.

There's good surfing, birdwatching and sailboarding at **Lake George**, 5km north of Beachport. **Canunda National Park**, with its giant sand dunes, is 22km south of town (see Troglodytes, Surfers & Spelunkers, p100).

In teensy Tantanoola, southeast of Millicent, the Tantanoola Hotel is home to the mythical **Tantanoola Tiger**. This moth-eaten, glass-eyed beast (actually an Assyrian wolf) was shot in 1895 after chewing on a few local sheep. Some were disappointed the killer was a lowly hound – presumed to have escaped from a shipwreck – and not the more glamorous Bengal tiger rumoured to have escaped from a travelling circus in the early 1880s.

See p100 for details on the Tantanoola Caves Conservation Park.

Sleeping & Eating

Beachport gets busy as a woodpecker in summer, so it's worth booking your accommodation well in advance. The Beachport visitors centre (opposite) and **Millicent visitors centre** (☎ 8733 0904; www.wattlerange.sa.gov.au; 1 Mt Gambier St, Millicent; ☾ 9am-5pm Mon-Fri, 10am-4pm Sat & Sun) are good starting points.

ourpick **Bompas** (☎ 8735 8333; www.bompas.com .au; 3 Railway Tce; dm/d from $35/85) Brilliant Bompas is an all-in-one small hotel and cosy licensed restaurant-cafe (meals $9 to $29, open for breakfast, lunch and dinner). Dorms have TVs, and all rooms are generously sized and strewn with modern art. If you're after a double try No 3 ($145) – it's more expensive but worth it for the million-dollar water views and deep balcony. Menu offerings downstairs include curries, lasagne and lamb shanks, with local and imported beers. The owners live on site, and call you 'Honey' and 'Darl' whether they know you or not.

Beachport Motor Inn (☎ 8735 8070; beachport motel@bigpond.com; 13 Railway Tce; d/unit from $90/105, extra person $15) Within two minutes' walk of the town beach, this little, U-shaped motel has neat and compact rooms and is pretty good value. It's 40 years old, but still in good nick. Free DVDs; units sleep five.

Southern Ocean Tourist Park (☎ 8735 8153; sotp@bigpond.net.au; Somerville St; unpowered/powered sites $17/20, cabins from $60; ☒) This grassy, well-pruned park sits behind a slope in the town centre and has a great location for camping. Facilities include a laundry, ice, fuel, bait, cov-

ered barbecues, crayfish cookers and a good little playground, but feedback from readers hasn't been too flattering.

Entertainment

South Coast Cinema (☎ 8735 8262; 7 Railway Tce; tickets $10; ☾ shows Fri & Sat nights Dec-Feb, reduced winter hr) Mainstream flicks in an old hall on the main street.

MT GAMBIER
pop 24,500

Strung out along the flatlands below an extinct volcano, Mt Gambier is the Limestone Coast's major town and service hub, and the hometown of musical *bon vivant* Dave Graney. We can see why Dave might have wanted to get to Melbourne in a hurry: 'The Mount' can seem a grim place, short on urban virtues and with a huge derelict hospital glowering over the rooftops. Revheads cruise the main drag as needless traffic lights blink from green to red.

But it's not what's above the streets that makes Mt Gambier special – it's the deep Blue Lake and the sinkholes and caves that worm their way though the limestone beneath the town. Amazing!

Information

Mt Gambier visitors centre (☎ 1800 087 187, 8724 9750; www.mountgambiertourism.com.au; Jubilee Hwy E; ☾ 9am-5pm) The biggest and most comprehensive in the region. Chipper staff have the low-down on local sights, activities and accommodation, and can show you a 20-minute video on the town. The Mt Gambier Discovery Centre (p100) is here too.

Department for Environment & Heritage (☎ 8735 1177; www.environment.sa.gov.au; 11 Helen St; ☾ 8.45am-5pm Mon-Fri)

Sights & Activities

Mt Gambier's big-ticket item is the luminous, 75m-deep **Blue Lake** (John Watson Dr; admission free; ☾ 24hr) which turns an almost implausible hue of blue during summer. Perplexed scientists think it has to do with calcite crystals suspended in the water, which form at a faster rate during the warmer months. Consequently, if you visit between April and November, the lake will look much like any other – a steely grey. But even in winter it makes for a scenic drive (or sweaty jog) around the encircling road. **Aquifer Tours** (☎ 8723 1199; www.aquifertours .com; cnr Bay Rd & John Watson Dr; adult/child/family $7/3/19;

LIMESTONE COAST

TROGLODYTES, SURFERS & SPELUNKERS

The geological history of the Limestone Coast is curious indeed, so clearly evidenced by the lakes and craters of **Mt Gambier** (p99) and the must-see **Naracoorte Caves National Park** (p106). But beyond these there's a cache of lesser-known coastal parks, water-filled sinkholes and caves to explore.

On the Mt Gambier road 13km north of Port MacDonnell, a steep footpath (20 minutes up) climbs **Mt Schank**, an extinct volcano. **Little Blue Lake**, 3km west of Mt Schank, is a brilliant swimming hole – icy cold even on scorching summer afternoons.

On the coast near the Victorian border the 547-hectare **Piccaninnie Ponds Conservation Park** (www.environment.sa.gov.au/parks/sanpr/piccaninnieponds) has walks, camping and reputedly the world's best freshwater dive feature: the **Cathedral**, a massive underwater cavern with 40m visibility. Permits and cave-diving qualifications are required for diving and snorkelling here, and further west at tiny **Ewen Ponds Conservation Park** (www.environment.sa.gov.au/parks/sanpr/ewenponds).

Back up the coast, 13km southwest of Millicent, the fabulous 9300-hectare **Canunda National Park** (www.environment.sa.gov.au/parks/sanpr/canunda) features giant sand dunes, craggy coastal scenery, wombats, walks, camping and 4WD tracks. Hardcore surfers carve up the breaks here, and in summer you can drive along the beach and through the dunes from Southend to Carpenter Rocks.

Another 6km southeast on the Princes Hwy, the 2000-hectare **Tantanoola Caves Conservation Park** (☎ 8734 4153; www.environment.sa.gov.au/parks/sanpr/tantanoolacaves; tours adult/concession/child/family $9/7.50/5.50/24.50; ⏲ 10am-4pm) has coastal caves formed in dolomite. Access by tour only.

For permits and further info, contact the Mt Gambier visitors centre (p99), the **Millicent visitors centre** (☎ 8733 0904; www.wattlerange.sa.gov.au; 1 Mt Gambier St, Millicent; ⏲ 9am-5pm Mon-Fri, 10am-4pm Sat & Sun), or the Mt Gambier office of the Department for Environment & Heritage (p99).

⏲ tours 9am-5pm Nov-Jan, to 2pm Feb-May & Sep-Oct, to noon Jun-Aug) runs hourly tours here. The 45-minute tours take you down to near the surface of the lake in a glass-panelled lift.

If the lake isn't blue, don't feel blue – cheer yourself up with a visit to the outstanding **Riddoch Art Gallery** (☎ 8723 9566; www.riddochart gallery.org.au; 8-10 Commercial St E; admission free; ⏲ 10am-5pm Tue-Fri, 11am-3pm Sat & Sun), one of Australia's best regional galleries. The sculpture, painting and visual-arts exhibitions here are invariably first rate.

Inside the Mt Gambier visitors centre (p99) is the **Mt Gambier Discovery Centre** (adult/child $10/5), which features a replica of the historic brig *Lady Nelson*. An audiovisual display focuses on the devastating impact of European settlement on the local Indigenous peoples, and the work of Christina Smith, who attempted to mediate between the settlers and local Aborigines.

The Mt Gambier district is famous for its limestone caves and sinkholes. **Engelbrecht Cave** (☎ 8725 5493, 0418-133 407; Jubilee Hwy W, entry off Chute St; tours adult/concession/child $7.50/6.50/4; ⏲ tours 9.30am-5.30pm Dec-Feb, to 3.30pm Mar-Nov) is a tour-accessible cave and popular cave-diving spot, extending 600m end-to-end beneath the sleepy suburbs of Mt Gambier.

The 45-minute tours depart on the half-hour. **Umpherston Sinkhole** (Jubilee Hwy E; admission free; ⏲ 24hr) is a fascinating pit that was once 'a pleasant resort in the heat of summer' on James Umpherston's estate, a rambling country acreage and mansion long since sub-divided and demolished. The Umpherstons used to row around a lake at the bottom, now also nonexistent. Ask at the visitors centre about volunteer-run tours.

To say that Mt Gambier is a hole is technically correct: right in the centre of town is **Cave Gardens** (cnr Bay Rd & Watson Tce; admission free; ⏲ 24hr), an amazing, 50m-deep sinkhole, with viewing platforms, gardens, dripping walls and the occasional suicidal shopping trolley at the bottom.

See above for details on other caves, walks, beaches and cave-diving and snorkelling opportunities in the area.

Sleeping

If nothing here takes your fancy, there are a heap of motels along Jubilee Hwy E, the road into town from Melbourne. Online, check out www.bnb.limestonecoast.com and www.mountgambieraccommodation.com.au for local apartment and B&B accommodation listings.

DETOUR: PORT MACDONNELL

Around 30km south of Mt Gambier, snoozy Port MacDonnell (population 700) is SA's southernmost town, and home to the state's largest crayfishing fleet. It was once a busy port, which explains the surprisingly hefty and handsome **Customs House** (1863).

More than 30 ships have come a cropper along the coast near here since 1844, which makes Port MacDonnell a popular dive site. Ask at the Mt Gambier visitors centre (p99) for details. The **Port MacDonnell & District Maritime Museum** (☎ 8738 7259, fax 8738 7340; 49 Meylin St; adult/concession/child $3.50/2/1; ☼ 12.30pm-4.30pm Wed, Fri & Sun, or by appointment) is a barnacle-encrusted trove of artefacts recovered from the shipwrecks.

Flamboyant 19th-century poet Adam Lindsay Gordon lived here in a little 1860 cottage called *Dingley Dell,* now part of **Dingley Dell Conservation Park** (☎ 8738 2221; www.environment.sa.gov .au/parks/sanpr/dingleydell; Dingley Dell Rd; adult/concession/child $2.50/1.50/1; ☼ 10am-4pm), which displays some of his musings and belongings.

There are a few unsophisticated places to stay and eat here, but you're probably better off day tripping from Mt Gambier.

Blue Lake Holiday Park (☎ 1800 676 028, 8725 9856; www.bluelakeholidaypark.com.au; Bay Rd; unpowered/powered sites $24/29, cabins/units/bungalows from $82/95/120; 🏊) Adjacent to the Blue Lake, a golf course and walking and cycling tracks, this amiable park has some natty grey-and-white cabins and well-weeded lawns. There are also spiffy new contemporary, self-contained 'retreats' (from $149) that sleep four.

Grand Central Motel (☎ 8725 8844; grandcentralmotel @hotmail.com; 6 Helen St; s/d/f $50/75/125; 🖥) A rock-solid, conveniently located cheapie whose managers are Mt Gambier born-and-bred, and can point you in the right direction on the town map. Rooms are nothing flash and bit pokey, but clean and well kept.

Arkana Motor Inn (☎ 8725 5433; www.arkanamotorinn .com.au; 201 Commercial St E; s/d/units $95/100/140; 🖥 🏊) The pick of the motels in the east end of town, the squat Arkana won't win any architectural awards but has bright, clean rooms and friendly managers. There's also a barbecue, cable TV, a heated pool, spa, and wireless internet.

Mt Gambier Hotel (☎ 8725 0611; www.gambierhotel .com.au; 2 Commercial St W; d from $110; 🖥) Upstairs at 'The G' is a collection of oddly configured pub rooms with kooky furnishings (little bit of art deco, little bit of '70s). But the location is primo, and the rooms are spacey and have spas and en suites. Redfins Seafood & Grill (see p102) is downstairs.

Park Hotel (☎ 8725 2430; www.parkhotel.com.au; 163 Commercial St W; d from $130; 🖥) In Mt Gambier's western wastelands, this old corner pub has spent a fortune renovating its half-dozen upstairs rooms. Polished timber floors, double glazing, marble bathrooms and coffee-and-cream colour schemes – a really slick product.

Colhurst House (☎ 8723 1309; www.colhursthouse .com.au; 3 Colhurst Pl, off Wyatt St; d incl breakfast from $135) Most locals don't know about Colhurst – it's up a laneway off a side street and you can't really see it from downtown Mt G. It's an 1878 mansion built by Welsh migrants, and manages to be old-fashioned without being twee. There's a gorgeous wrap-around balcony upstairs with great views over the rooftops. Cooked breakfasts, too.

Clarendon Chalets (☎ 8726 8306; www.clarendon chalets.com; Clarke Rd; d from $135, extra adult/child $30/20; 🖥) Up a spooky tree-lined driveway on a walnut farm 7km from town, these four alpine-style chalets will put you at bucolic ease (forget the spooky driveway). They're all fitted out with combustion fires, spas and barbecues – well worth the drive.

Eating

our pick **Bull Frogs** (☎ 8723 3933; 7 Percy St; lunch $9-19, dinner $16-40; ☼ lunch Mon-Sat, dinner daily; 🖥) Bull Frogs has injected some much-needed quality and worldliness into Mt Gambier's food scene. Spread over three floors of a fabulous old mill building (next to the Oatmill Cinema), this is the place for organic beef and lamb grills, boutique beers, Coonawarra wines, cocktails, trusty coffee and acoustic tunes on weekends. Hard to beat.

Banana Tree Cafe (☎ 8723 9393; 2/94 Commercial St E; mains $13-20; ☼ lunch & dinner; 🖥 Ⓥ) Wow – authentic Thai in Mt Gambier! A colourful, corner eatery with a Thai chef, serving chilli-laden dishes such as beef-and-basil

---

GREAT OCEAN ROAD

Mt Gambier is the last pit stop of any size as you head from the Limestone Coast into Victoria (or vice versa). From Mt Gambier you can put the foot down and boot it to Melbourne via Warrnambool, Colac and Geelong (a 426km dash along the Princes Hwy), or hit the coast at Warrnambool and take the legendary **Great Ocean Road** (www.greatoceanrd.org.au) to Geelong via the iconic 12 Apostles and a string of surf beaches, histrionic cliffs and photogenic coastal towns (a wiggly 600km from Mt Gambier to Melbourne over three days).

The Great Ocean Road has been compared to California's famous Hwy 1, and justly so. The road was hacked out of sheer cliffs by labourers put to work during the Great Depression – such a convoluted route that the whole coastline remained largely untouristed until the 1980s.

Along the way you can hit the surf at Jan Juc, Bells Beach or Wye River, fuel up in cafes at Apollo Bay and Lorne, check out the 12 Apostles, London Bridge and Loch Ard Gorge rock formations, and spy southern right wales offshore between July and October. Trundle down Cape Otway Rd to the heritage lighthouse – the steely ocean swell below will make you feel profoundly insignificant. Sleepy yet? Take your pick from a fabulous array of stylish B&Bs – everything from minimalist zen tree-houses to boomerang-shaped hillside bunkers.

---

stir-fry and a smokin' green chicken curry that will have a memorable effect on your innards.

Sage & Muntries (☎ 8724 8400; 78 Commercial St W; mains $16-40; ☺ lunch & dinner Mon-Sat; ☒ Ⓥ) An award-winning licensed cafe plating up enticing daily specials such as spicy sausages with mash and caramelised onions, plus steaming bowls of homemade pasta and Med-flavoured baguettes, salads and focaccias. Local wines by the bottle or glass (the nonlocal stuff doesn't sell!).

Redfins Seafood & Grill (☎ 8725 0611; 2 Commercial St W; mains $18-30; ☺ dinner Mon-Sat; ☒) Streetside at the Mt Gambier Hotel is Redfins, an upmarket dining room serving seafood and meaty mains (kangaroo, steak, chicken and veal). Coffin Bay oysters are a speciality (from $16 per dozen), done in five flavours: natural, Kilpatrick, Florentine, Virgin Mary or smoked salmon.

See also Flanagan's Irish Pub (below).

Drinking & Entertainment

Flanagan's Irish Pub (☎ 8725 1671; 6 Ferrers St) Flanagan's was allegedly the first Irish pub in SA. We're not going to argue with 'em, as they're by far the most palatable place to drink in the Mount. There's chunky pub food (mains $10 to $25, open for lunch and dinner), bands on Saturday night, snooker tables, cold Guinness and warm fires.

Oatmill Cinema (☎ 8724 9150; www.oatmill.com.au; 7 Percy St; tickets adult/concession/child $13.50/11/9.50) This three-screen cinema screens contemporary, top-selling flicks. All Tuesday tickets $9.

Sir Robert Helpmann Theatre (☎ 8723 8741; www .countryarts.org.au; Civic Centre, 10 Watson Tce; ☺ box office 9am-5pm Mon-Fri, 9.30am-12.30pm Sat) The Limestone Coast's major entertainment venue (528 bums on seats) always has something showing: Roy Orbison tributes, kids' afternoons, Indigenous film festivals and Antal Szalai and his Gypsy Orchestra!

Getting Around

For a taxi try **Lake City Taxis Co-op** (☎ 8723 0000). **McCormick's Bus Service** (☎ 8724 9978; ☺ runs Mon-Fri) serves three city routes; the visitors centre has timetables.

COONAWARRA WINE REGION

The Coonawarra is a dead-flat wine-making and agricultural region revolving around the 'saintly' town of Penola. Long-time locals protect the traditional Coonawarra Wine Region boundaries, which they see as being eroded by new wineries pushing further and further away from Penola. But near or far, the Cabernet Sauvignon from the area's 30-plus cellar doors is reliably divine. Online, have a look at www.coonawarra.org.

Also in the area is the flap-happy bird sanctuary of Bool Lagoon, and the amazing Naracoorte Caves, while the red-gum country between Mt Gambier and Bordertown has some of the richest fodder-growing and grazing land in SA.

TOP FIVE COONAWARRA WINERIES

When it comes to spicy Cabernet Sauvignon, it's just plain foolish to dispute the virtues of the Coonawarra Wine Region – the *terra rossa* (red earth) region between Penola and Naracoorte. The climate also produces some irresistible Shiraz and Chardonnay. Five of the best:

- **Balnaves of Coonawarra** (☎ 8737 2946; www.balnaves.com.au; Riddoch Hwy; ☉ 9am-5pm Mon-Fri, noon-5pm Sat & Sun) The tasting notes here ooze florid wine-speak (dark seaweed, leather or tobacco, anyone?), but even if your nosing skills aren't that subtle you'll enjoy the Cab Sav and Chardonnay.

- **Majella Wines** (☎ 8736 3055; www.majellawines.com.au; Lynn Rd; ☉ 10am-4.30pm) The family that runs Majella consists of fourth-generation Coonawarrans, so they know a thing or two about gutsy reds. Their Sparkling Shiraz and Riesling are unexpected bonuses. All the fruit comes from the estate's vineyards; truly homemade.

- **Rymill Coonawarra** (☎ 8736 5001; www.rymill.com.au; Riddoch Hwy; ☉ 10am-5pm) Down a long avenue of plane trees, Rymill rocks the local boat by turning out some of the best Sauvignon Blanc you'll ever taste. The modern cellar door is fronted by a statue of two duelling steeds – appropriately rebellious.

- **Wynns Coonawarra Estate** (☎ 8736 2225; www.wynns.com.au; Memorial Dr; ☉ 10am-5pm) The oldest Coonawarra winery, Wynns' cellar door dates from 1896 and was built by Penola pioneer John Riddoch. Top-quality Shiraz, fragrant Riesling and golden Chardonnay are the mainstays.

- **Zema Estate** (☎ 8736 3219; www.zema.com.au; Riddoch Hwy; ☉ 9am-5pm) A steadfast, traditional winery started by the Zema family in the early '80s. It's a low-key affair with a handmade vibe infusing the Shiraz and Cab Sav – well worth a visit.

PENOLA
pop 1670

A rural town on the way up (what a rarity!), Penola is the kind of place where you walk down the main street and five people say 'Hello!' before you get to the pub. The town has won fame for two things: firstly for its association with the Sisters of St Joseph of the Sacred Heart, the order cofounded by Mother Mary MacKillop in 1867 (see p104); and secondly for being smack-bang in the middle of the Coonawarra Wine Region – a prime base for a few days of wine-tinged indulgence. Online, check out www.penola.org.

Information

The **Penola visitors centre** (☎ 8737 2855; www.wattle range.sa.gov.au; 27 Arthur St; ☉ 9am-5pm Mon-Fri, 10am-4pm Sat & Sun) services the entire Coonawarra region. The John Riddoch Interpretative Centre (right) is also here.

Sights & Activities

The **Mary MacKillop Interpretative Centre** (☎ 8737 2092; www.mackillop-penola.com; cnr Portland St & Petticoat La; adult/child $5/free; ☉ 10am-4pm) is a snazzy new building with a gregarious entrance pergola – perhaps not as modest as Mary might have

liked! There's oodles of info on Australia's prospective saint (see also p104) here, plus the Woods-MacKillop Schoolhouse, the first school in Australia for children from lower socioeconomic backgrounds. The school was cofounded by Mary MacKillop and Father Julian Woods in 1866.

In the same building as the visitors centre, the **John Riddoch Interpretative Centre** (admission free) casts a web over local history back to the 1850s, including info on the local Pinejunga people and original Penola pastoralist Riddoch, who 'never gave in to misfortune' and was 'steady and persistent.' There's also an uninspiring display on natural gas, which is mined at nearby Kantook.

Riddoch's opulent house **Yallum Park** (Millicent Rd; admission $5; ☉ tours 2pm) is an Italian-style, two-storey mansion (1880) in original condition, right down to the William Morris wallpaper. Tours are run by the 90-year-old owner, who calls the visitors centre every morning to tell them if he's feeling up to it or not. If so, book at the visitors centre and make your own way there (it's 8km from town).

Diminutive **Petticoat Lane** was one of Penola's first streets. Most of the original

LIMESTONE COAST

AUSTRALIA'S SAINT-IN-WAITING

Mother Mary MacKillop (1842–1909) was beatified in 1995, and is now one step away from becoming Australia's first saint. To be canonised by the Catholic Church, you have to work two miracles. It's accepted that prayers to Mary helped cure a terminally ill woman in Melbourne, but a second miracle is yet to be sanctioned by the Vatican.

Born of Scottish-immigrant parents in Melbourne, Mary became a schoolteacher at 21. In 1866, when she was only 24, Mary and Father Julian Woods started Australia's first 'free' school at Penola, where fees were paid only by those who could afford them.

A fierce defender of equality, Mary MacKillop was cofounder of the Order of the Sisters of St Joseph of the Sacred Heart, the first Australian order of nuns committed to educating and caring for the poor. Mary took her vows at 26 in Adelaide. A year later, there were 30 sisters in SA running eight Josephite schools, an orphanage and a home for 'fallen' women. The following year they opened their first school in Queensland. All remarkable achievements by the single-minded Mary, but her unrelenting drive soon brought her into conflict with SA's Catholic religious hierarchy. In 1871 she was excommunicated, only to be reinstated five months later.

By the time of her death, Mary's order had founded 117 schools and 11 charitable homes in Australia and New Zealand. Many are still operating today, while around 1300 Josephite sisters keep up the good work.

buildings have been razed, but there are still a few old timber-slab houses and gnarly trees to see. The 1850 **Sharam's Cottage** (136 Petticoat La), was the first house in Penola and has interpretive panels in the garden out the back. Ask the visitors centre for access details if you want to have a look inside.

Coonawarra Discovery (☎ 1800 600 262, 8737 2449; www.coonawarradiscovery.com; tours per half-/full day $66/155) runs minibus winery tours of the region.

The annual **Penola Coonawarra Arts Festival** (☎ 8737 2855; www.artsfestival.com.au) in May promotes the cultural aspects of the town, along with the odd glass of wine…

Sleeping & Eating

There are plenty of historic cottages around Penola that have been refurbished as B&Bs. The free online accommodation-booking service, **Coonawarra Discovery** (☎ 1800 600 262, 8737 2449; www.coonawarradiscovery.com), has listings.

Penola Caravan Park (☎ 8737 2381; www.penola caravanpark.com.au; cnr Riddoch Hwy & South Tce; unpowered/powered/en suite sites $20/25/35, cabins from $80, linen $15) Don't expect any 'holiday' trimmings at this small, underwhelming park, but it's the cheapest place to stay within miles.

ourpick **Heyward's Royal Oak Hotel** (☎ 8737 2322; www.heywardshotel.com.au; 31 Church St; s $55, d & tw $88) The Royal Oak – a lace-trimmed, main-street megalith – is Penola's community hub. The rooms upstairs are a bit tatty and share bathrooms, but they're good

bang for your buck. Downstairs the huge tartan-carpeted dining room (mains $19 to 28, open for lunch and dinner) serves classy pub food (roo fillets with pepper crust and Cabernet glaze) and schnitzels as big as your head. Summery beer garden, too.

Coonawarra Motor Lodge (☎ 8737 2364; www .bushmansinn.com.au; 114 Church St; d/f $120/145; 🞬 🞮) On the way up the winery strip, this refurbished motel (splashes of chocolate and beige) occupies a compact, two-storey building overlooking a pool. There's also a restaurant here (mains $18 to $27), open for dinner from Monday to Saturday, serving fairly predictable pizza, pasta, lamb shanks and fish-and-chips.

Cobb & Co Cottages (☎ 8737 2526; www.cobbnco .com; 2 Portland St; d $130, extra adult/child $30/11; 🞬) A good family option is one of these three white-rendered, two-bedroom cottages with red corrugated-iron roofs. Great location, just back from the main street, but beware: frills, doilies and floral-print couches.

Chardonnay Lodge (☎ 8736 3309; www.chardonnay lodge.com.au; Riddoch Hwy; s/d from $132/156; 🞬 🞮) An odd choice of name (this is serious Cabernet Sauvignon territory) belies a pretty decent motel amid the Riddoch Hwy vines. Other pluses include disabled-access units, five walking-distance wineries and an on-site restaurant (mains $23 to $35, serving breakfast and dinner). Poplars Winery is across the road.

diVine (☎ 8737 2122; 39 Church Street; meals $7-15; ☺ breakfast & lunch; ⓥ)The busiest spot on the main street, diVine is a bright modern cafe serving baguettes, all-day breakfasts (try the pancakes with fresh strawberries, double cream and maple syrup) and great coffee. Nattering Penolans chew muffins and local cheeses, discussing the nuances of various vintages.

Poplars Winery (☎ 8736 3130; www.thepoplars winery.com; Riddoch Hwy; mains $13-27; ☺ breakfast & lunch; 🐾 ⓥ) A lofty, concrete-floored, glass-fronted food hall with an original 102-year-old Cabernet Sauvignon vine growing out the front. To eat: curries, pastas, salads or a tasty tour of the cheese bar. To drink: Cabernet Sauvignons, Merlots and Chardonnays.

Pipers of Penola (☎ 8737 3999; 58 Riddoch St, mains $28; ☺ lunch Fri-Sun, dinner Wed-Sat) This place is a winner: a classy, intimate dining room tastefully constructed inside an old Methodist church, with friendly staff and seasonal fare. The menu is studded with words such as 'galette', 'carpaccio' and 'rotollo' – seriously gourmet indicators! Reasonable prices, voluptuous wine glasses and awesome desserts.

NARACOORTE & AROUND
pop 5680

Settled in the 1840s, Naracoorte is a real old-timer as far as SA towns go, but there's not a whole lot o' shakin' going on here – its raison d'être is to act as service town for the surrounding agricultural and sheep-farming areas, which are increasingly being subsumed by grapevines. Still, it's an inoffensive country town, and its proximity to the Victorian border and the World Heritage–listed Naracoorte Caves makes it a practical pit stop.

Information

The optimistic **Naracoorte visitors centre** (☎ 1800 244 421, 8762 1399; www.naracoortelucindale .com; 36 MacDonnell St; ☺ 9am-5pm Mon-Fri, to 4pm Sat & Sun) is housed in an old flour mill, which also houses the Sheep's Back Museum.

Sights & Activities

Next to the visitors centre, the **Sheep's Back Museum** (☎ 8762 1399; 36 MacDonnell St; adult/child $5/2; ☺ 9am-5pm Mon-Fri, to 4pm Sat & Sun) has displays on the history of the SA wool industry from the 1840s to today, including a weird robotic shearing machine that never really caught on. Serious wool fetishists only.

For more sheep-shape indulgences, check out **Mini Jumbuck** (☎ 1800 088 834, 8762 3677; www .minijumbuk.com.au; 61 Smith St; ☺ 8.30am-5.30pm Mon-Fri, 9am-4pm Sat, 11am-4pm Sun), a brilliant shop producing and selling all things woolly: quilts, insoles, pillows and ug boots.

Coming into Naracoorte from Penola, turn west onto Bool Lagoon Rd 35km north of Penola. About 7km along is an acknowledged 'Wetland of International Importance' – the 3103-hectare **Bool Lagoon Game Reserve** (www .environment.sa.gov.au/parks/sanpr/boollagoon; admission per car $7.50), where 155 migrating and breeding bird species come to roost, including once-widespread brolgas. There are self-guided walks, campsites (per car $15) and boardwalks. Be careful driving through in October, particularly on Big Hill Rd, when breeding long-necked tortoises tend to wander across the roads in a sexy stupor.

The star of the emerging **Padthaway wine region** (www.padthawaywineregion.com), 50km north of Naracoorte, is **Padthaway Estate Winery** (☎ 8734 3031; www.padthawayhomestead.com.au; Riddoch Hwy; B&B d from $185; 1/2/3 courses $35/50/65; ☺ lunch & dinner) – a beautiful stone-and-wrought-iron homestead (1847) that looks like something out of *Gone with the Wind*. The homestead offers a cellar door (Shiraz, Chardonnay, Cabernet Sauvignon and sundry sparklings), a restaurant and upmarket accommodation.

Sleeping & Eating

Naracoorte Holiday Park (☎ 8762 2128; www.naracoorte holidaypark.com.au; 81 Park Tce; powered sites/vans/cabin $31/67/82, units from $96; 🐾 🖳) On the hill just to the north of Naracoorte, this park has myriad van, cabin and unit configurations. There's a fully chlorinated, free swimming lake next door – cool off after taking the 5km creek walking trail that loops past the park gates.

Country Roads Motor Inn (☎ 1800 088 363, 8762 3900; www.countryroadsnaracoorte.com.au; 20 Smith St; s/d/f $92/102/122; 🐾) Within walking distance of the town centre, this drive-in motel is the best one in Naracoorte, with immaculate, spacious brick-and-pine rooms. No sign of John Denver...

Kincraig Hotel (☎ 8762 2200; 158 Smith St; mains $15-28; ☺ lunch & dinner) The good ol' Kincraig is the best spot in town for slap-up pub grub. The bottomless bain-marie full of salads and veggies makes a meal in itself. Free pool and $4 pints on Thursday nights; cheap schnitzels on Tuesday.

LIMESTONE COAST

NARACOORTE CAVES NATIONAL PARK

About 12km southeast of Naracoorte, off the Penola road, is the only World Heritage–listed site in SA. The discovery of an ancient fossilised marsupial in these limestone caves raised palaeontologic eyebrows around the world, and featured in the BBC David Attenborough series *Life on Earth*.

The park visitors centre doubles as the impressive **Wonambi Fossil Centre** (☎ 8762 2340; www .naracoortecaves.sa.gov.au; Hynam-Caves Rd; adult/concession/child/family $7.50/6/4.50/20; ☉ 9am-5pm winter, to dusk summer) – a re-creation of the rainforest that covered this area 200,000 years ago. Follow a ramp down past life-sized reconstructions of extinct animals, including a marsupial lion, a giant echidna, *Diprotodon australis* (koala-meets–grizzly bear), and *Megalania prisca* – 500kg of bad-ass goanna. Some of the models grunt and move – a bit scary for young kids, but everyone else will dig it!

The 26 limestone **caves** here – including the Victoria Fossil Cave, Alexandra Cave, Blanche Cave, Bat Cave and Wet Cave – have bizarre formations of stalactites and stalagmites. Unless you're Bruce Wayne you can't actually access the Bat Cave, but at dusk during summer you can watch thousands of endangered southern bentwing bats exiting en masse to find dinner. Infrared TV cameras allow you to see them huddled up inside. You can check out the Wet Cave on a self-guided tour, but the others require ranger-guided tours.

Single-cave tours cost adult/concession/child/family $12/9.50/7.50/33; two-cave tours are $19.50/15.50/12/53. See the website for further tour and pricing info, including adventure tours of undeveloped caves (booking required).

There's also some great-value budget accommodation (bed in dormitory $15) here in an old stone house with a modern kitchen outbuilding.

Bringing the Bard to the belly of the Earth is **Shakespeare in the Caves** (☎ 0419 330 516; www.ozact .com), with annual performances of *Macbeth* and *A Midsummer Night's Dream* resonating through the stalagmites.

DUKES HIGHWAY

The last town on the SA side of the border is **Bordertown** (population 2590), the birthplace of former Labor prime minister Bob Hawke, aka 'the Silver Bodgie'. There's a bust of Bob outside the town hall. There's not much else to see or do here, but the town makes a handy pee-and-pie stop.

Near the Victorian border, the 207,941-hectare **Ngarkat Group of Conservation Parks** (www.environment.sa.gov.au/parks/sanpr/ngarkatgroup) comprises four parks: Scorpion Springs, Mt Shaugh, Mt Rescue and Ngarkat. The parks are home to a superb range of wildlife: echidnas, pygmy possums, dunnarts, kangaroos, lizards and birds. Walking tracks range from 10-minute strolls to five-hour hikes, and there's a good network of 4WD tracks.

Barossa Valley

'Barossa Valley' is a bit of a misnomer: the river running through here is the North Para, but that doesn't have quite the same ring to it! But forget about semantics. With its hot, dry summers and cool, moderate winters, the Barossa is one of the world's great wine regions – an absolute must for anyone with even the slightest interest in a good drop.

The Barossa Valley is compact – a 25km-long stretch of undulating hills – yet it manages to produce 21% of Australia's wine, mostly big, luscious and fruity reds. The 80-plus wineries here are within easy reach of one another, and make a no-fuss day trip from Adelaide, just 65km to the southwest. This accessibility, combined with the high-volume output, has fostered a mainstream, commercial scene reminiscent of California's Napa Valley (which is 16 years younger than the Barossa!). The long-established 'Barossa Barons' hold sway – big, ballsy and brassy – while sprightly young boutique wineries are harder to sniff out.

The wineries fuel the economies of the local towns, whose distinctly German heritage dates to 1842. Fleeing religious persecution in Prussia and Silesia, settlers (bringing their vine cuttings with them) created a Lutheran heartland where German traditions persist today. Gothic church steeples punctuate the valley skies, and town streets are lined with stone cottages. A dubious passion for oompah bands persists, as does an appetite for wurst, pretzels and sauerkraut.

So take a few days to immerse yourself in the valley's virtues. Eating and drinking here is a joy, and it's easy to avoid crowds by meandering along back roads; try palm-fringed Seppeltsfield Rd, the Marananga route to Bethany, and the back roads between Angaston and Tanunda.

BAROSSA VALLEY

HIGHLIGHTS

- Learning how to nose a Pinot and savour a Semillon at the **Barossa wineries** (p111)
- **Cycling** (p108) along vine-lined back roads, past historic churches and German farmhouses
- Loading up on calories at Tanunda's traditional German **bakery** (p112): *Brezel, Bienenstich* and mettwurst by the pound
- Counting palm trees along the surreal **Seppeltsfield Road** (p111)
- Surveying the scene from **Mengler Hill Lookout** (p110)
- Prancing around a maypole at the exuberant **Barossa Vintage Festival** (p109)
- Spilling a few secrets to someone at the other end of the **Whispering Wall** (p112)

Seppeltsfield Road

Tanunda ★

★ Mengler Hill Lookout

★ Whispering Wall

| ■ TELEPHONE CODE: ☎ 08 | ■ www.barossa.com | ■ www.winebarossa.com |

Accommodation

The Barossa is strewn with self-contained cottages and romantic hidey-holes offering the full spa-bath and champagne treatment. Most of these weekenders are around Tanunda and are pretty pricey (usually $150 per night and above, often with a two-night minimum), but are worth it for a few decadent days. Book ahead during holidays and festivals, when rates can get ugly. The Barossa visitors centre (opposite) books accommodation, or try **Getaways Reservation Service** (☎ 1300 136 970; www.getaways.net.au) or **BnB Booking Service** (☎ 1800 227 677; www.bnbbookings.com).

Tours

There's a day-trippin' smorgasbord of Barossa tours operating from Adelaide (just 90 minutes away) that swing through the main tourist sights, as well as a few wineries. For those with a real zeal for wine, stick with the smaller Adelaide companies and tour operators based in the valley – they visit more wineries and can access smaller cellar doors not always open to the coach hordes. Most Barossa Valley tour operators also offer Adelaide pick-ups; rates listed here are per person for local departures.

Balloon Adventures (☎ 08-8389 3195; www.balloonadventures.com.au; adult/child $300/195) Fly the sky in a hot-air balloon and sail serenely over the valley. One-hour flights depart Tanunda and include a sparkling wine breakfast. Daily flights, weather permitting.

Barossa Classic Cycle Tours (☎ 0427-000 957; www.bccycletours.com.au; tours $225 per day, less for bigger groups) One- and two-day cycling tours of the valley, covering around 30km per day. Accommodation extra.

Barossa Epicurean Tours (☎ 08-8564 2191, 0402-989 647; www.barossatours.com.au; full-/half-day tours $90/60) Good-value, small-group tours visiting the wineries of your choice and Mengler Hill Lookout, plus sundry food and cheese tastings.

Barossa Experience Tours (☎ 08-8563 3248, 0418-809 313; www.barossavalleytours.com; full-/half-day tours $105/75) Local small-group operator whisking you around the major sites, including churches, lookouts and a selection of wineries. The Food & Wine Experience ($210) includes lunch, cheese tastings and a glass of plonk.

Barossa Valley Tours (☎ 08-8563 3587, 0417-852 453; www.barossavalleytour.com; full-day tours from $85) Another local operator that will spin you around the major sights and stop for a two-course lunch. Adelaide pick-ups available.

Barossa Wine Lovers Tours (☎ 08-8263 1633; tours incl lunch from $65) This tour takes in several wineries, lookouts, shops and heritage buildings – a good blend.

Bikeabout (☎ 0413-525 733; www.bikeabout.com.au) Cycling day trips to the Barossa Valley ($75).

Groovy Grape Getaways (☎ 1800 661 177, 08-8440 1640; www.groovygrape.com.au; full-day tours $75) Backpacker day tours to the Barossa including the Whispering Wall, Big Rocking Horse, a few wineries and a barbecue lunch.

Prime Mini Tours (☎ 1300 667 650, 08-8556 6117; www.primeminitours.com; tours from $70) Adelaide-based company offering four full-day Barossa tours, all of which include lunch, four or five wineries and pit stops at sights such as the Whispering Wall and the Big Rocking Horse. Good value.

See p54 for more Adelaide-based tour companies who run excursions into the Barossa.

Getting There & Away

There are several routes from Adelaide; the most direct is along Main North Rd through Elizabeth and Gawler. If you're coming from the east and want to tour the wineries before hitting Adelaide, the scenic route via Springton and Eden Valley to Angaston is a sure bet.

Barossa Valley Coaches (☎ 08-8564 3022; www.bvcoach.com) runs an Adelaide-to-Angaston return route twice daily (once on Sunday), stopping at Lyndoch ($14.50, 1½ hours), Tanunda ($18, 1¾ hours), Nuriootpa ($19.50, two hours) and Angaston ($21, 2¼ hours).

Getting Around

The Barossa is pretty good for **cycling**, with routes trundling past a few wineries. The Barossa visitors centre (opposite) hires out bikes from $44 per eight hours (six hours on weekends), and can point you towards the best routes. You can also rent bikes from Tanunda Caravan & Tourist Park (p111; per half-/full day $18.50/30).

Running between Nuriootpa and Tanunda, the short-and-sweet, cross-country **Para Road Wine Path** passes four wineries and is technically a walking trail, but you can tackle it on a mountain bike.

Barossa Valley Taxis (☎ 08-8563 3600) has a 24-hour daily service that runs throughout the valley. From Tanunda the cost is around $20 to Angaston and $15 to Nuriootpa.

See Barossa Valley Coaches (above) for bus links between Lyndoch, Tanunda, Nuriootpa and Angaston.

FESTIVALS & EVENTS

The Barossa knows how to host a whizz-bang festival or two; here's a handful of the best. Check with the Barossa visitors centre (below) for specific dates as these often change from year to year.

January
Tour Down Under (www.tourdownunder.com.au) The Barossa leg of the Tour Down Under sees international cyclists sweating for supremacy.

February
Barossa Under the Stars (www.barossaunderthestars.com.au) Spare tickets for this event are as rare as bad Barossa Shiraz. Wine-slurping picnickers watch middle-of-the-road crooners such as Chris Isaak, Cliff Richard and Shirley Bassie.
A Day on the Green (www.adayonthegreen.com.au) Peter Lehmann Wines hosts this mature-age mosh-pit event (without the mosh pit). Acts such as Simply Red and Kate Ceberano.

April
Barossa Vintage Festival (www.barossavintagefestival.com.au) A colourful, week-long festival with music, maypole dancing, parades, wineries' tug-of-war contests etc; begins Easter Sunday in odd-numbered years. Much mirth and grape juice.

September
Barossa Wine Show (www.barossa.com) A key industry event with presentation dinner and lip-smacking public tastings.

October
Barossa Music Festival (www.barossa.org) Picnics, wine (naturally), theatre and bands playing classical music and jazz. Intimate venues include wineries, barrel halls and historic churches.

TANUNDA
pop 4690

At the centre of the valley both geographically and socially, Tanunda is the Barossa's main tourist town. Despite a steady deluge of visitors, Tanunda manages to morph the practicality of Nuriootpa with the charm of Angaston without a sniff of self-importance. There are a few attractions and artsy shops along Murray St, the main road through town, but the wineries are what you're here for – sip, sip, sip!

Information

Barossa visitors centre (☎ 1300 852 982, 8563 0600; www.barossa.com; 66-68 Murray St, Tanunda; ☺ 9am-5pm Mon-Fri, 10am-4pm Sat & Sun) The low-down on the valley, plus internet access, bike hire (see opposite) and accommodation bookings.

Raven's Parlour Bookshop (☎ 8563 3455; ravens@esc.net.au; 32A Murray St; ☺ 10am-5.30pm) Mooch through these comprehensive shelves of new books and secondhand (not so) dusty bargains.

Sights & Activities

Tanunda is flush with historic buildings, including the **cottages** around Goat Sq on John St. This was the *Ziegenmarkt,* a meeting and market place, laid out in 1842 as Tanunda's original town centre. Austere old Lutheran churches in Tanunda include the 1849 **Tabor Church** (79 Murray St), the 1868 **St John's Church** (11 Jane Pl), and the modest but elegant **Langmeil Lutheran Church** (Maria St) built in 1838.

Access to the **Barossa Valley Historical Museum** (☎ 8563 0507; 47 Murray St; adult/concession/child $2/1/50c; ☺ 10am-4pm) is via a secondhand bookshop out the front. Inside are displays of bone-handled cutlery, butter-making gear, photos of top-hatted locals, a recreated colonial bedroom and an amazing map of Germany pinpointing the homelands of Barossa settlers. The Indigenous coverage could use a little help.

The **Barossa Regional Gallery** (☎ 0428-322 871; www.freewebs.com/barossagallery; 3 Basedow Rd; admission free; ☺ 11am-4pm Tue-Sun) has an eclectic collection of paintings, crafts and touring exhibitions, plus an impressive set of organ

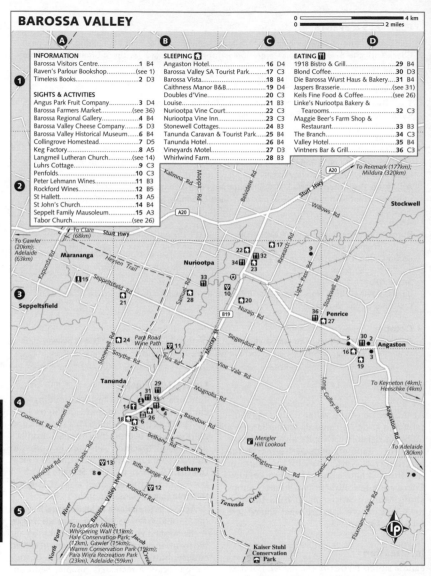

BAROSSA VALLEY

pipes at the back of the room. There's also a small memorial of photos of Barossa WWI and WWII veterans upstairs.

You can watch honest-to-goodness coopers make and repair wine barrels at the **Keg Factory** (☎ 8563 3012; www.thekegfactory.com.au; St Halletts Rd; admission free; ⏰ 10am-4pm), 4km south of town. They stop for a 45-minute lunch around noon.

From Tanunda, take the scenic route to Angaston via Bethany and hazy valley views from **Mengler Hill Lookout** (just ignore the naff sculptures in the foreground). The road tracks through beautiful rural country, studded with huge eucalypts. Also en route is the 390-hectare **Kaiserstuhl Conservation Park** (p114), with some ace views and walking tracks.

TOP FIVE BAROSSA VALLEY WINERIES

From the moment Johann Gramp planted the valley's first grapes on his property at Jacob's Creek in 1847, the Barossa Valley was destined to become a major Australian wine region. The valley is best known for Shiraz, with Riesling the dominant white. There are around 80 vineyards here and 60 cellar doors, ranging from boutique wine rooms to monstrous complexes; most are owned by multinationals. It's impossible to distil 80 down to five, but we did try:

- **Henschke** (☎ 8564 8223; www.henschke.com.au; Henschke Rd, Keyneton; ☼ 9am-4.30pm Mon-Fri,to noon Sat) Henschke, 11km southeast of Angaston in the Eden Valley, is known for its iconic Hill of Grace red, but most of the wines here are classics. Its first vintage was in 1868!

- **Penfolds** (☎ 8568 9408; www.penfolds.com.au; Tanunda Rd, Nuriootpa; ☼ 10am-5pm) You know the name. Book ahead for the 'Make your own Blend' tour ($55) or 'Taste of Grange' tour ($150), which allows you to slide some Grange Hermitage across your lips.

- **Peter Lehmann Wines** (☎ 8563 2100; www.peterlehmannwines.com.au; Para Rd, Tanunda; ☼ 9.30am-5pm Mon-Fri, 10.30am-4.30pm Sat & Sun) The multiaward-winning Shiraz and Riesling vintages here (oh, and the Semillon) are probably the most consistent and affordable wines in the Barossa. Buy a bottle and have a picnic in the grounds.

- **Rockford Wines** (☎ 8563 2720; www.rockfordwines.com.au; Krondorf Rd, Tanunda; ☼ 11am-5pm) This 1850s winery uses traditional winemaking methods and produces a small range of superb wines, including sparkling reds. The Black Shiraz is a smooth and spicy killer; the cellar door, in a beautiful old stable, is picturesque.

- **St Hallett** (☎ 8563 7000; www.sthallett.com.au; St Hallett's Rd, Tanunda; ☼ 10am-5pm) Using only Barossa grapes, St Hallet produces reasonably priced but consistently good whites (try the Poacher's Blend) and the excellent Gamekeeper's Reserve Shiraz-Grenache. Unpretentious and great value for money.

Other worthy detours include the **Para Road Wine Path** (p108) and **Seppeltsfield Road** (www.seppeltsfieldroad.com), an incongruous avenue of huge palm trees meandering through the vineyards. Beyond Marananga the palm rows veer off the roadside and track up a hill to the **Seppelt Family Mausoleum** – a Grecian shrine fronted by chunky Doric columns.

Sleeping

Tanunda Caravan & Tourist Park (☎ 8563 2784; www.tanundacaravantouristpark.com.au; Barossa Valley Hwy; unpowered/powered sites $21/26, vans from $52, cabins with/without bathroom from $80/62; ☷ 💻) This spacious park is an easy amble from central Tanunda, and is dotted with mature trees offering a little shade for your hangover. Facilities include a playground, barbecues, laundry, bike hire (see p108) and disabled-access units and bathrooms. Skip the weary on-site vans.

Tanunda Hotel (☎ 8563 2030; www.tanundapub.com; 51 Murray St; d without/with bathroom $70/80; ☷) Opened in 1846, this boisterous ol' pub in the centre of town is a real community centre. Rooms are good value and clean, but nothing out of the ordinary. Downstairs, Duran Duran wails from the jukebox and schnitzels fall off the edges of plates (mains $12 to $26, open for lunch and dinner).

Valley Motel (☎ 8563 2039; fax 8563 3830; 73 Murray St; s/d $90/110, d with spa $125; ☷) There are only five brick-and-stone rooms here (the smallest motel in Australia?), but they're spotless, modern and great value for the Barossa. The motel wing is out the back of the Valley Hotel (see p112), if you're keen for a bite or a beer.

Barossa Vista (☎ 0423-019 353; www.barossavista.com; 1b Murray St; d incl breakfast from $240; ☷) Going seriously upmarket, this three-bedroom 1919 villa doesn't look much externally, but inside it's a different story: leather couches, red, charcoal and mahogany colours, big-screen TV, open fire, espresso machine, wireless internet, iPod dock and beaut barbecue deck with valley views. Book an en suite double, or book the whole house.

Stonewell Cottages (☎ 0417-848 977; www.stonewellcottages.com.au; Stonewell Rd, Tanunda; cottages d incl breakfast from $255; ☷) These romantic, waterfront spa retreats are surrounded by vines and offer unbeatable privacy, comfort and serenity along

---

DETOUR: LYNDOCH & THE BAROSSA GOLDFIELDS

Lyndoch (population 1830) is an unassuming working town 13km south of Tanunda. There's not much here for marauding visitors, but it's worth a pit stop for the legendary **Lyndoch Bakery & Restaurant** (☎ 8524 4424; Barossa Valley Hwy; items $4-18; ⊙ lunch), a traditional German-style bakery. Load up on handmade rye bread, pretzels and pastries then hit the road again. Or, if you're here in November, check out the **Lyndoch Lavender Festival** (www.lyndochlavenderfarm.com.au).

Head 8km south from Lyndoch towards Williamstown, turn west for 5km, then take Goldfields Rd for 4km to **Para Wirra Recreation Park** (www.environment.sa.gov.au; admission per car $7.50). Here you'll find the **Barossa goldfields** which, in the late 1860s, boomed with 4000 diggers chasing nugget-shaped dreams. Three tonnes of gold was unearthed, with small amounts found until the 1930s. There's a walking track around the diggings at Victoria Hill and at the North Tunnel, which was partially excavated in 1895.

About 7km southwest of Lyndoch, the Barossa Reservoir dam is better known as the **Whispering Wall**. The huge concrete curve has amazing acoustics: whispers at one end of the wall can be heard clearly 150m away at the other. The perfect spot to propose?

---

with generous lashings of wine, port and edible goodies. Pet ducks waddle around rusty old ploughs as waterbirds splash down in the reservoir.

Eating

Keils Fine Food & Coffee (☎ 8563 1468; Shop 1, 63-67 Murray St; meals $4-10 ⊙ breakfast & lunch; ⊠ Ⓥ) Sidestep the coffee mums and their prams, spurn the ugly, humming drinks fridge and place your order for homemade baguettes, soups, quiches, pies, wraps, quality teas and the punchiest coffee in town.

Barossa Wurst Haus Bakery (☎ 8563 3598; 86a Murray St; meals $7-20; ⊙ breakfast & lunch) This fast-not-flashy bakery serves mettwurst (Bavarian sausage) rolls, cheeses, pies, cakes, strudel, *Brezel* (pretzels) and all-day breakfasts. It's hard to go past a traditional German roll with kransky sausage, sauerkraut and mustard, or the *Bayern Schmaus* (Bavarian feast). An emasculating display of phallic wursts dangles above the counter.

Jaspers Brasserie (☎ 8563 0990; 90 Murray St; mains $9-16; ⊙ breakfast & lunch daily, dinner Sat & Sun; ⊠) In a gorgeous old stone-fronted house at a skew-whiff angle to the road, this main-street, mainstream eatery serves big breakfasts, pizzas, burgers, lasagne, focaccias, bruschetta and salads. Kids' menu and dedicated kids' play room, too.

Valley Hotel (☎ 8563 2039; 73 Murray St; mains $14-30; ⊙ lunch & dinner; ⊠) The bistro at this affable pub (where the local footy and netball teams drink) is kid-friendly and really good value. Daily specials include the likes of chicken curry and peppercorn-crusted rump steak.

Order a hefty 500g T-bone and fuel up for tomorrow's endeavours.

1918 Bistro & Grill (☎ 8563 0405; 94 Murray St; mains $24-29; ⊙ lunch & dinner; ⊠) An enduring restaurant in a lovely old villa, the 1918 is set back from the main street beneath the boughs of a massive Norfolk Island pine. It's a sassy affair serving adventurous mains such as caramelised pork belly with steamed scallop dumplings, star-anise broth and coconut caramel. Book a veranda table for a long lunch.

See also Tanunda Hotel (p111).

NURIOOTPA

pop 5030

Along an endless main street at the northern end of the valley, Nuriootpa is the Barossa's commercial centre. It's not as immediately endearing as Tanunda or Angaston, but has a certain agrarian appeal. Lutheran spirit runs deep in 'Nuri': signs say, 'God has invested in you – are you showing any interest?' There are some affordable places to stay here, and a couple of good eateries – not a bad place to base yourself if you're on a budget.

Sights & Activities

There are some low-speed walking trails along the **North Para River**, which slides through town.

About 3km east of Nuriootpa, **Luhrs Cottage** (☎ 8562 3840; Immanuel Way, Light Pass Rd; admission by donation; ⊙ 9.30am-3.30pm Mon-Fri, 10am-4pm Sat & Sun) is a four-room 'pug' cottage (made from mud and straw), built in 1845 for Johann Luhrs, the town's first schoolteacher. It's now a museum, decked out in trad German style.

Sleeping & Eating

Barossa Valley SA Tourist Park (☎ 8562 1404; www
.barossatouristpark.com.au; Penrice Rd; unpowered/powered sites
$22/25, cabins with/without bathroom from $56/47; ⚟ 🖳)
There are at least six different kinds of cabins
at this shady park, lined with pine trees next
to the Nuriootpa football oval (go Tigers!). All
cabins have TVs, fridges, cooking facilities and
small balconies. Out the front is the 'Beginning
of Caravanning' – a 1931 truck with a house
glued on its back. Bike hire is $30 per day.

Doubles d'Vine (☎ 8562 2260; www.doublesdvine
.com.au; Barossa Valley Hwy; cottage/lodge d $80/70; ⚟ 🐾)
Affordable Barossa accommodation at last!
About 1.5km south of town is this self-
contained, unpretentious cottage and separate
'lodge' (a renovated apricot shed) with two en
suite doubles and shared lounge and kitchen.
Both have wood heaters, barbecues and access
to the pool. Reduced rates for two nights or
more; bike hire (guests only) $25 per day.

Nuriootpa Vine Inn & Vine Court (☎ 8562 2133;
www.vineinn.com.au; 14 & 49 Murray St; s/d $105/120 &
s/d $85/95; ⚟ 🐾) These two regulation mo-
tels share reception at the Vine Inn pub
(14 Murray St), out the back of which are
the better, pricier rooms and the swimming
pool. The pub bistro (mains $10 to $19)
serves lunch and dinner amid bright lights,
palms and pokies.

Whirlwind Farm (☎ 8562 2637; www.whirlwindbb
.com; Samuel Rd; s/d incl breakfast from $130/150; ⚟)
Surrounded by vineyards and native shrubs,
this farmhouse B&B has a private guest wing
with exposed timber beams, separate guest
entry and two country-style rooms. Snooze
on the wide veranda and contemplate a
day's successful (or imminent) wine touring.
Maggie Beer's Farm Shop is next door.

Louise (☎ 8562 2722; www.thelouise.com.au;
Seppeltsfield Rd, Marananga; d from $395; ⚟ 🐾) If
you're here for a special occasion – a lottery
win or bank robbery perhaps – you might
want to splash out on a night at The Louise,
a stunning complex of luxury, contemporary
suites on Seppeltsfield Rd between Nuriootpa
and Tanunda. The equally stunning restaurant (two/three courses $67/95, degustation
menu $190 per person, open for Sunday
lunch and dinner nightly) is generally the
domain of house guests, but you can book
a table (well in advance) for an upmarket
meal. Wireless internet throughout.

Maggie Beer's Farm Shop (☎ 8562 4477; www.maggie
beer.com.au; Pheasant Farm Rd, off Samuel Rd; items $4-200;
⚟ 10.30am-5pm; ⚟ 🇻) Celebrity SA gourmand
Maggie (have you seen her on *The Cook & The
Chef* on ABC TV?) has been hugely successful
with her range of condiments, preserves and
pâtés. The vibe here isn't as relaxed as it used
to be (there's a hint of 'empire' about proceed-
ings), but stop by for some tastings, an ice
cream or a hamper of delicious bites.

Linke's Nuriootpa Bakery & Tearooms (☎ 8562
1129; 40 Murray St; light meals $6-12; ⚟ breakfast & lunch
Mon-Sat; ⚟ 🇻) There are a few traditional
German offerings here, such as double-cut
fritz rolls and *Bienenstich* (a decadently
creamy pastry), plus regulation baguettes,
sandwiches, pies and pasties.

The Branch (☎ 8562 4561; 15 Murray St; mains $16-33;
⚟ breakfast & lunch daily, dinner Wed-Sat; ⚟) A cool
conversion of an old redbrick bank on the
main street is the backdrop for select Asian
and Euro offerings such as Kapunda saltbush lamb madras, Thai crispy beef salad,
burgers and risottos. The best coffee in town
to boot, and a well-considered wine and beer
list (local and imported).

ANGASTON
pop 2215

Photo-worthy Angaston was named after
George Fife Angas, a pioneering Barossa
pastoralist. An agricultural vibe persists, as
there are relatively few wineries on the town
doorstep: cows graze in paddocks down the
end of every street, and there's a vague whiff
of fertiliser in the air. Along the main drag
are two pubs, some terrific eateries and
a few B&Bs in old stone cottages (check
for double glazing and ghosts – we had a
sleepless night!).

Information

Open daily, **Timeless Books** (☎ 8564 2222; time
lessbooks@internode.on.net; 48 Murray St; ⚟ 10am-5.30pm
Mon-Sat, 10.30am-5pm Sun) has a great selection of
new and secondhand books and CDs (and a
beautiful pressed-tin ceiling!).

Sights & Activities

On the main street, the **Barossa Valley Cheese
Company** (☎ 8564 3636; ww.bvcc.ck.au; 67B Murray St;
⚟ 10am-5pm Mon-Fri, 10am-4pm Sat, 11am-3pm Sun)
is a fabulous stink room, selling handmade
cheeses from local cows and goats. Tastings
are free, but it's unlikely you'll leave without buying a wedge of the Washington
Washed Rind.

DESPERATELY SEEKING SOLITUDE

For a little grape-free time away from the vines, you can't beat the Barossa's regional parks, with walking tracks for everyone from Sunday strollers to hardcore bushwalkers. Ask at the Barossa visitors centre (p109) for maps, or the **Department for Environment & Heritage** (☎ 8280 7048; www.environment.sa.gov.au; Humbug Scrub Rd, One Tree Hill) at Parra Wirra. The **Heysen Trail** (see p287) also passes through this region.

The 1417-hectare **Para Wirra Recreation Park** (www.environment.sa.gov.au/parks/sanpr/parrawirra; Humbug Scrub Rd, One Tree Hill; admission per car $7.50) sits in the northern Mt Lofty Ranges and offers walking tracks and scenic drives with hill and valley views. There's disabled access, barbecues, sports ovals and tennis courts. Emus geek hopefully around picnic areas; western grey roos graze in the dusk.

The walking tracks in the 191-hectare **Hale Conservation Park** (www.environment.sa.gov.au/parks /sanpr/hale; Mt Pleasant Rd, Williamstown; admission free) are steeper and more challenging, although well worth the effort. Keep your eyes open for short-beaked echidnas!

The nearby 363-hectare **Warren Conservation Park** (www.environment.sa.gov.au/parks/sanpr/warren; Watts Gully Rd, Kersbrook; admission free) is a tranquil paradise of wattles, banksias, heaths and hakeas in spring, plus eucalypts including pink, blue and statuesque river red gums.

En route from Mengler Hill to Angaston is the turn-off for the 390-hectare **Kaiserstuhl Conservation Park** (www.environment.sa.gov.au/parks/sanpr/kaiserstuhl; Tanunda Creek Rd, Angaston; admission free), known for some excellent walks. The Stringybark Loop Trail (2.4km) and Wallowa Loop Trail (6.5km) start at the park entrance, and there are fantastic views from atop the Barossa Ranges. Look out for Nankeen kestrels, brown hawks and western grey roos.

Further up the street, **Angas Park Fruit Company** (☎ 8561 0800; www.angaspark.com.au; 3 Murray St; ☺ 9am-5pm Mon-Sat, 10am-5pm Sun) turns out sensational glacé fruit, chocolates, nuts, jams, chutneys and sauces. Watch shower-capped workers pitting prunes and trying to keep up with the conveyor belt.

The **Barossa Farmers Market** (☎ 0402-026 882; www.barossafarmersmarket.com; cnr Stockwell & Nuriootpa Rds; ☺ 7.30-11.30am Sat) happens every Saturday near Vintners Bar & Grill (opposite).

About 6km southeast of town, the lavish **Collingrove Homestead** (☎ 8564 2061; www.collingrove homestead.com.au; Eden Valley-Angaston Rd; tours adult/ concession $10/5; ☺ 1-4.30pm Mon-Fri, noon-4.30pm Sat & Sun) was built by George Angas' son John in 1856. Now owned by the National Trust, the rambling house is still furnished with the family's original antiques. Thirty-minute tours run at 1.30pm, 2.30pm and 3.30pm daily, plus 12.30pm on weekends. Regroup afterwards over Devonshire tea ($10), or consider a night in the B&B wing (doubles from $250).

Sleeping & Eating

Angaston is normally much quieter than Tanunda, so when the streets overflow with wine fiends, check here for accommodation before going further afield.

Vineyards Motel (☎ 8564 2404; www.vineyards motel.com.au; cnr Stockwell & Nuriootpa Rds; d/unit from $90/150; ☒ ▯) Across the road from Vintners, this '70s motel still has the original purple-and-red carpet and yellow-glass windows – so rude and uncool it's retro-cool! Renovations are rumoured, so get in quick before they purge the psychedelia. The units sleep six.

Caithness Manor B&B (☎ 8564 2761; www.caithness .com.au; 12 Hill St W; d incl breakfast from $175; ☒) The sign here says 'Ceud Mile Faille', Gaelic for '100,000 Welcomes'. The house is actually a refurbished girls' school, but there's not an ink stain or spitball in sight – just two cottage-style, ground-floor units with hillside views over the town (especially from the pool!).

Angaston Hotel (☎ 8564 2428; 60 Murray St; mains $8-20; ☺ lunch & dinner) The better looking of the town's two pubs, the friendly Angaston serves budget bar meals (sub-$10 burgers and sandwiches) and the cheapest steaks this side of Argentina. And check out the mural in the dining room! The bog-basic pub rooms up-stairs were still going cheap when we visited (single/double $50/70), but were about to be overhauled – expect a price hike.

Blond Coffee (☎ 8564 3444; 60 Murray St; mains $9-16; ☺ breakfast & lunch; ☒ Ⓥ) An elegant, breezy room with huge windows facing the main street, Blond serves nutty coffee and all-day cafe fare, including an awesome bacon-and-cheese club sandwich. There's also a cheese and smallgoods counter, and wall full of local produce (vinegar, olive oil, biscuits and confectionery). Fake-blonde Botox tourists share the window seats with down-to-earth regulars.

Vintners Bar & Grill (☎ 8564 2488; cnr Stockwell & Nuriootpa Rds; mains $21-35; ☻ lunch daily, dinner Mon-Sat; ☒) One of the Barossa's landmark res-taurants, Vintners stresses simple elegance in both food and atmosphere. The dining room has an open fire, vineyard views and bolts of crisp white linen. Menus concentrate on local produce: try the pan-fried Kangaroo Island haloumi or the Caesar salad with Barossa bacon. Plenty of local wines, and outdoor seating too.

See also Collingrove Homestead (opposite).

Flinders Ranges

Known simply as 'the Flinders', this ancient mountain range (once higher than the Himalayas) is an iconic South Australian environment. Jagged peaks and escarpments rise up north of Port Augusta and track a further 400km north to Mt Hopeless, before faltering down into the Strzelecki Desert. The colours here are remarkable: as the day stretches out, the mountains shift from mauve mornings to midday chocolates and ochre red sunsets.

But the physical virtues of the ranges are only part of the story. Before Europeans arrived, the Flinders were prized by the Adnyamathanha peoples for their red ochres, which had medicinal and ritual uses. Sacred caves, rock paintings and carvings exist throughout the region.

In the wake of white exploration came villages, farms, country pubs and cattle stations, which seem to define the Australian outback identity. The Flinders were once a vital trade route into the Northern Territory, with the old *Ghan* railway clattering through. When the train tracks were rerouted and the Stuart Hwy made it quicker to get to Alice Springs, the Flinders took a back seat: ruins of sunstruck farms and abandoned mines pepper the region's hills and gullies.

This is also a tale of two ranges. The cooler Southern Ranges are studded with stands of river red gums. Here, country hamlets have cherubic appeal and wheat farming endures in the face of climate change. In the arid Northern Ranges, the desert takes a hold: the scenery here is stark, desolate and very beautiful. Cattle grids, emus and fast lizards cross the hot highway; homesteads have deep verandas and slow-spinning windmills. Even as you fly by at 110km/h, time here still…passes…slowly.

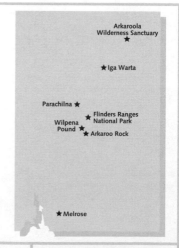

HIGHLIGHTS

- Careening off the Mawson Trail into gorgeous **Melrose** (p119), the Flinders' oldest town
- Paying your respects to the sacred Aboriginal paintings at **Arkaroo Rock** (p124)
- Spotting yellow-footed rock wallabies, emus and roos in **Flinders Ranges National Park** (p125)
- Hiking up to the lofty, desolate rim of **Wilpena Pound** (p125)
- Pulling into the **Prairie Hotel** (p128) in far-flung Parachilna for some 'feral' antipasto and a cold beer
- Learning about Adnyamathanha history and culture at the Aboriginal-run **Iga Warta** (p129)
- Reaching the end of the road and sliding into the swimming pool at **Arkaroola Wilderness Sanctuary** (p129)

★ Arkaroola Wilderness Sanctuary

★ Iga Warta

Parachilna ★

★ Flinders Ranges National Park

Wilpena Pound ★

★ Arkaroo Rock

★ Melrose

■ TELEPHONE CODE: ☎ 08 ■ www.flindersranges.com ■ www.flindersoutback.com

FLINDERS RANGES

National Parks

The Flinders is hot and dry in summer, but during the rest of the year there's magical bushwalking to be had in the area's national parks. If you're planning to visit all the parks hereabouts (including the Flinders Ranges, Mt Remarkable and Vulkathunha-Gammon Ranges parks), get hold of a Holiday Pass (per vehicle with/without camping $50/30), valid for two months. You can purchase one from the Department for Environment & Heritage in Port Augusta (p137), the Wilpena Pound visitors centre (p125), or online at www.environment.sa.gov.au/parks/visitor/onlinepass.html.

Alternatively, a single-park day pass costs $7.50 per vehicle, available from park rangers or at self-registration centres as you enter the parks. There's camping at Mt Remarkable (p121), Vulkathunha-Gammon Ranges (p128) and Flinders Ranges national parks (p127), with bush camping at several other spots too. You don't have to rough it, though, as there are cabins at Alligator Gorge (p121) and Mambray Creek (p121), and the plush Wilpena Pound Resort (p126).

Tours

The following Flinders Ranges tours run from Adelaide; others depart Port Augusta (see p137), Quorn (p122), Hawker (p124), Wilpena Pound (p126) and Arkaroola (p129). Definitely book ahead as tours are very popular; some (particularly flights) require minimum numbers.

Arabunna Tours (☎ 8675 8351; www.southaustralia.com/S9008383.aspx; 7-day tour $1050) Aboriginal-owned company offering cultural tours from Adelaide to the Flinders Ranges, Marree, Oodnadatta Track and Lake Eyre.

Bookabee Tours (☎ 8235 9954, 0408-209 593; www.bookabee.com.au; 4-/5-day tours $1930/2380) Highly rated Indigenous-run tours to the Flinders Ranges and outback, including quality accommodation, meals, cultural tours, activities & interpretation.

Ecotrek (☎ 8346 4155; www.ecotrek.com; 7-day tour $1548) Excellent all-inclusive tours walking the best sections of the Flinders, with soft beds, hot showers and food and wine at the end of each day.

Swagabout Tours (☎ 0408-845 378; www.swagabouttours.com.au) Dependable tours with the option of staying in hotels or camping under the stars. The Adelaide-to-Alice Springs trips (five-/seven-/nine-/10-day tours camping $1350/1850/2400/2690, hotels $1920/2675/3450/3850) take in the Flinders Ranges, Oodnadatta Track, Dalhousie Springs and Uluru. Dedicated Flinders Ranges trips (three/four days camping $650/1000, hotels $870/1300) include

Quorn and Wilpena (plus Arkaroola and Blinman on the four-day jaunt), and can be extended to Coober Pedy.

Other major operators swinging through the Flinders:

Adventure Tours Australia (☎ 1300 654 604, 8132 8130; www.adventuretours.com.au)

Groovy Grape (☎ 1800 661 177, 8440 1640; www.groovygrape.com.au)

Wayward Bus (☎ 1300 653 510, 8132 8230; www.waywardbus.com.au)

Getting There & Around

BUS

Premier Stateliner (☎ 8415 5555; www.premierstateliner.com.au) buses run at least twice daily from Adelaide to Port Augusta ($47, four hours) at the base of the Southern Flinders ranges. From here, **Yorke Peninsula Coaches** (☎ 8821 2755; www.ypcoaches.com.au) runs a Friday bus to Quorn ($6, 45 minutes) and Wilmington ($8, 1¼ hours). Yorke Peninsula Coaches also runs a Thursday bus from Port Pirie (south of Port Augusta) to Melrose ($8, 1¼ hours) and Wilmington ($9, 1½ hours); and a bus from Port Pirie to Laura ($4, 20 minutes) and Wirrabarra ($7, one hour) on the second and fourth Monday of the month.

Gulf Getaways (☎ 1800 170 170, 08-8642 6827; www.gulfgetaways.com.au) runs a Port Augusta–to-Wilpena shuttle on Fridays and Sundays, stopping at Quorn ($20, 30 minutes), Hawker ($40, 1¼ hours) and Wilpena Pound ($50, 2¼ hours).

CAR & MOTORCYCLE

The Flinders Ranges are accessed from Adelaide by sealed roads off Hwy 1 and Main North Rd, and via the Barrier Hwy from New South Wales (NSW). If you're coming from NSW, you can also turn off the Barrier Hwy at Yunta and take gravel-surfaced roads to Wilpena Pound, Gammon Ranges National Park and Arkaroola. The major roads to Quorn, Hawker, Wilpena Pound, Leigh Creek and the Southern Ranges towns are all sealed. At the time of research the road between Parachilna to Blinman was being sealed, but the roads between Blinman and Wilpena and into Arkaroola were still gravel (fine in a 2WD car if you take 'em slow).

Anyone planning to travel off the main roads, particularly in the north, should be prepared for a dearth of drinking water, shops and service stations. If you're heading

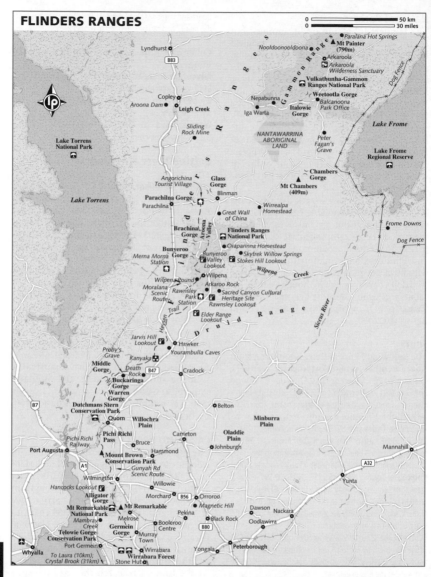

FLINDERS RANGES

0 — 50 km
0 — 30 miles

Lyndhurst
B83

Paralana Hot Springs
Mt Painter (790m)
Nooldoonooldoona
Arkaroola
Arkaroola Wilderness Sanctuary
Vulkathunha-Gammon Ranges National Park
Gammon Ranges
Dog Fence
Copley
Aroona Dam
Leigh Creek
Nepabunna
Weetootla Gorge
Balcanoona Park Office
Sliding Rock Mine
Iga Warta
Italowie Gorge
Lake Frome
Lake Torrens National Park
NANTAWARRINA ABORIGINAL LAND
Peter Fagan's Grave
Lake Frome Regional Reserve
Angorichina Tourist Village
Glass Gorge
Blinman
Chambers Gorge
Mt Chambers (409m)
Parachilna Gorge
Parachilna
Great Wall of China
Wirrealpa Homestead
Frome Downs
Brachina Gorge
Aroona Valley
Flinders Ranges National Park
Dog Fence
Lake Torrens
Bunyeroo Gorge
Merna Morra Station
Oraparinna Homestead
Skytrek Willow Springs
Bunyeroo Valley Lookout
Stokes Hill Lookout
Wilpena Pound
Wilpena
Wilpena Creek
Moralana Scenic Route
Rawnsley Park Station
Arkaroo Rock
Sacred Canyon Cultural Heritage Site
Rawnsley Lookout
Sliectas River
Elder Range Lookout
Druid Range
Jarvis Hill Lookout
Hawker
Proby's Grave
Yourambulla Caves
Middle Gorge
Death Rock
Kanyaka
Cradock
B847
Buckaringa Gorge
Warren Gorge
Dutchmans Stern Conservation Park
Belton
Minburra Plain
87
Quorn
Willochra Plain
Pichi Richi Railway
Pichi Richi Pass
Bruce
Carrieton
Oladdie Plain
Johnburgh
Mannahill
Port Augusta
Mount Brown Conservation Park
Hammond
A1
Gunyah Rd Scenic Route
A32
Wilmington
Willowie
Yunta
Hancocks Lookout
Morchard
B56
Orroroo
Alligator Gorge
Mt Remarkable National Park
Mt Remarkable
Melrose
Magnetic Hill
Dawson
Nackara
Mambray Creek
Pekina
Black Rock
Oodlawirra
Germein Gorge
Booleroo Centre
B80
Telowie Gorge Conservation Park
Murray Town
Port Germein
Yongala
Peterborough
Whyalla
To Laura (10km); Crystal Brook (31km)
Wirrabara
Wirrabara Forest
Stone Hut

---

further north than Leigh Creek, see p308 for advice on driving in outback conditions.

TRAIN

The restored **Pichi Richi Railway** (☎ 1800 440 101, 08-8648 6598; www.prr.org.au) connects Quorn to Port Augusta on a scenic trip. See Quorn (p123) for details.

SOUTHERN RANGES

The Southern Ranges extend from just north of Port Augusta to just south of Hawker, and eastwards towards Wirrabara and Laura. This is genteel farming country, with mannered villages and wheat farms in the south and long-established sheep stations in the north. Towering above it all, Mt Remarkable (with its own national park) is the ultimate immovable object.

LAURA TO WIRRABARA
Heading north from Adelaide along Main North Rd, you enter the Southern Ranges near **Laura** (population 500), emerging from the wheat fields like Superman's Smallville (all civic pride and 1950s prosperity). There's not a lot to do here, but the long, geranium-adorned main street has a supermarket, chemist, bakery, bank, post office…even a jeweller! If you want to stay the night, try **Laura Brewery B&B** (☎ 08-8663 2251; www.laurabrewery.com.au; 8 West Tce; d $140; 🐕), occupying an (you guessed it) old brewery done up in cottagey style.

About 10km further north, **Stone Hut** (population 290) doesn't have much on offer other than the amazing **Old Bakery** (☎ 8673 2165; www .oldbakerystonehut.com.au; Main North Rd; items $4-10; 🕑 7am-6pm; 🐕 🅅), which makes legendary chunky beef pies, slices, quandong tart, lemon-myrtle biscuits and monolithic lamingtons (and decent coffee). There's accommodation here too: a three-bed unit out the back, and five new corrugated-iron cabins with kitchenettes and bathrooms (doubles from $150).

Nine kilometres further on is **Wirrabara** (population 270), a lazy, sun-stroked town showing the faded prosperity of former times. About 7km to the west, **Wirrabara Forest** (☎ 8668 4163; www.forestry.sa.gov.au; Forest Rd; admission free; 🕑 office 12.30-4.30pm Mon, Tue, Thu & Fri, forest dawn-dusk) was once noted for its huge river red gums, logged mercilessly for jetty timbers and railway sleepers. The massive **King Tree** somehow evaded the saws (with an 11.5m circumference, maybe it was just too big!). There are some great walks here, including part of the Heysen Trail (p287) and a forest circuit (12km, five hours). About 4km into the forest is the basic **Ippinitchie Campground** (camping per 2 people $12); pay at the office on your way in.

Also in Wirrabara Forest, 7.5km from Wirrabara itself, the 16-bed **Wirrabara Old Schoolhouse YHA** (☎ 8414 3000; www.yha.com.au; Forest Rd; entire schoolhouse per night from $110) has basic facilities in an old stone schoolhouse; they'll tell you where to collect the key when you book. A little further along Forest Rd is **Taralee Orchards** (☎ 8668 4343; www.taralee.com.au; Forest Rd; d $110, extra adult/child $25/20), where you can stay in solar-powered comfort amid groves of biodynamic stone fruit. The two cottages here have full kitchens and an unlimited supply of apricot jam!

About 10km north of Wirrabara you can turn left and noodle through **Germein Gorge** towards Port Germein.

MELROSE
pop 200
If you've been kicking dust around the parched Northern Ranges for a while, you may well utter the phrase, 'Praise be to Melrose!' as you arrive here: a tiny town, snug under the elbow of the 960m Mt Remarkable, with the perfect mix of well-preserved architecture, a cracking-good pub, quality accommodation, a cafe, parks with ACTUAL GRASS and an inoffensive serving of 'quaint'. Established in 1853 when a copper mine opened for business nearby, Melrose is the oldest town in the Flinders. The police station here once had 70 horses and a jurisdiction extending all the way to the Timor Sea! These days you're more likely to see cyclists than steeds: the Mawson Trail (p287) wheels right through town.

Sights & Activities
The 1862 police station now houses the National Trust **Melrose Courthouse Heritage Centre** (☎ 8666 2141; www.heritageaustralia.com .au; 21 Stuart St; adult/concession/child/family $5/4/2/14, tours by appointment $8; 🕑 2-5pm), featuring ye olde photographs, gaol cells, stables and a Nukunu Aboriginal display. Opening hours are subject to change – call ahead.

In the back streets is the astonishing old **Jacka's Brewery** (cnr Mount & Lambert Sts), the derelict remains of an 1878 flour mill which then became a brewery between 1893 and 1934. It's a spooky sandstone structure, three stories taller than anything else in Melrose.

You can explore **Mt Remarkable National Park** (see p120) on an easy 3km track from the caravan park up to a **war memorial**, then back via an abandoned **copper mine** (Melrose's *raison d'être*). If you're feeling chipper, launch yourself up to the Mt Remarkable summit (see p121).

About 14km north of Melrose, a turn-off on the west leads to the old **Spring Creek Mine**, crumbling stone remnants of the copper boom.

Over the Edge (☎ 8666 2222; www.otesports.com.au; 6 Stuart St; bike hire per day $25-100; 🕑 9am-5pm Thu-Mon)

GOYDER'S LINE

Just off Main North Rd 3km north of Melrose is a monument heralding the presence of **Goyder's Line**. In 1865, George Woodroffe Goyder drew an imaginary line across the map of South Australia, delineating drought-prone land to the north and agriculturally viable land (with more than 10in of annual rain) to the south. The line arcs up from the Victorian border through Burra and Orroroo, darts down through Melrose, across the top of the Yorke Peninsula and slices off the Eyre Peninsula about halfway up. Over time, George W's estimations have proved reliable – farmers ignored his advice at their peril – but all this was before climate change. Where would he draw the line today?

---

hires out bikes for the Mawson Trail, and can straighten your spokes and take a gander at your gears.

See also Bluey Blundstone's Blacksmith Shop (right).

Sleeping & Eating

Melrose Caravan Park (☎ 8666 2060; mcp@rbe.net.au; Joe's Rd; dm $15, unpowered/powered sites $15/20, cabins $45-100;) Down by a babbling brook (well, when it rains in winter, anyway) with huge river red gums, this small, tidy park has bush campsites and a range of self-contained cabins (all with TVs and cooking facilities – the cheaper ones are sans bathrooms). The 12km return hike up Mt Remarkable starts on the back doorstep. Next door is a converted agricultural shed with basic dorm facilities (no air-con).

Mt Remarkable Cottage (☎ 8666 2171; www.mt remarkablecottage.com; off Melrose-Wilmington Rd; d $70, extra adult/child $15/10;) This two-bedroom, converted pottery studio is down a 1.5km dirt road off Main North Rd, 4km north of Melrose. It's about as close as you can get to Mt Remarkable without burrowing into it! There's a wood fire, full kitchen and cosy lounge so you can make yourself at home. Goannas stomp through the surrounding scrub.

Melrose Holiday Units (☎ 8666 2021; fulloo@central online.com.au; Whitby St; d from $80;) An unremarkable but affordable collection of green-painted, two-bedroom log cabins, with barbecues and kitchens. A no-frills overnighter.

ourpick **North Star Hotel** (☎ 8666 2110; www .northstarhotel.com.au; Nott St; r $90-160, trucks $140-160, ste $195-225;) As welcome as a summer downpour, the 150-year-old North Star (sister-pub to the Prairie Hotel in Parachilna – see p128) is renovated in city-meets-woolshed style. Sit under the hessian-sack ceiling and spinning fans for a fresh menu (mains $10 to $29, open for lunch Wednesday to Sunday, dinner Thursday to Saturday), great coffee and cold Flinders Ranges beer (try the Fargher Lager). Accommodation ranges from rooms in the place next door (TPND) to plush suites above the pub and surprisingly cool metal-clad cabins built on two old trucks out the back.

Bluey Blundstone's Blacksmith Shop (☎ 8666 2173; blueys@chariot.net.au; 32 Stuart St; d barn/cottage $120/135, extra adult/child $40/20) This place is a museum – an 1865 blacksmith shop authentically reconstructed by a NSW couple who breathed a bellows-full of life into the old girl. Through a tiny door is a modest cafe (mains $10 to $16, open for lunch Thursday to Tuesday) and accommodation in an eccentrically renovated barn (sleeps six) and a cosy cottage (sleeps two). Expect pressed-tin doors, corrugated-iron dados, lanterns, nooks, crannies and an old record player with a few discs to spin.

MT REMARKABLE NATIONAL PARK

Hikers and bush-boffins rave about this steep, jaggedy, 16,000-hectare park straddling the ranges between Melrose and Wilmington. Bushwalking is the main lure, with various tracks (including part of the Heysen Trail) meandering through isolated gorges and past rock outcrops; keep an eye out for fat goannas, yellow-footed rock wallabies, kookaburras and luridly coloured corellas along the way.

The **Park Office** (☎ 8634 7068; www.environment .sa.gov.au/parks/sanpr/mountremarkable; admission per car $7.50; office 8.30am-4.30pm) is at Mambray Creek, a right turn off Hwy 1 about 21km north of Port Germein, where you can pay the entry fee. If you're coming along the inland route (Main North Rd between Melrose and Wilmington), there's an honour box at Alligator Gorge. Both stations have brochures detailing camping and walking in the park.

Sights & Activities

In the park's north, **Alligator Gorge** is an 11km rattle across from Wilmington. From the car park here, you can take a short, steep walk

(2km, two hours) down into the craggy gorge (no sign of any 'gators), or continue on the ring route (9km, four hours) which has two camping spots along the way. Some other walks include **Hidden Gorge** (18km, seven hours) and **Mambray Creek** (13km, seven hours).

Peak-baggers will want to head straight to the track starting behind Melrose Caravan Park (opposite), and sweat the 960m to the summit of **Mt Remarkable** (12km return, five hours). The mountain is high enough to receive a (very) occasional smattering of snow – the views from the top are predictability brilliant. The Heysen Trail (see p287) tracks down from the summit along the Mt Remarkable Range into Wilmington.

The other main base from which to explore is **Mambray Creek**, off Hwy 1 between Port Germein and Port Augusta. A web of **walking tracks** heads off into the ranges from here – the return walk to Alligator Gorge (26km, 10 hours) is the most gut busting, but Davey's Gully (2.5km, one hour) is (literally and metaphorically) a walk in the park.

Sleeping

There are two **lodges** in the park: at Mambray Creek (sleeps four; per night $42) and Alligator Gorge (sleeping eight; per night $85). Both are solar powered, but Alligator Gorge has better cooking facilities and showers. Book through the Park Office.

There's plenty of **bush camping** (per car $15) including Longhill Camp, 10 minutes' walk from the Alligator Gorge car park, or you can drive north on a bumpy dirt road to Stony Creek Camp. Mambray Creek camping ground has the best facilities including wheelchair access and water.

WILMINGTON
pop 220

Originally called 'Beautiful Valley', Wilmington is barren in contrast to neighbouring Melrose. The town evolved around the 1879 Wilmington Hotel, a Cobb & Co staging post, and soon became a key agricultural centre. These days it's a pit stop for Heysen Trail walkers, but beyond the pub don't expect much more than some jacarandas, a couple of sparrows and a few tumbleweeds.

Sights & Activities

The **Wilmington Toy Museum** (☎ 8667 5276; www .websouth.com.au/toymuseum; cnr Third & Main Sts; adult/ child $4/free; ☒ 9.30am-5.30pm) is a semineglected collection of old tin toys, model planes, Meccano constructions, model trains, hubcaps and soft-drink cans – worth a look if you've got the kids in tow.

From here it's an easy drive to the **Alligator Gorge** section of Mt Remarkable National Park (see opposite). Alternatively, for a wide panorama over the western foothills to Spencer Gulf, take the road from Wilmington to Port Augusta for 3km, then the 7km detour to **Hancocks Lookout**.

If you're heading for Quorn, the **Gunyah Rd Scenic Route** is a bendy, 26km alternative to the bitumen road further east. It takes you through the eastern foothills of **Mt Brown Conservation Park** (www.environment.sa.gov.au/parks /sanpr/mountbrown) where you can hike to the summit (12km return, six hours), with beaut views along the way.

Sleeping & Eating

Beautiful Valley Caravan Park (☎ 8667 5197; www .beautifulvalley.com.au; Main Rd; unpowered/powered sites $17/22, on-site vans $30, cabins $47-65, linen $10; ☒ ☒) About 1.5km south of town on the road to Melrose is this serviceable park, with a good mix of cabins, a camp kitchen and a pool for those searing, dusty Wilmington afternoons.

Wilmington Hotel (☎ 8667 5154; wilmington hotel@hotmail.com; Main St; s/d $35/60) Darts, Akubra hats and Jimmy Barnes singing *Working Class Man* on the jukebox – not quite how it was when this place was built in 1879, but appealingly 'country' just the same. Spartan but clean pub rooms upstairs; basic meals downstairs (mains $12 to $24, open for lunch daily, dinner Monday to Saturday).

QUORN
pop 1010

You'd be forgiven for thinking Quorn is a film set after the crew has gone home – it's a cinematographic little town on the edge of the outback, with more jeering crows than people. Wheat farming took off here in 1875, and the town prospered with the arrival of the Great Northern Railway from Port Augusta. Quorn remained an important railroad junction until trains into the Flinders were cut in 1970. Driving around town you might see an old fella wave from his verandah shade, or a willy-willy (mini-tornado) gather momentum then dissipate into a column of sand, growing ever fainter.

Information

Flinders Ranges visitors centre (☎ 8648 6419; www .flindersranges.com; 3 Seventh St; ⊙ 9am-5pm; 💻) Maps, brochures, internet access and advice.

Sights & Activities

Quorn's streetscapes are a real history lesson, especially **Railway Tce** – a once-busy main street but now a quiet (but enduringly grand) thoroughfare. Pick up the *Old Quorn Walking Tour* brochure from the visitors centre for a tour of the town's old buildings, some of which have featured in iconic Australian films such as *Gallipoli* and *Sunday Too Far Away*.

A fragment of the long-defunct Great Northern Railway now conveys the **Pichi Richi Railway** (see opposite), a historic train running through Pichi Richi Pass to/from Port Augusta on Saturday.

Kicking off at nearby Woolshed Flat (ask at the visitors centre for directions), the **Waukarie Creek Trail** (9km, five hours) meets up with part of the Heysen Trail (see p287) and passes through copses of red gum and wattle. Look out for hollow trees once used as shelters by the Adnyamathanha people.

Tours

Pichi Richi Camel Tours (☎ 8648 6640, 0429-998 044; www.pichirichicameltours.com) Saddle up on a 'ship of the desert' for a one-hour ride ($35) or a longer half-/full-day camel-back tour ($95/175) through the country around Quorn. Overnight safaris and sunset and moonlight rides also available.

Quorn Adventures (www.quornadventures.com) Collaborative website listing tour operators and 4WD tracks in and around Quorn.

Wallaby Tracks Adventure Tours (☎ 0428-486 655; www.wallabytracks.com) Small group 4WD tours through the Southern Ranges (half-day $110) or extending north to Wilpena Pound (full day $160), departing either Quorn or Port Augusta.

Sleeping & Eating

Quorn Caravan Park (☎ 8648 6206; www.quorncaravan park.com.au; 8 Silo Rd; unpowered/powered sites $18/22, cabins $50-80; 🐾) Fully keyed in to climate change, this passionately run park on the (usually dry) Pinkerton Creek is hell-bent on reducing emissions and restoring native habitat.

Recovering from collisions with traffic, a few lazy roos lounge about under the red gums. Spotless cabins and shady sites.

Austral Inn (☎ 8648 6017; www.australinn.com.au; 16 Railway Tce, d motel/pub from $70/100; 🐾) This is the place to find the other travellers in town, but there's more than a few locals at the bar giving the jukebox a workout and chatting with the publican. The pub rooms are renovated – simple and clean with new linen – while the motel rooms are more '80s than the menu (standard country-pub fare with a twist: try the 'bush & bay' – local roo with Port Pirie prawns – or a mighty camel schnitzel). The pub is purportedly above an old well, so if it's been raining watch out for mozzies (you'll hear them coming like light aircraft).

Old Willows Country Estate (☎ 8648 6391; www .flindersranges.com/bis/oldwillowa.htm; 32 Eighth St; s/d $80/130) Stripped-back country elegance abounds at this renovated stone villa. It's a five-minute walk from town, and sleeps plenty of bods (for eight slumberers it's only $280!). Polished floorboards, antique brass beds and romantic/practical mozzie nets.

Quandong Apartments (☎ 8648 6155, 0432-113 473; www.quandongapartments.com; 31 First St; d $150; 🐾) Next door to the Quandong Café (and run by the same folks), these two self-contained apartments have full kitchens, big TVs, quality linen and mod-Asian touches. Rates come down with stays of two nights or more.

our pick **Quandong Café** (☎ 8648 6155; 31 First St; mains $6-12; ⊙ breakfast & lunch mid-Mar–mid-Dec; 🐾) A traditional country cafe with creaky floorboards and spinning ceiling fans, serving big breakfasts and light lunches. Try a generously adorned 'railway sleeper' (like a pizza sub), or a massive slab of lemon meringue or quandong pie. Good old-fashioned country value!

Transcontinental Hotel (☎ 8648 6076; transhotel@ bigpond.com.au; 15 Railway Tce; mains $12-20; ⊙ lunch & dinner; 🐾) The second-best pub in town (there are four of 'em…yes, four), the 'Trannie' serves no-fuss pub grub in a low-key dining room. A good sign: the barman eats here when he's finished his shift ('We've got a good chef here…he's bloody good'). There's a handful of basic pub rooms upstairs (singles/doubles $32/54), but they're usually booked out.

For self-caterers, the town supermarket is **Quorn IGA** (☎ 8648 6081; 2 Seventh St; ⊙ 8am-6pm Mon-Fri, 9am-4.30pm Sat & Sun).

DETOUR: BUCKARINGA SCENIC DRIVE

This 56km unsealed road heads north from Quorn along the eastern foothills. First up (7km from Quorn) is **Dutchmans Stern Conservation Park** (www.environment.sa.gov.au/parks/sanpr/thedutchmans stern), named after a bluff that resembles the rump of an 18th-century Dutch ship. The Heysen Trail (p287) runs through the park, and you can climb the bluff via a circular track (four hours, 8.2km) ascending through saltbush and native cranberry trees.

Continuing on, things get gorgeous: **Warren Gorge**, **Buckaringa Gorge** and **Middle Gorge** crop into view. There's bush camping at Warren Gorge, and a good rock-climbing spot too. Encompassing Buckaringa and Middle Gorges, **Buckaringa Sanctuary** (☎ 08-9380 9633; www .australianwildlife.org; admission free; ☼ 24hr) is a 2000-hectare wildlife reserve run by the Australian Wildlife Conservancy. Keep your peepers peeled for the rare yellow-footed rock wallaby.

The route continues on past **Proby's Grave** where Hugh Proby, founder of the Kanyaka settlement, rests his bones. The route then meets the main road to Hawker 34km north of Quorn.

Getting There & Away

The **Pichi Richi Railway** (☎ 1800 440 101, 8648 6598; www.prr.org.au) runs between Port Augusta and Quorn (one-way adult/concession/child/family $45/42/17/107, 2½ hours) on Saturday.

QUORN TO HAWKER

Derelict ruins of early settlements litter the Quorn–Hawker road, the most impressive of which is **Kanyaka**, just off the road 41km from Quorn. The remains of the 16-room Kanyaka Homestead and a collation of stone outbuildings are all that survives of the once-thriving sheep station, founded in 1851. There's a small, sad graveyard occupied by the Proby clan, the Scottish settlers who built the homestead.

From the ruins you can take a 10-minute walk to the old woolshed. The track continues about 1.5km to a waterhole, loomed over by a massive boulder called **Death Rock**. The story goes that local Aborigines once placed their dying kinsfolk here to see out their last hours.

NORTHERN RANGES

Worlds away from the domesticated Southern Ranges, the lonesome, sunburnt scrublands that stretch between Hawker and the Strzelecki Desert contain three of the finest conservation areas in all of South Australia (SA): Flinders Ranges National Park, Vulkathunha-Gammon Ranges National Park and the Arkaroola Wildlife Sanctuary. Each of these parks is of immense importance to the local Adnyamathanha Aboriginal people. Note

that mobile-phone reception north of Hawker is patchy at best.

HAWKER
pop 300

Hawker is the last outpost of civilisation before Wilpena Pound, 55km to the north. Much like Quorn, Hawker has seen better days…and it's hard to say if those days were all that good, but at least the old *Ghan* train stopped here. These days Hawker is a pancake-flat, pit-stop town with ostrich eggs 'blown and ready to decorate' in the local cafe, and quite possibly the world's most helpful petrol station. There's an ATM here too. Online, check out www.hawkersa.info.

Information

Flinders Ranges Accommodation Booking Service
(FRABS; ☎ 1800 777 880, 8648 4022; www.frabs.com.au) The deliciously named FRABS can help with bookings for rural cottages and shearers' quarters on outback stations around Hawker.

Teague's Hawker Motors & visitors centre
(☎ 8648 4014, 8648 4022; www.hawkermotors.com.au; cnr Wilpena & Cradock Rds; ☼ 7.30am-6pm; ☐) The town's petrol station (fill up if you're heading north) is also the visitors centre, with brochures, books, DVDs and info on the outback and Flinders Ranges (check out the seismograph in the corner!). Its *Discover Hawker* booklet ($2) has all the local info.

Sights & Activities

It's not so much what's in Hawker that's interesting – it's more what's around it – but if you like your great outdoors inside (and a little bit eccentric), **Wilpena Panorama** (☎ 8648 4071; www.wilpenapanorama.com; cnr Wilpena & Cradock

FLINDERS RANGES

Rds; adult/child $5.50/3; ⏰ 9am-5pm Mon-Sat, noon-4pm Sun) is a large circular room with a painting of Wilpena Pound surrounding you on all sides. There's a second monster mural of the Elder Range next door; combined admission costs $7.50/4 per adult/child.

Yourambulla Caves, 12km south of Hawker, have detailed Aboriginal rock paintings (including emu tracks), with three sites open to visitors. **Yourambulla Peak**, a half-hour walk from the car park, is the most accessible spot to check out the paintings.

Tours

Derek's 4WD Tours (☎ 0417-475 770; www.dereks 4wdtours.com; tours half-/full day from $105/160) For off-road action, Derek does several good trips with an environmental bent, including to Bunyeroo and Brachina gorges.

Skytrek Willow Springs (☎ 8648 0016; www.sky trekwillowsprings.com.au) This working outback sheep station runs six-hour self-drive tours of its rugged Skytrek route ($55 per vehicle), or staff can hook you up with a tour operator. There's an array of self-contained cabin accommodation here too ($45 to $160 per double).

Sleeping & Eating

Hawker Caravan Park (☎ 8648 4006; www.hawker big4holidaypark.com.au; cnr Wilpena Rd & Chace View Tce; unpowered/powered sites $24/26, en suite sites $30-36, cabins $86-120; ⚡ 🖳) At the Wilpena end of town, this upbeat acreage with generous sites and a range of cabins is the pick of Hawker's two caravan parks. The pool comes as sweet relief on a hot afternoon!

Hawker Hotel-Motel (☎ 8648 4102; hawhotmot@ internode.on.net; 80 Elder Tce; s/d pub $35/55, motel $70/80; ⚡) This budget-conscious pub has no-frills hotel rooms in an adjoining wing, plus a row of dated motel rooms out the back. Bar meals (mains $14 to $21, open for lunch and dinner daily) go heavy on the meat.

Chapmanton Outback Motel (☎ 8648 4100; fax 8648 4109; 1 Wilpena Rd; s/d/units $95/105/120; ⚡) This drive-up motel offers the best rooms in town. The two-bedroom units are good value for families, and the local swimming pool is just across the street.

Hawker General Store Café (☎ 8648 4005; cnr Wilpena & Cradock Rds; meals $4-12; ⏰ breakfast & lunch Mon-Fri, plus Sat & Sun Mar-Nov; ⚡) A jack-of-all-trades shop serving steak sangers, cooked breakfasts, cakes, coffee and quandong smoothies. You can also stock up on camping supplies, fruit-and-veg and groceries.

Sightseer's Curiosity Café Gallery (☎ 8648 4475; 66 Elder Tce; meals $7-12; ⏰ lunch Tue-Sun Nov-Feb, longer hr Mar-Oct; ⚡) For a quick-grab meal (burgers, sandwiches, cakes and coffee), this takeaway joint is a safe bet. The local art isn't a must see… They also have self-contained accommodation in the 1882 house next door (double $120).

Old Ghan Restaurant (☎ 8648 4176; Leigh Creek Rd; mains $20-28; ⏰ lunch & dinner Thu-Sat, closed Jan-Feb; ⚡) In the old *Ghan* railway station on the outskirts of town, this restaurant is about as upmarket as Hawker gets. Expect mains such as barramundi with quince-and-orange glaze, and grilled chicken breast with mango curry sauce.

See also Skytrek Willow Springs (left).

HAWKER TO WILPENA

With desert hills and lorikeets in equal measure, rangy **Rawnsley Park Station** (☎ reception 8648 0008, caravan park/YHA 8648 0030; www.rawnsleypark.com .au; Wilpena Rd; unpowered/powered sites $20/29, dm $33; cabins/units/villas from $82/112/340; ⚡ 🖳), 35km from Hawker, runs the whole gamut of accommodation from tent sites to luxe eco-villas. The YHA has set up shop in the caravan park section, commandeering some of the cabins as dorms. Also on offer is a range of outback activities including sheep-shearing demos (per adult/child/family $16/8/40), 4WD tours (per half-/full day $115/175), mountain-bike hire (per hour $15), and bushwalking (from 30 minutes to four hours). Scenic flights also wing up from the airstrip here (per 30 minutes $110). The **Woolshed Restaurant** (☎ 8648 0126; mains $12-28; ⏰ lunch & dinner, closed Feb) does bang-up bush tucker, plus curries, *tajines* (Moroccan stews), seafood and pizzas. Take a peek inside the glassed woolshed next door, used for shearing.

Around 40km from Hawker, **Arkaroo Rock** is a sacred Aboriginal site. On the underside of a huge fallen boulder, the art here features reptile and human figures in charcoal, birdlime and yellow and red ochre. Once used for initiation ceremonies, this is one of the Flinders' most significant Aboriginal cultural sites. It's a short(ish) return walk from the car park (2km, one hour).

As you truck towards Wilpena Pound, the towering rifts of the **Elder Range** and **Rawnsley Bluff** crop up to the east. On the southern end of Flinders Ranges National Park 41km from Hawker, **Rawnsley Lookout** has ace views of bluffs and cliffs to the northwest, and the **Chace Range** to the south.

FLINDERS RANGES NATIONAL PARK

One of SA's most treasured parks, **Flinders Ranges National Park** (www.environment.sa.gov.au/parks/sanpr/flindersranges; admission per car $7.50) is laced with craggy gorges, saw-toothed ranges, abandoned homesteads, Aboriginal sites, hyperactive wildlife and, after it rains, carpets of wildflowers. The park's big-ticket drawcard is the 80 sq km natural basin **Wilpena Pound** – a sunken elliptical valley ringed by gnarled ridges of rock (don't let anyone tell you it's a meteorite crater!).

Thanks to conservation efforts, this is the perfect place to spy grey kangaroos and geeky families of emus, both visible from the road. Rosellas, galahs, lorikeets and wedge-tailed eagles circle the skies, and keep your eyes peeled for nocturnal dunnarts (marsupial mice) and rare yellow-footed rock wallabies (look for the stripy tail).

The **Wilpena Pound visitors centre** (☎ 1800 805 802, 8648 0004; www.wilpenapound.com.au; Wilpena Rd; ☷ 8am-5.30pm; ☐) is on the road into the Wilpena Pound Resort (and staffed by the same dudes). This is the place for info on the park and the surrounding district, internet access and bike hire (per half-/full day $20/40). You can also book scenic flights (see p126), 4WD tours and guided walks here. If you didn't pay your park-entry fees at the self-registration booth a few kilometres back down the road, cough up the lucre here ($7.50 per vehicle).

Sights & Activities

The unmissable **Wilpena Pound** is only accessible in a vehicle on the Wilpena Pound Resort **shuttle bus** (return adult/concession/child/family $4/2.50/2.50/9), which drops you near the old **Wilpena Station**, within 1km of the **Wangarra Lookout**. From the lookout you can see why the Adnyamathanha people believed the Pound to be the joined bodies of two *akurra* (giant snakes), with St Mary Peak the head of one. *Wilpena* (or 'bent fingers') describes the shape of the two ridges twisting together. The shuttle runs at 9am, 11am, 1pm, 3pm and 5pm, dropping people off and coming straight back (so if you take the 5pm shuttle and want more than a cursory look around, you'll miss the return bus). Otherwise it's a three-hour, 8km return walk between the resort and lookout.

DETOUR: MORALANA SCENIC DRIVE

This sneaky, unsealed 28km back route between the Wilpena and Leigh Creek roads takes in railway ruins, lookouts and the rust red mountain scenery of the Elder and Wilpena Pound ranges. If you're heading north from Wilpena to Leigh Creek (or the other way around), it'll save you having to backtrack through Hawker. The turn-off is 24km north of Hawker on the Wilpena road (46km on the Leigh Creek road).

Rock hounds might want to drive the 20km **Brachina Gorge Geological Trail**, starring an amazing layering of exposed sedimentary rock, covering 120 million years of the Earth's history. Grab a brochure from the visitors centre.

The **Bunyeroo-Brachina-Aroona Scenic Drive** is a 110km round trip, passing by Bunyeroo Valley, Brachina Gorge, Aroona Valley and **Stokes Hill Lookout**. Short walks along the way make for a vigorous day trip, with a stop at **Bunyeroo Valley Lookout** a camera-conducive must. The drive starts north of Wilpena off the road to Blinman.

Just beyond the park's southeast corner, a one-hour, 1km return walk leads to the **Sacred Canyon Cultural Heritage Site**, with Aboriginal art rock galleries featuring animal tracks and designs.

BUSHWALKING

Before you make happy trails, ensure you've got enough water, sunscreen and a big hat, and tell someone where you're going and when you plan to get back. Pick up a copy of the *Bushwalking in Flinders Ranges National Park* brochure/map from the visitors centre, which details 17 walks in the park. Nine of the walks kick off at Wilpena Pound Resort, or you can shave a few kilometres off by taking the shuttle bus (see left) further into the Pound. Walks range from short, family-friendly walks to longer full-day (or overnight) epics.

For a really good look at Wilpena, the walk up to **Tanderra Saddle** on the ridge of **St Mary Peak** on the Pound's rim is brilliant, though it's a thigh-pounding scramble at times. The Adnyamathanha people request that you restrict your climbing to the ridge and don't climb St Mary Peak itself, due to its traditional significance to them (see p126). The return walk to the saddle (15km, six hours) from the shuttle

FLINDERS RANGES

ABORIGINAL AUSTRALIA: ADNYAMATHANHA DREAMING

Land and nature are integral to the culture of the traditional owners of the Flinders Ranges. The people collectively called Adnyamathanha (or 'Hill People') are actually a collection of the Wailpi, Kuyani, Jadliaura, Piladappa and Pangkala tribes, who exchanged and elaborated on stories to explain their spectacular local geography.

The walls of Ikara (Wilpena Pound), for example, are the bodies of two *akurra* (giant snakes), who coiled around Ikara during an initiation ceremony, eating most of the participants. The snakes were so full after their feast they couldn't move and willed themselves to die, creating the landmark. Because of its traditional significance, the Adnyamathanha prefer that visitors don't climb St Mary Peak, reputed to be the head of the female snake.

In another story another *akurra* drank Lake Frome dry, then wove his way across the land creating creeks and gorges. Wherever he stopped he created a large waterhole, including Arkaroola Springs. The sun warmed the salty water in his stomach causing it to rumble, a noise that can still be heard today in the form of underground spring water flowing.

Colour is essential to the Adnyamathanha as they use the area's red ochre in traditional ceremonies and medicine. Traditional stories purport that the vivid orange colour is from the *marrukurli*, dangerous dogs who were killed by Adnu, the bearded dragon. When Adnu killed the black *marrukurli* the sun went out and he was forced to throw his boomerang in every direction to reawaken the sun. It was only when he threw it to the east that the sun returned. Meanwhile the blood of the *marrukurli* had seeped into the earth to create sacred ochre deposits.

---

drop-off point opens up some good views of the ABC Ranges and Wilpena. If you have time, take the longer outside track for some even more eye-popping vistas. You can keep going on the round trip (22km, nine hours), camping overnight at **Cooinda Camp** then heading back via Wilpena Station the next day.

The track up to **Mt Ohlssen Bagge** (6½km, four hours) is a quick but tough hike that rewards the sweaty hiker with a stunning panorama. Good short walks include the stroll to Hills Homestead (6½km, two hours), or the dash up to the **Wilpena Solar Power Station** (500m, 30 minutes), which keeps the beer cold at Wilpena Pound Resort.

In the park's north (50km north of Wilpena Pound Resort), the **Aroona Ruins** – including a restored pug-and-pine hut – are the launch pad for a few less-trampled walks. The **Yuluna Hike** (8km, four hours) weaves through a painterly stretch of the ABC Ranges that once tickled the fancy of South Australian landscape artist Hans Heysen. On the challenging **Aroona-Youngoona Track** (one-way 15½km, seven hours), you follow a route used by early shepherds, with views of the Trezona and Heysen Ranges, before cooling your boots overnight at Youngoona campsite.

Tours

For 4WD park tours, contact Derek's 4WD Tours (p124), Rawnsley Park Station (p124), Skytrek Willow Springs (p124) or Wilpena

Pound Resort (below). Wilpena Pound Resort also runs guided walks into the Pound.

Central Air Services (☎ 8648 0008, 8648 0040; flights 20min/30min/1hr $125/145/215) Up, up and away over Wilpena Pound. Flights depart both Wilpena Pound Resort and Rawnsley Park Station. Bookings through Wilpena Pound visitors centre (p125) or Rawnsley Park Station (p124). Extended flights and transfers also available.

Sleeping & Eating

Unless you have a tent, there's no cheap accommodation at Wilpena Pound itself.

Wilpena Pound Resort (☎ 1800 805 802, 8648 0004; www.wilpenapound.com.au; Wilpena Rd; unpowered/powered sites $20/28, permanent tent with/without linen $90/65, s/d from $170/195; ❄ 🖳 🖳) This resort is already pretty plush, but it's slated for an upgrade (which will probably include prices). Accommodation includes motel-style rooms, more upmarket self-contained suites in clusters of six, and a great (although hugely popular) campsite. If you didn't bring your own camping gear, there are permanent tents sleeping four. Purchase your camping permit at the visitors centre (p125), which also has a store selling petrol and basic groceries (you'll pay through the nose for bottled water). The visitors centre also books scenic flights with Central Air Services (see above), 4WD tours (morning and afternoon per adult child $135/100) and short 1.5km to 3km guided walks into Wilpena Pound ($35 to $50 per person). And don't miss a swim in the pool, happy hour at the bar (5pm to 6pm), and dinner at the excellent bistro (mains $20 to $30 – the roo is the best we've ever had!).

Within the national park (ie outside the resort), **bush camping areas** (per car $10) have basic facilities; permits are available from either the visitors centre (p125) or self-service booths along the way. **Trezona**, **Aroona** and **Brachina East** have creek-side sites among big gum trees, while **Youngoona** in the park's north is a good base for walks. Remote **Wilkawillina** is certainly the quietest.

BLINMAN & AROUND
pop 30

Ubercute **Blinman** owes its existence to the discovery of copper and the smelter built here in 1903. But the boom soon went bust, and today Blinman's main claim to fame is as SA's highest town (610m above sea level). Online, check out www.blinman.org.au. To get to Blinman you can take the 59km unsealed road north from Wilpena (OK for 2WD cars), or the 31km road east from Parachilna en route to Leigh Creek, which was being sealed at the time of research.

Most of the structures at the **Blinman Mine** (☎ 8648 4370; adult/family $4/10, key deposit $10) – on a hillock about 1km to the north – have been developed with lookouts and information boards showing how ore was formed, mined and treated. Pick up a key from the Blinman General Store to access some of the mine shafts (the rest of the site is free).

There are several day trips you can do on the (generally) good dirt roads around Blinman, including a loop through Flinders Ranges National Park via Aroona Valley and Brachina Gorge. About 7km further on is the **Great Wall of China**, a low ridge topped with a wall-like layer of sandstone.

The rough track to **Chambers Gorge** turns off the Arkaroola road 64km northeast of Blinman. The gorge is surrounded by hefty gum trees and tan-coloured dolomite cliffs, with small rock pools and galleries of **Aboriginal rock carvings**. To reach the carvings from the car park, walk 8.3km up the gorge on your left from the main road – the first major gallery is 350m upstream and on your left just before a small waterfall. A 2WD will get you to the carvings, but you'll need a 4WD with good clearance to access the main gorge. It's a

scramble to the top of **Mt Chambers**, with views of **Lake Frome** and along the ranges to **Mt Painter** and Wilpena in the south.

The road between Blinman and Parachilna tracks through **Parachilna Gorge**, where you'll find good camping and chill-out spots along the creek (oh, and the mandatory astounding views). The northern end of the Heysen Trail (p287) starts/finishes here.

From Angorichina Tourist Village (below) near Parachilna Gorge, take the **Blinman Pools Walk** (6km, five hours) which follows a spring-fed creek past abandoned dugouts, river red gums and cypress pines.

Sleeping & Eating

Blinman Hotel (☎ 8648 4867; blinman@senet.com.au; Mine Rd, Blinman; unpowered/powered sites $10/20, d hotel/motel/cottage $110/135/135; 🐾 🖳) Chunky slate floors, old-time photographs and capacious luxury rooms collide at this renovated 1869 boozer. The kitchen (mains $14 to $24, open for lunch and dinner) serves up bush-hewn delights such as saltbush-wrapped chicken breast, seared kangaroo fillet and char-grilled eucalyptus lamb, and the beer is always cold – well worth a detour! There are raggedy tent and caravan sites out the back.

Angorichina Tourist Village (☎ 8648 4842; www .angorichinavillage.com.au; Parachilna Gorge; unpowered/powered sites $20/24, on-site vans s/d from $28/38, dm $18, cabins from $75; 🐾) About 3km east of Parachilna Gorge, this rambling joint has a whole mix of accommodation (though dorm beds are often booked up by backpacker tours). The store sells fuel and can fix your flat. 'Real people only, no Yuppies' is the slogan (hide your Lacoste T-shirt and Ray-bans in the boot).

Wild Lime Café & Gallery (☎ 8648 4679; Old Schoolhouse, Mine Rd, Blinman; mains $10-20; ☯ breakfast & lunch Tue-Sun, daily school holidays; 🐾) Run by a jeweller and a painter on the run from suburban Melbourne, this place is a welcome surprise, serving reliable coffee, soups, salads, pies, pasties and great cakes. The art is for sale, but don't expect any fevered sales pitches (also a welcome surprise).

HAWKER TO LEIGH CREEK

From Hawker the road follows the rail line that ferries coal from Leigh Creek Coal Field to the Port Augusta power stations. Around 46km along the road, you can turn off to stay at **Merna Mora Station** (☎ 8648 4717; www.mernamora.com.au;

Hawker-Leigh Creek Rd; d $70, extra adult/child $11/5.50, linen $8; 🍴), a beautiful cattle station with plenty of wilderness, a few curious ruins and undomesticated wildlife to boot. The turn-off is at the intersection for the Moralana Scenic Route (see p125).

Another 36km from Merna Mora Station, **Parachilna** (population somewhere between four and seven) is an essential Flinders Ranges destination. Aside from a few shacks, a phone booth and some rusty wrecks, the only thing here is a legendary hotel.

our pick **Prairie Hotel** (☎ 8648 4844; www.prairie hotel.com.au; Parachilna; cabin s $45-100, d $60-120, hotel d $175-320; 🍴 🖳). It's looking just a tad weary, but it's still a world-class stay with semi-subterranean suites in a slick extension out the back. Across the road the Overflow has basic cabins (the pricier ones have bathrooms and are self-contained). Don't miss a meal and a cold Fargher Lager (or five) in the pub (mains $16 to $28, open for lunch and dinner): try the feral mixed grill (camel sausage, kangaroo fillet, emu and bacon). We arrived at 10.42am: 'Too early for a beer!? Whose rules are those?' asked the barman.

LEIGH CREEK & COPLEY

Coal was first mined at **Leigh Creek** (population 700) in 1888, but it wasn't until the 1940s that commercial production got into full swing, supplying the Port Augusta power stations (which in turn supply 40% of SA's electricity). In the early 1980s the previously nonexistent town of Leigh Creek was built by the state government: blooming out of the desert, it's an odd, Canberra-like oasis of leafy landscaping and cul-de-sacs (or is that culs-de-sac?). The **Leigh Creek visitors centre** (☎ 8675 2723; lcvic@internode.on.net; 13 Black Oak Dr; 🕙 9am-5pm; 🖳) is the place to head for the local low-down.

The **Leigh Creek Tavern** (☎ 8675 2025; leighcreek tavern@flinderspower.com.au; Leigh Creek Town Shopping Centre; motel s/d $110/135, cabins s/d/f $80/95/120; 🍴) is the hub of town life, offering jaunty '80s-style motel rooms, cabins and miner-sized meals in the bistro (mains $10 to $27, open for lunch and dinner). Sunday night is pizza night; Wednesday night it's schnitzels ahoy!

About 6km north of Leigh Creek is the sweet little nothingness of **Copley** (population 80). The main attraction here (aside from the photogenic junk yard) is the **Quandong Café & Bush Bakery** (☎ 8675 2683; Railway Tce; meals $6-16; 🕙 breakfast & lunch) – stop for a quandong pie but not much else.

Conversely, **Copley Caravan Park** (☎ 8675 2288; www.copleycaravan.com.au; Railway Tce W; unpowered/powered sites $20/25, cabins d $60-130; 🍴) is a going concern: a small, immaculate park that does a bonfire cook-up for guests.

Heading north from Copley, it's 33km to **Lyndhurst**, where the bitumen peters out. From here it's 80km to **Marree**, the start (or end) point of the famous **Oodnadatta Track** (see p145).

VULKATHUNHA-GAMMON RANGES NATIONAL PARK

Blanketing 128,200 desert hectares, the remote **Vulkathunha-Gammon Ranges National Park** (www .environment.sa.gov.au/parks/sanpr/vulkathunha_gammon ranges) has deep gorges, rugged ranges and gorgeous gum-lined creeks. Most of the park is difficult to access (4WDs are near-compulsory) and has limited facilities. The rangers hang out at the **Balcanoona Park Office** (☎ 8648 0049), 99km from Copley.

Sights & Activities

From the park's entrance it's 22km to **Italowie Gorge**, which has two campsites with self-registration. At Balcanoona, information signs in the big old shearing shed detail the park's cultural and natural history.

Grindells Hut is in a striking area with expansive views and stark ridges all around. You can reach it on a 4WD track off the Arkaroola road or by walking through **Weetootla Gorge**. The hike is worthwhile, but it's 13km return (you might want to stay the night at Grindells Hut; see below); if you leave early in the morning you've a good chance of seeing yellow-footed rock wallabies. Check with the ranger before attempting to drive or walk in this area.

Sleeping

There are six **bush-camping areas** (per car $5) including Italowie Gorge, Grindells Hut, Weetootla Gorge and Arcoona Bluff. Pick up camping permits at Balcanoona Park HQ. Two huts can be booked at the ranger's office: **Grindells Hut** (up to 8 people $120) and **Balcanoona Shearer's Quarters** (up to 18 people $220). These prices give you exclusive use of the huts, regardless of how many people are staying. You'll need a 4WD to get to Grindells Hut.

See also Iga Warta (opposite).

FLINDERS RANGES

ABORIGINAL AUSTRALIA: IGA WARTA

About 60km east of Copley on the way into Vulkathunha-Gammon Ranges National Park is a superb, Indigenous-run place.

our pick **Iga Warta** (☎ 8648 3737; www.igawarta.com; Arkaroola Rd; unpowered sites $22, tents/bunkhouses/cabins/safari tents d $36/36/104/150, tours $75-138, cultural experiences $25-52; ⬚ ⬚) Iga Warta offers 4WD and bushwalking tours, and cultural experiences focusing on the surrounding country and Indigenous history. Bush-tucker walks and campfire stories are conducted by members of the Coulthard family, who founded this centre based on their father's vision to share their Adnyamathanha culture with all Australians. Accommodation is open to all comers (the safari tents are lovely!).

Immediately after Iga Warta is **Nepabunna**, an Adnyamathanha community that manages the land just before the park.

ARKAROOLA

Once a sheep station and now a privately operated wildlife reserve and tourist resort, **Arkaroola Wilderness Sanctuary** (☎ 1800 676 042, 8648 4848; www.arkaroola.com.au) is a far-flung (129km east of Copley on unsealed roads) and utterly spectacular part of the Flinders Ranges. The **visitors centre** (⊗ 9am-5pm) has displays on local natural history, including a scientific explanation of the tremors that often shake things up hereabouts (there's a seismological recording station here too).

At the tour desk at reception you can book guided or tag-along **tours** (drives and walks), or you can express your individuality over 100km of graded, generally single-lane tracks. Most areas are accessible in a 2WD car, with some hiking to pump up your pulse. If you're feeling *really* physical there's a web of cool **bushwalks** here too; brochures are available from the visitors centre.

The absolute must-do highlight of Arkaroola is the four-hour 4WD **Ridgetop Tour** (per person $99) through wild mountain country, complete with white-knuckle climbs and descents towards the freakish Sillers Lookout. Once you've extracted your fingernails from your seat, look for wedge-tailed eagles and yellow-footed rock wallabies. Alternatively, stargaze at galaxies far, far away on the **Tour the Universe** (per person $40) observatory tour, where you peek through high-powered telescopes. You can also take a **scenic flights** (per person from $99) here, swooping over Lake Frome or winging as far afield as Innamincka's Dig Tree.

The **resort** (☎ 1800 676 042, 8648 4848; www.arkaroola.com.au; Arkaroola Rd Camp; unpowered/powered sites $15/20, cabins $40, lodges $65-175; ⬚ ⬚) includes a motel complex and caravan park. Campsites range from dusty hilltop spots to creekside corners. Comfortable cabins are a good budget bet, while air-con lodges are a self-contained paradise. Other facilities include a woody bar-restaurant (mains $15 to $30, open for breakfast, lunch and dinner), a small supermarket and a service station.

Adelaide to Erldunda: Stuart Highway

No doubt about it: the Adelaide-to-Darwin drive up the middle of central Australia is a classic Australian road trip. The South Australian leg starts with a seductive swing through the vineyards of the Clare Valley, then a dash up Hwy 1 to Port Augusta, from where the Stuart Hwy shoots gun-barrel straight into the desert.

Far less commercial and brassy than the Barossa Valley further south, the Clare Valley produces some of the world's best Riesling. Here in the Mid North – perhaps South Australia's most underrated region – charismatic sandstone villages crop up unexpectedly among rounded hills, patchwork wheaten plains, tilled fields and ranks of grapevines under the sun.

Back on Hwy 1, Port Augusta squats at the base of the Flinders Ranges, looking optimistically at the highway and wondering if anyone's going to stop today. In fact, someone usually does – the 'Crossroads of Australia' has become a busy conference venue, with more motels than you can poke a pillow at. The town's revitalised Spencer Gulf waterfront is an added drawcard.

But what this chapter (and indeed this book) is really about is the Big Drive North. Heading into the red heart of Australia on the Stuart Hwy, Woomera is the first pit stop, with its dark legacy of nuclear tests and shiny collection of leftover rockets. Further north, the opal-mining town of Coober Pedy is an absolute one-off: a desolate human aberration amid the blistering, arid plains. If you're feeling gung-ho, tackle a section of the iconic Oodnadatta Track, a rugged outback alternative to the Stuart Hwy tarmac. Along the way are warm desert springs, the gargantuan Lake Eyre and some amazing old outback pubs.

HIGHLIGHTS

- Knock-knock-knocking on cellar doors as you pedal along the Clare Valley **Riesling Trail** (p134)
- Wondering how the hell they managed to collect all this stuff at Mintaro's **Martindale Hall** (p134)
- Bending your elbow at the bar of the famous **Rising Sun Hotel** (p134) in Auburn
- Checking out the collection of leftover military paraphernalia in **Woomera** (p139)
- Noodling through the mullock for opals in **Coober Pedy** (p141)
- Ogling the vivid colours of the **Painted Desert** (p143)
- Deflating your tyres a tad for a smoother ride along the rough 'n' ready **Oodnadatta Track** (p145)
- Stopping at the **South Australia/Northern Territory border** (p146) and wondering how on Earth you ended up here…

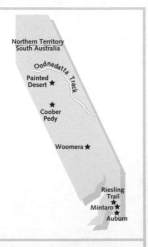

- TELEPHONE CODE: ☎ 08
- www.clarevalley.com.au
- www.opalcapitaloftheworld.com.au

National Parks
Department for Environment & Heritage
(☎ 1800 816 078; www.environmen t.sa.gov.au/parks; 9am-5pm Mon-Fri) Adelaide (☎ 08-8821 2270; 91-97 Grenfell St); Clare (☎ 08-8841 3400; 6/17 Lennon St); Port Augusta (☎ 08-8648 5300; upstairs, 9 MacKay St; 9am-5pm Mon-Fri) Contact point for regional park information.

The best way to explore the outback environment is to purchase a **Desert Parks Pass** (www.environment.sa.gov.au/parks/visitor/desertPrice .html; per car $105), allowing access to nine outback parks, with a map and handbook included. Aside from the DEH offices listed above, passes are available online or from the following outlets:

Mt Dare Hotel (☎ 08-8670 7835; Mt Dare, Witjira National Park)

Pink Roadhouse (p145) In Oodnadatta.

Royal Automobile Association of South Australia (p47) In Adelaide.

Russ Driver & Co (☎ 08-8952 1087; 58 Sargent St, Alice Springs)

Teague's Hawker Motors & visitors centre (p123) In Hawker.

Trading Post (☎ 08-8675 9900; Innamincka)

Underground Books (p141) In Coober Pedy.

Wadlata Outback Centre (p137) In Port Augusta.

Tours
Outback tours are a great way to go, particularly if you're not used to driving epic offroad distances. Clare Valley tours are much less challenging! The following options are all ex-Adelaide; see p54 for more. Other tours depart Port Augusta (see p137) and Coober Pedy (p143).

Arabunna Tours (☎ 08-8675 8351; www .southaustralia.com/S9008383.aspx; 7-day tour $1050) Aboriginal-owned company offering cultural tours from Adelaide to the Flinders Ranges, Marree, Oodnadatta Track and Lake Eyre.

Big Country Safaris (☎ 08-8538 7105; www.big countrysafaris.com.au; 12-day tour from $1860) Operator offering small-group outback-camping 4WD tours that take in the Simpson Desert, Coober Pedy and the Birdsville Track.

Bookabee Tours (☎ 08-8235 9954, 0408-209 593; www.bookabee.com.au; 4-/5-day tours $1930/2380) Highly rated Indigenous-run tours to the Flinders Ranges and outback, including quality accommodation, meals, cultural tours, activities & interpretation.

Clare Valley Experiences (☎ 08-8842 1880; www .clarevalleyexperiences.com; tours up to 4 people $220)

Choose-your-own-adventure Clare tours in a flash Merc to stretch your hedonistic muscles.

Clare Valley Tours (☎ 08-8843 8066, 0418-832 812; www.cvtours.com.au; 4/6hr tours $86/100) Minibus tours through the Mid North, taking in the Clare wineries, Martindale Hall and Burra.

Great Australian Cattle Drive (☎ 08-8303 2220; www.cattledrive.com.au) In 2010 this epic outback cattle drive will hoof through Coober Pedy, Marree and William Creek. Planning was in the early stages at the time of research; check the website for updates on how to participate.

Just Cruisin 4WD Tours (☎ 08-8383 0962; www .justcruisin4wdtours.com.au; 13-day tour $6650) Aboriginal cultural tours visiting outback Indigenous communities, sites and guides en route from Adelaide to Uluru (Ayers Rock). A 25-day epic Adelaide-to-Darwin tour is also on the cards ($8500).

Swagabout Tours (☎ 0408-845 378; www.swagabout tours.com.au) Dependable tours with the option of staying in hotels or camping under the stars. Its Adelaide-to–Alice Springs trips (five-/seven-/nine-/10-day tours camping $1350/1850/2400/2690, in hotels $1920/2675/3450/3850) take in the Clare Valley, Flinders Ranges, Oodnadatta Track, Dalhousie Springs and Uluru. It also runs one-/two-day Clare Valley trips ($120/440).

Other major operators plying outback routes:
Adventure Tours Australia (☎ 1300 654 604, 8132 8130; www.adventuretours.com.au)

Groovy Grape (☎ 1800 661 177, 8440 1640; www .groovygrape.com.au)

Wayward Bus (☎ 1300 653 510, 8132 8230; www .waywardbus.com.au)

Getting There & Away
AIR
Regional Express (☎ 13 17 13; www.regionalexpress.com .au) flies daily between Adelaide and Coober Pedy ($199, two hours).

BUS
Premier Stateliner (☎ 08-8415 5555; www.premier stateliner.com.au) buses run at least twice daily from Adelaide to Port Augusta ($47, four hours). From Port Augusta, buses continue to Whyalla ($19, one hour) and Port Lincoln ($65, 4½ hours) and Ceduna ($108, 6½ hours). Note: Ceduna buses only run on Monday, Wednesday, Thursday and Friday.

Yorke Peninsula Coaches (☎ 08-8821 2755; www .ypcoaches.com.au) depart Adelaide daily for Auburn ($21, 2¼ hours) and Clare ($29, 2¾ hours), extending to Burra ($29, 3¼

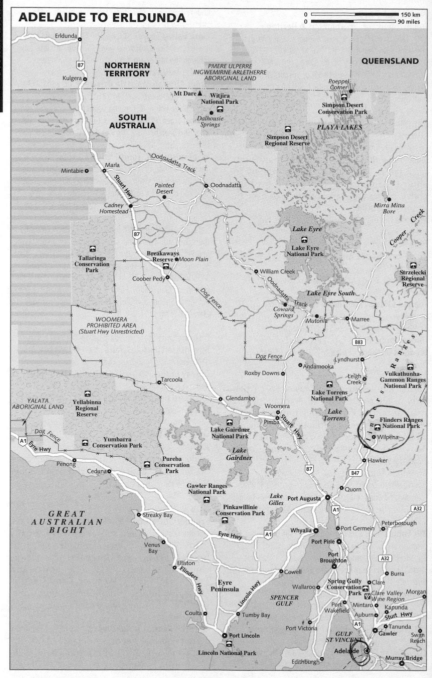

ADELAIDE TO ERLDUNDA

0 — 150 km
0 — 90 miles

Erldunda

87

NORTHERN TERRITORY

Kulgera

PMERE ULPERRE INGWEMIRNE ARLETHERRE ABORIGINAL LAND

QUEENSLAND

Mt Dare ▲ Witjira National Park

Poeppel Corner

SOUTH AUSTRALIA

Dalhousie Springs

Simpson Desert Conservation Park

PLAYA LAKES

Marla

Oodnadatta Track

Simpson Desert Regional Reserve

Mintabie

Painted Desert

Oodnadatta

Mirra Mitta Bore

Cooper Creek

Cadney Homestead

87

Lake Eyre

Lake Eyre National Park

Tallaringa Conservation Park

Breakaways Reserve ●Moon Plain

Dog Fence

Coober Pedy

● William Creek

Oodnadatta Track

Strzelecki Regional Reserve

Lake Eyre South

WOOMERA PROHIBITED AREA (Stuart Hwy Unrestricted)

Coward Springs

Mutonia

Marree

B83

Dog Fence

Lyndhurst

Vulkathunha-Gammon Ranges National Park

Tarcoola

Roxby Downs

● Andamooka

Leigh Creek

YALATA ABORIGINAL LAND

Yellabinna Regional Reserve

Glendambo

Woomera

Pimba

Lake Torrens National Park

Lake Torrens

Flinders Ranges National Park

Dog Fence

A1

Eyre Hwy

Yumbarra Conservation Park

● Wilpena

Penong

Ceduna

Pureba Conservation Park

Lake Gairdner National Park

Lake Gairdner

● Hawker

87

B47

GREAT AUSTRALIAN BIGHT

Gawler Ranges National Park

Pinkawillinie Conservation Park

Lake Gilles

Port Augusta

Quorn

A1

A32

Streaky Bay

Eyre Hwy

Whyalla

● Port Germein

Peterborough

Venus Bay

A1

Port Pirie

A32

Elliston

Flinders Hwy

Cowell

Port Broughton

● Burra

Eyre Peninsula

Lincoln Hwy

Wallaroo

Spring Gully Conservation Park

Clare

Clare Valley Wine Region

Morgan

Coulta

Tumby Bay

SPENCER GULF

Port Wakefield

Mintaro

Kapunda

Auburn

Stuart Hwy

Port Lincoln

Port Victoria

GULF ST VINCENT

● Tanunda

Gawler

Swan Reach

Lincoln National Park

A1

Edithburgh

Adelaide

Murray Bridge

hours) on Monday and Thursday. Buses also run between Port Augusta and Quorn ($6, 45 minutes).

Greyhound Australia (☎ 1300 473 946; www .greyhound.com.au) operates daily coaches from Adelaide to Alice Springs ($280, 19½ hours), stopping at Pimba ($119, seven hours), Glendambo ($132, 8¼ hours) and Coober Pedy ($168, 10½ hours). Internet fares are much reduced (eg Coober Pedy $94; Alice Springs $157).

CAR & MOTORCYCLE
Hwy 1 runs north from Adelaide to Port Augusta, continuing north into the Northern Territory as the Stuart Hwy. Fuel and accommodation facilities are dotted along the highway at Pimba (171km from Port Augusta), Glendambo (285km), Coober Pedy (535km), Cadney Homestead (689km), Marla (771km) and Kulgera in the NT (949km). Pimba, Coober Pedy and Marla have 24-hour fuel sales. The unsealed Oodnadatta Track (p145) links Marla with Marree in the northern Flinders Ranges. See p308 for outback driving tips.

To access the Clare Valley, head for Gawler then take route 32, which becomes the Barrier Hwy into NSW.

TRAIN
The famous *Ghan* train connects Adelaide with Darwin via Port Augusta and Alice Springs. The *Indian Pacific* (between Perth and Sydney) connects with the *Ghan* at Port Augusta. See p303 for details.

For a more scenic trip, **Pichi Richi Railway** (☎ 1800 440 101, 08-8648 6598; www.prr.org.au; one-way adult/concession/child/family $45/42/17/107) runs the 2½ hour journey between Port Augusta and Quorn in the Flinders Ranges on Saturdays.

CLARE VALLEY

Before you hit the main highway north, take a couple of days to check out the Clare Valley, about two hours north of Adelaide. At the centre of the fertile Mid North agricultural district, the skinny valley produces world-class Rieslings and reds. This is gorgeous countryside, with open skies, rounded hills, stands of large gums and wind rippling over wheat fields. The towns around here date from the 1840s, many built to service the Burra copper mines.

Accommodation
Refurbished B&Bs and self-contained cottages prevail around the valley, but unless you get a good package try and avoid staying here on weekends; Friday and Saturday night rates verge on outright greed.

AUBURN
pop 320
Sleepy, 1849 Auburn – the Clare Valley's southernmost village – is a leave-the-back-door-open-and-the-keys-in-the-ignition kinda town, with a time-warp vibe that makes you feel like you're in an old black-and-white photograph. The streets are defined by beautifully preserved, hand-built stone buildings, and cottage gardens overflow with untidy blooms. Pick up a copy of the *Walk With History at Auburn* brochure from the Clare visitors centre (p135).

Now on the main route to the valley's wineries, Auburn initially serviced bullockies and South American muleteers whose wagons – up to 100 a day – trundled between Burra's copper mines and Port Wakefield.

Clare Valley's largest winery **Taylors Wines** (see p135) lurks on the edge of town, while the brilliant 25km **Riesling Trail** (p134) starts (or ends) at the restored Auburn train station.

Cogwebs (☎ 8849 2380; www.cogwebs.com.au; 30 Main North Rd; ⏰ 8am-6pm Thu-Tue) offers internet access (per 30 minutes/hour $4/6) and bike hire (per half-/full day $25/40).

Sleeping & Eating
Auburn Shiraz Motel (☎ 8849 2125; www.auburnshiraz motel.com.au; Main North Rd; s $68-78, d $80-90; ⚡) This small motel on the Adelaide side of town has been proudly renovated with Shiraz-coloured render and Cabernet-coloured doors. There are nine bright, spotless units and friendly hosts – great value.

Amy's House (☎ 0408-492 281; www.amyshouse.com .au; cnr Church & Elder Sts; d $190; ⚡) A short walk to the Rising Sun Hotel, Amy's comprises two self-contained, corrugated-iron units with yolk-yellow shutters and wood heaters. Attached to the owner's house across the street is the bourgeois Autumn Suite – a roomy motel-style option. Multinight specials stoop as low as $120 per night. Wireless internet available; breakfast provisions supplied.

Rising Sun Hotel (☎ 8849 2015; rising@capri.net.au; Main North Rd; mains $14-18; ☷ lunch & dinner; ☒) This classic 1850 pub has a huge rep for its atmosphere, food and accommodation. En suite hotel rooms and cottage mews rooms out the back (doubles from $90/115 respectively) have solid occupancy – book well in advance (dinner and overnight packages a speciality). The pub food is unpretentious but unremarkable, and (disconcertingly) there was only one Clare Valley wine available by the glass when we visited.

Cygnets at Auburn (☎ 8849 2030; www.cygnetsatauburn.com.au; Main North Rd; mains $18-29; ☷ breakfast & lunch daily, dinner Thu-Sun Dec-Mar, Fri & Sat Apr-Nov; ☒) This gourmet restaurant/provedore serves and stocks local produce matched with Clare Valley wines. There's a wine-and-tapas bar for grazers, the best coffee in town, and delicious mains such as caramelised pear and blue cheese bruschetta. A good-value B&B wing is out the back (from $120 midweek).

MINTARO
pop 230

A few kilometres up the road from Auburn, heritage-listed Mintaro (founded 1849) is a stone village that could have been lifted out of the Cotswolds (England) and plonked into the Australian bush. There are very few architectural intrusions from the '40s, '50s, '60s or '70s – the whole place seems to have been largely left to its own devices through the last century. A fact for your next trivia night: Mintaro slate is used internationally in the manufacture of billiard tables.

Hedge your bets at **Mintaro Maze** (☎ 8843 9012; www.mintaromaze.com; Jacka Rd; adult/child $7/5; ☷ 10am-4pm Mon-Thu & school holidays) as you try and find your way into the middle and back out again.

There's nowhere else in the world quite like **Martindale Hall** (☎ 8843 9088; www.martindalehall.com; Manoora Rd; adult/concession/child $10/7.50/2.50; ☷ 11am-4pm Mon-Fri, noon-4pm Sat & Sun), an astonishing 1880 manor 3km from Mintaro. Built for young pastoralist Edmund Bowman Jnr who subsequently partied away the family fortune (OK, so drought and plummeting wool prices played a part…but it was mostly the partying), the manor features original furnishings, a magnificent blackwood staircase, Mintaro-slate billiard table and a museumlike smoking room. The hall starred as Appleyard College in the 1975 Peter Weir film *Picnic at*

THE RIESLING TRAIL

Following the course of a disused railway line between Auburn and Clare, the fabulous **Riesling Trail** (www.southaustraliantrails.com.au) is 25km of wines, wheels & wonderment. It's primarily a cycling trail, but the gentle gradient means you can walk or push a pram along it just as easily. It's a two-hour dash end-to-end on a bike, but why hurry? There are three loop-track detours to explore and dozens of cellar doors to tempt you along the way.

Clare Valley Taxis (☎ 0419-847 900) can drop you off or pick you up anywhere along the trail. For bike hire, see Clare Valley Cycle Hire (opposite) and Cogwebs (p133).

Hanging Rock. B&B and DB&B packages allow you to spend a spooky night here ($110 and $230 respectively; *Mirandaaa…*).

Sleeping & Eating

The Clare visitors centre (opposite) can help with Mintaro accommodation suggestions and bookings. Martindale Hall (left) also has accommodation.

Mintaro Mews (☎ 8843 9001; www.chariot.net.au/~minmews; Burra St; d $145-210; ☒ ☒) Often the first place in Mintaro to get booked out, this quaint retreat has a variety of rustic motelstyle rooms and a restaurant (three courses $45, open for dinner) with a self-select wine cellar. Accommodation and meal packages are great value.

our pick **Magpie & Stump Hotel** (☎ 8843 9014; Burra St; meals $7-25; ☷ lunch daily, dinner Mon-Sat) The old Magpie & Stump was first licensed in 1851, and was a vital rehydration point for the copper carriers travelling between Burra and Port Wakefield. Schnitzels and steaks, log fires, pool table, Mintaro slate floors, a beer garden and a lazy black dog – the perfect pub?

Reilly's Wines & Restaurant (☎ 8843 9013; www.reillyswines.com; Burra St; mains $15-25; ☷ 10am-5pm; ☒) Reilly's started life as a shop for an Irish cobbler in 1856, and has been a winery since the '90s. An organic veggie garden out the back supplies the attached restaurant, which is decorated with local art and serves creative Mod Oz (antipasto, rabbit terrine, veggie lasagne). The owners also rent out a three-bedroom house and three one-bedroom units on Hill St (doubles from $130).

CLARE
pop 3070

Named after County Clare in Ireland, this 1842 town is the biggest in the valley, but it's a little thin on charm. All the requisite services are here (post, supermarket, fuel, internet etc), but you'll have a more interesting Clare experience sleeping out of town.

Information

Clare Valley visitors centre (☎ 1800 242 131, 8842 2131; www.clarevalley.com.au; cnr Spring Gully & Main North Rd; ☯ 9am-5pm Mon-Fri, 10am-4pm Sat & Sun; 🖳) This shiny new centre has local info and internet access, and handles accommodation bookings.

Domain Internet Café (☎ 8842 4166; 202 Main North Rd; per 15min $3; ☯ 2.30-5.30pm Mon-Fri) Internet access.

Sights & Activities

Most folks are here for the wine, but Clare does have some worthy heritage-listed buildings. Pick up the *Clare Historic Walk* pamphlet from the visitors centre.

The 1850 cop-shop and courthouse is now the **Old Police Station Museum** (☎ 8842 2376; www.nationaltrustsa.org.au; adult/concession/child $2/1.50/50c; ☯ 10am-noon & 2-4pm Sat & Sun), displaying Victorian clothing, old photos, furniture and domestic bits and pieces.

Festivals here are big fun: the **Clare Valley Gourmet Weekend** (☎ 8843 4222; www.southaustralia.com) in May is a frenzy of wine, food and music, while the **Clare Show** (☎ 8842 2374) in October is the largest one-day show in SA.

About 3km southwest of Sevenhill, the 400-hectare **Spring Gully Conservation Park** (☎ 8892 3025; www.environment.sa.gov.au/parks/sanpr/springully; admission free) features blue-gum forest, red stringybarks and 18m-high winter waterfalls. There are plenty of bird twitters, critters and trails too.

Hit the **Riesling Trail** (opposite) with **Clare Valley Cycle Hire** (☎ 8842 2782, 0418-802 077; www.clarevalleycyclehire.com.au; 32 Victoria Rd; bike hire per half/full day $17/25; ☯ 8am-5pm). The operators will also collect and freight any wine you buy en route – bless their cotton socks!

Sleeping & Eating

Clare Caravan Park (☎ 8842 2724; www.clarecaravanpark.com.au; Main North Rd; unpowered/powered sites $20/27, cabins from $80; ☯ 🖳) This huge, dogmatically run park 4km south of town towards Auburn has

---

TOP FIVE CLARE VALLEY WINERIES

Despite a warm climate, the Clare Valley's cool microclimates (around rivers, creeks and gullies) noticeably affect the wines, enabling Clare Valley whites to be laid down for long periods and still be brilliant. The valley produces some of the best Riesling going around, plus grand Semillon and Shiraz. Our favourite cellar doors:

■ **Annie's Lane** (☎ 8843 2204; www.annieslane.com.au; Quelltaler Rd, Watervale; ☯ 9am-5pm Mon-Fri, 10am-4pm Sat & Sun) Annie's flagship wines are Copper Trail Shiraz and Riesling. The attached winery museum and art gallery contain personal touches such as the VE Day closure notice from WWII.

■ **Knappstein** (☎ 8842 2600; www.knappsteinwines.com.au; 2 Pioneer Ave, Clare; ☯ 9am-5pm Mon-Fri, 11am-5pm Sat, to 4pm Sun) Taking a minimal-intervention approach to winemaking, Knappstein has built quite a name for itself. Shiraz and Riesling steal the show, but it also makes a mighty fine Semillon–Sauvignon Blanc blend (and beer!).

■ **Pikes** (☎ 8843 4370; www.pikeswines.com.au; Polish Hill River Rd, Sevenhill; ☯ 10am-4pm) The industrious Pike family has been producing wine since 1886, so they know a thing or two about Riesling (and Shiraz, Sangiovese, Pinot Grigio, Viognier…). A beautiful cellar door, with Bella the wine dog.

■ **Skillogalee** (☎ 8843 4311; www.skillogalee.com; Trevarrick Rd, Sevenhill; ☯ 10am-5pm) Quite possibly our favourite SA winery (OK, so it is our favourite), Skillogalee is a small family outfit known for its spicy Shiraz, fabulous food and top-notch Riesling (a glass of which is like a summer kiss). Kick back with a long, lazy lunch on the veranda (mains $20 to $30). There's some classy accommodation here too (see p136).

■ **Taylors Wines** (☎ 8849 1111; www.taylorswines.com.au; Taylors Rd, Auburn; ☯ 9am-5pm Mon-Fri, 10am-5pm Sat, 10am-4pm Sun) Sure, it's a massive nation-wide operation with a heinous mock-castle cellar door, but the wine here is fit for royalty (love the Cab Sav).

DETOUR: BURRA

Bursting at the seams with historic sites, **Burra** (population 1110), 43km northeast of Clare, was a copper-mining boomtown with a burgeoning Cornish community between 1847 and 1877. Towns such as Mintaro and Auburn serviced miners travelling between Burra and Port Wakefield, from where the copper was shipped. The miners had it tough here, excavating dugouts for themselves and their families to live in.

Burra visitors centre (☎ 8892 2154; www.visitburra.com; 2 Market Sq; ☒ 9am-5pm) sells the self-guided Burra Heritage Pass ($20) providing admission (via a key) to eight historic sights, and the Burra Museum Pass ($15). A two-pass combo costs $30. The visitors centre also handles bike hire (per half/full day $35/20) and accommodation bookings.

---

secluded sites, all en suite cabins, a creek and giant gum trees. There's also an in-ground pool and bike hire (per day $25).

Clare Valley Cabins (☎ 8842 1155; www.clarevalley cabins.com.au; Hubbe Rd; d from $99; ☒) At this 52-acre property 6km north of Clare, secluded cabins come in a variety of packages with breakfast and barbecue provisions. It also has an 1860 stone chapel to sleep/pray/confess in (double from $120 per night).

Clare Valley Motel (☎ 8842 2799; clarevalleymotel@ bigpond.com; 74a Main North Rd; d $105-154; ☒ ☒) Looking like some kind of ranch from Vermont, this huge place has four different wings, offering basic motel rooms up to swish spa suites. The restaurant (mains $25 to $27) serves dinner nightly (except Sunday). Wireless internet available.

Batunga B&B (☎ 8843 0120; www.battunga.com.au; Watervale; d incl breakfast $160, extra adult/child $50/40) On a 200-acre farm over the hills 2km west of Watervale (it's a little hard to find – ask for directions), Batunga has four modern apartments in two stone cottages with Mintaro slate floors, barbecues, kitchenettes and wood fires. This is beautiful country – undulating farmland studded with huge eucalypts.

our pick Skillogalee (☎ 8843 4270; www.skillo galee.com; Trevarrick Rd, Sevenhill; d incl breakfast $190-350; ☒ ☒) Not far from Skillogalee's cellar door and restaurant (p135) is a luxurious three-bedroom stone house and two hillside cedar cottages sleeping four and six. Rates drop the longer you stay and the more people you cram in – grab some mates and treat yourself!

Citadel (☎ 8842 1453; Main North Rd; mains $12-18; ☒ lunch Sat & Sun, dinner Wed-Sun; ☒) Before it was an upmarket pizza joint, an old bloke lived here with no electricity and dirt floors! Things have improved: expect tasty pasta and even better pizzas. Takeaways welcome.

Clare Hotel (☎ 8842 2816; 244 Main North Rd; mains $13-25; ☒ lunch & dinner) The Clare (aka the 'Middle Pub') cooks up the best pub food in town, to the blaring soundtrack of horse racing and TVs simultaneously showing all available channels. There are also budget pub rooms upstairs (single/double $30/70) with shared bathrooms.

Salt n Vines Bar & Bistro (☎ 8842 1796; Wendouree Rd; mains $22-48; ☒ lunch & dinner; ☒) This mod, airy hillside bar-restaurant has a broad, sunny balcony – the perfect setting for a bottle of local Riesling and an indulgent seafood platter for two (surprisingly good this far inland!). Kids' menu and grown-up desserts, too.

HIGHWAY ONE

There's not much along this route to grab your attention, but Hwy 1 is the quickest route north to the Stuart Hwy. Take Main North Rd from North Adelaide (the extension of O'Connell St, which then becomes Port Wakefield Rd) and just keep on going! Tyre warehouses and motels soon give way to market gardens then wheat fields.

Between 1847 and 1877, **Port Wakefield** (population 600) was where the copper miners from Burra (above) delivered their payload to waiting ships. These days a spill of ugly roadhouses and fast-food joints makes the town a useful pit stop, but not much more than that. A billboard advertising a new retirement subdivision declares, 'Where the land ends, life begins!' – but we suspect it's the other way around…

Gargantuan lead- and zinc-smelting complexes and grain terminals dominate everything about **Port Pirie** (population 18,000): skyline, economy, culture, environment…

The best bet is to keep your foot down, and admire the bottom end of the Flinders Ranges cragging into view to the north.

The big-ticket item in **Port Germein** (population 250) at the head of Gulf St Vincent is Australia's longest straight wooden jetty (purportedly 1646m, but some sources say 1676m or 1680m – measure it yourself!). Tractors drag marooned boats back from the end of the jetty when the tide is out. It's a good spot for fishing, especially for blue swimmer crabs.

PORT AUGUSTA
pop 13,900

About 300km north of Adelaide at the top of Spencer Gulf (no more than a few hundred metres wide here), Port Augusta proudly calls itself the 'Crossroads of Australia'. The town earned this moniker when shipping booms in the 1880s made it a trading hub, a position reinforced when it became HQ for the Perth–Sydney Transcontinental Railway. From here, highways roll west across the Nullarbor into Western Australia, north to Alice Springs and Darwin, south to Adelaide, and east to Broken Hill and Sydney.

A slew of fast-food joints and petrol stations and a huge prison greet you as you arrive from the south, but the old town centre (southwest off Victoria Pde) has much more appeal, with some elegant old buildings and a revitalised waterfront: locals cast lines into the blue, and Indigenous kids back-flip off jetties. The town has had problems with drinking on the streets (which remain a dry zone), but the vibe is far from menacing.

Information
Department for Environment & Heritage
(☎ 8648 5300; upstairs, 9 Mackay St; ☼ 9am-5pm Mon-Fri) Information, maps and road-condition updates for the Flinders Ranges and outback.
Port Augusta Hospital (☎ 8648 5500; www.country healthsa.sa.gov.au; Hospital Rd; ☼ 24hr) Accident and emergency.
Port Augusta Public Library (☎ 8641 9151; 4 Mackay St; ☼ 9am-6pm Mon-Wed & Fri, to 8pm Thu, 10am-1pm Sat, 2-5pm Sun) Free internet access; booking required.
Port Augusta visitors centre (☎ 8641 9193; www .portaugusta.sa.gov.au; 41 Flinders Tce; ☼ 9am-5.30pm Mon-Fri, 10am-4pm Sat & Sun) Inside the Wadlata Outback Centre, this is the major information outlet for the Flinders Ranges, outback and Eyre Peninsula.

Sights & Activities
The highlights of the **Wadlata Outback Centre** (☎ 8641 9193; www.wadlata.sa.gov.au; 41 Flinders Tce; adult/concession/child/family $11/10/7/24.50; ☼ 9am-5.30pm Mon-Fri, 10am-4pm Sat & Sun) are the old transcontinental train carriage and the Outback Tunnel of Time, tracing Aboriginal and European histories using audiovisual displays, interactive exhibits and a distressingly big snake. Next door is the **Fountain Gallery** (☎ 8641 9175; www.portaugusta.sa.gov.au; 43 Flinders Tce; admission free; ☼ 10am-4pm Mon-Sat), an intimate space in a gracious old stone house showing works by local and Indigenous artists.

Just north of town the excellent **Australian Arid Lands Botanic Garden** (☎ 8641 1049; www .australian-aridlands-botanic-garden.org; Stuart Hwy; admission free; ☼ 9am-5pm Mon-Fri, 10am-4pm Sat & Sun) has 250 hectares of sandhills, clay flats and desert fauna. You can explore on your own, or take a guided tour (tours 10am Monday to Friday, adult/concession/child $6.50/6/5).

Port Augusta Aquatic & Outdoor Adventure Centre (☎ 8642 2699, 0427-722 450; paa.oac@bigpond.com; cnr Gibson & El Alamein Sts; ☼ 8am-8pm Oct-Mar, by appointment Apr-Sep) has lessons and gear rental for kayaking, windsurfing, fishing, rock-climbing, abseiling, snorkelling, orienteering, bushwalking, sailing…

On Saturdays, trainspotters can hitch a ride on the **Pichi Richi Railway** (☎ 1800 440 101, 8648 6598; www.prr.org.au; return adult/concession/child/family $71/66/23/16) between Port Augusta and Quorn. It's a 2½ hour journey each way.

For a local history hit, grab the two-hour *Heritage Walk* brochure from the visitors centre, taking in historic sites such as the Troopers Barracks (1860) and Corinthian-columned Town Hall (1887).

Tours
Blue Emu Tours (☎ 0439-346 120; www.blueemu tours.com.au) Half- and full-day Flinders Ranges tours ($98/180), plus Port Augusta area tours ($55 per hour).
Flinders Ranges Water Cruises (☎ 8642 2488, 0438-857 001; www.augustawestside.com.au; cruises per person from $45) Two-hour morning eco-cruises to the top of the Gulf, and two-hour sunset cruises with a Flinders Ranges focus. 'Cruise & Snooze' packages available with Comfort Inn Augusta Westside (see p138).
Gulf Getaways (☎ 8642 6827, 0408-445 133; www .gulfgetaways.com.au; 12-14 Victoria Pde; per person cruises incl lunch $45) Runs a 2½-hour eco-cruise on the Spencer Gulf, checking out mangroves, dolphins and birdlife.

Wallaby Tracks Adventure Tours (☎ 0428-486 655; www.wallabytracks.com) Small-group 4WD tours through the Southern Flinders Ranges (half-day $110) or extending north to Wilpena Pound (full day $160), departing Port Augusta.

Sleeping

Shoreline Caravan Park (☎ 8642 2965; www.shore linecaravanpark.com.au; Gardiner Ave; unpowered/powered sites $22/25, dm/cabin $18/55, units $65-85; ⊠ ⓡ) It's a grassless, dusty site a fair way from town, but the budget cabins here are beaut, plus there are simple four-bed dorm units for budgeteers.

Hotel Flinders (☎ 8642 2544; www.thehotelflinders .com; 39 Commercial Rd; motel dm/s/d/tr $22/55/70/80; ⊠) This central, 130-year-old pub has a variety of basic rooms upstairs and some clean but weirdly configured motel rooms off to one side. Some of the pub rooms have private bathrooms, TVs and bar fridges. The Cena on Chapel dining room here (see right) is pretty good, too.

Augusta Hotel (☎ 8642 2701; hotelaugusta@hotmail .com; 1 Loudon Rd; s & d $50) Renovated upstairs pub rooms across the Gulf from town. The owners live on-site, so no funny business, OK? Not a bad bistro downstairs (mains $19 to $28, open for lunch and dinner).

Comfort Inn Augusta Westside (☎ 8642 2488; www.augustawestside.com.au; 3 Loudon Rd; s $99-165, d $115-165; ⊠ ⓡ) A U-shaped complex of 20 standard motel rooms, just across the skinny upper reach of Spencer Gulf from downtown PA. Excuse the floral bedspreads for free satellite TV, swimming pool and spas in the better rooms.

Best Western Standpipe (☎ 8642 4033; www.stand pipe.com.au; cnr Stuart Hwy & Hwy 1; s/d/tr/f/apt $115/1 25/135/160/240; ⊠ ▢ ⓡ) Attracting government delegates and business types with its comfortable 1980s-ish units, this must be the only accommodation in SA that charges less on weekends (singles and doubles $77 and $84 respectively). The staff are professional and friendly, the restaurant is awesome (right), and there's an 18-hole golf course next door.

Oasis Apartments (☎ 1800 008 648, 8648 9000; www.majestichotels.com.au; foreshore, Marryatt St; apt $135-190; ⊠ ▢ ⓡ) A group of 75 luxury units with jaunty designs, right by the water. All rooms have washing machines, dryers, TVs, fridges, microwaves and natty flashes of interior design (big grey floor tiles and lime-coloured laminex splashbacks). Nice one!

Eating

Hot Peppers (☎ 8642 2549; 34 Commercial Rd; meals $5-10; ✷ breakfast & lunch Mon-Sat; ⊠) A light-hearted, yellow-fronted local cafe serving homemade nosh such as quiches, doorstop sandwiches and salads, plus the best (only?) espresso in town.

Gottabe Fish (☎ 8641 3777; 6 Marryatt St; meals $7-14; ✷ lunch & dinner) Here at the top of Spencer Gulf, you expect quality seafood. This sweaty takeaway joint serves fresh kingfish, snapper, King George whiting, prawns, butterfish and Smoky Bay oysters, plus burgers, yiros and steak sandwiches.

Cena on Chapel (☎ 8642 2544; Hotel Flinders, 39 Commercial Rd; mains $15-25; ✷ lunch & dinner; ⊠) The enormous Hotel Flinders dining room assumes Italian graces, plating up lasagne, cannelloni, scaloppine, pizza and pasta done 12 ways (try the *puttanesca*: capers, anchovies, spring onions, chilli, olives and tomato).

our pick **Best Western Standpipe** (☎ 8642 4033; cnr Stuart Hwy & Hwy 1; mains $15-30; ✷ lunch & dinner; ⊠) Unbelievable! An authentic Indian restaurant (with Indian chefs) on the edge of the South Australian desert! Beneath the lofty ceilings of the Standpipe motel's dining room you can sweat it out over a sensational beef vindaloo or Malabar seafood curry, or trad steaks, schnitzels, kangaroo fillets and seafood. The best place to eat in Port Augusta, hands down.

Self-caterers can check out **Coles** (☎ 8642 6722; cnr Jervois & Marryatt Sts; ✷ 6am-10pm).

Entertainment

Cinema Augusta (☎ 8648 8999; www.countryarts.org .au; 9 Carlton Pl; tickets adult/child $13/9; ✷ Thu-Sun) screens all the big flicks, plus the occasional Australian Film Commission release or event.

STUART HIGHWAY

Tracking north from Port Augusta, the Stuart Hwy was named after explorer John McDouall Stuart, whose expeditions in SA and the NT took him through much of the country traversed by the highway today; you might hear the name 'Explorer's Way' used instead. You hit the NT border 930km from Port Augusta, after which it's 294km to Alice Springs. En route are some isolated, offbeat SA towns, worth a visit if not a holiday. On the highway, watch out for road trains and

ON THE ROAD AGAIN

Driving through the outback from Adelaide to Darwin (or the other way around) is a truly epic road trip – like the song goes, it's a wide open road! Here are our tips for the best beds, bites and musical accompaniments en route to keep the wheels a-turnin':

Sleepy?

- **Oasis Apartments** (opposite) A slick, urbane retreat on the Port Augusta waterfront.
- **Radeka's Downunder Underground Backpackers & Motel** (p143) A warren of underground motel rooms and dorms in Coober Pedy.
- **Desert Rose Inn** (p184) A purpose-built budget-motel winner in Alice Springs.
- **Mataranka Homestead Resort** (p217) Camping, dorm rooms, cabins and motel units – plus a thermal pool!
- **Mt Bundy Station** (p234) Horse-riding, fishing and country smiles near Adelaide River (oh, and beds too).

Hungry?

- **Best Western Standpipe** (opposite) Wildly satisfying Indian curries in Port Augusta.
- **Red Sand Art Gallery** (p207) Espresso coffee in the middle of nowhere (well, Ti Tree actually).
- **Wauchope Hotel** (p208) Excellent outback counter meals.
- **Fran's Devonshire Tea House** (p215) Swing into Fran's in Larrimah for Devonshire teas (how much like Devon is Larrimah?) and homemade camel and buffalo pies.
- **Lazy Lizard Tavern** (p232) Pine Creek's tavern is big on steaks and barra.

Crank It Up!

- *Gurrumul* by Geoffrey Gurrumul Yunupingu (2008) – Haunting, pared-back acoustica from Northeast Arnhem Land's favourite son, sung in his native Yolngu language
- *Diesel & Dust* by Midnight Oil (1988) – The definitive Oils album spotlights Indigenous land rights and the outback
- *Great Southern Land* by Icehouse (1982) – A nostalgia-evoking Australian classic
- *Blow* by Marshall Whyler (2000) – Hypnotic didgeridoo-trance album from the NT didge master
- *Wide Open Road* by the Triffids (1986) – A dreamy road song full of evocative imagery that'll send you up the highway feeling like you've done this before…

transporters hauling oversize mining equipment to Roxby Downs. Before you leave, pick up a copy of the *Australia's Explorer's Way* info map from Adelaide's South Australian Visitor & Travel Centre (p50).

WOOMERA

pop 300

An 8km detour off the Stuart Hwy from **Pimba** (485km from Adelaide), Woomera set up shop in 1946 as the headquarters for experimental British rocket and nuclear tests, exploded nearby at notorious sites such as Maralinga and Emu. Local Indigenous tribes suffered greatly from nuclear fallout. These days Woomera is a drab, oddly artificial government town that's been making news as a proposed low-level nuclear waste dump and for its controversial refugee detention centre (now closed). It remains an active Department of Defence test site.

In the middle of town, the small **Woomera Heritage Centre** (☎ 1300 761 620, 8673 7042; www .woomera.com.au; Dewrang Ave; adult/child $6/3; ⏱ 9am-5pm Mar-Nov, 10am-2pm Dec-Feb) doubles as the visitors centre and has interesting museum displays on Woomera's past and present roles. Out the front is the **Lions Club Aircraft & Missile Park**, studded with rocket remnants. Most of the rockets meet expectations, but some of the missiles are surprisingly small – amazing when you consider the damage they could wreak.

Continue north through Woomera for around 90km (sealed road) and you'll hit **Roxby Downs** (population 4500; www.roxby downs.com), a bizarrely affluent desert town servicing the massive Olympic Dam Mine, which digs up untold amounts of copper, silver, gold and (distressingly) uranium.

Sleeping & Eating

Woomera Travellers' Village (☎ 8673 7800; www .woomera.com; Old Pimba Rd; unpowered/powered sites $20/24, cabins & units $50-75; 🔀) This affable place near the town entrance has a well-maintained range of budget accommodation; the cheaper cabins and units share bathroom facilities. BYO linen.

Eldo Hotel (☎ 8673 7867; www.eldohotel.com.au; Kotara Ave; d with/without bathroom $90/80; 🔀 🔊) Originally built to house rocket scientists, the plush Eldo (an acronym for the European Launcher Development Organisation) has comfortable budget and motel-style rooms, and serves meaty à la carte meals in the bistro (mains $15 to $30, open for lunch & dinner): try the kangaroo bratwurst snags!

WOOMERA TO COOBER PEDY

Around 115km northwest of Pimba and 245km shy of Coober Pedy, middle-of-nowhere **Glendambo** (population 30) was invented in 1982 as a Stuart Hwy service centre. This is the last fuel stop before Coober Pedy: the red desert flattens out and the low scrub hunkers down under the sun…so fill up!

You can bunk down at the oasislike **Glendambo Hotel-Motel** (☎ 8672 1030; www.glen dambooutback4x4.com.au; Stuart Hwy; unpowered/powered sites $20/24, s/d $85/90; 🔀 🔊) which has bars, a restaurant and a bunch of decent motel units for road-weary bodies. Out the back are some campsites without a huge amount of shade (shoot through before things heat up).

North of Glendambo the Stuart Hwy enters the government-owned **Woomera Prohibited Area** – the highway itself is unrestricted, but don't go wanderin' now, y'hear?

COOBER PEDY

pop 3500

Coming into Coober Pedy the dry, barren desert suddenly becomes riddled with holes and adjunct piles of dirt – reputedly more than a million around the township. The reason for all this rabid digging is opals – the 'fire in the stone' that's made this small town a mining mecca. This isn't to say it's also a tourist mecca – with swarms of flies, no trees, 50°C summer days, subzero winter nights, cave-dwelling locals and rusty car wrecks in every second front yard, you might think you've arrived in a postapocalyptic shithole – but it sure is an interesting place!

Coober Pedy is actually very cosmopolitan, with 44 nationalities represented. Greeks, Serbs, Croats and Italians form sizeable groups among the mining community, Indians and Sri Lankans run accommodation, and gem buyers come from as far off as Scotland and Hong Kong. The surrounding desert is jaw-droppingly desolate – a fact not overlooked by international film makers who've come here to shoot 'end of the world' epics such as *Mad Max III, Red Planet, Ground Zero, Pitch Black* and the slightly more believable *The Adventures of Priscilla, Queen of the Desert*.

Few people make their living solely from mining here, so there's a lot of 'career diversification'. This means the dude who drives the shuttle bus to the airport also loads the baggage onto the plane, mans the hotel reception desk and works his opal claim on weekends (so he can retire from his other jobs!).

Information

There are a few ATM machines in businesses around town, plus a Westpac branch (with ATM) on Hutchison St.

BOOM TOWN

Burrowing through tonnes of subterranean rock in pursuit of opal-coloured dreams requires a certain amount of blasting. The ready access to dynamite here has sometimes caused local spats to become, well…explosive. Coober Pedy miners have become so adept at making 'sausages' (homemade bombs) that a sign at the old cinema said, 'Explosives are not to be brought into this theatre' (perhaps they just wanted action movies to be a little more interactive…). The odd opinionated letter to the editor has even has resulted in the blowing up of the local newspaper office. Such incidents are rare, but some locals will tell you the real reason for living underground in Coober Pedy is to make their homes better bomb shelters.

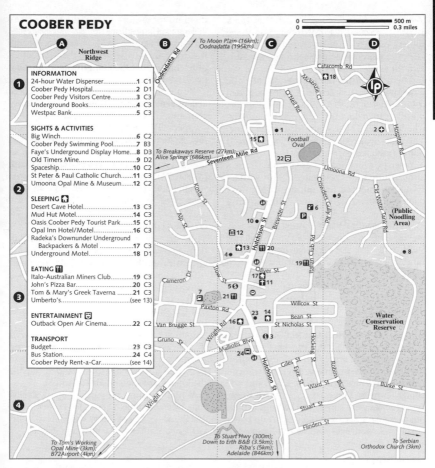

COOBER PEDY

0   500 m
0   0.3 miles

INFORMATION
24-hour Water Dispenser.................**1** C1
Coober Pedy Hospital....................**2** D1
Coober Pedy Visitors Centre...........**3** C3
Underground Books.......................**4** C3
Westpac Bank..............................**5** C3

SIGHTS & ACTIVITIES
Big Winch..................................**6** C2
Coober Pedy Swimming Pool...........**7** B3
Faye's Underground Display Home....**8** D3
Old Timers Mine..........................**9** D2
Spaceship..................................**10** C2
St Peter & Paul Catholic Church......**11** C3
Umoona Opal Mine & Museum......**12** C2

SLEEPING
Desert Cave Hotel........................**13** C3
Mud Hut Motel............................**14** C3
Oasis Coober Pedy Tourist Park......**15** C1
Opal Inn Hotel/Motel....................**16** C3
Radeka's Downunder Underground
  Backpackers & Motel..................**17** C3
Underground Motel.......................**18** D1

EATING
Italo-Australian Miners Club...........**19** C3
John's Pizza Bar...........................**20** C3
Tom & Mary's Greek Taverna **21** C3
Umberto's.................................(see 13)

ENTERTAINMENT
Outback Open Air Cinema..............**22** C2

TRANSPORT
Budget......................................**23** C3
Bus Station.................................**24** C4
Coober Pedy Rent-a-Car...............(see 14)

Northwest
Ridge

To Moon Plain (16km);
Oodnadatta (195km)

Catacomb Rd

To Breakaways Reserve (27km);
Alice Springs (686km)

Seventeen Mile Rd

To Tom's Working
Opal Mine (3km);
B72Airport (4km)

To Stuart Hwy (300km);
Down to Erth B&B (3.5km);
Riba's (5km);
Adelaide (846km)

To Serbian
Orthodox Church (3km)

24-hour water dispenser (Hutchison St; per 10L 20c) If you're headed into the desert, fill your canteens opposite the Oasis Tourist Park.

Coober Pedy Hospital (☎ 8672 5009; goddard.christine@asaugov.sa.gov.au; Hospital Rd; 24hr) Accident and emergency.

Coober Pedy visitors centre (☎ 1800 637 076, 8672 5298; www.opalcapitaloftheworld.com.au; Council offices, Hutchison St; 8.30am-5pm Mon-Fri, 10am-1pm Sat & Sun;) In addition to history displays and comprehensive tour and accommodation listings and prices, the centre offers visitors 30 minutes of free internet access.

Underground Books (☎ 8672 5558; undergroundbooks@bigpond.com; Post Office Hill Rd; 8.30am-5pm Mon-Fri, 10am-4pm Sat) The town's only bookshop also has loads of regional info.

Sights & Activities
OPAL MINING

Coober Pedy sweats with wide-eyed opal fever. The elusive gems are at the fore of everyone's consciousness, and there are hundreds of working mines around town – look for the telltale 'blowers' (big vacuum cleaners mounted on the backs of trucks) stirring up columns of white dust. If you're keen for a fossick, tour operators or locals may invite you out to their claim to 'noodle' through the mullock (waste pile) for stones. Watch out for unmarked shafts, and never wander around the fields at night.

The best place to check out a working excavation is **Tom's Working Opal Mine** (☎ 1800 196 500, 8672 3966; www.coobertours.com; Stuart Hwy;

tours adult/child/family $25/10/55; ☺ tours 10am, 2pm & 3.30pm), 3km southwest of town. You'll see miners continuing their search for the big vein, and visitors can noodle through the mullock for small fortunes.

The brilliant **Old Timers Mine** (☎ 8672 5555; www.oldtimersmine.com; Crowders Gully Rd; adult/concession/child/family $10/9/4.50/29; ☺ 9am-5pm) was mined in 1916 but then hidden by the miners, who left several opals embedded in the stone. The mine was rediscovered when a dugout home punched through into the labyrinth of tunnels, which make a great tour. There's also a museum, a re-created 1920s underground home and free mining-equipment demos (9.30am, 1.30pm and 3.30pm daily) to check out.

The **Umoona Opal Mine & Museum** (☎ 8672 5288; www.umoonaopalmine.com.au; Hutchison St; tours adult/child $10/5; ☺ 8am-7pm, tours 10am, noon, 2pm & 4pm) is a rambling complex in the centre of town, with informative mine tours, displays on desert ecology, geology and Aboriginal mythology and traditions, plus exhibitions on the early mining days.

DUGOUT HOMES & CHURCHES

It gets face-meltingly hot out here in summer, so it makes sense to live underground! Even when it's a stinker outside, subterranean temperatures never rise above 23°C, and air-conditioning isn't necessary. Many of the early **dugout homes** were simply worked-out mines, but these days they're usually excavated specifically as residences – some residents open them up for visitors. One of the best is **Faye's Underground Display Home** (☎ 1800 676 680, 8672 5029; Old Water Tank Rd; admission $5; ☺ 8am-5pm Mon-Sat), hand-dug by three women in the 1960s. It's a little chintzy, but the living-room swimming pool is a winner!

You can visit most of Coober Pedy's five **underground churches** – these are functioning churches, so be respectful of services and worshippers. The **Serbian Orthodox Church** (☎ 8672 3048; off Stuart Hwy; admission free; ☺ 11am-6pm) is the largest and most impressive, with carvings in the rock walls. The **St Peter & Paul Catholic Church** (☎ 8672 5011; Hutchison St; admission free; ☺ 10am-4pm) was the first church in Coober Pedy, and still has a sweet appeal.

OTHER STUFF

You can't miss the **Big Winch**, from which there are sweeping views over Coober Pedy and towards the Breakaways. An optimistic 'if' painted on the side of the big bucket sums up the town's spirit. Also here is a tree sculpture made from the remains of a burnt-out truck; it's quite possibly the only 'tree' in town.

Leftover sets and props from the movies that have been filmed here are littered around town. Check out the amazing **spaceship** from *Pitch Black*, which has crash-landed outside the Opal Cave shop on Hutchison St.

When the mercury nudges 50°C, **Coober Pedy Swimming Pool** (☎ 8672 5388; Paxton Rd; adult/child $5/2.50; ☺ 12.45pm-8.30pm Mon-Fri, 11am-8.30pm Sat & Sun) becomes a splashy human soup.

THE DOG FENCE

Erected as a barrier against sheep-killing dingoes, the 1.8m-high wire-mesh Dog Fence stretches thousands of kilometres across southeastern Australia, from the Nullarbor cliffs on the Great Australian Bight, across SA, into NSW, and on to Jimbour in southeast Queensland. Originally an astounding 8614km long, it was shortened to 5500km in 1980. You'll pass through it on the Stuart Hwy north of Coober Pedy.

Maintenance is an ongoing headache. The job is shared by individual landholders and state governments – the SA government alone spends upwards of $500,000 on annual upkeep. Parts of the fence are more than 100 years old and need replacing, and even the newest sections are under constant assault from emus, kangaroos, livestock, floods and shifting desert sands (not to mention dingoes).

A stretch of the Dog Fence starred in the 2002 Phillip Noyce film *Rabbit Proof Fence*. Set in Western Australia (WA), the film tells the story of two Aboriginal girls who are stolen from their families for domestic service. The girls try to steer their way home by following the fence across WA, but the film was actually shot along a particularly photogenic stretch of fence in SA.

For a more detailed study of the Dog Fence, read James Woodford's 2004 book *The Dog Fence* (see p20).

DETOUR: PAINTED DESERT

If you're headed for Oodnadatta and you can handle rough roads, turn off the Stuart Hwy at Cadney Homestead for a shorter run (172km) on dirt roads, rather than going via Marla (209km) or Coober Pedy (193km). As a bonus, you'll travel through the magical **Painted Desert** en route. The painterly colours here derive from sediments bedded down on the floor of a once-was inland sea. Minerals have eroded and leached from the hills, creating amazing striations and vivid flashes of red, orange, black and yellow. Bring your camera!

Tours

There are heaps of tour options that can take you around town or further afield. Most accommodation places also run town tours. Some of the many operators:

Arid Zone Tours (☎ 8672 5359, 0417-885 909; www .cooberpedy.info; tours per person from $55) Customised 4WD tours to anywhere you want to go, run by the experienced Merv: around town, Lake Eyre, Painted Desert, the Breakaways etc.

Desert Cave Tours (☎ 8672 5688; www.desertcave .com.au; 4hr tour adult/child $85/42.50) Arguably the most convenient tour, taking in town highlights and a few further out like the Dog Fence, Breakaways and Moon Plain. Departs from reception at the Desert Cave Hotel. Also on offer are four-hour 'Down 'N' Dirty' opal-digging tours (per person $98).

Desert Diversity Tours (☎ 1800 069 911, 8672 5226; www.desertdiversity.com) Coober Pedy–based full-day Painted Desert tours ($195) and mail-run tours to Oodnadatta and William Creek return ($175).

Explore the Outback (☎ 1800 064 244, 8634 7079; www.austcamel.com.au/explore.htm; 5-day trek $1612) Reliable camel treks and conservation-based desert tours north of William Creek. Can arrange transport from Coober Pedy.

Oasis Tours (☎ 8672 5169; 3hr tour adult/child $35/17.50) A good budget tour taking in the major town sights plus a little fossicking. Two-hour sunset Breakaways tours (adult/child $40/20) also swing by the Dog Fence and the Moon Plain.

Opal Air (☎ 8672 3067, 0427-304 599; www.opalair .com.au) A variety of flights, from a short town jaunt ($95) to an extensive overview of the Painted Desert ($290). Further afield you can check out Lake Eyre, Dalhousie Springs, Oodnadatta, Uluru or Alice Springs.

Radeka's Downunder Desert Breakaways Tour (☎ 1800 633 891, 8672 5223; www.radekadownunder .com.au; 4hr tour adult/child $50/25) A wandering tour that includes an underground home, fossicking, the Breakaways, an underground church, the Dog Fence and an active opal mine. See also Stargazing Tour, run by the same folks.

Stargazing Tour (☎ 1800 633 891, 8672 5223; www.radekadownunder.com.au; 1hr tour adult/child $30/15) Tired of messing around in the dirt? Explore the clear desert heavens on nightly trips out to Moon Plain. Minimum four people.

Stuart Range Tours (☎ 8672 5179; 3hr tour adult/ child $40/20, 4½hr tour adult/child $50/25) A budget-conscious option taking in the main sights and activities, including fossicking, an underground church and a working opal mine. The longer tours run in the afternoons and also visit the Dog Fence, Breakaways and Moon Plain.

Sleeping

Spending a night in Coober Pedy gives you the unique opportunity to sleep underground in dugout accommodation, from hand-carved hostels to machine-bored hotels. Underground places generally don't need air-con, so things can get a little stuffy! For nontroglodytes there are above-ground options too.

Riba's (☎ 8672 5614; www.camp-underground.com.au; William Creek Rd; underground/above-ground sites $24/16, powered sites $22, s/d $45/55; 💻) Around 5km from town, Riba's offers the unique option of underground camping! Extras include an underground TV lounge, budget rooms and nightly opal-mine tour (free for campers).

Opal Inn Hotel/Motel (☎ 8672 5054; www.opalinn .com.au; Hutchison St; unpowered/powered sites $20/27, hotel s/d $75/80, motel s/d/tr/q $115/125/135/145; ✴ 💻) The rambling Opal Inn is a jack-of-all-trades (we could say master of none…) with basic pub rooms with TVs and fridges; more sophisticated motel rooms; and a dusty caravan park out the back. The bistro (mains $15 to $29) does lunch from Monday to Saturday and dinner nightly, and the bar is the best place for a beer in town.

Oasis Coober Pedy Caravan Park (☎ 8672 5169; www.oasiscooberpedy.com.au; Seventeen Mile Rd; unpowered/powered sites $22/26, r/on-site vans $36/52, cabins $74-109; ✴ 💻 ⚐) There are a few places to camp in Coober Pedy, but this place is reasonably central and has the most shade, as well as a swimming pool and TV room inside two big cylindrical storage tanks. An affordable tour runs daily (see left).

our pick Radeka's Downunder Underground Backpackers & Motel (☎ 1800 633 891, 8672 5223; www.radekadownunder.com.au; Hutchison St; dm $25, d & tw $65, motel units $125; ✴ 💻) The owners started excavating this place in 1960 – they haven't found much opal, but have ended up with a beaut backpackers! On multiple levels down 6.5m below the surface are Coober Pedy's best budget beds, plus good individual rooms and motel units. The shared kitchen is handy for self-caterers, and there's a bar, barbecue, snooker room and laundry. Desert and stargazing tours also available (see p143).

Underground Motel (☎ 8672 5324; www.theunder groundmotel.com.au; Catacomb Rd; s/d/f incl light breakfast from $85/95/105, extra adult/child $30/16) Choose between standard rooms and suites (with separate lounge and kitchen) at this serviceable spot with a broad panorama towards the Breakaways. It's a fair walk from town, but friendly and affordable.

Mud Hut Motel (☎ 8672 3003; www.mudhutmotel .com.au; St Nicholas St; s/d/units $120/140/200; ✖ ⬚) The rustic-looking walls here are actually rammed earth, and despite the grubby name this is one of the cleanest places in town. The two-bedroom units are well serviced with cooktops, fridges and silent air-conditioning. The in-house restaurant does dinner most nights (mains $27 to $31).

Down to Erth B&B (☎ 8672 5762; www.downtoerth .com.au; Monument Rd; s & d incl breakfast $150, extra person $25; ⬚) A real dugout gem 4km from town, where you can do your own thing in a private, subterranean two-bedroom bunker. There's a shady plunge pool for cooling off after a day exploring the Earth, and a telescope for exploring the universe.

Desert Cave Hotel (☎ 8672 5688; www.desertcave .com.au; Hutchison St; d $218, extra person $35; ✖ ⬚ ⬚) For a much-needed shot of desert luxury – plus a pool, gym, in-house movies, formidable minibar and great restaurant (see right) – the 'world's only underground international hotel' won't disappoint. The staff is supercourteous and there are plenty of tours on offer (see p143). Above-ground rooms also available.

Eating

John's Pizza Bar (☎ 8672 5561; Hutchison St; meals $4-30; ✖ breakfast, lunch & dinner; ✖) You can't go past John's, serving up table-sized pizzas, hearty pastas and heat-beating gelato. Grills, salads, burgers, yiros and fish-and-chips also available. Sit inside, order some takeaway, or pull up a seat with the bedraggled pot plants by the street.

Italo-Australian Miners Club (IAMC; ☎ 8672 5102; Italian Club Rd; mains $10-15; ✖ dinner Wed-Sat; ✖) Vinyl chairs reflect the sunset at this elevated

local watering hole, attracting beer-bellies most nights. Meals (monster steaks, schnitzels and damn fine pastas) make an appetising appearance from Wednesday to Saturday nights.

Tom & Mary's Greek Taverna (☎ 8672 5622; Hutchison St; meals $15-25; ✖ lunch & dinner; ✖) This busy Greek diner does everything from a superb moussaka to yiros, seafood, Greek salads and pastas with Hellenic zing. Sit back with a cold Coopers or retsina as the red sun sets on another dusty day in Coober Pedy.

Umberto's (☎ 8672 5688; Hutchison St; mains $25-46; ✖ dinner; ✖) The Desert Cave Hotel's rooftop restaurant maintains the quality with first-class dishes such as wallaby shanks with vegetables and char-grilled tomato stew, and its 'essential tastes of the outback' platter: char-grilled kangaroo, camel, emu and beef with bush chutney and hand-cut fries. Swift service, moody desert views and a motivating wine list.

Entertainment

Catch the newest releases at the big **Outback Open Air Cinema** (☎ 1800 637 076; Umoona Rd; per car or walk-in $12; ✖ shows from 8pm Sat Feb-Nov), a volunteer-run drive-in.

Getting Around

The Desert Cave Hotel runs a shuttle van into town from the airport ($10). You can rent cars, 4WDs and campervans here (cars from around $70 per day, with additional fees for distances over 100km):

Budget (☎ 8672 5333; www.budget.com.au; 100 Hutchison St) Opposite the Opal Inn.

Coober Pedy Rent-a-Car (☎ 8672 3003; Mud Hut Motel, St Nicholas St)

AROUND COOBER PEDY

The **Breakaways Reserve** is a stark but colourful area of arid hills and scarps 27km away on a rough road north of Coober Pedy – turn off the highway 22km west of town. You can drive to a lookout in a conventional vehicle and check out the white-and-yellow mesa called the **Castle**, which featured in *Mad Max III* and *The Adventures of Priscilla, Queen of the Desert*. Entry permits ($2.20 per person) are available at the visitors centre in Coober Pedy (see p141).

An interesting 70km loop on mainly unsealed road from Coober Pedy takes in the Breakaways, the **Dog Fence** and the tablelike **Moon Plain** on the Coober Pedy-Oodnadatta Rd. If it's been raining, you'll need a 4WD.

THE OODNADATTA TRACK

The legendary, lonesome Oodnadatta Track is an unsealed, 615km road between Marla on the Stuart Hwy, and Marree on the northern fringe of the Flinders Ranges. The track traces the route of the old Overland Telegraph Line and the Great Northern Railway (which closed in 1980), passing ruined railway huts, train sidings and telegraph stations en route. **Lake Eyre** (the world's sixth-largest lake) is just off the road, and scattered along the way are oases fed by the Great Artesian Basin (the track's nickname is the 'String of Springs'). The landscape here is amazingly diverse: through dunes and red gibber plains near Coward Springs, across saltbush flats around William Creek, to the floodplains of the Algebra and Neales Rivers south of Marla.

The Oodnadatta is a rough, rocky and sandy track that's subject to closure after rains, and stray camels wandering across your path. It's best tackled in a 4WD, but you can do it in a sturdy conventional car if you take it slowly (we even saw a car towing a caravan on our trip!). Carry plenty of bottled water, deflate your tyres to 25psi to avoid punctures, and take a satellite phone or UHF CB radio with you in case you break down. If you're really keen, fit a set of cheap Chinese high-profile tyres to your car (around $80 per tyre) to give you a little more ground clearance. Before you set out, check track conditions with the Pink Roadhouse in Oodnadatta (see following), the Coober Pedy visitors centre (p141), the Royal Automobile Association in Adelaide (p47) or online at www.transport.sa.gov.au. If you're finding the dust and dirt heavy going, there are escape routes to Coober Pedy on the Stuart Hwy from William Creek and Oodnadatta. Fuel, accommodation and meals are all available at Marree, William Creek, Oodnadatta and Marla.

Sleepy **Marree** (population 380) was once a vital hub for Afghan camel teams and the Great Northern Railway. The **Oasis Town Centre Caravan Park & Motel** (☎ 8675 8352; Railway Tce; unpowered/powered sites $16/20, s/d $40/60; ✹) has campsites and a camp kitchen, as well as motel-style rooms with TVs and fridges. Alternatively, the 100-year-old **Marree Hotel** (☎ 8675 8344; marreepub@ bigpond.com; Railway Tce; pub s/d $45/70, motel $75/100; ✹ ✹) has decent pub rooms and brand-new motel units out the back. Both businesses can organise flights out over Lake Eyre and **Marree Man**, the 4.2km-long outline of a Pitjantjatjara Aboriginal warrior etched into the desert near Lake Eyre, which is beginning to wash away. It was only discovered in 1988, and no one seems to know who created it.

About 60km from Marree, the old township of Alberrie Creek has become a sculpture park called **Mutonia** (admission by donation; ◷ 24hr), featuring a gate made from a Kombi van cut in half and several planes welded together with their tails buried in the ground to form 'Planehenge'.

Some 130km from Marree, **Coward Springs Campground** (☎ 8675 8336; www.cowardsprings .com.au; unpowered sites $16) is the first stop at the old Coward Springs railway siding. You can soak yourself silly in a natural hot-spring tub made from old rail sleepers, or take a **camel trek** (per person per day from $200) to Lake Eyre from here.

In another 70km you'll hit **William Creek** (population six), best enjoyed in the weather-beaten **William Creek Hotel** (☎ 8670 7880; www.williamcreekhotel.net.au; unpowered/powered sites $16/20, cabins s/d $60/70, motel s/d $65/95; ✹), an iconic 1887 pub with a dusty campground and modest cabins and motel rooms. Also on offer are fuel, cold beer, basic provisions, meals and spare tyres.

Oodnadatta (population 150) is where the main road and the old railway line diverged. The heart of the town today is the **Pink Roadhouse** (☎ 1800 802 074, 8670 7822; www.pinkroadhouse .com.au; ◷ 8am-5.30pm), an excellent source of track info, plus it serves meals (try the impressive 'Oodnaburger'). It also runs the attached **caravan park** (unpowered/powered sites $15/25, budget cabins s/d/tr $45/60/70, self-contained cabins s/d $80/95; ✹ ✹) which has basic camping through to self-contained cabins.

From Oodnadatta it's 209km to Marla or detour north to the 771,000-hectare **Witjira National Park** (www.environment.sa.gov.au/parks/sanpr/witjira), on the western verge of the Simpson Desert.

For detailed track info, pick up the *Oodnadatta Track – String of Springs* booklet from the South Australian Tourism Commission, and the *Travel the Oodnadatta Track* brochure produced by the Pink Roadhouse. See p308 for more outback driving tips.

NORTH TO THE NORTHERN TERRITORY

From Coober Pedy the Stuart Hwy beats a flat track north into the desert. Around 82km south of Marla and 151km north of Coober Pedy, **Cadney Homestead** (☎ 8670 7994; www.cadney homestead.com.au; Stuart Hwy; unpowered/powered sites $14/20, d cabin/motel $55/97; ⚇ ⚑) has caravan and tent sites, serviceable motel rooms and basic (no linen) cabins. It also has the desert essentials – petrol, puncture repairs, takeaways, cold beer, ATM, swimming pool etc – and can organise Painted Desert tours.

In mulga scrub about 82km on from Cadney Homestead, **Marla** (population 245) replaced Oodnadatta as the official regional centre when the *Ghan* railway line was rerouted in 1980. **Marla Travellers Rest** (☎ 8670 7001; Stuart Hwy; unpowered/powered sites $10/18, d $90; ⚇ ⚑) has fuel, a good range of motel rooms, campsites, an all-day cafe and a supermarket for self-caterers.

Frontier-style **Mintabie** (population 250) is an opal field settlement on Aboriginal land 35km west of Marla. If you're stuck out here for some reason, there's a general store, restaurant and basic caravan park.

From Marla the NT border is another 180km, with a fuel stop 20km beyond that in Kulgera. At the border itself there's a **border sign** where tour groups stop for happy snaps.

KULGERA

pop 50

The small settlement of Kulgera, 20km north of the SA border, is your first pit stop in the Territory. From here the gravel Goyder Stock Route (Finke-Kulgera Rd) heads off east for the 150km trip to Finke and the centre of the continent (see p203). The busy pub-roadhouse and **police station** (☎ 8956 0974) here services the outlying Pitjantjatjara Aboriginal community and pastoral leases.

Kulgera Roadhouse (☎ 8956 0973, fax 8956 0807; Stuart Hwy; unpowered/powered sites $11/15, dm $30, budget r $50, s/d $85/110; ⚇ 6am-11pm; ⚇ ⚑) has an expansive camping area, basic backpacker rooms with share facilities, and comfortable motel rooms with TV, fridge and air-con.

The roadhouse has a no-frills **dining room** (mains $12 to 18), a **bar** (⚇ 11am-11pm), an ATM, and stocks a limited range of groceries.

ERLDUNDA

pop 50

Erldunda is a sprawling roadhouse and motel complex on the Stuart Hwy at the point where the Lasseter Hwy branches off to Uluru (244km west). It's 74km north of Kulgera and 200km south of Alice Springs.

Desert Oaks Motel & Caravan Park (☎ 8956 0984; www.desertoaksresort.com; cnr Stuart & Lasseter Hwys; unpowered/powered sites $20/28, budget s/d/tr/q $35/52/65/70, motel s/d $89/107; ⚇ ⚇ ⚑) gets a fair bit of traffic – presumably people who underestimated the distance to Uluru – and as such it's better than your average roadhouse accommodation. The shady grassed camping area has a pool, tennis court and barbecues. The three air-con backpacker cabins have four beds each with communal facilities, and the modern motel units are well equipped with TV, fridge and en suite.

In addition to accommodation, bistro meals are available in the **Ringers Inn** (mains $15-19; ⚇ 10am-11pm), while the **roadhouse** (⚇ 7am-8.30pm) does a brisk trade in takeaway food and groceries. Fuel and vehicle parts are available from 6.30am to 10pm.

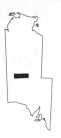

Uluru-Kata Tjuta

Australia's most recognisable natural wonder, Uluru (Ayers Rock), draws tourists from around the world like moths to a big red flame. A close encounter with the Rock exposes a multi-faceted stone possessing many more contours, fissures and formations than the emblematic loaf of bread lit by the setting sun. Your first view from the Lasseter Hwy is of a gradually sloping mound. As you approach from the park entrance, past the sunset viewing area, you get the characteristic postcard profile. As you drive or walk around the rock you will discover waves of smooth stone, honeycomb ulcers, vertebra-like ridges and spillways that link rock pool after rock pool. Surely there would be few better spectacles than storm waters cascading off the dimpled surface of Uluru.

Nearby is the mystical clutch of stone siblings, Kata Tjuta (the Olgas). The 36 textured, pink red domes flaunt their amazing curves in the concentrated light of sunset. Deeply cleaved with narrow gorges and decorated with occasional tufts of vegetation, the revelation is as much biological as geological. Little wonder that these intriguing formations hold sacred secrets known only to the initiated.

These monumental landforms that so spectacularly interrupt the wide horizons have drawn people for millennia. Creation stories and sacred sites abound around the arid lands of Uluru and Kata Tjuta; home for thousands of years to the Pitjantjatjara and Yankunytjatjara Aboriginal peoples. Thanks to the current custodians and traditional owners you have the chance to hear these stories and share in the wonder of an ancient culture.

HIGHLIGHTS

- Reveal the concealed details and experience the immense presence of the Rock on the **Uluru base walk** (p155)
- Enter the colossal and sacred defile of **Walpa Gorge** (p157) separating two of Kata Tjuta's mightiest domes
- Discover the Dreaming and the richness of Anangu culture and tjukurpa (lore), at the **Uluru-Kata Tjuta Cultural Centre** (p154)
- Gather at the **Uluru sunset viewing area** (p156) as the setting sun briefly ignites the monolith with an incredible radiance
- Wander quietly through Kata Tjuta's eerie **Valley of the Winds** (p157)
- Gaze at a billion brilliant stars studded in the black desert sky at the **Night Sky Show** (p158)

Valley of the Winds • Walpa Gorge ★★ • ★ Night Sky Show • Uluru sunset viewing area • ★★ Uluru base walk • Uluru-Kata Tjuta Cultural Centre

---

- TELEPHONE CODE: ☎ 08
- www.environment.gov.au/parks /uluru
- www.ayersrockresort .com.au

LASSETER HIGHWAY

Named after prospector and explorer Harold Lasseter who spent half his life searching for a lost gold reef, the Lasseter Hwy links the Stuart Hwy with Uluru-Kata Tjuta National Park. The 244km sealed road strikes west from Erldunda and takes less than three hours to cover.

MT EBENEZER

The first stop along the highway is Mt Ebenezer, an Aboriginal-owned station 56km west of the Stuart Hwy in the shadow of the Basedow Range and Mt Ebenezer to the north. The roadhouse is the art-and-craft outlet for the local Imanpa Aboriginal community and prices here are very competitive. A small gallery shows a picture board of local artists along with paintings ($30 to $45 for small pieces, up to $700 for larger ones), wood carvings and printed T-shirts.

At **Mt Ebenezer Roadhouse** (☎ 8956 2904; Lasseter Hwy; camping free, powered sites per person $10, dm/s/d $20/88/98; ☯ 8am-10pm; ☒) the camping area is a bit parched, though the facilities are adequate and the motel-style rooms have en suites. Meals are available (mains $15 to $25).

MT CONNER

Mt Conner, the large mesa that looms 350m out of the desert floor about 20km south of the highway, is the outback's most photographed red herring. On first sighting many people mistake this for Uluru, but other than being a large mass protruding from a vast plain, it bears no resemblance. With a base circumference of around 32km, it is much larger than Uluru. There's a rest area and panoramic lookout towards Mt Conner on the highway 26km beyond the Luritja Rd turn-off.

Mt Conner lies within Curtin Springs Station and there is no public access, except by joining an organised tour. **Uncles Tours** (☎ 8956 2916; www.unclestours.com.au; half-/full-day tours $100/185,2hr sunset tour $60, climb $100), departing from Curtin Springs Roadhouse, has informative tours out to Mt Conner, across saltpans and to the old station homestead. The six-hour return Mt Conner climb requires a decent level of fitness and all tours require a minimum of two passengers.

CURTIN SPRINGS

A further 52km from the Luritja Rd turn-off to Kings Canyon is Curtin Springs, the last stop before reaching Yulara, about 80km away. The roadhouse here gets plenty of traffic and can be quite lively.

Curtain Springs Wayside Inn (☎ 8956 2906; www .curtinsprings.com; Lasseter Hwy; camping free, powered sites $25, budget cabin s/d without bathroom $60/80, d $135-200; ☒ ☐) is a popular accommodation alternative for those not wishing to pay the resort prices at Yulara. You can pitch a tent in the camping ground for free, and the various configurations of cabins are well maintained. There's a licensed restaurant (mains $16 to $25), a small store, takeaway food and fuel.

ULURU-KATA TJUTA NATIONAL PARK

For most visitors to Australia, a visit to Uluru is high on the list of 'must-sees', and for many Australians this World Heritage–listed icon has attained the status of a pilgrimage.

The park offers much more than just the chance to see the Rock. Along with the equally (some say more) impressive Kata Tjuta (the Olgas), the area is of deep cultural significance to the local Pitjantjatjara and Yankunytjatjara Aboriginal peoples (who refer to themselves as Anangu).

Although many tour groups zip through the area in 24 hours, it's recommended to spend at least the three days allowed for the park pass. There's plenty to see and do: meandering walks, guided tours, desert culture and, of course, the many aspects and changeable moods of the great monolith itself. The resort village of Yulara offers a range of accommodation and dining, though be prepared for premium prices reflecting the remote locale.

Aboriginal Heritage

Archaeological evidence suggests that Aboriginal people have inhabited this part of Australia for at least 10,000 years. According to tjukurpa (Aboriginal lore derived from the Creation) all landscape features were made by ancestral beings, and the Anangu today are the descendants of the ancestral beings and custodians of the land.

According to Anangu legend, Uluru was built by two boys who played in the mud after rain; it is at the centre of a number of Dreaming tracks that criss-cross central Australia.

The Anangu officially own the national park, which is leased to **Parks Australia** (www.environment .gov.au/parks/uluru/index.html), the Commonwealth government's national parks body, on a 99-year lease. The traditional owners receive annual rent plus a percentage of the park-entrance fees to go towards community projects such as health and education.

European History

The first white man to venture into the area was Ernest Giles, during his attempted crossing from the Overland Telegraph Line to the west of the continent in 1872. His party had travelled west from Watarrka and sighted Kata Tjuta, which he named Mt Ferdinand after his financier, the noted botanist Baron Ferdinand von Mueller. However, von Mueller later changed the name to Mt Olga, after Queen Olga of Wurttemberg.

The following year a party led by William Gosse set out to cross to the west. He named Mt Conner and, sighting a hill to the west, stated this:

The hill, as I approached, presented a most peculiar appearance, the upper portion being covered with holes or caves. When I got clear of the sandhills, and was only two miles distant, and the hill, for the first time, coming fairly into view, what was my astonishment to find it was one immense rock rising abruptly from the plain… I have named this Ayers Rock, after Sir Henry Ayers the premier of South Australia.

The early explorers were followed by pastoralists, missionaries, doggers (dingo hunters) and various adventurers. Among these was one Harold Lasseter, who insisted he had found a fabulously rich gold reef in the Petermann Ranges to the west in 1901. He died a lonely death in the same ranges in 1931 trying to rediscover it.

As European activity in the area increased, so did the contact and conflict between the two cultures. With the combined effects of stock grazing and drought, the Anangu found their hunting and gathering options becoming increasingly scarce, which in turn led to a dependence on the white economy. In the 1920s the three governments of Western Australia, South Australia and the Northern Territory set aside a reserve (the Great Central Aboriginal Reserve) for Aboriginal people. The Anangu shunned this and other reserves, preferring instead to maintain traditional practices.

By 1950 a dirt road had been pushed through from the east and tourism started to develop in the area. As early as 1951 the fledgling Connellan Airways applied for permission to build an airstrip near Uluru, which resulted in the area of Uluru and Kata Tjuta being excised from the reserve in 1958 for use as a national park.

By the 1970s it was clear that planning was required for the development of the area. Between 1931 and 1946 only 22 people were known to have climbed Uluru. In 1969 about 23,000 people visited the area. Ten years later the figure was 65,000 and now the annual visitor figures are approaching 500,000.

Increased tourism activity over the years led to Aboriginal anxiety about the desecration of important sites by tourists. The Federal government was approached for assistance and by 1973 Aboriginal people had become involved with the management of the park. In 1983, following renewed calls from traditional owners for title to the land, the federal government announced that freehold title to the national park would be granted and the park leased back to what is now Parks Australia for a period of 99 years. The transfer of ownership took place on 26 October 1985.

Geology

The Rock itself is 3.6km long by 2.4km wide, stands 348m above the surrounding dunes and measures 9.4km around the base. It is made up of a type of coarse-grained sandstone known as arkose, which was formed from sediment from eroded granite mountains. Kata Tjuta, on the other hand, is a conglomerate of granite and basalt gravel glued together by mud and sand.

The sedimentary beds that make up both Uluru and Kata Tjuta formations were laid down over about 600 million years, in a shallow sea in what geologists call the Amadeus Basin. Various periods of uplift caused the beds to buckle, fold and lift

ULURU-KATA TJUTA

ULURU-KATA TJUTA NATIONAL PARK & AROUND

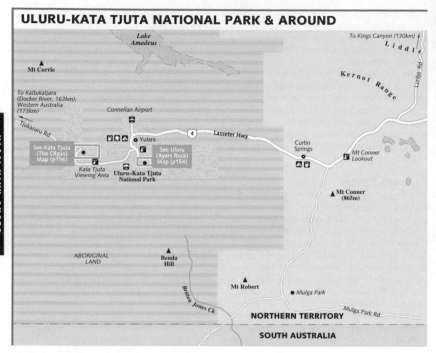

above sea level; those that form Uluru were turned so that they are now almost vertical, while at Kata Tjuta they were tilted about 20°C. For the last 300 million years wind, water and sand have sculpted the surface, leaving what we see today. It's believed that Uluru extends up to 5km beneath the surface.

Climate

The park is in the centre of the arid zone, with an average annual rainfall of around 220mm. The most likely time for rain and thunderstorms is during the hotter months (November to March), but drought is not uncommon and a year or two may go by without rain.

Many people are surprised at how cold it gets at Uluru in winter. Daytime temperatures from May to October can be pleasant, but clear nights often see the temperature plunge to below freezing – campers, be prepared!

In summer it can be scorching, with temperatures peaking during February and March and reaching up to 45°C. Usually the summer maximum is around 30°C to 35°C.

Wildlife
ANIMALS

Although the arid country around Uluru doesn't look very fertile, it is home to a wide variety of animals – the fact that most of the tjukurpa sites within the park are animal related is evidence of that. Anangu knowledge of ecosystems and animal behaviour has proven invaluable to wildlife-conservation programs.

The most common native mammals include red kangaroos, euros, dingoes and small marsupials such as dunnarts and marsupial moles. The moles have become specialised desert dwellers – they are blind and use their short, strong limbs to burrow through the loose sand, feeding on insect larvae and small reptiles.

The once-common rufous hare-wallaby (known as *mala* to Anangu) is classified extinct in the wild, wiped out by European settlement and feral predators. However, in 2005 25 animals were reintroduced to the Uluru-Kata Tjuta National Park, protected by a 170 hectare feral-proof enclosure. By 2008 the population had more than doubled.

limit the amount of accumulated vegetation. Park managers re-create the 'mosaic' pattern of small burns that occurred before European settlement to avoid unrestrained 'hot' fires, which can result from long fire-free periods.

Information

The park is open from half an hour before sunrise until sunset daily (varying between 5am to 9pm in summer and 6.30am to 7.30pm in winter). Three-day entry permits to the **national park** (adult/child $25/free) are available at the drive-through park-entry station on the road from Yulara.

There are picnic and toilet facilities at Uluru (at the Cultural Centre and near the Mala car park) and at Kata Tjuta.

Uluru-Kata Tjuta Cultural Centre (☎ 8956 1128; ☺ 7am-6pm; information desk ☺ 8am-noon, 1-5pm) Just 1km before the Rock, this should be your first stop for information on the park. Along with cultural displays and galleries, there's an information desk in the Nintiringkupai building where you can speak to park rangers and pick up the informative *Visitor Guide*, leaflets and walking notes. See p154 for more information on the centre.

Visitors Centre (☎ 8957 7377; ☺ 9am-5.30pm) The visitors centre at Yulara is also a good source of park information.

Tours

BUS TOURS

Yulara's **Tour & Information Centre** (☎ 8956 2240; Yulara Shopping Centre; ☺ 8am-8.30pm) houses several local tour operators.

AAT-King's (☎ 8956 2171; www.aatkings.com) has the biggest range of coach tour options departing Yulara. You can choose from a range of half- and full-day tours, or buy one of a selection of three-day tour passes (from adult/child $200/98). Check the website or ask at the Tour & Information Centre for details.

Discovery Ecotours (☎ 8956 2563; www.ecotours.com.au) has small-group day tours around Uluru for $115 and Kata Tjuta for $84. There's also a seven-hour tour to **Cave Hill**, across the South Australian border in Pitjantjatjara land, including lunch for $237.

CAMEL TOURS

Uluru Camel Tours (☎ 1800 806 499; www.ananguwaai.com.au; off Yulara Dr, Yulara; short rides adult/child $10/5; ☺ 10.30am-noon), owned by Anangu Tours, has a small museum and short but interesting (if you've never been on a camel before) rides. The most popular ride, however, is the

Most of the park's mammals are active only at night, but you're bound to see birds. Crested pigeons are common around Yulara and while walking round the Rock you'll probably see colourful galahs, budgerigars and zebra finches. A checklist of birds found within the park is available from the Uluru-Kata Tjuta Cultural Centre (see p154).

PLANTS

The plants of the red sand plains of central Australia – mainly spinifex grasses, mulga bushes (acacia) and desert oak trees – are well adapted to the harsh, dry climate. These plants remain virtually dormant during times of drought and shoot into action after rain.

Except in times of severe drought, numerous grevilleas and fuchsias thrive in the sand dunes, and late winter and early spring (August to September) usually turn on a showy display of wildflowers. Common eucalypts found in the area include the Centralian bloodwood, the river red gum and the blue mallee.

As in the Top End, Aboriginal people in central Australia used fire to manage the land. Controlled burns encourage regrowth and

ABORIGINAL AUSTRALIA: TJUKURPA

Tjukurpa (pronounced chook-or-pa) refers to the spiritual heritage of the Anangu people. Within it are creation stories associated with Uluru. The most important creation ancestors to the Anangu are the **Mala** (rufous hare-wallaby), the **Kuniya** (woma python), the **Liru** (brown snake) and **Lungkata** (blue-tongue lizard), and evidence of their activities can be seen in features of the Rock.

Mala

The Mala travelled from the Yuendumu area to Uluru for *inma* (ceremonies). The men climbed to the top of Uluru to plant a ceremonial pole, while the women collected and prepared food at Taputji, a small isolated rock on the northeastern side.

During the ceremonies, the Mala were invited by the Wintalka (mulga seed) men to attend dance ceremonies away to the west. Already committed to their own celebrations, the Mala refused and the angered Wintalka created a nasty dingolike creature (Kurpany), which sneaked up on the women's dancing ceremonies at Tjukatjapi on the northern side of the Rock. The frightened women fled right into the middle of the men's secret ceremony, ruining it, and in the confusion a Mala man was killed and eaten by Kurpany. The remaining Mala fled south towards the Musgrave Ranges.

Kuniya & Liru

The tjukurpa tells of how Kuniya came from the east to hatch her young at Uluru. While she was camped at Taputji, she was attacked by a group of Liru, who had been angered by Kuniya's nephew. At Mutitjulu she came across a Liru warrior and performed a ritual dance, mustering great forces. In an effort to dispel this terrifying force she picked up a handful of sand and let it fall to the ground. The vegetation where the sand fell was poisoned and today remains unusable to Anangu.

The force within her remained strong and a great battle with Liru was fought. She hit him on the head, trying to inflict a 'sorry cut', but overcome with anger she hit him a second time, killing him. The two wounds received by Liru can be seen as the vertical cracks on the Rock near Mutitjulu.

Lungkata

Lungkata (blue-tongue lizard man) found an emu, which had been wounded by other hunters, at the base of the Rock. He finished it off and started to cook it. The original hunters, two Bellbird brothers, found Lungkata and asked him if he had seen their emu. He lied, saying he hadn't seen it, but the hunters did not believe him and chased him around the base of the Rock. While being pursued Lungkata dropped pieces of emu meat, and these are seen as the fractured slabs of sandstone just west of Mutitjulu, and at Kalaya Tjunta (emu thigh) on the southeastern side of Uluru, where a spur of Rock is seen as the emu's thigh.

Camel to Sunrise, a 2½-hour tour with billy tea, and the sunset equivalent with champagne or beer. Both cost $99 per person. At noon daily between April and October the Camel Express ($65, 45 minutes) trudges through the desert to a view of both Uluru and Kata Tjuta.

CULTURAL TOURS

To gain a true insight into the significance of the Rock through the eyes of the traditional owners, check out **Anangu Tours** (☎ 8956 2123; www.ananguwaai.com.au). Owned and operated by Anangu from the Mutitjulu community, these tours are the ultimate cultural experience at Uluru, and give you a greater understanding of Aboriginal culture.

The 4½-hour Aboriginal Uluru Tour starts with sunrise over Uluru and breakfast at the Cultural Centre, then takes in the Liru walk to the base, Aboriginal culture, and demonstrations of bush skills and spear-throwing. It departs daily and costs $127/85 for adults/children.

The Kuniya Sunset Tour ($106/69) leaves at 2.30pm (3.30pm between November and February) and includes a visit to Mutitjulu Waterhole and the Cultural Centre, finish-

---

ABORIGINAL AUSTRALIA: SPEAKING ANANGU

Visiting the Cultural Centre or taking an Anangu tour, you'll hear a number of words in the Pitjantjatjara language, the most prominent Anangu dialect. Here's a brief glossary of commonly used words:

inma	dance, ceremony	**pila**	spinifex plains
itjanu	flower	**piranpa**	non-Aboriginal people
kali	boomerang	**piti**	wooden bowl
karu	creek	**puli**	rock
kulata	hunting spear	**puti**	woodland or bushland
kuniya	woma python	**tali**	sand dunes
kurpany	devil dog	**tatintja**	climb
liru	brown snake	**tjara**	shield
mala	rufous hare-wallaby	**tjukuritja**	creation ancestors
miru	spear thrower	**tjukurpa**	creation law, *stories*
nganampa	ours	**walpa**	wind
ngura	all of us	**wana**	digging stick
Nguraritja	traditional owner	**wari**	cold
palya	OK, hello, goodbye	**wiya**	no, don't

---

ing with a sunset viewing. If you have your own transport you can choose to skip the preliminaries and join any of the tours at the Cultural Centre for $63/32.

Another option is the Mala walk ($79/53) at 9am, which starts with a vehicle tour of the Rock then a guided Mala walk. Finally there's a three-hour dot-painting workshop ($79/56) at the Cultural Centre.

DINING TOURS

Sounds of Silence (☎ 8296 8010; www.ayersrockresort.com.au/sounds-of-silence; adult/child $155/77), Snappily dressed waiters serve sparkling wine and canapés on a desert dune with stunning sunset views of Uluru and Kata Tjuta, accompanied by the droning of a lone didgeridoo. Then you retire to your table in the desert for a buffet of gourmet Aussie food and wine as the night descends. Afterwards, the startlingly clear night sky is dissected and explained with the help of a telescope and an astronomer.

If you're more of a morning person, try the **Desert Awakenings 4WD Tour** (☎ 8296 8010; www.ayersrockresort.com.au; adult/child $137/106). This tour starts with a predawn excursion to a secluded dune where you watch sunrise on Uluru and Kata Tjuta and then enjoy a bush breakfast. From the dune you are taken to Uluru where you are guided through the Cultural Centre and taken on a walk to Mutitjulu Waterhole.

Neither tour is really suitable for children under 10 years. Bookings are essential and pick up/drop off from your accommodation is included.

MOTORCYCLE TOURS

Sunrise and sunset tours to Uluru and/or Kata Tjuta can also be done on the back of a Harley-Davidson with **Uluru Motorcycle Tours** (☎ 8956 2019; www.ulurucycles.com; rides $50-295). Experienced riders would prefer the **self-drive tours** (2/3/5/10hr $275/355/455/650), which require a $2500 deposit and full motorcycle licence.

SCENIC FLIGHTS

The view from the ground is one thing, but from the air it's something else – just be aware that flights must maintain a certain distance from the Rock itself. Bookings are essential (preferably a day in advance) and flights may be cancelled if weather conditions aren't suitable. The following operators can be booked at the Tour & Information Centre in Yulara. If you're wondering whether to go up by chopper or plane, the light plane gives you more time in the air and is slightly cheaper, but the helicopter flies lower, offering a better all-round view. There are no child concessions.

Ayers Rock Helicopters (☎ 8956 2077; $100-580) offers a 15-minute buzz over the Rock ($110), a 30-minute Uluru-Kata Tjuta flight ($220) or longer flights to Mt Connor or Kings Canyon.

Ayers Rock Scenic Flights (☎ 8956 2345; www.ayersrockflights.com.au; flights $165-600) has a 40-minute

ULURU-KATA TJUTA

plane flight over the Rock and Kata Tjuta for $165; Uluru, Kata-Tjuta, Lake Amadeus and Kings Canyon is $390.

Professional Helicopter Services (PHS; ☎ 8956 2003; www.phs.com.au; flights $115-830) has short flights over the Rock from $115, Uluru and the Olgas for $220, and the works, including Lake Amadeus and Kings Canyon, for $830.

TOURS FROM ALICE SPRINGS
There's a whole gamut of tours to Uluru from Alice Springs; see p182 for a list of operators. Check out the company's vehicles, group size (and ages), accommodation, types of meals and whether it includes park entry (most don't).

ULURU (AYERS ROCK)
No matter how many times you've seen it in postcards; nothing quite prepares you for the real thing. The first sight of Uluru will astound even the most jaded, road-weary traveller. The remote desert location, the rich cultural significance and the renowned changing colours of the Rock combine to create an unforgettable attraction.

Sights & Activities
ULURU-KATA TJUTA CULTURAL CENTRE
To gain an understanding of the culture and lifestyle of the traditional owners and their relationship with the land, the superb **Cultural Centre** (☎ 8956 3138; ⏱ 7am-6pm, last entry 5.30pm) should not be missed. This is also the place to pick up the free *Visitor Guide & Maps* brochure.

The two innovative rammed-earth and timber buildings here represent the ancestral figures of Kuniya (woma python) and Liru (brown snake) and contained within them are inspiring displays with multilingual information. Entering from the car park you pass murals of Anangu art and interpretive displays relating to tjukurpa with detailed information on ancestral *stories*, ceremonies and bush foods. The next building houses the Nintiringkupai display, focusing on the modern history and joint management of the national park, as well as flora, fauna and Aboriginal tools. If you're thinking of souveniring something from the park, check out the pile of rocks and letters from people around the world who – in a fit of guilt or

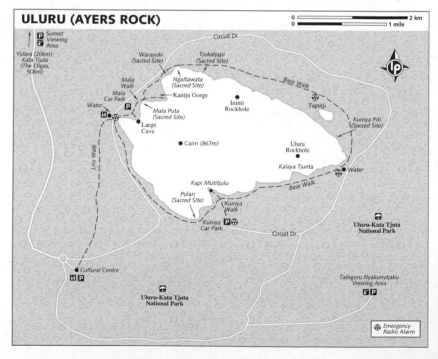

ULURU (AYERS ROCK)

0   2 km
0   1 mile

Sunset Viewing Area

Yulara (20km); Kata Tjuta (The Olgas, 50km)

Circuit Dr

Warayuki (Sacred Site)

Tjukatjapi (Sacred Site)

Base Walk

Mala Walk

Ngaltawata (Sacred Site)

Mala Car Park

Kantju Gorge

Ininti Rockhole

Taputji

Water

Mala Puta (Sacred Site)

Kuniya Piti (Sacred Site)

Large Cave

Liru Walk

Cairn (867m)

Uluru Rockhole

Kalaya Tjunta

Water

Kapi Mutitjulu

Base Walk

Pulari (Sacred Site)

Kuniya Walk

Kuniya Car Park

Circuit Dr

Uluru-Kata Tjuta National Park

Cultural Centre

Talnguru Nyakunytjaku Viewing Area

Uluru-Kata Tjuta National Park

Emergency Radio Alarm

ULURU-KATA TJUTA

A QUESTION OF CLIMBING

Of the 450,000-plus visitors to Uluru each year, there are no definitive figures on how many actually climb the Rock. For many people, the climb is regarded as a rite of passage, a pilgrimage to conquer the mighty monolith and a reason to visit.

But for the traditional owners, the Anangu, Uluru is a sacred place. The path up the side of the Rock is part of the route taken by the Mala ancestors on their arrival at Uluru and has great spiritual significance – and is not to be trampled by human feet. When you arrive at Uluru you'll see a sign from the Anangu saying 'We don't climb' and a request that you don't climb either.

Apart from the cultural significance, the Anangu are the custodians of these lands and take responsibility for the safety of visitors. Any injuries or deaths that occur on the Rock (and they do occur – check out the memorial plaques at the base) are a source of distress and sadness to them. For similar reasons of public safety, Parks Australia would (unofficially) prefer that people didn't climb. It's a very steep and taxing ascent, not to be taken lightly, and each year there are several costly air rescues, mostly from people suffering heart attacks. Furthermore, Parks Australia must constantly monitor the climb and close it on days when the temperature is forecast to reach 36°C or strong winds are expected.

So if the Anangu don't want people to climb and Parks Australia would prefer to see it closed, why does it remain open? The answer is tourism. The tourism industry believes visitor numbers would drop significantly – at least initially – if the climb was closed, particularly from overseas visitors thinking there is nothing else to do at Uluru.

The debate has grown louder in recent years and many believe the climb will eventually be closed for good. Until then, it remains a personal decision and a question of respect. Before deciding, visit the Cultural Centre and perhaps take an Anangu tour. You might just change your mind.

---

superstition – have returned rocks after taking them! Removing natural objects from the park is prohibited anyway.

Also in the complex are two art galleries and a souvenir shop (see p156), and **Ininti Café** (meals $5-10; 7am-5.15pm;) serving breakfast, sandwiches, hot food (including emu pies!) and drinks.

WALKING

There are several walking tracks around Uluru, with an emphasis on Anangu cultural significance. Informative walks, guided by both park rangers and Anangu Tours, delve into local tjukurpa *stories*, plants, wildlife and geology. Several areas of spiritual significance to Anangu are off-limits to visitors and should not be photographed – these are marked with fences and signs.

The *Visitor Guide & Maps* brochure, which can be picked up at the Cultural Centre if you didn't receive it when you paid admission to the park, gives details on the following self-guided walks (except the climb).

Base walk (9.4km loop, three to four hourrs, medium) A highlight for many. Circumnavigate the base of the Rock's mass and let it conquer you, as you peer at the caves and art sites along the way. It's an easy stroll but quite long, so plan to go in the early morning or mid-afternoon.

Liru walk (4km return, 1½ hours, easy) This walking track links the Cultural Centre with the start of the Mala walk and climb, and passes a number of significant Anangu sites. It's wheelchair accessible in dry weather.

Mala walk (2km return, one hour, easy) From the base of the climbing point, interpretative signs explain the tjukurpa of the Mala. At Kantju Gorge you can either continue on the base walk or return to the car park. A ranger-guided walk along this route departs at 10am daily (8am in summer) from the car park. It's wheelchair accessible.

Kuniya walk (1km return, 45 minutes, easy) A short walk from the car park on the southern side leads to the only permanent waterhole, Mutitjulu, with links to the Kuniya and Liru tjukurpa. It's wheelchair accessible.

The climb (1.6km return, about two hours, difficult) If you insist on climbing (see above), take note of the warnings. It's a demanding climb and there have been numerous deaths from falls and heart attacks. Plan to go early in the day, take plenty of water and be prepared to turn around if it all gets too much. The first part of the walk is by far the steepest and most arduous, and there's a chain to hold onto. After that it's a relatively easy (and safe) walk across the top of the rock to a cairn. The view is panoramic – you can easily see Kata Tjuta and Mt Conner. The climb is often closed due to strong winds, rain, mist and Anangu business, and from 8am on days forecast to reach 36°C or more.

SUNSET & SUNRISE VIEWING AREAS
About halfway between Yulara and Uluru the **sunset viewing area** has plenty of car-parking space, although in peak season you'll have to arrive early to snare a space. You can't miss it – dozens of cars and buses unload camera-toting tourists from about an hour before sunset. It provides a superb view of the most recognised face of the rock in all its colour-changing glory.

The **Talnguru Nyakunytaku viewing area** should be operational by the time you read this. This new area provides a different perspective of Uluru to the postcard profile, and will be of interest for more than just sunrise.

Shopping
There are two art galleries and a souvenir outlet in the Uluru-Kata Tjuta Cultural Centre.

Ininti Souvenirs (☎ 8956 2214; ⏰ 7am-5.15pm), Attached to the cafe, Ininti sells souvenirs such as T-shirts, ceramics, hats, CDs and a variety of books on Uluru, Aboriginal culture, biographies, bush foods and the flora and fauna of the area.

Maruku Arts (☎ 8956 2558; www.maruku.com .au; ⏰ 8.30am-5.30pm) This place is an art-and-craft gallery owned by about 20 Anangu communities from across central Australia (including Mutitjulu). Here you will find

dot paintings ($700 to $2500) and all sorts of carved wooden pieces such as *piti* (large bowls), *kulata* (hunting spears), *miru* (spear throwers) and *wana* (digging sticks). There are also carved animals and music sticks. You can usually see artists at work each morning from Monday to Friday.

Walkatjara Art (⏰ 8.30am-5.30pm) A working art centre owned by the Mutitjulu community, it focuses on paintings and ceramics created by women from Mutitjulu.

KATA TJUTA (THE OLGAS)
No journey to Uluru is complete without a visit to Kata Tjuta, 35km or so west of the Rock or 53km by road from Yulara. Kata Tjuta means 'many heads', and there are 36 domed rocks shoulder to shoulder forming deep valleys and steep-sided gorges. The tallest rock, Mt Olga, at 1066m above sea level, is nearly 200m higher than Uluru. Kata Tjuta is of great significance to Anangu and is associated with a number of tjukurpa *stories* relating to secret men's initiation ceremonies. Though it lacks the star status of Uluru, this congregation of monolithic rocks is equally impressive and many visitors find it even more captivating. The Valley of the Winds walk is one of the most challenging and rewarding in the national park.

The main car park, close to the western edge of Kata Tjuta, has shade shelters, picnic tables and toilets.

Just to the west is a turn-off from the main access road, where you'll find the **sunset viewing area** with picnic tables and toilets. The views

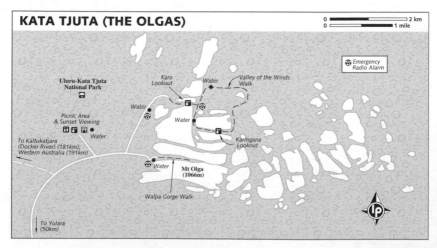

KATA TJUTA (THE OLGAS)

0 ————— 2 km
0 ————— 1 mile

Emergency Radio Alarm

Uluru-Kata Tjuta National Park

Karu Lookout

Water

Valley of the Winds Walk

Water

Water

Water

Picnic Area & Sunset Viewing

Water

Karingana Lookout

To Kaltukatjara (Docker River) (181km); Western Australia (191km)

Water

Mt Olga (1066m)

Walpa Gorge Walk

To Yulara (50km)

here are just as colourful as Uluru as the setting sun illuminates the domes in vibrant, rich reds – but without the crowds.

Sights & Activities

WALKING

There are two marked trails at Kata Tjuta, both of which are well worth the effort.

Walpa Gorge (Tatintjawiya; 2.6km return, 45 minutes, easy) This is a short signposted track leading to a boardwalk into the extraordinary, sheer-sided Walpa (Olga) Gorge from the car park. In the afternoon the sun floods the gorge.

Valley of the Winds (7.4km loop, three hours, medium) Many rate this as the most interesting walk in the park and it's hard to disagree. The track winds through the gorges giving excellent views of the domes and traversing varied terrain. Although not difficult, it requires a reasonable level of fitness, sturdy footwear and plenty of water. Starting this walk at first light may reward you with a track to yourself, enabling you to listen to the country and appreciate the sounds of the wind and the bird calls carried up the valley. The track is closed from the Karu Lookout from 11am on days forecast to reach 36°C or more.

KATA TJUTA VIEWING AREAS

Along the road between Yulara and Kata Tjuta there is a marked **dune viewing area**. From the car park a 300m boardwalk through the dunes leads to a viewing platform with sweeping views over the surrounding dune country, with Kata Tjuta seemingly marching to the west and Uluru visible on the eastern horizon. This is the best place to see Kata Tjuta at sunrise. Interpretive signs here outline the features of the complex dune environment. The **sunset viewing** area is just west of Kata Tjuta (there's a signposted turn-off to the car park).

YULARA

pop 2080 (including Mutitjulu)

Yulara (the Anangu word means 'place of the howling dingo') is the service village for the national park and has effectively turned one of the world's most remote and least hospitable regions into a comfortable – even luxurious – place to stay. Lying just outside the national park, 20km from Uluru and 53km from Kata Tjuta, the complex is the closest base for exploring the area's renowned attractions.

Information

The *Resort Guide*, with a list of facilities and a map, is a useful sheet available from the visitors centre and hotel desks. Most of Yulara's facilities are in the shopping centre. There's a community noticeboard outside the post office with local job vacancies. As well as the services listed here, there are souvenir shops, a photo lab and a hairdresser.

Wheelchair access is possible throughout Yulara Resort.

BOOKSHOPS

Ayers Rock Newsagency (☎ 8956 2177; ◔ 8am-9pm) Stocks interstate papers, magazines and souvenir books on Australia.

EMERGENCY

Ambulance (☎ 0420 101 403)
Police station (☎ 8956 2166)

INTERNET ACCESS

Most accommodation has internet access.
Tour & Information Centre (per 10min $2; ◔ 8am-8pm) Coin-operated terminals in the resort shopping centre.
Internet cafe (Outback Pioneer Hotel; per 10min $2; ◔ 5am-11pm) In the backpacker common room.

MEDICAL SERVICES

There's no pharmacy in Yulara, but the supermarket stocks basic pharmaceutical products.

Royal Flying Doctor Service medical centre (☎ 8956 2286; ◔ 9am-noon & 2-5pm Mon-Fri, 10-11am Sat & Sun) This is the resort's medical centre and ambulance service.

MONEY

ANZ bank (☎ 8956 2070; ◔ 9.30am-4pm Mon-Thu, to 5pm Fri) Currency exchange and 24-hour ATM.

POST

Post office (☎ 8956 2288; ◔ 9am-6.30pm Mon-Fri, 10am-2pm Sat & Sun) Opposite the supermarket, this is also an agent for the Commonwealth and NAB banks. Payphones are outside.

TOURIST INFORMATION

Tour & Information Centre (☎ 8957 7324; ◔ 8am-8pm) The hub for booking any sort of tours and hire cars.
Visitors centre (☎ 8957 7377; ◔ 9am-5pm) The visitors centre acts as a tourist office, with helpful staff and postings on the weather forecast and sunrise and sunset times. There's a display on the geology, wildlife, history and Aboriginal lore of the region. To get the most out of it, take the free audio tour (available in several languages).

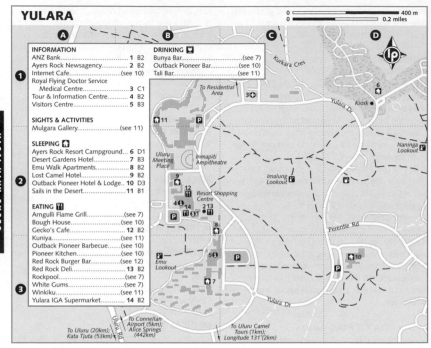

YULARA

0 — 400 m
0 — 0.2 miles

INFORMATION		
ANZ Bank	**1**	B2
Ayers Rock Newsagency	**2**	B2
Internet Cafe	(see 10)	
Royal Flying Doctor Service		
Medical Centre	**3**	C1
Tour & Information Centre	**4**	B2
Visitors Centre	**5**	B3

SIGHTS & ACTIVITIES	
Mulgara Gallery	(see 11)

SLEEPING		
Ayers Rock Resort Campground	**6**	D1
Desert Gardens Hotel	**7**	B3
Emu Walk Apartments	**8**	B2
Lost Camel Hotel	**9**	B2
Outback Pioneer Hotel & Lodge	**10**	D3
Sails in the Desert	**11**	B1

EATING		
Arngulli Flame Grill	(see 7)	
Bough House	(see 10)	
Gecko's Cafe	**12**	B2
Kuniya	(see 11)	
Outback Pioneer Barbecue	(see 10)	
Pioneer Kitchen	(see 10)	
Red Rock Burger Bar	(see 12)	
Red Rock Deli	**13**	B2
Rockpool	(see 7)	
White Gums	(see 7)	
Winkiku	(see 11)	
Yulara IGA Supermarket	**14**	B2

DRINKING	
Bunya Bar	(see 7)
Outback Pioneer Bar	(see 10)
Tali Bar	(see 11)

To Residential Area

Kurkara Cres

Yulara Dr — Kiosk

Naninga Lookout

Uluru Meeting Place — Inmapiti Ampitheatre

Imalung Lookout

Resort Shopping Centre

Perentie Rd

Emu Lookout

Yulara Dr

To Connellan Airport (5km); Alice Springs (442km)

To Uluru (20km); Kata Tjuta (53km)

To Uluru Camel Tours (1km); Longitude 131 (2km)

Sights & Activities

When not visiting the park, most people will be content to spend their day lounging by the hotel pool, but there are some short **walking tracks** on Yulara's elevated dunes. Also check out the **Mulgara Gallery** in the lobby of the Sails in the Desert Hotel, where quality handmade Australian arts and crafts inspired by the landscape are displayed.

Each evening the **Night Sky Show** (☎ 8956 2563; www.ecotours.com.au; adult/child/family $33/25/95) provides an informative look at Anangu and Greek astrological legends, along with stunning views of the outback night sky through telescopes and binoculars. There are trips in English at 8.30pm and in Japanese at 9.15pm year-round, with further English sessions at 7.30pm from May to August and 10.15pm from September to April. Pick up/return from accommodation is included.

Sleeping

All of the accommodation in Yulara, including the camping ground and hostel, is owned by the Voyages Ayers Rock Resort. Even with almost 5000 beds, you should reserve all accommodation, especially during school holidays. Bookings can be made through **central reservations** (☎ 1300 134 044; www.ayersrockresort.com.au). The switchboard number at Yulara is ☎ 8957 7888. Accommodation is priced at a premium so search for internet deals and ask about discounts for stays of three days or more.

If you have your own transport, **Curtain Springs Station** (p148) may tempt you with free camping and relatively inexpensive accommodation.

The following are high season (July to November) prices. At all other times they're at least 10% lower.

BUDGET

Ayers Rock Resort Campground (☎ 8956 7001; camp .ground@ayersrockresort.com.au; unpowered/powered sites $31/36, permanent tents $90, cabins $150; ⏰ reception 7am-9pm; ✖ ☐ ⌨) Yulara's saviour for the budget-conscious and anyone with a tent, swag or caravan, this ground is set among native gardens interspersed with manicured patches of green grass. There are good facilities including a camp kitchen, free barbecues, laundry and a reasonably well-stocked kiosk. The permanent tents have two single beds and a table and very little room for anything else. And although the air-con cabins sleep six and have cooking facilities, they're rather small (no en suite) and would only really suit a young family.

Outback Pioneer Hotel & Lodge (☎ 8957 7605; dm/q $34/168; ✕ ▣ ☎) With a lively bar, plenty of food, and a range of accommodation, this is the budget choice for noncampers. The complex has two 20-bed YHA backpacker dorms and four-bed (2 double bunks) budget cabins with fridge and TV. All have shared bathrooms. With a cosy common room, internet cafe and the village pub, this is a bit of a social hub. The communal kitchen is top notch.

MIDRANGE & TOP END

It's definitely worth asking for standby discounts at the resort's more expensive options. As well, bona fide Territorians can usually secure a discount by flashing their driver's license.

Outback Pioneer Hotel & Lodge (☎ 8957 7605; budget d $210, without bathroom $184, standard d $412; ✕ ▣ ☎) The hotel section of this complex has budget and standard motel-style rooms with TVs and tea and coffee facilities. There are various configurations that sleep up to four people. Children under 12 are free, while extra adults (anybody over 12 years!) are charged $38. The standard rooms also have a kitchenette.

Lost Camel Hotel (☎ 8957 7605; d $412; ✕ ▣ ☎) This bright boutique hotel has been redesigned as a romantic couples' hangout with bold colours and Aboriginal designs. The rooms are modern but rather compact, with an en suite squeezed in behind the bed. Note that there are no TVs in the rooms. Outside distractions include the superb central pool, the TV lounge and the bar.

Emu Walk Apartments (☎ 8956 7714; 1-/2-bed apt $458/552; ✕) For a family group looking for self-contained accommodation, Emu Walk is the pick of the bunch. The apartments are not fancy, but they're bright and comfy and have a lounge with TV, one or two bedrooms (accommodating four or six people), and a fully equipped kitchen with washer and dryer. Rates are for two adults in the single bedroom apartment and for four adults in the double bedroom apartment. Extra persons over 12 years are charged $38.

Desert Gardens Hotel (☎ 8957 7714; d $458, deluxe with desert/Uluru view $520/560; ✕ ▣ ☎) One of

the Yulara originals, this ageing hotel has spacious rooms, in-house movies, a very pleasant pool, a restaurant and a bar. The deluxe rooms feature a balcony with desert or Uluru views.

Sails in the Desert (☎ 8956 2200; standard d $560, deluxe spa d $654, ste $898; ✕ ▣ ☎) Until Longitude came along, this five-star hotel was the top property in Yulara and it still maintains a high standard. The lovely pool area, with its signature sails, is exclusive to guests and there are tennis courts, a health spa, casual and formal restaurants and a piano bar. The deluxe spa rooms feature a balcony spa and several rooms (even standard rooms) offer a view of Uluru – request such a room when booking.

Longitude 131° (☎ 8957 7888; www.longitude131 .com.au; 2 nights s/d $3400/4200; ✕ ▣ ☎) For those who can afford it, this is the last word in luxury. There are just 15 stylish 'tents' (raised steel-constructed rooms with a canvas tent-style roof), each facing the northern side of the Rock and providing exquisite luxury and intimacy. The Rock views, which open out from your doorstep, are unbeatable. The plush lounge–dining area also offers elevated views and an open bar. All activities, meals, drinks and tours are included in the price and there's a minimum two-night stay.

Eating

Most eateries in Yulara are attached to accommodation places. At several of those with buffets, kids eat free with a paying adult, which can help cut costs for families.

RESTAURANTS

Gecko's Cafe (☎ 8956 2562; mains $17-28; ☺ lunch & dinner; ✕ Ⓥ) In the resort shopping centre, Gecko's is a casual, licensed restaurant and bar that is not attached to any accommodation. There's a bright and bustling air-con section as well as tables outside overlooking the central courtyard and around the veranda. The menu features a large range of salads, gourmet wood-fired pizzas and more substantial Mediterranean-inspired chicken dishes, seafood, steak and burgers.

Outback Pioneer Barbecue (Outback Pioneer Hotel & Lodge; barbecue $18-26; ☺ dinner) This do-it-yourself barbecue is easily the most popular informal dining experience in Yulara. Choose from kangaroo, barramundi, beef or veggie burger, cook it up on the barbecue and help yourself to the generous salad bar (salad bar only costs $16). There's a boisterous atmosphere in the bar most nights, and the main drawback is the long queue for the barbecues.

White Gums (☎ 8957 7888; Desert Gardens Hotel; dinner mains $20-35; ☺ breakfast & dinner; ⊠) It's mainly the hotel's guests who enjoy the big buffet breakfast and return at night for an à la carte dinner featuring fusion cuisine with Asian, Mediterranean and Australian themes.

Winkiku (☎ 8956 2200; Sails in the Desert; breakfast buffet $25-35, dinner buffet $60; ☺ breakfast & dinner; ⊠) In one of Yulara's five-star hotels, this casual-yet-stylish restaurant does extravagant buffets with seafood, a meat carvery, and all the trimmings and desserts you can imagine. Kids (under 12) eat free, so it can work out as good value for fecund families.

Bough House (☎ 8956 2170; Outback Pioneer Lodge; breakfast/dinner buffets $28/47; ⊠) Another smorgasbord special, this family-friendly, country-style place overlooks the pool at the Outback Pioneer and has buffet spreads for breakfast and dinner. The dinner choices feature Australian fare – kangaroo, emu, crocodile and barramundi. Kids under 12 eat free, so collect a bunch and bring 'em along.

Rockpool (☎ 8956 2200; Sails in the Desert; tapas $45; ☺ dinner) Beside the pool and under the sails, this casual, alfresco eatery provides delicious Mediterranean and Asian snacks and some decadent desserts.

Kuniya (☎ 8956 2200; Sails in the Desert Hotel; mains $45-60; ☺ dinner; ⊠) Yulara's most sophisticated restaurant, Kuniya is the place for romantic candlelit dinners and special occasions. The walls are adorned with contemporary Australian art and the inspired menu features Aussie cuisine infused with native ingredients. Dress smartly and note that reservations are essential.

Arngulli Flame Grill (☎ 8957 7888; Desert Gardens Hotel; 2/3 courses $49/59; ☺ dinner; ⊠) This seasonal, set-price restaurant features flame-grilled meats and seafood, though note that premium cuts of steak attract a surcharge on the set prices.

CAFES & TAKEAWAY
Red Rock Deli (Resort Shopping Centre; snacks $4-10; ☺ 8am-4pm) Chilly mornings see the folks lining up here for steaming hot espresso and croissants. There're also muffins and sticky cakes for a calorie infusion, and filled paninis, wraps and baguettes for a guilt-free lunch.

Red Rock Burger Bar (Resort Shopping Centre; burgers $6.50-10; ☺ lunch) This is the place to head for a no-fuss burger and chips on the run.

Pioneer Kitchen (Outback Pioneer Lodge; mains $10-17; ☺ lunch & dinner) This hole-in-the-wall serves up edible burgers, chips and pizzas to hungry backpackers, but it won't win any gourmet awards.

SELF-CATERING
Yulara IGA Supermarket (Resort Shopping Centre; ☺ 8am-9pm) This well-stocked supermarket has a delicatessen and also sells picnic portions, fresh fruit and vegetables, meat, groceries, ice and camping supplies at reasonable prices.

Drinking
Takeaway alcohol is only available from the bar of the **Outback Pioneer Hotel** (☺ 6-10pm), and in order to mke a purchase you'll need a room key or camping permit to prove you're a guest at the resort. When the sun sets on Uluru, evening entertainment can be found in a handful of hotel bars.

Outback Pioneer Bar (Outback Pioneer Lodge; ☎ 8957 7605; ☺ 10am-midnight) If you're after a cold beer and a game of pool in a rowdy, convivial environment, this open-air bar is the social centre of Yulara. There's live entertainment every night – usually a guitar-twanging country singer – and plenty of chances to meet travellers and locals at the long bench tables.

Tali Bar (Sails in the Desert Hotel; ☺ 10am-1am) At this elegant little piano bar you can try cocktails ($15 to $20) inspired by the landscape, such as 'valley of the winds' and 'desert oasis', while listening to the tinkling ivories and overlooking the pool area. Dress standards rise as the sun sets.

Bunya Bar (Desert Gardens Hotel; ☺ 11am-midnight) The lobby bar at the Desert Gardens has chess and games tables in a rather sterile cigar-lounge setting. There's also a bar at this hotel's pool.

GETTING THERE & AWAY
Air
Connellan Airport is roughly 5km from Yulara. **Qantas** (13 13 13; www.qantas.com.au) has direct flights from Alice Springs ($160, one hour), Cairns ($400, three hours), Melbourne ($300, three hours), Perth ($215, 2¼ hours) and Sydney ($280, 3½ hours). Check the website for the latest deals.

Bus

Daily shuttle connections (listed as minitours) between Alice Springs and Yulara are run by **AAT Kings** (☎ 1300 556100; www.aatkings.com) and cost adult/child $135/68. **Austour** (☎ 1800 335009; www .austour.com.au) run the cheapest daily connections between Alice Springs and Uluru ($120/60). At the time of research, there were no direct services between Adelaide and Yulara.

Car

Renting a car in Alice Springs to go down to Uluru and back is a reasonable option between a group, but shop around and make sure you get unlimited kilometres (or a reasonable kilometre deal – you'll travel at least 1000km). Some operators offer special two- or three-day rental deals, but expect to pay at least $100 a day for a small car. See p191 for a list of operators. Alternatively you can hire a vehicle in Yulara. **Hertz** (☎ 8956 2244) has a desk at the Tour & Information Centre (p157), which also has phones direct to the **Avis** (☎ 8956 2266) and **Thrifty** (☎ 8956 2030) desks at Connellan Airport.

There's a **service station** (☎ 8956 2229; ⏰ 7am-9pm) up the road from the Outback Pioneer Hotel & Lodge that sells all types of fuel, snacks, maps and ice; a mechanic is on duty every day.

GETTING AROUND
To/From the Airport

A free shuttle bus meets all flights and drops off at all accommodation points around the resort; pick-up is 90 minutes before your flight.

Around Yulara

A free shuttle bus loops through the resort – stopping at all accommodation points and the shopping centre – every 15 minutes from 10.30am to 6pm and from 6.30pm to 12.30am daily.

Bike hire is available at the **Ayers Rock Resort Camp Ground** (☎ 8957 7001; per hr $7, per half-/full-day $15/20, deposit $200 or credit card; ⏰ 7am-8pm).

Around the National Park

Uluru Express (☎ 8956 2152; www.uluruexpress.com.au) runs shuttles to Uluru and back at sunrise and sunset (adult/child $45/25), and during the day ($40/20). Morning shuttles to Kata Tjuta cost $60/35; afternoon shuttles include a stop for the Uluru sunset and cost $65/35. There are also two-day ($145/70) and three-day ($160/70) passes that allow unlimited use of the service. Fares do not include the park-entry fee.

Uluru to Alice Springs

Moving on from Uluru (Ayers Rock) there are few routes from which to choose. Of course you can head straight back to the Stuart Hwy at Erldunda for the quick, smooth run north to Alice. However, this route can easily be supplemented with an out-and-back visit to Kings Canyon without getting off the tarmac. From Kings Canyon, experienced drivers in well-prepared vehicles can venture forth on a couple of rough-and-ready outback roads. The Red Centre Way, incorporating the Mereenie Loop Rd, is the shortest route from Kings Canyon to Alice Springs, while the equally corrugated Ernest Giles Rd strikes east to meet up with the Stuart Hwy about 70km north of Erldunda.

The major drawcard in this region is the stunning, sheer-walled Kings Canyon of Watarrka National Park in the George Gill Range. Here visitors can embark on several short walks in and around the canyon exploring fascinating geological formations, panoramic vistas and cool, shaded refuges with permanent water.

Beyond Kings Canyon, as you approach Alice Springs on the corrugated Mereenie Loop Rd, you can make side trips to the ancient crater of Tnorala (Gosse Bluff), the historic mission of Hermannsburg, and the lost worlds of Finke Gorge National Park. To explore Finke Gorge National Park you'll definitely need a 4WD. The highlight of this remote quarter is the luxuriant Palm Valley. Exploring these extraordinary places and camping under the stars gives the traveller a true appreciation of the rugged beauty and isolation of this region.

HIGHLIGHTS

- Walking the **Kings Canyon rim walk** (p166) as the setting sun warms the sheer red cliffs
- Tackling the 4WD track to camp under the stars and slender palms at the amazing and secluded **Palm Valley** (p169)
- Inspecting the poignant buildings and central Australian art before sampling a strudel at historic **Hermannsburg** (p168)
- Capturing the changing hues of **Rainbow Valley** (p164) as the sun sets on this other-worldly geological formation
- Taking the challenging short cut from Kings Canyon to Alice Springs on the lonely **Mereenie Loop Road** p167)
- Riding a swaying camel or straddling a revving quad bike at **Kings Creek Station** (p166)
- Exploring Australia's oldest river, the Finke, on the challenging 4WD route through **Finke Gorge** (p170)

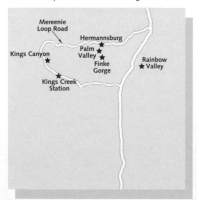

- TELEPHONE CODE: ☎ 08
- www.nreta.gov.au

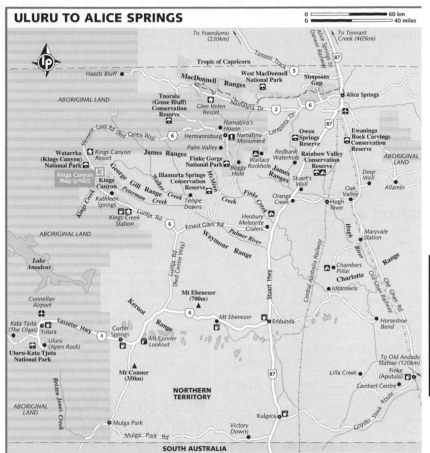

ULURU TO ALICE SPRINGS

ULURU TO ALICE SPRINGS

ERLDUNDA TO ALICE SPRINGS

For those wanting to take a fully sealed road route to Alice Springs the only option is to head east from Uluru and Yulara to the Stuart Hwy at Erldunda (see p148) and then strike north. The diversions are few and far between, though they do make a welcome break from staring at the wobbly black strip winding out beyond the windscreen. You can inspect impact craters from an extraterrestrial invasion, ride a camel, or turn off to Rainbow Valley for a spectacular sunset before heading into Alice Springs.

ERNEST GILES ROAD

The unsealed Ernest Giles Rd heads west from the Stuart Hwy about 70km north of Erldunda. This is one of the shorter routes to Kings Canyon (the other being the Mereenie Loop Rd) from Alice, but it's hard on vehicles (and drivers) and impassable after heavy rain. About 100km from the Stuart Hwy the track joins the Luritja Rd (p165), which is sealed for the final 95km to Kings Canyon. Beyond the Henbury Meteorite Craters turn-off, the Ernest Giles Rd is not recommended for 2WDs.

Henbury Meteorite Craters Conservation Reserve

Eleven kilometres west of the Stuart Hwy, a corrugated track on the right leads 5km to a cluster of 12 small craters in an exposed, stony plain. About 4500 years ago a meteorite clocking a scorching 40,000km/h broke up as it entered the earth's atmosphere. The craters were formed when the fragments hit the ground – the largest of the craters is 180m wide and 15m deep, and was formed by a piece of rock about the size of a 44-gallon drum.

The facts are interesting, but it's only worth a detour if you have a deep interest in this sort of thing. NASA once used the craters for training astronauts.

The exposed **camping ground** (adult/child/family $3.30/1.65/7.70) here is on stony ground, has no water, and is pretty grim.

STUART'S WELL

Stuart's Well is about 120km north of Erldunda and 90km south of Alice Springs, where the Stuart Hwy passes through a gap in the James Ranges. It's well worth stopping in at the roadhouse for a beer and to browse the walls of photos and memorabilia covering the history of the development of Kings Canyon by the Cotterill family. You might also catch Dinky the famous singing dingo – rescued and raised from a pup by owner Jim Cotterill. Dinky entertains tourists by tiptoeing across the piano and howling a few notes!

The main attraction here though is **Camels Australia** (☎ 8956 0925; www.camels-australia.com .au), founded by central Australia's 'camel king', Noel Fullerton. It's a good opportunity to take a short camel ride (adult/child $5/4 around the yard, $25/20 for 30 minutes, $40/30 for one hour, and $165 for one day), but the serious stuff is the extended outback safaris from three ($500) to five days ($800) through the gaps and gorges of the James Ranges. Meals, swag accommodation and camel are included.

Jim's Place (☎ 8956 0808; unpowered/powered sites $17/20, budget r with own swag/supplied linen $15/30, s/d cabins with en suite $70/85; mains $15-30; ⏰ 9am-8.30pm; ✖ 🖵 🕿), next door to the camel farm, is a roadhouse run by central Australian identity Jim Cotterill. The Cotterill family, Jim and his late father Jack, opened up Kings Canyon to tourism, cutting a road through from their Wallara Ranch in the 1960s – the truck used to clear the roads sits out front. There's a monument to Jack at Kings Canyon and

Jim is a fountain of knowledge on the area. Jim's has a shaded camping ground, pool and spa, a store with basic provisions and a licensed restaurant.

RAINBOW VALLEY CONSERVATION RESERVE

The turn-off to Rainbow Valley is only 15km north of Stuarts Well (77km south of Alice Springs) along the Stuart Hwy. From there it is 24km along a 4WD road to the car park and camping area. The attraction at Rainbow Valley is a series of sandstone bluffs and cliffs that blaze then blush in a shifting show of ochre red, orange and purple as the sun sets. If you're lucky enough to visit after some rain, the whole scene is stunningly reflected in the foreground claypans.

The reserve is important to the southern Arrernte people, and the large rock massif known as Ewerre in the south of the reserve is a registered sacred site. There's a sunset-viewing platform and a 10-minute walk skirts the claypan and leads around the foot of the bluff to **mushroom rock**.

The small **camping ground** (adult/child/family $3.30/1.65/7.70) has picnic tables, a pit toilet and gas barbecues. It's a bit exposed, with little shade and no water, but the setting is superb and perfectly positioned for sunset viewing.

RED CENTRE WAY & KINGS CANYON

The Red Centre Way connects Uluru with Alice Springs via the Lasseter Hwy, Luritja Rd, Mereenie Loop Rd and, finally, with a choice of the Namatjira or Larapinta Drs. At the time of research the Namatjira Dr was being progressively sealed, which will complete a fully sealed 'inner loop' with the Larapinta Dr. The plan for sealing the Mereenie Loop Rd is one of the biggest talking points in Alice – and has been for a very long time. Locals aren't holding their breath, and neither should you.

The main attraction along this route is, of course, Kings Canyon, and the drive beyond the canyon along the Mereenie Loop Rd offers a challenging outback driving experience.

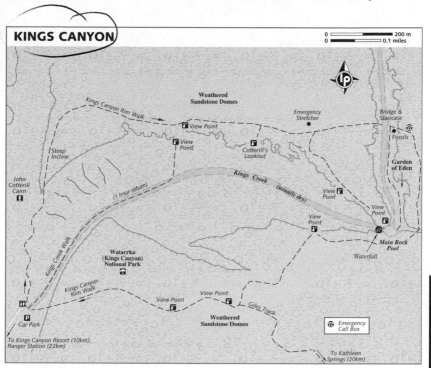

KINGS CANYON

0 ——————— 200 m
0 ——————— 0.1 miles

Weathered Sandstone Domes

Kings Canyon Rim Walk

View Point

View Point

Emergency Stretcher

Bridge & Staircase

Fossils

Steep Incline

Cotterill's Lookout

Garden of Eden

John Cotterill Cairn

Kings Creek (usually dry)

(1 hour return)

View Point

View Point

View Point

Kings Creek Walk

Watarrka (Kings Canyon) National Park

Main Rock Pool

Waterfall

Kings Canyon Rim Walk

View Point

View Point

View Point

Giles Track

Weathered Sandstone Domes

Emergency Call Box

Car Park

To Kings Canyon Resort (10km); Ranger Station (22km)

To Kathleen Springs (20km)

LURITJA ROAD

The sealed Luritja Rd leaves the Lasseter Hwy 136km east of Yulara. After 67km you reach the intersection with the Ernest Giles Rd, an unsealed road heading directly east, across the Palmer River, and past the Henbury Meteorite Craters Conservation Reserve (p163) to link up with the Stuart Highway 140km south of Alice.

Past the Ernest Giles Rd intersection, the Luritja Rd swings northwest as the escarpment of the George Gill range comes into view. Kings Creek Station appears on the left after 58km and it is another 36km to the Kings Canyon turn-off.

KINGS CANYON & WATARRKA NATIONAL PARK

The western half of the George Gill Range is protected by Watarrka National Park, which includes one of central Australia's greatest attractions – the sheer, 100m-high walls of **Kings Canyon**.

The name Watarrka refers to the area around the Kuninga (western quoll or native cat) Dreaming Trail, which passes through the park. More than 600 plant species have been recorded in the park, giving it the highest plant diversity of any place in Australia's arid zone. At the head of the 1km gorge is the spring-fed **Garden of Eden**, where a moist microclimate shelters a variety of plants. The gorge is carved from a dominating sandstone plateau, crowned in many places by bizarre, weathered sandstone domes.

History

The Luritja Aboriginal people have lived in this area for at least 20,000 years. There are sacred sites and three communities of Aboriginal people living within the park.

In 1872 Ernest Giles named the George Gill Range after his brother-in-law, who also helped fund the expedition. Here he found desperately needed water. Giles also named Kings Creek after his friend Fielder King. Being the first European to explore the area, Giles had first option on applying for a pastoral lease, which he did in 1874. It covered almost 1000 sq miles and included the area of the present park.

WALKING THE CANYON RIM

The **Kings Canyon Rim walk** (6km loop, three to four hours, medium) is a fabulous walk that not only offers an awesome view into the canyon from several angles, but also takes you through a diverse range of terrain and geological features. From the canyon car park it begins with a short, steep climb up a rocky slope (about 20 minutes), which is the only 'difficult' part of the walk. From here the trail skirts the western rim of the canyon with stunning views of the sheer eastern cliff faces. Here you see fascinating ripple rock, ancient-looking cypress pines and the first of the curious 'beehive' domes: weathered sandstone outcrops which to the Luritja represent the men of the Kuniya Dreaming.

A 600m detour leads to Cotterill's Lookout with spectacular views directly down into the canyon. The trail then descends down wooden stairs into the Garden of Eden, a narrow gorge leading to a lush oasis of ferns and prehistoric cycads ending at a tranquil pool. The walk continues around the eastern side of the canyon rim, then crosses a swarm of beehive domes before descending via stone steps (starting at Kestrel Falls lookout) to the car park.

Although the walk is not difficult, a reasonable level of fitness is required, as is plenty of water and a hat. Watch your step around the rim of the canyon – the cliffs are unfenced and the wind can be strong.

Pastoralist William Liddle took up a lease and established Angas Downs Station in 1929. The first tourism venture in the area was set up by Jack Cotterill in 1960 on Angas Downs Station, and was run from here until the formation of the park in 1989.

Information

General information is available at the receptions at Kings Creek Station and Kings Canyon Resort. Both places sell fuel. At the resort you can access the **internet** (Desert Oaks Cafe; 10am-9pm), and buy groceries and Mereenie Loop Passes at the **service station** (7am-7pm) within the resort's shopping precinct.

Sights & Activities

There's a **sunset-viewing area** 1km short of the canyon car park. Toilets, water and information are available at the car park from where several walks start. From May to October there are ranger-guided **walks** on Thursday and Saturday starting from the Kings Canyon car park.

BUSHWALKING

The canyon rim walk is one of the best short walks in central Australia – see the boxed text, above.

Kings Creek walk (2km return, one hour, easy) A short stroll along the rocky bed of Kings Creek leads to a raised platform with amphitheatre-like views of the towering canyon rim. There is wheelchair access for the first 700m.

Kathleen Springs walk (2.5km return, one hour, easy) A wheelchair-accessible path leads from the car park (17km

southeast of the canyon turn-off) to a beautiful spring-fed rock pool at the base of the range. This permanent waterhole was important to the nomadic Luritja people and harboured abundant food plants, such as the native fig and plum bush. There is a picnic ground with gas barbecues, shade, water and toilets.

Giles track (22km one-way, overnight, easy) If you have more time, this lovely marked trail follows the George Gill Range from Kathleen Springs to Kings Canyon (one-way only), partly in the footsteps of explorer Ernest Giles. There's plenty of wildlife to be seen, particularly around the waterholes. It's possible to do part of this track as a day walk from Lilla (Reedy Creek), about halfway along the trail. You need to be fully self-sufficient in both food and water and overnight walkers should register (1300 650 730). There's a designated camping ground along the ridge above Lilla.

QUAD BIKE & CAMEL RIDES

Kings Creek Station (opposite) offers **quadbiking** (30min/1hr/2½hr $67/78/176), riders must be over 16 years; and more sedate **camel rides** (5min $7, 15min $15, 1hr sunrise or sunset ride adult/child $50/40).

SCENIC FLIGHTS

Helicopter flights from Kings Canyon Resort with **Professional Helicopter Services** (PHS, 8956 7873) cost $115 for a 15-minute trip over the canyon and $220 for 30 minutes over the canyon and George Gill Range.

Kings Creek Helicopters (8956 7886; flights per person $45-380) has flights from Kings Creek Station, including a short buzz in the local area for $45, Petermann Pound ($110, 15 minutes) or Kings Canyon ($220, 30 minutes).

ABORIGINAL AUSTRALIA: CONWAYS' KIDS

Ian Conway of Kings Creek Station grew up in Arrernte and Luritja country, his pedigree is of Arrernte and pioneer stock, and he speaks the lingo of the bush – straight talking. When Ian saw the desperate health and education needs of nearby cultural Aboriginal communities and how government funding was not reaching the people it was intended for, he decided to bypass the bureaucracy and break the spiral of hopelessness. With his wife Lyn, he set up a charitable trust, Conways' Kids (www.conwayskids.org.au) and approached private schools in Adelaide. The response to this grassroots approach was overwhelming – the kids from remote communities such as Ukarka are looked after in terms of boarding, health and private tuition to bring them up to speed. Ian says, 'These kids are the future for these communities, but they have to grapple with homesickness and massive culture shock'. In Ian's words the aim of the trust is 'To ensure cultural Aboriginal children of central Australia get the same chance of education as the children of wider Australia'.

Sleeping & Eating

our pick **Kings Creek Station** (☎ 8956 7474; www .kingscreekstation.com.au; Luritja Rd; campsites per adult/child $15.50/7.70, power $5.50, safari cabins s/d $95/145; ☒) This is a friendly, family-run alternative to the big resort. About 35km southeast of the Kings Canyon turn-off, it also offers something of a bush camping experience. Pleasant campsites are set among desert oaks. In a separate area are the 'safari cabins' (small canvas tents on a solid floor with bedding, heating and lighting), which come with cooked breakfast. Amenities are shared and there's a communal kitchen/barbecue/campfire area. For more upmarket accommodation located elsewhere on the station, see Kings Canyon Wilderness Lodge below.

Camel or quad-bike safaris and helicopter flights are also available. Fuel, ice, beer, wine, snacks, barbecue packs and limited supplies are available at the **shop** (☒ 7am-7pm).

Kings Canyon Resort (☎ 1800 089 622; www.kings canyonresort.com.au; Luritja Rd; unpowered/powered sites $27/33, dm $42, lodge/standard/deluxe d $104/344/428; ☒ ☒ ☒) Only about 10km from the canyon, this resort boasts a wide range of accommodation from campsites to deluxe rooms with patio spas. The grassy camping ground has plenty of shade, a pool (with bar), laundry and barbecues. The four-bed dorms and lodge rooms share kitchen and bathroom facilities. Thoughtful design of the hotel rooms gives you the feeling of being comfortably secluded in the bush. There are several dining options: the **Desert Oaks Cafe** (mains $8-15; ☒ 10am-3pm; ☒) has burgers and snacks; the **George Gill Bar** (mains $9-20; ☒ 3pm-late; ☒) does pizzas; the **Outback BBQ & Grill** (mains $29-35; ☒ dinner; ☒) has big steaks and live entertainment; and **Carmichael's**

(☒ breakfast & dinner; ☒) is a stylish buffet restaurant. A final option is **Sounds of Firelight** (☎ 1300 134 044; per person $139), a five-course, gourmet meal with drinks served under the stars around a campfire. This intimate bush dinner is similar to the Sounds of Silence dinner at Uluru (without the view), and is marketed as a romantic night out (restricted to 10 couples).

Kings Canyon Wilderness Lodge (☎ 1800 891 121; www.aptouring.com.au; Luritja Rd; tented cabins d $500; ☒) This new luxury retreat of 10 tented cabins with private en suite facilities is secreted in a pocket of Kings Creek Station. The very private, spacious cabins are set among grand desert oaks and a gourmet breakfast and dinner is included in the tariff. It's the perfect place to get away from it all, but if you get the urge to do a bit more, all the activities at Kings Creek Station are not too far away.

Getting There & Away

There are no regular commercial flights to Kings Canyon. **Austour** (☎ 1800 335 009; www.aus tour.com.au) runs the cheapest daily connections between Alice Springs and Kings Canyon (adult/child $110/60).

If you have your own vehicle, preferably 4WD, the most interesting route to/from Alice Springs is the 331km Mereenie Loop Rd and the West MacDonnells. An even more exciting route for well-prepared, experienced 4WDers is through the Finke Gorge National Park via the Ernest Giles Rd and Boggy Hole.

MEREENIE LOOP ROAD

The rugged Mereenie Loop Rd begins just beyond Kings Canyon Resort looping northwest then east to Katapata Gap, about 26km west

ULURU TO ALICE SPRINGS

of where Larapinta Dr links with Namatjira Dr. In dry conditions the road is suitable for conventional vehicles with good ground clearance, though there are deep sandy patches and countless corrugations (call ☎ 1800 246 199 for latest road conditions). Be aware that 2WD hire vehicles will not be covered by insurance on this road. The Northern Territory government is planning to seal the route; however, the project has been on the drawing board for quite a while. Fuel is available at Kings Canyon Resort, Hermannsburg and Glen Helen Resort.

To travel along this route, which passes through Aboriginal land, you need a **Mereenie Tour Pass** ($2.20), which is valid for one day and includes a souvenir booklet with details about the local Aboriginal culture and a route map. Passes are available at Kings Canyon Resort, Tourism Central Australia Visitor Information Centre in Alice Springs, Glen Helen Resort, and Hermannsburg.

There's a rest area at **Jump Up Lookout**, 28km from Kings Canyon Resort, but note that camping is not permitted anywhere along the Mereenie Loop. It takes around 3½ hours to travel the 204km from Kings Canyon Resort to Hermannsburg. The road travels through low scrub, sand dunes and bare rocky ridges. Artificial highlights include a skeletal tree bristling with discarded tyres and car-body parts, and makeshift road signs – a rusty old 44-gallon drum carries a warning to slow down: 'LIFT UM FOOT', soon followed by another reading 'PUTTUM BACK DOWN'!

About 156km from the resort, Namatjira Dr intersects from the north. Straight ahead on Larapinta Dr is Hermannsburg (44km), Finke Gorge National Park (66km) and Alice Springs (170km). Turn left for Tnorala (18km), Glen Helen Resort (73km) and Alice Springs (205km).

Tnorala (Gosse Bluff) Conservation Reserve

This remnant of a huge crater was blasted out of the earth when a comet plunged into the ground around 140 million years ago. The power of such an impact is almost impossible to comprehend – the 5km-diameter crater you see today was originally 2km below the impact surface, and is just the core of the original 20km-diameter crater.

The crater was named by Ernest Giles in 1872 after Harry Gosse, a telegraphist at the Alice Springs Telegraph Station. Tnorala is the Western Arrernte name for the crater, and in the local mythology is a traditional wooden baby carrier that crashed down from the sky during the Dreaming. The area is a registered sacred site.

Tnorala can also be approached from the north via Namatjira Dr and Tylers Lookout (p199), which provides a panoramic view of the crater. Access to Tnorala is 8km along a rough track, best tackled in a 4WD, which goes right into the crater. There's a picnic ground with pit toilet, but camping is not permitted. A Mereenie Tour Pass is required.

HERMANNSBURG
pop 460

The Aboriginal settlement of Hermannsburg (Ntaria), about 125km from Alice Springs, is famous as the one-time home of artist Albert Namatjira, the birthplace of anthropologist Ted Strehlow and the site of the Hermannsburg Mission.

Although the town is sited on restricted Aboriginal land, permits are not required to visit the mission, general store or supermarket, or to travel through. Groceries, fuel, Mereenie Tour Passes and takeaway food are available from **Ntaria Supermarket** (☎ 8956 7480; ⏲ 9am-5.30pm Mon-Sat, 10am-5.30pm Sun) on the main road into town. You'll also find an ATM and internet access here.

Hermannsburg Historic Precinct

In 1876, fresh from the Hermannsburg Mission Institute in Germany, pastors AH Kempe and WF Schwarz left Adelaide bound for central Australia. The journey was a testing introduction to the central Australian environment, and the pastors eventually arrived at the site of the mission 18 months later. In 1894 Pastor Carl Strehlow arrived. Strehlow learnt the Arrernte language, translated the New Testament into Arrernte and wrote a number of important works on the Arrernte people. His youngest son, Professor TGH (Ted) Strehlow, was born on the mission and spent more than 40 years studying the Arrernte people. The Arrernte entrusted him with many items of spiritual significance when they realised their traditional lifestyle was under threat. These items are under the care of the Strehlow Research Centre in Alice Springs (p177).

ALBERT NAMATJIRA

Australia's most renowned Aboriginal artist, Albert Namatjira (1902–59) lived at the Hermannsburg Lutheran Mission west of Alice Springs and was introduced to the art of European-style water-colour painting by Rex Batterbee in the 1930s.

Namatjira successfully captured the essence of central Australia using distinctive purple, blue and orange hues and a style heavily influenced by European art. At the time his paintings were seen solely as picturesque landscapes. However, it's now understood that they depicted important Dreaming sites to which he had a great cultural bond.

Namatjira supported many of his people with the income from his work, as was his obligation under traditional law. In 1957 he was the first Aboriginal person to be granted Australian citizenship. Due to this, he was permitted to buy alcohol at a time when it was illegal for Aboriginal people to do so. Remaining true to his kinship responsibilities, he broke non-Indigenous laws and in 1958 was jailed for six months for supplying alcohol to his community. Released from jail, he died the following year, aged 57.

Namatjira did much to change the extremely negative views of Aboriginal people that prevailed back then. At the same time, he paved the way for the Papunya Tula painting movement that emerged a decade after his death.

Just east of Hermannsburg is a monument to Albert Namatjira, and about 5km west of town is Namatjira House, a tiny stone cottage where Albert lived with his family for five years from 1944.

The whitewashed walls of the **mission** (☎ 8956 7402; adult/child/family $10/5/25; �) 9am-4pm Mar-Nov, 10am-4pm Dec-Feb) are shaded by majestic river red gums and old date palms. Among the low, stone buildings are a church, a school and various houses and outbuildings. The 'Manse' houses an art gallery and a history of the life and times of Albert Namatjira as well as examples of the work of 39 Hermannsburg artists.

The **Kata-Anga Tea Room** (meals $7-13; ☉ 9am-4pm), in the old missionary house, serves highly recommended apple strudel and Devonshire tea. Distinctive paintings and pottery by the locals is also on display here and is for sale.

FINKE GORGE NATIONAL PARK

Famous for its rare red cabbage palms, Finke Gorge National Park, south of Hermannsburg, is one of central Australia's premier wilderness reserves. The top-billing attraction is Palm Valley with its ribbon of tall palms and cycads, but the main gorge features high red cliffs, stately river red gums, cool waterholes and lovely walks.

For thousands of years, the Finke River formed part of an Aboriginal trade route that crossed Australia, bringing goods such as sacred red ochre from the south and pearl shell from the north to the central Australian tribes. The area around Hermannsburg was a major refuge for the Western Arrernte people in times of drought, thanks to the permanent water in soaks dug in the Finke River bed.

Access to the park follows the sandy bed of the Finke River and rocky tracks, and so a high-clearance 4WD is essential. If you don't have one, several tour operators go to Palm Valley from Alice Springs, see p182. The turn-off to Palm Valley starts about 1km west of the Hermannsburg turn-off on Larapinta Dr, while the turn-off to Finke Gorge starts about 50m east of the Hermannsburg turn-off.

Palm Valley

If you only have time to see one part of the park, don't miss Palm Valley (Mpulungkinya), where towering red cabbage palms shelter beneath stark sandstone cliffs.

Leaving the Finke River at its junction with Palm Creek, head west past an old ranger station and 1km further on you arrive at the Kalarranga car park. En route, a small information bay introduces some of the walks in the area. **Kalarranga**, also known as the Amphitheatre, is a semicircle of striking sandstone formations sculpted by a long-gone meander of Palm Creek. From Kalarranga, you soon pass the camping ground, and from here the track deteriorates into an extremely rough and rocky ride for the final 5km to Palm Valley. The valley is actually a narrow gorge that in places is literally choked with stands of red cabbage palms up to 25m high.

PALMS FROM THE PAST

The tall, slender palms that grace Palm Valley are a remarkable remnant from a time when central Australia enjoyed a much wetter climate. The seemingly incongruous palms and cycads survive here because of a reliable supply of water within the surrounding sandstone. The tall red cabbage palms (*Livistona mariae*) are found nowhere else in the world and grow in an area of about 60 sq km. To the Arrernte people the palms are associated with the Fire Dreaming. There are about 3000 mature palms in the wild, so rangers request that you stay on the marked trails out of the palm groves – the young palms are hard to see and can easily get trampled underfoot.

BUSHWALKING

The four marked walking tracks in the Palm Valley area are fairly gentle hikes, all suitable for families.

Kalarranga Lookout (1.5km return, 45 minutes, easy) The view over the Amphitheatre from this mushroomlike sandstone knob is striking. Dawn breaks beautifully here.

Arankaia walk (2km loop, one hr, easy) This walk traverses the valley, returning via the sandstone plateau where there are great views over the park.

Mpulungkinya track (5km loop, two hours, easy) This walk through Palm Valley passes dense stands of palms and offers excellent views down the gorge before joining the Arankaia walk on the return. It's the most popular walk in the park and is a good one to tackle in the morning or afternoon when animals descend into the gorge to drink and forage.

Mpaara track (5km loop, two hours, medium) From the Kalarranga car park, this loop track takes in the Finke River, Palm Bend and the rugged Amphitheatre. It leads you in the footsteps of two heroes from the Aboriginal Dreaming: Mpaara (Tawny Frogmouth Man) and Pangkalanya (Devil Man), whose various adventures are explained by signs along the way.

SLEEPING

Palm Valley Camping Ground (adult/child/family $6.60/3.30/15.40) Located beside Palm Creek, with views across to the red sandstone ridges, this is a superb camping ground with hot showers, gas barbecues, fireplaces and flush toilets. It's a popular spot, so it's worth arriving early to secure a site, especially on weekends. Remember to collect firewood before the park-entry sign. Rangers give free campfire talks here on Tuesday and Friday nights between May and October.

Finke Gorge

If you have a high-clearance 4WD and you're well prepared, there's a challenging route through the national park following the sandy bed of the Finke River. This is a remote and scenic drive to the Ernest Giles Rd, from where you can continue west to Kings Canyon (and Uluru), or east back to the Stuart Hwy. Because the rough track involves deep sand driving, it pays to travel with another vehicle – plenty of people have been bogged on the way to Boggy Hole!

The track leaves Larapinta Dr about 50m or so east of the main turn-off to Hermannsburg. It's about 32km (1½ hours) to **Boggy Hole**, a popular permanent waterhole and camping spot (no facilities). Nearby are the scant remains of a police camp set up in 1889 to protect pastoralists and stock. Another 37km brings you to the turnoff to **Illamurta Springs Conservation Reserve**, an isolated spring with ruins of a police camp 11km along the track.

In all it's about 100km from Hermannsburg to the Ernest Giles Rd – allow two days from Alice Springs. Register your trip at ☎ 1300 650 730 and check road conditions by calling ☎ 1800 246 199.

HERMANNSBURG TO ALICE SPRINGS

There are a couple of worthwhile detours along the route from Hermannsburg to Alice Springs. The first is to **Wallace Rockhole**, an outpost of Hermannsburg Mission.

Wallace Rockhole Tourist Park (☎ 8956 7993; www .wallacerockholetours.com.au; unpowered/powered sites per person $10/12, cabins d $130) has a pleasant camping area with good facilities, plus cabins with private bathrooms. Tours must be booked in advance and include a 1½-hour **rock art and bush medicine tour** (adult/child $10/8) and **bush tucker tag-along tours** ($50; minimum 6 people). The access road is unsealed, but suitable for 2WD vehicles.

Another interesting detour leaves Larapinta Dr 50km west of Alice Springs. This 50km 4WD route through **Owen Springs Reserve** follows the Hugh River through the old Owen Springs cattle station to the Stuart Hwy. It can easily be done as a loop day trip from Alice Springs, a total of about 160km, or there are bush campsites along the river. About 4km before you reach the Stuart Hwy there's a turn-off to **Redbank Waterhole**, a permanent waterhole where you can camp. Once on the highway it's an easy 45-minute drive back to Alice.

Alice Springs & Around

The Alice, as it's often known, sprang from humble beginnings as a lonely telegraph station on the continent-spanning Overland Telegraph Line (OTL) nearly 140 years ago. It is an outback town with a singular personality borne of its vibrant Aboriginal culture, tough pioneering past and, naturally, the inexorable, expansive outback stretching towards every horizon. No matter which direction you arrive from, or what mode of transport delivers you, this thriving town makes a sudden and welcome interruption to a long journey.

Although still famous for its remote location, this is no longer a lonely frontier town beyond the influence and trends of the coastal capitals or the wider world. Ignited by the boom in adventure tourism, the insatiable interest in contemporary Aboriginal art and improved access, the modernisation of Alice has been abrupt and confronting. For many travellers, international and Australian, Alice Springs is their first encounter with contemporary Indigenous Australia – with its enchanting art, mesmerising culture and its present-day challenges.

The Alice is a pit stop of relaxation and retail therapy for any big outback trip, and is the natural base for exploring central Australia. After all, Uluru-Kata Tjuta National Park is a *relatively* close four-hour drive away! The ruggedly beautiful MacDonnell Ranges stretch east and west from the town centre, and you don't have to venture far to find yourself among ochre red gorges, pastel-hued ranges and ghostly white gum trees – the romantic yet challenging landscape portrayed in a 19th-century explorer's diary or a Namatjira watercolour.

HIGHLIGHTS

- Breakfasting or brunching in **Todd Mall** (p187) before browsing contemporary Aboriginal art in central Australia's premier art galleries
- Uncovering the secret lives of desert fauna and examining a wedge-tailed eagle up close at the **Alice Springs Desert Park** (p175)
- Hiking one of Australia's great walks – the **Larapinta Trail** (p195) to camp under a billion stars and wake up an ancient landscape.
- Walking the superb track through the gorge and around the pound at **Ormiston Gorge** (p197)
- Exploring the birthplace of Alice at the **Telegraph Station Historical Reserve** (p178)
- Filing through the narrow cleft of **Standley Chasm** (p196) as the midday sun briefly warms the sheer red walls
- Imagining the ghosts of miners while exploring the old gold-mining town of **Arltunga** (p201)
- Cooling off in a waterhole after trekking through tranquil **Trephina Gorge** (p200)

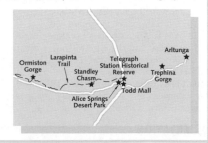

ALICE SPRINGS & AROUND

TELEPHONE CODE: ☎ 08   ■ www.centralaustraliantourism.com.au

ABORIGINAL AUSTRALIA: MPARNTWE

To the Arrernte people, the traditional owners of the Alice Springs area, this place is called Mparntwe. The heart of Mparntwe is the junction of the Charles (Anthelke Ulpeye) and Todd (Lhere Mparntwe) Rivers, just north of Anzac Hill (Untyeyetweleye). All the topographical features of the town were formed by the creative ancestral beings – known as the Yeperenye, Ntyarlke and Utnerrengatye Caterpillars – as they crawled across the landscape from Emily Gap (Anthwerrke), in the MacDonnell Ranges southeast of town.

To the west, Mt Gillen is Alhekulyele, the nose of the wild dog creator, where it lay down after an extended battle with an intruding dog from another area. Heavitree Gap (Ntaripe) is also of significance. As it was associated with men's ceremonies, women were traditionally not permitted to pass through here and had to take long detours to cross the ranges.

Alice Springs today has a sizeable Aboriginal community with strong links to the area, and native title over the area was recognised in 2000. If you want to see what's happening in one of the town camps, Hidden Valley, check out the website www.usmob.com.au.

ALICE SPRINGS

pop 26,305

HISTORY

Alice Springs began as a staging point on the OTL in 1871. A telegraph repeater station was built near a waterhole (though the water regularly retreats beneath the sand) in the otherwise-dry Todd River. The river was named after Charles Todd, Superintendent of Telegraphs in Adelaide, and the waterhole (mistaken for a spring) was named after Alice, his wife.

The taking up of pastoral leases in the central Australia, combined with the rush of miners who flocked to the gold and 'ruby' fields to the east, led to the establishment of Stuart a few kilometres south of the telegraph station in 1888. But the gold discovery didn't amount to much, the rubies turned out to be garnets and the railway from Adelaide took another 40 years to reach the town. When the railway finally reached Stuart in 1929, the non-Aboriginal population stood at about 30, and by the time the name was officially changed to Alice Springs in 1933, it had swollen to around 400.

In WWII Alice Springs became a major military base and the administrative centre of the Northern Territory (NT). The biggest boost to the Alice came with the sealing of the Stuart Hwy from Port Augusta in 1987, while the extension of the *Ghan* railway line from Alice to Darwin finally opened in 2004.

ORIENTATION

Alice Springs' town centre is a compact area just five streets wide, bordered by the (usually dry) Todd River to the east and the Stuart Hwy to the west. Todd St is the centre of the action; from Wills Tce to Gregory Tce it is a pedestrian mall featuring restaurants, art galleries and souvenir shops.

The striking MacDonnell Ranges form the town's backdrop and its southern boundary. A dramatic natural cutting, Heavitree Gap, allows the river, the highway and the famous *Ghan* railway to squeeze through the rock-strewn mountains and head south.

Larapinta Dr is the main road heading west, leading to the Araluen Cultural Centre, the Territory Wildlife Park, Hermannsburg, and (via Namatjira Dr) the famous red gorges of the West MacDonnell Ranges.

Greyhound Australia buses arrive at and depart the terminal office on Todd St. The train station is west of the Stuart Hwy in the town's light industrial area, and the airport is 15km south of town through Heavitree Gap.

Maps

For town maps of Alice Springs and outback road maps, your best bet is the visitor information centre (p175).

For a comprehensive range of topographical and road maps see **Desert Dwellers** (Map p173; ☎ 8953 2240; 38 Elder St; ☿ 9am-5pm Mon-Fri, to 2pm Sat).

INFORMATION

Bookshops

Bookmark It (Map p176; ☎ 8953 2465; Shop 1, 113 Todd St; ☿ 9am-5pm Mon-Fri, 10am-2pm Sat) Piles of secondhand books to sell and trade, including an extensive foreign-language section.

Dymocks (Map p176; ☎ 8952 9111; Alice Plaza, Todd Mall; ☿ 8.30am-5.30pm Mon-Fri, to 5pm Sat, 10am-3pm Sun)

ALICE SPRINGS

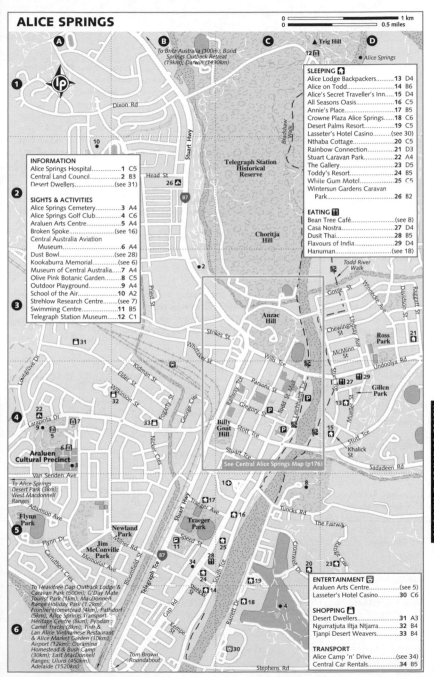

0 — 1 km
0 — 0.5 miles

INFORMATION
Alice Springs Hospital..............**1** C5
Central Land Council.............**2** B3
Desert Dwellers......................(see 31)

SIGHTS & ACTIVITIES
Alice Springs Cemetery............**3** A4
Alice Springs Golf Club.............**4** C6
Araluen Arts Centre...............**5** A4
Broken Spoke.....................(see 16)
Central Australia Aviation
Museum..........................**6** A4
Dust Bowl........................(see 28)
Kookaburra Memorial..............(see 6)
Museum of Central Australia.......**7** A4
Olive Pink Botanic Garden........**8** C5
Outdoor Playground..................**9** A4
School of the Air....................**10** A2
Strehlow Research Centre.........(see 7)
Swimming Centre..................**11** B5
Telegraph Station Museum......**12** C1

SLEEPING
Alice Lodge Backpackers..........**13** D4
Alice on Todd.....................**14** B6
Alice's Secret Traveller's Inn...**15** D4
All Seasons Oasis...................**16** C5
Annie's Place........................**17** B5
Crowne Plaza Alice Springs......**18** C6
Desert Palms Resort................**19** C5
Lasseter's Hotel Casino...........(see 30)
Nthaba Cottage....................**20** C5
Rainbow Connection...............**21** D3
Stuart Caravan Park................**22** A4
The Gallery..........................**23** D5
Toddy's Resort.....................**24** B5
White Gum Motel.................**25** C5
Wintersun Gardens Caravan
Park.................................**26** B2

EATING
Bean Tree Café.....................(see 8)
Casa Nostra.........................**27** D4
Dusit Thai............................**28** B5
Flavours of India...................**29** D4
Hanuman..............................(see 18)

ENTERTAINMENT
Araluen Arts Centre................(see 5)
Lasseter's Hotel Casino..........**30** C6

SHOPPING
Desert Dwellers.....................**31** A3
Ngurratjuta Iltja Ntjarra..........**32** B4
Tjanpi Desert Weavers............**33** B4

TRANSPORT
Alice Camp 'n' Drive.............(see 34)
Central Car Rentals................**34** B5

ALICE SPRINGS & AROUND

ALICE SPRINGS IN...

Two Days

Come face to face with the wild and elusive creatures of the central deserts at the **Alice Springs Desert Park** (opposite) in the morning. Allow a few hours to explore and make sure you don't miss the birds of prey show. Return to town to take a leisurely lunch on **Todd Mall** (p188) before spending a few hours perusing Alice's **Aboriginal art galleries** (p189). In the afternoon head to the **Olive Pink Botanic Garden** (p178) for a peaceful stroll and/or a relaxing coffee. Wander up **Anzac Hill** (p178) for a desert sunset over the town and nearby ranges. On day two, walk, cycle or drive out to the **Old Telegraph Station** (p178) in the morning and visit the **Araluen Cultural Precinct** (opposite) in the afternoon. Take in the **Sounds of Starlight** (p189) in the evening and a few beers at **Bojangles** (p188).

Four Days

Four days gives enough time to explore some of the sights in the ranges around town. In addition to the above, you could visit the **Royal Flying Doctor Service Base** (p178) and **School of the Air** (p179) to get a taste of remote outback life. Relive the caravans of yore by taking a sunset **camel ride** (p180), and, if it's not too hot, hire a bike to cycle out to **Simpsons Gap** (p194) on the dedicated **bike trail** (p180). Take a drive, and a picnic lunch, out to **Standley Chasm** (p196) and ramble through this remarkably narrow gorge.

One Week

With a week, you can explore the country a little further out of town. Drive through the West MacDonnell Ranges and camp out for a night at **Ormiston Gorge** (p197) or stay at **Glen Helen Resort** (p198). You can also head to the less-visited east side to explore the natural beauty of **Trephina Gorge** (p200) and the fascinating ghost town at **Arltunga** (p201).

Mainstream bookshop with a good selection of central Australian titles.

Red Kangaroo Books (Map p176; ☎ 8953 2137; 79 Todd Mall; ☺ 9am-5.30pm Mon-Fri, to 2pm Sat) Excellent bookshop specialising in central Australian titles: history, Aboriginal art, travel, novels, guidebooks and more.

Emergency

Ambulance (☎ 8951 6633 or ☎ 000)
Police (☎ 8951 8888 or ☎ 000)

Internet Access

Alice Springs Library (Map p176; ☎ 8950 0555; Gregory Tce; per 25min $3.60; ☺ 10am-6pm Mon, Tue & Thu, to 5pm Wed & Fri, 9am-1pm Sat, 1-5pm Sun).

JPG Computers (Map p176; ☎ 8952 2040; Coles Complex, Bath St; per hr $6; ☺ 9am-5.30pm Mon-Fri, 10am-2pm Sat)

Outback Email (Map p176; 2a Gregory Tce; per hr $3; ☺ 9am-6pm) Part of the Outback Travel Shop.

Todd Internet Café (Map p176; ☎ 8953 8355; Colocag Plaza, 76 Todd St; per hr $4; ☺ 10am-6pm)

Laundry

Alice Wash House Laundromat (Map p176; Railway Tce; per load $4; ☺ 6am-10pm)

Medical Services

Alice Springs Hospital (Map p173; ☎ 8951 7777; Gap Rd; ☺ 24hr)

Alice Springs Pharmacy (Map p176; ☎ 8952 1554; Shop 19 Yeperenye Shopping Centre, 36 Hartley St; ☺ 8.30am-7.30pm)

Money

Major banks with 24-hour ATMs such as ANZ, Commonwealth, National Australia and Westpac can be found in the town centre. There are also ATMs at the airport.

Permits

Mereenie Loop Passes and fossicking permits are available from the visitor information centre (opposite).

Central Land Council (Map p173; ☎ 8951 6211; www.clc.org.au; 31-33 Stuart Hwy ; PO Box 3321, NT 0871; ☺ 8.30am-noon & 2-4pm) For Aboriginal land permits and transit permits.

Outback Gems (Map p176; ☎ 8952 9299; Shop 2, Coles Complex, Bath St; ☺ 9am-5pm Mon-Fri, to 1pm Sat) This is the best place to get fossicking information and free fossicking permits.

Post

The **main post office** (Map p176; ☎ 13 13 18; 31-33 Hartley St; ☼ 8.15am-5pm Mon-Fri) has a Post Shop and a poste restante counter.

Tourist Information

Tourism Central Australia Visitor Information Centre (Map p176; ☎ 1800 645 199, 8952 5199; www.centralaustral iantourism.com; 60 Gregory Tce; ☼ 8.30am-5.30pm Mon-Fri, 9am-4pm Sat & Sun) is well located in the town centre. It has clued-up staff, a good selection of maps, and copious brochures on accommodation and touring options. Make sure you pick up copies of the free *Holiday & Visitor Guide* and *Welcome to Central Australia*, which are full of useful information and listings. Weather forecasts and current road conditions are posted on a wall, and Mereenie Loop Passes ($2) and fossicking permits (free) are issued here. National park notes, including for Larapinta Trail, are also available (ask at the counter). Tourism Central Australia desks are also found at the airport and train station.

Travel Agencies

Backpackers World Travel (Map p176; ☎ 8953 0666; Cnr Todd St & Gregory Tce; ☼ 9am-6pm Mon-Fri, to 12.30pm Sat).

Flight Centre (Map p176; ☎ 8953 4081; Yeperenye Shopping Centre, Hartley St; ☼ 9am-5.30pm Mon-Fri, 9.30am-12.30pm Sat)

SIGHTS

Alice Springs Desert Park

There's no better way to see what's really happening out there in the central deserts than to visit the fabulous **desert park** (off Map p173; ☎ 8951 8788; www.alicespringsdesertpark.com.au; Larapinta Dr; adult/ child/family $20/10/55; ☼ 7.30am-6pm, last entry 4.30pm). Abutting the ramparts of Mt Gillen 6km west of town, the park exhibits the living treasures of central Australia in a series of habitats: inland river, sand country, and woodland.

The excellent **nocturnal house** displays 20 arid-zone mammal species, half of which are endangered or extinct in mainland Australia. Once your eyes adjust to the darkness you can spot the bilby, quoll and a plethora of snakes and lizards such as the aptly named thorny devil. To capture the desert at its night-time best join the guided **nocturnal tour** ($50; ☼ 6.50pm Mon & Thu).

Walk-through aviaries feature water birds and colourful desert parrots, but the free-flying **birds of prey show** (☼ shows 10am & 3.30pm), featuring Australian kestrels, kites and awe-some wedge-tailed eagles, is the avian highlight. Twitchers and early risers well enjoy the dawn **bird walkabout** (per person$30; ☎ Wed & Sat), a birdwatching tour accompanied by experts and breakfast.

To get the most out of the park, pick up a free audio guide with commentary in several languages, or join one of the free ranger talks held at various exhibits throughout the day. There are free barbecues, a picnic area and a **cafe** (☼ 9am-5.30pm). The gift shop hires out strollers and wheelchairs, and the park is wheelchair accessible.

If you don't have your own wheels, use **Desert Park Transfers** (☎ 1800 806 641; www.tailor madetours.com.au; adult/child/family $38/26/124). It operates five times daily during park hours (between 7.30am and 6pm) and the cost includes park entry and pick-up and drop-off at your accommodation.

Araluen Cultural Precinct

You can easily spend a few hours exploring this **cultural precinct** (Map p173; ☎ 8951 1120; www .nt.gov.au/nreta/arts/ascp; Larapinta Dr; adult/child/family $10/7/30), which combines an art centre with a compact and fascinating natural-history museum, an aviation museum, an enthralling memorial to the *Kookaburra* air crash, and a historical cemetery. The precinct sits on the site of Alice Springs' first aerodrome, about 2km west of the town centre – you can wander around freely outside, but the 'precinct pass', available at the Araluen Arts Centre, gives entry to all the attractions here.

ARALUEN ARTS CENTRE

The **arts centre** (Map p173; ☎ 8952 5022, box office ☎ 8951 1122; www.araluencentre.com.au; ☼ 10am-4pm Mon-Fri, 11am-4pm Sat & Sun) has four galleries and is the town's performing-arts centre. Beautiful stained-glass windows grace the foyer – the largest window features the Honey Ant Dreaming (a popular central Australian theme) designed by local artist Wenten Rubuntja. Other windows were designed by Aboriginal students of Yirara College. A large painting by Clifford Possum Tjapaltjarri was commissioned for the centre and is reproduced on the exterior eastern wall.

The Albert Namatjira gallery features original paintings by Namatjira, other Hermannsburg School artists and Rex Batterbee (the man who introduced Namatjira to watercolours), along with early Papunya works. Other galleries

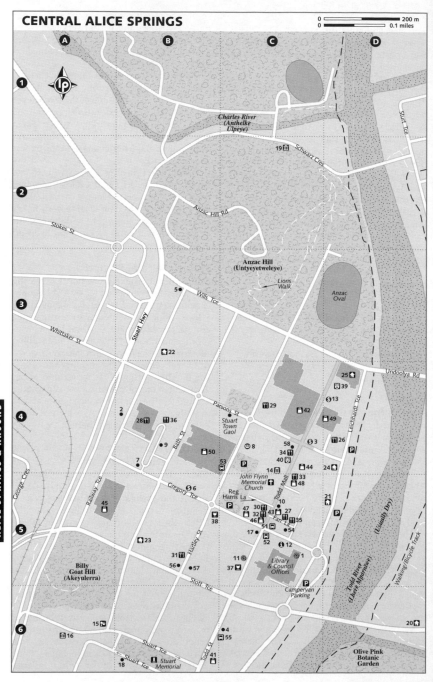

CENTRAL ALICE SPRINGS

showcase art from the Central Desert region, contemporary art and travelling exhibitions.

On the path between the centre and the Museum of Central Australia is the walk-through Yeperenye Sculpture, which tells the *story* of the Caterpillar ancestors, complete with commentary and sound effects.

MUSEUM OF CENTRAL AUSTRALIA
Housed in a building partly constructed of a massive rammed-earth wall, the **museum** (Map p173; ☎ 8951 1121; ⏰ 10am-5pm) boasts a small but fascinating natural-history collection. Among the exhibits you'll find the imposing skeleton of an extinct flightless bird, and good display extraterrestrial rocks with information on meteorites and NT's famous craters.

Housed in the same building, the **Strehlow Research Centre** (Map p173; ☎ 8951 1111; ⏰ 10am-5pm) commemorates the work of Professor Ted Strehlow among the Arrernte people. Strehlow was born in Hermannsburg and returned years later to study Arrernte language and culture. His legacy is the most comprehensive collection of *tjurunga* (Aboriginal spirit artefacts) in the country – entrusted to Strehlow for safe-keeping by the Arrernte people when they feared their traditional life was under threat. These items cannot be viewed by an uninitiated male or *any* female, and are kept in a vault in the centre.

CENTRAL AUSTRALIA AVIATION MUSEUM & KOOKABURRA MEMORIAL
The former Connellan Air hangar is now a **museum** (Map p173; Memorial Ave; admission free; ⏰ 9am-5pm Mon-Fri, 10am-5pm Sat & Sun) housing an assortment of old planes and engines. There are exhibits on pioneer aviation in the Territory including Royal Flying Doctor (RFDS) planes.

The highlight of the museum, however, is in the small building outside the hangar where you'll find the wreck of the tiny *Kookaburra*, and its tragic tale. The two-man plane crashed into the Tanami Desert in 1929 while out searching for Charles Kingsford-Smith and his copilot Charles Ulim, who had gone down in their plane, the *Southern Cross*. The *Kookaburra* pilots Keith Anderson and Bob Hitchcock perished in the desert while Kingsford-Smith and Ulim were rescued.

ALICE SPRINGS CEMETERY
Adjacent to the aviation museum is the old town **cemetery** (Map p173; ⏰ dawn-dusk), which contains the graves of prominent locals.

ALICE SPRINGS & AROUND

The most famous grave is that of Albert Namatjira. This interesting headstone was erected in 1994, and features a terracotta-tile mural of three of Namatjira's Dreaming sites in the MacDonnell Ranges. Harold Lasseter, who perished in 1931 while trying to rediscover the rich gold reef he found west of Ayers Rock 20 years earlier, has a prominent headstone. Anthropologist Olive Pink is buried facing the opposite direction to the others – a rebel to the end.

Telegraph Station Historical Reserve

Alice Springs was born out of the OTL, so a visit to the **Telegraph Station Historical Reserve** (Map p173; ☎ 8952 3993; adult/child/family $7.80/4.30/21; ✆ 8am-9pm, museum 8.30am-5pm), 4km north of town, is a step back to the town's European beginnings. Built along the line in the 1870s, the station was constructed of local stone and continued to operate until 1932. It then served as a welfare home for children of mixed ancestry until 1963. The buildings have been faithfully restored to give an idea of what life was like for the small community here. The main telegraph office has working equipment inside.

Short **guided tours** (phone to confirm times) operate roughly every half-hour between 9.15am and 4.30pm from April to October; there's also an informative map available. Ranger-led walks operate between June and August, and the blacksmith's shop is occasionally fired up for demonstrations.

Nearby is the original Alice 'springs', a semipermanent waterhole (Thereyurre to the Arrernte people) in the Todd River bed. It is not really a spring, but water accumulates here and even if it appears dry, water can usually be found beneath the sand.

There's a grassy picnic area outside the station museum with barbecues, tables and shady gum trees, and a number of **walking tracks** radiate from the reserve. The best is the 30-minute loop to Trig Hill, returning via the original station cemetery.

It's an easy 4km walk or ride from the Alice town centre – just follow the path north along the Todd River's west bank. If you're driving, the station is signposted off the Stuart Hwy about 2km north of Anzac Hill.

Olive Pink Botanic Garden

Just across the Todd River from the town centre, the **Olive Pink Botanic Garden** (Map p173; ☎ 8952 2154; www.opbg.com.au; Tuncks Rd; admission by donation; ✆ 10am-6pm) has a landscaped and labelled collection of central Australian shrubs and trees, featuring some pleasant minibushwalks, sculptures and a very tempting alfresco cafe. The **visitors centre** (✆ 10am-4pm) has exhibits on the evolution and ecology of arid-zone plants, and their traditional use by Aboriginal people. You can also read about the life of the garden's eccentric founder, the prominent anthropologist and botanical artist Olive Pink (1884–1975), who was an early campaigner for Indigenous rights. Pink named trees in the garden after government officials, and if any of them failed to please her, she would stop watering their particular tree. Walks from the visitors centre include the **Hill Walk** (35 minutes return), which offers views over the town.

The excellent **Bean Tree Cafe** (p187) serves gourmet fare, coffee and cakes in a delightful garden setting.

Anzac Hill

For a panoramic view over Alice, take a hike or a drive to the top of Anzac Hill (Map p176), preferably just before sunset. From the WWI memorial there's a 360-degree view over the township and down to Heavitree Gap, while the burnished MacDonnell Ranges stretch east and west. Aboriginal people call the hill Untyeyetweleye (onjeea-*toolia*), the site of the Corkwood Dreaming of a woman who lived alone on the hill. On the southern edge of the town centre you can see the small rise of **Billy Goat Hill** (Akeyulerra; Map p176). Here the Two Sisters Dreaming passed on their way north through the area, and the hill is now a registered sacred site.

You can walk the short, sharp ascent to the top along the **Lions Walk** from Wills Tce, or there's vehicle access and parking from the northwestern side.

At the northern foot of Anzac Hill is the RSL Club with its **War Museum** (Map p176; ☎ 8952 2868; Schwarz Cres; admission free; ✆ 10am-6pm), which features a collection of firearms, medals and photos of Alice Springs and the bombing of Darwin during WWII.

Royal Flying Doctor Service Base

The **base** (Map p176; ☎ 8952 1129; www.flyingdoctor.net; Stuart Tce; adult/child $7/3.50; ✆ 9am-4pm Mon-Sat, 1-4pm Sun) amply demonstrates the vision and work of the Royal Flying Doctor Service (RFDS), which changed the way people lived in remote inland Australia. Established in 1939, the Alice Springs RFDS base still operates remote medical clinics for isolated communities.

Entry to the base is by a half-hour tour, which includes a video presentation and a peek into an operational control room. Then you can wander through the museum with model planes, a cockpit simulator and some ancient medical and radio gear (including an early pedal radio).

The adjoining **cafe** (🕙 9am-4.45pm Mon-Sat) serves light meals, cakes and drinks.

School of the Air

The **School of the Air** (Map p173; ☎ 8951 6834; www .assoa.nt.edu.au; 80 Head St; adult/child/family $6.50/4.50/18; 🕙 8.30am-4.30pm Mon-Sat, 1.30-4.30pm Sun), about 3km north of the town centre, is another of those innovations born out of necessity in the remote outback. Started in 1951, this was the first school of its type in Australia, broadcasting lessons to children over an area of 1.3 million sq km. While transmissions were originally all done over high-frequency radio, satellite internet connections and webcams now mean students and teachers can study in a 'virtual classroom'. You get a guided tour of the centre and during school terms you can view a live class broadcast from 8.30am to 2.30pm Monday to Friday, or recorded lessons at other times.

Alice Springs Reptile Centre

Featuring Australia's most poisonous snakes, as well as frilled lizards, bearded dragons and thorny devils, the **Reptile Centre** (Map p176; ☎ 8952 8900; www.reptilecentre.com.au; 9 Stuart Tce; adult/child $12/6; 🕙 9.30am-5pm) is the safest place to come face to face with some of central Australia's most intriguing cold-blooded critters. It's possible to handle a python and get a kiss from a blue-tongue lizard during the handling demonstrations (usually 11am, 1pm and 3pm). Outside is an enclosure that's home to a formidable-looking perentie (Australia's largest lizard) and Terry, a 3.3m-long saltwater crocodile.

National Pioneer Women's Hall of Fame

A tribute to Australia's pioneering women the **hall of fame** (Map p176; ☎ 8952 9006; www.pioneer women.com.au; 2 Stuart Tce; adult/child $6.50/3; 🕙 10am-5pm) is in the former Alice Springs Gaol, very near the Royal Flying Doctor base. Behind the high walls and rolls of barbed wire are stories of the exploits and achievements of women from all over the country, including a large pictorial display on 'Women First in Their Field' in politics, sport, law, the arts and other endeavours. Among the luminaries are Pat O'Shane, Australia's first Aboriginal barrister, and sports stars Cathy Freeman, Evonne Goolagong Cawley and Dawn Fraser. 'Women at the Heart' celebrates outback heroines such as Olive Pink and Ida Standley and many unsung achievers. You can wander among the cells, which are being developed as an attraction in their own right.

Alice Springs Transport Heritage Centre

At the MacDonnell siding, about 10km south of Alice and 1km west of the Stuart Hwy, are a couple of museums dedicated to big trucks and old trains. If you want to visit both the museums, consider the **half-day tour** (☎ 8955 5047; tour $55; 🕙 10am-2pm); which includes entry, a guide and lunch.

The **Old Ghan Rail Museum** (off Map p173; ☎ 8955 5047; 1 Norris Bell Ave; adult/child/family $8/5/23; 🕙 9am-5pm) has a collection of restored *Ghan* locos and carriages to please train buffs and anyone interested in this pioneering railway (originally called the *Afghan Express* after the cameleers who forged the route). There's also an ad hoc collection of railway memorabilia in the lovely Stuart railway station. The station also incorporates the Old Ghan Tea Rooms, which recreate the atmosphere of railway retiring rooms of yore.

If big trucks are more your thing, the **National Road Transport Hall of Fame** (off Map p173; ☎ 8952 7161; www.roadtransporthall.com; 2 Norris Bell Ave; adult/child/family $12/6/28; 🕙 9am-5pm) has a fabulous collection, including a few ancient road trains. There are over 100 restored trucks and vintage cars, including many of the outback pioneering vehicles. Here you'll find a 1964 B61 Mack truck, old Studebakers, Buicks and a 1911 Model T Ford. Admission includes entry to the **Kenworth Dealer Hall of Fame** (more trucks) and is valid for two days, so take your time.

Adelaide House

Built in the 1920s as the Australian Inland Mission hospital, **Adelaide House** (Map p176; ☎ 8952 1856; Todd Mall; admission by donation; 🕙 10am-4pm Mon-Fri, to noon Sat) was the first hospital in central Australia, designed by the founding flying doctor Reverend John Flynn, and built of local stone and timber carted from

ALICE SPRINGS & AROUND

Oodnadatta in South Australia. Since 1998 the building has been preserved as a memorial museum with displays of photographs and implements of the pioneering medical work undertaken in remote areas. At the rear of the building stands a small shed housing the original 'pedal radio' invented by Alfred Traeger.

ACTIVITIES
Bowling
Alice's imaginatively named tenpin bowling alley, the **Dust Bowl** (Map p173; ☎ 8952 5051; 29 Gap Rd; weekday/weekend per game $7/$10; ⏰ noon-late) stays open till the last bowlers depart and there's a kiosk and **bar** (⏰ 6-10pm).

Bushwalking
If you really want to get to know this country, head out to the bush. Several easy walks radiate from the Olive Pink Botanical Gardens and the Telegraph Station, including the Telegraph Station to Simpsons Gap route, which is also the first stage of the Larapinta Trail (p195).

Central Australian Bushwalkers (http://home.austarnet.com.au/longwalk) is a group of local bushwalkers that schedules a wide variety of walks in the area, particularly the West MacDonnell Ranges, from March to November.

If you're keen to tackle part of the Larapinta Trail but don't have your own equipment, **Lone Dingo Adventure** (☎ 8953 3866; cnr Todd Mall & Gregory Tce) can put together packs of camping and hiking gear for hire, as well as Global Positioning System (GPS) and emergency position-indicating radio beacon (EPIRB) equipment (see p190).

Camel Riding
Camels played an integral part in pioneering central Australia, and travellers can relive some of that adventure. At the **Frontier Homestead** (off Map p173; ☎ 8953 0444; www.cameltours.com.au; Ross Hwy) you can take a half-day adventure (one hour of riding) along the Todd River (adult/child $55/35), or take a camel to dinner or breakfast (see opposite). The homestead is on the Ross Hwy about 5km southeast of Heavitree Gap, and incorporates a small and interesting museum.

Pyndan Camel Tracks (off Map p173; ☎ 0416 170 164; www.cameltracks.com; Jane Rd) has one-hour rides just south of the MacDonnell Ranges (adult/child $40/20), as well as half-day rides ($95) and an overnight ride, including dinner and breakfast and a night in a swag, for $245. Prices include transfers from Alice Springs accommodation.

Cycling
Alice Springs is flat and perfect for cycling. Recommended rides include the excellent track beside the Todd River to the Telegraph Station, west to the Alice Springs Desert Park, or further out on the designated cycle path to Simpsons Gap. For a map of cycling and walking paths, pick up a copy of Active in Alice from the visitor information centre.

Alice Bike Hire (☎ 0407 324 697; half-/full day $15/25) Drop-off/pick-up service, mountain bikes, kids' bikes and baby seats available.

Broken Spoke (Map p173; ☎ 8953 8744; 10 Gap Rd; half-/full day $25/35; ⏰ 9am-6pm Mon-Fri, to 2pm Sat) Sells and hires bicycles, stocks accessories and does repairs. Hire bikes include cruisers and tandems.

Golf
Alice has a mostly green 18-hole golf course with a striking backdrop of the decidedly ungreen MacDonnell Ranges. The **Alice Springs Golf Club** (Map p173; ☎ 8952 1921; Cromwell Dr; course fees 9/18 holes $25/40, club hire half/full set $18/25; ⏰ 6.30am-11pm) is just east of the Todd River.

Hot-Air Ballooning
Floating high above the desert at sunrise is an unforgettable way to start the day. Daily dawn balloon flights take off some distance south of the MacDonnell Ranges and all include a sparkling wine breakfast. Children pay about 30% less and there are discounts for backpackers, especially if you book through a hostel. Pick-up and drop off from accommodation in Alice are included in the rates. However, the mandatory insurance is an additional fee – $25 to $30 per person.

Ballooning Downunder (☎ 1800 801 601, 8952 8816; www.ballooningdownunder.com.au; 30min flight $230)

Outback Ballooning (☎ 1800 809 790; www.outbackballooning.com.au; 30-/60min flight $230/360)

Spinifex Ballooning (☎ 1800 677 893, 8953 4800; www.balloonflights.com.au; 30min flight $230).

Quad-biking
For a thrill on four wheels you can't beat these go-anywhere bikes, which are automatic, pretty stable and don't require a licence or previous experience. Pick-up and drop-off at your accommodation is included.

Outback Quad Adventures (☎ 89530697; www
.oqa.com.au; tours per person $115-330) Guided tours
(minimum 2½ hours) go out on Undoolya Station. The
overnight tour ($330) includes camping out with dinner
and breakfast.

Swimming
Almost without exception, all places to stay
have a swimming pool; however, if you want
to do laps head to the local **Swimming Centre**
(Map p173; ☎ 8953 4633; Speed St; adult/child $3.30/1.70;
⏱ 6am-7pm Mon-Fri, 10am-7pm Sat & Sun).

ALICE FOR CHILDREN
If the idea of seeing a python wrap itself
around your precious offspring appeals then
head for the **Reptile Centre** (p179), where regular hands-on shows are sure to excite would-
be crocodile hunters. For a slightly more
sedate wildlife encounter, the **Alice Springs
Desert Park** (p175) west of town is an entertaining and educational experience for the
whole family. Don't miss taking the kids to
the **Heavitree Gap Outback Lodge** (p185) on the
southern edge of town any time after 4pm
to handfeed the rock wallabies that climb
down from the ranges. Apart from the wallaby pellets, it's free!

A **camel ride** (opposite) is sure to capture
their imagination, with the bonus that after an
hour in the saddle they may never pester you
to ride a camel again. There's a spacious **outdoor playground** (Map p173) at Frank McEllister
Park next to the Araluen Arts Centre on
Larapinta Dr, with energy-sapping rides, free
barbecues and a BMX track.

TOURS
Alice Springs is the hub of central Australian
tourism and all roads – and tours – start
and end here. There are daily trips by bus
or 4WD to one or more of the major attractions: Uluru-Kata Tjuta National Park, Kings
Canyon and Watarrka National Park, Palm
Valley, and the West and East MacDonnells,
with less frequent tours to places such as
Rainbow Valley and Chambers Pillar. The
visitor information centre (p175) has details on most of the organised tours from
Alice Springs. You can also book most
tours through your accommodation, or try
the travel-company shopfronts, such as the
Outback Travel Shop (Map p176; ☎ 8955 5288; www
.outbacktravelshop.com.au; 2a Gregory Tce), which often
have standby discounts.

Town Tours
Alice Wanderer (☎ 1800 722 111; 8952 2111; www
.alicewanderer.com.au) has 'hop on – hop off'
town tours for $40, which continually cir-
cuit around town. The ticket is valid for
two days.

Foot Falcon (☎ 0427 569 531; www.footfalcon.com;
tours $30) has excellent morning, evening and
afternoon walking tours of the Alice covering Aboriginal history, historical buildings
and tales of the early days.

Aboriginal Cultural Tours
Aboriginal Art & Culture Centre (Map p176; ☎ 8952
3408; www.aboriginalart.com.au; 125 Todd St; half-/full day
$95/170) offers the chance to meet Aboriginal
people and learn about their culture. Tours
include a bushwalk, dance performance
and didgeridoo lesson (see also p189).
Full-day trips can be customised to suit
your interest.

Alice Springs Aboriginal Culture Tours (☎ 1800
089 644; www.aboriginalculturetours.com.au; $99; ⏱ tours
10am) offer a three-hour tour of Alice Springs
and nearby Emily and Jessie Gaps where a
local guide describes sacred sites and traditional Arrernte culture. It's followed by
a 'tastes of the Outback' lunch at the Red
Ochre Grill (p187).

Alice Wanderer (☎ 1800 722 111; 8952 2111; www
.alicewanderer.com.au) has half-day tours to the
Santa Teresa Aboriginal community and
Keringke art centre for $130.

Beanies, Baskets & Bushtucker (☎ 0408 436 928;
tours $77) offers the opportunity to sit with
Pitjantjatjara women around a campfire in
the Alice Springs Desert Park to learn grass
weaving and beanie crochet, while listening
to *stories* and tasting bush tucker.

Dreamtime Tours (☎ 8955 5095; www.rstours.com
.au; adult/child $84/42, self-drive $66/33; ⏱ 8.30-11.30am)
has the popular three-hour 'Dreamtime &
Bushtucker Tour', where you can meet
Warlpiri Aboriginal people and learn a little about their traditional life. As it caters for
large bus groups it can be impersonal, but
you can tag along with your own vehicle.

Dining Tours
Take a Camel out to Breakfast or Dinner (☎ 8953
0444; www.cameltours.com.au; Ross Hwy; breakfast adult/
child $89/53, dinner adult/child $115/85) combines a
one-hour camel ride with a barbecue breakfast or three-course dinner at the Frontier
Homestead (opposite).

GAY & LESBIAN ALICE

For an outback town, Alice Springs has a surprisingly conspicuous and strong gay and lesbian community. Your first port of call is www.aliceiswonderland.com, the home of the **Alice IS Wonderland** gay and lesbian festival (opposite). Closely associated with the festival is Phil Walcott, the gregarious owner of **Rainbow Connection** (Map p173; ☎ 8952 6441; 22-24 Raggatt St; r from $155; ✕ ✿) Alice's gay-friendly guesthouse. This B&B has four rooms, three of which are in a separate house with its own kitchen, lounge and bathroom. The other room is a funky boutique double room with en suite, earthy tones, TV and fridge.

Cafe Mediterranean Bar Doppio (p188), just off Todd Mall, is lesbian-owned and a great place to mingle and check out the alternative scene.

Red Centre Dreaming (☎ 1800 896 119; www.aurora resorts.com.au; Palm Circuit; adult/child $105/55; ✿ 7-10pm), at the Heavitree Gap Outback Lodge (p185), is a three-course 'Territorian' buffet feed (including drinks) with Aboriginal dancing, music and *story*-telling.

Scenic Flights

The following operate from Alice Springs airport:

Alice Springs Aero Club (☎ 8955 5200; www.alicespring saeroclub.com.au) operates scenic flights over the Alice and MacDonnell Ranges from $235 per person.

Alice Springs Helicopters (☎ 8952 9800; www.anh.com.au) has several options including brief flights over Alice ($110), and longer flights over Simpsons Gap ($285) and the West MacDonnell Ranges ($995).

Murray Cosson's Australian Outback Flights (☎ 8953 1444; www.australianoutbackflights.com.au) seasonally operates flights over Alice Springs ($175), as well as the West MacDonnell Ranges (1½ hours $375), Kings Canyon including lunch and canyon walk (eight hours $560), and Uluru and Kata Tjuta (full day $900). All prices are per person with two passengers. For three or four passengers the per-person cost is less.

Tours Departing Alice Springs

Numerous operators run tours of one, two or more days to Uluru, Kata Tjuta and Kings Canyon. These vary from all-inclusive camping trips to upmarket tours with luxury-hotel accommodation. Check out the company's vehicles, group size (and ages), accommodation, types of meals and whether it includes park entry (most don't) or attracts a fuel surcharge.

Note that the major sites of the East and West MacDonnell Ranges can be seen in a day or two and with two or more people you may get a better deal hiring a small car than taking a tour.

AAT Kings (☎ 8952 1700; www.aatkings.com) An established operation with some very long day tours to Uluru adult/child ($199/100), Palm Valley ($139/70) and Kings Canyon (199/100) for those short of time. This really means a long time in a bus seat, however. It also runs a daily shuttle between Alice Springs and Yulara ($135/68) and between Alice Springs and Kings Canyon ($138/69).

Adventure Tours Australia (☎ 8981 4255; www.adventuretours.com.au) Another established outfit with a variety of vehicles and tour options including two-/three-day trips of Uluru, Kata Tjuta and Kings Canyon from $325/495. Group sizes can be larger than others.

Alice Wanderer (☎ 1800 722 111; www.alicewanderer.com.au) Full-day tours into the West MacDonnell Ranges as far as Glen Helen Gorge, including morning tea and lunch cost adult/child $105/75, and a half-day trip to Simpsons Gap and Standley Chasm costs $62/42. There is also a full-day tour into Palm Valley, including morning tea and lunch for adult/child $105/75.

Austour (☎ 1800 335009; www.austour.com.au) Here you'll find the cheapest daily connections between Alice Springs and Uluru (adult/child $120/60) and between Alice Springs and Kings Canyon ($110/60). Two-day tours to Uluru and Kings Canyon start at $400 (excluding park-entry fee).

Emu Run Tours (☎ 8953 7057; www.emurun.com.au) Day tours to Uluru cost $199 and two-day tours to Uluru and Kings Canyon cost $440. Prices include park entry fees. There are also recommended small-group day tours through the West MacDonnell Ranges or Palm Valley for $100, including morning tea, lunch and entrance fees.

Mulga's Adventures (☎ 1800 359 089; www.mulgas.com.au), Departing from Annie's Place (p184), this three-day tour to Uluru is popular with backpackers. It's certainly cheap ($250) and includes bush camping and stops at Kings Canyon and a camel farm.

Ossies Outback 4WD Tours (☎ 8952 2308; www.ossies.com.au) Ossies promise to get you further off the beaten track than most other tours. There are several excellent 4WD tours, including a three-day trip that goes

ALICE SPRINGS & AROUND

through Finke Gorge National Park to Kings Canyon and Uluru. It costs from $1650 depending on the accommodation option selected. Other trips include a three-day Simpson Desert tour with Chambers Pillar, Old Andado and Mt Dare ($975), and there is a day trip to Owen Springs and Rainbow Valley ($135).

Outback Experience (☎ 8953 2666; www.outback experience.com.au) Run by knowledgeable local Leigh Goldsmith; covers Chambers Pillar and Rainbow Valley in a day for $148, and East MacDonnells for $130.

Palm Valley Tours (☎ 8952 0022; www.palmvalley tours.com.au) Offers one-/two-day ($135/325) small-group tours into Palm Valley and Hermannsburg. The two-day tour also includes Tnorala (Gosse Bluff) and Ormiston Gorge.

Path Tours (☎ 8952 0525; www.pathtoursadventure .com) As well as offering half- ($159) and full-day ($189) tours to the East and West MacDonnell Ranges, you have the option of tailoring your own excursions.

Rock Tour (☎ 1800 246 345; www.therocktour .com.au) Has recommended three-day (two nights) camping safaris ($295) that visit Kings Canyon, Curtain Springs and the 'rock' and Kata Tjuta.

Wayoutback (☎ 8952 4324; www.wayoutback .au) Runs three-day 4WD safaris that traverse 4WD tracks to Uluru and Kings Canyon for $565, and five-day safaris that top it up with the Palm Valley and West MacDonnells for $885.

Wildway (☎ 8953 7045; www.wildway.com.au) Three-day Uluru and Kings Canyon tours for $390, including sleeping bags, park entry and meals.

FESTIVALS & EVENTS
MARCH & APRIL
Alice IS Wonderland Festival (www.aliceiswonder land.com) The gay and lesbian community hits the town in this post–Mardi Gras festival.

Heritage Week The emphasis is on the town's European past during this week of reenactments, displays and demonstrations of old skills, usually held in late April.

MAY
Alice Springs Cup Carnival (www.alicespringsturfclub .org.au) The highlight of the autumn racing carnival is the Alice Springs Cup held on the holiday on first Monday in May.

Bangtail Muster A parade of floats along Todd Mall followed by a sports carnival, also held on the first Monday in May.

JUNE & JULY
Finke Desert Race (www.finkedesertrace.com.au) Motorcyclists and buggy drivers vie to take out the title in this crazy race over 240km from Alice Springs along the Old

---

DRY RIVERS & DESERT SHIPS

They say if you see the Todd River flow three times in your life you're a local, but a lack of water doesn't stop the sports-and-beer-loving people of the Alice having a good time.

Every September (since 1962) the town gears up for one of central Australia's most famous sports events – the **Henley-on-Todd Regatta**. Borrowing its name from the even more famous English boat race, the star attractions are 'boat' races along the sandy bed of the dry Todd River. The 'boats' are bottomless and the crews race barefoot with their lightweight craft hauled up around their waists. No oars, coxes or winged keels are required here, just a swift pair of heels. There are numerous race categories and the boats come in all shapes and sizes – yachts with sails, kayaks, flat-bottom boats pushed through the sand using shovels instead of oars and even a bath-tub derby where contestants carry a passenger in a bath-tub to the finish! Add to that a sand-ski race, a tug-of-war, and – just to flavour it with a little surf carnival atmosphere in the desert – a 'surf rescue' and iron-man and -woman events! (For the record, the races have been cancelled at least once owing to water in the river!)

But for curious visitors to the Alice, much of the real entertainment can be found outside the actual racing. Locals dress up in oddball outfits, a procession of boats and floats winds its way through the streets and, like all good outback happenings, the booze flows freely and partying goes well into the night. Entry to the event is $12/5 (adult/child), with 10% of profits going to a different charity each year. For information and annual dates, check out the website www .henleyontodd.com.au.

Another hilarious and entertaining race day in Alice Springs is the **Camel Cup**, held in mid-July at Blatherskite Park, south of the Gap. As well as the races, where the gangly legs of those ships of the desert make a surprisingly swift bid for the finish line, there are stalls, rides, music, plenty of drinking and a carnival atmosphere. And what would a race day be without fashions on the fields and the judging for Mr and Miss Camel Cup? It's a great family day out; entry is $15/5 (adult/child). For more information, check out www.camelcup.com.au.

ALICE SPRINGS & AROUND

South Rd to Finke; the following day they race back again! It's held on the Queen's Birthday weekend in June.

Beanie Festival (www.beaniefest.org) An Alice Springs festival with cult status, this event in late June/early July honours the woollen beanie with colourful entries from around Australia and abroad; there are prizes, exhibitions and workshops at the Araluen Art Centre.

Alice Springs Show (www.alice-springs.com.au) The annual agricultural show on the first weekend in July has the usual rides and attractions, as well as local business displays.

Camel Cup (www.camelcup.com.au) Camel races extraordinaire – see Dry Rivers & Desert Ships, p183.

AUGUST

Alice Springs Rodeo Yee-ha! Bareback bull-riding, steer wrestling, calf roping and ladies' barrel races are some of the events at the rodeo at Blatherskite Park.

Old Timers Fete An Alice institution; the Old Timers Village hosts this huge fete on the second Saturday of August.

SEPTEMBER & OCTOBER

Henley-on-Todd Regatta (www.henleyontodd.com.au) Boats with legs – see Dry Rivers & Desert Ships, p183.

Alice Desert Festival (www.alicedesertfestival.com.au) This arts and cultural festival features central Australian art, music, dancing, exhibitions and street performers.

Desert Mob Month-long exhibition of Central Desert artists.

SLEEPING

Alice Springs boasts a wide range of accommodation: there are numerous caravan parks and hostels, as well as midrange motels, atmospheric B&Bs and luxury hotels. We recommend you book ahead during the peak season (June to September) and during festivals (see p183).

Budget

HOSTELS

There's plenty of backpacker accommodation in Alice, but you'll still need to book ahead if you want a private room. Most places have dorm beds and motel-style doubles, swimming pools, complimentary 'coffee and toast' breakfasts and internet connections. Ask about VIP/YHA/Nomads discounts.

Alice's Secret Traveller's Inn (Map p173; ☎ 1800 783 633, 8952 8686; www.asecret.com.au; 6 Khalick St; dm $20-24, s/tw/d $42/54/62; 🐾 💻 🏊) Just across the Todd River from town, this is a recommended 'hideaway' hostel where you can relax around the pool, strum a guitar, puff on a didge or play a game of badminton in the garden. Rooms in the dongas are a bit of a squeeze,

and those in the big old house are simple, comfortable and clean.

Toddy's Resort (Map p173; ☎ 1800 027 027; www .toddys.com.au; 39-41 Gap Rd; dm $20-26, d $58-90; 🐾 💻 🏊) Toddy's is a rambling place encompassing two properties and a huge variety of rooms. There are basic four-, six- and eight-bed dorms, family rooms, budget doubles and motel doubles. Toddy's is popular with groups and there's a party atmosphere, spurred on by the all-you-can-eat meals at the outdoor bar every evening. Although there are plenty of beds, the motel-style rooms can be hard to get (book ahead).

Pioneer YHA Hostel (Map p176; ☎ 8952 8855; www .yha.com.au; cnr Leichhardt Tce & Parsons St; dm $20-29, tw & d $65-73, q $98; 🐾 💻 🏊) In the old Pioneer outdoor cinema right in the centre of town, location is the biggest bonus here but it's also spotlessly clean, friendly and well run. The comfortable doubles share bathrooms. There's a good-sized kitchen, common room with internet and a pleasant outdoor area around a small pool.

Alice Lodge Backpackers (Map p173; ☎ 1800 351 925; www.alicelodge.com.au; 4 Mueller St; dm $22-25, d $63; 🐾 💻 🏊) Across the river, about a 10-minute walk from town in a quiet neighbourhood, is this small, relaxed hostel. There are three-, four- and eight-bed dorms as well as comfortable doubles and twins. Rooms, beds and the facilities are kept clean and the management is friendly and helpful.

Annie's Place (Map p173; ☎ 8952 1549, 1800 359 089; www.anniesplace.com.au; 4 Traeger Ave; dm $22, d or tw $65; 🐾 💻 🏊) Alice's most popular hostel has a cosy feel with converted motel rooms (all with bathroom and some with a fridge) around a central pool. Rooms vary in quality and cleanliness issues are occasionally raised by readers, so check a few rooms before settling in. Apart from a poky kitchen, the facilities are excellent and the lively Travellers Café & Bar (dinner meals for guests are $5 to $12) is a winner.

HOTELS & MOTELS

our pick Desert Rose Inn (Map p176; ☎ 8952 1411; www .desertroseinn.com.au; 15 Railway Tce; budget s/d $45/50, motel s/d from $85; 🐾 💻 🏊) The Desert Rose makes a great alternative to the hostel experience in a conveniently central location. The purpose-built budget rooms have two beds plus a shower in the room. No more walking down the corridor in your towel! There are other budget rooms with double beds, fridges and TVs, and larger rooms with full en suites. You will definitely find a room to your liking, as well as a well-equipped kitchen and hassle-free management.

Todd Tavern (Map p176; ☎ 8952 1255; www.todd tavern.com.au; 1 Todd Mall; d with/without bathroom $70/50; ✿) In the heart of town at the top end of Todd Mall, the rooms above Todd Tavern are motel quality at a budget price. The only downside is the lingering odour of cigarettes in some rooms and noise from the pub – mainly Thursday to Sunday. As long as you're not the early-to-bed type it's great value.

CAMPING & CARAVAN PARKS

Most caravan parks are on the outskirts of Alice, but that's still relatively close to the centre. All have barbecues, a laundry, swimming pool and shop with basic provisions, as well as cabins.

Heavitree Gap Outback Lodge & Caravan Park (off Map p173; ☎ 1800 896 119, 8950 4444; www.aurora resorts.com.au; Palm Circuit; unpowered/powered sites $20/22, d $123-135; ✿ ▣ ▣) Although the camping area is a bit of a side issue at this resort, it's still the pick of the bunch, nestled at the foot of the ranges where rock wallabies descend for an evening feed. There's a dump point, wash bay and good shade. The old-fashioned kitchenette rooms are cheaper than the lodge rooms, making them even better value with their basic cooking facilities and ability to sleep six people. The backpacker rooms sleep four and next door is a pub.

MacDonnell Range Holiday Park (off Map p173; ☎ 1800 808 373; www.macrange.com.au; Palm Place; unpowered/powered sites $32/36, cabins d $68-172; ✿ ▣ ▣) Probably Alice's biggest and best-kept, this facility-packed park has grassy sites, spotless amenities, recreation rooms, adventure playgrounds and plenty of activities for restless youngsters. Cabins range from simple affairs with no linen or en suite, to two-bedroom villas.

Also recommended:

G'Day Mate Tourist Park (off Map p173; ☎ 8952 9589; Palm Circuit; unpowered/powered sites $24/28, cabins from $85; ▣) Friendly, though a little tight on space.

Stuart Caravan Park (Map p173; ☎ 8952 2547; www.stuartcaravanpark.com.au; Larapinta Dr; unpowered/powered sites $22/28, cabins $70-140; ▣ ▣) Opposite the cultural precinct 2km west of town.

Wintersun Gardens Caravan Park (Map p173; ☎ 8952 4080; www.wintersun.com.au; Stuart Hwy; unpowered/powered sites $23/29, cabins $88-120; ▣) About 2km north of the town centre.

Midrange

There's plenty of hotels, motels and self-contained apartments in this range, plus a small selection of B&Bs.

HOTELS & MOTELS

White Gum Motel (Map p173; ☎ 8952 5144; www .whitegum.com.au; 17 Gap Rd; s/d/tr/q $95/110/125/140; ✿ ▣ ▣) This impeccable motel is conveniently located a few minutes' walk from the mall, and perfect if you want a reasonably priced room with your own full kitchen. The spacious, old-fashioned rooms are fully self-contained, clean as a whistle and ideal for families.

All Seasons Oasis (Map p173; ☎ 8952 1444; www .allseasons.com.au; 10 Gap Rd; d from $110; ✿ ▣ ▣) The large, central pool shaded with sails surrounded by palm-shaded lawn convincingly creates an oasis experience. The well-appointed rooms are conventional and comfortable and there are numerous tour groups coming and going attesting to its popularity. Facilities include a relaxing bar and restaurant and wheelchair-accessible rooms. The best rates are available from the website.

Alice on Todd (Map p173; ☎ 8953 8033; www.aliceon todd.com; cnr Strehlow St & South Tce; studio $115, 1-/2-bedroom apt $140/175; ✿ ▣) This attractive and secure apartment complex on the banks of the Todd River offers modern, self-contained rooms with kitchen and lounge. The two-bedroom apartments sleep up to six people, and the well-treed, landscaped grounds have a barbecue area, children's playground, and games room with a pool table. These private, balconied rooms are perfect for families and couples alike, and standby and long-term rates are available.

Elkira Motel (Map p176; ☎ 1800 809 252; 65 Bath St; elkira@bestwestern.com.au; budget s/d $100/120, standard s/d $110/130, deluxe s/d $125/145; ✿ ▣) Elkira is a modest, midpriced motel, with a decent restaurant, a central but quiet location and comfortable if unexceptional rooms. The budget rooms are rather poky whereas some of the deluxe rooms have a kitchenette.

Desert Palms Resort (Map p173; ☎ 8952 5977; 1800 678 037; www.desertpalms.com.au; 74 Barrett Dr; s/d villas from $120/135; ✿ ▣ ▣) A world away from the average motel, this is one of the most relaxing places in town, with palms positioned for seclusion and cascades of bougainvillea pouring over balconies. The rows of Indonesian-style villas add to the exotic feel, with cathedral ceilings and tropical-style furnishings. Each has a kitchenette, tiny en suite, TV, breakfast bar and private balcony. The island swimming pool is a big hit with kids.

Lasseter's Hotel Casino (Map p173; ☎ 1800 808 975, 8950 7777; www.lhc.com.au; 93 Barrett Dr; d from $140, ste $250; ❄ 🖳 🖭) Despite all the flashiness of its attached casino, Lasseter's is surprisingly good value if you score one of its special deals. The 140 rooms are bright and spacious with all the mod cons, and the suites come with private spa, bar and a view of the ranges. And you get free golf at the nearby club, along with a brilliant gym, pool and tennis courts.

Aurora Alice Springs (Map p176; ☎ 1800 089 644; www.auroraresorts.com.au; 11 Leichhardt Tce; standard/deluxe/executive d $160/180/250; ❄ 🖳 🖭) Right in the town centre (the 'back' door opens out onto Todd Mall), this modern hotel has a wonderful relaxed atmosphere and an excellent restaurant, the Red Ochre Grill (opposite). Standard rooms are nondescript but spotless and well appointed with fridge, phone and free in-house movies.

BED & BREAKFASTS AND FARMSTAYS

Alice has a handful of B&Bs offering an alternative to the motel experience, especially for couples.

Pathdorf (off Map p173; ☎ 8952 0525; www.pathtoursadventure.com; 107 Heath Rd; d $100-160; ❄ 🖭) For privacy it would be hard to beat the self-contained stone cottage in the sprawling grounds of this rural B&B. Although only a 10-minute drive through Heavitree Gap from the centre of town, Pathdorf is decidedly bucolic, bordering the Todd River with a backdrop of the MacDonnell Ranges. The main house has an en suite apartment and three single rooms. Have a game of tennis, hire a bike, or just sit by the pool in the native garden. The owner is an experienced tour guide and avid birdwatcher and there are discounts for longer stays.

The Gallery (Map p173; ☎ 8953 3514; thegallery@outbacktravelshop.com.au; 16 Range Cres; d $130-170; ❄) Overlooking the golf course in a quiet part of town, this beautiful stone house is an oasis of peace. Play a game of snooker, relax in the elevated lounge or on the outdoor decking and admire the artworks on

the walls. There are three guest rooms with shared facilities. The owners are a mine of local knowledge and speak five languages.

Nthaba Cottage (Map p173; ☎ 8952 9003; www.nthabacottage.com.au; 83 Cromwell Dr; s/d $145/185; ❄) This attractive family home tucked into Alice's exclusive Golf Course estate, on the east side of town, has a beautiful garden with a separate, self-contained cottage giving ample privacy. A room in the house may also be available if the cottage is booked.

Bond Springs Outback Retreat (off Map p173; ☎ 8952 9888; www.outbackretreat.com.au; 0871; 2-/3-bedroom cottage from $230/280; ❄ 🖭) This is the closest you'll come to experiencing outback station life while still being a short drive from Alice. Although you're on a working cattle station the accommodation is exclusive and very private, with two separate self-contained cottages (refurbished stockman's quarters). Modern comforts are matched by traditional furnishings, giving them a bona fide country feel. A full breakfast is included but the rest is self-catering, so stock up in Alice before you arrive. To get here, drive 15km north of Alice along the Stuart Hwy, turn right at the sign and continue a further 7km.

Top End

Crowne Plaza Alice Springs (Map p173; ☎ 8950 8000; www.crowneplaza.com.au; Barrett Dr; d from $165, ste $250-295; ❄ 🖳 🖭) With spacious resort-style facilities and attentive service, this is one of Alice's best hotels. Choose from the garden-view rooms or the better mountain range–view rooms – all have a balcony or patio, TV, minibar, safe, free movies and bath-tubs. A pleasant pool and spa, well-equipped gym and sauna, tennis courts and one of Alice's best restaurants, Hanuman (see opposite), complete the picture.

Alice Springs Resort (Map p176; ☎ 8951 4545; www.voyages.com.au; 34 Stott Tce; d standard/superior/deluxe $150/180/240; ❄ 🖳 🖭) With a circle of double-storey buildings arranged around a swath of lawns and gumtrees, Alice Springs Resort is very stylish and relaxed. Modern, well-appointed rooms are spacious with TV, minibar and writing desk; the deluxe 'River Gum' rooms have a balcony or veranda and a bath-tub. There's a seafood restaurant, albeit a long way from the sea, and a cool pool terrace with a poolside bar.

Ooraminna Homestead & Bush Camp (off Map p200; ☎ 8953 0170; www.ooraminnahomestead.com.au; off Old South Rd; s swag $140, d incl meals $500) This homestead is only 30km south of Alice and offers a genuine outback station experience. Roll out a swag (provided) or stay in style in the secluded stone or timber cabins converted from buildings originally constructed for a movie set (one is an old gaol!). The cabins have four-poster beds made from desert oak and modern bathrooms. You can relax on the veranda of the family homestead, which has a bar and dining room, or take a station tour or go bushwalking.

EATING
Tourism has brought Alice a relatively diverse dining scene where you can sample seared kangaroo, wood-fired pizza, or a Thai curry, but of course if it's a 2kg slab of beef you are after, Alice also won't disappoint. For fine dining the top-end hotel restaurants can't be beaten, and for casual breakfasts, brunches and lunches Todd Mall is the place to head. For an out-there outback experience, take a camel to dinner (see Dining Tours, p181).

Restaurants
Thai Room (Map p176; ☎ 8952 0191; Fan Lane; mains $9.50 21; ☯ lunch Mon-Fri, dinner Mon-Sat; ☒ Ⓥ) For adequately spiced and reasonably priced Southeast Asian food, duck down tiny Fan Lane off Todd Mall. The lunch menu of laksa, pad Thai, curry and rice is a bargain and this unassuming little eatery is one of very few BYO restaurants in Alice.

Flavours of India (Map p173; ☎ 8952 3721; 20 Undoolya Rd; mains $14-20; ☯ dinner; ☒ Ⓥ) The decor is far from Taj Mahal exotica but the food is inexpensive (most mains around $15) and aromatic. The menu features the usual list of temptations, namely tandoori, butter chicken, rogan josh and biryani, plus a good range of vegetarian dishes. Though fully licensed BYO is also possible.

Tinh & Lan Alice Vietnamese Restaurant (off Map p173; ☎ 8952 8396; 1900 Heffernan Rd; mains $14-20; ☯ lunch & dinner Tue-Sun; ☒ Ⓥ) Follow the signs off Colonel Rose Dr to reach this excellent Vietnamese restaurant about 14km south of town. The alfresco market-garden setting, atmospherically illuminated with lanterns, is impressive and there is an indoor dining room if preferred. All the favourites – spring rolls, rice paper rolls, pho and noodles – are deliciously prepared and the ingredients, growing all around you, couldn't be fresher.

Casa Nostra (Map p173; ☎ 8952 6749; cnr Undoolya Rd & Sturt Tce; mains $14-28; ☯ dinner; ☒) Casa Nostra is an unpretentious and popular slice of Italiana just across the river from the town centre. With thin-crust pizza, generous portions of pasta and a selection of chicken and beef mains you won't be leaving hungry. Enjoy the informal, bustling atmosphere with attentive, genial staff, red-and-white checked tablecloths, and plastic grapes hanging from the bar – you get the picture. Note that it's BYO vino.

Red Ochre Grill (Map p176; ☎ 8952 9614; Todd Mall; mains $10-31; ☒) With innovative fusion cuisine featuring outback meats, as well as traditional favourites, the Red Ochre is one of the more popular eateries on Todd Mall. Breakfast and all-day brunch (burgers, wraps and salads) are served in the courtyard. Dinner in the restaurant – which is framed by superb Ken Duncan outback photography – usually features Aussie fauna infused with bush spices as well as conventionally interpreted dishes of chicken, lamb, barramundi and beef.

Dusit Thai (Map p176; ☎ 8952 8882; 29 Gap Rd; mains $20-28; ☯ dinner; ☒ Ⓥ) A Thai restaurant which also dabbles (successfully) with Indian curries, Dusit Thai is not cheap but the dishes are generous and well executed. The seafood dishes we tried, namely soft-shell crab, barramundi with ginger, and black pepper calamari were all delicious. Reasonably priced wine can be purchased by the bottle or glass, and the ability to send the kids next door to the Dust Bowl bowling alley (p180) is an added bonus.

our pick Hanuman (Map p173; ☎ 8953 7188; www .hanuman.com.au; Crowne Plaza Alice Springs, Barrett Dr; mains $14-30; ☯ lunch Mon-Fri, dinner; ☒ Ⓥ) In hues of deep purple, stylish Hanuman is decorated to transport you on a journey along the spice route with Thai- and Indian-influenced cuisine. The delicate Thai entrees, including the stuffed trumpet mushrooms and the signature dish of oysters, lemongrass and basil, are a real triumph. Although the menu is ostensibly Thai, featuring beef, chicken, seafood, jasmine rice and noodles, there are enough Indian dishes to satisfy a curry craving. There are several vegetarian offerings and Indian breads, but strangely no basmati rice.

Lane (Map p176; ☎ 8952 5522; 58 Todd Mall; mains $18-32; ☯ breakfast Sat & Sun, lunch & dinner Tue-Sun; ☒) The Lane has stood proud on Todd Mall for many years as the place for a casual after-work drink, tapas and romantic dinner for two. The Lane also works as a morning-coffee and casual- lunch stop, with the stylish restaurant seating spilling out on to Todd Mall. Although undergoing management changes at the time we visited, the wood-fired pizzas and Mediterranean à la carte mains were still inspiring and the inventive tapas menu set to return. The service is usually excellent and there's often live entertainment on weekends.

Overlanders Steakhouse (Map p176; ☎ 8952 2159; www.overlanders.com.au; 72 Hartley St; mains $20-40; ☺ dinner; ☒) A local institution for huge steaks of all kinds, Overlanders is an over-the-top representation of all things outback. Amid the drovers' decor – saddles, cowboy hats, branding irons – you can sample buffalo, kangaroo, crocodile, camel, emu and barramundi. The famous 'Drover's Blowout' ($65) is a four-course meal that includes soup, a platter of the Aussie meats, choice of steak or barra, and dessert. The bar is fully licensed and you can further stretch the belly with a Darwin stubby.

Pubs

Todd Tavern (Map p176; ☎ 8952 1255; 1 Todd Mall; meals $11-24; ☺ lunch & dinner; ☒) The Todd Tavern is hard to beat for traditional pub fare served the old-fashioned way – big. There's the usual burgers and nachos to soak up a beer throughout the day, and savvy appetites will join the feeding frenzy at the Sunday roast ($12.50). It's also family friendly (children's meals around $8.50) and look out for daily specials, such as Thursday night schnitzels ($7) and movie-and-meal deals ($20) on Monday (the cinema is next door).

Bojangles (Map p176; ☎ 8952 2873; 80 Todd St; mains $14-26; ☺ lunch & dinner; ☒) With its rustic tables hewn from railway sleepers, cowhide seats and walls dripping with stockman's regalia and bush memorabilia, Bo's has bags of 'yee haa' atmosphere and a surprisingly gourmet 'Territorian' menu. Start with crocodile spring rolls to prepare for the main assault of king-size steaks, bourbon-beef ribs, or camel-and-stout pie. Friday and Saturday nights are usually lively, though Bo's can be bursting with thirsty backpackers any night of the week.

Firkin & Hound (Map p176; ☎ 8953 3033; 21 Hartley St; mains $15-25; ☺ lunch & dinner; ☒) The Firkin delivers a typical pommy-pub menu in cosy surrounds – perfect for warming up a cold winter night. Before choosing hearty bangers and mash, the huge beef-and-Guinness pie or beer-battered fish-and-chips, check the daily specials of soup, pizza and pasta.

Cafes

Bean Tree Café (Map p173; ☎ 8952 0190; Olive Pink Botanic Garden, Tuncks Rd; mains $9-12; ☺ 10am-4pm Tue-Sun) The Bean Tree is a perfect retreat in the peaceful grounds of the Olive Pink Botanic Garden. Amid the birdsong and under the shady boughs select from a small but always changing selection of tasty, wholesome dishes – kangaroo and rocket salad, Thai chicken pot pie, BLT etc. It also does refreshing, creamy iced coffees.

Café Mediterranean Bar Doppio (Map p176; ☎ 8952 6525; Fan Lane; meals $10-17; ☺ breakfast & lunch; Ⓥ) In a tiny arcade off Todd Mall, this busy but spacious cafe serves up generous portions of wholesome, nourishing food. There are cooked breakfasts, focaccias, felafel rolls, curries, great coffee, fresh juices and more. The walls and windows are a fount of knowledge on Alice's art/alternative/gay and lesbian scenes.

Red Dog Cafe (Map p176; ☎ 8953 1353; 64 Todd Mall; mains $12-15; ☺ breakfast & lunch) Decent mugs of good coffee, eggs, pancakes, and tables spreading out onto the mall make this the perfect place for breakfast. Try the full 'bushman's breakfast' ($15.50) and you won't need lunch. But if you do, they have an excellent range of chicken burgers ($15).

Sporties Café & Restaurant (Map p176; ☎ 8953 0953; Todd Mall; mains $15-35; ☒) With tables on Todd Mall and a bar and restaurant inside, this is a good spot for a lunchtime feed – filling focaccias, baguettes, crepes, pasta – or just a beer or coffee. The broad menu also has steaks and pub-style meals. The atmosphere inside is more airport-lounge than cosy, but sports lovers will enjoy the paraphernalia.

Quick Eats

Wicked Kneads (Map p176; Coles Complex, Bath St; pastries $3-4.50, focaccias $8.50; ☺ 7am-4pm) With some of Alice's best pies (15 varieties), quiches, cakes and a sandwich bar, this excellent bakery is perfect for a budget lunch and coffee.

The shopping malls – Yeperenye Shopping Centre (Map p176) and Alice Plaza (Map p176) – have food courts with cafes, bakeries, fast food and various ready-made dishes. Alice also has most of the big fast food chains: look for your favourite sign.

Self-Catering

Large supermarkets include **Woolworths** (Map p176; Yeperenye Shopping Centre; ☺ 7am-midnight Mon-Sat, to 10pm Sun) and **Coles** (Map p176; Coles Complex, cnr Gregory & Railway Tce; ☺ 24hr).

Afghan Traders (Map p176; ☎ 8955 5560; 9.30am-5.30pm Mon-Fri, 9am-2pm Sat), in a lane off Parsons St behind the ANZ bank, is worth the search for its excellent range of organic and health foods. Fresh vegies and Asian greens can be had at Tinh and Lan Ngyuen's **Alice Market Garden** (off Map p173; Lot 1900 Heffernan Rd; 8am-6pm), about 14km south of town via Colonel Rose Dr.

DRINKING

Outside of the tourist hotels, Alice has a small range of pubs, bars and cafes, all of which double as eating places.

Bojangles (Map p176; ☎ 8952 2873; www.boslive saloon.com.au; 80 Todd St; 11.30am-late) Behind the swinging saloon doors, with a contrived 'wild west meets Aussie outback' theme, Bojangles is easily the most popular pub in town, beloved of backpacker groups and jumping most nights of the week.

Firkin & Hound (Map p176; ☎ 8953 3033; 21 Hartley St; 11.30am-1am) The Firkin is Alice's sole British-themed pub. Snug booths, large TV and a dozen or so beers on tap make up what's essentially a local drinking hole.

Todd Tavern (Map p176; ☎ 8952 1255; 1 Todd Mall; 10am-midnight) This long-standing, typically Aussie pub is the true 'local' in Alice. There's a lively bar, pokies, pub grub and occasional live music on weekends.

Uncles Tavern (Map p176; ☎ 8952 8977; All Seasons Diplomat Hotel, cnr Gregory Tce & Hartley St; noon-10.30pm) Though it doesn't look much now, this was the site of Alice's premier hotel. The history of the grand, art deco Hotel Alice Springs and its larger-than-life owner 'Uncle' Ly Underdown is displayed on the walls of this unassuming watering hole. Old Ly Underwood was held in high esteem by both black and white during less tolerant times, and his legacy continues here.

ENTERTAINMENT

The gig guide in the entertainment section of the *Centralian Advocate*, published every Tuesday and Friday, lists what's on in and around town.

Theatre & Cinemas

Sounds of Starlight Theatre (Map p176; ☎ 8953 0826; www.soundsofstarlight.com; 40 Todd Mall; adult/concession/family $30/25/90; 8pm Tue, Fri & Sat Apr-Nov) Andrew Langford's didgeridoo performances have become an Alice institution, with a crescendo of lights and sound effects evoking the spirit of the outback. The surprising versatility of the didgeridoo is accompanied by drums and keyboards and wonderful photography for this 1½-hour show.

Araluen Arts Centre (Map p176; ☎ 8952 5022, bookings ☎ 8951 1122; www.araluencentre.com.au; Larapinta Dr) The cultural heart of Alice, the 500-seat Araluen Theatre hosts a diverse range of performers on national tours, from dance troupes to comedians. The Art House Cinema screens every Sunday evening (adult/child $12/10). The website has an events calendar.

Alice Springs Cinema (Map p176; ☎ 8952 4999; Todd Mall; adult/child $14.50/10, Tue $10/8) This multiscreen cinema shows latest-release movies between 10am and 9pm. Some hostels offer discount movie-ticket deals.

Story Wall (Map p176; Adelaide House; Todd Mall; ☎ showsThu & Fri nights) Park yourself on the grass outside Adelaide House and enjoy free films pertaining to central Australia's heritage screened on an adjacent building's wall.

Casino

Lasseter's Hotel Casino (Map p173; ☎ 8950 7777; 93 Barrett Dr; 10am-3am Sun-Thu, to 4am Fri & Sat, gaming tables from 2pm) Clouds of smoke, electronic beeps and garish carpets are typical of any pokie-infested venue, and along with the usual games there's a two-up ring, live music and the Juicy Rump restaurant.

SHOPPING

Todd Mall is the shopping hub and just off here you'll find the main indoor shopping malls, Alice Plaza (Map p176) and Springs Plaza (Map p176). A block away is Yeperenye Shopping Centre (Map p176). For general items, Kmart (Map p176) is well stocked.

Aboriginal Arts & Crafts

Alice is the centre for Aboriginal arts and crafts from all over central Australia. The places owned and run by community art centres ensure that a better slice of the proceeds goes to the artist and artist's community.

Aboriginal Art & Culture Centre (Map p176; ☎ 8952 3408; www.aboriginalaustralia.com.au; 125 Todd St; 9am-5pm) Established by southern Arrernte people, this is a good first stop. The small shop offers one-hour didgeridoo lessons ($20) and has a range of authentic central Australian art and artefacts, such as woodcarvings and paintings, plus didgeridoos from the Top End.

Central Australian Aboriginal Media Association (CAAMA; Map p176; ☎ 8951 9711; www.caama.com.au; 79 Todd Mall; ☉ 9am-5pm Mon-Fri, to 1pm Sat) Here you will find most of the CDs recorded by central Australia's Aboriginal musicians. The CAAMA studio, which has its own radio network (8KIN FM), is just down the road at 101 Todd St. As well as CDs the shop in the mall stocks Aboriginal-design printed material, T-shirts, jewellery and other Indigenous-themed items.

Ngurratjuta Iltja Ntjarra (Map p173; ☎ 8951 1953; www.ngurart.com.au; 29 Wilkinson St; ☉ 9am-3.30pm Mon-Fri) The 'many hands' art centre is a small gallery and studio for visiting artists from all over central Australia. Watercolour and dot paintings are reasonably priced here ($200 to $500) and you buy directly from the artists. You can see artists at work from Monday to Thursday, 10am to 3pm.

Papunya Tula Artists (Map p176; ☎ 8952 4731; www.papunyatula.com.au; 63 Todd Mall; ☉ 9am-5pm Mon-Fri, 10am-2pm Sat) The Western Desert art movement began at Papunya in 1971 and today this Aboriginal-owned and operated centre displays some of the most sought-after artworks in central Australia. The bright gallery is a great place to get a feel for quality Aboriginal art. Papunya Tula works with around 120 artists, most painting in Kintore in the far west.

Tjanpi Desert Weavers (Map p173; ☎ 8958 2377; www.tjanpi.com.au; 3 Wilkinson St; ☉ 10am-4pm, closed Jan) This small enterprise employs and supports central desert women from remote communities and helps keep their culture alive. The women collect traditional materials and weave baskets and fascinating sculptural fibre art. All profits feed back to the local communities.

There are also plenty of commercial outlets for quality (and otherwise) Aboriginal art. The following are reputable.

Gallery Gondwana (Map p176; ☎ 8953 1577; www.gallerygondwana.com.au; 43 Todd Mall; ☉ 9.30am-6pm Mon-Fri, 10am-5pm Sat) Gondwana is a respected, well-established gallery, recognised for dealing directly with community art centres and artists. Quality works from leading and emerging Central and Western Desert artists include examples from Yuendumu and Utopia.

Mbantua Gallery (Map p176; ☎ 8952 5571; www.mbantua.com.au; 71 Gregory Tce; ☉ 9am-6pm Mon-Fri, 9.30am-5pm Sat) This privately owned gallery

was being extended through to Todd Mall at the time we visited. The renovations include a cafe and plenty of wall space to exhibit the extensive collection of works from the renowned Utopia region, as well as watercolour landscapes from the Namatjira school. The upstairs Educational & Permanent Collection (adult/child $4.60/3.30) is a superb cultural exhibition space with panels explaining Aboriginal mythology, lifestyle, ceremonies, and customs of marriage and death.

Outdoor Equipment

Desert Dwellers (Map p173; ☎ 8953 2240; 38 Elder St; ☉ 9am-5pm Mon-Fri, to 2pm Sat) has just about everything you need to equip yourself for an outback jaunt – maps, swags, tents, sleeping bags, portable fridges, stoves, camp ovens, Larapinta Trail Packs and more.

Lone Dingo Adventure (Map p176; ☎ 8953 3866; cnr Todd Mall & Gregory Tce; ☉ 9am-6pm Mon-Fri, to 4pm Sat, 10am-2pm Sun) has a variety of hiking and camping gear from rucksacks and sleeping bags to maps, Global Positioning System (GPS) units and emergency position-indicating radio beacons (EPIRBs).

Markets

Todd Mall Market (Todd Mall; ☉ 9am-1pm every 2nd Sun, May-Dec) Craft markets, food stalls, clothing, Aboriginal art, jewellery and knick-knack stalls line Todd Mall every second Sunday. It's a colourful atmosphere with music, sizzling snacks and a few bargains.

GETTING THERE & AWAY
Air

Alice Springs is well connected by air, with Qantas and Tiger Airways operating daily flights to/from capital cities. One-way fares from Alice include Yulara ($160), Adelaide ($250), Melbourne ($310), Darwin ($270), Sydney (from $270), Brisbane (from $310), and Perth (from $330). Check websites for latest timetables and fare offers.

Although you will probably have more luck with a call centre or web page, Qantas and Tiger have representatives at the airport:

Qantas (☎ 13 13 13, 8950 5211; www.qantas.com.au)
Tiger Airways (☎ 9335 3033; www.tigerairways.com.au)

Bus

Greyhound Australia (☎ 13 14 99; www.greyhound.com.au; Shop 3, 113 Todd St; office ☉ 8.30am-11.30am, 1.30pm-4pm

Mon-Fri) has regular services from Alice Springs (check website for timetables). Buses arrive at, and depart from, the Greyhound office in Todd St.

Destination	Duration (hr)	One-way fare ($)
Adelaide	20	280
Coober Pedy	8	165
Darwin	22	315
Katherine	16½	255
Tennant Creek	6½	160

Austour (☎ 1800 335009; www.austour.com.au) runs the cheapest daily connections between Alice Springs and Yulara (adult/child $120/60) and between Alice Springs and Kings Canyon ($110/60). Daily connections between Alice Springs and Yulara are also run by **AAT Kings** (☎ 8952 1700; www.aatkings.com) and cost ($135/68). AAT Kings also has a daily service from Kings Canyon to Alice Springs ($138/69), but not in the opposite direction.

Backpacker buses roam to and from Alice Springs, providing a party atmosphere and a chance to see some of the sights on the way. **Desert Venturer** (☎ 1300 858 059; www.desertventurer.com.au) plies the route from Alice to Cairns via the Plenty Hwy. The three-day coach trip costs $396 plus $85 for meals. **Groovy Grape Getaways Australia** (☎ 1800 661 177; www.groovygrape.com.au) plies the route from Alice to Adelaide, overnighting in Coober Pedy, for $195.

Car

Alice Springs is a long way from anywhere, although the roads to the north and south are sealed and in good condition.

CAR RENTAL

All the major companies have offices in Alice Springs, and Avis, Budget, Europcar, Hertz and Territory Thrifty also have counters at the airport. Prices drop by about 20% in the low season (November to April) but try to avoid deals with 100km daily limits if you plan exploring well outside Alice.

A conventional (2WD) vehicle will get you to most sights in the MacDonnell Ranges and out to Uluru and Kings Canyon via sealed roads. If you want to go further afield, say to Chambers Pillar, Finke Gorge or even the Mereenie Loop Rd, a 4WD is essential. Prices depend on the size of vehicle and length of hire, and not all companies offer unlimited kilometres. Insurance excess is also much higher for 4WD vehicles. Shop around as early as possible.

Alice Camp 'n' Drive (Map p173; ☎ 8952 0099; www.alicecampndrive.com; 48 Gap Rd) Provides vehicles fully equipped for camping with swags (or tents), sleeping bags, cooking gear, chairs etc. Rates include unlimited kilometres, and vehicles can be dropped off at your accommodation.

Avis (Map p176; ☎ 8953 5533; Coles Shopping Complex, Gregory Tce)

Budget (Map p176; ☎ 8952 8899; www.budget.com.au; Shop 6, Capricornia Centre, Gregory Tce)

Central Car Rentals (Map p173; ☎ 8952 0098; www.centralcarrentals.com.au; 48 Gap Rd) A local operator (associated with Alice Camp 'n' Drive) with 2WD and 4WD vehicles that can be equipped with camping gear. Unlimited kilometres rates are available.

Europcar (☎ 131390; www.europcarnt.com.au) At airport only.

Hertz (Map p176; ☎ 8952 2644; www.hertznt.com; 76 Hartley St)

Territory Thrifty Car Rental (Map p176; ☎ 8952 9999; www.rentacar.com.au; cnr Stott Tce & Hartley St)

CAMPERVAN RENTAL

Hiring a campervan gives you a bed on wheels and it's also possible to hire camping equipment with the vehicle.

Britz Australia (off Map p173; ☎ 1800 331 454; www.britz.com.au; cnr Stuart Hwy & Power St) Big range of campervans and motor homes including 2WD and 4WD with unlimited kilometres. This is also the base for **Maui** (www.maui.com.au) and **Backpacker** (www.backpackercampervans.com).

Train

The *Ghan* between Adelaide, Alice Springs and Darwin is a classic way to enter or leave the Territory. There are two services weekly in each direction throughout the year; Adelaide-bound trains depart from Alice Springs at 12.45pm on Thursday and 3.15pm Saturday. Heading north to Darwin, trains depart from Alice Springs at 6pm on Monday and Wednesday. Northbound the train stops at Katherine for four hours on Tuesday morning, allowing a quick visit to the gorge.

It's a popular service, especially during winter, and bookings are essential – contact **Trainways** (☎ 13 21 47; www.trainways.com.au), or book through **Travel World** (Map p176; ☎ 8953 0488; Todd Mall).

ALICE SPRINGS & AROUND

The **train station** (Map p173) is at the end of George Crescent off Larapinta Drive.

GETTING AROUND
To/From the Airport

Alice Springs airport is 15km south of the town, which is about $30 by taxi – there's a free taxi phone outside the terminal. The **airport shuttle** (☎ 8953 0310; one-way 1/2/3 persons $17/29/33) meets flights and drops off passengers at city accommodation. Leaving town it departs from outside the ticket office on Gregory Tce, near the corner of Todd St (Map p176), but also picks up from all accommodation; book a day in advance.

Bicycle

For details on bike hire, see Cycling, p180.

Car & Motorcycle

Parking is free (with time restrictions) in Alice but the central area can get pretty congested on weekdays. The easiest places to find a space are in the car parks of the Coles and Kmart complexes (three-hour limit). Campervans and trailers can park on Leichhardt Tce just north of the Stott Tce roundabout.

Public Transport

Asbus (☎ 8950 0500), the local bus network, runs four routes that depart from outside the Yeperenye Shopping Centre on Hartley St:

West Route (No 1) Goes along Larapinta Dr, with a daily detour (Route 1C) for the cultural precinct. Route 1C leaves at 9.45am and returns at 3.35pm.

East Route (No 2) East to the residential area along Undoolya Rd.

North Route (No 3) Heads north along the Stuart Hwy and passes the School of the Air.

South Route (No 4) Runs along Gap Rd – past many of the hotels and hostels – through Heavitree Gap and along Palm Circuit (useful for the southern caravan parks).

Buses run approximately every 1½ hours from 7.45am to 6pm Monday to Friday and 9am to 12.45pm Saturday. A three-hour ticket costs adult/child or concession $2/50c.

ALICE WANDERER

A hop-on, hop-off bus service, **Alice Wanderer** (☎ 1800 722 111, 8952 2111; www.alicewanderer.com.au; adult/child $40/30; ⏰ 9am-4pm) covers 11 major sights, including the Telegraph Station, School of the Air, Cultural Precinct, Olive

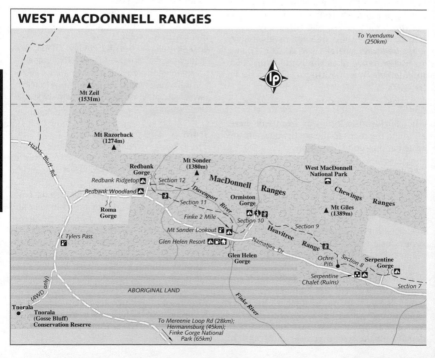

WEST MACDONNELL RANGES

Pink Botanic Garden, RFDS Base and Ghan Museum, complete with commentary. The ticket is valid for two days and the circuit runs every 70 minutes from the southern end of Todd Mall. You can also arrange pick-up from your accommodation before the 9am departure.

Taxi

To order a taxi, call ☎ 13 10 08 or ☎ 8952 1877. Taxis congregate on Gregory Tce near the tourist office.

WEST MACDONNELL NATIONAL PARK

The ancient, weather-beaten MacDonnell Ranges stretch 400km across the desert. Alice Springs lies where the Todd River bisects the range through Heavitree Gap, creating the East and West MacDonnells. Though not particularly high, this range provides dramatic relief from the surrounding plains and exhibits an artist's pallette of colour and texture. Its hidden-world topography harbours rare wildlife and poignant Aboriginal heritage and it's all accessible from Alice Springs.

The West MacDonnell National Park protects a significant part of this range, from the Stuart Hwy just north of Alice Springs to Mt Zeil, 170km to the west. Within its boundaries are beautiful, brick-red gorges, cool waterholes and camping grounds, plus a network of trails for bushwalkers.

In dry conditions all the attractions are accessible to 2WD vehicles, and most can be visited in several short day trips or one long day trip from Alice. To get the most out of the area, it's best to camp or stay at Glen Helen Resort for at least one night. Namatjira Dr turns off Larapinta Dr and is sealed as far as Tylers Pass. Work is ongoing to seal it the entire way to the Larapinta Dr west of Hermannsburg – making the so-called Inner Loop back to Alice.

Wildlife

To the casual observer the wildlife of the ranges can be difficult to appreciate (let alone see), but dwelling in the rocky crevices and around the waterholes is a diverse fauna –

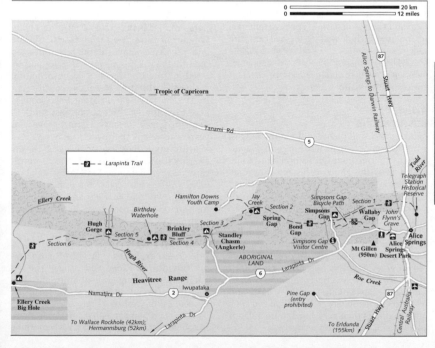

some 167 species of bird, 85 species of reptile, 23 species of native mammal, five species of frog and various fish are found in this area.

Most mammals are shy and for the most part nocturnal, but if you're out and about in the late afternoon keep an eye out for black-footed rock wallabies foraging among the rocks at Standley Chasm or Ormiston Gorge, as well as euros and red kangaroos grazing in more open country.

Although arid, the ranges are blessed with a great variety of plants, including the majestic ghost gums and, in sheltered and moist settings, relics of ancient rainforests, such as the MacDonnell Ranges cycad.

Information

There are (not always manned) national-park visitors centres at **Simpsons Gap** (☎ 8955 0310; ◷ 5am-8pm) and **Ormiston Gorge** (☎ 8956 7799). and each main site throughout the park has information signs describing the geology, Aboriginal lore and local wildlife.

Fuel is available at Glen Helen Resort.

GUIDED WALKS & TALKS

During the main tourist season (May to October), Parks & Wildlife rangers conduct free scheduled 'walks and talks' at Simpsons Gap and Ormiston Gorge. The program varies, but may include walks, a themed campfire talk or a slide show – check with **Parks & Wildlife** (☎ 8951 8211; www.nt.gov.au/nreta/parks/walks/guided walks.html) for times and locations, or check at the respective visitors centres.

Activities
BUSHWALKING

Walkers will find plenty to do in the ranges, from a 10-minute stroll into Simpsons Gap to the superb four-hour Ormiston Pound walk. Don't miss the short walks into Standley Chasm or Redbank Gorge. Serious walkers should consider the tough eight-hour-return walk to the summit of Mt Sonder, or plan to walk part of the Larapinta Trail.

For long-distance walkers, the problem lies in getting to or from the various trailheads. **Alice Wanderer** (☎ 8952 2111; www.alicewanderer.com .au) provides transfers to nine access points. Rates for two passengers include $80 to Simpsons Gap, $100 to Standley Chasm and $210 to Ormiston Gorge, but if you can get a seat on one of their scheduled tours it drops to $30, $35, and $60, respectively.

Glen Helen Resort (☎ 8956 7495; www.glenhelen.com .au) also runs transfers between Alice Springs and Glen Helen Gorge and the trailheads.

CYCLING

The **Simpsons Gap Bicycle Path** offers the chance for a smooth and traffic-free bush ride. The sealed cycling path between Flynn's Grave on Larapinta Dr and Simpsons Gap wanders 17km along timbered creek flats and over low rocky hills. It's an easy one- to two-hour ride and, if you add the 7km by road from Alice to the start of the path, you can make the 50km return trip in a comfortable day.

There are several bush picnic spots en route, information signs and excellent views of Mt Gillen, Rungutjirba Ridge and the rugged Alice Valley. The path is open only during daylight hours, so head out in the early morning and return in the afternoon. Water is available 3.5km from the start and at Simpsons Gap; always carry a water bottle.

Tours

See p182 for a list of companies that run tours to the West MacDonnell National Park.

JOHN FLYNN'S GRAVE

About 7km west of Alice Springs along Larapinta Dr is the grave of Dr John Flynn, founder of the Royal Flying Doctor Service and the Australian Inland Mission, who died in 1951. The grave itself is topped by a red granite boulder and the information shelter tells the story of a rocky controversy. In 1952, a large round stone was brought here from the Devil's Marbles just south of Tennant Creek to mark Flynn's grave. For years afterwards the owners (Kaytetye and Warumungu peoples) of this sacred site (Karlukarlu) lobbied to have the stone returned. Eventually the local Arrernte community offered to replace the stone with one of their own, and in 1999 an official swap took place – the rock from Karlukarlu was returned to its rightful place.

SIMPSONS GAP

Roe Creek exploited a fault in the quartzite Rungutjirba Ridge and gouged the red gorge and towering cliffs of Simpsons Gap, the first of many impressive cracks in the ranges, 24km west of Alice.

The area is popular with picnickers and also has some excellent short walks. Early morning

LARAPINTA TRAIL

The 230km Larapinta Trail extends along the backbone of the West MacDonnell Ranges and is one of Australia's great long-distance walks. It's split into 12 stages or sections of between 13km and 31km, starting from the Telegraph Station Museum at Alice Springs to Mt Sonder (1380m), the fourth-highest peak in the Northern Territory. Note that several sections take two days to complete. Along its length, the trail passes the permanent waterholes at Simpsons Gap, Standley Chasm (Angkerle), Ellery Creek, Ormiston Gorge and Redbank Gorge. Although this is described as a desert walk, in fact there's lots of vegetation, amazing rocky outcrops and a booklist of birdlife.

The first section's 24km stretch to Simpson Gap is particularly spectacular, alternating between the ridge and the foot of the range and passing a number of smaller gaps and waterholes along the way. Section 3, a short 14km stretch from Jay Creek to Standley Chasm, is even better, departing the idyllic Jay Creek camping ground and following a twisting cut through the range then offering alternative high- and low-altitude routes, before descending the dramatically narrow, rocky and picturesque gorge that leads into Standley Chasm. Sections 4 and 5 follow high ridges with wonderful views, descending into Stuart Pass and a series of challenging gorges. Section 9 is one of the tougher parts of the trail since there are no reliable water sources along the 29km, two-day walk. The final stages make a fitting finale to the classic walk. From Ormiston Gorge the trail leads to the Finke River before climbing to the summit of Mt Sonder with spectacular views in all directions.

There are more than 20 designated camping areas, and water sources on most stages. The trail is best walked in the cooler months from April to September since summer in the centre can be incredibly hot and the waterholes are more likely to have dried up.

To complete the entire distance takes nearly three weeks, which is far too long to carry supplies, particularly since you must carry plenty of water. It's best to walk the trail in sections with resupply points along the way.

Several companies offer organised walks of varying lengths on the trail. **Trek Larapinta** (☎ 1300 724 795; www.treklarapinta.com.au), run by Shane Fewtrell, offers fully guided and catered walks from $1200 for a six-day walk from Ormiston to Mt Sonder, to $1860 for a nine-day trek. The mother of all walks – the 19-day end-to-end – costs $3960 and is scheduled once a year. Check the website for upcoming walks. **World Expeditions** (☎ 1300 720 000; www.worldexpeditions.com.au) has seven-day treks for $1800 which cherry pick sections along the trail.

Trail notes and maps are available from the **Parks & Wildlife Service** (www www.nt.gov.au/nreta /parks/walks/larapinta/walking.html), though it is also recommended that you purchase a Larapinta Trail Pack ($45) from outdoor-equipment shops in Alice Springs (p190). All walkers should register their names and itinerary on ☎ 1300 650 730. And don't forget to deregister. Sections are graded as medium (suitable for people who walk regularly), hard (rough trail suitable for people with bushwalking experience), and very hard (rough trail, frequent steep ascents and descents, suitable for people with extensive bushwalking experience), but each stage will have some easy and some challenging sections.

Larapinta Trail Sections

Section	Trail	Distance (km)	Duration (hr)	Rating
1	Alice Springs Telegraph Station to Simpsons Gap	24	9	medium
2	Simpsons Gap to Jay Creek	25	9	medium
3	Jay Creek to Standley Chasm (Angkerle)	14	7	hard
4	Standley Chasm to Birthday Waterhole	18	11	very hard
5	Birthday Waterhole to Hugh Gorge	16	9½	very hard
6	Hugh Gorge to Ellery Creek	31	10	medium
7	Ellery Creek to Serpentine Gorge	14	6½	hard
8	Serpentine Gorge to Serpentine Chalet Dam	14	6½	hard
9	Serpentine Chalet Dam to Ormiston Gorge	29	15	hard
10	Ormiston Gorge to Finke River	10	5	medium
11	Finke River to Redbank Gorge	25	12	hard
12	Redbank Gorge to Mt Sonder and return	16	8	hard

and late afternoon are the best times to see the black-footed rock wallabies that live among the jumble of boulders in the gap. To the Arrernte people, Simpsons Gap is known as Rungutjirba, the home of Giant Goanna ancestral beings.

The park entrance (open 5am to 8pm) and **visitors centre** (☎ 8955 0310), about 1km in from Larapinta Dr, has displays on local wildlife, drinking water, toilets and free gas barbecues. At the entrance to the gap itself are more toilets, picnic tables and gas barbecues. From here it's a 20-minute return walk along the (usually) dry creek bed to the gap and a small waterhole.

Bushwalking

Apart from the short walk into the gap itself, there are some pleasant and not-too-strenuous walks around Simpsons Gap. You can also do day walks on the first two sections of the Larapinta Trail – peaceful **Bond Gap** (to the west) and **Wallaby Gap** (to the east).

Ghost Gum walk (1km return, 15 minutes, easy) This brief stroll starts at the visitors centre and is lined with information boards describing some of the vegetation of the area, including a beautiful 200-year-old ghost gum.

Cassia Hill (1.5km loop, 45 minutes, easy to medium) About halfway between the visitors centre and the gap, this loop walk meanders through groves of witchetty bush and mulga, then up a moderate hill for views of the ranges.

Woodland trail (17km return, seven hours, medium) This walk starts about 2km from the visitors centre and passes through Rocky Gap to Bond Gap.

STANDLEY CHASM (ANGKERLE)

From the Simpsons Gap turn-off, you cross Aboriginal land for the next 30km to spectacular **Standley Chasm** (Angkerle; ☎ 8956 7440; adult/senior & child $8/6.50; camping $3; ⏱ 8am-6pm). This part of the MacDonnells is owned and managed by the nearby community of Iwupataka. Its English name honours Ida Standley, the first schoolteacher in Alice Springs in 1914.

The school for Aboriginal children was moved to Jay Creek (now Iwupataka) in 1925 and Mrs Standley was the first non-Aboriginal woman to visit the chasm.

The chasm was formed where a tributary of the Finke River wore a narrow cleft through the surrounding sandstone. In places the smooth vertical walls rise to 80m and at its widest the chasm is 9m across. It's cool and dark on the chasm floor, and for about an hour either side of midday the red stone walls are briefly warmed by sunlight.

The kiosk at the site sells snacks and drinks; there are picnic tables, wood barbecues (bring your own wood), campsites and toilets near the car park.

Bushwalking

Main chasm walk (1.6km return, 30 minutes, easy) The trail up the rocky gully from the kiosk to the extraordinary sheer-walled chasm features moisture-loving river red gums, cycads and ferns, creating an unexpected lushness.

Second chasm walk (2.4km return, one hour, medium) Scramble over the rocks at the end of the main chasm. At the far end turn left, then follow the creek bed for a further 300m before returning. You need to scramble over boulders and tree trunks here, making it more challenging than the main walk.

Larapinta Hill (1.5km return, 45 minutes, hard) From the main chasm track, this signposted trail – part of the Larapinta Trail – climbs to a lookout (signposted as Jay Creek).

Loop Walk (2.5km loop, one hour, medium) Follow the signposted trail from the southern side of the kiosk and return via the main road.

ELLERY CREEK BIG HOLE

Just under 90km from Alice Springs on Namatjira Dr, Ellery Creek Big Hole is a popular swimming hole in summer but, as it's shaded by the high cliffs of Ellery Gorge, the water is freezing for much of the year.

Ellery Creek was named by explorer Ernest Giles in 1872 after a Victorian astronomer. The Aboriginal name for the waterhole is Udepata, and it was an important gathering point along a couple of Dreaming trails that pass through the area.

The **Dolomite Walk** (20 minutes return) is worth the detour. An information shelter at the car park explains the area's geological history, which is exposed in the creek banks downstream from the waterhole.

Within easy reach of the waterhole is a small, often crowded **camping ground** (sites per adult/child/family $3.30/1.65/7.70) with gas barbecues, tables, a pit toilet and limited shade.

SERPENTINE GORGE

About 11km further along Namatjira Dr a rough gravel track leads to the Serpentine Gorge car park. From here it's a 1.3km walk along the sandy creek bed to the gorge and its waterholes, which sustain some rare plants, such as the Centralian flannel flower.

A waterhole blocks access to the entrance of the narrow gorge, which snakes for over 2km through the Heavitree Range. The stunning

---

ABORIGINAL AUSTRALIA: THE MAGIC OF OCHRE

Ochre was an important commodity in traditional Aboriginal life, where it was used medicinally and traded. Red ochre mixed with grease and eucalyptus leaves became an effective decongestant balm, and white ochre was believed to have magical powers – it was mixed with water and then blown from the mouth, a practice which was said to cool the sun and calm the wind. Ochre was also used extensively for body decoration and in painting. Red ochre was used in important ceremonies such as the initiation of young men.

Ochre from the West MacDonnells was occasionally traded as far south as the Pitjantjatjara communities of South Australia. It was dampened and pressed into bricks or rolled into balls for easy transport.

The different coloured layers and swirls of the Ochre Pits were created by layers of deposited silt containing varying amounts of iron being compressed, folded and buckled over millions of years.

---

scenery of cycads and a second water-filled cleft can also be enjoyed from a lookout above the main entrance.

SERPENTINE CHALET RUINS

Continuing on from Serpentine Gorge you soon arrive at the Serpentine Chalet turn-off. A rough track leads to the ruins of this early 1960s tourism venture. Visitors would travel all day from Alice Springs to reach the chalet.

Lack of water caused the chalet to close after only a couple of years and all that remain are the concrete foundations and floor slabs. These days travellers stop in for the bush **campsites** (free) scattered along the track to and beyond the original site. The first five sites are accessible to 2WD vehicles, the last six to 4WD vehicles only.

A roadside stop between here and the Ochre Pits takes you up to a **lookout** over the ranges, with picnic tables, pit barbecues and a water tank.

OCHRE PITS

A little further along the highway, a car park and boardwalk (disabled access) leads about 300m to the Ochre Pits, a site that has been used by the local Arrernte people for centuries. Small deposits of yellow ochre are still used occasionally for ceremonial decoration, though the remaining ochre here is generally of poor quality and modern materials have largely replaced natural ochre. The picnic area has free gas barbecues.

A three-hour-return walk takes you to scenic **Inarlanga Pass** at the foot of the Heavitree Range. The track passes through some rather uninspiring country, though there is some interest in the gorge and the old Serpentine

Chalet dam, an hour's walk to the east along the Larapinta Trail.

ORMISTON GORGE

The soaring red cliffs, brilliant ghost gums, and peaceful waterhole at Ormiston Gorge combine to form some of the grandest scenery in the central ranges, and the Ormiston Pound walk is a highlight of the park. There's a **visitors centre** (☎ 8956 7799; ☾ 5am-8pm) with information panels, a **kiosk** (☾ 10am-4pm), and an excellent camping ground. Free ranger talks are given here four days a week from May to October – ask at the visitors centre for a program.

Ormiston Gorge is a haven for wildlife enthusiasts, thanks to the variety of habitats – mulga woodland, spinifex slopes, large river red gums and permanent water. The waterhole is part of the Aboriginal Emu Dreaming and is a registered sacred site. Although the water is pretty cold, it's still a popular summer swimming spot. Climb the steps to the Ghost Gum Lookout for an awesome view over the gorge and ranges.

The turn-off to the gorge is 26km on from the Ochre Pits and only 4km east of Glen Helen, then a further 8km along a sealed road to the car park and camping area.

Bushwalking

This part of the park has some of the best short walks in the MacDonnell Ranges. The *Walks of Ormiston Gorge & Pound* leaflet, available from Parks & Wildlife, gives more details.

Waterhole (400m return, 10 minutes, easy) Signs along this short stroll explain Aboriginal lore and the wildlife of the waterholes.

Ghost Gum Lookout (2km return, 30 minutes, medium) Climb the many steps of the western cliffs to the lone ghost gum standing sentinel at this lookout. There are superb views down to the gorge itself.

Ghost Gum walk (2km loop, 1½ hours, medium) Follow the track to the Ghost Gum Lookout and return along the floor of the gorge.

Pound walk (7km loop, three to four hours, medium) This superb walk climbs to an elevated spinifex-clad gap in the range, passes into remote Ormiston Pound then follows the floor of the gorge back to the camping ground. Do it first thing in the morning in an anticlockwise direction so you can enjoy a sunlit view of the big cliffs, or do the Ghost Gum walk first and link with the Pound walk; take plenty of water.

Longer walks to **Bowman's Gap** (18km return, one to two days, medium) and **Mt Giles** (31km return, two to three days, difficult), which includes a 600m ascent of Mt Giles, can be tackled by experienced bushwalkers. The view at dawn across Ormiston Pound from Mt Giles to Mt Sonder is sensational.

Sleeping

Ormiston Gorge Camping Ground (adult/child/family $6.60/3.30/15.40) The ritziest of the West MacDonnell National Park's sites, this camping ground is right next to the gorge car park. There are hot showers, toilets (with disabled facilities), picnic tables and free gas barbecues. Get here early for a site as caravans and campervans crowd out many spots.

GLEN HELEN GORGE & HOMESTEAD

The large waterhole at Glen Helen Gorge, 135km from Alice Springs, has been carved through the Pacoota Range by the Finke River. To the Arrernte people the gorge is a sacred site known as Yapulpa, and is part of the Carpet Snake Dreaming. In 1872 Ernest Giles was the first European to explore the area and the pastoral lease was first taken up by prominent pastoralists Grant and Stokes. In 1876 their surveyor, Richard Warburton, named the station (and gorge) after Grant's eldest daughter.

In 1901 the station was bought by Fred Raggatt and remnants from that time, such as the timber meat-house, still survive. The homestead on its current site was originally built in 1905. In 1992 the property was purchased by the Ngurratjuta/Pmara Ntjarra Aboriginal Corporation.

A 10-minute stroll takes you from the car park to the gorge entrance, where you can admire the 65m-high cliffs, but if you want to go further you'll have to either swim through the waterhole or climb around it. The rugged cliffs positively radiate in the late afternoon sun – you can enjoy them over a beer from the back veranda of the Glen Helen Homestead.

Just west of the Finke River crossing on Namatjira Dr is the turn-off to the **Mt Sonder lookout** with an evocative view of the reclining mountain made famous in Albert Namatjira's watercolours. First light illuminates Mt Sonder beautifully.

Finke Two Mile Camping Ground offers free bush camping sites on the Finke River, upstream from the crossing on Namatjira Drive. You'll need a 4WD to get to it and there are no facilities, but the views and atmosphere are hard to beat – it's popular with weekenders from Alice. The turn-off is not signposted but is to the north of Namatjira Dr just past Glen Helen Resort.

Sleeping & Eating

Glen Helen Resort (☎ 8956 7489; www.glenhelen.com.au; Namatjira Dr; unpowered/powered sites $24/30, dm $30, d $160-180). The looming red cliffs provide a dramatic backdrop to the Glen Helen Homestead, the centrepiece of this popular outback resort on the edge of the national park. You can pitch a tent in the shady grounds, stay in a backpackers lodge, or do it in comfort in one of the pricey motel rooms. The back veranda is an idyllic place to unwind, and there's a lively pub with pool table and live music (Thursday to Monday, April to November). The excellent Namatjira Restaurant features bush-tucker and conventional meals (dinners $22 to $32), an open fire and walls adorned with prints and originals by the Namatjira family. Otherwise, you can grab a bite at the resort's roadhouse (breakfast and lunch $5 to $15). There are also helicopter flights from the homestead ranging from $50 to $375, with the $125 Ormiston Gorge flight representing the best value.

REDBANK GORGE

Well known to locals but often overlooked by visitors who have had their fill of gorges, Redbank is another scenic detour at the western end of the ranges, reached via a rugged 4WD road. There are two camping grounds here where you can really find bush solitude.

The Redbank Gorge turn-off is about 20km west of Glen Helen, then it's 5km north to the car park. From here it's another 15-minute walk up a rocky creek bed to the gorge itself.

Redbank Gorge is extremely narrow, with polished, multihued walls that close over your head and block out the sky. To traverse the gorge you must clamber and float along the freezing deep pools with an air mattress. The colours and cathedral atmosphere are magnificent. Allow two hours to get to the end, and then you'll need to walk and float back. Except in summer, swimming the gorge is not recommended – the icy water can cause cramps or hypothermia.

Bushwalking

Redbank Gorge is the starting point for Section 12 of the Larapinta Trail to nearby Mt Sonder. The walk along the ridge from the gorge to the summit of **Mt Sonder** (16km return, eight hours, difficult) will appeal to fit, well-prepared walkers. After the constructed trail ends, markers show the way along the ridge where the track rises from 680m to 1380m. Some locals regard this as the finest walk in the West MacDonnells and a highlight of the trail. The superb view from the summit of Mt Sonder and the sense of achievement are ample reward. Camping is not permitted on the summit, so start early.

Sleeping

There are two bush-camping grounds along the rough track to Redbank Gorge.

Redbank Woodland Camping Ground (adult/child/family $3.30/1.65/7.70) A few kilometres back from the gorge car park, this large, shady camping ground is on a creek flat with well-spaced sites, fireplaces (no wood provided), free gas barbecues and picnic tables.

Redbank Ridgetop Camping Ground (adult/child/family $3.30/1.65/7.70) Much closer to the gorge, this is a small, intimate camping ground with stony sites and basic facilities – a pit toilet and fireplaces.

TYLERS PASS LOOKOUT

Sixteen kilometres beyond the Redbank Gorge turn-off Namatjira Dr swings south and 26km from the turn-off you reach Tylers Pass Lookout. This is an ideal ridge from which to view **Tnorala** (Gosse Bluff), a deep red impact crater. The scientific and Dreaming explanations for this impressive formation that erupts from the surrounding plain is explained on panels at the viewing shelter. For information on exploring Tnorala, see p168.

Namatjira Dr continues south of Tylers Pass for 26km to intersect with Larapinta Dr from where you can turn back to Alice and visit Hermannsburg (p168), or turn right and take the Mereenie Loop Rd (p167) to Kings Canyon (p165).

EAST MACDONNELL RANGES

Although overshadowed by the more popular West MacDonnells, the East MacDonnell Ranges are no less picturesque and, with fewer visitors, can even be a more enjoyable outback experience. Access is via the Ross Hwy, which snakes east for 78km from Alice to Ross River. It is a scenic drive skirting high ridges and hills drained by gum-lined creeks. Along the way you pass several small reserves where you can explore scenic gorges, Aboriginal culture and abandoned mines.

The road is sealed, though it is only a single lane for significant sections, for the 78km to Ross River Resort. The gold-mining ghost town of Arltunga is 33km off the Ross Hwy along an unsealed road that can be quite rough, but it's usually OK for 2WD vehicles in dry conditions. An alternative return route via Claraville, Ambalindum and the Garden homesteads to the Stuart Hwy is recommended for 4WDs only.

Access to John Hayes Rockhole (in Trephina Gorge Nature Park), N'Dhala Gorge and Ruby Gap is by 4WD only.

Although most of the attractions out this way can be seen in a single day, you may find it more rewarding to take it slowly and plan to camp overnight at Trephina, Arltunga or Ruby Gap. Apart from the Ross River Resort, camping is the only accommodation option.

EMILY & JESSIE GAPS NATURE PARK

Following the Ross Hwy east of the Stuart Hwy for 10km you arrive at **Emily Gap**, the first of two scenic gaps in the Heavitree Range. How these features got their English names has been lost in time, but both gaps are associated with an Arrernte Caterpillar Dreaming trail.

The highlight here is the stylised **rock paintings** on the gorge walls. Known to the Arrernte as Anthwerrke, this is one of the most important Aboriginal sites in the Alice

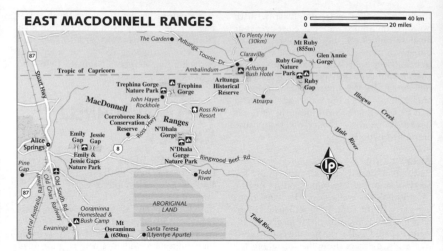

EAST MACDONNELL RANGES

Springs area, as it was from here that the Caterpillar Ancestral Beings of Mparntwe (Alice Springs) originated.

Jessie Gap, 8km further on, is an equally scenic gorge and a good place for a picnic. Both sites are popular swimming holes and have toilets. Camping is not permitted.

Bushwalking

Sweeping panoramas extend from the high, narrow ridge **walk** (8km one way, 2½ hours, unmarked, medium) between Emily and Jessie Gaps. Look out for wildlife, such as euros, black-footed rock wallabies and wedge-tailed eagles. The trick is to get someone to drop you off at Emily Gap, and then have them continue on to Jessie Gap to get the picnic ready.

CORROBOREE ROCK CONSERVATION RESERVE

Past Jessie Gap, you drive over eroded flats, with the East MacDonnell Ranges looming large on your left. Corroboree Rock, 41km from Alice Springs, is one of a number of unusual tan-coloured dolomite hills that are scattered over the valley floor.

A small cave in this dog-toothed outcrop was once used by local Aboriginal people as a storehouse for sacred objects. It is a registered sacred site and part of the Perentie Dreaming. Despite the name, it's doubted whether the rock was ever used as a corroboree area, owing to the lack of water in the vicinity.

There's a picnic ground, toilets, and a short **walking track** around the base of the rock.

TREPHINA GORGE NATURE PARK

About 60km from Alice Springs you cross the sandy bed of **Benstead Creek** and a lovely parade of river red gums, which continues for the 6km from the creek crossing to the Trephina Gorge turn-off.

If you only have time for a couple of stops in the East MacDonnell Ranges, make Trephina Gorge Nature Park, 3km north of the Ross Hwy, one of them. The contrasts are spectacular, between the sweep of pale sand in the dry river beds, rich orange, red and purple tones of the valley walls, white tree trunks with eucalyptus green foliage and the blue sky. There are also some excellent walks, swimming holes, wildlife and secluded camping areas. The main attractions are the gorge itself, **Trephina Bluff** and **John Hayes Rockhole**, a permanent waterhole reached by a rough 4WD track.

Trephina Gorge makes a great spot to set up camp for a day or so. Visit the waterhole early in the morning and you'll usually spot black-footed rock wallabies leaping about on the rock face.

There is a **ranger** (☎ 8956 9765) stationed in the park and an emergency call box at the ranger station.

Bushwalking

There are several good walks here, ranging from a short stroll to a five-hour hike. A short signposted walk along the entrance road leads to a magnificent ghost gum, estimated to be 300 years old. The following marked trails are outlined in the *Walks of Trephina Gorge Nature Park* brochure, which is available at the park entrance:

Trephina Gorge walk (2km loop, 45 minutes, easy)
Skirting along the edge of the gorge, the trail drops to the sandy creek bed then loops back to the starting point.

Panorama walk (3km loop, one hour, easy) Great views over Trephina Gorge and examples of bizarre, twisted rock strata are highlights of this walk.

Chain of Ponds walk (4km loop, 1½ hours, medium)
From the John Hayes Rockhole camping ground, this walk leads through the gorge, past rock pools and up to a lookout above the gorge. It requires some climbing and scrambling, and it's impassable after heavy rain.

Ridgetop walk (10km one way, five hours, difficult)
This marked trail traverses the ridges from Trephina Gorge to the delightful John Hayes Rockhole, a few kilometres to the west. Here a section of deep gorge holds a series of waterholes long after the more exposed sections have dried up. The walk offers splendid views and isolation. The 8km return leg along the road takes about two hours.

Sleeping

There are **camping grounds** (adult/child/family $3.30/1.65/7.70) at Trephina Gorge, the Bluff and John Hayes Rockhole. The **Trephina Gorge Camping Ground** is in a timbered gully a short stroll from the main attraction, and has 10 sites, running water, pit toilets (one with disabled access), gas barbecues, fireplaces and picnic tables. It's suitable for caravans and campervans. The **Bluff Camping Ground** has similar facilities (eight sites), but a more spectacular creek-bank setting under tall gums in front of a towering red ridge. The **John Hayes Rockhole Camping Ground** is just three basic sites with toilets beside a rocky creek down from the waterhole. The rough road here gives a real feeling of remoteness. There's no reliable freshwater supply here – fill up at the other campsites.

N'DHALA GORGE NATURE PARK

The highway continues from the Trephina Gorge turn-off towards Ross River. Look out for the roadside shrine dedicated to a local biker who died in an accident here in 1998.

Shortly before reaching Ross River you come to the 4WD track to N'Dhala Gorge Nature Park, where over 5900 ancient **rock carvings** (petroglyphs) decorate a deep, narrow gorge. The 11km access track winds down the picturesque **Ross River valley**, where a number of sandy crossings make this a bad idea for 2WD vehicles.

The rock carvings at N'Dhala (known to the eastern Arrernte people as Irlwentye) are of two major types: finely pecked, where a stone hammer has been used to strike a sharp chisel such as a bone or rock; and pounded, where a stone has been hit directly on the rock face. The carvings, which are not always easy to spot, are thought to have been made in the last 2000 years, though some could be as old as 10,000 years. Common designs featured in the carvings are circular and featherlike patterns, and these are thought to relate to the Caterpillar Dreaming. A **walking trail** (1.5km return, 45 minutes, easy) passes the main rock carvings, though you can continue further down the river bed.

The **camping ground** (adult/child/family $3.30/1.65/7.70) at the gorge entrance has fireplaces (collect your own wood), tables and a pit toilet. Shade here is limited and there is no reliable water source.

ROSS RIVER RESORT

The old Ross River Homestead has a pretty setting beside the Ross River. It's 9km along the continuation of the Ross Hwy past the Arltunga turn-off. Incidentally, if the words 'Ross River' strike the fear of fever into you, rest assured that the name was derived from Ross River in Townsville (Queensland).

With its secluded setting, birdlife, accommodation and bistro-bar, **Ross River Resort** (☎ 8956 9711; www.rossriverresort.com.au; unpowered/powered site $24/30, bunkhouse $22, d cabin $120; 🛇 🖢) offers an oasis of comfort and a great place to unwind. The air-con cabins have en suites, and there's a pool and spa, plus a store with fuel. It's worth the detour to check out the old homestead and maybe grab lunch or a beer in the Stockman's Bar, but it may pay to ring first and check that it is open.

ARLTUNGA HISTORICAL RESERVE

This historical site of crumbling buildings, abandoned mine shafts and rusting mining machinery is all that is left of central Australia's first official town – a gold-rush settlement that was once home to nearly 300 people.

The first 12km of the Arltunga Rd passes through scenic **Bitter Springs Gorge**, where red quartzite ridges tower above dolomite hills. This was the route taken by miners as they walked from Alice Springs to the goldfields at the turn of the last century. The road can

ALICE SPRINGS & AROUND

be rough and is impassable after heavy rain. About 1km before the Arltunga Historical Reserve, you pass the Arltunga Bush Hotel and camping ground, before arriving at the visitors centre in the reserve itself.

Fossicking is not permitted at Arltunga, but there is a **fossicking reserve** in a gully just to the south where you may (with luck and a permit) find some gold.

From Arltunga it is possible to do a loop back to Alice Springs along Arltunga Tourist Drive, or to join up with the Plenty Hwy along a 4WD track.

Information

The **visitors centre** (☎ 8956 9770; ◷ 8am-5pm) has interesting displays of old mining machinery and historical photographs. A free 20-minute slide show describes the reserve and its history. Drinking water is available and there are toilets (including facilities for the disabled). Pick up brochures and fact sheets for the self-guided walks through the reserve.

Sights & Activities

Arltunga's history is fascinating and the area gives an idea of what life must have been like for the early diggers. The main sites are scattered over a wide area and you'll need a vehicle to get between them. Ranger-guided tours, which include cranking up a battery, are usually conducted on Sunday between May and August.

RUBY RUSH

Ruby Gap was named after a frantic ruby rush in the late 1880s. David Lindsay, an explorer and surveyor who came through this way while leading an expedition from Adelaide to Port Darwin, saw ruby red stones in the dry bed of the Hale River, glittering in the afternoon sun. The whole dream crashed overnight when it was found that the 'rubies' were relatively worthless garnets (albeit high grade), but not before some 200 hopeful prospectors had made the arduous trek from the railhead at Oodnadatta.

However, the rush led to the chance discovery in 1887 of alluvial gold at Paddy's Rockhole, known as Annurra Ntinga to the local Eastern Arrernte peoples, and later Anglicised to **Arltunga**.

Allow half an hour to walk around the **Government works** area, where the best collection of dry-stone buildings survives. A short walk (1.5km, 15 minutes) leads to the **old police station**, or you can drive there.

Two mines are open in this area, but a torch (flashlight) is essential to explore them. At the **MacDonnell Range Reef Mine** you can climb down steel ladders and explore about 50m of tunnels between two shafts. The **Golden Chance Mine** boasts several old dry-stone miners' huts.

At the crossroads there's an old **cemetery**, plus the ruins of the old bakehouse; this was the site surveyed for the township that never eventuated. **Joker Gorge** features more old stone buildings and a good view reached by a 200m path up a hill.

Another short self-guided walk leads to the **Great Western Mine**. After climbing some steep ridges with great views to the east, the road ends at **White Range Cemetery**, the resting place of Joseph Hele, the first man to find gold here.

Sleeping

Camping is not permitted within the reserve, but the nearby **Arltunga Bush Hotel** (☎ 8956 9797; sites per adult/child $8/4) has showers, toilets, barbecue pits and picnic tables. Fees are collected in the late afternoon. The bar was open for drinks Thursday to Monday at the time of writing, but wasn't serving meals.

RUBY GAP NATURE PARK

This little-visited and remote park, accessible only by 4WD, is a challenging but rewarding detour to some of the wildest gorge and river scenery in central Australia. The waterholes at Glen Annie Gorge are usually deep enough for a cooling dip.

It is essential to get a map from Parks & Wildlife, and to **register** (☎ 1300 650 730) in Alice Springs before setting out – and de-register when you return. Do not attempt the trip if you are inexperienced, especially in summer, or after heavy rain. Carry sufficient water and, as the last 5km is through boggy sand (deflate tyres), a shovel and jack may come in useful.

Allow two hours each way for the trip. The park is managed by the **Arltunga ranger station** (☎ 8956 9770), so check road conditions there or in Alice before heading out here. The rangers suggest leaving the park in the event of rain –

DETOUR: THE CENTRE OF THE CONTINENT

If you think that you are in the middle of nowhere, you're wrong – you are in the middle of Australia. A signposted sandy track leaves Finke-Kulgera Rd about 23km west of Finke, and runs 14km to the **Lambert Centre**, Australia's geographical heart. To mark the spot there's a dinky 5m-high replica of the flagpole, complete with Australian flag, that sits atop Parliament House in Canberra. If you picked Australia up at its centre of gravity, it would balance here at latitude 25°36'36.4"S and longitude 134°21'17.3"E. You can add your name to the visitors book if you like.

The track is quite sandy and narrow in patches, so a 4WD is recommended. There are two parallel tracks so stick to the left. From the turn-off it is 6km to the Mulga bore, then 8km west to the site.

---

travellers in the past have had their car stuck at Ruby Gap for a month!

There are no marked walking trails, but you can make the rugged walk by the river bed to Glen Annie Gorge. Although there are no camping facilities in the park, camping is permitted anywhere along the river – bring in your own firewood and water.

SOUTHEAST OF ALICE SPRINGS

The southeastern corner of the NT is dominated by the vast Simpson Desert, one of the toughest, driest and most inhospitable parts of Australia. Although it's possible to travel in a 2WD vehicle some of the way down the Old South Rd, which runs close to the old *Ghan* railway line, the main attractions – Chambers Pillar, Lambert Centre and the Old Andado Track – are accessible only to high clearance 4WD vehicles.

ALICE SPRINGS TO FINKE

The Old South Rd, also known as Maryvale Rd, turns off the Stuart Hwy 12km south of Alice Springs. At Rodinga the road splits, continuing south to Maryvale Station, the Titjikala Aboriginal community and the turnoff to Chambers Pillar, or southeast to Finke (Apatula). The road to Maryvale is quite rough in patches, but is fine for conventional vehicles in dry conditions. After that it's 4WD only. At the Rodinga siding the Finke Track heads for 133km to Finke. This forms part of the Simpson Desert Loop via New Crown, Andado Homestead and north to Alice along the Old Andado Track.

Ewaninga Rock Carvings Conservation Reserve

This small conservation reserve 39km out of Alice protects an outcrop of sandstone next to a claypan sacred to Arrernte people, and known to them as Napatika. The rock carvings found here and at N'Dhala Gorge are thought to have been made by Aboriginal people who lived here before those currently in the centre, between 1000 and 5000 years ago. The carvings, which include concentric circles and animal tracks, are chiselled into the soft rock, but their meanings are either lost in time or are regarded as too sacred for the uninitiated.

There's an easy 20-minute loop walk with informative signs leading from a picnic area with wood barbecues and pit toilets.

Titjikala & Maryvale Station

Continuing past the turn-off to Finke for 13km brings you to **Maryvale Station** (☎ 8956 0989; ☺ 9am-5pm) where you can get fuel, drinks and basic supplies.

Just past the store is the small Titjikala Aboriginal community, which you can visit without a permit. Drop into the **Titjikala Art Centre** (☎ 8956 0788; www.titjikala.com.au; ☺ 8am-5pm Mon-Thu) where local artists create dot paintings, wire sculptures, screen prints and woodcarvings.

Gunya Titjikala (☎ 8347 1159, 1300 135 657; www .gunya.com.au; d $1300) provides the opportunity for an intimate outback experience with traditional Aboriginal hosts. The luxury canvas tents are perched on platforms overlooking the desert and meals are a fusion of gourmet and local bush tucker. Itineraries are customised depending on visitors' interests – art, culture, bush tucker or landscape. Half the profits go to the Titjikala Foundation for community health and education projects.

Chambers Pillar

From Maryvale Station a rough 4WD-only road heads southwest for 44km to **Chambers Pillar Historic Reserve**. The last 10km is through sand drifts and dunes.

Towering nearly 50m above the plain, the pillar is all that's left of a layer of sandstone that formed 350 million years ago. Early explorers used it as a navigational beacon; their names and the dates of their visits are carved into the base of the soft rock. Unfortunately, it also bears the work of less-worthy graffiti artists – there are hefty fines for adding your own name.

Like many central Australian sights, the pillar is at its photogenic best at sunset and sunrise. Since it's a tough drive to get here, the best idea is to arrive an hour or two before sunset and camp overnight.

To Arrernte, Chambers Pillar is the remains of Itirkawara, a powerful Gecko Ancestral Being who killed some of his ancestors and took a girl of the wrong skin group. They were banished to the desert where both turned to stone – the girl became **Castle Rock**, about 500m away.

The **camping ground** (adult/child/family $3.30/1.65/7.70), in an attractive grove of desert oaks, has pit toilets, tables and fireplaces – bring water and firewood.

Finke (Apatula)

Back on the main track, the road turns southeast on the Finke Track at the ruins of the Rodinga siding. Now you're in real 4WD territory for the 140km to the Aboriginal community of Apatula (better known as Finke). The narrow track here follows the old railway line through red sand. This is the route followed in the annual Finke Desert Race (see p183).

Eventually you cross the wide sandy bed of the Finke River and arrive in the small town of Finke, which started life as a railway siding and gradually grew to have a European population of about 60. With the opening of the new *Ghan* line further west in 1982, administration of the town was taken over by the Apatula Aboriginal community.

The **community store** (☎ 8956 0968; ⏲ 9am-noon & 2-4pm Mon-Fri, 9am-noon Sat) sells fuel, supplies, and local art.

Apatula is linked to the Stuart Hwy, 150km to the west, by the Kulgera-Finke Rd, a reasonably well-maintained dirt road sometimes known as the Goyder Stock Route. It's a fairly dull stretch of road, although the Lambert Centre makes an interesting diversion.

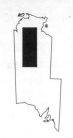

Alice Springs to Katherine

The epic journey from Alice Springs to Katherine – the Territory's biggest towns after Darwin – bridges the gap between the arid Red Centre and the tropical Top End. This is true outback: flat and straight for most of the way as the Stuart Hwy snakes 1180km northwards and at times you'll think there's precious little out there. But every stretch of desert has its own tale to tell.

The highway roughly follows the route of explorer John McDouall Stuart and parallels the *Ghan* railway line. Reminders of the historic Overland Telegraph Line (OTL) and WWII staging posts pop up from time to time. There are diversions from the bitumen highway: northeast of Alice are the Utopia Homelands, a rich source of Aboriginal art, while to the northwest the Tanami Track heads off through Aboriginal land and stark desert to Western Australia. Curious roadside stops and offbeat roadhouses dot the main highway, inviting you to pull in for a beer. More surreal though, is the Devil's Marbles, a stunning landscape of giant spherical granite boulders piled up beside the highway.

Tennant Creek, a town with a proud mining past, boasts a fine Aboriginal cultural centre and is a good place to break the journey. To the east are the Barkly Tablelands, vast open grasslands and cattle country.

Further north, Daly Waters has a notable outback pub worth calling into, and by now you're well into the tropical Top End. As if to prove it, Mataranka welcomes you with a lush oasis of thermal pools, before you finally reach a measure of 'civilisation' again at Katherine.

HIGHLIGHTS

- Wandering among the precarious balancing boulders at **Devil's Marbles Conservation Reserve** (p208) at sunset
- Delving into a mine shaft and reliving mining history at Tennant Creek's **Battery Hill Mining Centre** (p209)
- Absorbing Aboriginal culture, learning the history and hearing the stories at **Nyinkka Nyunyu** (p209) in Tennant Creek
- Pulling in for a beer and a barra burger at the **Daly Waters Pub** (p215)
- Soaking in the sublime thermal springs of the Elsey National Park near **Mataranka** (p216)
- Exploring Aboriginal culture and art on a guided tour at **Manyallaluk** (p218).

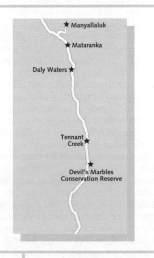

★ Manyallaluk
★ Mataranka
Daly Waters ★
Tennant Creek ★
★ Devil's Marbles Conservation Reserve

■ TELEPHONE CODE: ☎ 08   ■ www.barklyarts.com.au   ■ www.barklytourism.com.au

ALICE SPRINGS TO KATHERINE

DETOUR: TANAMI ROAD

Spearing 1000km through some of the Territory's most remote country, the name of this road/track has become synonymous with isolated outback driving. The Tanami Rd connects Alice Springs with Halls Creek in Western Australia (WA) and is essentially a short cut between central Australia and the Kimberley.

The Tanami Desert is the traditional homeland of the Warlpiri Aboriginal people, and for much of its length the road passes through Aboriginal land. Permits are not required for travel on the Tanami Rd or to visit the local community of Yuendumu. At Yuendumu, home of the famous **Bush Mechanics** (www.bushmechanics.com), it's worth popping into the **Warlukurlangu Art Centre** (☎ 8956 4133; www.warlu.com; ☯ 9am-6pm Mon-Fri, weekends by appointment), a locally owned venture specialising in acrylic paintings, screen prints, etchings and crafts.

In dry conditions it's possible to cover the Tanami Rd in a well-prepared 2WD vehicle. The Northern Territory section is wide and usually well graded (sealed almost to Tilmouth Well), but between the WA border and Halls Creek some sandy patches and creek crossings require care and a high-clearance vehicle is advisable. After rain (which is rare), sections of the track around Sturt Creek and Billiluna can become impassable. In any case, this is no Sunday drive, so stock up with spares and supplies and notify someone of your plans.

Accommodation, food and fuel are available at Tilmouth Well (188km from Alice Springs), Yuendumu (288km), Rabbit Flat Roadhouse (590km; open Friday to Monday only), Billiluna (850km; business hours only) and Halls Creek (1020km). The best map is Wesprint's *Tanami Track* 1:1 000 000, a double-sided sheet covering the track from Alice Springs to Halls Creek with GPS locations and places of interest.

NORTH OF ALICE SPRINGS

The Stuart Hwy snakes out of Alice Springs, weaving through the low, scrubby outliers of the MacDonnell Ranges before straightening out for the long haul north. About 21km north of Alice is the turn-off for the Tanami Rd (see above), an adventurers' road connecting the Red Centre with the Kimberley.

A further 11km brings you to the marker for the **Tropic of Capricorn**, a skeletal globe augmented with information boards. Although this marks the line of 23°44'S latitude, it's a long way north (around Newcastle Waters) before you'll feel the transition from the dry centre to the seasonally wet tropics. Veering east off the Stuart Hwy, about 70km north of Alice, is the Plenty Hwy, which heads to the fossicking grounds of the **Harts Range** and across the northern fringes of the Simpson Desert to Boulia in Western Queensland, a mere 742km away.

The **Native Gap Conservation Reserve** is a small gap in the Hann Range, 110km north of Alice Springs. This is a registered sacred site, known to the local Aboriginal people as Arulte Artwatye. Here you will find a shady rest stop (no water or camping) beside the road.

After another 19km the highway crosses the small **Ryan Well Historic Reserve**, which preserves the ruins of a well and the Glen Maggie Homestead.

AILERON

The first major stop on this drive comes 138km north of Alice Springs, where the Aileron roadhouse sits next to the homestead of Aileron Station. The tall fella out the back is Charlie Quartpot, the Anmatyerre man. At the time of writing work had started on Charlie's family – a woman and child – to be constructed beside the nearby Outback Art Gallery. The curious can walk up for a closer look and find answers to any questions they might have about a 12m man in a loincloth.

The roadhouse and homestead house a surprisingly large collection of some 200 works by the Namatjira family, including about 10 painted by Albert. The **Outback Art Gallery** (☎ 8956 9111; ☯ 8am-5pm Mon-Sat, 10am-4pm Sun) sells inexpensive watercolours and dot paintings by the local Anmatyerre community, as well as paintings from the Warlpiri community of Yuendumu. If you're lucky you may see artists at work.

Aileron Hotel Roadhouse (☎ 8956 9703; www.aileron roadhouse.com.au; campsites per person $10, dm/s/d $36/98/100; mains $10-20; ☯ 7am-10pm Mon-Sat, to 9pm Sun; ☒ ☲) has campsites (occasionally grassed, power available till 10pm), a 10-bed dorm and decent motel units. There's an ATM, bar, supplies shop and a licensed restaurant.

TI TREE & AROUND

About 12km south of Ti Tree, **Red Centre Farm** (☎ 8956 9828; www.redcentrefarm.com; ☽ 9am-7pm), otherwise known as 'Shatto Mango', is an essential stop if you're interested in sampling some unique Territory wines or have a sudden desire for cool mango ice cream. It's one of about a dozen farms growing table grapes and mangoes thanks to water provided by subartesian bores. The small store (tin shed), just off the highway, sells a diverse range of mango and grape products, including toppings, chutneys, marinades and the aforementioned delicious mango ice cream. However, the star attraction is the range of wines, ports and liqueurs, with free tastings. They sell for $15 to $20.

The tiny town of **Ti Tree**, 193km north of Alice Springs, is a service centre for the surrounding Aboriginal communities, including nearby Pmara Jutunta and Utopia (200km east). The town, originally called Tea Tree Wells after the tea tree–lined waterhole about 300m west of the roadhouse, began as a settlement on the OTL.

Ti Tree Roadhouse (☎ 8956 9741; unpowered/powered campsites $14/20, budget s/d $55/65, motel s/d $75/90; mains $16-24; ☽ 6am-10pm Mon-Sat, to 9pm Sun; ⊠) has a range of accommodation, including budget rooms with shared facilities and motel rooms with TV, fridge and air-con. Flo's Bar serves bistro meals, and has a pool table and ATM.

Red Sand Art Gallery (☎ 8956 9738; www.redsandart .com.au; ☽ 8am-5pm), just west of the highway and roadhouse, is an excellent repository for artworks from the surrounding 1800 sq km Utopia homelands. Artists work in-house occasionally; prices for a didgeridoo run from $150 to $550 and dot paintings cost from $900 to $9000. There's a **café** (meals $4-7) serving sandwiches, rolls, pies and drinks; most notably espresso coffee.

CENTRAL MT STUART HISTORICAL RESERVE

A cairn beside the Stuart Hwy 20km north of Ti Tree commemorates John McDouall Stuart's naming of Central Mt Stuart, a hill about 12km to the northwest.

Stuart thought he had reached the centre of Australia (although he was a fair way off; see Lambert Centre, p203, for the true geographical centre), and named the 'mountain' Central Mt Sturt after his former expedition leader and friend, Charles Sturt. The name was later changed to honour Stuart himself.

BARROW CREEK

Historical Barrow Creek sits next to the Stuart Hwy, where the road passes through a dramatic gap in the Watt Range about 70km north of Central Mt Stuart. Beside the Barrow Creek Hotel is one of the original **telegraph stations** on the OTL from Port Augusta to Darwin (11 stations were built and four remain in the Territory). Built in 1872, it operated as a repeater station and post office until made redundant in 1980. In addition to the main building, there's a blacksmith shop and wagon shed. An unstable roof meant entry into the station was prohibited at the time we visited; in any case there's nothing to see inside.

In February 1874 the telegraph station, under stationmaster James Stapleton, was attacked by a group of Kaytetye Aboriginal men. Stapleton and a linesman were killed; their graves are close to the station. The attack came as something of a surprise as Stapleton had adopted a fairly enlightened (for the times) approach to the local Aboriginal population. The South Australian government authorised a punitive expedition that led to the deaths of at least 50 Aboriginal people.

Sleeping & Eating

Barrow Creek Hotel & Roadhouse (☎ 8956 9753; Stuart Hwy; powered campsites $10, s/d $45/60; mains $10-20; ☽ 7am-midnight) One of the highway's friendliest outback pubs, the rustic Barrow Creek Hotel opened in 1932. The walls are adorned with all manner of drawings, cartoons and banknotes – ringers (shearers) would leave a banknote on the wall with their name on it so that they would have enough for a drink the next time they passed through. Now travellers and passers-by follow suit. There are only three rooms (with share bathrooms) available so book ahead. Fuel is available from 7am to 11pm, and main meals are served from 6pm to 8pm, but you can get snacks, burgers and steak sandwiches throughout the day.

WYCLIFFE WELL

Unearthly happenings abound at Wycliffe Well, 93km north of Barrow Creek, where a spate of UFO sightings has been documented. The well referred to in the name dates from 1872. During WWII a 2-hectare vegetable farm was established here to supply the troops further up the Stuart Hwy.

DETOUR: DAVENPORT RANGE NATIONAL PARK

To detour off the Track in this region requires a good deal of preparation and planning and a 4WD, but the rewards are worth the effort. The proposed **Davenport Range National Park**, east of Wauchope, protects a series of permanent waterholes – an ancient, isolated watercourse that is a vital refuge for birds and mammals and a home to some hardy fish.

The Davenports are not the most spectacular mountain range on earth, but they are among the oldest, as their eroded peaks are all that remains of the 1800-million-year-old geological formations.

The **Whistleduck Creek** area and the **Old Police Station Waterhole** are the only places in this 1120-sq-km proposed national park that can be visited. Both can be reached by 4WD vehicle from the Stuart Hwy (91km and 170km, respectively) via the track to Kurundi and Epenarra Stations, which leaves the Stuart Hwy at Bonney Well, 90km south of Tennant Creek. Alternatively, Old Police Station Waterhole can be accessed from the south (also 170km via the Murray Downs station track, which heads east off the Stuart Hwy about 40km north of Barrow Creek). Access is by high-clearance 4WD only. This is very remote country and tracks are not signposted.

The **camping grounds** (adult/child/family $3.30/1.65/7.70) at Whistleduck Creek and Old Police Station Waterhole have pit toilets and no other facilities. All visitors must be completely self-sufficient. Fuel is available at Kurundi, Epenarra and **Murray Downs** (☎ 8964 1958) stations. Roads can be flooded between December and March; for information about conditions phone the **police station** (☎ 8964 1959) at Ali Curung. For the latest park information contact the Visitor Information Centre at Tennant Creek (opposite).

Wycliffe Well Roadhouse & Holiday Park (☎ 8964 1966; www.wycliffe.com.au; unpowered/powered sites $22/26, budget s/d $30/38, donga s/d $55/68, cabins s/d $99/112; ⏲ 6.30am-9pm; ✗ ☐ ⊠) is said to be on a cross-section of ley lines (energy lines), meaning that any UFOs flying around will pass directly overhead. There's an indoor pool, laundry, barbecues, camp kitchen and a restaurant with Chinese and roadhouse meals (mains $16 to $18). You can read all about the UFO sightings while sampling the enormous variety of international beers available at the bar – and ponder the association between alcohol and aliens.

WAUCHOPE

The settlement of Wauchope (*war*-kup) is little more than a fuel stop by the highway, about 17km north of Wycliffe Well and 10km south of the Devil's Marbles. The pub dates back to the 1930s, and the 'town' owes its existence to the discovery of wolfram (tungsten) in the area in 1914. At its height, around 50 miners worked the small but rich field 12km east of here. After WWI the price of wolfram halved almost overnight as the British no longer needed it in their war effort, and the Wauchope field became unviable. The price of wolfram revived in the late 1930s in the build-up to WWII, and it was at this time that the pub was established. For a second time a war finished and the market for wolfram collapsed. Before long the fields were deserted

and Wauchope became the small highway stop that it is today.

Wauchope Hotel (☎ 8964 1963; Stuart Hwy; unpowered/powered campsites $14/18, s $40, cabin s/d $70/80; ✗ ⊠) is a handy place to stay near the Devil's Marbles. The budget rooms are spotless dongas and the more expensive doubles are comfortable en suite cabins. Tent camping is on lush lawn, whereas caravans make do with dust-free, crushed basalt stones. As well as a pool, there's a tennis court and pleasant beer garden. The restaurant serves excellent meals (mains $12 to $20) – there's usually a good-value special on offer. Otherwise, there's a barbecue in the camping ground. Fuel is available from 6am to 11pm. Bicycle hire is available if you feel like pedalling the 10km to the Devil's Marbles.

DEVIL'S MARBLES CONSERVATION RESERVE

The huge boulders that appear beside the Stuart Hwy about 393km north of Alice Springs and about 105km south of Tennant Creek are known as the Devil's Marbles. This geological phenomenon is particularly beautiful at sunrise and sunset, when these oddballs glow warmly.

How and what? Over an estimated 1640 million years a huge granite block criss-crossed with fault lines eroded into slabs roughly 3m to 7m square. The extreme desert temperatures forced the expansion and contraction of the blocks, and slabs flaked off, like the skin of an onion. With corners rounded off by eons of erosion, the result is a stunning clutch of granite eggs. Some appear to have been stacked in precarious piles, others stand alone balanced at unlikely angles – they look as if a good shove could send them tumbling.

The area is a registered sacred site known as Karlukarlu to the local Warumungu people. Several Dreaming trails cross the area, and the rocks are believed to be the eggs of the Rainbow Serpent.

The **self-guided loop walk** (20 minutes) starts at the car park and is enlivened with interpretive signs and diagrams. Along the way it passes an amazing 4m-high boulder that has been neatly split in half – as if by a giant carving knife.

The **camping ground** (adult/child/family $3.30/1.65/7.70), around the eastern side of the boulders, has remarkably hard ground and really fills up in the afternoon. There are pit toilets, a shade shelter and a fireplace (BYO firewood).

Tours to the Marbles are run from Tennant Creek. If you don't want to camp, there's decent budget accommodation and good meals at Wauchope (see opposite).

TENNANT CREEK
pop 2019

Tennant Creek is the only town of any size between Alice Springs, 511km to the south, and Katherine, 680km to the north. Many travellers spend a night here to break up the long drive, make a bus connection, and see the town's few attractions.

History

Known as Jurnkurakurr to the Warumungu people, Tennant Creek is at the intersection of a number of Dreaming trails and adjacent to a sacred site associated with the spiky-tailed goanna.

John McDouall Stuart passed through here on an expedition in 1860 before turning back at Attack Creek some distance north. He named the creek, which is about 10km north of town, after John Tennant, a prominent South Australian pastoralist.

A repeater station for the OTL was set up in Tennant Creek in the 1870s. The story goes that the town itself was established 12km south of the repeater station because that was where a wagon carrying beer broke down in the early 1930s. Rather than find another way to take the beer to the people, the people went to the beer and that's where the town has stayed. The truth is far more prosaic: the town was established as the result of a small gold rush around the same time. In 1932, a Warumungu man found a rock containing traces of gold and showed it to a group of men who formed a syndicate and began mining and prospecting. By WWII there were some 100 small mines in operation.

However, the gold rush was short-lived and the town might well have gone the way of a number of 'boom and bust' towns in the Territory, except that viable quantities of copper were found in the 1950s. New technology led to further mining and one mine, Nobles Nob (16km east of town) ranks among Australia's richest. It was the country's biggest open-cut gold mine until mining ceased in 1985. More recent gold-mining ventures have operated discontinuously depending on metal prices, and exploration continues in the region today.

Orientation & Information

Tennant Creek sprawls along the Stuart Hwy, which is called Paterson St as it passes through town. You'll find the most places to stay, a few places to eat, ANZ and Westpac banks with ATMs and a supermarket along here. There are also two roadhouses, a pub and post office.

Central Land Council (☎ 8962 2343; 63 Paterson St) Assists with permits to cross Aboriginal land.

Enterprise Electrics (☎ 8962 2064; 62 Paterson St) Sells long-distance bus tickets and, should regular flights return to Tennant Creek, air tickets.

Leading Edge Computers (☎ 8962 3907; 145 Paterson St; per 20min $2; ☼ 9am-5pm Mon-Fri, to 12.30pm Sat) Internet access.

Police station (☎ 8962 4444; Paterson St)

Tennant Creek Hospital (☎ 8962 4399; Schmidt St) A couple of blocks west of Paterson St.

Tennant Creek Library (☎ 8962 0050; Peko Rd; per 30min $2; ☼ 9am-5pm Mon, 1-5pm Tue, 10am-5pm Wed-Fri, to noon Sat) Internet access.

Tennant Creek Visitor Information Centre (☎ 8962 1281; www.barklytourism.com.au; Peko Rd; ☼ 9am-5pm) Located 2km east of town at the Battery Hill Mining Centre.

Sights

Nyinkka Nyunyu (☎ 8962 2221; www.nyinkkanyunyu.com.au; Paterson St; adult/child/family $10/5/20; ☼ 8am-5pm Mon-Fri & 9am-4pm Sat May-Sep, 9am-5pm Mon-Fri

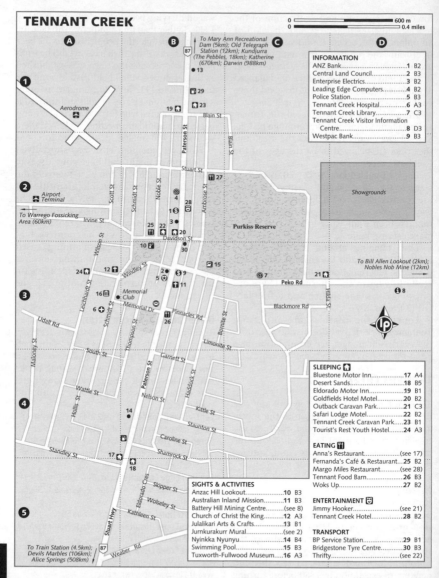

TENNANT CREEK

INFORMATION
ANZ Bank	1 B2
Central Land Council	2 B3
Enterprise Electrics	3 B2
Leading Edge Computers	4 B2
Police Station	5 B3
Tennant Creek Hospital	6 A3
Tennant Creek Library	7 C3
Tennant Creek Visitor Information Centre	8 D3
Westpac Bank	9 B3

SIGHTS & ACTIVITIES
Anza Hill Lookout	10 B3
Australian Inland Mission	11 B3
Battery Hill Mining Centre	(see 8)
Church of Christ the King	12 A3
Julalikari Arts & Crafts	13 B1
Jurnkurakurr Mural	(see 2)
Nyinkka Nyunyu	14 B4
Swimming Pool	15 B3
Tuxworth-Fullwood Museum	16 A3

SLEEPING
Bluestone Motor Inn	17 A4
Desert Sands	18 B5
Eldorado Motor Inn	19 B1
Goldfields Hotel Motel	20 B2
Outback Caravan Park	21 C3
Safari Lodge Motel	22 B2
Tennant Creek Caravan Park	23 B1
Tourist's Rest Youth Hostel	24 A3

EATING
Anna's Restaurant	(see 17)
Fernanda's Café & Restaurant	25 B2
Margo Miles Restaurant	(see 28)
Tennant Food Barn	26 B3
Woks Up	27 B2

ENTERTAINMENT
Jimmy Hooker	(see 21)
Tennant Creek Hotel	28 B2

TRANSPORT
BP Service Station	29 B1
Bridgestone Tyre Centre	30 B3
Thrifty	(see 22)

& 10am-2pm Sat Oct-Apr, to 2pm Sun year-round) is an excellent Aboriginal art and culture centre, with absorbing displays on contemporary art, traditional objects (many returned by the Victorian and South Australian museums), bush medicine and regional history. Nyinkka Nyunyu is located beside a sacred site of the spiky-tailed goanna, or Nyinkka. There's an

indigenous garden, which is sometimes the venue for ceremonies and performances, and the Jajjikari Café, which sells espresso coffee, muffins, burgers and focaccias.

Also worth visiting is the **Julalikari Arts & Crafts** (☎ 8962 2163; ☀ 8am-noon Mon-Fri), also known as the Pink Palace, in the Ngalpa Ngalpa community (also known as Mulga

Camp) at the northern end of town. Here you can see Aboriginal women painting traditional and contemporary art, chat to the artists and purchase directly from the painter or one of her colleagues.

Gold-bearing ore was originally crushed and treated at what is now **Battery Hill Mining Centre** (☎ 8962 1281; Peko Rd; adult/child/family $30/20/60; ⊙ 9am-5pm), 1.5km east of town. There are **underground mine tours** (⊙ 9.30am & 2.30pm) and surface tours of the 10-head **battery** (⊙ 11am & 4pm). In addition there is a superb **Minerals Museum** and you can try your hand at gold panning. The admission price gives access to all of the above, or you can just choose one of the tours (adult/child/family $22/15/55), visit the Minerals and Social History Museums only (adult/family $5/10), or just go panning ($5 per person).

The **Jurnkurakurr Mural** (63 Paterson St), on the wall of the Central Land Council building, was painted by the local Aboriginal people. It depicts Dreamings from this area – among them the snake, white cockatoo, crow, budgerigar, fire and lightning.

Across from the Memorial Club, the small **Tuxworth-Fullwood Museum** (☎ 8962 2340; Schmidt St; admission $2.20; ⊙ 2-4pm Mon-Fri) dates from 1942 when it was built as an army hospital. Until 1978 it was used as an outpatients' clinic for the hospital next door. There are displays of local memorabilia and a re-creation of a miner's camp.

The 1936 **Church of Christ the King** (Windley St) and the **Australian Inland Mission** (Uniting Church; Paterson St), just south of Peko Rd, are both constructed of corrugated iron. The latter was built in the 1930s by the Sidney Williams Co. which supplied numerous prefabricated, steel-frame, corrugated-iron buildings for the Territory.

The small **Anzac Hill lookout**, off Davidson St opposite the Safari Lodge Motel, offers a view over the town.

About 12km north of town, you'll see the lovely stone buildings of the old **Telegraph Station**, just off the highway. Built in 1872, this is one of only four of the original 11 stations remaining in the Territory (the others are at Barrow Creek, Alice Springs and Powell Creek). This was the most northerly station to be provisioned from Adelaide, and the supplies were brought by camel from the railhead at Oodnadatta. The station's telegraph functions ceased in 1935 when a new office opened in the town itself, but it was in use until 1950

as a linesman's residence and until 1985 as a station homestead. It is an interesting and pleasant spot that's well worth a wander around. To see inside, you need to get a key ($20 deposit) from the visitor information centre, the Outback Caravan Park or Three Ways Roadhouse.

Just north of the Telegraph Station is the turn-off west to **Kundjarra** (The Pebbles), a formation of granite boulders like a miniaturised version of the better-known Devil's Marbles found 100km south. It's a sacred women's Dreaming site of the Warumungu people. Access is 6km along a good dirt road, and it's best enjoyed at sunset or sunrise.

The **Bill Allen Lookout**, about 2km east of Battery Hill, looks over the town and the McDouall Ranges to the north, and has signboards explaining the sights.

Activities

If you're into fossicking, head for **Warrego Fossicking Area**, about 60km west of town along the Warrego road. Note that a (free) permit must be obtained from the visitor information centre.

If you are in need of a cool dip, head to the outdoor **swimming pool** (Peko Rd; adult/child $2.60/1.30; ⊙ 10am-6.30pm).

About 5km north of town is the **Mary Ann Recreational Dam**, a beaut spot for a swim and a picnic. A bicycle track runs next to the highway to the turn-off and then it's a further 1.5km.

Tours

Devil's Marbles Tours (☎ 0418-891 711) runs tours ($88 with lunch) out to (you guessed it) the Devil's Marbles. Aboriginal-guided tours of the garden at **Nyinkka Nyunyu** (see p209) cost $15 per person. More extensive tours of the surrounding bush can be organised.

Festivals & Events

Tennant Creek plays host to the **Tennant Creek Show** (July) and the **Tennant Creek Cup** (August). The **Desert Harmony Arts Festival** (August/September) is a celebration of Tennant Creek's diverse culture through music, art, street parades and markets.

Sleeping

BUDGET

Tourist's Rest Youth Hostel (☎ 8962 2719; www.tourist rest.com.au; cnr Leichhardt & Windley Sts; dm/d $18/38;

ABORIGINAL AUSTRALIA: OPENING TENNANT CREEK'S SHUTTERS

Tennant Creek is known as Jurnkurakurr to the local Warumungu people and almost half of the town's population is of Aboriginal descent. As well as Warumungu, there are Warlmanpa and Wambaya (from north of Tennant Creek), and Warlpiri (from the west). When the town is in the news it is usually for the wrong reasons – unemployment, alcoholism and violence, and the shuttered windows and shopfronts tell their own story. But there is also a lot that is positive happening here.

The innovative art and cultural centre of **Nyinkka Nyunyu** (pronounced ny-ink-a ny-oo ny-oo, p209) greets travellers with the words, 'Don't be frightened, come in'. It's a genuine greeting yet it also acknowledges ingrained cultural barriers. As well as a museum, art gallery, shop and cafe, there are personalised tours of the indigenous flora garden, or into the surrounding bush with Aboriginal guides. Learning about bush tucker, ceremonies and Dreaming stories as well as contemporary life from the guides is even more enthralling than the excellent recorded commentaries in the centre.

On the northern fringe of town, it's hard to miss Ngalpa Ngalpa, the town camp. And though it doesn't look all that inviting, you wouldn't want to miss the opportunity to visit the Pink Palace, aka **Julalikari Arts & Crafts** (p209), right at the camp's entrance. It's best to visit the art centre around mid-morning to find the artists, all women, at work. It's not all painting, but the bright images, be they dot paintings or striking naïve renditions of birds, do grab the eye. The artists' experiences vary – town, mission, traditional – and so does the art. Contemporary issues are as popular as landforms or traditional stories. Several artists from here have attained national recognition. Annie Grant, one of the senior supervisors and an accomplished artist, showed us around, introducing artists and explaining the art and the cooperative nature of the art centre. Her ultrafine dot work and intricate squiggles reveal a very steady hand, and when she isn't painting Annie is organising the canvases and paints for the other artists. If you do decide to buy art from here you can be assured that the proceeds go firstly to the artist, with a percentage used to keep the artists supplied with canvas and paint and other media.

⚄ ▭ ▣) This small, friendly and slightly ramshackle hostel has bright, clean rooms, free breakfast and VIP discounts. The hostel can organise tours of the goldmines and Devil's Marbles and pick-up from the bus stop.

Tennant Creek Caravan Park (☎ 8962 2325; tennantvanpark@bigpond.com.au; Paterson St; unpowered/powered sites $20/25, dm $35, cabin d $55-80; ⚄ ▣) On the northern edge of town, this is a pet-friendly park with lots of shade, drive-through sites, a camp kitchen and top-notch amenities.

Outback Caravan Park (☎ 8962 2459; www.outbacktennantcreek.com.au; Peko Rd; unpowered/powered sites $21/27, cabins $60-115, serviced apartments $95-180; ⚄ ▣) About 1km east of town, this is a pleasant shady park with a kiosk, 'refreshment' garden, camp kitchen, fuel and the irrepressible Jimmy Hooker (see opposite). It's worth paying the few extra dollars for the en suite cabins; the cheapest cost $75 and there are discounts for bookings for more than three nights. The serviced apartments are outside the park, closer to town.

MIDRANGE

Goldfields Hotel Motel (☎ 8962 2030; fax 8962 3288; 113 Paterson St; s/d $75/85) The Goldfields has the cheapest motel rooms in town. The rooms are clean and comfortable and, most importantly, they are sufficiently removed from the somewhat rowdy pub for a good night's sleep.

Safari Lodge Motel (☎ 8962 2207; safari@switch.com.au; Davidson St; s/d $80/90; ⚄) Part of the Budget chain, this motel is centrally located, family run and recently accredited as environmentally friendly. The rooms are fairly standard with phone, fridge and TV, and there's also an outdoor spa.

Desert Sands (☎ 8962 1346; www.desertsands.com.au; 780 Paterson St; s/d from $85/95, additional persons $10; ⚄ ▣) The Desert Sands offers enormous units (sleeping three to eight) each with a fully equipped kitchen, TV (with in-house movies), and a bathroom with a washing machine. This motel is at the southern end of Paterson Street and is excellent value.

Eldorado Motor Inn (☎ 8962 2402; fax 8962 3034; 192 Paterson St; s/d from $99/108; ✲ ✲) On the highway at the northern end of town, this unspectacular brick complex of 80 comfortable, well-appointed units surrounds a pool and includes a licensed restaurant.

Bluestone Motor Inn (☎ 8962 2617; bluestone@ internode.on.net; 1 Paterson St; standard/deluxe d $100/123; ✲ ✲) At the southern end of town, this 3½-star motel has very comfortable standard rooms with all the expected facilities. In addition there are very spacious hexagonal deluxe rooms with queen-size beds and a sofa. There are wheelchair units, and the licensed Anna's Restaurant (below) here is one of Tennant Creek's best.

Eating

Woks Up (☎ 8962 3888; Ambrose St; mains $9-18; ✲ dinner; ✲) Inside the fortress that is the Sporties Club you'll find one of the Territory's best Chinese diners with an immense menu and generous portions.

our pick **Fernanda's Café & Restaurant** (☎ 8962 3999; 1 Noble St; mains $9-25; ✲ lunch & dinner; ✲) Tucked inside the Tennant Creek squash courts (yes squash courts) is this surprising Mediterranean-themed, licensed restaurant. Among the offerings is Moroccan kangaroo with roasted vegetables drizzled in honey-yoghurt glaze and herb oil. The speciality of the house would have to be the Portuguese seafood hotpot. For lighter lunches there are salads, dips, curries, pastas and nachos and Territory-sized burgers.

Margo Miles Restaurant (☎ 8962 2227; Tennant Creek Hotel, 146 Paterson St; mains $13-24; ✲ lunch & dinner Wed-Sun; ✲) This pleasant pub-restaurant is a welcome change from the roadhouse dining rooms up and down the Track. Choose a drink from the reasonably priced selection in the Faye Lewis Bar, sit down in the period dining room and peruse the specials board. Select a steak, seafood, pasta, Thai or gourmet pizza from the menu. The pizzas are the best in town.

Anna's Restaurant (☎ 8962 2617; Bluestone Motor Inn, 1 Paterson St; mains $24-29; ✲ dinner; ✲) This is a casual licensed restaurant with a mouth-watering selection of old favourites cooked with care and a minimum of fuss – rack of lamb, hefty steaks and barramundi. There is a user-friendly kids' menu ($10.50) and one or two vegetarian options always available.

Tennant Food Barn (☎ 8962 2296; 185 Paterson St) Opposite the post office, this supermarket can supply your self-catering needs.

Entertainment

Jimmy Hooker (☎ 8962 2459; Outback Caravan Park, Peko Rd; admission $5; ✲ 7.30pm) Jimmy is a Tennant Creek institution. He is a bush poet, yarn spinner and mine of information on bush tucker, which he will bring along for you to taste.

Tennant Creek Hotel (☎ 8962 2006; 146 Paterson St) Jackson's Bar opens at 10am and the Faye Lewis Bar takes the evening shift with occasional live entertainment on Thursday, Friday and Saturday night.

Getting There & Around

At the time of writing there were no regular air services to Tennant Creek, and the only flying option is to contact a regional charter operator such as **Outback Airlines** (www.outbackairlines.com.au).

All long-distance buses stop at the **BP Service Station** (☎ 8962 2626; 218 Paterson St). **Greyhound Australia** (☎ 13 14 99; www.greyhound.com.au) has regular buses from Tennant Creek to Alice Springs ($160, six hours), Katherine ($165, 8½ hours), Darwin ($225, 14 hours) and Mt Isa ($135, eight hours).

The weekly *Ghan* rail link between Alice Springs and Darwin can drop off passengers in Tennant Creek, although few people stop here and cars can't be loaded or offloaded. It's actually cheaper to travel to Darwin from here than it is from Katherine, far to the north – see p302 for details of fares and timetables. The train station is about 6km south of town and there is no shuttle service. Instead, call for a taxi (☎ 8962 3626, 0432-289 369; ✲ 6am-5.30pm).

Car hire is available from **Thrifty** (☎ 8962 2207; Safari Lodge Motel, Davidson St), while for tyres and tyre repairs head to **Bridgestone Tyre Centre** (☎ 8962 2361; Paterson St).

TENNANT CREEK TO KATHERINE

It's 670km from Tennant Creek to Katherine, the next big town up the Track. Along the way are roadhouses, historic settlements with links to the old rail line and Overland Telegraph, oddball pubs and the soothing thermal springs of Mataranka. On this leg of the trip you'll begin to get the feel of the gradual transition from the dry Centre to the moist humidity of the Top End, and the sparse desert vegetation is eventually replaced by thick scrub.

DETOUR: NEWCASTLE WATERS

A former droving town, **Newcastle Waters** lies at the intersection of northern Australia's two most important stock routes – the Murranji and the Barkly. Today is virtually a ghost town, the only permanent inhabitants being the families of employees from Newcastle Waters Station. The turn-off is 25km north of Elliott, then it's just 3km west of the Stuart Hwy.

In recognition of the need for permanent water along the stock routes, Newcastle Waters was made the depot for a bore-sinking team in 1917. Once the 13 bores along the Murranji were operational in 1924, use of the route increased steadily.

The town site for Newcastle Waters was leased from the station by the government in 1930 and a store and pub were built, followed by a telegraph repeater station in 1942. The town's death knell was the demise of the drovers in the early 1960s, with the advent of road transport for moving stock, and the fact that the Stuart Hwy bypassed the town.

Only a few buildings remain on what was once the main street. The rustic **Junction Hotel**, built in 1932 out of abandoned windmills, was the town's focus. The other notable building is **Jones Store**, also known as George Man Fong's house, which was restored by the National Trust in 1988 and houses a small unstaffed museum with information and photos of the town's heyday, including a few interesting anecdotes.

Heading out of Tennant Creek, the Stuart Hwy continues its ramrod-straight path north. After 26km you come to the important Three Ways junction – important, that is, if you're heading east on the Barkly Hwy to Queensland. From the roadhouse here it's 643km to Mt Isa, the first major town in Queensland, with only the Barkly Homestead and Camooweal in between.

About 48km further north the highway crosses **Attack Creek**, where there is a memorial to explorer John McDouall Stuart. The creek was named because Stuart's party was turned back by hostile Warumungu Aboriginal men here during his first attempt at a south–north crossing of the continent in 1860.

A further 30km along is **Banka Banka Station** (☎ 8964 4511; Stuart Hwy; campsites $6 per person), a friendly oasis with a grassy camping ground shaded by yellow flame trees.

Next stop, **Renner Springs** is a roadhouse on what is generally accepted as being the dividing line between the dry centre and the seasonally wet Top End. The often-monotonous country is relieved around here by the Ashburton Range, which parallels the highway for some distance either side of Renner Springs. **Renner Springs Desert Inn** (☎ 8964 4505; www.rennerspringshotel.com.au; Stuart Hwy; unpowered/powered sites $15/20, d $80-85; 🛇 🖵 🞿) is housed in an army hut removed after WWII from the staging camp at Banka Banka Station to the south. It's built entirely of corrugated iron – even the bar.

About halfway between Alice Springs and Darwin, **Elliott** is a small and unassuming town with roadhouses (with accommodation and groceries), and a nine-hole golf course that boasts real grass greens.

A further 25km north of Elliott is the turnoff to the ghost town of Newcastle Waters (see above). Another 80km on from that, **Dunmarra Wayside Inn** has a friendly restaurant-bar and a reptile display (with live snakes), as well as the usual fuel, refreshments and takeaway. Just north of here, the Buchanan Hwy is an unsealed beef road that heads west to Top Springs and the Buntine Hwy (to Halls Creek in Western Australia).

Daly Waters

Thiss is undoubtedly the most popular stop along the Stuart Hwy between Tennant Creek and Mataranka, mainly due to a little outback pub that's made a big name for itself. The historic settlement of Daly Waters lies 4km west of the Stuart Hwy, just past the turn-off to the Carpentaria Hwy.

Although most people stop purely for a night at the pub, Daly Waters has an intriguing history. On John McDouall Stuart's third attempt to cross the continent from south to north, he came across the small creek here, which he named in honour of the then-governor of South Australia. About 1km from the pub is a signposted turn-off to the sorry remains of a tree where Stuart carved a large letter 'S'. In 1872 the OTL came through and a repeater station was built. In the 1890s a pub sprang up, catering for drovers using Daly Waters as a camp on the overland stock route between Queensland and the Kimberley. The current building dates from the late 1920s and, from the outside at least, looks much the same as it would have then – it lays claim to the title of 'oldest pub in the Territory', as its liquor licence has been used continuously since 1893. In the early 1930s Qantas used Daly Waters as a refuelling stop on the Singapore leg of its Sydney–London run. The airstrip became one of the major stops in northern Australia.

The RAAF also used Daly Waters as a refuelling stop for its bombers en route to Singapore, and in 1942 established a base here. It was in constant use throughout the war, and the restored hangar now belongs to the National Trust and has a small aviation display.

Daly Waters Pub (☎ 8975 9927; www.dalywaterspub .com; unpowered/powered sites $10/18, dm/d $15/50, cabins $75-95; ✖ ☒) has become a bit of a legend along the Track, although it may be a bit too popular for its own good. The once-motley collection of memorabilia – bras to banknotes, business cards and old drivers licences – has now been stapled in an orderly fashion around the pub walls and on our visit the bar closed at 11pm. Still, the staff tells us it stays open late 'most nights' in the Dry. Every evening from April to September there's the popular beef 'n' barra barbecue ($25), along with entertainment from the 'Chook Man' or a visiting country muso. Otherwise, hearty meals (mains $10to $25), including the filling barra burger, are served. Beside the pub is a dustbowl camping ground with a bit of shade – book ahead or arrive early to secure a powered site. Accommodation ranges from basic dongas to spacious self-contained cabins.

The **Daly Waters Campdraft, Show & Rodeo**, in mid-September, is the social event of the year, with a dance held at the pub on the Saturday evening.

Back on the highway at Daly Waters Junction, the **Hi-Way Inn** (☎ 8975 9925; cnr Stuart & Carpentaria Hwy; unpowered/powered sites $14/20, dm $45, budget d $70, s/d $85/95; ✖ ▢ ☒) also has accommodation, fuel, internet ($2 for 15 minutes) and food. From here, the Carpentaria Hwy heads east to Cape Crawford, Borroloola and the Gulf of Carpentaria.

Larrimah
pop 20

It's an easy 100km or so up the highway to the tiny settlement of Larrimah, one of many towns along the highway that served as important bases during WWII, and there are still reminders of that era around town. There's a cracking outback pub, a roadhouse and some good home-cooked food to keep you going.

The North Australian Railway terminated at the settlement of Birdum Creek, 8km south of Larrimah – pretty much in the middle of nowhere. As Birdum was subject to flooding, the army established Larrimah as a staging camp on the highway during WWII. In 1942 the Royal Australian Air Force (RAAF) started work on Gorrie Airfield, 10km north of Larrimah. It became one of the largest in the Pacific and was the base for 6500 military personnel. Following WWII, Larrimah's population fell to less than 50. The Birdum Hotel was dismantled and moved to its current location in Larrimah, while the rest of the settlement was abandoned. In 1976 the railway line closed as it had long since become uneconomical to run. All this is explained at the small but excellent **museum** (☎ 8975 9771; Mahoney St; admission by donation; ☽ always open) in the former telegraph repeater station opposite the Larrimah Hotel, with displays on the railway and WWII.

In early September, the **Back to Birdum Festival** is a celebration of the old rail days, with section cars running from Larrimah to Birdum along the original line and festivities taking place around a replica of the old pub.

SLEEPING & EATING
Larrimah Hotel (☎ 8975 9931; unpowered/powered sites $10/15, d $40-45; ✖ ☒) Otherwise known as the Pink Panther Pub (ask behind the bar for the story, but the bedraggled oversized Pink Panther next to the giant Darwin stubby may hold a clue), this quirky outback pub offers a rustic bar experience and a menagerie of donkeys, birds and crocs next door. The owners are a mine of local information and have developed the old rail line – up to Birdum. The camping ground is a little exposed, the pool is the size of a bath-tub and the rooms are basic, but it's a clean and friendly place. Counter meals (mains $12 to $20) at lunch and dinner are served in the shady bar area or in the period dining room.

ourpick Fran's Devonshire Tea House (☎ 8975 9945; Stuart Hwy, Larrimah; meals $7-12; ☽ 8am-5pm) It's hard to miss the convoluted collection of black-and-white signs directing you to Fran's kitchen, which is right beside the highway. This is the place to stop for a filling homemade camel or buffalo pie, roast lamb with damper, or just a Devonshire tea or fresh coffee. Fran is passionate about her food and insists that every dish is a meal in itself and it 'ain't no roadhouse food'.

Mataranka & Elsey National Park
pop 425

With its soothing, warm thermal springs set in lush pockets of palms and tropical vegetation, you'd be mad not to pull into Mataranka for at least a few hours to soak away those miles of road travel.

Mataranka itself is a small town (pop 250) on the highway 60km north of Larrimah, with a roadhouse, pub, cafe and museum, and there are several good camping and cabin accommodation places east of the highway close to the springs in Elsey National Park.

The first European explorers through this region were Ludwig Leichhardt (1845) and John McDouall Stuart (1862). When AC Gregory came through in 1856 on his exploratory journey from Victoria River Depot (Timber Creek), he named Elsey Creek after Joseph Elsey, a young surgeon and naturalist in his party. The name went on to became famous as Elsey Station (established in 1881) – the setting for *We of the Never Never*.

The **Back to the Never Never Festival** takes place in Mataranka in May and includes an art show, rodeo and bush poetry recitals.

The **Mataranka Rural Transaction Centre** (☎ 8975 4576; ✆ 9am-4.30pm Mon-Fri) is the post office agent and has internet access ($2 per 15 minutes).

SIGHTS & ACTIVITIES

The 138-sq-km **Elsey National Park** surrounds the Mataranka Homestead and takes in the Little Roper River and a long stretch of the Roper River, with monsoon forests along its banks. On the eastern edge of the park are colourful tufa limestone formations, which form the Mataranka Falls. The Roper River section of the park is reached along the 20km stretch of John Hauser Dr, which turns off Homestead Rd, while the Bitter Springs section is along Martins Rd.

The area is the site of some Dreaming trails of the Yangman and Mangarayi peoples. Mataranka Station was selected as an experimental sheep station in 1912. The sheep did not prosper and were removed in 1919, but cattle did better and some of the yards are still standing at 12 Mile Yards.

Mataranka's famous crystal-clear **thermal pool** is about 10km east of town. The turn-off to the hot springs is 1.5km south of Mataranka, and then it's 8km along the bitumen Homestead Rd. The warm, mineral-rich waters flow from Rainbow Spring into a landscaped pool surrounded by rainforest palms. Don't expect the secluded tranquillity of other hot springs in the Top End; the pool is reached via a short boardwalk from the touristy Mataranka Homestead Resort and can get pretty crowded. There's no need to worry about the freshness of the water, however, as it comes out of the ground at more than 16,000L per minute at a temperature of 34°C.

About 200m away (follow the boardwalk) is the **Waterhouse River**, where you can walk along the banks, or rent canoes for $10 an hour. **Stevie's Hole**, a natural swimming hole in the cooler Waterhouse River, about 1.5km from the homestead, is rarely crowded.

Outside the homestead entrance is a replica of the **Elsey Station Homestead**, which was made for the filming of *We of the Never Never* (shown daily at noon in the main homestead), and now houses historical displays.

John Hauser Drive is a sealed road branching off Homestead Rd and leads to a camping area at 12 Mile Yards. A few kilometres along, the **Botanic Walk** (1.5km, one hour, easy) passes through dense vegetation bordering a creek and has interpretive signs explaining the Aboriginal uses of various species. **Korowan Walk** (4.1km one way, two hours, easy) follows the scenic Roper River downstream from Mulurark, through 12 Mile Yards (1km) to a set of small cascades and Mataranka Falls. There are some tranquil and safe **swimming spots** along the Roper River at 4 Mile, Mulurark and 12 Mile Yards. Freshwater crocs inhabit the river but it is safe to swim above the falls. Fishing is also permitted here.

From Mataranka town, take the Martins Rd turn-off to reach **Bitter Springs**, a serene, palm-fringed thermal pool along the Little Roper River. Its language name is *Korran*, part of the Black Cockatoo Dreaming, but its less tasteful name was derived from the high mineral content that makes the water unpleasant to drink. The incredible blue colour of the 34°C water is due to dissolved limestone particles. A **walking trail** (900m loop, 15 minutes) circles the spring and has viewing platforms into palm and paperbark forests. You can jump in at one end and take a therapeutic swim downstream

JEANNIE GUNN

Probably the most famous woman in the history of the Territory is Jeannie Gunn. Originally from Melbourne, where she had run a school for young ladies, she arrived in the Territory in 1902 with her husband, Aeneas, who had already spent some years there and was returning to take up the manager's position at Elsey Station.

It was a brave move on the part of Jeannie as at that time there were very few European women living in the Territory, especially on isolated cattle stations. They made the trip from Darwin to Elsey Station over several weeks during the Wet.

Station life was tough, but Jeannie adapted to it and eventually gained the respect of the men working there. She also gained a good understanding of the local Aboriginal people, a number of whom worked on the station.

Only a year after their arrival at Elsey, Aeneas contracted malarial dysentery and died. Jeannie returned to Melbourne and soon after recorded her experiences of the Top End in the novel *We of the Never Never*, published in 1908. She was a keen observer of the minutiae of station life, and her observations captured the imagination of the people down south who led such a different existence. These days, however, her depiction of Aboriginal people seems somewhat patronising.

Jeannie was awarded an OBE in 1939 for her contribution to Australian literature, and died in Melbourne in 1961 at the age of 91.

Her book remains one of the classics of outback literature, recording in detail the lives of the early pioneers, and was made into a film in 1981.

---

to the bridge. There are information boards, toilets and gas barbecues near the car park.

In town, the **Never Never Museum** (Stuart Hwy; adult/child $2.50/1; 8.30am-4.30pm Mon-Fri) has displays on the OTL, as well as WWII and railway paraphernalia.

About 7km off the Stuart Hwy, 7km south of the Roper Hwy turn-off, **Elsey Cemetery** is the final resting place of a number of the real-life characters portrayed in the novel *We of the Never Never*. Among them are Aeneas Gunn, the manager of the station and husband of Jeannie Gunn, the book's author. The site of the original homestead, as near as can be determined, is 500m or so beyond the cemetery, by the bridge over the Elsey Creek. A plaque and cairn mark the spot.

SLEEPING & EATING

Jalmurark Camping Ground (adult/child/family $6.60/3.30/16) Located at 12 Mile Yards, this national-park campground has lots of grass and shade and access to the Roper River and walking trails. There are solar hot showers and gas barbecues, and you can hire canoes here when the kiosk is staffed. Generators are not allowed.

Mataranka Homestead Resort (8975 4544; Homestead Rd; unpowered/powered site $20/24, dm $19, motel d $89, cabins $115;) Only metres from the main thermal pool and with a range of accommodation, this is a popular place to stay or to call into for lunch and a quick soak. The large camping ground is a bit dusty but has shady areas, good amenities and barbecues. The fan-cooled hostel rooms are pretty basic but comfortable enough, and linen is provided. The air-con motel rooms have fridge, TV and bathroom, while the cabins have a kitchenette and sleep up to six people. Book ahead. The resort's Garden Bistro (mains $16 to $25) churns out steaks, fish and chicken dishes in the evening, while Jeanie's Kitchen (mains $5 to $13) serves burgers and snacks in the open-sided Maluka's Bar.

Down Martins Rd towards Bitter Springs are a couple of good options.

Mataranka Cabins (8975 4838; www.mataranka cabins.com.au; Martins Rd, Bitter Springs; unpowered/powered sites $20/24, cabins $110;) On the banks of the Little Roper River, only a few hundred metres from Bitter Springs thermal pool, this quiet bush setting has some amazing termite mounds adorning the front paddock. The secluded, open-plan cabins are equipped with linen, bathrooms and kitchens, and accommodate up to six people.

Territory Manor (8975 4516; www.territorymanor motelcaravanparkmataranka.com; Martins Rd; unpowered/powered sites $20/24, s/d $89/103;) About 300m off the highway on the road to Bitter Springs, this place has ample shady sites and attractive rammed-earth motel rooms. The restaurant

ALICE SPRINGS TO KATHERINE

GHUNMARN & MANYALLALUK CULTURAL CENTRES

If you're interested in seeing genuine Aboriginal art produced by local communities, it's worth detouring off the Stuart Hwy to these two remote cultural centres.

The small community of Beswick is reached via the sealed Central Arnhem Hwy 56km east of the Stuart Hwy on the southern fringes of Arnhem Land. Here you'll find the **Ghunmarn Cultural Centre** (☎ 8977 4250; www.djilpinarts.org.au; Beswick; ⊙ 10am-4pm Mon-Fri Apr-Nov), opened in 2007, and displaying local artworks, prints, carvings, weaving and didgeridoos from western Arnhem Land. The centre also features the Blanasi Collection, a permanent exhibition of works by elders from the Western Arnhem Land region. Visitors are welcome to visit the centre without a permit – call ahead to check that it's open.

A very special festival at Beswick is **Walking with Spirits**, magical performances of traditional corroborees staged in conjunction with the Australian Shakespeare Company. It's held on the first weekend in August. Camping is possible at Beswick Falls over this weekend but advance bookings are essential (see p224).

Abutting the eastern edge of Nitmiluk National Park, the southern edge of Kakadu and the western edge of Arnhem Land, the former 3000-sq-km Eva Valley cattle station is now home to the Jawoyn community of **Manyallaluk**. Unlike Beswick, Manyallaluk can only be visited as part of a guided **cultural tour** (☎ 1800 644 727, 8975 4727; self-drive adult/child $135/78, incl transfers to/from Katherine $177/88; ⊙ Wed-Sun Apr-Oct). On these highly regarded one-day tours you'll learn about traditional bush tucker and medicine, spear throwing and how to play a didgeridoo from Indigenous Jawoyn guides. Lunch and billy tea is included.

Manyallaluk Art & Craft Centre has excellent art and crafts at competitive prices, and is included in the tours. No permits are needed to visit the community, but alcohol is prohibited.

There's a **camping ground** (unpowered/powered sites $12/18) with grassy sites, and a community store with basic supplies.

The turn-off to Manyallaluk is 15km along the Central Arnhem Hwy, then 35km along a well-maintained, all-season gravel road. Both Manyallaluk and Beswick are around a 90-minute drive from Katherine.

(mains $15 to $20) serves huge steaks, fresh barramundi and delicious desserts. Call in to see the spectacular barramundi-feeding sessions at 9.30am and 1pm daily.

Stockyard Gallery (☎ 8975 4530; Stuart Hwy; snacks $3-10; ⊙ 9am-4pm; ❸ Ⓥ) In town, this casual cafe is a little gem. There's a delicious range of homemade snacks such as focaccias and sandwiches, cakes and muffins. Finish with fresh plunger coffee, a divine mango smoothie or the unusual bush-orange ice cream. The art gallery here has Aboriginal art, jewellery and books; and information on the region is also available.

Cutta Cutta Caves Nature Park

Just off the highway 78km northwest of Mataranka and only 28km from Katherine, Cutta Cutta is the only cave system open to the public in the Territory. The 1499-hectare **Cutta Cutta Caves Nature Park** (☎ 8972 1940; adult/child $14.50/7.25; ⊙ 8.30am-4.30pm, guided tours 9am, 10am, 11am, 1pm, 2pm & 3pm) protects this extensive karst (limestone) landscape. The caves have a unique ecology and you'll be sharing the space with brown tree snakes, plus the endangered ghost bats and orange horseshoe bats that they feed on, 15m below the ground. During the Dry, however, the bats move into the far recesses of the caves and visitors have little chance of seeing them.

Cutta Cutta is a Jawoyn name meaning many stars; it was taboo for Aborigines to enter the cave, which they believed was where the stars were kept during the day. The first European person to see the cave was a local stockman in 1900, after whom it was known as Smith's Cave.

The only way to enter the caves is with a 45-minute guided tour run from the kiosk. There are limited numbers on each tour, so it's worth booking ahead. Tours also run out of Katherine.

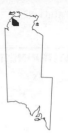

Katherine to Darwin

The final leg of the Stuart Hwy odyssey, this is true 'Top End' country. The heavy rains of the Wet create permanent water sources here, starting with the powerful Katherine River and continuing up to the crocodile- and barramundi-infested Daly and Adelaide river systems. The desert landscape is replaced with woodland savannah and tropical vegetation, the humidity moves up a notch and the locals become a little more laid-back.

Katherine itself is the Territory's third-largest settlement, a transcontinental crossroads and a good place to browse Indigenous art and stock up for the trip. More importantly, it's the gateway to Nitmiluk National Park where you can canoe or boat through sublime sandstone gorges or bushwalk to rock-art sites. Although not covered in this book, the Victoria Hwy heads southwest towards the border with Western Australia (WA), passing some dramatic scenery and little-visited national parks.

The Stuart Hwy to the north passes through a handful of old mining towns – most notably Pine Creek, where the Kakadu Hwy peels off to the northeast, and Adelaide River. Detours from here will carry you deep into barramundi fishing country at Daly River, to natural hot springs, historic sites and hidden waterfalls.

But the main attraction north of Katherine is Litchfield National Park, a superb pocket of bushland where waterfalls tumble over ranges into idyllic swimming holes. It's a beautiful place to camp and chill out for a few days.

HIGHLIGHTS

- Paddling a canoe along an ancient course beneath the spectacular walls of **Katherine Gorge** (p227)

- Bushwalking the **Jatbula Trail** (p229) from Katherine Gorge to Leliyn (Edith Falls)

- Camping, bushwalking and swimming in the wonderful waterfall-fed pools of **Litchfield National Park** (p235)

- Soaking in the natural thermal waters of **Douglas Hot Springs** (p233)

- Fishing for the famed Top End barramundi on the **Daly River** (p233)

- Spotting all of the Territory's normally elusive wildlife at the excellent **Territory Wildlife Park** (p239).

- TELEPHONE CODE: ☎ 08   ■ www.visitkatherine.com.au   ■ www.nt.gov.au/nreta/parks

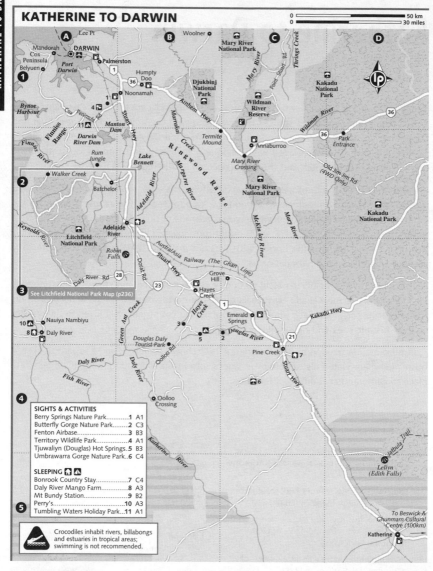

KATHERINE TO DARWIN

0 — 50 km
0 — 30 miles

SIGHTS & ACTIVITIES
Berry Springs Nature Park............1 A1
Butterfly Gorge Nature Park........2 C3
Fenton Airbase...........................3 B3
Territory Wildlife Park................4 A1
Tjuwaliyn (Douglas) Hot Springs.5 B3
Umbrawarra Gorge Nature Park..6 C4

SLEEPING
Bonrook Country Stay.................7 C4
Daly River Mango Farm..............8 A3
Mt Bundy Station.......................9 B2
Perry's.....................................10 A3
Tumbling Waters Holiday Park...11 A1

See Litchfield National Park Map (p236)

Crocodiles inhabit rivers, billabongs and estuaries in tropical areas; swimming is not recommended.

KATHERINE

pop 5850

Katherine is considered a big town in this part of the world and you'll certainly feel like you've arrived somewhere after the long trip up the highway. Its namesake river is the first permanent running water on the road north from Alice Springs. In the wet season the river swells dramatically and has been responsible for some devastating floods – the worst in memory occurred on Australia Day 1998, when rising waters inundated the surrounding countryside and left a mark up to 2m high on buildings in Katherine.

Katherine is probably best known for the Nitmiluk (Katherine Gorge) National Park to the north, and the town makes an obvious base, with plenty of accommodation options and some decent restaurants. Katherine also has quite a few attractions of its own, including a thriving Indigenous arts community, thermal springs and a few museums. The Stuart Hwy forms the main street through town – possibly one of the only streets in Australia that pipes music from loudspeakers day and night. It's a disconcerting mix of country and retro pop – whether you like it or not!

HISTORY

The Katherine area is the traditional home of the Jawoyn and Dagoman Aboriginal people. Following land claims they have received the title to large parcels of land, including Nitmiluk National Park.

The first Europeans through the area were those in the expedition of Ludwig Leichhardt in 1844. The river was named the Catherine by John McDouall Stuart in 1862, but for some reason the current spelling was adopted. As was so often the case with Territory towns, it was the construction of the Overland Telegraph Line (OTL) and the establishment of a telegraph station that really got the town going.

Pastoral ventures soon followed, one of the most notable being the establishment of Springvale Station by Alfred Giles in 1878. Although his attempts at sheep and cattle farming were not outrageously successful, he laid the foundations for the cattle industry in the Katherine region.

The town found its current site when the railway bridge over the Katherine River was opened in 1926. During WWII, Katherine became a major defence-force base, and it even received a bit of attention from the Japanese when nine bombers raided the town in March 1942.

ORIENTATION

Katherine's main street, Katherine Tce, is the Stuart Hwy as it runs through town. Giles St, the road to Katherine Gorge, branches off to the northeast in the middle of town. Murphy Street branches west off the Stuart Hwy to become the Victoria Hwy (for Victoria River, Timber Creek and WA), part of Hwy 1 around Australia.

Long-distance buses pull into the transit centre and 24-hour BP station, diagonally opposite the information centre.

INFORMATION
Bookshops
Katherine Book Exchange (☎ 8971 1246; Railway Tce; ◷ 1-5pm Mon & Wed, 9am-1pm Tue & Fri, 1-3pm Sat, 10am-noon Sun) Secondhand books for buy, sell and swap.
Katherine Books (☎ 8972 2530; shop 10, Oasis Shopping Centre)

Emergency
Police station (☎ 8972 0111; Stuart Hwy) Two kilometres southeast of the town centre.

Internet Access
Didj Shop Internet Cafe (☎ 0415-461 759; www .didj.com.au; cnr Giles St & Railway Tce; per 15min/hr $2/6; ◷ 10am-7pm Mon-Sat, plus 11am-3pm Sun Apr-Oct only) Katherine's best internet cafe – log on, order fine coffee and chat with the gregarious owner. Buy a coffee and get 15 minutes internet free. Access for laptops.
Katherine Art Gallery (☎ 8971 1051; 12 Katherine Tce; per 15min $2; ◷ 9am-6pm) Coin-op internet at this Aboriginal art and craft shop.
Katherine Library (☎ 8971 1188; Randazzo centre, Katherine Tce; per 30min $3; ◷ 10am-5pm Wed-Fri, to 1pm Sat, 8.30am-5pm Tue)

Medical Services
Katherine Hospital (☎ 8973 9211; Giles St) In case of emergency, the hospital is about 2.5km north of the town centre.

Post
Main post office (☎ 13 13 18; 13 Katherine Tce) Corner Giles St; post restante and public phones at the front.

Tourist Information
Katherine Visitor Information Centre (☎ 8972 2650; www.visitkatherine.com.au; cnr Lindsay St & Katherine Tce; ◷ 8.30am-5pm Mon-Fri, 9am-2pm Sat & Sun, to 5pm May-Oct) Modern, air-con information centre stocking information on all areas of the Northern Territory; plenty of parking off Lindsay St.
Northern Land Council (☎ 8971 9802; 5 Katherine Tce) If you wish to drive along the Central Arnhem Hwy towards Nhulunbuy, a permit from the Northern Land Council is required.
Parks & Wildlife office (☎ 8973 8888; 32 Giles St) National park information notes are available here.

KATHERINE

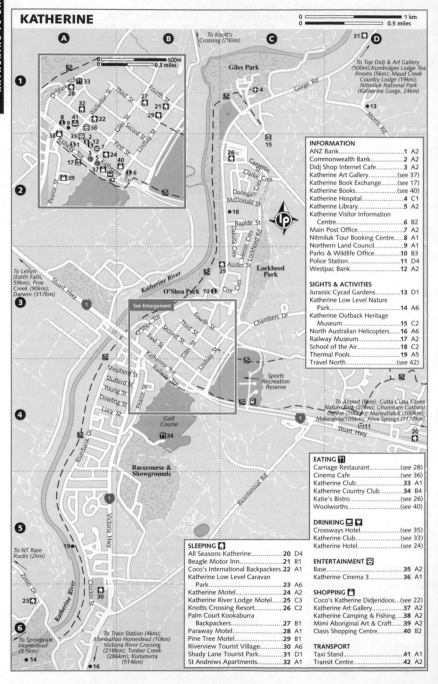

INFORMATION
ANZ Bank	1 A2
Commonwealth Bank	2 A2
Didj Shop Internet Cafe	3 A2
Katherine Art Gallery	(see 37)
Katherine Book Exchange	(see 17)
Katherine Books	(see 40)
Katherine Hospital	4 C1
Katherine Library	5 A2
Katherine Visitor Information Centre	6 B2
Main Post Office	7 A2
Nitmiluk Tour Booking Centre	8 A1
Northern Land Council	9 A1
Parks & Wildlife Office	10 B3
Police Station	11 D4
Westpac Bank	12 A2

SIGHTS & ACTIVITIES
Jurassic Cycad Gardens	13 D1
Katherine Low Level Nature Park	14 A6
Katherine Outback Heritage Museum	15 C2
North Australian Helicopters	16 A6
Railway Museum	17 A2
School of the Air	18 C2
Thermal Pools	19 A5
Travel North	(see 42)

EATING
Carriage Restaurant	(see 28)
Cinema Cafe	(see 36)
Katherine Club	33 A1
Katherine Country Club	34 B4
Katie's Bistro	(see 26)
Woolworths	(see 40)

DRINKING
Crossways Hotel	(see 35)
Katherine Club	(see 33)
Katherine Hotel	(see 24)

ENTERTAINMENT
Base	35 A2
Katherine Cinema 3	36 A1

SHOPPING
Coco's Katherine Didjeridoos	(see 22)
Katherine Art Gallery	37 A2
Katherine Camping & Fishing	38 A2
Mimi Aboriginal Art & Craft	39 A2
Oasis Shopping Centre	40 B2

TRANSPORT
Taxi Stand	41 A1
Transit Centre	42 A2

SLEEPING
All Seasons Katherine	20 D4
Beagle Motor Inn	21 B1
Coco's International Backpackers	22 A1
Katherine Low Level Caravan Park	23 A6
Katherine Motel	24 A2
Katherine River Lodge Motel	25 C3
Knotts Crossing Resort	26 C2
Palm Court Kookaburra Backpackers	27 B1
Paraway Motel	28 A1
Pine Tree Motel	29 B1
Riverview Tourist Village	30 A6
Shady Lane Tourist Park	31 D1
St Andrews Apartments	32 A1

ABORIGINAL AUSTRALIA: JAWOYN COUNTRY

The area to the north and east of Katherine is Jawoyn country. One of the largest Aboriginal groups in the Top End, the Jawoyn have successfully made land claims in recent years, including Nitmiluk National Park and the southern part of Kakadu National Park. Today, many Jawoyn are based in Katherine town, but also at Barunga and Beswick. To the west and south you'll find the traditional lands of the Wardaman people, sometimes referred to as Lightning Brothers country.

Katherine has a vibrant arts community and is one of the best places in the Territory to shop for a locally made didgeridoo, an instrument traditionally associated with the Top End. Also worth visiting are the Manyallaluk and Ghunmarn cultural centres (p218) southeast of Katherine. Good places for local Indigenous insights:

- **Mimi Aboriginal Art & Craft** (p226).
- **Coco's Katherine Didjeridoos** (p226)
- **Top Didj & Art Gallery** (p226)
- **Nitmiluk Centre** (p230)
- **Barunga Festival p224**
- **Walking with Spirits** (p224)

SIGHTS & ACTIVITIES

Katherine has enough sights to keep you busy for the day. For details of Aboriginal art galleries, see Shopping (p226).

Katherine Outback Heritage Museum (☎ 8972 3945; Gorge Rd; adult/child $5/2; ☿ 9am-4pm) is in the old airport terminal, about 3km from town on the road to the gorge. The original Gypsy Moth biplane flown by Dr Clyde Fenton, the first Flying Doctor, is housed here. There's a good selection of historical photos, including a display on the 1998 flood.

At the **School of the Air** (☎ 8972 1833; www .schools.nt.edu.au/ksa; Giles St; adult/child $5/2; ☿ Mar-Nov), 1.5km from the town centre, you can listen into a class and see how kids in the remote outback are educated in the virtual world. Guided tours are held at 9am, 10am and 11am on weekdays and bookings are preferred.

Jurassic Cycad Gardens (☎ 0417-623 014; www .cycadinternational.com.au; 61 Morris Rd; adult/child/family $10/5/25; ☿ 8am-6pm Tue-Sun) is home to over 200 species of prehistoric cycads, collected and seeded from around Australia and overseas. A self-guided tour through the remarkable maze of rare plants also takes you past baobabs, rock figs, ferns and cacti. The attached cafe is a good place for breakfast or lunch.

Katherine's **Railway Museum** (Railway Tce; admission $2 donation; ☿ 1-4pm Mon-Fri May-Oct) is a tiny display on railway history in the original station building (1926) one block back from the main street. The other half of the building is occupied by the Katherine Book Exchange.

Alfred Giles established **Springvale Homestead** (☎ 8972 1355; Shadforth Rd) in 1879 after he drove 2000 cattle and horses and 12,000 head of sheep from Adelaide to the site in 19 months. It claims to be the oldest cattle station in the Northern Territory. The stone homestead still stands by the river, about 7km southwest of town, and the surrounding riverside property is now a caravan and camping resort. There's a free tour of the homestead at 3pm daily (except Monday) from May to October. Canoes are available for hire from $11 an hour or $21 for a half-day.

The 105-hectare **Katherine Low Level Nature Park** is 4km south of town, just off the Victoria Hwy. It's a lovely spot on the banks of Katherine River, with a popular dry-season swimming hole. There are picnic tables, gas barbecues and toilets here. A cycle-walking path along the southern bank of the river connects the park with town and the **thermal pools**. Floating in the clear, warm (32°C) waters past pandanus palms to the rapids area is serene. The pools are also accessible from the Victoria Hwy via Murray St, a few kilometres south of town, or there's wheelchair access from Croker St – if the gate is closed call ☎ 1800 653 142 for the combination-lock code.

TOURS

Katherine offers a diverse range of tours. You can delve into local history or Aboriginal art and culture, fly, cruise or walk in the region. For Nitmiluk National Park tours see p230.

Most tours can be booked through the visitors centre, or Travel North.

Crocodile Night Adventure (☎ 1800 089 103; adult/child $55/29; ⏰ 6.30pm May-Oct) At Springvale Homestead, this evening cruise seeks out crocs and other nocturnal wildlife on the Katherine River. Includes barbecue dinner and drinks.

Gecko Canoeing (☎ 1800 634 319, 8972 2224; www .geckocanoeing.com.au) Exhilarating guided canoe trips on the more remote stretches of the Katherine River. Trips vary from one/three days ($195/720) on the Katherine River to expeditions of up to seven days on the Baines, Wickham and Victoria Rivers. A five-day hike along the Jatbula Trail in Nitmiluk National Park costs $995. Gecko also runs eco tours to Kakadu, Litchfield and Mataranka.

Katherine Town Tour (☎ 8971 9999; adult/child $62/32; ⏰ Tue, Wed, Fri & Sat) Half-day tours of local and regional attractions, including Springvale Homestead.

Manyallaluk Tours (☎ 8972 2294) Excellent Aboriginal cultural tours at Manyallaluk, about 100km from Katherine. A one-day cultural experience (adult/child $177/88) departing from Katherine includes a bush-tucker and bush-medicine walk, lunch, and painting and craft activities. The self-drive option is $135/78.

North Australian Helicopters (☎ 1800 621 717; www.northaustralianhelicopters.com.au; Victoria Hwy) Scenic flights from a 10-minute Town Tour ($65) to flights over Katherine Gorge (from $220).

Travel North (☎ 1800 089 103; www.travelnorth.com .au; Transit Centre, Katherine Tce) Katherine's main tour operator has a range of tours to Kakadu, Arnhem Land, Litchfield, Manyallaluk, Mataranka and the Katherine region. Also booking agent for the *Ghan* and Greyhound.

FESTIVALS & EVENTS
MAY
Katherine Country Music Muster (www.kcmm.com .au) Features plenty of live music in the pubs and entertainment at a site on Gorge Rd over the May Day long weekend.

Katherine Races Race meeting at the Katherine Showgrounds, followed by a rodeo.

JUNE & JULY
Katherine Canoe Marathon This one-day 47km race organised by the Red Cross on the Queen's Birthday long weekend in June is the Territory's only canoe race.

Barunga Festival (www.barungafestival.com.au) Also held during the Queen's Birthday long weekend in June, Barunga, 80km southeast of Katherine, hosts Aboriginal performers from around 40 communities. There are displays of traditional arts and crafts, as well as dancing and athletics competitions.

Katherine District Show (www.katherineshow.org.au) An annual agricultural show held at the Katherine Show Grounds with rides, stalls and lots of animals.

AUGUST & SEPTEMBER
Walking with Spirits (www.djilpinarts.org.au) This two-day Indigenous cultural festival is held at Beswick Falls, about 130km from Katherine. In a magical setting, traditional dance and music is combined with theatre, films and a light show. Camping is allowed at the site (only during the festival). A 4WD is recommended for the last 20km to the falls, or a shuttle bus runs from Beswick.

Flying Fox Art & Cultural Festival A three-week festival of music, art and dance featuring local artists and performers, dragon-boat races and a street parade.

SLEEPING
Budget
Katherine has only a couple of hostels, but there are lots of campgrounds around town and a few motels that fall into the budget category.

HOSTELS
Coco's International Backpackers (☎ 8971 2889; www.21firstst.com; 21 First St; camping per person $13, dm $23) With travellers lounging around amid tents in the backyard, idly strumming on guitars and swapping outback tales, you'll feel like you've walked into an old Asian overland bolthole here. Coco's is a real backpackers, a converted home where the owner chats with the guests and offers sage advice on didgeridoos from his tin-0shed gallery. Aboriginal artists are often here painting didgeridoos.

Palm Court Kookaburra Backpackers (☎ 1800 626 722; www.travelnorth.com.au; cnr Third & Giles Sts; dm $24, tw or d $54; ✖ 🅿 🖥) This well-equipped backpacker hostel is a welcoming place where they pack 'em in to the retired motel rooms. Each room has a bathroom, fridge and TV; there are four-to eight-bed dorms or twin/double rooms.

MOTELS
Beagle Motor Inn (☎ 8972 3998; cnr Lindsay & Fourth Sts; s/d $68/78; ✖ 🅿) Katherine's cheapest motel is a bit worn and weary, with '50s-style rooms around a car park and a tiny pool. Some cheaper rooms have share bathrooms, but it's a friendly enough place to crash for the night and there's a licensed restaurant.

Katherine River Lodge Motel (☎ 8971 0266; www.katherineriverlodge.net; 50 Giles St; d $79-89, f $100; ✖ 🅿 🖥) One of Katherine's best-value motels, this large complex has spotless rooms in a lush tropical garden. The attached Cheeky Croc Restaurant (mains $17 to $29) serves filling meals from Tuesday to Sunday, including $6.50 kids' meals. Perfect for families.

CAMPING & CARAVAN PARKS

Springvale Homestead (☎ 8972 1355; www.travelnorth
.com.au; Shadforth Rd; unpowered/powered sites $10/25,
s/tw $51/61; ✖ ▣) This historic homestead is
a lovely place to camp in a real bushland setting by the Katherine River. There's plenty of
space, a palm-shaded pool and a bistro open
in the evening. Rooms are motel style and
there are free tours of the homestead at 3pm
daily in the Dry.

Shady Lane Tourist Park (☎ 8971 0491; www.shady
lanetouristpark.com.au; Gorge Rd; unpowered/powered sites
$26/28, cabins $110-140; ✖ ▣) A friendly, well-
run park about 6km out of the town centre
towards Nitmiluk. A range of spotless cabins
and clean amenities, and the camp kitchen
has a fridge and gas barbecues.

Katherine Low Level Caravan Park (☎ 8972
3962; www.katherinelowlevel.com.au; Shadforth Rd; un-
powered/powered sites $27/30, cabins $130; ✖ ▣)
Across the river, off the Victoria Hwy about
5km from town, this sprawling manicured
park has plenty of shady sites, a great swimming pool adjoining a bar and bistro, and
spotless amenities.

Also recommended:

Manbulloo Homestead Caravan Park (☎ 8972
1559; www.manbulloohomesteadcaravanpark.com.au; off
Victoria Hwy; unpowered/powered sites $18/22, motel/
cabin $80/120) Peaceful cattle station property 12km
southwest of Katherine.

Riverview Tourist Village (☎ 8972 1011; www.river
viewtouristvillage.com.au; 440 Victoria Hwy; unpowered/
powered sites $21/26.50, budget cabins $69-79, motel d
$89, cabins from $95; ✖ ▣) Convenient to the thermal
pools but hugging the Victoria Hwy, this pet-friendly park
has a good range of cabins and shady sites.

Midrange

Knott's Crossing Resort (☎ 1800 222 511, 8972 2511;
www.knottscrossing.com.au; cnr Cameron & Giles Sts; powered sites $30, cabins from $95, motel d from $142; ✖ ▣)
Knott's Crossing is more a motel and cabin
resort than camping, but it's a great spot for
caravans and campervans as all sites have private en suite and it's close to town. Set amid
lush tropical gardens, everything is packed
pretty tightly here but it's very well run with a
day spa, bar and the excellent Katie's Bistro.

Katherine Motel (☎ 8972 1622; www.katherine
motel.com; 3 Giles St; s/d from $95/112; ✖ ▣) Just
back from the main street, it doesn't come
more central, though the motel is behind the
rowdy Katherine Hotel. Budget rooms are
pretty basic or you can pay a bit more for

deluxe rooms with some extra furniture and
a fridge. There's wi-fi and a nice pool.

Paraway Motel (☎ 8972 2644; www.parawaymotel
.com.au; O'Shea Tce; d $110-150; ✖ ▣) This smart
motel is as neat as a pin and its quiet location is handy to the main-street shopping.
Standard motel rooms are spotless and comfortable and there are spa rooms. There's also
the popular Carriage Restaurant.

Pine Tree Motel (☎ 8972 2533; pinetree2@bigpond
.com; 3 Third St; d $132, ✖ ▣) The Pine Tree is a
comfortable chain motel with spacious rooms
orbiting a central garden and pool. Licensed
restaurant, poolside barbecue and wi-fi.

All Seasons Katherine (☎ 1300 65 65 65, 8972 1744;
www.accorhotels.com.au; Stuart Hwy; powered sites $25-28,
d $142-152; ✖ ▣ ▣) This is Katherine's top
motel, although it has a dull location just
off the highway 4km southeast of town. The
standard rooms are a bit small – the spacious
queen-size deluxe doubles are worth paying
the extra $10 for. Adjacent is a pleasant cara-
van park (powered sites only) with barbecues,
gardens and a tennis court.

our pick **Maud Creek Country Lodge** (☎ 8971 1814;
www.maudcreeklodge.com.au; Gorge Rd; d $156, cottage
$186; ✖ ▣) Set on a former cattle run just
6km from the gorge, this peaceful farmstay
puts you in touch with nature. The property reaches down to the river and is ideal
for bushwalking, birdwatching and fishing.
The three immaculate adjoining lodge rooms
share a communal kitchen and TV lounge,
but better still is the private self-contained
cottage. It's all set in a lush tropical garden
with pool, gazebo and mahogany trees. A
continental breakfast is included and each
room has a minibar with drinks proudly kept
at town prices.

St Andrews Apartments (☎ 1800 686106; www.st
andrewsapts.com.au; 27 First St; apt $170-240; ✖ ▣) In
the heart of town, these serviced apartments
are great for families or if you pine for a few
home comforts. Spotless and contemporary,
the two-bedroom apartments sleep four (six
if you use the sofa bed), and come with fully
equipped kitchen and lounge-dining area.

EATING

Katherine has a handful of reasonably good
cafes, pubs and motel restaurants. Locals tend
to eat out at clubs such as the **Katherine Country
Club** (☎ 8972 1276; 3034 Pearce St; mains $12-25; ☑ lunch
& dinner; ✖), overlooking the nine-hole golf
course; and the **Katherine Club** (☎ 8972 1250;

cnr Second St & O'Shea Tce; mains $15-20; ☺ lunch Tue-Fri, dinner Tue-Sat; ☒), closer to the town centre. They're nothing fancy but you can rely on inexpensive and satisfying bistro meals such as steak, schnitzel and barra, and kids are welcome.

Cinema Cafe (☎ 8971 0594; 20 First St; meals $5-15; ☺ 8am-3pm Mon, to 5pm Tue-Thu, to 8pm Fri & Sat, 8.30-11.30am Sun; ☒ Ⓥ) This simple cafe, unsurprisingly attached to the cinema, is a local meeting spot and a good place for coffee, all-day breakfast or light lunches such as burgers or sandwiches.

our pick **Kumbidgee Lodge Tea Rooms** (☎ 8971 0699; Gorge Rd; mains $7-18; ☺ 7am-8.30pm; ☒) On the road to Nitmiluk, 10km from Katherine, Kumbidgee is a tranquil spot with a big deck overlooking a small pond and a few pet goats to keep the kids happy. It's a great spot to indulge in a hearty 'bush breakfast' ($13) or a Devonshire tea while catching up with the rest of the world in the newspapers. The Sunday buffet breakfast ($12) is a popular local outing. It's also well known for its barramundi dishes and is BYO.

Katie's Bistro (☎ 8972 2511; Knotts Crossing Resort, cnr Giles & Cameron Sts; mains $19-38; ☺ breakfast & dinner; ☒) This intimate little bistro at Knotts Crossing Resort is locally regarded as one of Katherine's best. Wagyu beef, lobster and prawn pasta, and grilled outback camel grace the eclectic menu, and you can eat inside or alfresco by the pool.

Carriage Restaurant (☎ 8972 2644; Paraway Motel, O'Shea Tce; mains $27-35; ☺ dinner Wed-Sun; ☒) The Carriage specialises in stone-grill cooking, where the meat of your choice is brought to your table on heated stone. Also on the menu is grilled barramundi and Asian spiced pork loin. The outdoor seating area with high-backed wicker chairs is much more atmospheric than the dining room. It's pricey but popular, so book ahead.

To stock up on groceries, head to **Woolworth's** (Oasis Shopping Centre, Katherine Tce; ☺ 7am-10pm). The Oasis Shopping Centre also has a liquor shop and a bakery.

DRINKING & ENTERTAINMENT

If you're buying takeaway alcohol, it's worth knowing the rules here. Drinking in public places is banned, alcohol is only sold between 2pm and 8pm weekdays and Sunday, and noon and 8pm Saturday, and photo ID must be shown to purchase alcohol.

Katherine Tce, the main drag, has two fairly rowdy pubs a block apart. **Katherine Hotel** (☎ 8972 1622; cnr Katherine Tce & Giles St) has occasional live bands and a giant barnlike beer garden at the back.

Crossways Hotel (☎ 8972 1022; 23 Katherine Tce) also has a big breezy beer garden and Katherine's only nightclub, the **Base** (☺ 9pm-4am Fri & Sat), which kicks off around 1am and can get pretty messy.

For a quieter drink, try the **Katherine Club** (☎ 8972 1250; cnr Second St & O'Shea Tce), which has two bars, pool tables and live music on weekends.

Katherine Cinema 3 (☎ 8971 2555; www.katherine cinemas.com.au; 20 First St; adult/child $13/8) screens current-release movies, usually from Wednesday to Sunday.

SHOPPING

Mimi Aboriginal Art & Craft (☎ 8971 0036; www .mimiarts.com; 6 Pearce St; ☺ 8.30am-4.30pm Mon-Fri) This Aboriginal-owned co-op sells quality art and crafts from the Katherine, Arnhem Land and Kimberley regions.

Coco's Katherine Didjeridoos (☎ 8971 2889; 21 First St) Coco sells didgeridoos in a variety of keys (A to G) from a shed next to his hostel (p224) and will happily demonstrate their sounds and uses.

Katherine Art Gallery (☎ 8971 1051; www.katherine artgallery.com.au; 12 Katherine Tce) Wide range of art, didgeridoos and carvings from the Katherine area as well as the central deserts and Arnhem Land.

Top Didj & Art Gallery (☎ 8971 2751; 3045 Jaensch Rd; ☺ 9am-6pm May-Oct) Run by the owners of the Katherine Art Gallery, this is a good place to meet Indigenous artists at work in the backyard, along with the pet emu. The gallery displays quality works from around the Territory.

NT Rare Rocks (☎ 8971 0889; 1809 Zimin Dr) All sorts of souvenirs, jewellery and crafts made from unusual polished rocks such as zebra stone and rainbow siltstone, as well as gems and crystals.

Katherine Camping & Fishing (☎ 8972 3456; cnr Katherine Tce & Victoria Hwy) A big range of camping gear, caravan accessories and fishing gear.

GETTING THERE & AWAY
AIR

Katherine's airport is 11km south of town and shared with the Tindal air-force base. **Airnorth** (☎ 1800 627 474) and a number of other companies fly charters to/from Katherine from Darwin and Alice Springs and other destinations in the Territory.

BUS

Katherine is a major road junction in this part of the Territory: apart from the Stuart Hwy tracking north and south, the Victoria Hwy heads west from here to Kununurra in WA. **Greyhound Australia** (☎ 1300 473 946; www.greyhound .com.au) has regular services between Darwin and Alice Springs, Queensland or WA. All buses stop at Katherine's **Transit Centre** (☎ 8971 9999; 6 Katherine Tce). Typical one-way fares from Katherine include Darwin ($84, four hours), Alice Springs ($253, 16 hours), Tennant Creek ($166, 8½ hours) and Kununurra ($130, five hours).

TRAIN

The *Ghan* train travels between Adelaide and Darwin twice a week, stopping at Katherine for four hours – enough for a whistlestop tour to Katherine Gorge; see p303 for timetable and fare details. Katherine train station is off the Victoria Hwy, 9km southwest of town. **Travel North** (☎ 8971 9999; Transit Centre) runs shuttles between the station and town.

GETTING AROUND

The town centre is compact enough to walk around, although most sights, such as the thermal pools and museum, are a bit far apart. Katherine is more or less flat and cycling is a good way to get around – unfortunately there was nowhere to hire a bike at the time of research. Palm Court Kookaburra Backpackers (p224) may have some by the time you read this.

Taxis congregate at a stand near the corner of Warburton and First Sts. Alternatively, call **Katherine Taxis** (☎ 8972 177).

AROUND KATHERINE

NITMILUK (KATHERINE GORGE) NATIONAL PARK

Spectacular Katherine Gorge forms the backbone of this 2920-sq-km park, about 30km from Katherine. A series of 13 deep sandstone gorges has been carved out by the Katherine River on its journey from Arnhem Land to the Timor Sea. It is a hauntingly beautiful place – though it can get crowded in peak season – and a must-see from Katherine. In the Dry the tranquil river is perfect for a paddle, but in the Wet the deep, still waters and dividing rapids are engulfed by an awesome torrent that churns through the gorge. Plan to spend at least a full day, canoeing or cruising on the river and bushwalking.

The lesser-known Leliyn (Edith Falls), also part of Nitmiluk, is accessible from the Stuart Hwy, 40km north of Katherine (see p231). Leliyn has a lovely swimming hole, waterfalls and walking trails. Access roads to both sections of the park are sealed, but may be cut off for short periods during the wet season.

What was once Katherine Gorge National Park was proclaimed in 1962. In 1989 the Jawoyn Aboriginal people gained ownership following a land claim that had been lodged in the late 1970s. The name was changed to Nitmiluk and the land leased back to Parks & Wildlife. It is now managed by the Nitmiluk Board of Management, which has a Jawoyn majority, and traditional practices such as hunting, food gathering and ceremonies are still carried out in the park. Nitmiluk is the Jawoyn name for the Cicada Dreaming, which takes in the area from the Nitmiluk Centre up to the end of the first gorge.

Information

The **Nitmiluk Centre** (☎ 1800 089 103, 8972 1253; www.nitmiluktours.com.au; ☼ 7am-7pm May-Aug, to 4pm Sep-Apr) has excellent displays and information on the park's geology, wildlife, the traditional owners (the Jawoyn) and European history. There's also a desk for **Parks & Wildlife** (☎ 8972 1886), which has information sheets on a wide range of marked walking tracks that start here and traverse the picturesque country south of the gorge. Some of the tracks pass Aboriginal rock paintings up to 7000 years old. The more detailed *Guide to Nitmiluk (Katherine Gorge) National Park* ($6.60) is also available here. Registration for overnight walks and camping permits ($3.30 per person per night) is from 7am to 1pm; canoeing permits are also issued. Check at the centre for information on ranger talks.

The Nitmiluk Centre, camping ground and boat tours are all wheelchair accessible.

NITMILUK (KATHERINE GORGE)

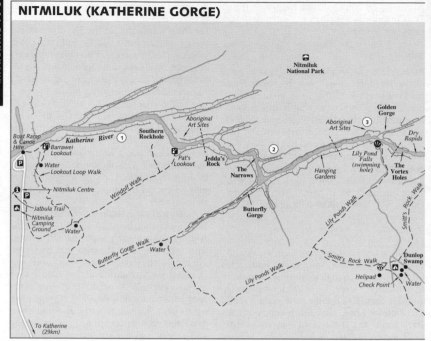

Nitmiluk National Park

Katherine River

Boat Ramp & Canoe Hire
Barrawei Lookout
Water
Lookout Loop Walk
Nitmiluk Centre
Jatbula Trail
Nitmiluk Camping Ground
Water

Southern Rockhole

Aboriginal Art Sites

Pat's Lookout
Jedda's Rock
The Narrows

Windolf Walk

Butterfly Gorge

Butterfly Gorge Walk
Water

Aboriginal Art Sites

Golden Gorge

Dry Rapids

Lily Pond Falls (swimming hole)
The Vortex Holes

Hanging Gardens

Hanging Gardens

Lily Ponds Walk

Smitt's Rock Walk

Smitt's Rock Walk
Dunlop Swamp

Helipad
Check Point

Water

To Katherine (29km)

Activities

SWIMMING

The gorge is usually safe for swimming in the Dry and there's a designated swimming platform near the picnic area. However, it's probably best enjoyed by taking a canoe and finding your own space somewhere upstream.

In the Wet the gorge is closed to boats and canoes. The only crocodiles around are generally the freshwater variety; however, Parks & Wildlife staff will advise if the situation is otherwise.

BUSHWALKING

The park has around 120km of walking tracks, ranging from short strolls to the 58km one-way Jatbula Trail to Leliyn (Edith Falls).

Walkers setting out on any overnight walk must register and deregister at the Nitmiluk Centre. There's a $50 refundable deposit for any overnight walk and a camping fee of $3.30 per person per night. For day walks, registration is not necessary, but you should inform someone of your intentions, and you can voluntarily register with the ranger. Don't forget to deregister on return.

The main walks, all of which are clearly marked, are listed here. Note that all distances are return (measured from the Nitmiluk Centre), and that times will vary depending on the individual and the weather.

Barrawei (Lookout) Loop (3.7km loop, one hour, medium) A short, steep climb with good views over the Katherine River.

Windolf (8.4km return, three hours, medium) A good walk that features a swimming spot at the southern rockhole near the end of the first gorge.

Butterfly Gorge (12km return, 4½ hours, difficult) A shady walk through a pocket of monsoon rainforest, often with butterflies, leads to midway along the second gorge and a deep-water swimming spot.

Lily Ponds (20km return, 6½ hours, difficult) This walk leads to Lily Pond Falls, at the far end of the third gorge. Ask at the Nitmiluk Centre for an update on the swimming hole here.

Smitt's Rock (24km return, 8½ hours, difficult) A rugged trek that takes you to Smitt's Rock near the start of the fifth gorge. There are excellent gorge views along the way, and you can swim and camp overnight at Dunlop Swamp.

Eighth Gorge (33km return, overnight, difficult) Most of the way this trail is actually well away from the edge of the gorge, only coming down to it at the end.

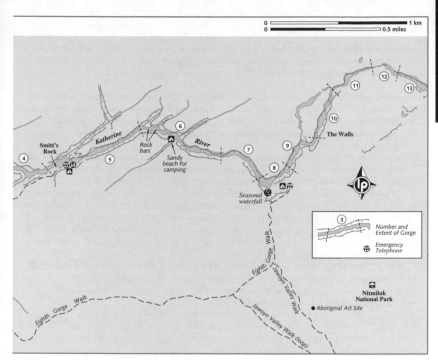

Jawoyn Valley (40km loop, overnight, difficult) A wilderness loop trail leading off the Eighth Gorge walk into a valley with rock outcrops and rock-art galleries.

Jatbula Trail (58km, four to five days, difficult) This walk to Leliyn (Edith Falls) climbs the Arnhem Land escarpment, taking in features such as the swamp-fed Biddlecombe Cascades, Crystal Falls, the Amphitheatre and the Sweetwater Pool. This walk can only be done one way (ie you can't walk from Leliyn to Katherine Gorge) and a minimum of two people are required to do the walk. A ferry service ($5) takes you across the gorge to begin this walk.

CANOEING

Nothing beats exploring the gorges in your own boat, and lots of travellers canoe at least as far as the first or second gorge. Bear in mind the intensity of the sun and heat, and the fact that you may have to carry your canoe over the rock bars and rapids that separate the gorges. Pick up the *Canoeing Guide* (which shows points of interest along the way, such as rock art, waterfalls and plantlife) at the Nitmiluk Centre (p227).

Nitmiluk Tours (☎ 8972 1253) hires out single/double canoes for a half-day ($40/59, departing 8am and 12.30pm) or full day ($51/76, departing 8am), including the use of a splash-proof drum for cameras and other gear (it's not fully waterproof), a map and a life jacket. The half-day hire only allows you to paddle up the first gorge; with the full day you can get up as far as the fourth gorge depending on your level of fitness – start early. The canoe shed is at the boat ramp by the main car park, about 500m beyond the Nitmiluk Centre (p227).

You also can be a little more adventurous and take the canoes out overnight for $98 per person, plus $3.30 for an overnight camping permit – there are campsites at the fifth, sixth, eighth and ninth gorges. Bookings are essential as overnight permits are limited and there is a $60 deposit. Don't take this trip lightly though – see p230. It's also possible to use your own canoe in the gorge for a registration fee of $5.50 per person per day, plus a refundable $50 deposit.

FISHING

There are more than 40 species of fish in the river (including barramundi), which makes fishing, by lure only, popular here. Fishing gear is available in Katherine; ask the locals for location tips.

PADDLING KATHERINE GORGE

Canoeing up beautiful Katherine Gorge may seem like a leisurely paddle, but it's not for the faint-hearted and if you're planning on camping, you'll definitely have to carry that canoe at some point. Leonie Starnawski took to the water and found out the true meaning of portage.

The staff members laughed and told us we'd sink. They then produced garbage bags for our surplus gear, of which we filled about three. We informed our sole male companion (to his shock) that he'd have to go without a tent that night – it was, after all, supposed to be an 'under the stars adventure'. The two waterproof canisters would hold our jumpers, food and camera equipment, just barely.

Thus unburdened we threw ourselves, four sleeping bags, the waterproof canisters, a gas cooker, and a backpack (containing not much more than a pillow and some pasta) into two double canoes and we were away…with no idea what we had let ourselves in for.

We knew we had to canoe at least as far as the fifth gorge, as it was the first camping point. We'd added up the paddling times and this mysterious 'portage', of which we knew little, and they amounted to only four and a half hours. Although we had zero canoeing experience and the staff had told us little, we were optimistic, brazen even. Not so the bloke at the end of the pier, who upon seeing our 'skills' deemed it necessary to shout out instructions: 'paddle left to turn right'. It was about 11am.

Portage, we learned, means clambering up and over piles of sharp and slippery rocks carrying all the gear we thought we needed – and a bloody heavy canoe. We were soaked through – the beige cargo pants worn by our usually immaculate Polish girlfriend had turned transparent – but it was 30-something degrees and no time for pride.

Six or so exhausting hours later we landed on the beach of the sixth gorge; cut, bruised and unamused. But after a rest and a bug-infested pasta meal, we were sleepily content. The stars were out, we had the beach to ourselves, we were warm and untroubled by mosquitoes. We didn't yet know that sometime the next day we would fail to turn in to the sixth gorge portage point in time, hit some rapids, capsize our canoe and end up in the water with everything we owned. As the information sheet says, 'it's an encounter you will never forget'. I, for one, can't wait to do it again.

Leonie Starnawski is a Lonely Planet staff member

Tours

GORGE CRUISES

A popular way to see far into the gorge is on one of the numerous cruises run by **Nitmiluk Tours** (☎ 1300 146 743, 8972 1253; www.nitmiluktours.com .au). Bookings on some cruises can be tight in the peak season, so it's a good idea to make a reservation the day before.

The two-hour cruise (adult/child $53/30) goes to the second gorge and visits a rock-art gallery (including 800m walk). Departures are at 9am, 11am, 1pm and 3pm daily year-round. There's wheelchair access to the top of the first gorge only. The four-hour cruise (adult/child $69/32) goes to the third gorge and includes refreshments and a chance to swim. Cruises leave at 9am daily from April to November, plus at 11am and 1pm May to August. Finally, there's the full-day eight-hour trip (adult or child $110), which takes you up to the fifth gorge,

involves walking about 5km and includes a barbecue lunch and refreshments. It departs at 8am daily from May to October.

There's also a more leisurely dawn breakfast cruise (adult/child $59/47, 7am April to November) with a full buffet breakfast; a two-hour lunch cruise (adult/child $69/40, noon Monday to Saturday); and a sunset cruise (adult/child $116/101, 4.30pm Wednesday and Friday to Monday, April to November), with a candlelit buffet dinner and sparkling wine.

SCENIC FLIGHTS

Nitmiluk Helicopter Tours (☎ 1300 146 743; www.air bournesolutions.com.au; flights per person from $75) has a variety of flights ranging from an eight-minute buzz over the first three gorges ($75 per person) to an 18-minute flight over all 13 gorges ($165). The Adventure Swim Tour ($285) drops you at a secluded swimming hole for an hour or so, and there are broader tours that take in Aboriginal rock-art sites, Kakadu and a cattle station. Book at the Nitmiluk Centre (opposite).

Sleeping & Eating
A luxury Indigenous-owned and -operated resort called Cicada Lodge was due to open in the park early in 2009.

Nitmiluk Caravan Park (☎ 8972 1253; unpowered/powered sites $19/24, safari tent $80; ⬚) This park has plenty of grass and shade and is well equipped with hot showers, toilets, barbecues and laundry. Wallabies and goannas are frequent visitors. There's a 'tent village' here with permanent safari tents sleeping two people, with camp beds and linen provided: the package is good value as it includes dinner at the bistro and return transfers from Katherine.

Nitmiluk Bistro (☎ 8972 1253; Nitmiluk Centre; mains $12-20; ◷ breakfast, lunch & dinner; ⬚) Relaxing on the broad timber deck at this licensed cafe is a great way to unwind after a walk, cruise or canoeing trip. Full breakfasts, snacks and lunches, such as burgers and salads, are on offer.

Getting There & Away
It's 30km by sealed road from Katherine to the Nitmiluk Centre (opposite), and a few hundred metres further to the car park, where the gorge begins and the cruises start.

Daily **transfers** (return adult/child $24/12) between Katherine and the gorge run from the Nitmiluk Tour Booking Centre in Katherine and pick up at local accommodation places on request. From April to September they leave Katherine at 8am, 12.15pm and 4pm, returning from Nitmiluk at 9am, 1pm and 5pm. From October to March they leave at 8am and 4pm, returning at 9am and 5pm. Seats are usually booked with cruise bookings.

NORTH OF KATHERINE

KATHERINE TO LITCHFIELD NATIONAL PARK
The highway continues northwest from Katherine and, although Darwin is the next town of any real size, there's plenty to see. North of the old mining town of Pine Creek the highway starts to pass through more undulating landscape, revealing occasional views stretching north towards Litchfield and Kakadu, and west of Hayes Creek is an interesting detour to the Douglas–Daly River region.

Leliyn (Edith Falls)
Although within Nitmiluk National Park (see p227), Leliyn is included here because it's accessed off the Stuart Hwy 40km north of Katherine and a further 20km along a sealed road to the falls and camping ground. The falls themselves cascade into the lowest of three large pools; it's a beautiful, safe place for swimming and a ranger is stationed here throughout the year.

The **Leliyn Trail** (2.6km loop, 1½ hours) climbs into escarpment country through grevillea and spinifex and past scenic lookouts (Bemang is best in the afternoon) to the Upper Pool, where the **Sweetwater Pool Trail** (8.6km return, three to five hours, medium) branches off. The peaceful Sweetwater Pool has a small camping site; overnight permits are available at the kiosk.

The Parks & Wildlife **camping ground** (☎ 8975 4869; adult/child/family $8.80/4.50/20) at the main pool has grassy sites, lots of shade, toilets, showers, a laundry and disabled facilities. Fees are paid at the **kiosk** (◷ 8am-6pm), which sells snacks and basic supplies. Nearby is a picnic area with gas barbecues and tables.

Nitmiluk Tours (☎ 8972 1253; www.nitmiluk.com.au) has transfers from Katherine (one way/return $35/45) daily from May to September and by request from October to March.

Umbrawarra Gorge Nature Park
The tranquil Umbrawarra Gorge Nature Park features some Aboriginal rock-art sites, small sandy beaches and safe swimming in the rock pools. The turn-off is about 3km south of Pine Creek; it's then 22km along a dirt road (often impassable in the Wet) to the park. Although passable to 2WD vehicles in the Dry, it can get very rough and corrugated. The creek stops flowing late in the dry season.

In Aboriginal legend, the gorge is the Dreaming site of *Kuna-ngarrk-ngarrk*, the white-bellied sea-eagle. Here he caught and ate a barramundi; the white flakes in the granite rock are said to be the scales of the barra, and the quartz outcrops are the eagle's droppings. Rock art can be seen along the gorge walls at its eastern end.

There's a basic **camping ground** (adult/child/family $3.30/1.65/7.70) with tables, pit toilet and fireplaces.

Pine Creek
pop 256

A short detour off the Stuart Hwy, Pine Creek was once the scene of a frantic gold rush and although the open-cut mine here ceased in 1995, today there's a new influx of mine workers from the recently opened gold and iron ore mines nearby. A few of the old 19th century timber and corrugated-iron buildings still survive and there are museums devoted to the town's history and the railway that started here in 1889.

The town itself is 1km or so off the highway, which gives it a sleepy atmosphere, undisturbed by the road trains thundering up and down the highway. It's a reasonably popular stopover since the Kakadu Hwy to Cooinda and Jabiru meets the Stuart Hwy here.

HISTORY

In the early 1870s labourers working on the OTL found gold here, sparking a rush that was to last nearly 20 years. Chinese workers were brought in to do much of the tough mining work and it was not long before more Chinese began arriving under their own steam, eventually outnumbering Europeans 15 to one. By 1889 Pine Creek had become the terminus of the newly built North Australian Railway.

SIGHTS

Dating from 1888, the **railway station** (admission free; daily) has a display on the Darwin to Pine Creek railway (1889–1976). The lovingly restored steam engine, built in Manchester in 1877, sits in its own enclosure next to the museum.

Pine Creek Museum (Railway Tce; adult/child $2.20/free; 11am-5pm Mon-Fri, to 1pm Sat & Sun May-Oct), in an old mining warden's residence, has mining memorabilia and a mineral collection, plus old telegraph equipment and bric-a-brac.

You can drive or walk up the short-but-steep hill off Moule St to a **lookout** overlooking the old open-cut mine, now full of water.

SLEEPING & EATING

The opening of mines in the area has put a strain on accommodation in Pine Creek

as mine workers take up the best beds, but there are three caravan and camping sites in town.

Lazy Lizard Tourist Park & Tavern (☎ 8976 1224; unpowered/powered sites $15/20;) The small but well-grassed camping area at the Lazy Lizard is really only secondary to the pulsing pub next door (mains $16 to $32; lunch and dinner). The open-sided bar, which is supported by carved ironwood pillars, is a great local watering hole and the kitchen here serves top-notch pub food that leans heavily towards NT favourites: big steaks and barra dishes.

Pine Creek Hotel-Motel (☎ 8976 1288; 40 Moule St; s/d/tr $90/110/125;) If you call ahead you should be able to get basic, comfortable in a room at the motel behind the Pine Creek Hotel.

Bonrook Country Stay (☎ 8976 1232; www.bonrook.com; Stuart Hwy; s/d $50/60, deluxe d $85-120, f $120;) Just 8km south of town, this tranquil B&B has a beautiful setting on a wild horse sanctuary where the brumbies are free to roam. The spotless rooms have no TV and no phone – just the sound of the wind in the trees and the birds outside. There's plenty of opportunity to relax in the spa pools and barbecue area.

Mayse's Cafe (☎ 8976 1241; Moule St; meals $4-12; 7am-3pm) Mayse's works hard to have an identity with a Hollywood-memorabilia theme and various pop-culture mementos. Its namesake, Mayse Young, was a one-time publican of the Pine Creek pub. Her autobiography *No Place for a Woman* is on sale at the cafe. The food is reasonable and the mango smoothies and homemade iced coffee worth stopping for.

Hayes Creek

Hayes Creek, 54km north of Pine Creek, is little more than a roadside stop. This is also a junction where you can detour off the Stuart Hwy and take an interesting alternative route to Adelaide River via the sealed Old Stuart Hwy (Dorat Rd).

Hayes Creek Holiday Park (☎ 8978 2430; www.hayescreek.com.au; 455 Stuart Hwy; unpowered/powered sites $18/28, motel d $70;) has friendly, authentic charm with a lovely camping ground that's rarely crowded. There's a spring-fed waterhole nearby and a rocky escarpment that catches the evening sun. The roadhouse has a bar and bistro.

DETOUR: HAYES CREEK TO ADELAIDE RIVER VIA DOUGLAS DALY REGION

From Hayes Creek you can continue on the Stuart Hwy northwest for 60km to Adelaide River, or turn off to one of the Territory's best natural hot springs and an interesting drive along the convoluted original Stuart Hwy.

Dorat Rd turns west off the main highway 6km north of Hayes Creek. After 5km, turn south on the sealed Oolloo Rd which leads to Douglas Daly Park and Oolloo Crossing. Historical reminders of WWII include the remains of **Fenton Airbase** which was headquarters to a large number of American and Australian air-force personnel. It's reached down a rough, deeply rutted track (best for 4WDs) and there's not much left to see. Further south is a turnoff to the old **airfield** with the remains of a former aircraft 'graveyard' here, where damaged war birds were left to rust in peace.

Tjuwaliyn (Douglas) Hot Springs

The hot springs at Tjuwaliyn are part of Wagiman country and a great place to spend the afternoon swimming or to camp overnight. Drive 35km down Oolloo Rd then 7km down a dirt track (passable to 2WD vehicles). The hot springs themselves are piping at 40°C to 60°C – too hot for bathing – but where these waters mix with the Douglas River there are some fine shallow bathing spots – check the water temperature first. The **camping ground** (adult/child/family $6.60/3.30/16) here has pit toilets, barbecues, picnic tables and drinking water.

Butterfly Gorge Nature Park

A 4WD track stretches 17km beyond Tjuwaliyn Hot Springs to Butterfly Gorge Nature Park. True to its name, butterflies sometimes swarm in the gorge, which is reached via a short walking track through a tall paperbark forest from the car park. The gorge is a 70m-deep gash cut through the sandstone escarpment by the Douglas River. There are numerous rock pools, the large one at the base of the gorge being a popular swimming hole.

Dorat Road

Back on Dorat Rd, after about 30km you pass the Daly River Rd turnoff which leads to Daly River and the Nauiya Aboriginal community. Continuing on you'll feel like you're on a roller coaster as the narrow bitumen road twists, turns and dips sharply past old mining sites and smouldering scrub. After about 15km is the turn-off to **Robin Falls**, a picturesque little waterfall that tumbles into a two-tier plunge pool. From the car park it's a 10-minute scramble along a rocky path (wear closed shoes) to the falls. Back on Dorat Rd it's 15km to Adelaide River and the Stuart Hwy.

Daly River

The Daly River is considered some of the best barramundi fishing country in the Territory and the hub is this small community 117km southwest of Hayes Creek, reached by a narrow sealed road off the Old Stuart Hwy.

Most of the population lives in the Nauiya Nambiyu Aboriginal community, a few kilometres before Daly River Crossing. There's a shop and fuel here and visitors are welcome without a permit, but note that this is a dry community (no alcohol). The main attraction here is **Merrepen Arts** (☎ 8978 2533; www .merrepenarts.com; ☼ 10am-5pm), a gallery displaying locally made arts and crafts including etchings, screen printing, acrylic paintings, carvings, weaving and textiles. You can usually see artists at work in the mornings.

The **Merrepen Arts Festival**, held on the first weekend in June, celebrates arts and music from communities around the district, such as Nauiya, Wadeye and Peppimenarti.

At Daly River itself is the **Daly River Roadside Inn** (☎ 8978 2418), a boisterous pub with basic rooms, a small campground and meals and fuel available.

SLEEPING

There are bush campsites along the Daly River but watch out for crocs – the river is infested with salties.

The best places to stay are the various tourist parks and fishing camps, which are split into two main areas. All of these places offer guided fishing tours from around $250 per person per day – what you're really paying for is for local knowledge. Down Wooliana Rd, about 4.5km before the turn-off to Nauiya, is a string of fishing camps near the river, while past the Daly River Crossing are two more excellent fishing retreats.

Perry's (☎ 8978 2452; www.dalyriver.com; Mayo Park; unpowered/powered sites $24/30; 🖳 🛋) This is a very peaceful place to get away from it all with 2km of river frontage and gardens where or-phaned wallabies bound around. Dick Perry is a well-known fishing expert and operates guided trips.

Daly River Mango Farm (☎ 1800 000 576, 8978 2464; www.mangofarm.com.au; unpowered/powered sites $24/30, budget d $100-150, cabins $120-180; 🕃 🛋) Signposted 9km from the river crossing, this welcoming place is right on the banks of the river. Once the site of a Jesuit mission, and the first mango farm in Australia, its magnificent grove of 90-year-old mango trees shades the grassy camping ground.

Adelaide River
pop 190
Adelaide River is another small Stuart Hwy stop with a big history. It was an impor-tant point on the OTL, the North Australia Railway, and as a rest camp and supply depot during WWII.

The **Railway Museum** (☎ 8976 7101; admission $2 donation; ⏰ 9am-4pm May-Oct, variable hr Nov-Apr), near the Daly River Rd turn-off, is part of the historic rail precinct. It also acts as an information centre.

Well signposted east of the highway just north of the river, the **Adelaide River War Cemetery** is the largest war cemetery in the country. The rows of simple headstones hon-our those killed in the Japanese air raids dur-ing WWII. There are a few picnic tables and gas barbecues in a tranquil park along the river bank here.

SLEEPING & EATING
ourpick **Mt Bundy Station** (☎ 8976 7009; www.mt bundy.com.au; Haynes Rd; unpowered/powered sites $20/24, s/d $35/70, cottage from $165, B&B $260; 🕃 🛋) If you're into horse riding, fishing or just relaxing with some country-style hospitality, Mt Bundy is the perfect detour, just 3km off the highway before Adelaide River. Original station build-ings are now a spotless 20-bed bunkhouse with kitchen and a separate cottage sleeping six. Up on the hill in the family residence are two beautiful boutique B&B rooms where you

can enjoy sunset drinks and panoramic views from the balcony. There are plenty of animals on the property: guided horse riding costs from $35 for a half-hour to $100 for a half-day, and overnight treks can be arranged.

Adelaide River Inn (☎ 8976 7047; unpowered/pow-ered sites $15/20, cabins $120; 🕃 🛋) Dominating the highway just north of the bridge, an affable little pub hides behind the roadhouse with a compact caravan park and camping area. The pub is worth stopping in for a beer – on the corner of the bar stands Charlie the water buffalo, who lived here in relative obscurity until shooting to fame in *Crocodile Dundee*. When he died the owner had him stuffed for posterity. The Diggers Bistro serves moun-tainous pub food (mains $17 to $22) such as steaks and barra with chips all day.

Batchelor
pop 480
The small, neatly laid out little town of Batchelor lies 12km west of the Stuart Hwy. It was established in 1952 to service Australia's first uranium mine, Rum Jungle, which closed in 1971. Today it serves as the main gateway to Litchfield National Park and is also home to the Batchelor Institute for Indigenous Education, an excellent art centre and some fine accommodation.

Across the road from the general store is a small **visitors centre** (⏰ 8.30am-5pm) with bro-chures and information on Litchfield.

For free internet access try the **Batchelor Library** (Batchelor Institute; ☎ 1800 677 095; Nurndina St; ⏰ 10am-8pm Mon, 8am-8pm Tue-Thu, to 4pm Fri, 1-4.30pm Sun, closed Sat).

The **Coomalie Cultural Centre** (☎ 8939 7404; www .coomaliaculturalcentre.com; cnr Awillia Rd & Nurndina Sts; ⏰ 10am-5pm Tue-Sat Apr-Sep, 1to 4pm Tue-Fri Oct-Mar) displays and sells a range of Indigenous art and crafts from throughout the Territory and runs an artist-in-residence program, so you'll often see artists at work.

The **Batchelor Butterfly & Petting Farm** (☎ 8976 0199; www.butterflyfarm.net; 8 Meneling Rd; adult/child/fam-ily $10/5/25; ⏰ 9am-4.30pm) is a pleasant diversion, with large walk-through enclosures full of but-terflies (including the beautiful electric blue Ulysses), pigs, rabbits, peacocks and galahs. Great for kids.

SLEEPING & EATING
Although most travellers are naturally headed into Litchfield, this gateway town offers some

quality accommodation. The **Batchelor General Store** (☎ 8976 0450; ☽ 7am-6pm) has a well-stocked supermarket, takeaway shop, newsagent and post office.

Batchelor Resort (☎ 8976 0166; www.batchelor-resort .com; 37-49 Rum Jungle Rd; unpowered/powered sites $24/30-50, self-contained cabins $115, motel d $168; ⊠ ⊠ ⊑) On the edge of town, this impressive resort complex has a sprawling caravan park with en suite sites and cabins, and a separate motel section. It's good for families, with an 18-hole mini golf course, bird-feeding and two pools. There are two licensed resorts, a bar and a shop selling groceries and Batchelor's only takeaway alcohol.

Batchelor Butterfly & Bird Farm (☎ 8976 0199; www.butterflyfarm.net; 8 Meneling Rd; d $85-95, f $150, bungalow $160; ⊠ ⊑ ⊠) The enthusiastic owner here has been busy building Batchelor's quirkiest accommodation for years now. The self-contained house behind the butterfly enclosure has three colourful rooms with hand-crafted mahogany beds, and there's a pair of cosy en suite bungalows that sleep up to four. Call into the **cafe** (mains $12-23; ☽ 8am-8.30pm; ⓥ) for some comfort food such as nasi goreng, lentil burgers and garlic prawns – it's all very Zen with Buddha statues, sitar music and wicker chairs on the shaded deck.

our pick **Historic Retreat B&B** (☎ 8976 0554; www .historicretreat.com.au; 19 Pinaroo Cres; d $120-180; ⊠) The beautifully restored former home of Rum Jungle mine managers, this elevated tropical-style place has louvred windows, polished floorboards, vintage furniture and your own 'butler'. The five guest rooms share two bathrooms and a modern well-equipped kitchen, with a 'silver service' breakfast included.

Rum Jungle Bungalows (☎ 8976 0555; www.rumjungle bungalows.com.au; 10 Meneling Rd; d $140; ⊠ ⊑ ⊠) Lush tropical gardens veil the six modern Bali-inspired bungalows in this intimate space. Each has a patio, bathroom, TV and fridge and comes with tropical breakfast. Two bungalows can sleep a family of four.

Beyond Batchelor, on the road to Litchfield, are two caravan parks that make good bases for day trips into the park.

Banyan Tree Caravan & Tourist Park (☎ 8976 0330; www.banyan-tree.com.au; Litchfield Park Rd; unpowered/ powered sites $17/20, budget r $65, cabins $110-135; ⊠ ⊠) Located 11km from Batchelor, this place has grassy, shaded sites and clean brightly-painted cabins.

Litchfield Tourist & Van Park (☎ 8976 0070; www .litchfieldtouristpark.com.au; Litchfield Park Rd; unpowered/

powered sites $18/24, cabins $75-105; ⊠ ⊠) Just 2km further on, the standout feature here is the two-bedroom ranch-style house that you can rent for $500 (it sleeps 15!) or for $105 per couple,and the highly regarded **Leslee's on Litchfield Restaurant** (mains $12-23; ☽ 8am-8pm)

LITCHFIELD NATIONAL PARK

It may not be as well known as Kakadu, but many Territory locals rate Litchfield even higher. It's certainly one of the best places in the Top End for swimming, with waterfalls plunging into gorgeous swimming holes, but also for bushwalking, camping and 4WDing.

The 1500-sq-km national park encloses much of the spectacular Tabletop Range, a wide sandstone plateau mostly surrounded by cliffs. The waterfalls that pour off the edge of this plateau are a highlight of the park, feeding crystal-clear cascades and croc-free plunge pools. Top dips are at Florence Falls, Buley Rockhole and the large pool at Wangi Falls. Along the way you'll discover unusual termite mounds, curious sandstone formations and superb bushwalking country. National Parks campsites near the swimming holes are complemented by a number of commercial caravan parks just outside the park boundary. If Litchfield does have a drawback, it's that it can get incredibly crowded, especially on dry season weekends or holidays. Try to time your visit for a weekday.

Information

There's a small visitors centre at Batchelor (opposite), and an information bay 5km inside the park's eastern boundary with a map showing walks and road closures. Informative signboards at most sites explain geology, flora and fauna, and Aboriginal activity.

A ranger is stationed near the northern entrance to the park, but should only be contacted in an emergency. During the Dry the rangers conduct a number of talks; activities aimed at increasing your enjoyment and knowledge of the park. The schedule is published in the widely available *Come Alive in Territory Parks* and should be posted at the information bays on the way into the park and at Wangi Falls. There are emergency call devices (ECD) at Florence, Tolmer, Wangi and Tjaynera Falls.

Sights
MAGNETIC TERMITE MOUNDS
About 17km from the eastern boundary of the park is a field of curious termite mounds that are all aligned roughly north–south. A small

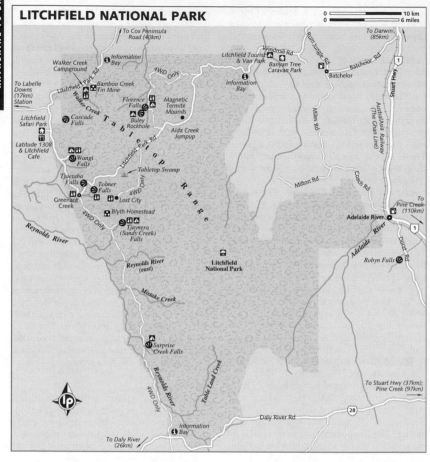

LITCHFIELD NATIONAL PARK

boardwalk takes you out close to some of the mounds, and an excellent information display explains how and why the mounds came to be. Nearby are some giant mounds of the aptly named cathedral termites.

BULEY ROCKHOLE & FLORENCE FALLS

Almost immediately after the termite mounds, the road climbs the escarpment up the Aida Creek Jumpup and after 6km you come to the Florence Falls turn-off on the eastern edge of the plateau. The falls lie in a pocket of monsoon forest 5km off the road.

Buley Rockhole is a very popular swimming spot of bubbling horizontal cascades and pools, with toilets and picnic tables. A track from the day-use car park (3.2km return,

1½ hours including swim) follows Florence Creek to Florence Falls.

Florence Falls has a walking track (with wheelchair access), 200m from the car park, that leads to a lookout over the gorgeous twin falls and an idyllic plunge pool. This excellent swimming hole is reached via a boardwalk and staircase (500m, 15 minutes) or via the Shady Creek walk (1.8km return, one hour including swim), which features small pools near several picturesque picnic areas upstream. The best route is to take the boardwalk down and Shady Creek walk back, via the Monsoon Forest Garden and Savannah Woodland Garden. There's also a trail that links to the longer Tabletop Track, which encircles the Tabletop Range.

LOST CITY

Erosion of softer soils, gouged out of the plateau, has left these more resistant sandstone columns and blocks that, with a little imagination, resemble ruined buildings. There's a short walk around the 'city', but no facilities or water. The Lost City turn-off is 4.2km from the Florence Falls turn-off. The 10.5km (30 minutes) access track is 4WD only.

TABLETOP SWAMP

About 5km past the Lost City turn-off a track to the left leads a few hundred metres to Tabletop Swamp. This small, paperbark-ringed wetland supports water birds, such as green pygmy geese and large egrets, and there are honeyeaters feeding on the paperbark blossom. A short walk goes around the swamp and there are picnic tables.

TOLMER FALLS

The Tolmer Falls turn-off is 6km past the swamp. Here the escarpment offers sweeping views over the tropical woodland stretching away to the horizon. The falls, which cascade spectacularly into a deep, narrow gorge, screen a series of caves that form the largest known breeding site for the endangered orange horseshoe bat and ghost bat.

Access to the falls has been restricted to protect the habitat, and there is no swimming at this site. A 400m walking track (with wheelchair access) leads to the falls lookout. From here the track continues to complete a loop (1.6km, 45 minutes) back to the car park, passing beautiful, small rock pools above the falls.

GREENANT CREEK & TJAETABA FALLS

Another 2km along the main road is the access road to Greenant Creek, which has a picnic area, toilets and an excellent walking trail (2.7km return, one hour) to Tjaetaba Falls. The pretty falls area is sacred to local Aboriginal people and swimming is not permitted in the creek below the falls.

BLYTH HOMESTEAD RUINS, TJAYNERA FALLS & SURPRISE CREEK FALLS

Just 1km beyond the Greenant Creek turn-off is the turn-off to Tjaynera (Sandy Creek) Falls, which lie 9km off the road along a corrugated 4WD track with a couple of water crossings and speed humps.

Only 700m in is a major water crossing through the fast-flowing Tolmer River.

Around 5.5km down the track is the turn-off for Blyth Homestead, a further 1.5km and one more river crossing away. This 'homestead' was built in 1929 by the Sargent family, and it remained in use until the area was declared a national park in 1986.

Back on the main track the road forks after 2km. The left (eastern) fork heads to Tjaynera Falls (1.5km) with a good camping ground, while the right fork continues south to Surprise Creek Falls and the Daly River Rd. The 3.4km (1½ hours) return walk to Tjaynera Falls meanders through cycad-filled gullies and paperbark forest. The plunge pool here is deep, cool and far less crowded than the more easily accessible sites.

Surprise Creek Falls is a further 13km south through the isolated southern reaches of the park. This track is the last to be opened after the Wet, as it cuts through a swamp and the Reynolds River. Never swim in the Reynolds River as saltwater crocodiles may be lurking. There's a short walk at the falls to a series of waterholes that lead into a deep pool, which is perfect for a refreshing dip. Camping is free at Surprise Creek Falls.

The southern 4WD-only track eventually links up with the Daly River Rd, 17km beyond Surprise Creek.

WANGI FALLS

The main road through the park continues north from the Tjaynera turn-off another 6.5km to the turn-off to Litchfield's most popular attraction – Wangi Falls (pronounced *wong*-guy), 1.5km along a side road. This area can really become overrun on weekends – arrive early before the tour buses do.

The falls here flow year-round and fill a beautiful plunge pool that is great for swimming. Although the pool looks safe enough, the currents can be strong. Beside the pool a sign points out the dangers, and markers indicate when the water is considered too high to be safe. There's an emergency telephone at the car park. Excellent visibility makes it a great spot for snorkelling.

A marked walking trail (1.6km return, one hour) takes you up and over the falls for a fine view. There's a boardwalk over the two river crossings that turn into the falls, but it's quite a steep walk in places.

Near the car park is the **Bark Shelter** (✤ 8.30am-4pm), a tent gallery displaying local Aboriginal art.

There are barbecues (BYO wood), tables and a kiosk in the picnic area, and a campsite nearby.

WALKER & BAMBOO CREEKS

After passing the accommodation that sits just outside the park's boundary (Litchfield Tourist Precinct), the road loops back into the park, and after about 12km there's a turn-off to Walker Creek that leads 600m to a picnic area with tables and pit fires by the creek. A rock-pool walk (3.5km, one hour) leads upstream along a fern-fringed river to a rock-pool swimming area.

At Bamboo Creek, a further 1.5km up the main road, the well-preserved ruins of the tin mines that operated here in the 1940s provide an insight into the working conditions of the miners. It's well worth a look – there are informative signs and a loop walk (600m, 20 minutes).

It's only another 3km to the northern boundary of the park, and from there it's around 42km of corrugated dirt road to the Cox Peninsula Rd.

Tours

Numerous companies offer trips to Litchfield from Darwin, ranging from small-group tours that uncover the uncrowded gems to backpacker buses that blitz the popular waterholes. Most day tours cost from $80 to $130, which includes pick-up from your accommodation, guided tour of various sights, at least one swim, morning tea and lunch. Other tours include croc jumping on the Adelaide River or a stop at the Territory Wildlife Park (see opposite).

Albatross Helicopters (☎ 8988 5081, or Litchfield Cafe 8978 2077; www.albatrosshelicopters.com.au), based near Litchfield Cafe, has various tours over Litchfield and the Daly River region, starting from $175 per person for a 15-minute flight.

Labelle Adventures (☎ 8978 2330; www.labelle adventures.com.au) has cruises on the sublime private McKeddies Billabong, including a brief tour of the Labelle Downs cattle station ($50) at 10am; and half-day barra fishing charters ($250 per person) on the same billabong. Most accommodation and information places in Litchfield can make bookings. It's reached via a 17km well-maintained unsealed road that's usually suitable for 2WD vehicles. Accommodation is also available (see opposite).

Sleeping & Eating

Camping is well set up at Litchfield with official national parks sites near the best swimming spots. It's on a first-come first-served basis: pay at the registration box and take a ticket as the ranger will most likely come calling. Camping is free at Surprise Creek Falls.

Walker Creek camping ground (adult/child/family $3.30/1.65/7.70) This camping place is a secluded, walk-in bush camp with a swimming area, tables and pit fires. Campers have to lug their own gear upstream from the car park, so it's not as busy as other sites. Individual sites must be booked on the reservation board in the car park.

Buley Rockhole (adult/child/family $6.60/3.30/16) The rockhole has a nice 2WD-access campground (no caravans) with toilets and pit fires, with easy access to the swimming hole.

Florence Falls (adult/child/family $6.60/3.30/16) This spot has two camping grounds, one with 2WD access, the other 4WD-only access. Cold showers and disabled facilities are available at the 2WD camping ground.

Tjaynera Falls (adult/child/family $6.60/3.30/16) This falls has a camping ground with hot showers, flushing toilets and pit fires (BYO wood).

Wangi Falls camping ground (adult/child $6.60/3.30) Well set up with hot showers and facilities for the disabled, the large, stony sites here are good for vans, but make tent camping a bit uncomfortable. The kiosk (☑ 8am-5.30pm May-Oct, to 4pm Nov-Apr) sells snacks, barbecue packs, ice cream, ice and mosquito repellent.

Other privately owned places are available in the so-called Litchfield Tourism Precinct, 4km north of Wangi Falls and down a short dirt road.

Litchfield Safari Camp (☎ 8978 2185; www.litch fieldsafaricamp.com.au; unpowered/powered sites $20/30, safari tents without/with bathroom $110/130) Shady grassed sites make this a good alternative to Litchfield's bush-camping sites, especially if you want power (generator). The spacious safari tents are great value as they comfortably sleep up to four people and come with fridge, fan and cooking utensils.

Latitude 1308 & Litchfield Cafe (☎ 8978 2077; www .litchfieldcafe.com.au; mains $16-26; ☒ V) Most people come here for the excellent licensed garden cafe, which serves up great comfort food throughout the day. Filo parcels such as chicken, mango and macadamia are popular for lunch, or you could go for a meal of grilled barra or roo fillet, topped with good coffee and a wicked mango cheesecake. In a nearby bush clearing, Latitude 1308 is an intimate group of safari tents rented only on a full-board basis (single/double B&B including dinner $145/215).

our pick **Labelle Downs Station** (☎ 8978 2330; www .labelleadventures.com.au; unpowered/powered sites $20/25) For a taste of outback station life, Labelle Downs is well worth a detour. Although well outside the park boundaries, this 100,000-hectare cattle station is only 17km from the turn-off just north of Wangi Falls. Wallabies abound and there's a peaceful atmosphere around the camping area (book ahead for the limited powered sites). The owners run cruises on their private billabong as well as barra-fishing trips.

LITCHFIELD TO DARWIN
If you're in a 2WD hire vehicle it's best to backtrack via the sealed road through Batchelor and on to the Stuart Hwy north to Darwin. From the highway turn-off it's 85km to Darwin. If you have a 4WD or your own 2WD vehicle and don't mind shaking it up a bit, the back road from Litchfield to Darwin continues on past the Wangi Falls turnoff, running out of sealed road just past the Walker Creek turnoff. The 50km road from here to the Cox Peninsula Rd is passable to conventional vehicles in the Dry but can be rough and corrugated depending on when it was last graded. Travel time is roughly the same whichever way you go (about two hours), but one reason to take the back road is to stop at the Territory Wildlife Park and Berry Springs. Either way, once you reach Noonamah on the Stuart Hwy, you start to see the residential sprawl of outer Darwin and finally leave the outback behind.

Not long after you hit the bitumen on the Cox Peninsula Rd you come to **Tumbling Waters Holiday Park** (☎ 8988 6255; www.tumblingwatersholiday park.com.au; Cox Peninsula Rd; unpowered/powered sites $18/22, cabins $65-110), a friendly family resort

in a beautiful setting about 10km west of Berry Springs. Facilities include a bar, camp kitchen, pool, wireless internet, a freshwater croc display and a free deckchair cinema on Wednesday and Saturday night.

Territory Wildlife Park
Much like the Alice Springs Desert Park, the **Territory Wildlife Park** (☎ 8988 7200; www.territory wildlifepark.com.au; Cox Peninsula Rd; adult/concession/child/ family $20/14/10/55; ☹ 8.30am-6pm, last admission 4pm) showcases the best of Aussie wildlife in a state-of-the-art open-air zoo. You can spend years looking around in the wild and still not see half of what's on display here.

Highlights include the **Flight Deck**, where birds of prey display their intelligence and dexterity – don't miss one of the free-flying birds-of-prey demonstrations at 10am and 3pm daily; the **nocturnal house**, where you can observe nocturnal fauna such as bilbies and bats; 11 habitat **aviaries**, each representing a different habitat from mangroves to woodland; and a huge **walk-through aviary**, representing a monsoon rainforest. Pride of place must go to the **aquarium**, where a walk-through clear tunnel puts you among giant barramundi, stingray, sawfish, saratoga and a score of others, while a separate tank holds a 3.8m saltwater crocodile. To see everything you can either walk around the 4km perimeter road, or hop on and off the shuttle trains that run every 15 to 20 minutes and stop at all the exhibits.

Berry Springs Nature Park
This **nature park** (admission free; ☹ 8am-6.30pm) is a great place for a swim and a picnic. There's a thermal waterfall, spring-fed pools ringed with paperbarks and pandanus palms, and abundant birdlife. Bring a mask and snorkel to check out the teeming aquatic life.

From Berry Springs it's around 55km to Darwin.

Darwin & Around

Australia's only tropical capital, Darwin gazes out confidently across the Timor Sea. It's closer to Bali than Bondi, and many from the southern states still see it as some strange frontier outpost or jumping-off point for Kakadu National Park. But Darwin is a surprisingly affluent, cosmopolitan, youthful and vibrant city, thanks in part to an economic boom fuelled by the mining industry and tourism. It's a city on the move: property prices are up, unemployment is down and multimillion-dollar development projects are in full swing. Still, there's a small-town feel about Darwin, and a laconic, relaxed vibe that fits with the tropical climate.

Whether this is the start or end of your central Australian odyssey, Darwin has plenty to offer the traveller. Boats sail on the harbour, chairs and tables spill out of streetside restaurants and bars, museums reveal the city's absorbing past and galleries showcase the region's rich Indigenous art. Darwin's cosmopolitan mix – over 50 nationalities are seamlessly represented here – is typified by the wonderful Asian markets held throughout the dry season. While the future looks bright, there are lessons and legacies from the past. Darwin has endured total makeovers several times since its settlement in 1861, thanks to more than a few destructive cyclones and a barrage of Japanese bombs during WWII.

Nature is well and truly part of Darwin's backyard – the famous national parks of Kakadu and Litchfield are a few hours' drive away and the unique Tiwi Islands a boat ride away. For locals the perfect weekend is going fishing for barra with a tinny and an esky full of beer.

A steady stream of travellers passes through Darwin, but rather than using it as a stepping stone, take some time to hang around and appreciate this tropical city.

HIGHLIGHTS

- Sunset and sizzling satay at the exotic stalls of the Thursday and Sunday **Mindil Beach Sunset Market** (p259)
- Taking the Sea Cat to Mandorah and enjoying a beer and a view of the city from the **Mandorah Beach Hotel** (p262)
- Hearing the howling of Cyclone Tracy and exploring Aboriginal art at the free **Museum & Art Gallery of the Northern Territory** (p243)
- Hand-feeding bread rolls to the ravenous schools of wild fish at **Aquascene** (p243)
- Wining, dining and winding down on the waterfront marina at stylish **Cullen Bay** (p254)
- Reclining under the stars with a movie and a picnic at the classic **Deckchair Cinema** (p258)

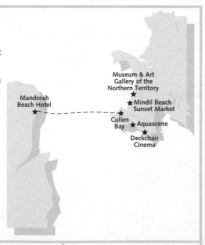

Mandorah Beach Hotel ★
Museum & Art Gallery of the Northern Territory ★
★ Mindil Beach Sunset Market
Cullen Bay ★ Aquascene
★ Deckchair Cinema

■ TELEPHONE CODE: ☎ 08   ■ www.tourismtopend.com.au   ■ www.darcity.nt.gov.au

DARWIN

pop 66,300

ORIENTATION

Darwin sits at the end of a peninsula poking into the turquoise waters of Port Darwin. The main shopping, accommodation, wining and dining area is a compact grid along the parallel Mitchell, Smith and Cavenagh Sts, including the pedestrianised Smith St Mall and the intersecting Knuckey St.

Long-distance buses pull in to the Transit Centre off Mitchell St in the city centre. Most places of interest to travellers in central Darwin are within two or three blocks of the Transit Centre or Smith St Mall, or a short distance north in the 'suburbs' of Cullen Bay, Fannie Bay, East Point and Parap. Darwin's airport is 12km northeast of the centre, while the train station is about 15km to the east, near Berrimah.

INFORMATION

Bookshops

Angus & Robertson (Map pp244-5; ☎ 8941 3489; 18 The Galleria, Smith St Mall) Stocks a broad range of fiction, nonfiction, Australiana and travel books.
Read Back Book Exchange (Map pp244-5; ☎ 8981 0099; 32 Smith St Mall) Secondhand books, CDs and videos.

Emergency

Ambulance (☎ 000)
Fire (☎ 000)
Lifeline (☎ 13 11 14)
Poisons Information Centre (☎ 13 11 26; ☺ 24hr) Advice on poisons, bites and marine stingers.
Police (☎ 000 or 13 14 44)

Internet Access

Hotels and hostels generally have their own terminals. The numerous internet cafes in the CBD charge between $2 and $5 an hour.
Global Gossip (Map pp244-5; ☎ 8942 3044; 44 Mitchell St; ☺ 9am-midnight Mon-Sat, to 11pm Sun) Darwin's busiest internet cafe with space for laptops and full phone and scanning services.
Northern Territory Library (Map pp244-5; ☎ 1800 019 155; Parliament House, Mitchell St; ☺ 10am-6pm Mon-Fri, 1-5pm Sat & Sun) You'll need to book in advance for a terminal, but access is free and wi-fi available.

Maps

NT General Store (Map pp244-5; ☎ 8981 8242; 42 Cavenagh St) Stocks maps and guidebooks.

Medical Services

Travellers Medical & Vaccination Centre (Map pp244-5; ☎ 8981 7492; 1st fl, 43 Cavenagh St; appointments ☺ 8.30am-noon & 1.30-5pm Mon-Fri)
Royal Darwin Hospital (Map p242; ☎ 8920 6011; Rocklands Dr, Tiwi)

Money

The four major banks have branches with ATMs all over the city centre.
ANZ (Map pp244-5; ☎ 8982 3510; 69 Smith St)
Commonwealth Bank (Map pp244-5; ☎ 8982 8707; 66 Smith St) ATM outside the Youth Shack on Mitchell St.
National Australia Bank (Map pp244-5; ☎ 13 22 65; 82 Mitchell St)
Westpac (Map pp244-5; ☎ 13 20 32; 24 Smith St) ATM near Chilli's Backpackers.

Permits

If you are travelling through Aboriginal land you'll need a permit, though if you're going on an organised tour, the tour company will organise your permits.
Northern Land Council (Map pp244-5; ☎ 8920 5100; www.nlc.org.au; 45 Mitchell St) Issues permits for Arnhem Land.
Tiwi Land Council (Map p242; ☎ 8981 4898; www.tiwilandcouncil.net.au; Armidale St, Stuart Park) Issues permits for the Tiwi Islands.

Post

Main post office (Map pp244-5; ☎ 13 13 18; 48 Cavenagh St; ☺ 9am-5pm Mon-Fri, to 12.30pm Sat) You can send packages by sea or air, and there's an efficient poste restante.

Tourist Information

Noticeboards and tour desks in most of the hotels and hostels run the gamut of advertisements for tours, buying and selling vehicles, rides and travel companions. There's an information and accommodation-booking desk at the airport.
Tourism Top End (Map pp244-5; ☎ 8980 6000; www.tourismtopend.com.au; 6 Bennett St; ☺ 8.30am-5.30pm Mon-Fri, 9am-3pm Sat, 10am-3pm Sun) Stocks hundreds of brochures and can book tours or accommodation for businesses within its association. Free publications include *Destination Darwin & the Top End*, published twice yearly, and *The Top End Holiday Guide*, an annual guide to regional attractions. A full range of fact sheets on Top End national parks is also available.

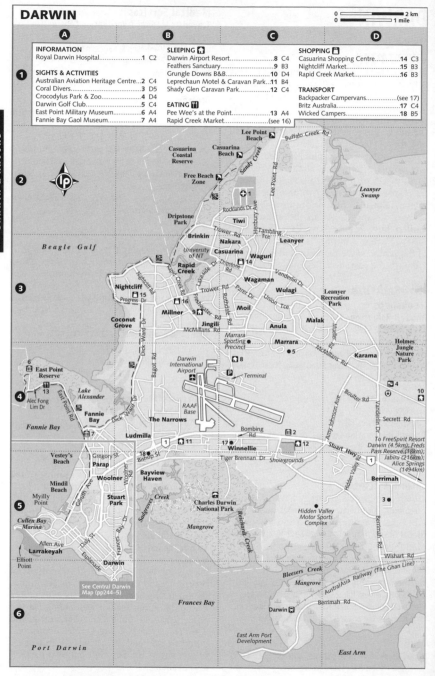

DARWIN

0 ————— 2 km
0 ————— 1 mile

INFORMATION
Royal Darwin Hospital.....................1 C2

SIGHTS & ACTIVITIES
Australian Aviation Heritage Centre...2 C4
Coral Divers.................................3 D5
Crocodylus Park & Zoo....................4 D4
Darwin Golf Club...........................5 C4
East Point Military Museum..............6 A4
Fannie Bay Gaol Museum.................7 A4

SLEEPING
Darwin Airport Resort.....................8 C4
Feathers Sanctuary........................9 B3
Grungle Downs B&B.......................10 D4
Leprechaun Motel & Caravan Park...11 B4
Shady Glen Caravan Park...............12 C4

EATING
Pee Wee's at the Point..................13 A4
Rapid Creek Market....................(see 16)

SHOPPING
Casuarina Shopping Centre............14 C3
Nightcliff Market..........................15 B3
Rapid Creek Market......................16 B3

TRANSPORT
Backpacker Campervans.............(see 17)
Britz Australia.............................17 C4
Wicked Campers..........................18 B5

Travel Agencies

To make a book or confirm flights, bus and train travel, there's no shortage of agents in Darwin.

Backpackers World Travel (Map pp244-5; ☎ 8941 5100; www.backpackersworld.com.au; Shop 9, 21 Knuckey St)

Flight Centre (Map pp244-5; ☎ 8941 8002; www.flight centre.com.au; 24 Cavenagh St)

Qantas Travel (Map pp244-5; ☎ 13 13 13; 16 Bennett St)

SIGHTS
Museum & Art Gallery of the Northern Territory

Don't miss this excellent **museum and art gallery** (Map pp244-5; ☎ 8999 8264; www.magnt.nt.gov.au; Conacher St, Fannie Bay; admission free; ☯ 9am-5pm Mon-Fri, 10am-5pm Sat & Sun, closed holidays), about 4km north of the city centre. The eclectic collection is beautifully presented and just enough to take in with a single visit. A highlight is the Aboriginal art collection, which provides an excellent introduction to many different styles, although its focus is on the art of the Top End. The collection is particularly strong in carvings and *pukumani* (decorated burial poles) from the Tiwi Islands, and bark paintings from Arnhem Land.

An entire room is devoted to Cyclone Tracy in a display that graphically illustrates life before and after the disaster. You can stand in a darkened room and listen to the whirring sound of Tracy at full throttle – a sound you won't forget in a hurry. The cavernous Maritime Gallery houses an assortment of weird and wonderful craft from the nearby islands and Indonesia, as well as a pearling lugger and a Vietnamese refugee boat.

Pride of place among the stuffed animals undoubtedly goes to 'Sweetheart', a 5m-long, 780kg saltwater crocodile, which became a Top End personality after attacking several fishing dinghies on the Finniss River south of Darwin. The locally focused natural history section is well set out into different habitats.

The museum has a good bookshop and the Cornucopia Museum Café (p257) is a great lunch spot. Buses 4 and 6 travel close by, or get here on the Tour Tub or along the bicycle path from the city centre.

Aquascene

Hundreds of fish head to shore at high tide each day to feast on the bread at **Aquascene** (Map pp244-5; ☎ 8981 7837; www.aquascene.com.au; 28 Doctors Gully Rd; adult/child/family $8/5/20), near the corner of Daly St and the Esplanade. It's quite a 'loaves and fishes' experience to be surrounded by schools of green milkfish (some 1.5m in length) thrashing around and snapping at the soggy morsels. More sedate mullet, batfish, rays, catfish and quite a few other species join in. Children love it. Phone ahead or check in *This Week in Darwin* for feeding times. Aquascene is an easy walk from the north end of the Esplanade.

Crocosaurus Cove

If the tourists won't go out to see the crocs, then bring the crocs to the tourists. Right in the middle of Mitchell St, **Crocosaurus Cove** (Map pp244-5; ☎ 8981 7522; www.crocosauruscove.com; 58 Mitchell St; adult/child $28/16; ☯ 8am-8pm, last admission 6pm) is as up close and personal as you'll ever want to get to these amazing creatures. Six of the largest crocs in captivity can be seen in state-of-art aquariums and pools. You can be lowered right into a pool with Snowy, a 600kg 'albino' saltie in the transparent 'Cage of Death' (one/two people $120/160). If that's too scary, there's another pool where you can swim with a clear tank wall separating you from another big croc. Other aquariums feature barramundi, turtles and sting rays, and there's an enormous reptile house.

George Brown Botanic Gardens

The 42-hectare **Botanic Gardens** (Map pp244-5; ☎ 8981 1958; admission free; ☯ 7am-7pm daily) showcases plants from the Top End and around the world. Of particular interest are the monsoon vine forest, the mangroves and coastal plants habitat, baobabs and a magnificent collection of native and exotic palms and cycads. The pleasant gardens are a splendid place for a walk, particularly in the cool of the morning.

Many of the plants here were traditionally used by the Larrakia Aboriginal people, and self-guiding Aboriginal plant use trails have been set up – pick up a brochure at the gardens' **Information Centre** (☯ 8am-4pm Mon-Fri, 8.30am-4pm Sat & Sun) near the Geranium St entry.

It's an easy 2km bicycle ride out to the gardens from the centre of town along Gilruth Ave and Gardens Rd, or there's another entrance off Geranium St, which runs off the Stuart Hwy in Stuart Park.

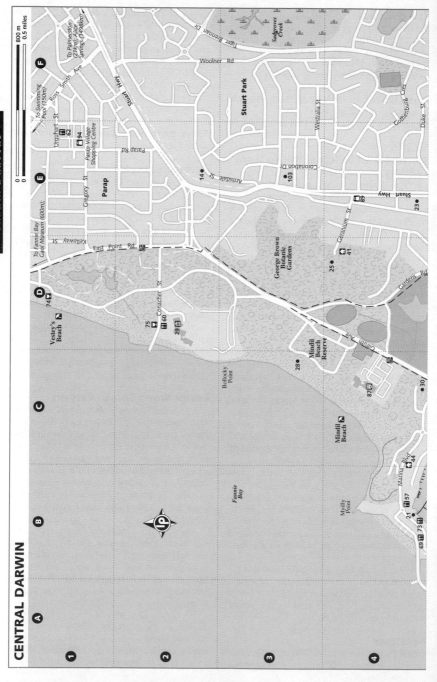

CENTRAL DARWIN

DARWIN & AROUND

Fannie Bay

Mindil Beach

Myilly Point

Mindil Beach Reserve

George Brown Botanic Gardens

Bullocky Point

Vestey's Beach

Stuart Park

Parap

To Fannie Bay Gaol Museum (600m);

To Swimming Pool (150m)

To Palmerston (21km); Alice Spring (1498km)

Tiger Brennan Dr

Sadgroves Creek

Woolner Rd

Ross Smith Ave

Urquhart St

Gregory St

Kellaway St

East Point Rd

Conacher St

Stuart Hwy

Parap Rd

Parap Village Shopping Centre

Armidale St

Westralia St

Coronation Dr

Cothenburg Cres

Duke St

Stuart Hwy

Geranium St

Gardens Rd

Gilruth Ave

Marina Blvd

800 m
0.5 miles

DARWIN & AROUND

Parliament House & Supreme Court

Dominating the edge of town just south of Smith St Mall is cubelike **Parliament House** (Map pp244-5; tour bookings ☎ 8946 1430; ☉ 8am-6pm, tours 9am & 11am Sat), dubbed 'the wedding cake', and the adjoining Supreme Court buildings.

The grand parliament building was opened in 1994 and drew much criticism for 'lacking outback ambience'. But, perhaps more appropriately, it owes something to Southeast Asian architecture and evokes the grandeur of colonial buildings worldwide. It's worth wading through the strict security check to wander through the cavernous interior to the secluded cafe, Speakers Corner, which opens out to a garden terrace with impressive views.

The building also houses the subterranean **Northern Territory Library** (☉ 10am-6pm Mon-Fri, 1-5pm Sat & Sun).

The nearby **Supreme Court** (Map pp244-5; ☉ 8am-5.30pm Mon-Fri) is chiefly of interest for the fine artwork on display inside. A mosaic by Aboriginal artist Nora Napaltjari Nelson lines the floor. Called *Milky Way Dreaming*, its construction used some 700,000 pieces of Venetian glass. Also on display is *Kooralia and the Seven Sisters*, a rug woven by Tim Leura Tjapaltjarri that was the centre of a copyright

CYCLONE TRACY

The statistics of this natural disaster are frightening. Cyclone Tracy built up over Christmas Eve 1974 and by midnight the winds began to reach their full fury. At 3.05am the airport's anemometer failed, just after it recorded a wind speed of 217km/h. It's thought the peak wind speeds were as high as 280km/h. In all, 66 people died. Of Darwin's 11,200 houses, 50% to 60% were destroyed either totally or beyond repair, and only 400 survived relatively intact.

Much criticism was levelled at the design and construction of Darwin's houses, but plenty of places at least a century old, and built as solidly as you could ask for, also toppled before the awesome winds. The new and rebuilt houses have been cyclone-proofed with steel reinforcements and roofs that are firmly pinned down.

Most people say that next time a cyclone is forecast, they'll jump straight into their cars and head down the Track – and come back afterwards to find out if their houses really were cyclone-proof! For the full story, see the exhibit at the Museum & Art Gallery of Northern Territory.

dispute and marked a landmark decision in favour of an Aboriginal artist.

Wharf Precinct

Bold development of Darwin Harbour is well underway. Due to be finished in 2009, the billion-dollar Darwin City Waterfront development will feature a new cruise-ship terminal, luxury hotels, boutique restaurants and shopping, and a wave pool. The new convention centre was already up and running during our visit. In the meantime, the old **Stokes Hill Wharf** is well worth an afternoon promenade. It's a short stroll down from the Survivors' Lookout at the end of Smith St, past the WWII Oil-Storage Tunnels and the Indo-Pacific Marine Exhibition.

At the end of the jetty an old warehouse houses a food centre that's ideal for an alfresco lunch, cool afternoon beer or a seafood dinner as the sun sets over the harbour. Several harbour cruises and a jet boat also leaves from the wharf.

WWII OIL-STORAGE TUNNELS

You can escape from the heat of the day and relive your Hitchcockian fantasies by walking through the **oil-storage tunnels** (Map pp244-5; ☎ 8985 6333; adult/child $5/3; ⏰ 9am-4pm May-Sep, to 1pm Tue-Sun Oct, Nov, Jan, Mar & Apr, closed Dec & Feb). After Japanese air raids destroyed above-ground oil tanks near Stokes Hill Wharf, five oil-storage tunnels were dug by hand into the rock cliff. It was an ambitious project that ultimately failed because of the high water table and seepage, and the tunnels were never used. Tunnels 5 (171m long) and 6 (78m) are open to the public, and on the walls there's a series of interesting wartime photos.

INDO-PACIFIC MARINE EXHIBITION

This excellent **marine aquarium** (Map pp244-5; ☎ 8981 1294; www.indopacificmarine.com.au; Kitchener Dr; adult/child/family $18/8/44; ⏰ 10am 5pm Apr-Oct, 9am-1pm & 10am-5pm Sat & Sun Nov-Mar) gives you a close encounter with the denizens at the bottom of Darwin Harbour. Each small tank is a complete ecosystem, with only the occasional extra fish introduced as food for some of the predators, such as stonefish or the bizarre angler fish. Box jellyfish are occasionally on display, as well as sea horses, clownfish and butterfly fish. The living coral reef display is especially impressive. Admission includes a guided tour.

Also recommended here is **Coral Reef by Night** (adult/child $104/55; ⏰ shows 7pm Wed, Fri & Sun), which includes a tour of the aquarium, seafood dinner and impressive illuminated night show.

AUSTRALIAN PEARLING EXHIBITION

Next door to the aquarium, the **Australian Pearling Exhibition** (Map pp244-5; ☎ 8981 1294; Kitchener Dr; adult/child/family $6.60/3.30/17; ⏰ 10am-5pm) has excellent displays and informative videos on the harvesting, farming and culture of pearl oysters in the Top End. You can also experience life underwater inside a simulated diving helmet.

Fannie Bay Gaol Museum

The original buildings of this interesting **museum** (Map pp244-5; ☎ 8999 8920; cnr East Point Rd & Ross Smith Ave; admission free; ⏰ 10am-4.30pm) were erected in 1883, and the grounds housed Darwin's main jail for nearly 100 years. Among its locally famous inmates was Harold Nelson, who lobbied for political representation and eventually became the NT's first member of parliament.

You can wander around the grounds and enter the old cells and see the gallows constructed for two hangings in 1952. The sorry tale behind the hangings is graphically illustrated inside. There's also a minimum security section, used at various times for juvenile delinquents, lepers and Vietnamese refugees. The jail closed in 1979, when a new maximum security lock-up opened at Berrimah.

Buses 4 and 6 from the city centre pass nearby the museum; it's also on the Tour Tub route.

East Point Reserve

North of Fannie Bay, this spit of land is particularly good in the late afternoon when wallabies emerge to feed and you can watch the sun set over the bay. On the northern side there are some wartime gun emplacements and the military museum. The beach is worth combing for scattered coral fragments and other interesting debris.

Lake Alexander, a small, recreational saltwater lake, was made so people could enjoy a swim year-round without having to worry about box jellyfish. There's a good children's playground and picnic areas with barbecues. A 1.5km **mangrove boardwalk** (8am-6pm) leads off from the car park. Signs explain the uses the Larrakia people made of mangrove communities.

EAST POINT MILITARY MUSEUM

Devoted to Darwin's WWII experiences, this fascinating little **museum** (Map p242; ☎ 8981 9702; adult/child/family $10/5/28; 9.30am-5pm) is north of Fannie Bay within East Point Reserve. Inside there's a 15-minute video on the bombing of Darwin, and cabinets showing various weapons and wartime photos. One curio is a captured Bible in Japanese.

Outside there's an assortment of military hardware – check out the ball turret, about the size of a large beach ball, from an American B24 Liberator. The centrepiece is a concrete emplacement housing a replica 9.2in gun. The original massive gun could lob a shell weighing 172kg over a distance of 27km, although it was not installed and tested until 1945, by which time the war was all but over! Ironically, the gun was sold for scrap to a Japanese salvage company in 1960.

Myilly Point Historic Precinct

At the far northern end of Smith St is this small but important precinct of four houses built in the 1930s. The houses were designed for the tropical climate by the Northern Territory Principal Architect, BCG Burnett, who came to Darwin in 1937 after spending many years working as an architect in China. The small elevated point was a prime residential spot as it had fine views and enjoyed sea breezes, and so it was here that the top civil and military officials were housed.

The houses are now on the Register of the National Estate, and one of them, Burnett House, operates as a **museum** (Map pp244-5; ☎ 8981 2848; admission by donation; 10am-1pm Mon-Sat). There's a tantalisingly colonial high tea ($7.50) in the gardens on Sunday afternoon from 3.30pm to 6pm.

Crocodylus Park & Zoo

This **wildlife park** (Map p242; ☎ 8947 2510; www.croco dyluspark.com; McMillans Rd, Berrimah; adult/child/family $27.50/13.50/70; 9am-5pm, tours 10am, noon, 2pm & 3.30pm) showcases hundreds of crocs and a mini-zoo comprising lions, tigers, a Persian leopard and other big cats, spider monkeys, marmosets, cassowaries and large birds. Allow about two hours to look around the whole park, and you should time your visit with a tour, which includes a feeding demonstration.

The park is about 15km from the city centre. Take bus 5 or 9 from Darwin.

Australian Aviation Heritage Centre

Darwin's **aviation museum** (Map p242; ☎ 8947 2145; www.darwinsairwar.com.au; 557 Stuart Hwy, Winnellie; adult/child/family $12/7/30; 9am-5pm), about 10km from the centre, is one for military aircraft nuts. The huge hangar is crammed with aircraft, engines and wartime displays. The centrepiece is a mammoth B52 bomber – one of only a few of its kind displayed outside the USA – which has somehow been squeezed inside. It dwarfs the other aircraft, which include a Japanese Zero fighter shot down in 1942 and the remains of a RAAF Mirage jet that crashed in a nearby swamp. Short videos on the bombing of Darwin and the mighty B52 run daily and are available for purchase. Free guided tours commence at 10am and 2pm. It's worth a look for the B52 alone.

Buses 5 and 8 run along the Stuart Hwy and it's on the route of the Tour Tub.

DARWIN & AROUND

DARWIN SUNSETS

Darwin enjoys some magical sunsets over the bay. Here are some of the best spots to watch the sun sink into the Timor Sea.

- Mindil Beach (below)
- Stokes Hill Wharf (p247)
- Mandorah Beach Hotel (p262)
- Darwin Sailing Club (p257)
- Dripstone Cliffs, Casuarina Coastal Reserve (below)
- Deck of a boat during a harbour cruise (p251)

Casuarina Coastal Reserve

Sites of Aboriginal and historical significance are preserved in the coastal reserve, a stretch of fine, sandy beaches and sandstone cliffs between Rapid Creek and Lee Point. The rock offshore is a registered sacred site known to the Larrakia as *Dariba Nunggalinya*. It is said that interference with the rock led to Cyclone Tracy.

There's a popular sunset lookout along the way at Dripstone Cliffs.

ACTIVITIES
Beaches & Swimming

Darwin is no beach paradise – naturally enough the harbour has no surf – but along the convoluted coastline north of the city centre is a string of sandy beaches. The most popular are **Mindil** and **Vestey's** on Fannie Bay. Further north, a stretch of the 7km **Casuarina Beach** is an official nude beach. Darwin's swimming beaches tend to be far enough away from mangrove creeks to make the threat of meeting a crocodile very remote. However, the potential is always there for the unlucky or unwary swimmer. A bigger problem is the deadly box jellyfish, which makes swimming decidedly unhealthy between October and May. June to September is considered 'safe', but Darwin Hospital has records of stings occurring every month of the year, so take notice of any current warnings.

Cycling

Darwin is great for cycling. A series of bike tracks covers most of the city, with the main one running from the northern end of Cavenagh St to Fannie Bay, Coconut Grove,

Nightcliff and Casuarina. At Fannie Bay, a side track heads out to the East Point Reserve. Most hostels hire out bicycles for $12 to $20 per day for a mountain bike, or try **Darwin Scooter Hire** (Map pp244-5; ☎ 8941 2434; 29 Stuart Hwy) which has mountain bikes for $20 a day ($100 deposit required).

Diving

The Japanese bombs of WWII and Cyclone Tracy have contributed an array of wrecks to the floor of Darwin Harbour. Over the years, coral has encrusted these artificial reefs and attracted myriad colourful marine life. On the downside Darwin experiences massive tides, which churn the sea floor and restrict diving times, so you will need to plan ahead to catch the best conditions (only during neap tides).

Cullen Bay Dive (Map pp244-5; ☎ 8981 3049; www.dive darwin.com; 66 Marina Blvd, Cullen Bay Marina) conducts PADI-affiliated instruction courses and wreck dives throughout the year.

Coral Divers (Map p242; ☎ 8981 2686; www.coral divers.com.au; 26 Makagon Rd, Berrimah) has advanced courses such as nitrox and technical diving, with IANTD courses starting at $400.

Fishing

Fishing is another word for living for many inhabitants and visitors to the Top End, and Darwin is blessed with some great fishing spots. There's no shortage of charter operations taking anglers into the harbour or beyond for some outback barra action or blue-water sports fishing among the islands. Half-/full-day charters cost around $120/240 per person and most leave from Cullen Bay Marina. Fishing charter brochures occupy a dedicated stand at Tourism Top End (p241).

Golf

For a serious round of golf, head to the **Darwin Golf Club** (Map p242; ☎ 8927 1015; www.darwingolfclub .com.au; Links Rd, Marrara; 9/18 holes $17.50/27), just past the airport in Marrara. If you just want a quick hit, **Garden Park Golf Links** (Map pp244-5; ☎ 8981 6365; Gardens Rd) is a basic nine-hole course centrally located near the Botanic Gardens.

Sailing

The **Darwin Sailing Club** (Map pp244-5; ☎ 8981 1700; www.dwnsail.com.au; Atkins Dr, Fannie Bay) is a good place to meet local yachties, as well as an excellent place to watch the sunset over a beer. Although you can't charter boats here, there is a noticeboard advertising crewing needs and detailing the seasonal race program. Temporary membership is available free on the spot.

The **Winter School of Sailing** (☎ 8981 9368, 0417-818 257; www.darwinsailingschool.com.au; 3hr sailing session $60, overnight cruise from $120, courses from $230) sails the harbour in *Zanzibar*, an 11.6m sloop berthed at Cullen Bay Marina. Regular crewing sessions are held on Wednesday afternoon. Check the website for a timetable of training courses.

Skydiving

Top End Tandems (☎ 0417 190 140; www.topendtandems .com.au; tandem jumps from $310) has tandem skydives starting at Darwin Airport and landing at Lee Point Reserve.

Jet-boating

If a harbour cruise is too tame, jump on **Oz Jet Boats** (Map pp244-5; ☎ 1300 13 55 95; www.ozjetboating.com .au; adult/child $50/30) for a thrilling ride around the harbour. Departs from Stokes Hill Wharf.

DARWIN FOR CHILDREN

Outdoorsy Darwin is great for children. At the top of the list would have to be **Aquascene** (p243) where kids of all ages will be thrilled to hand-feed torpedolike milkfish and schools of their more demure cousins – getting a soaking is part of the fun. More fishy delights await at the **Indo-Pacific Marine Exhibition** (p247) where aspiring deep-sea divers can stick their faces into the viewing bubbles and check out life on the sea floor. There's more fun with an educational spin at the **Museum & Art Gallery of the Northern Territory** (p243), where kids can interact with many displays and get hands-on with bugs and microscopes in the Teach & Explore Room.

The **George Brown Botanic Gardens** (p243) has plenty of shade and space, as well as a Children's Evolutionary Playground where curious minds can grapple with plant evolution. The Top End crocs have never been closer than Darwin's fabulous **Crocosaurus Cove** (p243) where even kids can safely come face-to-face with big salties. More hands-on is **Crocodylus Park & Zoo** (p248), where kids can handle baby crocs and see feeding demos.

Older kids especially will enjoy harbour cruise (opposite) or a more exhilarating jet-boat ride (above).

Not too far out of town are a couple of superb wildlife attractions. Don't miss the birds-of-prey flight show at the **Territory Wildlife Park** (p239), where the kids can also look a 4m-long crocodile or a barrel-size barramundi right in the eye. Wide eyes and gasps are sure to accompany the jumping crocs at **Adelaide River Crossing** (p264), where deadly reptiles do their best Flipper impersonation.

TOURS

There are dozens of tours in and around Darwin, and lots of combinations covering Kakadu, Arnhem Land, Litchfield and further afield. Tourism Top End (p241) is the best place to start looking and asking questions. It gets busy so it helps to know roughly what you want before you start queuing. You can also book tours and accommodation from here. Remember that many tours run less frequently (or not at all) in the wet season.

City Sights

Darwin Day Tours (☎ 1300 721 365; www.aussie adventure.com.au) Runs an afternoon city tour (adult/child $59/30; ☽ tours 2pm), which takes in all the major attractions, including Stokes Hill Wharf, the Museum & Art Gallery and East Point Reserve, and can be linked with a sunset harbour cruise ($99/48).

Darwin Walking & Bicycle Tours (☎ 8942 1022; www.darwinwalkingtours.com.au) Two-/three-hour guided walks of local attractions for $25/35 (children free) and three-hour bike tours ($40) that take you out to Fannie Bay and East Point; depart from Ducks Nuts Bar & Grill (p257).

Double Decker Tours (☎ 0416 140903; www .doubledeckertours.com.au; night tour $50; ☽ tours 5-10pm Sat) Evening pub crawl on an open double-decker bus with food and a drink at each venue; departs from the Cavanagh (p257). One for the backpackers.

Night Sky Adventures (☎ 1300 883 545; www .nightskyadventures.com.au; East Point Reserve; adult/child $55/40; ☽ tours Fri-Wed Apr-Oct) Guided stargazing tour using telescope and binoculars at East Point Reserve. Barbecue included.

Tour Tub (☎ 8985 6322; www.tourtub.com.au; adult/child $30/20; ☽ tours 9am-4pm, closed Dec) This open-sided hop-on-hop-off minibus tours around the various Darwin sights throughout the day. In the city centre it leaves from Knuckey St, near the end of the Smith St Mall, on the hour. Sites visited include Crocosaurus Cove, Aquascene (only at fish-feeding times), WWII Oil-Storage Tunnels (admission included), Indo-Pacific Marine and Wharf Precinct, the museum & art gallery, East Point and the military museum, Fannie Bay Gaol Museum, Parap Market (Saturday only) and the Botanic Gardens.

Harbour Cruises

Between April and October there are plenty of boats based at the Cullen Bay Marina and Stokes Hill Wharf to take you on a cruise of the harbour. You'll find their glossy brochures at Tourism Top End (p241).

Anniki (☎ 8941 4000; www.australianharbourcruises.com.au; adult/child $60/40) Three-hour sunset cruises on this historical pearling lugger depart at 4.45pm from Cullen Bay and include sparkling wine and nibbles. You might recognise the ship from the film *Australia*.

Darwin Harbour Cruises (Map pp244–5; ☎ 8942 3131; www.darwinharbourcruises.com.au) Variety of cruises from Stokes Hill Wharf. The 20m schooner *Tumlaren* does a three-hour barbeque lunch cruise at noon (adult/child $70/42), and a sunset cruise departing at 5pm ($60/39). The 30m schooner *Alfred Noble* has a full-dinner tour departing at 5.45pm ($90/59).

Spirit of Darwin (☎ 8981 3711; www.spiritofdarwin.net; adult/child $40/18) Fully licensed air-con motorcatamaran does a two-hour sightseeing cruise at 1.40pm and a sunset cruise at 5.30pm daily. Departs Cullen Bay Marina.

Sunset Sail (☎ 0408-795 567; www.sailnt.com.au; adult/child $60/45) This three-hour afternoon cruise aboard the catamaran *Daymirri* departs from Stokes Hill Wharf. Refreshments are included but BYO alcohol.

Beyond Darwin

Lots of companies run trips that take in croc jumping at Adelaide River, Kakadu National Park, Arnhem Land and Litchfield; some operators can take you as far as Alice Springs, Adelaide and Broome.

Adventure Tours (Map pp244–5; ☎ 8132 8230; www.adventuretours.com.au; shop 2, 52 Mitchell St) Range of 4WD tours to suit the adventurous backpacker crowd. Litchfield day tour is $95; two-/three-day Kakadu tours $375/475; as well as longer tours.

Aussie Adventure (Map pp244–5; ☎ 1300 721 365; www.aussieadventure.com.au; shop 6, 52 Mitchell St) Trips include half-day Territory Wildlife Park (adult/child $66/33); jumping-croc cruise ($92/46); Kakadu ($179/90); and Litchfield ($117/59).

Kakadu Dreams (Map pp244–5; ☎ 1800 813 266; www.kakadudreams.com.au; 50 Mitchell St) Backpacker day tours to Litchfield ($80), and two-/three-/five-day trips to Kakadu ($350/460/680).

Sacred Earth Safaris (☎ 8981 8420; www.sacredearthsafaris.com.au) Multiday small-group camping tours to Kakadu, Arnhem Land and the Kimberley. Two-day 4WD Kakadu tour starts at $565, the five-day Top End tour is $1850.

Wallaroo Eco Tours (☎ 8983 2699; www.litchfielddaytours.com) Small-group tours to Litchfield National Park (per person $120).

FESTIVALS & EVENTS

Darwin has plenty of tropical colour and flair when it comes to local festivals. Most of these take place in the Dry; check with Tourism Top End (p241) for exact dates.

MAY

Arafura Games (www.arafuragames.nt.gov.au) Darwin is the host to this biennial sporting event (odd-numbered years) that attracts competitors from Australasia, Asia and the Pacific Islands.

Freds Pass Rural Show (www.fredspass.org) A very popular agricultural show at the Freds Pass Reserve, McMinns Lagoon, south of Palmerston.

JULY

Beer Can Regatta (www.beercanregatta.org.au) An utterly insane and typically Territorian festival that features races for boats made out of beer cans. It takes places at Mindil Beach and is a good fun day.

Darwin Cup Carnival (www.darwinturfclub.org.au) The Darwin Cup racing carnival takes place in July and August at the Darwin Turf Club in Fannie Bay. The highlight of the eight-day program is the running of the Darwin Cup, along with all the fashions and social outings.

Darwin Fringe Festival (www.darwinfringe.com.au) Showcases eclectic, local performing and visual arts at venues including Browns Mart Theatre.

Royal Darwin Show (www.darwinshow.com.au) This agricultural show takes place at the showgrounds in Winnellie on the last weekend of the month. Activities include all the usual rides, as well as demonstrations and competitions.

Sail Indonesia (www.sailindonesia.net) Darwin is the starting point for this fiercely contested yacht race, which draws an international field of contestants.

AUGUST

Darwin Aboriginal Art Fair (www.darwinaboriginalartfair.com.au) Held at the convention centre, this two-day festival showcases Indigenous art from communities throughout the NT.

Darwin Festival (www.darwinfestival.org.au) This mainly outdoor arts and culture festival reflects the city's large Aboriginal and Asian populations and runs for about two weeks.

Darwin Rodeo (☎ 0412-892 224) Yee ha! The whips crack as local and international teams compete in numerous events of bull riding and horsemanship at the Robbie Robbins Reserve in Berrimah.

SLEEPING

Darwin has a good range of accommodation, most of it handy to the CBD, but finding a bed in the peak May-to-September period can be difficult at short notice – book ahead, at least for the first night. As a result, accommodation prices vary greatly with the season and demand. Prices given here are for high season, but expect big discounts between November and March, especially for midrange and top-end accommodation.

Budget

Darwin has about a dozen centrally located backpacker hostels, including a few party places on Mitchell St. If you want a quieter stay, choose one a bit further out – they're still walking distance to the action. If the backpacker scene isn't for you, there are a few cheap lodges and motels that fall into the budget sphere.

Caravan parks are scattered around the outer suburbs. Some campervanners attempt to stay overnight at parking areas along the beach around Fannie Bay and East Point Reserve, but it's illegal and council officers frequently dish out fines.

HOSTELS

Hostel facilities usually include communal kitchen, pool and laundry facilities. Some offer airport, bus or train station pick-ups with advance bookings, and most give YHA/VIP discounts.

Cavenagh (Map pp244–5; ☎ 1300 851 198, 8941 6383; www.thecavenagh.com; 12 Cavenagh St; dm $22-27, motel d $159; ✖ 🖳 🙊) The Cav is as much motel as hostel – the four to 12-bed dorms are in converted motel rooms that wrap around a huge central pool. It's a sociable place with a perpetual pool-party atmosphere, a popular bar-restaurant and central location, with the Roma Bar cafe right across the road.

Globetrotters YHA (Map pp244–5; ☎ 8981 5385; www.yha.com.au; 97 Mitchell St; dm $24-30, d $83; 🙊 ✖ 🖳) One of the newer additions to the hostel scene, Globetrotters is in a converted motel, so all rooms (including dorms) have en suites, and they're built around a decent pool. Kitchen and TV room are tiny, but there's the Globies Bar, with cheap meals and entertainment, attached.

Frogshollow Backpackers (Map pp244–5; ☎ 1800 068 686; www.frogs-hollow.com.au; 27 Lindsay St; dm $24-30, d without/with bathroom $75/100; ✖ 🖳 🙊) Set in a lush garden opposite parkland, Frogshollow is an easy walk to the city centre but far enough away to have a relaxed atmosphere. The swimming pool and spa in the garden and a pool table in the common area give it a sociable feel and facilities, including

kitchen and laundry, are good. Dorms can be a bit cramped.

Banyan View Lodge (Map pp244–5; ☎ 8981 8644; www.banyanviewlodge.com.au; 119 Mitchell St; dm $25, s/d without bathroom $60/70, d $120; ✖ 🙊) The Banyan View suits travellers not into the party scene. It's a big YWCA that welcomes men and has no curfew. Spacious rooms are clean and well kept and all have air-con.

Gecko Lodge (Map pp244–5; ☎ 1800 811 250; www.geckolodge.com.au; 146 Mitchell St; dm $25-29, tw & d without bathroom $75-92; ✖ 🖳 🙊) Want to stay away from the Mitchell St madness? In a pair of well-worn elevated houses halfway to Mindil Beach, this small, personable hostel offers a relaxing stay and a place to park a campervan, which attracts a few long-termers and savvy backpackers. The main house has a pool and the better rooms, while the 'House Next Door' has a roomy living room and kitchen. There's bike hire and a free pancake breakfast.

Youth Shack (Map pp244–5; ☎ 1300 793 302; www.youthshack.com.au; 69 Mitchell St; dm $29, tw & d without bathroom $77; ⏲ 24hr reception; ✖ 🖳 🙊) At one end of the Transit Centre, this popular hostel has a large open kitchen and meals area overlooking a pool big enough to actually swim in. Rooms are a little tired but clean, and the staff are consistently praised for being friendly and helpful.

Chilli's (Map pp244–5; ☎ 1800 351 313; www.chillis.com.au; 69A Mitchell St; dm $29, tw & d without bathroom $77, d $82; ✖ 🖳) Run by the same crew as the Youth Shack – note the colour coordination – Chilli's is a funky place with a small sundeck and spa (use the pool next door), a pool table, an air-con TV room and a breezy kitchen and meals area overlooking Mitchell St. Rooms are compact but clean.

Melaleuca on Mitchell (Map pp244–5; ☎ 1300 723 437; www.melaleucaonmitchell.com.au; 52 Mitchell St; dm $30, d without/with bathroom $95/115; ✖ 🖳 🙊) The highlight at this busy backpackers is the bopping rooftop bar and pool area overlooking Mitchell St – complete with waterfall spa and big-screen TV. The modern hostel is immaculate but a little sterile with its stark white walls and sparse rooms. Facilities are A1 though and it's very secure – the 3rd floor is female only.

CAMPING & CARAVAN PARKS

The following caravan parks are within about 10km of the city centre.

Leprechaun Motel & Caravan Park (Map p242; ☎ 8984 3400; 378 Stuart Hwy, Winnellie; unpowered/

powered sites $22/27, motel s/d $85/95; ❄️ 🖵) The closest caravan park to the city centre is relatively small and simple, but also the cheapest around, and the motel is reasonable value.

Shady Glen Caravan Park (Map p242; ☎ 1800 662 253; 8984 3330; www.shadyglen.com.au; cnr Farrell Cres & Stuart Hwy; unpowered & powered sites $29, r $59-79, cabins $90-180; ❄️ 🖵) Shady by name… Well-treed caravan park with immaculate facilities, camp kitchen, licensed shop and friendly staff.

FreeSpirit Resort Darwin (off Map p242; ☎ 1800 350888; www.freespiritresorts.com.au; 901 Stuart Hwy, Berrimah; unpowered/powered sites $30/38, cabins $110-220; ❄️ 🖵 💻) Impressive park with loads of facilities, including wi-fi from the terrace area and three pools.

Midrange

You'll find a range of motels, good-value serviced apartments and a sprinkling of homely family-run B&Bs, but they're not exactly thick on the ground so book ahead in high season.

B&BS

Grungle Downs B&B (Map p242; ☎ 8947 4440; www.grungledowns.com.au; 945 McMillans Rd, Knuckey Lagoon; d $120-165, cottage $400; ❄️ 🖵) Set on a five-acre property, this beautiful rural retreat seems a world away from the city but is not that far and handy to Crocodylus Park and the airport. Relax in the guest lounge, extensive gardens or by the pool. There are four lodge rooms (one with en suite) and a gorgeous two-bedroom cottage.

our pick Steeles at Larrakeyah (Map pp244-5; ☎ 8941 3636; www.steeles-at-larrakeyah.com.au; 4 Zealandia Cres, Larrakeyah; d $165-185; ❄️ 🖵) Some B&Bs are business and others feel like staying with friends; Steeles is the latter. With a perfect residential location midway between the city centre, Cullen Bay and Mindil Beach, the three rooms in this pleasant Spanish Mission–style home are equipped with air-con, TV, fridge and private entrance. Enjoy breakfast in the tropical garden.

HOTELS & MOTELS

Barramundi Lodge (Map pp244-5; ☎ 8941 6466; www.barramundilodge.com.au; 4 Gardens Rd, The Gardens; s/d without bathroom $50/100; ❄️ 🖵) Relatively quiet, secure and comfortable, Barramundi Lodge is a touch above most backpacker places but still caters to a budget crowd. Spotless and spacious, the old-fashioned, louvre-windowed rooms have a TV and kitchenette, though the bathrooms are all communal. There's a laundry and a

pool lounge area with a barbecue. It's close to the Botanical Gardens and Mindil Beach.

Ashton Lodge (Map pp244-5; ☎ 8941 4866; www.ashtonlodge.com.au; 48 Mitchell St; d without bathroom without/with air-con $65/85, d $140; ❄️ 🖵) This warren of compact rooms is squeezed in behind the Wisdom Bar & Grill in the thick of the action. The cheapest rooms are tiny and there's lots of blue in the decor, but it's very clean and secure.

Value Inn (Map pp244-5; ☎ 8981 4733; www.valueinn.com.au; 50 Mitchell St; d $130; ❄️ 🖵) In the thick of the Mitchell St action but quiet and comfortable, Value Inn lives up to its name. En suite rooms are small but sleep up to three and have fridge, TV and air-con.

Poinciana Inn (Map pp244-5; ☎ 8981 8111; www.poincianainn.com.au; cnr Mitchell & McLachlan Sts; d $160; ❄️ 🖵) Poinciana is unexceptional but undoubtedly central, with the hub of Mitchell St a short walk away. Motel rooms are neat with phone, fridge and TV; extra features include wi-fi and free in-house movies.

Darwin Airport Resort (Map p242; ☎ 1800 600 975; www.darwinairportresort.com.au; cnr Henry Wrigley & Sir Norman Brierly Dr; d $155-205; ❄️ 🖵 💻) If you really must stay near the airport – and it's really not that far from town – this is a good choice of accommodation. A variety of rooms, from fully appointed business suites to rather whimsical-looking bungalows, are set around an impressive pool and landscaped gardens.

APARTMENTS

There are a number of serviced apartments in Darwin that are good value for stays of a week or more – certainly more homely than the big hotels – but you'll need to book well ahead in high season. Some of these seem like top-end prices but fit here because they sleep four to six people. There are often significant discounts in the wet season.

Palms City Resort (Map pp244-5; ☎ 1800 829 211, 8982 9200; www.citypalms.com; 64 the Esplanade; motel d $165-175, villa d $180-265; ❄️ 🖵) Palm-filled gardens and a fabulous location at the southern end of the Esplanade. The superior motel rooms are worth the extra $10 for the extra space. The villas with solid-timber finishes and louvred windows orbit a central pool, while the executive villas with outdoor spa are pure luxury.

Peninsular Apartment Hotel (Map pp244-5; ☎ 1800 808 564; www.peninsularapartments.com; 115 Smith St; d/tr/f $180/190/240; ❄️ 🖵) The self-contained apartments here are ageing but not bad value, and the location is close to the city centre. There's a bar and shaded pool downstairs.

Alatai Holiday Apartments (Map pp244-5; ☎ 1800 628 833, 8981 5188; www.alataiapartments.com.au; cnr McMinn & Finniss Sts; studio/apt $190/295; ✷ ☎) This well-kept, leafy complex built around a swimming pool offers a peaceful and private stay at the northern edge of the city centre. The compact studios sleep two, while roomy two-bedroom apartments have their own kitchen and laundry and sleep up to six. There's a garden cafe and a licensed Chinese restaurant.

Cullen Bay Resorts (Map pp244-5; ☎ 1800 625 533; www.cullenbayresortsdarwin.com.au; 26-32 Marina Blvd; hotel d $150, 1-/2-bedroom apt $240/290; ✷ ☎) Cullen Bay is (or was) Darwin's prime waterfront location and this pair of twin apartment towers boasts million-dollar views over the marina and harbour. You'll pay more than the prices listed here for water views but the slick hotel rooms and spacious apartments are decent value.

Botanic Gardens Apartments (Map pp244-5; ☎ 8946 0300; www.botanicgardens.com.au; 17 Geranium St, Stuart Park; motel d $195, apt $245-395; ✷ ☎) Location, location. In a unique and peaceful location nudging up against the Botanic Gardens, the motel rooms and roomy one-, two- and three-bedroom apartments here are enveloped in palms and lush tropical gardens, and there are two fabulous pools to cool off in. The best apartment rooms boast prestigious views over the Botanic Gardens to the Timor Sea.

Top End

Most of Darwin's high-rise top-dollar hotels are around the city centre and along the Esplanade, hogging the prime water views across the park. By the time you read this a new luxury hotel complex should be open at the wharf precinct. High-season rack rates are listed here, but these are mostly fiction – booking through agents, online or even walk-in should get you a lower rate.

Frontier Hotel (Map pp244-5; ☎ 8981 5333; www.frontierdarwin.com.au; 3 Buffalo Crt; d $185, apt $225; ✷ ☎) Towering above other places on the northern edge of town, this block of spacious, stylish rooms boasts excellent views, particularly from the 6th-floor apartments. There's a bar and the rooftop restaurant has stunning harbour views across the golf course.

Novotel Atrium (Map pp244-5; ☎ 8941 0755; www.noveldarwin.com.au; 100 the Esplanade; d $200-275, 2-bedroom apt from $295; ✷ ☐ ☎) With an impressive namesake atrium, the Novotel is one of Darwin's finest business hotels and has fine views from the upper floors. The well-appointed rooms are arranged around the verdant atrium, at the bottom of which is the Zest Restaurant and a cocktail bar swathed in palms and vines.

Mantra Esplanade (Map pp244-5; ☎ 1300 881 686, 8943 4333; www.mantra.com.au; 88 the Esplanade; d from $230, apt $310-750; ✷ ☐ ☎) This four-star tower of contemporary style has slick hotel rooms and one- to three-bedroom apartments if you really need to spread your wings. Stunning harbour views cost top dollar but the city views are pretty good too. Good business and conference facilities including wi-fi.

Feathers Sanctuary (Map p242; ☎ 8985 2144; www.featherssanctuary.com; 49a Freshwater Rd, Jingili; d $275; ✷) A perfect retreat for bird enthusiasts and nature lovers, Feathers has beautifully designed timber-and-iron cottages with semi-open-air bathrooms and luxurious interiors. The lush gardens have a private aviary breeding some rare birds, and a waterhole – a setting that belies the proximity to the city. Rates include breakfast.

EATING

When it comes to dining, Darwin doesn't pretend to be a Melbourne or Sydney, but it does have by far the best culinary scene between here and Adelaide. Restaurants and cafes make the most of the tropical ambience with alfresco seating and the quality and diversity of produce tops anywhere else in the NT. Savour the exotic and innovative creations at the city's top restaurants, or embark on a culinary jaunt through Asia as you investigate the fast, cheap and varied delights that sizzle and smoke at any of Darwin's bustling multicultural markets (see p259).

A few pubs also entice backpackers off the pavement with free barbecues and cheap meals to soak up the beer. Some of the best deals are at the Vic and Shenannigans – see Drinking (p257) for more information.

Apart from the many city centre restaurants and cafes, Cullen Bay has a hip waterfront dining scene, while the food centre at the end of Stokes Hill Wharf provides cheap and cheerful fish-and-chips and Asian stir-fries, and there are a few gems hidden in the suburbs north of the city.

Restaurants
CITY CENTRE & WHARF PRECINCT

Vietnam Saigon Star (Map pp244-5; ☎ 8981 1420; shop 4, 21 Smith St; mains $5-20; ☒ lunch & dinner Mon-Fri, dinner Sat & Sun; ☒) Surprisingly, this is Darwin's only truly Vietnamese restaurant, with a typically extensive menu. It's quick, clean and inexpensive with rice-paper rolls, beef, pork, chicken and seafood dishes with a multitude of sauces. Vegetarians are well catered for and there are good-value lunch specials.

Monsoons (Map pp244-5; ☎ 8941 7188; www.monsoons.net.au; 46 Mitchell St; mains $13-30; ☒) The old Rourke's Drift pub has been completely remodelled into a sassy restaurant-bar with an oriental/Indian feel – all dark wood, high-back chairs and bamboo blinds. The bar is enormous, the terrace relatively small and the fusion menu features meze plates, lamb kofta and crispy-skin duckling.

Tim's Surf'n'Turf (Map pp244-5; ☎ 8981 1024; 10 Litchfield St; mains $14-30; ☒ lunch Mon-Fri, dinner daily; ☒) Tim's is a long-standing Darwin diner where you can enjoy good-value seafood, steak, schnitzels and pasta in a relaxed, quiet setting – it's squirrelled away in a city backstreet. Specialities include the seafood platter and the surf'n'turf steak. Lunch is great value with all meals at $12.50. It's fully licensed.

Nirvana (Map pp244-5; ☎ 8981 2025; 6 Dashwood Cr; mains $15-30; ☒ dinner Mon-Sat; ☒) Excellent Thai, Malaysian and Indian dishes are only part of the story at Nirvana – it's also one of Darwin's best small live-music venues for jazz and blues. It doesn't look much from the outside, but entering via the fortresslike Smith St door is an intimate warren of rooms with booth seating and oriental decor. Enjoy a Thai green curry, nasi goreng or fish masala with your music.

Ducks Nuts Bar & Grill (Map pp244-5; ☎ 8942 2122; www.ducksnuts.com.au; 76 Mitchell St; mains $15-35; ☒) Slick bistro delivering clever fusion of Top End produce with that Asian-Mediterranean blend we like to claim as Modern Australian. Try the red Thai duck shank and banana curry, barra wrap or succulent lamb shanks. The attached Bar Espresso coffee shop delivers good brekkies and caffeinated brews.

ourpick Hanuman (Map pp244-5; ☎ 8941 3500; 28 Mitchell St; mains $16-32; ☒ lunch Mon-Fri, dinner daily; ☒ Ⓥ) Ask most locals where to find Darwin's top fine-dining experience and the answer is usually Hanuman. Sophisticated but not stuffy or pretentious, enticing aromas of innovative Indian and Thai Nonya dishes waft from the kitchen to the stylish open dining room and deck. The signature dish is oysters bathed in lemongrass, chilli and coriander, or the *meen mooli* – reef fish in coconut and curry leaves – but the menu is broad with exotic vegetarian choices and banquets available.

Moorish Café (Map pp244-5; ☎ 8991 0010; 37 Knuckey St; tapas $7-11, mains $24-32; ☒ Mon-Sat; ☒) Seductive aromas emanate from this divine cafe fusing North African, Mediterranean and Middle Eastern delights. It's especially popular with the lunchtime crowd for its tantalising tapas and lunch specials, but it's an atmospheric place for dinner, with classical Spanish guitar on Tuesdays, salsa dancing Thursdays and belly dancers on Saturday nights. Signature dishes include the *tagine* of the day, vegetarian paella, North African meatballs or Portuguese seafood hotpot with homemade bread.

Char Restaurant (Map pp244-5; ☎ 8981 4544; www.charrestaurant.com.au; cnr Esplanade & Knuckey St; mains $25-40; ☒ lunch & dinner Mon-Fri, dinner Sat & Sun; ☒) In the historic Admiralty House on the Esplanade, Char is the latest addition to Darwin's culinary landscape. The speciality here is chargrilled steaks, aged, grain-fed and cooked to perfection, but there's also a range of seafood, a crab-and-croc lasagne and a thoughtful vegetarian menu. Great wine list too.

Crustaceans (Map pp244-5; ☎ 8981 8658; Stokes Hill Wharf; mains $25-55; ☒ dinner Mon-Sat; ☒) This highly regarded but rather touristy seafood restaurant perches on the end of Stokes Hill Wharf, where diners can enjoy sunset and views over Frances Bay. Fresh fish, mud crabs, lobster, crocodile and oysters grace the tables and are accompanied by a first-rate wine list.

CULLEN BAY

Buzz Cafe (Map pp244-5; ☎ 8941 1141; 48 Marina Blvd, Cullen Bay; mains $15-35; ☒ lunch & dinner, also breakfast on weekends; ☒) This chic bar-restaurant furnished in Indonesian teak and Mt Bromo lava has a super multilevel deck overlooking the marina and makes a lovely, sunny spot for a lazy lunch and a few drinks. Meals are Mod Oz, with some excellent salads and dishes to share. The men's toilets reveal all.

Yots Greek Taverna (Map pp244-5; ☎ 8981 4433; 54 Marina Blvd, Cullen Bay; mains $24-34; ☒ lunch & dinner; ☒ Ⓥ) With a prime deck overlooking the marina, Yots serves up classic Greek and Mediterranean fare from saganaki and souvlaki to moussaka and spanakopita, along with barramundi and prawn dishes – the Greco

---

DARWIN'S SATAY KING

Darwin's Asian-style food markets are an institution, and whether it's the Mindil Beach Sunset Market (p259) on Thursday and Sunday evenings or Parap Market on a Saturday morning, you can bet you'll find Darwin's 'satay king', Bobby Wiviseno, fanning the flames of his smoking brazier.

Bobby was one of the originals who founded the Mindil Markets back in 1986. What started with around 20 stalls has now ballooned to hundreds and in peak season up to 15,000 people flock to the Thursday-night event.

'We proposed the idea as something for the people to have a gateway to Asia,' he said. Bobby first arrived in Darwin in 1979 from Jakarta, Indonesia, but unlike many migrants it was supposed to be temporary. 'I came for a holiday for one week. Three days later I applied for a job here. Darwin is unique. Here the mixed culture between all nations is marvellous. It's the friendliest city in Australia.'

Bobby's tips for a good time in Darwin naturally include visiting all the local markets, as all have a different atmosphere, and to go fishing on the harbour.

Explaining his longevity behind the satay stand, Bobby pays tribute to his wife Annie: 'She's my backbone. Without her, I can't survive.'

---

barramundi is served on spinach with baked lemon potatoes and a caper sauce. Excellent wine list and there's a cheaper lunch menu.

Seadogs (Map pp244-5; ☎ 8941 2877; Marina Blvd; mains $16-24; ❤ lunch & dinner Tue-Sun; ✖) It may not front the marina, but the meals are cheaper at this popular local restaurant specialising in pizza, pasta, risotto and a few prawn and calamari dishes.

PARAP & EAST POINT

Most people visit Parap for the Saturday-morning markets, but the shopping centre has some fine restaurants, cafes and galleries.

Saffrron (Map pp244-5; ☎ 8981 2383; shop 14, 34 Parap Rd, Parap; mains $14-20; ❤ dinner Wed-Sun; ✖ Ⓥ) Saffrron is Darwin's newest Indian restaurant, a contemporary but intimate dining experience. The menu spans the sub-continent, from rich butter chicken to Kerala lamb curry or Goan beef vindaloo. There are plenty of vegetarian choices and traditional India sweets such as *kulfi* (ice cream) and *lassi* (yoghurt drink).

Pee Wee's at the Point (Map p242; ☎ 8981 6868; Alec Fong Lim Dr, East Point Reserve; mains $25-46; ❤ dinner; ✖) Pee Wee's has an unbeatable location with sweeping views over the harbour to East Point. Grilled saltwater barra, lamb rump and tempura bug tails top the Mod Oz menu, and there's a thoughtful vegetarian list. Bookings are recommended.

Cafes & Quick Eats

Darwin has a growing number of cool cafes serving good coffee and snacks. There are also several food courts tucked away in the arcade off Smith St Mall.

Relish (Map pp244-5; ☎ 8941 1900; shop 1, 35 Cavenagh St; meals $4.50-8; ❤ breakfast & lunch Mon-Fri; ✖) Hip hole-in-the-wall cafe with a good dose of acoustic music, local artworks and magazines. Gourmet melts, ciabattas, focaccias and salads dominate the blackboard and there's good coffee or spicy chai.

Cyclone Cafe (Map pp244-5; ☎ 8941 1992; 8 Urquhart St, Parap; meals $5-9; ❤ 7.30am-3pm Mon-Fri, 8.30am-1pm Sat; ✖) Possibly the best coffee in Darwin is brewed at this unassuming local haunt in Parap. The simple corrugated-iron decor harks back to a simpler time, the coffee is strong and aromatic (try the hyper-cino), and there's some great breakfast and lunch fare such as croissants, burritos and cheese melts.

Banyan Tree Cafe (Map pp244-5; ☎ 8981 8577; shop 14, 69 Mitchell St; mains $5-12; ❤ 5.30am-2pm; ✖) At the Transit Centre, the Banyan deserves a mention for its ultra-early breakfasts – ideal if you have an early bus.

Indian Cafe (Map pp244-5; ☎ 8941 0752; 1/15 Knuckey St; mains $7.50; ❤ lunch & dinner; ✖ Ⓥ) Cheap and cheerful, this hole-in-the-wall curry joint has $7.50 two-curries-and-rice meal deals, eat in or take away.

Rendezvous Café (Map pp244-5; ☎ 8981 9231; shop 6, Star Village Arcade, 32 Smith St Mall; mains $7-14; ❤ lunch Mon-Sat, dinner Tue-Sat; ✖ Ⓥ) Tucked away in a quiet arcade off Smith St – look for signboards on the Mall – this Thai and Malaysian BYO cafe has achieved legendary laksa status.

Roma Bar (Map pp244-5; ☎ 8981 6729; 9-11 Cavenagh St; mains $7-16; ☻ breakfast & lunch; ☷) Once dubbed the 'Kremlin' by Gough Whitlam, Roma has long been a local institution and meeting place for lefties, literati and business types. Well away from the bustle of Mitchell St, the free wi-fi is a bonus, the coffee and juices are great, and you can get anything from a muesli and eggs for breakfast to excellent focaccias and wraps for lunch.

Boatshed Coffee House (Map pp244-5; ☎ 8981 0200; 54-56 Marina Blvd, Cullen Bay; mains $5-23; ☻ 7.30am-4pm) Occupying a funky breezeway in Cullen Bay with nautical theme (the central bar is shaped like an Indonesian fishing boat), the Boatshed serves up good coffee, all-day breakfasts and imaginative lunches from a steaming bowl of mussels to Portuguese chicken. It shares some space with the Boardwalk Cafe, overlooking the marina. Wi-fi available.

Cornucopia Museum Café (Map pp244-5; ☎ 8981 1002; Conacher St, Fannie Bay; mains $9-30; ☻ 9am-5pm; ☷) This is a great place for coffee or lunch after a visit to the attached museum (p243). Tempting focaccias, pastas, burgers, crepes, coffee-and-cake deals and cooling iced coffee or chocolate can be enjoyed out on the deck or in the air-conditioned interior.

Self-Catering

There are two large supermarkets in town centre. **Coles** (Map pp244-5; ☎ 8941 8055; Mitchell Centre, 55-59 Mitchell St) is open 24 hours, while **Woolworths** (Map pp244-5; ☎ 8941 6111; cnr Cavenagh & Whitfield Sts) is open until midnight most nights.

Parap Fine Foods (Map pp244-5; ☎ 8981 8597; 40 Parap Rd, Parap) is a gourmet food hall in the Parap shopping centre stocking organic and health foods, deli items and wine – perfect for a picnic.

DRINKING

Drinking is big business in tropical Darwin and the city has dozens of pubs and terrace bars that make the most of sunny afternoons and balmy evenings. Virtually all bars double as restaurants. Mitchell St has the densest concentration of bars popular with travellers, all within a short walk of each other.

Tap on Mitchell (Map pp244-5; ☎ 8981 5521; www .thetap.com.au; 58 Mitchell St; ☻ 8am-10pm) One of the busiest of the terrace bars, the Tap is always buzzing and there are inexpensive meals of nachos, burgers and calamari to complement a good range of wine and beers.

Wisdom Bar & Grill (Map pp244-5; ☎ 8941 4866; www .wisdombar.com; 48 Mitchell St) Bright blue walls, velour couches and a nice terrace with a tree growing out of it add up to a more intimate version of the Tap. There's an extensive menu of bar food.

Victoria Hotel (the Vic; Map pp244-5; ☎ 8981 4011; 27 Smith St) The Vic is a good place for a drink but these days it's more of an all-round backpacker entertainment venue – see p258.

Top End Hotel (Map pp244-5; ☎ 8981 6511; cnr Mitchell & Daly Sts) Popular with locals, this busy little entertainment enclave has several clubs and bars, including Lizards Outdoor Bar & Grill, with its lush tropical beer garden, the Rock 'n' Country Bar, with pool tables on the deck, Elvis posters and guitars stuck to the roof (Darwin's version of the Hard Rock Cafe!) and the Beehive Nightclub.

Darwin Ski Club (Map pp244-5; ☎ 8981 6630; Conacher St, Fannie Bay) Leave Mitchell St behind and head for a sublime sunset at this laid-back water-ski club on Vestey's Beach. The view through the palm trees from the beer garden is sublime and there are often live bands. Interstate or international visitors get issued with a free membership.

Darwin Sailing Club (Map pp244-5; ☎ 8981 1700; www.dnwsail.com.au; Atkins Dr, Fannie Bay; mains $10-32; ☻ noon-11pm) More upmarket than the ski club, the sailing club is always filled with yachties and families enjoying the sunset over the Timor Sea. Expansive beachfront garden, kids' playground and a good range of pasta, Asian curries, burgers and seafood at the Waterfront Bistro.

Shenannigans (Map pp244-5; ☎ 8981 2100; www.shen annigans.com.au; 69 Mitchell St) Darwin has a few Irish-theme pubs, but Shenannigans mixes it up with a big Mitchell St terrace, good food and big party nights.

Other popular city watering holes:

Cavenagh (Map pp244-5; ☎ 8941 6383; www.the cavenagh.com; 12 Cavenagh St) Popular backpackers' and sports bar, the Cav also serves up good food.

Ducks Nuts Bar & Grill (Map pp244-5; ☎ 8942 2122; 76 Mitchell St) A big backlit cocktail bar, regular live music and the swanky Tzars vodka bar give the Ducks Nuts plenty of cred.

Mandorah Beach Hotel (☎ 8978 5044; mandorah beachhotel@bigpond.com) Reached in just 20 minutes by the ferry from Cullen Bay, the Mandorah pub is well worth a visit for a beer and a meal with views back across the bay to Darwin city – see p262.

DARWIN & AROUND

ENTERTAINMENT

Darwin's balmy nights invite a bit of late-night exploration and while there are only a handful of nightclubs, you'll find something on every night of the week. There's also a thriving arts and entertainment scene of theatre, film and concerts.

Find up-to-date entertainment listings for live music and other attractions in the free what's on guide *Off the Leash*.

Top End Arts (www.topendarts.com.au) lists events happening around town, as does **Darwin Community Arts** (www.darwincommunityarts.org.au). Keep an eye out for bills posted on noticeboards and telegraph poles that advertise dance and full-moon parties.

Live Music

Just about every pub and bar in town has some form of live music, mostly on Friday and Saturday nights. Some places also keep their microphones busy with karaoke and DJs on other nights.

Victoria Hotel (the Vic; Map pp244–5; ☎ 8981 4011; 27 Smith St) The Vic has loads of history – the stone building on the Mall dates from 1890 – but it's hard to see it these days. This is Darwin's favourite backpacker pub and goes off every night of the week. Dirt-cheap meals draw the travellers into the upstairs Banjos Bar, and they stay for the pool tables, DJs and dance floor. Downstairs is a happening bar with a pub quiz on Monday, table dancing, live bands and DJs.

Nirvana (Map pp244–5; ☎ 8981 2025; Smith St; ⏲ from 6.30pm Mon-Sat) Behind an imposing doorway, this cosy restaurant-bar has live jazz/blues every Thursday, Friday and Saturday night and a open-mic jam session every Tuesday. As well as meals, bar snacks are available at reasonable prices.

Ducks Nuts Bar & Grill (Map pp244–5; ☎ 8942 2122; www.ducksnuts.com.au; 76 Mitchell St) Live band every Friday night and occasional Sunday sessions.

Nightclubs

Discovery & Lost Arc (Map pp244–5; ☎ 8942 3300; www.discoverynightclub.com; 89 Mitchell St; ⏲ 9pm-4am Fri & Sat) Discovery is Darwin's biggest nightclub and dance venue with three levels playing techno, hip-hop and R&B tunes. Lost Arc is the neonlit chill-out bar opening on to Mitchell St, but it starts to rock after 10pm.

Throb (Map pp244–5; ☎ 8942 3435; www.throbnightclub.com.au; 64 Smith St; admission $10; ⏲ 11pm-4am Fri&Sat)

Darwin's premier gay- and lesbian-friendly nightclub and cocktail bar, Throb attracts partygoers of all genders and persuasions for its hot DJs and cool atmosphere. Hosts drag shows and touring live acts.

Cinemas

Deckchair Cinema (Map pp244–5; ☎ 8981 0700; www.deckchaircinema.com; Jervois Rd, Wharf Precinct; adult/child/family $13/6/30; box office ⏲ from 6.30pm Apr-Nov) During the Dry, the Darwin Film Society runs this fabulous outdoor cinema below the southern end of the Esplanade. Watch a movie under the stars while reclining in a deckchair – bring a cushion for real comfort. There's a licensed bar serving food or you can bring your own picnic (no BYO alcohol). There's usually a double feature on Friday and Saturday ($20/9/45). If you're walking, the best way to get here is via the Damoe Ra walkway at the southern end of Bicentennial Park – follow the signs.

Darwin City Cinemas (Map pp244–5; ☎ 981 5999; 76 Mitchell St; adult/child $15/10.50) This is the city's large cinema complex, screening the latest-release films across five theatres. Head down on Tropical Tuesday for $9 entry (all day).

Theatre

Darwin Entertainment Centre (Map pp244–5; ☎ 8980 3333; www.darwinentertainment.com.au; 93 Mitchell St; box office ⏲ 10am-5.30pm Mon-Fri & 1hr prior to shows) Darwin's main community arts venue houses the Playhouse and Studio Theatres, and hosts events from fashion-award nights to plays, rock operas, comedies and concerts. Check the website for upcoming shows.

Brown's Mart (Map pp244–5; ☎ 8981 5522; www.brownsmart.com.au; Harry Chan Ave) This historic venue features live theatre performances, music and short films. An arty crowd congregates here for Bamboo Lounge.

Casino

Skycity Darwin (Map pp244–5; ☎ 8943 8888; www.skycitydarwin.com.au; Gilruth Ave) On Mindil Beach, this is Darwin's flashy casino complex with accommodation, three restaurants and all the card tables, roulette wheels and pokie machines you need – all the tools to help you lose your shirt (or win your fortune); and to ensure you have one to lose there's a dress code, which means no singlets, thongs or scruffy clothing.

SHOPPING

You'll find specialist shops for outdoor gear, cameras and photographic equipment, books, fishing tackle, fashion clothing and more in Darwin's central business district. Many chain stores are represented at the large Casuarina Shopping Centre (Map p242). A visit to one of Darwin's fabulous outdoor markets (below) is an 'essential' for all shopaholics.

Arts & Crafts

The city centre has a good range of outlets and galleries selling arts and crafts from the Top End, such as bark paintings from Arnhem Land, and carvings and screen prints by the Tiwi people of Bathurst and Melville Islands. It's worth having a browse in a couple of galleries to build some knowledge of artists and prices, and to recognise the regional differences in art. Some of the best galleries:

24HR Art (☎ 8981 5368; www.24hrart.org.au; Vimy Lane, Parap Village Shopping Centre; ☷ 10am-4pm Wed-Fri, to 2pm Sat) Changing exhibitions by the Northern Territory Centre for Contemporary Art.

Aboriginal Fine Arts (Map pp244-5; ☎ 8981 1315; www.aaia.com.au; 1st fl, cnr Mitchell & Knuckey Sts) Displays and sells art from Arnhem Land and the Central Desert region, including the work of high-profile artists such as 'Lofty' Bardayal Nadjamerrek.

Framed (Map pp244-5; ☎ 8981 2994; www.framed.com.au; 55 Stuart Hwy, Stuart Park) Framed presents a fine range of arts and crafts in its gallery near Botanic Gardens entrance. The eclectic and ever-changing range is typically Territorian and tropical, and includes contemporary Aboriginal art, pottery, jewellery and exquisitely carved furniture.

Karen Brown Gallery (Map pp244-5; ☎ 8981 9985; www.karenbrowngallery.com; 1/22 Mitchell St) Commercial gallery specialising in changing exhibitions of contemporary Aboriginal art.

Maningrida Arts & Culture (Map pp244-5; ☎ 8981 4122; www.maningrida.com; shop 1, 32 Mitchell St) Features didgeridoos, weavings and paintings from the Kunibidji community at Maningrida on the banks of the Liverpool River, Arnhem Land.

Mason Gallery (Map pp244-5; ☎ 8981 9622; www.masongallery.com.au; shop 7, 21 Cavenagh St) Features bold dot paintings from the Western Desert regions of Papunya, Kintore and Kiwirrkura, and the Central Desert region of Utopia.

Territory Colours (Map pp244-5; ☎ 8981 1803; www.territorycolours.com; 21 Knuckey St) Contemporary paintings and crafts, including glass, porcelain and wood from local artists; features the work of contemporary Indigenous artist Harold Thomas.

DARWIN'S MAGICAL MARKETS

As the sun heads towards the horizon on Thursday and Sunday, half of Darwin descends on **Mindil Beach Sunset Market** (Map pp244-5; ☎ 8981 3454; www.mindil.com.au; off Gilruth Ave; 5-10pm Thu & 4-9pm Sun May-Oct) with tables, chairs, rugs, grog and kids to settle under the coconut palms for sunset and decide which of the tantalising food-stall aromas has the greatest allure. Food is the main attraction and it spans the globe from Thai, Sri Lankan, Indian, Chinese and Malaysian to Brazilian, Greek, Portuguese and more, all at around $5 to $8 a serve. Top it off with fresh fruit salad, decadent cakes or luscious crepes. But it's only half the fun: arts and crafts stalls bulge with handmade jewellery, fabulous rainbow tie-died clothes, Aboriginal artefacts, and wares from Indonesia and Thailand. Patrons peruse and promenade, or stop for a pummelling massage or to listen to rhythmic live music. Mindil Beach is about 2km from the city centre. Buses 4 and 6 go past the market area or you can catch a shuttle ($2).

Similar stalls (you'll recognise many of the stallholders) can be found at various suburban markets from Friday to Sunday.

- **Parap Village Market** (Map pp244-5; ☎ 8942 0805; Parap Village Shopping Centre; ☷ 8am-2pm Sat) This compact but crowded market is a local favourite every Saturday with the full gamut of Southeast Asian cuisine, as well as plenty of ingredients to cook up your own storm.

- **Nightcliff Market** (Map p242; Pavonia Way; ☷ 8am-2pm Sun) Another popular community market, north of the city in the Nightcliff Shopping Centre. Lots of craft stalls, secondhand goods and designer clothing.

- **Rapid Creek Market** (Map p242; Trower Rd; ☷ 5-10pm Fri, 8am-2pm Sun) Darwin's oldest market is another Asian marketplace, with a tremendous range of tropical fruit and vegetables mingled with a heady mixture of spices and swirling satay smoke. Among the fresh produce you can also find book stalls, bric-a-brac and purveyors of everything from sharks' teeth to mango smoothies.

DARWIN & AROUND

Outdoor Equipment

NT General Store (Map pp244-5; ☎ 8981 8242; 42 Cavenagh St) For camping-equipment needs, this is one of the best places with shelves piled high with clothing, tents and bush gear. It also has a great range of guidebooks and maps.

GETTING THERE & AWAY
Air

Domestic flights connect Darwin with all other Australian capital cities, as well as Alice Springs, Broome, Cairns, Kununurra and various regions throughout the Top End. A few international flights to Asian destinations also leave Darwin. Check websites for current fares.

Apart from the following major carriers, smaller routes are flown by local operators; ask a travel agent.

Airnorth (☎ 1800 627 474; www.airnorth.com.au) Small airline serving the Top End region and some international destinations including Broome, Gove/Nhulunbuy, Kununurra, Dili (East Timor) and Denpasar (Indonesia).

Jetstar (☎ 13 15 38; www.jetstar.com) Direct flights to Melbourne, Sydney, Brisbane, Cairns and Adelaide, as well as international flights to Singapore and Ho Chi Minh City (Vietnam).

Qantas (☎ 13 13 13; www.qantas.com.au) Direct daily services to Adelaide, Alice Springs, Brisbane, Cairns, Melbourne, Perth and Sydney.

Skywest (☎ 1300 66 00 88; www.skywest.com.au) Direct flights to Perth and Broome.

Virgin Blue (☎ 13 67 89; www.virginblue.com.au) Direct flights only to Brisbane; for other cities, connect through Brisbane.

Boat

Sea Cat (Map pp244-5; ☎ 8941 1991; www.seacat.com.au; adult/child/family return $20.50/10.50/60) runs a regular ferry service to and from Mandorah, a 20-minute ride across the bay (see p262). The same company runs the **Arafura Pearl** (adult/child $259/189; ⊙ 7.30am Mon, Wed & Fri) ferry to the Tiwi Islands (see opposite). Both services depart from Cullen Bay ferry terminal.

Bus

There's only one road in and out of Darwin and long-distance bus services are operated by **Greyhound Australia** (Map pp244-5; ☎ 1300 473 946; www.greyhound.com.au; Transit Centre, 69 Mitchell St). At least one service per day travels up and down the Stuart Hwy. Buses depart from the rear of the Transit Centre and stop at various points down the Stuart Hwy, including Pine Creek ($65, three hours), Katherine ($84, 4½ hours), Mataranka ($106, seven hours), Tennant Creek ($225, 14½ hours) and Alice Springs ($314, 22 hours).

For Kakadu, there's a daily return service from Darwin to Cooinda ($74, 4½ hours) via Jabiru ($53, 3½ hours). There's no service to Litchfield.

Car & Campervan

For driving around Darwin, conventional vehicles are cheap enough, but most companies offer only 100km free and around Darwin 100km won't get you very far. The prices invariably drop for longer rentals for both 2WD and 4WD vehicles. Rates start at around $35 per day for a small car with 100km per day.

There are also plenty of 4WD vehicles available in Darwin, but you usually have to book ahead, and fees and deposits are higher than for 2WD vehicles. Larger companies offer one-way rentals plus better mileage deals for more expensive vehicles. Campervans are a great option for touring around the NT and you generally get unlimited kilometres even for short rentals. Prices start at around $50 a day for a basic camper or $80 to $100 for a three-berth hi-top camper, to $200-plus for the bigger mobile homes or 4WD bushcampers. Additional insurance cover or excess reduction costs extra.

Most rental companies are open every day and have agents in the city centre. Avis, Budget, Hertz and Thrifty all have offices at the airport.

Advance Car Rentals (Map pp244-5; ☎ 8981 2999; www.advancecar.com.au; 86 Mitchell St) Small local operator with some good deals.

Avis (Map pp244-5; ☎ 8981 9922; www.avis.com; 89 Smith St)

Backpacker Campervans (Map p242; ☎ 8981 2081; www.backpackercampervans.com.au; 17 Bombing Rd, Winnellie) At the same depot as Britz, this is a budget outfit with small campers and hi-tops at reasonable rates.

Britz Australia (Map p242; ☎ 8981 2081; www.britz .com.au; 17 Bombing Rd, Winnellie) Britz is a reliable outfit with a big range of campervans and motorhomes, including the 4WD bushcampers.

Budget (Map pp244-5; ☎ 8981 9800; www.budget .com.au; cnr Daly St & Doctors Gully Rd)

Europcar (Map pp244-5; ☎ 8941 0300; www.europcar .com.au; 77 Cavenagh St)

Hertz (Map pp244-5; ☎ 8941 0944; www.hertz.com.au; cnr Smith & Daly Sts)

Thrifty (Map pp244-5; ☎ 8924 0000; www.rentacar .com.au; 64 Stuart Hwy, Stuart Park)

Travellers Auto Barn (Map pp244-5; ☎ 8941 7700; www.travellers-autobarn.com.au; 13 Daly St) Campervan specialist.

Wicked Campers (Map p242; ☎ 1800 24 68 69; www .wickedcampers.com.au; 34 Bishop St, Woolner) Colourfully painted small campers aimed at backpackers.

Train

The famous *Ghan* train operates weekly (twice weekly May to July) between Adelaide and Darwin via Alice Springs. The Darwin terminus is located on Berrimah Rd, about 18km or 20 minutes from the city centre. A taxi fare into the centre is about $30, though there is a shuttle service to/from the Transit Centre for $10. See p303 for fare details. Bookings (recommended) can be made through **Trainways** (☎ 13 21 47; www.trainways.com.au).

GETTING AROUND
To/From the Airport

Darwin International Airport (Map p242; ☎ 8920 1805) is about 12km northeast of the centre of town, and handles both international

---

TIWI ISLANDS

The Tiwi Islands – Bathurst and Melville Islands – lie about 80km north of Darwin, and are home to the Tiwi Aboriginal people. The Tiwis ('We People') have a distinct culture and today are well known for producing vibrant art and the odd champion Aussie Rules football player.

Tourism is restricted on the islands and for most tourists the only way to visit is on one of the daily organised tours from Darwin (see below).

The Tiwis' island homes kept them fairly isolated from mainland developments until the 20th century, and their culture has retained several unique features. Perhaps the best known are the *pukumani* (burial poles), carved and painted with symbolic and mythological figures, which are erected around graves. More recently the Tiwi have turned their hands to art for sale – carving, painting, textile screen printing, batik and pottery using traditional designs and motifs. The Bima Wear textile factory was set up in 1969 to employ Tiwi women, and today makes many bright fabrics in distinctive designs.

The main settlement on the islands is **Nguiu**, in the southeast of Bathurst Island, which was founded in 1911 as a Catholic mission. On Melville Island the settlements are **Pularumpi** and **Milikapiti**.

The majority of the 2700 Tiwi Islanders live on Bathurst Island (there's about 900 people on Melville Island). Most follow a mainly nontraditional lifestyle, but they still hunt dugong and gather turtle eggs, and hunting and gathering usually supplements the mainland diet a couple of times a week. Tiwis also go back to their traditional lands on Melville Island for a few weeks each year to teach and to learn traditional culture. Descendants of the Japanese pearl divers who regularly visited here early this century also live on Melville Island.

Aussie Rules football is a passion among the islanders and one of the biggest events of the year (the only time it's possible to visit without a permit) is the Tiwi football grand-final day in late March. Given the large numbers of people coming across from the mainland for the event, it's still best to organise this through a tour or book well ahead for the *Arafura Pearl*.

Tours

Tiwi Tours (☎ 1300 721 365, 8923 6523; www.aussieadventure.com.au) runs fascinating one- and two-day Tiwi Island tours, although interaction with the local Tiwi community tends to be limited to your guides and the local workshops and showrooms. A one-day tour (adult/child $414/212) to Bathurst Island includes a charter flight, permit, lunch, tea and damper with Tiwi women, craft workshops, and visits to the early Catholic mission buildings, the Patakijiyali Museum and a *pukumani* burial site. It departs daily from April to November.

The two-day tour ($704/544) includes overnight camping in a remote location and allows you to get a better experience of the people, culture and the islands environment, with wildlife spotting and searching for turtles' nests. The tour operates on Tuesday from May to October.

Arafura Pearl (Map pp244-5; ☎ 8941 1991; www.seacat.com.au; adult/child $259/189; ⏰ tours 7.30am Mon, Wed & Fri, Mar-Nov) is a cheaper alternative to flying, with daily catamaran tours run in association with Tiwi Tours. Leaving Cullen Bay ferry terminal at 7.30am and returning at 5pm, the trip takes about two hours, and you spend all of the land time in Nguiu, visiting the church, museum, Tiwi Design and Ngaruwanajirri Art Community. There's an additional permit charge of $16.50 per person.

and domestic flights. **Darwin Airport Shuttle** (☎ 1800 358 945, 8981 5066) will pick up or drop off almost anywhere in central Darwin for $11. When leaving Darwin book a day before departure. A taxi fare into the centre is about $22, so two or more travellers might as well take a cab.

Public Transport

Darwinbus (Map pp244-5; ☎ 8924 7666; Harry Chan Ave) runs a comprehensive bus network that departs from the City Bus Interchange, opposite Brown's Mart. Buses enter the city along Mitchell St and leave along Cavenagh St.

A $2 adult ticket gives unlimited travel on the bus network for three hours (validate your ticket when you first get on). Daily ($5) and weekly ($15) travel cards are also available from bus interchanges, some newsagencies and Tourism Top End (p241). Bus 4 (to Fannie Bay, Nightcliff, Rapid Creek and Casuarina) and bus 6 (Fannie Bay, Parap and Stuart Park) are useful for getting to Aquascene, the Botanic Gardens, Mindil Beach, the Museum & Art Gallery of the Northern Territory, Fannie Bay Gaol Museum, East Point and the markets.

The **Tour Tub** (☎ 8985 6322; www.tourtub.com .au) hop-on-hop-off minibus tours Darwin's sights throughout the day; see p250.

Scooter

Darwin Scooter Hire (Map pp244-5; ☎ 0418 892 885; www .thescootershop.com.au; 29 Stuart Hwy), rents out 50cc scooters for $30/40 per two/four hours or $50 per day. Motorbikes are also available for hire, along with bicycles.

Taxi

Taxis wait along Knuckey St, diagonally opposite the north end of Smith St Mall, and are usually easy to flag down. Phone **Darwin Radio Taxis** (☎ 13 10 08).

AROUND DARWIN
Mandorah

A low-key, relaxed residential beach suburb, Mandorah looks out across the harbour at Darwin. It sits on the tip of Cox Peninsula, 128km by road from Darwin but only 6km across the harbour by regular ferry. The main reason to visit is for the ferry ride across the harbour and a few drinks or dinner at the superfriendly pub. The nearby Wagait Aboriginal community numbers around 400 residents.

The **Mandorah Beach Hotel** (☎ 8978 5044; man dorahbeachhotel@bigpond.com; d $88, f $110; 🅿 🏊) has sublime views over the beach and turquoise water to Darwin. All rooms in the refurbished motel have a fridge, TV and air-con. Even if you don't stay the night, the pub and restaurant are great. Hearty meals ($10 to $25) are available for lunch and dinner and there's live music some weekends in season.

The **Sea Cat** (Map pp244-5; ☎ 8941 1991; www.sea cat.com.au; adult/child/family return fare $20.50/10.50/60) operates about a dozen daily services, with the first departure from the Cullen Bay Marina in Darwin at 6.30am and the last at 10pm (midnight on Friday and Saturday). The last ferry from Mandorah is at 10.20pm (12.20am on Friday and Saturday nights).

DARWIN TO KAKADU

Heading south for 34km out of the city, the Arnhem Hwy branches left off the Stuart Hwy towards Kakadu National Park and Arnhem Land. There's a whole chunk of the Top End to see between here and there – open wetlands, crocodile-infested rivers, brilliant barra fishing and welcoming roadhouses. You could make the main stops in a day, but with more time it's worth exploring the Adelaide River and Mary River wetlands. The highway crosses these two major rivers, which are probably best known to tourists for the acrobatic antics of the resident saltwater crocodiles, but better known to locals and serious anglers as a fishing paradise.

Greyhound Australia (Map pp244-5; ☎ 1300 473 946; www.greyhound.com.au; Transit Centre, 69 Mitchell St, Darwin) buses run between Darwin and Cooinda daily ($74, 4½ hours), stopping at Jabiru and numerous accommodation places along the way.

Where the Arnhem Hwy branches off the Stuart Hwy, the **Didgeridoo Hut & Art Gallery** (☎ 8988 4457; www.didgeridoohut.com.au; 1 Arnhem Hwy) is an Aboriginal-owned venture where you can watch artists from Kakadu and Arnhem Land at work and purchase Indigenous arts and crafts, particularly a wide range of didgeridoos.

HUMPTY DOO
pop 5413
Only 10km along the highway you come to a small but spread-out town with the unlikely

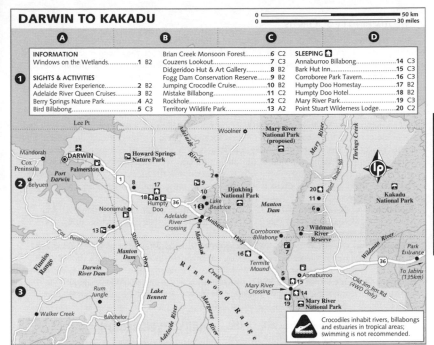

DARWIN TO KAKADU

0   50 km
0   30 miles

INFORMATION
Windows on the Wetlands.................1 B2

SIGHTS & ACTIVITIES
Adelaide River Experience................2 B2
Adelaide River Queen Cruises........3 B2
Berry Springs Nature Park................4 A2
Bird Billabong..................................5 C3

Brian Creek Monsoon Forest.............6 C2
Couzens Lookout...........................7 C3
Didgeridoo Hut & Art Gallery..........8 B2
Fogg Dam Conservation Reserve......9 B2
Jumping Crocodile Cruise...............10 B2
Mistake Billabong.........................11 C2
Rockhole....................................12 A2
Territory Wildlife Park...................13 A2

SLEEPING
Annaburroo Billabong....................14 C3
Bark Hut Inn...............................15 C3
Corroboree Park Tavern.................16 C3
Humpty Doo Homestay..................17 B2
Humpty Doo Hotel........................18 B2
Mary River Park...........................19 C3
Point Stuart Wilderness Lodge........20 C2

Crocodiles inhabit rivers, billabongs and estuaries in tropical areas; swimming is not recommended.

DARWIN & AROUND

name of Humpty Doo. You first pass a turn into a bland modern shopping centre, but continue further up the highway to the self-proclaimed 'world famous' **Humpty Doo Hotel** (☎ 8988 1372; www.humptydoohotel.com.au; Arnhem Hwy; d $80, cabins $95; ✷ ✷). It's a popular local that serves lunch and dinner ($12 to $20). There are big Sunday sessions and weekend local bands.

Humpty Doo Homestay (☎ 8988 1147; bmadent opend@austarnet.com.au; 45 Acacia Rd; cottage $100; ✷ ✷), 2.5km north of the Arnhem Hwy (turn left just past the pub), is a delightful fully equipped cottage set in tropical gardens, which sleeps up to four people comfortably. There's an outdoor barbecue area and pool, and there's plenty of local bird and animal life around – the owners help look after sick and injured wildlife.

ADELAIDE RIVER WETLANDS
Fogg Dam Conservation Reserve

About 15km beyond Humpty Doo is the turnoff to **Fogg Dam Conservation Reserve**, which lies 10km north of the highway. A carpet of green conceals most of the dam waters, which provide a wetland home to numerous water birds.

In the 1950s investors pumped a load of money into the Humpty Doo Rice Project, a scheme to turn the Adelaide River floodplains into a major rice-growing enterprise. It lasted just 10 years due to poor infrastructure and highly variable seasons; however, the dam quickly became an important dry-season refuge for wildlife. During the Dry you're likely to see plenty of white-bellied sea eagles, magpies geese, brolgas, jabirus, kingfishers, ibises and egrets. The reserve also contains large numbers of water pythons – which feed almost exclusively on the numerous dusky rats – plus a multitude of mosquitoes and saltwater crocodiles.

The road into the reserve goes right across the old low-lying dam wall. On the western side of the wall, the elevated **Pandanus Lookout** has interpretive signs and is a good spot to catch a sunset.

There are several other viewing platforms, and marked walks start at the reserve entry car park before the dam wall. The **Monsoon Forest Walk** (3.6km return, one hour) takes you through a variety of habitats, including monsoon and paperbark forests, then on

---

THE JUMPING CROC CIRCUS

Few people seem to be able to resist the sight of a 5m-long saltwater crocodile launching itself out of the water towards a hunk of meat. Like a well-trained circus act, these wild crocs know where to get a free feed and down on the Adelaide River, the croc-jumping show is guaranteed.

Jumping out of the water to grab prey is actually natural behaviour for crocs, usually to take surprised birds or animals from overhanging branches. They use their powerful tails to propel themselves up from a stationary start just below the surface, from where they can see their prey.

Croc-jumping cruises have been going on the Adelaide River for more than 20 years now and there are currently three operators at different locations along the river. The modus operandi is pretty similar – a crew member or lucky tourist gets to hold one end of a long stick that has a couple of metres of string attached to the other end. Tied to the end of the string is a very do-mestic-looking pork chop. Not exactly wild bush tucker, but the acrobatic crocs seem to love it. The whole thing is a bit of a circus really, but it is still a thoroughly amazing sight – have your camera at the ready.

Adelaide River Experience (☎ 8983 3224; www.adelaiderivercruises.com.au; Anzac Parade; adult/child $30/16; ☺ shows 9am, 11am, 1pm & 3pm) On a private stretch of river past the Fogg Dam turn-off. Also runs small-group full-day wildlife cruises.

Adelaide River Queen (☎ 8988 8144; www.jumpingcrocodilecruises.com.au; all cruises $25; ☺ shows 9am, 11am, 1pm & 3pm) Well-established operator on the highway just before Adelaide River Crossing. Licensed coffee shop.

Jumping Crocodile Cruise (☎ 8988 9077; www.jumpingcrocodile.com.au; adult/child/family $30/15/70; ☺ tours 9am, 11am, 1pm & 3pm) Along the Window on the Wetlands access road, this outfit runs one-hour tours.

---

to the floodplains. On the other side of the road, the **Woodlands to Waterlilies Walk** (2.2km return, 45 minutes) skirts the southern edge of the dam through woodlands that fringe the floodplains. You can walk along the dam wall to the **Pandanus Lookout** (2.2km return, 45 minutes) or drive it.

You may see northern quolls and black-footed bandicoots on the **nocturnal walks** (☎ 8988 8188) conducted by rangers during the Dry; bookings are essential.

Window on the Wetlands Visitors Centre

There aren't many hills in this pancake-flat region and Beatrice Hill, right beside the highway 3km past the Fogg Dam turnoff, is little more than a small bump. But it's the perfect elevation for **Windows on the Wetlands** (☎ 8988 8188; admission free; ☺ 7.30am-7pm), a modern structure full of static and interactive displays that give a great introduction to the wetland ecosystem, as well as the history of the local Aboriginal people: this area is known to the Limilngan-Wulna people as the place of the Turtle Dreaming. There are great views over the Adelaide River floodplain from the observation deck, and binoculars for studying the water birds on Lake Beatrice.

MARY RIVER REGION

Beyond the Adelaide River, the Arnhem Hwy passes through the Mary River region with the wetlands and wildlife of the (Proposed)Mary River National Park extending to the north.

Bird Billabong, just off the highway a few kilometres before Mary River Crossing, is a backflow billabong, filled by creeks flowing off the nearby Mt Bundy Hill during the Wet. It's 4km off the highway and accessible by 2WD year-round. The scenic **loop walk** (4.5km loop, 1½ hours) passes through tropical woodlands, with a backdrop of Mount Bundy granite rocks, and true to its name you'll see a variety of birdlife from the lookout.

A little further on is the emerald green **Mary River Billabong**, with a pleasant barbecue area (no camping), and from here a 4WD-only track leads deeper into the national park to Corroboree Billabong and Hardies Lagoon (25km) and Couzens camping area (37km).

Back on the Arnhem Hwy, it's 3km to **Mary River Crossing** where there's a small reserve with a boat ramp providing river access, a picnic ground and toilets. Further along are a few roadhouses and accommodation places before you reach Kakadu National Park.

Corroboree Park Tavern (☎ 8978 8920; Arnhem Hwy, Corroboree Park; unpowered/powered sites $10/18.50,

DETOUR: MARY RIVER NATIONAL PARK

For locals in the know, the (proposed) Mary River National Park is the perfect antidote to the well-touristed Kakadu. Covering the Mary River wetlands, it's a fabulous spot for fishing, birdwatching and wildlife-spotting. The main access road, the Point Stuart Rd, turns off the Arnhem Hwy 19km west of the Bark Hut Inn and leads north. It is 2WD-accessible in the Dry, sealed for the first 17km and unsealed for the 37km to Shady Camp. Access to the western side of the park is via Hardies (4WD) Track, which continues north from the Bird Billabong access road. The park's 4WD roads are closed during the Wet; for road information call ☎ 1800 246 199.

Sixteen kilometres north along the Point Stuart Rd, another dirt road heads west for 16km to **Couzens Lookout** on the Mary River. It offers great views, especially at sunset, and has a basic camping area. **Rockhole,** 1km further along, has a boat ramp, information boards, picnic tables and toilets.

Back on the Point Stuart Rd, about 9km north of the Couzens Lookout turn-off, another side-road heads west to the **Brian Creek Monsoon Forest**. About 400m along this road is a car park with an 800m walk leading to a small pocket of rainforest boasting an awesome strangler fig and plenty of hand-sized spiders that weave webs across the track.

Again back on the Point Stuart Rd, about 3km past the Brian Creek/Wildman turn-off, **Mistake Billabong** is an attractive wetland with a viewing platform and picnic ground. A further 7km brings you to Point Stuart Wilderness Lodge.

Another 18km brings you to **Shady Camp**, a popular fishing spot right on the Mary River where there are picnic tables, pit fires, toilets, campsites and a viewing platform. The grassy campsites under banyan trees are appealing, but armies of mosquitoes swarm in at dusk so come prepared. There is also a boat ramp and boat hire is available.

A two-hour **wetland cruise** ($35 per person; ⊙ 10am & 4pm) on Rockhole Billabong can be arranged from the Point Stuart Wilderness Lodge.

Point Stuart Wilderness Lodge (☎ 8978 8914; www.pointstuart.com.au; unpowered/powered sites $24/30, d from $85; ⊠ ▣ ▣) is part of an old cattle station and a great base from which to explore the Mary River region. Camp or stay in comfortable cabins, and there's a good bar and bistro serving breakfast, dinner and packed lunches. Boat hire is available and wetland cruises can be booked here. The lodge is easily accessed by 2WD, 1.5km off the Point Stuart Rd and 5km north of Mistake Billabong.

s/d cabin $55/70; ⊠ ▣) has lots of grassy camping space, cosy budget cabins, a store, bistro (mains $15 to $20) and a mini menagerie of pigs, an albino buffalo and Fred and Brutus the pet saltwater and freshwater crocs.

Mary River Park (☎ 1800 788 844, 8978 8877; www.maryriverpark.com.au; Arnhem Hwy, Mary River Crossing; unpowered/powered sites $22/30, cabins $99, deluxe cabins $199; ⊠ ▣), boasting 3km of Mary River frontage but a location just off the highway, is a fine bush retreat heading steadily upmarket. New owners have built a slick licensed restaurant (mains $10 to $30) and 10 small but comfortable units around a private pool to complement the cheaper cabins (which have en suites) and grassy camping area down by the river. Guided tours include a croc cruise ($45), sunset cruise ($80) and half-day fishing ($160); bookings essential.

Bark Hut Inn (☎ 8978 8988; Arnhem Hwy, Annaburroo; unpowered/powered sites $14/22, s/d/f $45/60/80; ⊠ ▣)

has a rustic bar adorned with boar and buffalo heads, and a remarkable little bullet collection, while the bistro (mains $15 to $23) serves hearty pub meals of kangaroo, barra, buffalo and plain old chicken. This is the last place to stock up on takeaway alcohol (albeit overpriced) – it's not available in Kakadu. There's camping out the back but the basic dongas leave much to be desired.

ourpick Annaburroo Billabong (☎ 8978 8971; Arnhem Hwy; unpowered sites per adult/family $7.50/20, cabins $70-150; ⊠) has a private billabong, bush camping sites, a wandering menagerie and friendly owners – it seems a world away from the highway only 2km down the road and is a great alternative to the roadhouses. The elevated African-style safari cabins with fridge and en suite are cosy, and there are cabins, lodge rooms and immaculate tin-and-bamboo amenity blocks. Free canoes for guests to paddle around the croc-free billabong.

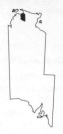

Kakadu National Park

Kakadu is much more than just a national park. It's an adventure into a natural and cultural landscape that almost defies description. Encompassing almost 20,000 sq km, it holds in its boundaries a spectacular ecosystem and a mind-blowing concentration of ancient rock art.

In just a few days you can cruise on billabongs bursting with crocodiles and birdlife, examine 25,000-year-old rock paintings with the help of an Indigenous guide, swim in pools at the foot of tumbling waterfalls and hike through ancient sandstone escarpment country.

Kakadu and neighbouring Arnhem Land epitomise the remarkable landscape and cultural heritage of the Top End. Each is a treasure house of natural history and Aboriginal art, and both are significant in terms of contemporary Indigenous culture and its connection with tradition. It's an acknowledgement of the elemental link between the Aboriginal custodians and the country they have nurtured, endured and respected for thousands of generations. The landscape is an ever-changing tapestry – periodically scorched and flooded, apparently desolate or obviously abundant depending on the season.

If Kakadu has a downside – in the dry season at least – it's that it's very popular. Resorts, camping grounds and rock-art sites can get very crowded in peak seasons, but this is a vast park and with a little adventurous spirit you can easily get off the beaten track and be alone with nature.

HIGHLIGHTS

- Watching the sun set over the floodplains from the rocky sentinel of **Ubirr** (p274)

- Viewing the exceptional Aboriginal rock-art galleries under the massive rock face of **Nourlangie** (p278)

- Discovering the rock art of Injalak Hill and visiting the art centre at **Gunbalanya** (p283)

- Spotting saltwater crocodiles and seeing remarkable birdlife on a dawn cruise of the **Yellow Water Wetlands** (p281)

- Visiting Kakadu's excellent and absorbing **Bowali Visitor Centre** (p271) and **Warradjan Aboriginal Cultural Centre** (p271)

- Rolling out a swag and **camping** (p273) under the stars at one of the many bush-camping sites

- Getting off the beaten track and **bushwalking** (p271) along the many park trails.

- TELEPHONE CODE: ☎ 08 | - www.environment.gov.au/parks/kakadu | - www.kakadunationalpark.com

HISTORY

Kakadu was proclaimed a national park in three stages. Stage One, the eastern and central part of the park (including Ubirr, Nourlangie, Jim Jim and Twin Falls and Yellow Water billabong), was declared in 1979. Stage Two, in the north, was declared in 1984 and gained World Heritage listing. Stage Three, in the south, was finally listed in 1991, bringing virtually the whole of the South Alligator River system within the park.

Aboriginal Heritage

It is known that Aboriginal people have lived in the Kakadu area for at least 23,000 years, and possibly up to 50,000 years. Artefacts such as stone tools and grindstones found at a number of sites indicate constant habitation in the area.

As in other parts of Australia, the people here led a hunter-gatherer existence, where men hunted and women gathered vegetable foods and seeds. They moved through the country as necessary, but never aimlessly, and along defined paths that had been used for generations in the search for food, water or other natural resources, such as ochre or spears.

Today the park is occupied by a number of different groups (or clans), each with a different language and often different traditional practices. They include the Gagudju, the Gundjehmi and the Jawoyn.

European Exploration

Although a number of vessels had sailed along the coast on exploratory voyages since the mid-17th century, it wasn't until Captain Phillip King made a number of voyages between 1818 and 1822 that any of the hinterland was investigated. King travelled up the East Alligator and South Alligator Rivers, and named them after mistaking the many saltwater crocs for alligators.

The first European to come through this area overland was the remarkable Prussian naturalist Ludwig Leichhardt, who set out from Queensland in October 1844 for Port Essington on the Cobourg Peninsula. He crossed the Arnhem Land plateau and the South Alligator River many months later before finally staggering into Port Essington, somewhat worse for wear, in December 1845.

Some 20 years later, a party led by experienced explorer John McKinlay was sent out by the South Australian government to find a better site than Escape Cliffs (by the Adelaide River mouth) for a northern settlement. McKinlay botched the expedition by not setting out until the middle of the wet season, which had been particularly severe that year. The party took months to travel just the relatively short distance to the East Alligator River, and ended up bailing out by shooting their horses, constructing a makeshift horse-hide raft and floating all the way back to Escape Cliffs!

In the 1890s a few Europeans started to make a living from shooting water buffalo for hides in the Alligator Rivers region. Foremost among these men was Paddy Cahill, who dominated European settlement in this area until 1925. In that year the Church Missionary Society was given permission by the government to establish a mission at Oenpelli, one of a number throughout the Arnhem Land Aboriginal Reserve, which had been established in 1921. By this stage any attempts to set up pastoral properties had failed and parts of the area had become vacant crown land.

In 1969 and 1972 the precursors to Kakadu, the Woolwonga and Alligator Rivers Wildlife Sanctuaries, were declared. These were followed in 1978 by the granting of some land titles to the traditional Aboriginal owners under the *Aboriginal Land Rights (NT) Act 1976*, and the proclamation of the Kakadu National Park in 1979.

WILDLIFE
Habitats & Plants

Kakadu's landforms, vegetation and wildlife are inextricably linked, and an understanding of one is virtually impossible without some appreciation of the others.

The Kakadu region has six major landforms: the Arnhem Land escarpment and plateau, coastal estuaries and tidal flats, riverine floodplains, lowlands, monsoon rainforests, and the southern hills. Each has its own distinctive mix of vegetation and animals. Over 1600 plant species have been recorded in the park, and a number of them are still used by the local Aboriginal people for food, bush medicine and other practical purposes.

The most obvious plant community here is the open woodland, so typical of the Top End, dominated by trees such as bloodwoods,

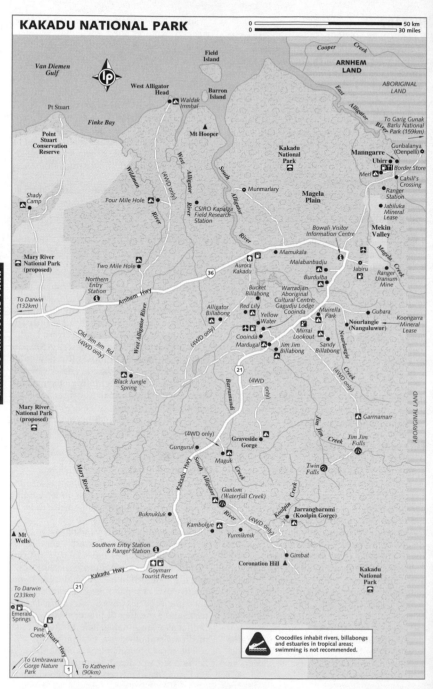

KAKADU NATIONAL PARK

0 ——— 50 km
0 ——— 30 miles

Cooper Creek

ARNHEM LAND

Van Diemen Gulf

Field Island

Barron Island

ABORIGINAL LAND

West Alligator Head

Waldak Irrmbal

To Garig Gunak Barlu National Park (159km)

Pt Stuart

Finke Bay

Mt Hooper

Gunbalanya (Oenpelli)

Manngarre

Ubirr

Border Store

Merl

Cahill's Crossing

Point Stuart Conservation Reserve

Kakadu National Park

Ranger Station

Shady Camp

Munmarlary

Magela Plain

Jabiluka Mineral Lease

Mekin Valley

Four Mile Hole

CSIRO Kapalga Field Research Station

Mary River National Park (proposed)

Bowali Visitor Information Centre

Magela Creek

Two Mile Hole

Mamukala

Malabanbadju

Burdulba

Aurora Kakadu

Jabiru

Ranger Uranium Mine

Northern Entry Station

Amhem Hwy

36

To Darwin (132km)

Bucket Billabong

Warradjan Aboriginal Cultural Centre, Gagudju Lodge Cooinda

Red Lily

Alligator Billabong

Yellow Water

Muirella Park

Gubara

Nourlangie (Nanguluwur)

Koongarra Mineral Lease

Old Jim Jim Rd (4WD only)

Cooinda

Mardugal

Mirrai Lookout

Jim Jim Billabong

Sandy Billabong

(4WD only)

Black Jungle Spring

Mary River National Park (proposed)

21

Barramundi

(4WD only)

Garnnamarr

ABORIGINAL LAND

(4WD only)

Gungurul

Graveside Gorge

Jim Jim Falls

Maguk

Twin Falls

Mary River

Gunlom (Waterfall Creek)

Koolpin

Jarrangbarnmi (Koolpin Gorge)

Buknukluk

Kambolgie

(4WD only)

Mt Wells

Yurmikmik

Southern Entry Station & Ranger Station

Gimbat

Coronation Hill

Kakadu National Park

To Darwin (233km)

Goymarr Tourist Resort

21

Kakadu Hwy

Emerald Springs

Pine Creek

Stuart Hwy

To Umbrawarra Gorge Nature Park

1

To Katherine (90km)

Crocodiles inhabit rivers, billabongs and estuaries in tropical areas; swimming is not recommended.

ABORIGINAL AUSTRALIA: BININJ & MUNGGUY COUNTRY

The name Kakadu comes from Gagudju, one of the languages spoken in the north of the region. Much of Kakadu is Aboriginal land, leased to the government for use as a national park. There are around 300 Aboriginal people living in several Aboriginal settlements in the park and in the township of Jabiru, and about one-third of the park rangers are Aboriginal. As such, Kakadu is one of the best places in the Northern Territory to learn about Indigenous culture. Collectively, the traditional owners are known as Bininj (in the north) and Mungguy (south), which translate simply as 'people'.

Opportunities include free ranger-guided tours of rock-art sites at Nourlangie and Ubirr (although the ranger may not be Indigenous) or a tour with one of the Aboriginal-owned operators. The tour of the rock-art sites at Injalak Hill, just outside the park boundary in Arnhem Land, is one not to be missed. Check out the following:

- Bowali Visitor Centre (p271)
- Injalak Arts & Crafts Centre (p283)
- Kakadu Animal Tracks (p272)
- Kakadu Culture Camp (p279)
- Magela Cultural & Heritage Tours (p272)
- Murdudjurl Kakadu (p273)
- Warradjan Aboriginal Cultural Centre (p271)

---

ironwood and the beautiful salmon gum. Between and under the trees are smaller shrubs, including native plums and tall (up to 2m high) spear grass. Pockets of monsoon rainforest grow in sheltered, well-watered sites, such as Butterfly Gorge. Along the main waterways grow lofty paperbarks and stands of pandanus, while the higher sandstone ridges are typically covered in spinifex grass and hardy shrubs such as grevilleas and acacias.

Animals

Kakadu has over 60 species of mammals, more than 280 bird species, 120 or so types of reptile, 25 species of frog, 55 freshwater fish species and at least 10,000 different kinds of insect. There are frequent additions to the list and a few of the rarer species are unique to the park. Most visitors see only a fraction of these creatures in a visit, since many of them are shy, nocturnal or scarce.

MAMMALS

Eight types of kangaroos and wallabies inhabit the park, mostly in the open forest and woodland areas, or on the fringes of the floodplains. Most commonly seen are agile wallabies – petite, fawn-coloured wallabies that rocket through the undergrowth or into the path of your car – and the large antilopine wallaroos, Kakadu's largest macropod. Those not

so often sighted include the short-eared rock wallabies, which can sometimes be seen at Ubirr first thing in the morning and at sunset. Also keep your eyes open for the enigmatic and beautiful black wallaroo at Nourlangie Rock, where individuals sometimes rest under shaded rock shelters.

Nocturnal northern brushtail possums, sugar gliders and northern brown bandicoots are also common in the woodlands. Kakadu is home to 28 bat species and is a key refuge for four rare varieties. At dusk, look out for huge fruit bats leaving their camps.

BIRDS

Kakadu's wetlands are famous for birdlife; keen birdwatchers should head straight for Nourlangie Rock or Gunlom to winkle out some of the rarer species before enjoying the water-bird spectacle. The greatest variety is seen just before the Wet, when masses of birds congregate at the shrinking waterholes, the migrants arrive from Asia and many species start their breeding cycle.

Kakadu is one of the chief refuges in Australia for several waterbird species, among them the magpie goose, green pygmy goose and Burdekin duck. Other fine water birds include pelicans, darters and the black-necked stork, or jabiru, with its distinctive red legs and iridescent blue-black plumage. Those with bright yellow eyes are females; the males have black eyes. Water birds are most easily seen at Mamukala and other wetlands, or on the Yellow Water cruise.

The open woodlands are home to yet more birds. You're quite likely to see rainbow bee-eaters, kingfishers, the long-tailed pheasant coucal and the endangered bustard, Australia's heaviest bird of flight, as well as gaudy parrots and cockatoos: look for raucous sulphur-crested white cockatoos in the paperbark trees and spectacular red-tailed black cockatoos on recently burnt ground. Raptors include majestic white-bellied sea eagles, which are often seen near inland waterways, while whistling and black kites are common. Count yourself lucky if you spot an emu in the park – and keep it to yourself, lest it ends up as bush tucker. At night you might hear barking owls calling (they sound just like dogs) and you will almost certainly hear the plaintive cry of the bush stone-curlew.

REPTILES

Kakadu is home to an extraordinary number of reptile species. Of the 120 species so far recorded, 11 are endemic, and the striking Oenpelli python was first seen by non-Aboriginal people only in 1976. The world's largest reptile – the estuarine or saltwater crocodile – is abundant in Kakadu. Several large specimens normally hang around Yellow Water. Both Twin and Jim Jim Falls have resident freshwater crocodiles, which are considered harmless. While it's quite a thrill to be so close to nature, all crocodiles are not to be meddled with on any account.

After the crocodiles, Kakadu's most famous reptilian inhabitant is probably the frilled lizard. These large members of the dragon family can grow to 1m in length and are a common sight during the Wet. Look for them sitting upright by the roadside, or scurrying away through the bush on their hind legs. You're more likely to spot one of the goanna species weaving along the trails or sliding through the water.

Although Kakadu has many snakes, most are nocturnal and rarely encountered. Several beautiful species of python include the olive python and the striking black-headed python. File snakes, so named because of the texture of the skin, live in permanent billabongs and are a favoured bush tucker.

INSECTS

If you're wondering what that enginelike sound droning across the wetlands at dusk is, don't ask – run for the repellent! The mosquitoes at Ubirr may just carry you away, and they seem to come equipped with hypodermic needles. Mozzies are the most noticeable insect in the park, although they become less menacing as you move south.

Termites are probably more abundant still, although their impressive earth mounds are much more obvious than the actual insects; these are northern Australia's answer to the vast grazing herds of Africa.

One of the most famous of the park's insect inhabitants is Leichhardt's grasshopper, a beautiful blue and orange insect that was not seen again by science until 130 years after its discovery in 1845. The Aboriginal people know them as Aljurr, the children of Namarrgon (Lightning Man), because they are said to call their father to start the storms before the Wet.

CLIMATE

The average maximum temperature in Kakadu is 34°C year-round. Broadly speaking, the Dry is from May to October and the Wet is from November to April; unsurprisingly, most of the average rainfall of 1600mm falls in the Wet. The transition from Dry to Wet transforms the Kakadu landscape: wetlands expand, rivers flood and unsealed roads become impassable, cutting off some highlights like Jim Jim Falls.

ORIENTATION

Kakadu National Park is huge. It's 145km from Darwin at its nearest boundary, and stretches another 130km from there across to the western edge of Arnhem Land. It is roughly rectangular and covers almost two million hectares.

Two main roads traverse the park (Arnhem Hwy and Kakadu Hwy), which are both sealed and accessible year-round. The 4WD-only Old Jim Jim Rd is an alternative access from the Arnhem Hwy, joining the Kakadu Hwy 7km south of Cooinda.

INFORMATION

Kakadu National Park (www.environment.gov.au/parks /kakadu; admission free) is open year-round. Access roads to Jim Jim and Twin Falls and to West Alligator Head are closed during the Wet,

KAKADU'S SEASONAL CYCLE

The Aboriginal people of Kakadu recognise six seasons in the annual climatic cycle. These seasons are marked not only by observed changes in the weather but also by its effect on plant growth and animal behaviour.

Gunmeleng This is the 'build-up' to the Wet, which starts in mid-October. Humidity increases and the temperatures rise to 35°C or more – and the number of mosquitoes, always high near water, rises to near-plague proportions. By November the thunderstorms have started, billabongs are replenished and the water birds and fish disperse. Traditionally this is when the Aboriginal people made their seasonal move from the floodplains to the shelter of the escarpment.

Gudjuek The Wet proper continues through January, February and March, with violent thunderstorms and an abundance of plant and animal life thriving in the hot, moist conditions. Most of Kakadu's rain falls during this period.

Banggereng In April, storms (known as 'knock 'em down' storms) flatten the spear grass, which during the course of the Wet has shot up to 2m in height.

Yekke The season of mists, when the air starts to dry out, extends from May to mid-June. The wetlands and waterfalls still have a lot of water and most of the tracks are open, and there aren't too many other visitors. The first firing of the countryside begins.

Wurrgeng & Gurrung The most comfortable time to visit Kakadu is during the late Dry in July and August. This is when wildlife, especially birds, gathers in large numbers around shrinking billabongs.

and attractions in the southern part of the park, such as Gunlom, are accessible only by 4WDs in the Wet.

Bowali Visitor Centre

Kakadu's main information centre, **Bowali Visitor Centre** (☎ 8938 1121; Kakadu Hwy, Jabiru; ☺ 8am-5pm) is a beautifully designed building of walk-through displays that sweep you across the land, explaining Kakadu's ecology from both cultural and conservation perspectives. It has good access and facilities for disabled visitors, a souvenir shop and a good cafe with espresso coffee and snacks.

The information desk has plenty of leaflets on various aspects of the park. A theatrette shows a 25-minute audiovisual presentation on the seasonal changes in the park (screened hourly from 9am to 4pm), and an excellent resource centre has a comprehensive selection of reference books and maps. Another theatrette shows documentaries about the park from 8.30am to 3.30pm daily.

The **Marrawuddi Gallery** (www.marrawuddi.com) sells a range of souvenirs and is well stocked with books on all things Kakadu. A couple of recommended purchases are 'Kakadu Bill' Neidjie's *A Story About Feeling*, which allows you to *feel* Kakadu, and Malcolm Arnold's *Birds of the Top End*.

The visitors centre is about 2.5km south of the Arnhem Hwy intersection. A 1km walk-

ing track connects it to Jabiru (20 minutes). Allow at least two hours to get the most out of a visit.

Warradjan Aboriginal Cultural Centre

This **cultural centre** (☎ 8975 0051; Yellow Water Area; ☺ 9am-5pm) near Cooinda gives an excellent insight into the culture of the park's traditional owners. The circular design of the building symbolises the way Aboriginal people sit in a circle when having a meeting, and is also reminiscent of the *warradjan* (pig-nosed turtle).

The displays depict creation *stories* when the *Nayuhyunggi* (first people) laid out the land and the laws, and the winding path you follow through the display symbolises the way the Rainbow Serpent moves through the country. It gives an introduction into the moiety (kin relationships) system and skin names (groups) of the region.

You can choose from 12 videos on Kakadu and aspects of the local culture. There's also a craft shop selling local art, didgeridoos and paintings, as well as T-shirts and refreshments.

Warradjan is an easy walk (1km, 15 minutes) from the Cooinda resort.

ACTIVITIES
Bushwalking

Kakadu has some amazing but challenging bushwalking country. Many people will be satisfied with the many marked tracks that range from 500m strolls to more demanding 12km loop walks, most of which are described in this chapter. For the more adventurous there are infinite possibilities, especially in the drier southern and eastern sections of the park.

Many of the ranger-led activities involve a guided walk along various tracks, and there is a *Park Notes* fact sheet for most, so you can easily do a self-guided walk. These sheets are available from the visitors centre and usually from a box at the start of each track. A bushwalking permit, available from the Bowali Visitor Centre (p271), is required for overnight walks. Topographic maps (also available from the visitors centre) are necessary for extended walks and must be submitted with a permit application. Allow one week for the permit to be issued.

The **Darwin Bushwalking Club** (www.bushwalking .org.au/dbc) welcomes visitors and may be able to help with information. It has walks most weekends, often in Kakadu. See the website for contacts phone numbers.

GUIDED WALKS & TALKS

A wonderful variety of informative and free activities is conducted by park staff during the Dry. The range includes: art-site talks at Ubirr and Nourlangie; guided walks at Ubirr, Nourlangie, Yellow Water, Mardugal, Maguk and Gunlom; and slide shows at various accommodation places. The schedule of activities differs somewhat from season to season; find out details from the Bowali Visitor Centre. Current times are also posted at the various sites.

Wetland & River Trips

Boat trips on the park's rivers and billabongs are a highlight of any visit to Kakadu. The most popular trip is the **Yellow Water cruise** at Cooinda (p281), a sublime wildlife-watching experience that takes you through some diverse wetlands habitats.

Equally good is the **Guluyambi cruise** (p275) on the East Alligator River near Ubirr. The emphasis here is on Aboriginal culture and the tour is led by an Aboriginal guide.

Kakadu Culture Camp (p279), based at the Muirella campground, has a night-time boat cruise on the Djarradjin Billabong, which opens up a whole new world of wildlife.

Scenic Flights

The view of Kakadu from the air is spectacular and a scenic flight is the only way to see the stunning Jim Jim and Twin Falls in the Wet. **Kakadu Air** (☎ 1800 089 113; www.kakaduair.com.au), at Jabiru and Cooinda, has 30-minute/one-hour fixed-wing flights for $100/175 per person. Helicopter tours, though more expensive, give a more exciting aerial perspective. They cost from $195 (20 minutes) to $425 (70 minutes) per person.

TOURS

There are loads of tours to Kakadu from Darwin (p251) and a few that start from inside the park. These range from comfortable air-con sightseeing to more rugged 4WD camping trips. Tours are certainly useful if you don't have a 4WD, or if you want the knowledge of a guide to enhance your experience.

A number of cultural tours from Kakadu also visit Arnhem Land, exploring Aboriginal land and pristine wilderness areas.

From Jabiru & Cooinda

The 4WD access road to Jim Jim and Twin Falls inhibits many from venturing to these beautiful spots. Most 4WD rental agreements stipulate that the vehicle must not be taken along this route. A couple of companies run trips out to Jim Jim and Twin Falls, including lunch and paddling gear, departing from Jabiru or Cooinda. Try **Top End Explorer Tours** (☎ 8979 3615; www.topendexplorertours.com; adult/child $159/135) or **Kakadu Gorge & Waterfall Tours** (☎ 8979 0111; www.gagudju-dreaming.com; adult/child $170/145).

Lord's Kakadu & Arnhemland Safaris (☎ 8948 2200; www.lords-safaris.com; adult/child $195/155) runs a one-day trip into Arnhem Land from Jabiru. The tour visits Gunbalanya (Oenpelli) with a guided walk around Injalak Hill. Lord's also has a range of multi-day trips covering Kakadu and Arnhem Land departing from Darwin.

Magela Cultural & Heritage Tours (☎ 8979 2548; www.kakadutours.com.au; adult/child $235/188) is an Aboriginal-owned and -operated day tour into northern Kakadu and Arnhem Land, including Injalak Hill and a cruise on Inkiyu billabong. Pick-up from Jabiru.

Kakadu Animal Tracks (☎ 8979 0145; www.animal tracks.com.au; adult/child $165/125), based at Cooinda, runs highly recommended tours combining a wildlife safari and Aboriginal cultural tour with an Indigenous guide. You'll see thousands of birds on the floodplains in the Dry, and get to hunt and gather, prepare and consume bush tucker and crunch on some green ants.

Murdudjurl Kakadu (☎ 8979 0145; www.murdudjurl kakadu.com.au; 2hr tour $75) is an Aboriginal-owned and -run cultural tour that takes you onto private land, where you can interact with the traditional owners, learn about bush tucker, basket weaving and painting. The two-hour tour departs from Gagudju Lodge in Cooinda on Monday, Wednesday, Friday and Saturday at 3pm.

Kakadu Fishing Tours (☎ 8979 2025; Jabiru; half-/full day $180/290) operates fishing tours on the South and East Alligator Rivers. **Yellow Waters Fishing Safaris** (☎ 0427 790004, 8979 0415; Cooinda; half-/full day $150/290) operates full- and half-day fishing tours on Yellow Water billabong. Lure and fly-fishing tackle is supplied on a 'replace if lost' basis.

Want to learn more about uranium? You can take a two-hour tour of the Ranger mine east of Jabiru, visiting the large open-cut mine and extraction plant (see p277).

SLEEPING

With the exception of camping grounds, accommodation prices in Kakadu can vary tremendously depending on the season – Dry-season prices (given here) are often as much as 50% above wet-season prices. With demand so high and accommodation limited, the resorts charge the earth for motel-style rooms in peak season.

Camping

Facilities at camping grounds operated by National Parks range from basic sites with pit toilets to full amenities blocks with solar hot showers, although there's no power at any of them. Some remote bush sites, usually accessible only by 4WD, have no facilities. Commercial camping areas with more facilities, such as restaurants and swimming pools, are attached to the various resorts at South Alligator, Jabiru and Cooinda. Camping outside designated areas requires a permit, available from Bowali Visitor Centre or online at www.environment.gov.au /parks/permits/kakadu-camping.html.

NATIONAL PARKS CAMPING GROUNDS

There are four main National Parks **camping grounds** (adult/child $5.40/free). These are at Merl, near Ubirr; Muirella Park, several kilometres south of the Nourlangie turn-off and then 6km off Kakadu Hwy; Mardugal, just off the high-way 1.5km south of the Cooinda turn-off; and Gunlom, 37km down a dirt road that branches off Kakadu Hwy near the southern entry gate. Only Mardugal is open during the Wet. All have pit fires, hot showers, flushing toilets, drinking water and a generator zone. These are the only sites that are really suitable for caravans. See the individual sections for more details.

National Parks provide 14 more basic camping grounds around the park at which there is no fee. They have fireplaces, some have pit toilets and at all of them you'll need to bring your own drinking water.

GETTING THERE & AROUND
Air

Although Jabiru has an airport, there are no scheduled commercial flights into Kakadu.

Bus

You can get from Darwin to Jabiru and Cooinda on scheduled bus services, but to explore further you're better off taking a tour or hiring your own vehicle.

Greyhound Australia (☎ 13 14 99; www.greyhound .com.au) has a daily service between Darwin and Cooinda via Jabiru. Buses reach the Yellow Water wetlands in time for the 1pm cruise, and depart after the cruise, 1½ hours later. The bus leaves Darwin at 8am and Jabiru at 11.30am, arriving at Cooinda at 12.40pm. It departs from Cooinda at 1.15pm and Jabiru at 2.30pm, and arrives in Darwin at 5.30pm. The one-way fare from Darwin to Jabiru is $53, and to Cooinda, $74.

Car

The flexibility of your own vehicle is the best way to explore Kakadu. It doesn't have to be a 4WD, since roads to most sites of interest are sealed, but a 4WD will give you greater freedom and is the only possible way to see Jim Jim or Twin Falls. Check if your rental agreement allows this. Sealed roads lead from Kakadu Hwy to Nourlangie, to the Muirella Park camping area and to Ubirr. Other roads are mostly dirt and blocked for varying periods during the Wet and early Dry.

ARNHEM HIGHWAY TO JABIRU

From the park's unmanned and unassuming north entry station, it's about 20km to a turn-off to the north which leads to basic campsites at **Two Mile Hole** (8km) and **Four Mile Hole** (38km) on the Wildman River, and

Waldak Irrmbal (West Alligator Head; 80km), which are all popular fishing spots. The track is suitable for conventional vehicles only in the Dry, and then only as far as Two Mile Hole.

About 35km further along the Arnhem Hwy, a turn-off to the south, again impassable to 2WD vehicles in the Wet, leads to campsites at **Alligator, Bucket** and **Red Lilly billabongs**, and on to the Kakadu Hwy.

South Alligator Area

The South Alligator River Crossing is on the Arnhem Hwy 64km into the park and 3km past Aurora Kakadu resort. There's a boat ramp at this popular fishing spot and a picnic area near the bridge. The resort has a bar, fuel and a well-stocked shop.

Close to the resort are a couple of easy walks:

Gu-ngarre Monsoon Rainforest (3.6km return, 90 minutes, easy) This flat circular walk skirts the Aurora resort through monsoon forest and woodlands before passing Anggardabal billabong. Interpretive signs show Aboriginal plant uses.

Mamukala Wetlands (3km, up to two hours, easy) This large wetland area, 11km past the Aurora Resort, is an excellent place to view water birds on the wetlands fringed with paperbark woodlands. It is at its best during September and October, when truly spectacular congregations can build up, including thousands of magpie geese. A short walk from the car park leads to a birdwatching hideout overlooking the wetlands, while the longer walk leads through the woodlands around the wetlands.

SLEEPING & EATING

Aurora Kakadu (☎ 1800 818 845; www.auroraresorts
.com.au; Arnhem Hwy; unpowered & powered sites per person $12, motel r $240-325; ✖ ▣ ▨) The first and only park accommodation along the Arnhem Hwy before you reach Jabiru, the Aurora Resort is set in lush, sprawling gardens with shady trees and plenty of birdlife. The camping area seems like a bit of an afterthought and is accessed via a separate driveway. The spacious motel rooms come with TV and fridge and are grouped in unusually designed circular buildings orbiting a lovely shaded pool and spa area, tennis court, laundry and gas barbecues.

The **Barra Kafe** (mains $10-18; ✇ 8am-4pm) serves up coffee and light meals – munch on a barra burger while watching the giant barramundi swimming around in the central aquarium. The **Wetlands Restaurant & Munmalary Bar** (mains $20-29; ✇ breakfast & dinner) offers steak, fish, lamb shanks and pasta dishes.

Ubirr

The turn-off to Ubirr is only a couple of kilometres before Jabiru and it's worth taking this detour in plenty of time for sunset to witness some of the most spectacular views in Kakadu. Ubirr is an outcrop of the Arnhem escarpment, famous for its extensive Aboriginal **rock-art galleries** (✇ 8.30am-dusk 1 Apr-30 Nov, 2pm-dusk 1 Dec-31 Mar), and there are dramatic late-afternoon views over the Nardab floodplains when the surrounding escarpment turns golden and the setting sun reflects across the mirrored wetlands. Of course, most visitors and tour groups come here for sunset, so the crowds can really build – if you have the time, consider visiting again in the morning or early afternoon when you might just have the place to yourself.

An easily followed path from the Ubirr car park takes you through the rock-art galleries. The highlight is the main gallery, which has a large array of well-preserved X-ray-style wallabies, possums, goannas, tortoises and fish, plus a couple of *balanda* (white men) with hands on hips, an intriguing Tasmanian tiger and Mimi figures. Also of major interest here is the Rainbow Serpent painting, and the picture of the Namarkan Sisters, shown with string pulled taut between their hands. The Ubirr paintings are in many different styles. They were painted starting from over 20,000 years ago right up to the 20th century.

Other activities in the Ubirr area include bushwalking (see below), fishing and cruises on the East Alligator River. All of the access roads are sealed, although low-lying areas may be inundated during the Wet. If you're camping, it's worth pencilling this in as an overnight stay.

This part of the park is as far east as you can go, and the East Alligator River marks the boundary with Arnhem Land. If you have a permit (see p276), Cahill's Crossing – a tidal ford – gives access to Arnhem Land and Gunbalanya (Oenpelli), plus Garig Gunak Barlu National Park on the Cobourg Peninsula. Take care when crossing the ford – vehicles are occasionally swept away – and on no account should you attempt to cross on foot as death by crocodile is a distinct possibility.

BUSHWALKING

There are four tracks in the Ubirr area:
Ubirr Art Site Walk (1km return, one hour, easy) This track loops around the rock-art galleries, and there's a

ROCK ART

Kakadu's extraordinary rock-art sites were critical to the park's World Heritage listing. The art is referred to as naturalistic – portraying the physical, social and cultural environment – and may depict animals that no longer exist, such as the thylacine at Ubirr. More than 5000 sites are known, the oldest dating from more than 20,000 years ago. The best of the accessible galleries are at Ubirr, Nourlangie and Nanguluwur, and across the park border at Gunbalanya (Oenpelli).

For the local Aboriginal people the rock-art sites are a major source of traditional knowledge and are used as their historical archives. The most recent paintings, some executed as recently as the 1980s, connect the local community with the artists. Older paintings are believed by many Aboriginal people to have been painted by spirit people, and depict *stories* that connect the people with creation legends and the development of Aboriginal law.

The majority of rock-art sites open to the public are relatively recent. The paintings, which often have layers of styles painted over one another, may depict hunting scenes, favoured prey, ceremonies or creation ancestors. The hauntingly beautiful stick figures are Mimi ancestral beings and are one of the oldest Aboriginal art styles.

The conservation of the Kakadu rock-art sites is a major part of the park management task because the natural, water-soluble ochres (paints) used are very susceptible to water damage. Drip-lines of small ridges of clear silicone rubber have been made on the rocks above the paintings to divert the water flow. The most accessible sites receive up to 4000 visitors a week, which presents the problem of dust damage. Boardwalks have been erected to keep the dust down and to keep people at a suitable distance from the paintings.

short-but-steep side track to a lookout with stunning panoramic views over the East Alligator River floodplain.

Manngarre Monsoon Rainforest Walk (1.5km return, 30 minutes, easy) Mainly sticking to a boardwalk, this walk starts by the boat ramp near the Border Store and winds through heavily shaded vegetation, palms and vines.

Bardedjilidji Sandstone Walk (2.5km, 90 minutes, easy) Starting from the upstream picnic area car park, this walk takes in wetland areas of the East Alligator River and some interesting eroded sandstone outliers of the Arnhem Land escarpment. Informative track notes point out many features on this walk.

Sandstone & River Bushwalk (6.5km, three hours, medium) This extension of the Bardedjilidji Walk features sandstone outcrops, paperbark swamps and river banks.

EAST ALLIGATOR RIVER CRUISE

Although not as well-known as the Yellow Waters cruise, the **Guluyambi Cruise** (☎ 1800 089 113; www.guluyambi.com.au; adult/child $45/25) on the East Alligator River is a whole different experience, more attuned to Indigenous culture than wildlife. An Aboriginal guide takes the 1¾-hour trip and the emphasis is on Aboriginal culture and relationship with the land.

Cruises depart from the upstream boat ramp at East Alligator at 9am, 11am, 1pm and 3pm daily from May to October. There's a free shuttle bus from the Border Store, where you can also book tickets. During the

Wet, Guluyambi operates day tours, including a cruise across the picturesque, flooded Magela Creek and a bus drive on to Ubirr (adult/child $127/99). It departs Jabiru at 10am daily and provides the only means by which visitors can get to Ubirr when it is at its waterlogged best.

SLEEPING & EATING

Merl Camping Ground (adult/child $5.40/free) The turn-off to this National Parks ground is about 1km before the Border Store. The figure-of-eight layout has a quiet zone and a generator-use zone with showers and toilets in the middle of each. There are lots of shady, secluded sites with fireplaces but it can get mighty busy at peak times, so secure a site or plan to get here straight after sunset at Ubirr. The mosquitoes are diabolical and no amount of repellent will save you! The site is closed in the Wet.

Border Store (☎ 8979 2474; meals $6-18; ☼ 8am-5.30pm Apr-Nov) Stocks a good range of groceries, snacks, light lunches, cooked breakfasts and takeaway food, as well as souvenirs and tour bookings. Alcohol is not available here, and neither is fuel. Sadly, the popular hostel here closed years ago. There are plans to rebuild accommodation here but it may be years in the making.

JABIRU

pop 1135

It may seem surprising to find a town of Jabiru's size and structure in the midst of a wilderness national park, but it exists solely because of the nearby uranium mine. Jabiru was built in 1982 to accommodate workers first at the Jabiluka mine and now the Ranger mine, and is not only the major service centre for Kakadu but a residential area where you can shop, picnic by the lake or play a round of golf.

Information

The Jabiru Plaza shopping centre off Flinders St has a good range of amenities. There's a branch of the Westpac Bank with an ATM, a Commonwealth Bank agency and a post office. Eftpos is available at both the supermarket and Mobil service station.

Jabiru Community Health Centre (☎ 8979 2018; Jabiru Plaza; ☾ 9am-noon & 1-4pm Mon & Wed, 8am-noon & 1-4pm Tue & Fri, 8am-noon Thu)

Jabiru Library (☎ 8979 2097; cnr Flinders St & Tasman Cres; per 20min $3; ☾ 10.30am-5.30pm Tue, to 4.30pm Wed-Fri, to 1.30pm Sat) Internet access available.

Kakadu Tours & Travel (☎ 8979 2548; www.kakadu tours.com.au; shop 6, Jabiru Plaza) Internet access $3 per 30 minutes. Tour and travel bookings.

Mobil service station (☎ 8979 2001; cnr Leichhardt St & Lakeside Dr; ☾ 6.30am-8.30pm) Fuel, mechanical repairs, camping gas, general groceries and ice.

Northern Land Council (☎ 8979 2410; www.nlc .org.au; Flinders St; ☾ 8am-1pm & 2-4.30pm Mon-Fri) Issues permits (adult/child $13.20/free) to visit Gunbalanya (Oenpelli), across the East Alligator River.

Police station (☎ 8979 2122; Tasman Cres) Opposite the shopping centre.

Sights & Activities

Even if you're not staying at the 'Croc' hotel, it's worth a wander through the **Ochre Gallery** in the foyer of the Gagudju Crocodile Holiday Inn. The gallery displays a range of quality works by local artists from Kakadu and Arnhem Land and all are for sale.

Lake Jabiru, just northeast of the centre, is an artificial lake (no swimming) with a pleasant picnic area, barbecues and a kids' playground. On the other side of town, a 1km walking

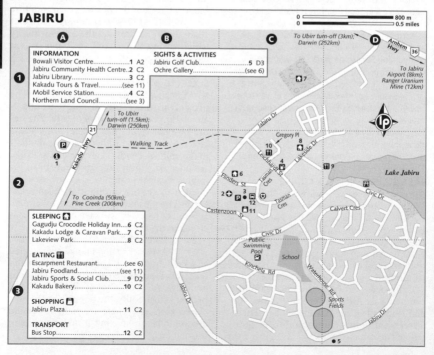

JABIRU

INFORMATION	
Bowali Visitor Centre	**1** A2
Jabiru Community Health Centre	**2** C2
Jabiru Library	**3** C2
Kakadu Tours & Travel	(see 11)
Mobil Service Station	**4** C2
Northern Land Council	(see 3)

SIGHTS & ACTIVITIES	
Jabiru Golf Club	**5** D3
Ochre Gallery	(see 6)

SLEEPING	
Gagudju Crocodile Holiday Inn	**6** C2
Kakadu Lodge & Caravan Park	**7** C1
Lakeview Park	**8** C2

EATING	
Escarpment Restaurant	(see 6)
Jabiru Foodland	(see 11)
Jabiru Sports & Social Club	**9** D2
Kakadu Bakery	**10** C2

| SHOPPING | |
| Jabiru Plaza | **11** C2 |

| TRANSPORT | |
| Bus Stop | **12** C2 |

To Ubirr turn-off (3km); Darwin (252km)

To Jabiru Airport (8km); Ranger Uranium Mine (12km)

To Ubirr turn-off (1.5km); Darwin (250km)

Walking Track

To Cooinda (50km); Pine Creek (200km)

Lake Jabiru

Gregory Pl

Jabiru Dr

Leichhardt Dr

Lakeside Dr

Tasman Cres

Flinders St

Castenzoon St

Tasman Cres

Civic Dr

Calvert Cres

Public Swimming Pool

Kinchela Rd

School

Civic Dr

Waterhouse Rd

Jabiru Dr

Sports Fields

URANIUM MINING

It's no small irony that some of the world's biggest deposits of uranium lie within one of Australia's most beautiful national parks. In 1953 uranium was discovered in the Kakadu region. Twelve small deposits in the southern reaches of the park were worked in the 1960s, but were abandoned following the declaration of Woolwonga Wildlife Sanctuary.

In 1970 three huge deposits – Ranger, Nabarlek and Koongarra – were found, followed by Jabiluka a year later. The Nabarlek deposit (in Arnhem Land) was mined in the late '70s, and the Ranger Uranium Mine started producing ore in 1981.

While all mining in the park has been controversial, it was Jabiluka that brought international attention to Kakadu and pitted conservationists and Indigenous owners against the government and mining companies. After uranium was discovered at Jabiluka in 1971, an agreement to mine was negotiated with the local Aboriginal peoples. Mine development was delayed until 1996 due to oscillating Federal government mining policy, by which time concern had grown that Aboriginal Elders had been coerced into signing the agreement.

The Jabiluka mine became the scene of sit-in demonstrations during 1998, which resulted in large-scale arrests. A Unesco delegation inspected the mine site and reported that it would endanger Kakadu's World Heritage listing, a finding later contradicted by an Independent Science Panel. In 2003, stockpiled ore was returned into the mine and the decline tunnel leading into the deposit was backfilled as the mining company moved into dialogue with the traditional landowners, the Mirrar people.

In February 2005 the current owners of the Jabiluka mining lease, Energy Resources of Australia (ERA), signed an agreement that gave the Mirrar the deciding vote on any resumption of this controversial mining project. Under the deal ERA is allowed to continue to explore the lease, subject to Mirrar consent. In addition, every four years ERA is allowed to ask the Mirrar to consider opening the mine, beginning in 2006. As the Mirrar have staged a David and Goliath–style battle against the mine's construction for many years, it's unlikely their position, based on cultural and environmental concerns, will change. Meanwhile, the Ranger mine – which is officially not part of the national park but is surrounded by it – is due to close in 2010, but the discovery of further deposits in late 2008 means it is possible the mine could remain operating for another five years, depending on the approval of government and the Northern Land Council.

trail off Jabiru Dr leads to the **Bowali Visitor Centre** (p271).

Jabiru Golf Club (☎ 8979 2575; www.jabirugolfclub .com.au; 9/18 holes $10/15) has a well-kept nine-hole course within a World Heritage–listed national park. You can play any time but club hire ($10) is available only after 3.30pm on weekdays and 10am weekends.

The **Ranger Uranium Mine Tour** (☎ 1800 089 113; adult/child $25/10; ☯ 9am, 11am & 1pm Mon-Sat) is an opportunity to see one of the park's controversial mining projects up close and learn some of the issues surrounding uranium mining. Guided tours leave from Jabiru airport, about 8km east of town.

Sleeping

Kakadu Lodge & Caravan Park (☎ 1800 811 154; www .auroraresorts.com.au; Jabiru Dr; unpowered/powered sites $26/32, cabins from $240; ☒ ☐ ☑) An impeccable resort with shady, grassy sites and a great lagoon-style swimming pool. Self-contained cabins sleep up to five people but are booked up well in advance. There's a kiosk, bar and bistro.

our pick **Lakeview Park** (☎ 8979 3144; www.lake viewkakadu.com.au; 27 Lakeside Dr; powered sites with bathroom $30, bungalow $95, d $110, cabin $195; ☒) Although there are no lake views as such, this beautifully landscaped, Aboriginal-owned park is a great place to stay, with a range of comfortable, tropical-themed bungalows set in lush gardens. The doubles share a communal kitchen, bathroom and lounge, and also come equipped with their own TV and fridge, while the 'bush bungalows' are elevated, stylish, safari-designed affairs that sleep up to four, with private external bathroom.

Gagudju Crocodile Holiday Inn (☎ 8979 9000; www .gagudju-dreaming.com; Flinders St; d from $300; ☒ ☐ ☑) Known locally as 'the Croc', this hotel is designed in the shape of a crocodile, which of course is obvious only when viewed from the air (or Google Earth). The rooms are clean and comfortable, if a little pedestrian for the price. Try for one on the ground floor opening out to the central pool. The artworks hanging in the Ochre Gallery in the foyer are worth inspecting.

Eating & Drinking

Jabiru at least gives you a choice of places to eat and drink. The shopping plaza has takeaway food and the well-stocked **Jabiru Foodland** (Jabiru Plaza; 9am-5.30pm Mon-Fri, to 3pm Sat, 10am-2pm Sun & public holidays), which also has a good range of camping equipment.

Kakadu Bakery (☎ 8979 2320; Gregory Pl; snacks $2-8; 6.30am-2pm Mon-Fri, 7am-2pm Sat, 9am-1pm Sun) This little gem of a bakery is definitely the place for breakfast, with a range of fresh bread, pies, pastries and delicious scrolls.

Jabiru Sports & Social Club (☎ 8979 2326; Lakeside Dr; mains $18-32; lunch daily, dinner Mon-Sat) Along with the golf club, this is the place to meet the locals over a beer. The bistro meals are generous and there's a nice outdoor deck overlooking the lake, along with sports on TV and a TAB (betting outlet).

Escarpment Restaurant (☎ 8979 9000; Flinders St; mains $26-34) Kakadu's top dining address is in the Gagudju Crocodile Inn. There are inspiring (or at least filling) buffets for breakfast ($28) and dinner ($55) – the latter includes seafood and carvery – as well as a la carte meals seasoned with bush ingredients. The bar is open till 11pm.

You can enjoy a drink at the bar of the Sports Club (sign in as a temporary member), Golf Club or licensed restaurants, but there is no takeaway alcohol available here or anywhere in Kakadu. If you want a drink back at the campsite, stock up in Darwin.

JABIRU TO COOINDA

From Jabiru, the Kakadu Hwy heads southwest for 204km to the Stuart Hwy at Pine Creek. Cooinda, the next major accommodation base, is 55km from Jabiru. Along the way are a couple of camping areas and the turn-off to the rock-art sites at Nourlangie.

About 17km along is the turn-off to **Malabanjbanjdju campground**, and a little further along the highway is another short access road to **Burdulba campground**. Both are free and have basic toilet facilities but no showers or drinking water. Between the two is the **Iligadjarr Floodplain Walk** (4km loop, 1½ hours, easy) along the grassy floodplain around Burdulba

billabong. The name refers to the ancestral file snakes that live in the billabong.

Nourlangie

The sight of this looming, mysterious, outlier of the Arnhem Land escarpment makes it easy to understand why it has been important to local Aboriginal people for so long. Its long, red, sandstone bulk slopes up from the surrounding woodland only to fall away at one end in sheer, stepped cliffs. Beneath is Kakadu's best-known collection of rock art.

The name Nourlangie is a corruption of *nawulandja*, an Aboriginal word that refers to an area bigger than the rock itself. You reach it at the end of a 9km sealed road, which turns east off the Kakadu Hwy. The road is open from 8am to sunset daily.

From the main car park the boardwalk takes you first to the **Anbangbang rock shelter**, which may have been used for 20,000 years as a refuge from heat, rain and the frequent wet-season thunderstorms. The shelter may have housed up to 30 people of the Warramal clan. Archaeological finds have revealed that the shelter was in almost constant use from about 6000 years ago to the time of European contact.

The **Anbangbang Gallery** is the main gallery and is accessible by wheelchair – elsewhere the track is steep in parts. The gallery here was repainted in the 1960s by Nayambolmi (also known as Barramundi Charlie), a respected artist, fisherman and hunter. The major character in the gallery is **Namondjok**, who broke traditional law by committing incest with one of his clan sisters. Next to Namondjok is **Namarrgon**, the Lightning Man, depicted here surrounded by an arc of lightning.

From the gallery a short walk takes you to the **Gunwarddehwarde Lookout**, which has a view of the Arnhem Land escarpment, and Lightning Dreaming (Namarrgon Djadjam), the home of Namarrgon.

BUSHWALKING

Nourlangie is one of the most visited parts of the park, and apart from the main gallery there are five other walking tracks at points along the access road.

Nawurlandja Lookout (600m return, 30 minutes, medium) This is just a short walk up a gradual slope, but it gives excellent views of the Nourlangie Rock area and is a good place to watch the sunset.

SHARING KAKADU STORIES

The Namarkan Sisters

The *story* of the Namarkan sisters is told to warn young children about the dangers of crocodiles. One day, the sisters were sitting together by a billabong when one of the sisters dived into the water, changed into a crocodile, then paddled back and frightened the life out of her sister. She then changed herself back and returned to her sister, who related how she had been terrified by a crocodile.

The first sister got such a kick out of this that she repeated the prank over and over. Finally the other sister realised what was going on and retaliated in the same way. The sisters then realised that if they were to turn themselves into crocodiles permanently, they could scare – and eat – anyone they pleased.

Today the Namarkan sisters are present in all crocodiles, evident in the lumps behind the eyes and their great skill and cunning as hunters.

The Rainbow Serpent

The *story* of the Rainbow Serpent is a common subject in Aboriginal traditions across Australia, although the *story* varies from place to place.

In Kakadu the serpent is a woman, Kuringali, who painted her image on the rock wall at Ubirr while on a journey through this area. This journey forms a creation path that links the places she visited: Ubirr, Manngarre, the East Alligator River and various places in Arnhem Land.

To the traditional owners of the park, Kuringali is the most powerful spirit. Although she spends most of her time resting in billabongs, if disturbed she can be very destructive, causing floods and earthquakes. One local *story* has it that she even eats people.

Anbangbang Billabong Walk (2.5km loop, 45 minutes, easy) This picturesque, lily-filled billabong lies close to Nourlangie, and the picnic tables dotted around its edge make it a popular lunch spot. The track circles the billabong and passes through paperbark swamp; start from any of the parking areas but walk clockwise for the best views of Nourlangie Rock with the billabong in the foreground.

Nanguluwur Gallery (3.5km return, 1½ hours, easy) This outstanding but little-visited rock-art gallery sees far fewer visitors than Nourlangie simply because it's further to walk to and has a gravel access road. Here the paintings cover most of the styles found in the park, including very early dynamic style work, X-ray work and a good example of 'contact art', a painting of a two-masted sailing ship towing a dinghy. The colours in the overhanging rock are also beautiful.

Gubara Pools (6km return, three hours, medium) Further along the same road from Nanguluwur is the turn-off to this walk, which winds 3km each way along a sandy path and skirts some clear pools in a patch of monsoon rainforest also known as Baroalba Springs. Remarkably, at least 14 species of freshwater fish are found in these small pools.

Barrk Sandstone Bushwalk (12km loop, 6 to 8 hours, difficult) This long day-walk will take you away from the crowds on a circuit of the Nourlangie area. Barrk is the male black wallaroo and you might see this elusive marsupial if you set out early. Starting at the Nourlangie car park, the demanding walk passes through the Anbangbang galleries before a steep climb to the top of Nourlangle Rock. Cross the flat top of the rock, weaving through sandstone pillars, before descending along a wet-season watercourse. The track then follows the rock's base past the Nanguluwur gallery and western cliffs before emerging at the car park.

Muirella Park

On a paperbark-lined billabong, **Muirella Park** (adult/child $5.40/free) is an excellent National Parks camping ground along a sealed road 6km off the Kakadu Hwy and 7km south of the Nourlangie Rock turn-off.

This is also the base for **Kakadu Culture Camp** (☎ 0428-792 048; www.kakaduculturecamp.com), which offers a number of excellent cultural and 'after dark' tours on Djarradjin Billabong. The Night Wildlife boat cruise (adult/child $49/30) is a two-hour evening cruise led by local Aboriginal guides. It runs from Monday to Friday in the Dry (every evening in June and July) from 6.20pm. Kakadu by Night (adult/child $179/119) includes a guided bush-tucker walk, campfire dinner and the night cruise, and runs every Wednesday night in the Dry.

Bubba Wetlands Walk (3.5km loop, 1½ hours, easy) starts near the Muirella Park camping ground (it's signposted), and skirts the edge of the Bubba Wetlands.

A 6km 4WD track leads from Muirella Park to a free bush-camping area at **Sandy Billabong**, which has basic toilet facilities only. It was here that a German tourist was tragically killed by a crocodile in 2002, so we don't recommend swimming.

Back on the Kakadu Hwy, 4km past the Muirella Park turn-off, **Mirrai Lookout** (3.6km return, 1½ hours, difficult) is a steep track that scales the relatively dizzy heights of Mt Cahill (120m); trees obscure some of the view.

Jim Jim & Twin Falls

Remote and spectacular, these two falls epitomise the rugged Top End. The 57km 4WD-only dry-season track that turns south off the Kakadu Hwy between the Nourlangie Rock and Cooinda turn-offs is lined by the escarpment and the last 9km is slow going.

Jim Jim Falls, a sheer 215m drop, is awesome after rain, but its waters shrink to a trickle by about June. Even so, the gorge is impressive at any time, and the plunge pool makes a great dry-season swimming hole (when it is croc-free). To reach the falls themselves requires a 1km scramble over rocks and tree trunks.

Twin Falls are reached via a bumpy 10km ride from Jim Jim camping ground, followed by an 800m boat shuttle through the snaking, forested gorge that cuts through 200m sandstone cliffs. The boat shuttle (adult/child return $12.50/free) – introduced because of the risk posed by crocodiles – leaves roughly every half hour between 7.30am and 4.30pm in the Dry. Tickets can be purchased at the Garrnamarr Camping Area near Jim Jim Falls, Bowali Visitor Centre (p271), Gagudju Crocodile Holiday Inn (p277), Gagudju Lodge Cooinda (opposite), Mardugal camping ground (opposite) and at Tourism Top End in Darwin (p241).

Twin Falls is more impressive for most visitors as it enjoys year-round flows. The flows of Jim Jim Creek at the Jim Jim camping area means the track is often impassable until well into the Dry. Markers indicate the depth in the middle of the creek, but these should be used as a rough guide only as wheel tracks in the sandy creek bed can mean the water is deeper than you think. If you are unsure, wait for a tour vehicle or someone else with local knowledge to cross before attempting it. This crossing is suitable only for high-clearance 4WDs equipped with a snorkel.

A few adventure tours regularly visit Jim Jim and Twin Falls (see p272). The road to both is often closed until well into May or even June, and road access to Twin Falls closes off in the early Wet. If the road is open, Jim Jim alone is worth the visit as there is usually plenty of water dropping over the cliffs. The only way to see the falls during the Wet is from the air.

Garrnamarr campground (adult/child $5.40/free), the camping area near Jim Jim, has showers and toilets.

BUSHWALKING

Some rough scrambling is all that's required to get the most out of these two magnificent waterfalls.

Budjmii Lookout (1km return, 45 minutes, medium) There are excellent escarpment views along this fairly rugged walk, which starts from the Jim Jim camping ground.

Jim Jim Falls (1km return, one hour, medium) This is more of a scramble than a walk, as you climb over and around boulders of increasing size as you approach the falls. It is definitely not suitable for small children unless you can carry them. Allow at least an hour for a swim in the fantastic plunge pool at the foot of the falls.

Barrk Malam (6km return, five hours, difficult) This is a very steep, marked trail up to the plateau above Jim Jim Falls. Carry plenty of water.

Plateau above Twin Falls (6km return, three hours, medium) This marked trail offers good views and the chance to swim (at your own risk) in pools above the falls.

COOINDA & YELLOW WATER

Cooinda is probably the most popular place to stay in Kakadu, thanks to the nearby Yellow Water wetland and the superb daily cruises. The turn-off to the Cooinda accommodation complex is about 50km down the Kakadu Hwy from its junction with the Arnhem Hwy. It's then 4.5km to the Warradjan Aboriginal Cultural Centre, a further 1km to the Yellow Water wetland turn-off, and about another 1km again to Cooinda.

A small **information centre and shop** (6am-9pm May-Oct, 6am-7.30pm Nov-Apr) at the resort sells basic foodstuffs, film, fishing gear, souvenirs and 24-hour fuel.

Yellow Water is an excellent place to watch the sunset, particularly in the Dry when the smoke from the many bushfires at this time of year turns the setting sun into a bright red fireball. Bring plenty of insect repellent with you as the mosquitoes can be voracious.

A highlight of many people's visit to Kakadu is the boat trip on the wetlands. The **Yellow Water Cruises** (☎ 8979 0145; www.gagudju -dreaming.com; adult/child 1½hr $50/35, 2hr $70/49) run six times daily from April to November and four times a day from December to March. From the covered boat, you glide through remarkably diverse waterways, spotting crocodiles sunning themselves on the banks and many species of water birds against a backdrop of vivid greens and a bright blue sky. The paperbark swamp, with the trees mirrored in the glassy water, is sublime. The dawn trip is definitely the best, especially for photography, but other trips throughout the day can be equally good, and the 4.30pm trip has the advantage of the sunset. Take mosquito repellent and sunscreen.

During the Dry, the two-hour cruise leaves at 6.45am, 9am and 4.30pm, while 1½-hour trips depart at 11.30am, 1.15pm and 2.45pm. During the Wet, only 1½-hour trips are available, leaving daily at 8.30am, 11.45am, 1.30pm and 3.30pm. Book tickets at Gagudju Lodge Cooinda (below); the shuttle bus to the jetty leaves from the resort.

Bushwalking

Yellow Water (1.5km return, one hour, easy) This walk is little more than a stroll along a raised boardwalk out to a small viewing platform over the wetland.

Mardugal Billabong (1km, 30 minutes, easy) Close to Mardugal camping area, a short walk takes you along the shore of Mardugal Billabong.

Gun-gardun (2km, 40 minutes, easy) Also near the Mardugal camping ground, this circular walk showcases woodlands – Kakadu's most widespread habitat.

Sleeping & Eating

Book ahead for accommodation and powered sites at the Cooinda resort – it gets pretty crowded in high season. Campers will usually find a spot and there's a National Parks camping area just south of Cooinda.

Gagudju Lodge Cooinda (☎ 8979 0145; www .gagudjulodgecooinda.com.au; unpowered/powered sites $15/35, dm $35, budget r $85, lodge r $285; ✖ ▢ ▨) This resort is a modern oasis. The large camping area has plenty of shade, but with 380 sites, facilities are still stretched at times. The budget air-con units are compact and comfortable, and share the camping ground amenities. The lodge rooms are spacious and comfortable, have satellite TV and sleep up to four people.

Barra Bar & Bistro (mains $6-25; ☒ 10am-10pm) This open-sided bar is the casual-dining option at Cooinda, with pizzas and snacks served throughout the day, along with good old steak and barra.

Mimi Restaurant (mains $26-36; ☒ breakfast & dinner) A more intimate night can be had in this slick contemporary restaurant by the pool, where the menu promises Atlantic salmon, marinated kangaroo rump and buffalo steak.

Just off the Kakadu Hwy, 2km south of the Cooinda turn-off, the National Parks **Mardugal** (adult/child $5.40/free) camping area is the only site not affected by the Wet. It's a nice, shady spot with showers, toilets and a generator zone.

COOINDA TO PINE CREEK

Just south of the Yellow Water and Cooinda turn-off, the Kakadu Hwy heads southwest out of the park to Pine Creek on the Stuart Hwy, about 160km away. The main detour before you leave the park is the dirt track to Gunlom, a wonderfully accessible camping area, waterfall and swimming hole, and there are plenty of bushwalks in the area.

About 45km south of Cooinda is the turn-off to the beautiful falls and pools of **Maguk** (Barramundi Gorge), 12km off the highway along a 4WD track, with a popular free campsite.

Another 5km along the highway brings you to the turn-off to **Gungurul**, a picnic area and basic camping ground that is 2WD accessible. Nearby, the highway crosses the South Alligator River, the traditional boundary between Jawoyn and Gagudju country.

After a further 37km along the highway, a turn-off on the left (east) leads 37km along a gravel road to **Gunlom** (Waterfall Creek). This is another superb escarpment waterfall and plunge pool, and the only one accessible to conventional vehicle. There is camping here and a lovely grassy picnic area with gas barbecues and tables shaded by salmon gums.

Southeast of Gunlom, accessible by 4WD only and requiring a permit, is **Jarrangbarnmi** (Koolpin Gorge) – a beautiful and little-visited gorge. An unmarked 2km track follows Koolpin Creek through the gorge to a series of pools and waterfalls. There's a rock-art site and safe swimming in the creek. You can download a permit application form from www.environment.gov.au/parks/permits /kakadu-jarrangbarnmi.html (allow seven days). This area is worth visiting as part of a tour, since the rock-art galleries are hard to find and permits are taken care of.

Bushwalking

The southern section of the park sees fewer visitors than further north, although Gunlom is a popular side trip and the car park here is sometimes full.

Gunlom Waterfall (1km return, one hour, difficult) This short but steep walk takes you to the top of the dramatic Gunlom Waterfall. It has incredible views and is a good place to look for rare escarpment wildlife, such as black wallaroos. There's also a short walk to the large pool at the base of the waterfall (200m), with disabled access. Another, to Murrill Billabong (1km), carries on to the bank of the South Alligator River (2.5km).

YURMIKMIK BUSHWALKS

Five walks of varying difficulty penetrate the southern stone country of the park from Yurmikmik, 5km south of the South Alligator River on the road to Gunlom. Some are day or half-day walks, while others are overnight and involve bush camping and navigational skills; these require permits and should be attempted only by experienced bushwalkers.

Boulder Creek Walk (2km loop, 45 minutes, medium) This is the easiest of the Yurmikmik walks and crosses Plum Tree Creek through woodlands and monsoon forest to return to the car park.

Yurmikmik Lookout Walk (5km return, 90 minutes, medium) The lookout gives fine views over Jawoyn country: the rugged ridges of the southern park area, the South Alligator River and the high, flat Marrawal Plateau.

Motor Car Falls Walk (7.5km return, three hours, medium) Named after the exploits of an old tin miner who drove his truck up here in 1946, this is actually a disused vehicle track. Markers lead to a plunge pool.

Motor Car Creek Walk (11km, seven hours, difficult) From Motor Car Falls, this is an unmarked section along the creek to the South Alligator River. It is essential to carry a topographic map and compass, and a camping permit is required.

Motor Car and Kurrundie Creek Circular Walk (14km, 10 hours, difficult) A topographic map, compass and camping permit are essential for this unmarked overnight walk. The effort will be repaid by remote and seldom-visited country along Kurrundie Creek, returning by the South Alligator River and Motor Car Creek.

Sleeping & Eating

National Parks operates the **Gunlom camping ground** (adult/child $5.40/free), a mostly shady area

with flush toilets, hot showers, water and gas barbecues. There's a separate generator area.

Goymarr Tourist Resort (☎ 8975 4564; Kakadu Hwy; unpowered/powered sites $14/25, dm $17, budget d $40, motel d from $100; ❄ ❑) Located just outside the park's southern boundary, the former Mary River Roadhouse has a variety of accommodation options, a bistro and a bar – if you're coming into Kakadu from the south, this is the last place to buy takeaway alcohol. There's a small information office and gallery showing Indigenous art for sale in a tin shed next to the roadhouse.

BEYOND KAKADU: ARNHEM LAND

Arnhem Land is a vast, overwhelming and mysterious corner of the Northern Territory (NT). About the size of the state of Victoria and with a population of only 16,000, this Aboriginal reserve is one of Australia's last great untouched wilderness areas.

The only settlements of any size are Nhulunbuy (Gove), on the peninsula at the northeastern corner, and Gunbalanya (Oenpelli), just across the East Alligator River from Kakadu National Park. To the north is the remote Cobourg Peninsula, most of which is preserved as Garig Gunak Barlu National Park and features the ruins of the ill-fated Victoria Settlement, some fine fishing and the world's largest wild herd of banteng, or Indonesian cattle.

Access to Arnhem Land is by permit only, numbers are strictly controlled and this is 4WD-only country. It has long been known for its superb fishing, but the 'stone country' – the Arnhem escarpment and its outliers – also hosts literally thousands of Aboriginal rock-art sites of incredible variety, age and interest.

A visit to Oenpelli, just across the East Alligator from Kakadu, is an easy introduction to Arnhem Land. Permits are easily obtained from the Northern Land Council in Jabiru (p276) and the access road is passable to conventional vehicles in the Dry. For more extensive trips into Arnhem Land you need to join a tour, stay at one of the expensive wilderness/fishing resorts, or join a volunteer project working with remote Aboriginal communities or conservation projects For information on volunteer work possibilities for tourists, see www.conservationvolunteers .com.au, www.worldexpeditions.com and www.redcross.org.au.

Tours

A number of tours visit Arnhem Land from Darwin, also picking up in Jabiru:

Arnhemlander (☎ 1800 089 113; www.arnhemlander .com.au; adult/child $195/156) For 4WD tours to the Mikinj Valley and Injalak Art Centre at Gunbalanya (Oenpelli).

Davidson's Arnhemland Safaris (☎ 8927 5240; www.arnhemland-safaris.com) Experienced operator taking tours to Mt Borradaile, north of Oenpelli. Meals, guided tours, fishing and accommodation in the comfortable safari camp are included in the daily price of around $450; transfers from Darwin can be arranged.

Gove Diving & Fishing Charters (☎ 8987 3445; www.govefish.com.au) Variety of fishing, diving and snorkelling, and wilderness trips from Nhulunbuy.

Lord's Kakadu & Arnhemland Safaris (☎ 8948 2200; www.lords-safaris.com; adult/child $195/155) Based in Kakadu; small-group 4WD tours to Gunbalanya (Oenpelli), including an Aboriginal guided walk to the Injalak Hill rock-art site, lunch and a scout around the Mikinj Valley.

Nomad (☎ 8987 8085; www.nomadcharters.com.au; tours $375-1800) Luxury small group tours from Nhulunbuy including fishing charters and cultural tours.

Venture North Australia (☎ 8927 5500; www .northernaustralia.com; 4-/5-day tour $1479/1960) Tours to remote areas, with expert guidance on rock art. It also has a safari camp near Smith Point on the Cobourg Peninsula.

GUNBALANYA (OENPELLI)
pop 880

Gunbalanya is a small Aboriginal community 17km into Arnhem Land across the East Alligator River from the Border Store in Kakadu. The drive in itself is worth it for that brilliant green wetlands and spectacular escarpments all around. Road access is possible only between May and October: check the tides at Cahill's Crossing on the East Alligator River before setting out so you don't get stuck on the other side.

A permit is required to visit the town, usually issued for visits to the **Injalak Arts & Crafts Centre** (☎ 8979 0190; www.injalak.com; ☺ 8am-5pm). At this centre, artists and craftspeople produce traditional paintings on bark and paper, plus didgeridoos, pandanus weavings and baskets, and screen-printed fabrics, either at the arts centre or on remote outstations throughout Arnhem Land. Prices here are wholesale – all sales benefit the artists and therefore the community. Credit cards are accepted and discounts are offered to YHA members.

As you walk around the veranda of the arts centre to see the artists at work (mornings only), peer out over the wetland at the rear to the escarpment and **Injalak Hill** (Long Tom Dreaming). Knowledgeable local guides lead tours to see the fine rock-art galleries here. The two-hour tours (bookings essential) cost $150 per group. Although it may be possible to join a tour as a walk-in, it's generally best to book a tour from Jabiru that includes the Injalak Hill walk.

You can obtain permits from the **Northern Land Council** (☎ 8979 2410; Flinders St, Jabiru; per person $12.50; ☺ 8am-4.30pm Mon-Fri), which issues them on the same day, although 24 hours' notice is appreciated.

Stone Country Festival (www.gunbalanya.org), in August, is an open day and cultural festival with traditional music, dancing, arts and crafts demonstrations. It's the only day you can visit Gunbalanya without a permit. Camping is allowed but strictly no alcohol.

DIRECTORY

Directory

ACCOMMODATION

As well as the usual slew of hotels, motels, caravan parks and youth hostels, central Australia offers some truly Aussie ways to spend the night. Roll out your swag under the desert stars, park your campervan at a remote cattle station, dream Shiraz-coloured dreams in a plush wine region B&B or blow a small fortune on a luxury 'tent' with views of Uluru.

In this book high-season prices are quoted unless indicated otherwise. Accommodation sections are divided into Budget (up to $80), Midrange ($80 to $160) and Top End (over $160).

In most areas you'll find seasonal price variations. In South Australia (SA) prices peak during summer (December to February) and school and public holidays (see p291). Outside these times discounts and lower

walk-in rates can be found. In the Northern Territory (NT) peak season (the Dry) is June to September, plus school and public holidays. April to May and October to November are quieter shoulder seasons up north, and summer (the Wet in the Top End) is the low season – prices can drop by as much as 30%. Book accommodation in advance in peak periods.

B&Bs

The atmosphere and privacy of B&Bs can be hard to top – everything from restored stone cottages to converted boat sheds, upmarket country houses, romantic escapes and simple bedrooms in family homes. The majority of B&Bs are 'self-catering', meaning breakfast provisions are provided for you to cook. Rates are typically in the $100 to $160 range, though they can climb much higher.

The South Australian Tourist Commission (SATC) publishes a B&B booklet. Online, try www.bandbfsa.com.au, www.bnbbookings.com, www.ozbedandbreakfast.com or www.bed-and-breakfast.au.com.

Camping

Bush camping at remote sites or in national parks is a highlight of any central Australian trip. Nights around a campfire under blanketing stars, listening to the sounds of the night, are unforgettable. In the desert, where rain is relatively rare and mosquitoes aren't an issue, you don't even need a tent – just slip into a swag (zipped canvas bedrolls with mattress, available from camping stores).

There are plenty of free camping places out here, including roadside rest areas. In

---

BOOK YOUR STAY ONLINE

For more accommodation reviews and recommendations by Lonely Planet authors, check out the online booking service at www.lonelyplanet.com/hotels. You'll find the true, insider lowdown on the best places to stay. Reviews are thorough and independent. Best of all, you can book online.

BUSH-CAMPING TIPS

▪ You need a permit to camp on Aboriginal land.

▪ Select your campsite carefully before nightfall, and for privacy and security choose a spot invisible from the road.

▪ Some trees (eg river red gums and desert oak) are notorious for dropping branches – don't camp under them.

▪ Ants live everywhere, and beware spiny seeds that can puncture groundsheets.

▪ Carry out your rubbish, don't bury it.

▪ Observe fire restrictions and ensure fires are safe.

▪ Don't chop down trees or branches to light fires; in national parks BYO firewood.

▪ Use a gas stove for cooking.

▪ Respect wildlife and observe crocodile warnings – camp at least 50m from suspect areas.

▪ Don't camp close enough to rivers or streams to pollute them – a safe distance is 20m.

---

national parks camping is usually only permitted in designated areas, where facilities can range from a fireplace and simple pit toilet to hot showers and free gas barbecues. Payment is made into honesty boxes ($6 to $12 per person).

Caravan Parks

Generally speaking, central Australia's caravan parks are well kept, conveniently located and excellent value, charging from $20 to $25 for two people camping, slightly more for a powered site. Most have basic cabins with shared facilities (from $50) and en suite cabins with cooking facilities ($70 to $120). Additional adults/children incur a small extra fee.

Most places have a camp kitchen, swimming pool, laundry, barbecues and a shop or kiosk, and all offer toilets and hot showers. You'll have no trouble finding a camping space, but it pays to book ahead for powered sites and cabins in peak season.

Unless otherwise indicated, the unpowered/powered campsite prices listed in this book are for two people.

Farm & Station Stays

For a true country experience, stay on a farm or working cattle station. Some let you kick back and watch workers raise a sweat; others rope you in to day-to-day chores. Most accommodation is very comfortable – B&B-style in the main homestead (dinner on request), or in self-contained cottages. Some farms

also provide budget outbuildings or shearers' quarters. Check the options online at www .farmstaysa.com.au, www.australiafarmhost .com and www.frabs.com.au.

Hostels

Hostels are a highly social and low-cost fixture of the central Australian accommodation scene. A dormitory bed costs around $20 to $28, and most also have comfortable private rooms from around $50 ($60 to $80 with en suite). Most hostels have kitchens with fridges, stoves, microwaves and cooking utensils, communal areas with TV, a laundry, internet access, travellers' noticeboards and tour-booking services. Some roadhouses and towns along major highways also have backpacker beds.

HOSTEL ORGANISATIONS

Australia-wide backpacker organisations:

Nomads World (☎ 1800 091 905, 02-9280 4110; www.nomadsworld.com) Relatively small organisation that runs pubs and hostels around the country. Membership for 12 months costs $34. Hostels in Adelaide, Darwin, Uluru, Kangaroo Island, Alice Springs and Kings Canyon.

VIP Backpacker (☎ 07-3395 6111; www.vipbackpackers .com) International organisation is affiliated with a dozen hostels in SA and the NT. A one-/two-year membership costs $43/57.

YHA (☎ 08-8981 6344; www.yha.com.au) The world's biggest youth-hostel network has 15 hostels in SA and the NT. A Hostelling International membership costs $42/82 for one/two years.

INDEPENDENT HOSTELS

Central Australia (particularly SA) has numerous independent hostels, fierce competition for the backpacker dollar prompting fairly high standards and enticements such as free breakfasts, supper and courtesy buses. Places range from rundown hotels trying to fill empty rooms, to converted motels where four- to six-bed units have a fridge, TV and bathroom. The best places tend to be the smaller, more intimate hostels where the owner is also the manager.

Independent backpacker establishments typically charge $20 to $26 for a dorm bed and $50 to $80 for a twin or double room (usually without bathroom).

Hotels & Motels

For comfortable, midrange accommodation, motels are the way to go. There are dozens of motels in cities and smaller towns, and many roadhouses also have motel accommodation. The average motel is a modern (but anonymous), low-rise affair with parking, swimming pool and tidy rooms with bathroom, fridge, tea/coffee facilities, TV, telephone and air-con. Expect to pay at least $60 for a double and up to $120 for more upmarket places.

Fancier hotels and resorts are all around SA but are limited to Darwin, Alice Springs, Yulara, Kings Canyon and Kakadu in the NT. Most have fabulous facilities and locations, but more than a few five-star places are clinical and corporate in atmosphere. Although rack rates are high, discounts and deals mean you'll rarely pay full price except in peak season.

Pubs

For the budget traveller, pubs ('hotels' that serve beer) are cheap, central options. Many pubs were built during boom times, so they're often the largest, most extravagant buildings in town. Some pubs have been restored as heritage buildings, but generally rooms remain small and old fashioned, with an amble down the hall to the bathroom. You can sometimes rent a single room at a country pub for little more than a hostel dorm, and you'll be in the centre of town to boot. If you're a light sleeper, never book a room above the bar, and be aware that pub rooms don't always have air-con.

Pub singles/doubles with shared facilities start around $40/60, more if you want a private bathroom. Few have a separate reception area – just ask at the bar. For women travellers, see p297.

Rental Accommodation

Serviced apartments and holiday flats resemble motels but usually contain cooking facilities – good value for longer stays. Holiday flats are found in holiday areas; serviced apartments in Darwin and Adelaide. In some holiday flats you provide your own sheets and bedding; others are fully equipped. See Sleeping sections in destination chapters for listings.

ACTIVITIES

In SA, there are plenty of opportunities for bushwalking, canoeing, cycling, sailing, diving, rock climbing, surfing and whale-watching. In the NT, the main games are bushwalking, fishing, swimming and wildlife-watching. See regional chapters for activity listings.

Major long-distance cycling and walking trails in SA:

Heysen Trail (www.heysentrail.asn.au) Australia's longest walking trail: 1200km between Cape Jervis on the Fleurieu Peninsula and Parachilna Gorge in the Flinders Ranges.

Kidman Trail (www.kidmantrail.org.au) A 10-section cycling and walking trail between Willunga on the Fleurieu Peninsula and Kapunda north of the Barossa Valley.

Mawson Trail (www.southaustraliantrails.com) A 900km bike trail between Adelaide and Blinman in the Flinders Ranges, via the Adelaide Hills and Clare Valley.

BUSINESS HOURS

Most shops and businesses open from 9am to 5pm or 6pm Monday to Friday, and close at either noon or 5pm on Saturday. In Adelaide and Darwin on Friday, doors stay open until 9pm. Supermarkets generally open from 7am until at least 8pm; some open 24 hours. Delis (general stores) also open late.

Banks are open from 9.30am to 4pm Monday to Thursday, and until 5pm on Friday. Post offices are open from 9am to 5pm Monday to Friday, but you can also buy stamps from newsagents and delis.

Restaurants typically open around noon for lunch and from 6pm for dinner. Restaurants typically serve until at least 9pm, later on Friday and Saturday. Adelaide and Darwin eateries keep longer hours. Cafes tend to be all-day affairs that either close around 5pm or continue their business into the night. Pubs usually serve food from noon to 2pm and from 6pm to 8pm. Pubs and bars often open for drinking at lunchtime and continue well into the evening, particularly from Thursday to Saturday.

Out on the highways, roadhouses and service stations remain open from around 8am to 10pm. Some service stations in town are open 24 hours for fuel, but don't count on it.

CHILDREN
Practicalities

You'll find public rooms where you go to feed babies or change nappies in most shopping centres; check with local visitors centres for details. As anywhere, children should be accompanied in all public toilets, including shopping centres.

Motels and some caravan parks have playgrounds and swimming pools, and can supply cots and baby baths. Top-end hotels and many (but not all) midrange hotels often accommodate children for free, but B&Bs are often child-free zones.

For babysitting, check under Baby Sitters and Child Care Centres in the *Yellow Pages*, or phone the local council for a list. **Dial-An-Angel** (☎ 08-8267 3700; www.dialanangel.com.au) provides nannies and babysitters in Adelaide.

Child concessions (and family rates) often apply for tours, admission fees, and air, bus and train transport, with some discounts as high as 50% off. However, the definition of 'child' can vary from under 12 to under 18 years.

Heat can be a problem while travelling in central Australia, especially in the hotter months, with relentless desert sun and high humidity in the Top End. Make sure kids are well covered up with a hat, SPF 30+ sunscreen and sunglasses. If you're out walking, factor in plenty of shady stops or visits to swimming pools and waterholes (if safe). Always carry plenty of water and drink regularly.

Medical services here are of a high standard, with items such as baby-food formula and nappies widely available (plan ahead if heading to remote regions). Major hire-car companies can supply booster seats, for which you'll be charged around $20 for up to three days' use, with an additional daily fee for longer periods.

Sights & Activities

Travelling with children in central Australia can be a joy – bush camping, short walks, stargazing, swimming and wildlife spotting are all healthy, family-friendly activities. Adelaide and Darwin have parklands with play equipment and nearby beaches, and most towns have a playground.

The biggest problem may be keeping the kids amused on long road trips. Portable DVD players or Play Station–type games (with headphones!) can help pass the kilometres, and books-on-tape (available at ABC Shops) are perfectly suited to long drives. At the very least, be sure to factor in regular rest stops.

For more ideas see Adelaide for Children (p53), Alice Springs for Children (p181) and Darwin for Children (p250). Lonely Planet's *Travel with Children* also contains useful information.

DIRECTORY

CLIMATE

Central Australia has three distinct climatic regions: temperate southern SA (cold, rainy winters and warm-to-hot summers), the arid central deserts (hot, dry days and cold nights), and the tropical Top End (wet in summer, dry in winter).

See When to Go (p17) for more seasonal info. For current forecasts, see the **Bureau of Meteorology** (www.bom.gov.au) website.

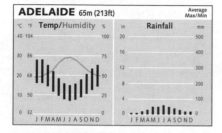

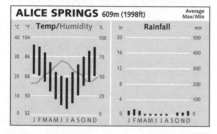

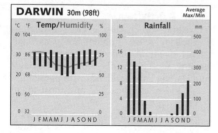

CUSTOMS

When entering Australia you can bring most articles in free of duty, provided that customs is satisfied they are for personal use and that you'll be taking them with you when you leave. There's a duty-free per-person quota of 2.25L of alcohol, 250 cigarettes and dutiable goods up to the value of A$900.

Narcotics, of course, are illegal, and customs inspectors and their highly trained hounds are diligent in sniffing them out. Quarantine regulations are strict, so you must declare all goods of animal or vegetable origin – wooden spoons, straw hats, the lot. Fresh food, particularly meat, cheese, fruit, vegetables, and flowers, is also prohibited. There are disposal bins located in the airport where you can dump any questionable items if you don't want to bother with an inspection.

For more information see Interstate Quarantine (p301), or contact the **Australian Quarantine & Inspection Service** (AQIS; ☎ 1800 020 504; www.aqis.gov.au) or **Australian Customs Service** (☎ 1300 363 263; www.customs.gov.au).

DANGERS & ANNOYANCES
Animal Hazards

For four to six months of the year (at least) you'll have to cope with those two banes of the Australian outdoors: the fly and the mosquito (mozzie). Flies aren't too bad in Adelaide, but they're more prevalent in the outback and the NT.

Flies emerge with the warmer spring weather (early September) and last until winter. Insect repellents such as Aerogard and Rid may also help to deter them. Mozzies are a menace in summer, especially near wetlands (they can pretty much lift you off the ground in Kakadu), and some species are carriers of viral infections (see p313). Try to keep your arms and legs covered as soon as the sun sets, and make liberal use of insect repellent.

Another serious hazard is animals straying onto the road, particularly kangaroos but also livestock. Vehicles travel fast on the main highways and kangaroos can and will hop from the side of the road in the blink of an eye. The worst time to travel is between dusk and dawn.

See p312 for information on sharks, snakes, spiders, jellyfish, crocodiles and stinging marine animals.

Bushfires

Bushfires are an annual event in SA. In hot, dry and windy weather, be extremely careful with any naked flame – cigarette butts thrown out of car windows have started many a fire – and make sure your fire's out before you decamp. On total-fire-ban days it's forbidden even to use a camping stove in the open – penalties are harsh. Campfires are banned in conservation areas during the Fire Danger Period (FDP), which varies from region to region but is usually from 1 November to 31 March (30 April in some places).

Bushwalkers should seek local advice before setting out. When a total fire ban is in place, delay your trip until the weather improves. If you're out in the bush and you see smoke, even a long distance away, take it seriously – bushfires move quickly and change direction with the wind. Go to the nearest open space, downhill if possible. A forested ridge, on the other hand, is the most dangerous place to be.

Crime

Central Australia is a relatively safe place to visit but you should still take reasonable precautions. Lock hotel rooms and cars, and don't leave your valuables unattended or visible through car windows. In Darwin, Alice Springs and Katherine, petty crime can be a problem, particularly late at night. Avoid walking alone in unlit areas.

In response to several reports of drugged drinks in pubs and clubs, authorities are advising women to refuse drinks offered by strangers in bars and to drink bottled alcohol rather than from a glass.

On the Road

As a rule, central Australian drivers are a courteous bunch, but risks can be posed by rural revheads, inner-city speedsters and fatigue- or alcohol-affected drivers. Take regular breaks to avoid fatigue and be aware of animals, which can be a real hazard on country roads, particularly at dusk.

If you're keen to explore the outback, do some careful planning and preparation. Driving on dirt roads can be tricky if you're not used to them, and travellers regularly encounter difficulties in the harsh outback conditions. The golden rules are to always carry plenty of water and tell someone where you're going. For more info on outback driving, see p308.

Swimming

Popular beaches are patrolled by surf lifesavers. Safe areas are marked by red-and-yellow flags. Even so, surf beaches can still be dangerous if you aren't used to the local conditions. Undertows (or 'rips') are the main problem. If you find yourself being carried out by a rip, don't panic or try to swim against the rip, which will exhaust you. In most cases the current stops within a couple of hundred metres of shore – you can then swim parallel to the shore for a short way to escape the rip and make your way back to land. If you swim between the flags, help should arrive quickly; raise your arm (and yell!) if you need help.

A number of people are paralysed every year by diving into waterholes or waves in shallow water and hitting the bottom – look before you leap.

DISCOUNT CARDS
Senior Cards

The **Seniors Card** (www.seniorscard.com.au) is available to permanent residents over the age of 60, giving discounts on everything from accommodation and tours to car hire and meals (with participating businesses, of course). The card is free and you can apply online. Even without a card, seniors with proof of age receive a discount on admission to many attractions in central Australia – ask at the ticket counter.

Student Cards

A student card entitles you to a wide range of discounts – from transport and tour charges to admission fees. The most common is the **International Student Identity Card** (ISIC; www.isiccard .com). To get one you need proof of full-time student status – unless, of course, you're buying it off the street in Bangkok. For that very reason, some airlines require a card or letter from your home university before giving student discounts.

The same organisation also produces the International Youth Travel Card (IYTC or Go25) with benefits equivalent to the ISIC, issued to people between 12 and 26 years of age and not full-time students. Another similar card is the International Teacher Identity Card (ITIC), available to teaching professionals.

All three cards are issued by student unions, hostelling organisations and student-travel companies.

EMBASSIES & CONSULATES

The principal diplomatic representations to Australia are in Canberra; some countries have also consular representation in Adelaide and Darwin:

Canada (☎ 02-6270 4000; www.dfait-maeci.gc.ca /australia; Commonwealth Ave, Canberra, ACT 2600)

France (☎ 02-6216 0100; www.ambafrance-au.org; 6 Perth Ave, Yarralumla, Canberra, ACT 2600)

Germany (☎ 02-6270 1911; www.germanembassy.org .au; 119 Empire Circuit, Yarralumla, Canberra, ACT 2600)

Indonesia Canberra (☎ 02-6250 8600; www.kbri -canberra.org.au; 8 Darwin Ave, Yarralumla, Canberra, ACT 2600); Darwin (Map pp244-5; ☎ 08-8943 0200; www.kri-darwin.org; 20 Harry Chan Ave, Darwin, NT 0800)

Ireland (☎ 02-6273 3022; canberraembassy@dfa.ie; 20 Arkana St, Yarralumla, Canberra, ACT 2600)

Italy (☎ 08-8337 0777; www.consadelaide.esteri .it/consolato_adelaide; 398 Payneham Rd, Glynde, Adelaide, SA 5070)

Japan (☎ 02-6273 3244; www.au.emb-japan.go.jp; 112 Empire Crt, Yarralumla, Canberra, ACT 2600)

Netherlands (☎ 08-8232 3855; www.netherlands.org .au; Level 1, 147 Frome St, Adelaide, SA 5000)

New Zealand (☎ 02-6270 4211; www.nzembassy.com; Commonwealth Ave, Canberra ACT 2600)

South Africa (☎ 02-6272 7300; www.sahc.org.au; cnr Rhodes Pl & State Circle, Yarralumla, Canberra, ACT 2600)

UK (☎ 1300 367 066, 08-8232 9817; www.britaus.net; 444-446 Pulteney St, Adelaide, SA 5000)

USA (☎ 02-6214 5600; http://canberra.usembassy.gov; Moonah Pl, Yarralumla, Canberra, ACT 2600)

FESTIVALS & EVENTS

Adelaide prides itself on being Australia's festival epicentre, in a state that excels in putting on a show – arts, music, culture, food and wine, or high-adrenaline sport. Annual events are listed in the events section on www.southaustralia.com.

The NT has some of Australia's wackiest festivals, including a boat race on a dry river in Alice Springs, and another in Darwin where the boats are made entirely of beer cans! There are also Aboriginal cultural festivals offering the chance to visit communities without a permit.

January
Tour Down Under (☎ 08-8463 4701; www.tourdown under.com.au) SA's six-stage version of the Tour de France.

February
Barossa Under the Stars (☎ 08-8563 0600; www .barossaunderthestars.com.au) A weekend of live entertainment (previous performers include Jimmy Barnes and Joe Cocker) and night picnics in the Barossa Valley (SA).

March
Adelaide Festival of Arts (☎ 08-8216 4444; www .adelaidefestival.com.au) Culture vultures absorb international and Australian dance, drama, opera and theatre performances at this popular biennial festival (even-numbered years).

Adelaide Fringe (☎ 08-8100 2000; www.adelaide fringe.com.au) Independent arts festival, second only to the Edinburgh Fringe.

Clipsal 500 (☎ 08-8212 8500; www.clipsal500.com .au) Mulleted bogans rejoice as Adelaide's streets become a four-day Holden-vs-Ford racing track.

Crush (☎ 1300 305 577; www.adelaidehillswine.com .au) Much fine quaffing at this Adelaide Hills wine festival.

WOMADelaide (☎ 08-8271 1488; www.womadelaide .com.au) One of the world's best live-music events, with more than 400 musicians and performers from around the globe.

April
Barossa Vintage Festival (☎ 08-8563 0600; www .barossavintagefestival.com.au) Biennial festival (odd-numbered years) with processions, maypole dancing, traditional dinners and muchos Barossa (SA) wine tasting.

May
Alice Springs Cup Carnival (☎ 08-8952 4977; www.alicespringsturfclub.org.au) Horseracing hoo-ha in the Red Centre.

Clare Valley Gourmet Weekend (☎ 08-8843 0222; www.southaustralia.com) Festival of fine wine and food put on by local wineries and some of SA's top restaurants.

June
Adelaide Cabaret Festival (☎ 08-8216 8600; www.adelaidefestivalcentre.com.au/adelaidecabaret) Unique cabaret festival supporting local and interstate music and theatre.

Barunga Festival (☎ 08-8971 1100; www.barunga festival.com.au) Aboriginal cultural and sports festival in Katherine. Music, dance, arts, crafts, football, athletics and spear throwing.

Finke Desert Race (☎ 08-8952 8886; www.finke desertrace.com.au) Two-day, off-road bike and car race through the desert from Alice Springs to the Apatula Community.

Sea & Vines Festival (☎ 08-8323 9944; www.seaand vines.com) Wine, seafood and live music in McLaren Vale (SA) wineries over the June long weekend. Can get insanely crowded.

July
Camel Cup (☎ 08-8952 6796; www.camelcup.com.au) Unpredictable camel racing (yes, camels) in Alice Springs.

Darwin Cup Carnival (☎ 08-8923 4222; www .darwinturfclub.org.au) The Fannie Bay racecourse erupts with thundering hoofs. Wear your best hat.

Darwin Fringe Festival (☎ 08-8981 5522; www .darwinfringe.com.au) Offbeat culture in the Top End: theatre, visual arts, dance, music and poetry.

NAIDOC Week (☎ 1800 079 098; www.naidoc.org.au) The National Aboriginal & Islander Day Observance Committee conducts performances, exhibitions and talks in communities around SA and the NT.

Royal Darwin Show (☎ 08-8984 3091; www.darwin show.com.au) How many prize cows and sheep shearers can you handle?

August

Beer Can Regatta (☎ 0409-823 871; www.beercan regatta.org.au) Sandy high jinks and beer-can boats at Darwin's Mindil Beach.

Darwin Festival (☎ 08-89434700; www.darwinfestival .org.au) Theatre, comedy, cabaret, dance, music, food and workshops – an artistic cavalcade!

Flying Fox Art & Cultural Festival (☎ 08-8972 5500; www.katherine.nt.gov.au) Katherine's 22-day arts and cultural festival.

Walking with Spirits Festival (www.djilpinarts.org .au) Traditional corroboree at Beswick (near Katherine) with music, dance, stories, puppetry and film.

September

AFL Grand Final (☎ 03-9643 1999; www.afl.com.au) Annual finale of the Australian Football League season. Will the Adelaide Crows or Port Adelaide win it this year?

City-to-Bay Fun Run (☎ 08-8232 6184; www.city -bay.org.au) A 12km dash from Adelaide to Glenelg. Better start training!

Henley-on-Todd Regatta (☎ 08-8952 6796; www .henleyontodd.com.au) Alice Springs' iconic boat races on the (usually) bone-dry Todd River.

Royal Adelaide Show (☎ 08-8210 5211; www.adelaide showground.com.au) A major seven-day agricultural festa.

Alice Desert Festival (www.alicedesertfestival.com .au) Central Australian art, music, dancing, exhibitions and street performers.

October

Barossa Music Festival (☎ 08-8564 2511; www.barossa .org) Food and wine hootenanny with jazz and classical music.

November

Adelaide Christmas Pageant (☎ 1300 655 276; www.cupageant.com.au) Adelaide institution – floats, bands and marching troupes hijack the city streets for a day in November.

GAY & LESBIAN TRAVELLERS

Attitudes towards homosexuality in SA are fairly relaxed, but as you'd expect, homophobia does rear its ugly head the further you travel into the outback. Adelaide has plenty of gay-friendly venues (see p61), and a dedicated annual gay and lesbian cultural festival, **Feast** (☎ 08-8231 4322; www.feast.org.au), held over three weeks in November. For info on the G&L scene, pick up a copy of **Blaze** (www.blaze.e-p.net .au) magazine, available around Adelaide, or contact the **Gay & Lesbian Counselling Service of SA Inc** (☎ 1800 182 233, 08-8422 8400; www.glcssa.org.au).

In the NT you'll find active gay and lesbian communities in Alice Springs (p182), though homophobic attitudes do exist beyond the main towns.

For general information, check out the **Gay Guide Australia** (www.gayguideaustralia.com), which has information on destinations, gay-friendly businesses, places to stay and nightlife. See also www.gaystayaustralia.com.

HOLIDAYS
Public Holidays

National and state public holidays observed in SA and the NT:

New Year's Day 1 January
Australia Day 26 January
Easter Good Friday to Easter Monday inclusive; March/April
Anzac Day 25 April
May Day 1st Monday in May (NT only)
Adelaide Cup Day 3rd Monday in May (SA only)
Queen's Birthday 2nd Monday in June
Picnic Day 1st Monday in August (NT only)
Labour Day 1st Monday in October (SA only)
Christmas Day 25 December
Boxing Day 26 December (NT only)
Proclamation Day 28 December (SA only)

School Holidays

The Christmas-holiday period is part of the long summer school vacation. This is low season in the NT, so you're unlikely to find crowds or accommodation booked out (but you will in SA). There are three other school-holiday periods during the year: from early to mid-April (including Easter), late June to mid-July, and late September to early October.

Local Holidays

Alice Springs Show Day 1st Friday in July
Tennant Creek Show Day 2nd Friday in July
Katherine Show Day 3rd Friday in July
Darwin Show Day 4th Friday in July

DIRECTORY

INSURANCE

A travel-insurance policy to cover theft, loss and medical problems is a stellar idea. Some policies offer lower and higher medical-expense options. There's a wide variety of policies available, so check the small print. Be sure that the policy covers ambulances or an emergency flight home – wrecking your ankle and having to be airlifted out of a gorge is costly. Some policies specifically exclude 'dangerous activities', which may include scuba diving, motorcycling or even trekking.

You may prefer a policy that pays doctors or hospitals directly rather than you having to pay on the spot then claim later. If you have to claim later, make sure you keep all documentation. Car-hire companies offer vehicle insurance.

See p308 for vehicle-insurance info.

INTERNET ACCESS
Access Points

Most public libraries have internet access, but generally they're provided for research needs, not for travellers to check their emails – so book ahead or tackle a cybercafe. You'll find plenty of internet cafes in Adelaide, Darwin, Alice, larger towns and pretty much anywhere that travellers congregate. The cost ranges from less than $6 an hour to $10 an hour. Most youth hostels can hook you up, as can many hotels and caravan parks.

Hooking Up

If you're bringing your palmtop or laptop, check with your Internet Service Provider (ISP) for access numbers you can dial into in central Australia. Most international ISPs have numbers for Adelaide and Darwin. Australia primarily uses the RJ-45 telephone plugs although you may see Telstra EXI-160 four-pin plugs – electronics shops such as Tandy and Dick Smith can help.

Wireless connections are increasingly popular throughout Australia, but don't count on wi-fi being available. Keep in mind, too, that your PC-card modem may not work in Australia. The safest option is to buy a reputable 'global' modem before you leave home or buy a local PC-card modem once you get to Australia. Also see p22.

LEGAL MATTERS

Most travellers will have no contact with the police or legal system. There's a significant police presence on the region's roads; they have the power to stop your car and see your licence (you're required to carry it), check your vehicle for roadworthiness, and insist that you take a breath test for alcohol.

First offenders caught with small amounts of illegal drugs are likely to receive a fine rather than go to jail, but the recording of a conviction against you may affect your visa status. Speaking of which, if you remain in Australia beyond the life of your visa, you'll officially be an 'overstayer' and could face detention and expulsion, then be prevented from returning to Australia for up to three years.

Legal aid is available only in serious cases; for Legal Aid office info see www.nla.aust.net.au. However, many solicitors do not charge for an initial consultation.

In the NT, the legal age for driving, voting and drinking is 18. The age of sexual consent is 16. In SA, you can drive when you're 16½, vote and drink at 18 and have consensual sex at 17.

MAPS

For detailed maps, try the **Royal Automobile Association of South Australia** (RAA; Map p48; ☎ 08-8202 4600; www.raa.net; 55 Hindmarsh Sq, Adelaide) or the **Automobile Association of the Northern Territory** (AANT; Map pp244-5; ☎ 08-8981 3837; www.aant.com.au; 79-81 Smith St, Darwin).

Hema (☎ 07-3340 0000; www.hemamaps.com.au) and **Westprint** (☎ 03-5391 1466; www.westprint.com.au) publish touring maps covering Adelaide to Darwin, central Australia, Kakadu, the Flinders Ranges and Kangaroo Island (among others places), plus 4WD and outback track maps. **Geoscience Australia** (☎ 1800 800 173; www.ga.gov.au) publishes large-scale topographic sheet maps for bushwalking and 4WD explorations.

Gregorys (☎ 1800 021 987, 02-9857 3700; www.gregorys-online.com) and **UBD** (☎ 1800 021 987, 08-8400 3242; www.ubd.com.au) both produce Adelaide street directories (around $30) that are useful if you intend to stay a while and do lots of city driving. Also, UBD has a street directory covering numerous country centres.

In SA, GPS systems and topographic maps are available from **Carto Graphics** (off Map p48; ☎ 08-8357 1777; www.cartographics.com.au; 147 Unley Rd, Unley, Adelaide) and the **Map Shop** (Map p48; ☎ 08-8231 2033; www.mapshop.net.au; 6 Peel St, Adelaide). The latter also provides special-interest maps and cycling and bushwalking guides (including Heysen and Mawson trail maps), which are also available at outdoor shops. You can also hire a GPS in Alice Springs at **Central Comms** (Map p176; ☎ 08-8952 2388; www.centralcomms. com.au; cnr Stuart Hwy & Wills Tce, Alice Springs), or rent one from the major car-hire companies (see p306; Darwin and Adelaide only, subject to availability).

MONEY

Australia's currency is the Australian dollar, comprising 100 cents. There are 5c, 10c, 20c, 50c, $1 and $2 coins, and $5, $10, $20, $50 and $100 notes. In this book, unless otherwise stated, prices listed are in Australian dollars.

The Aussie dollar has fluctuated in recent years. It nosedived below US50c in 2001, soared to nearly US$1 in 2008 and since then has settled somewhere in between. See Quick Reference (inside front cover) for exchange rates, and Getting Started (p18) for information on costs.

ATMs & Eftpos

There are 24-hour ATMs in most substantial towns in SA and the NT (including Yulara at Uluru and Jabiru and Cooinda in Kakadu National Park). All accept cards from other Australian banks, and most are linked to international networks. ATMs can also be found in roadhouses along the Stuart Hwy.

Most service stations and supermarkets have Electronic Funds Transfer at Point of Sale (Eftpos) facilities allowing you to make purchases and even draw out cash with your credit or debit card. Always have some cash in reserve in case these facilities aren't operating.

Credit & Debit Cards

Credit cards (especially Visa and MasterCard) are widely accepted throughout Australia for everything from a hostel bed to an adventure tour. A credit card is essential if you want to hire a car, and can also be used for cash advances at banks and from ATMs (depending on the card). Diners and AmEx cards are not widely accepted.

A debit card allows you to draw money directly from your home bank account using ATMs, banks or Eftpos machines. Any card connected to the international banking network – Cirrus, Maestro, Plus and Eurocard – should work with your PIN (Personal Identification Number). Expect substantial fees.

Taxes & Refunds

The Goods and Services Tax (GST) is a flat 10% tax on all Australian goods and services, with some exceptions such as basic food items (milk, bread, fruit and vegetables etc). By law, the tax is included in the quoted or shelf prices. All prices in this book are GST inclusive.

If you purchase new or secondhand goods with a minimum value of $300 from any one supplier within 30 days of departure from Australia, you're entitled to a refund of GST paid under the Tourist Refund Scheme (TRS). Contact the **Australian Customs Service** (☎ 1800 228 227; www.customs.gov.au) for more details.

Tipping

Tipping is far from ingrained in Australian society, and most people in the outback don't bother. The only place where tipping is considered normal is restaurants, where 10% of the bill is reasonable for good service. Taxi drivers don't expect tips, but rounding up to the nearest dollar is the done thing.

Travellers Cheques & Moneychangers

Changing travellers cheques (AmEx, Travelex and Thomas Cook, and foreign currency) at most banks is easy. There are also exchange bureaux at Adelaide, Darwin and Alice Springs airports and downtown in these cities. Commissions and fees for changing foreign-currency cheques varies, so it's worth shopping around. Buying travellers cheques in Australian dollars is a good option: these can be exchanged immediately at banks without conversion from foreign currencies, commissions or fees. Present your passport for identification when cashing travellers cheques.

Foreign currency can also be exchanged in most banks and at currency-exchange bureaux.

POST

Australia's postal services are reasonably cheap and efficient. It costs 55c to send a standard letter or postcard within Australia. **Australia Post** (☎ 13 13 18; www.auspost.com.au) divides international destinations for letters into two regions: airmail letters up to 50g to Asia-Pacific/Rest of the World cost $1.40/2.05. Postcards (up to 20g) to any country cost

$1.35. Contact Australia Post or check the website for details of parcel costs.

All post offices will hold mail for visitors, and the main post offices in Adelaide, Darwin, Alice Springs and Katherine have poste restante sections. You need to provide some form of identification (such as a passport) to collect mail. Post offices are open from 9am to 5pm Monday to Friday, and you can also buy stamps at some newsagencies.

SHOPPING

There are plenty of things for sale in central Australia that are definitely not worth buying: plastic boomerangs, fake Aboriginal ashtrays and T-shirts, and all manner of other terrible souvenirs. Most of these come from Taiwan, China or Korea; before buying anything, make sure it was actually made here!

Indigenous Art

Buying authentic Aboriginal art or artefacts supports Indigenous cultures. Unfortunately, much so-called Indigenous art in souvenir shops is just plain fake. Admittedly it is often difficult to tell whether an item is genuine, but it's worth trying to find out. Look for the 'Label of Authenticity', or ask to see artists' biographical informations. You can also ask how much of the sale price is returned to the artist. If a vendor can't comply, keep walking. Try to buy artefacts either directly from community art-and-craft centres, or from Indigenous-owned galleries. This way you can ensure items are genuine and that your money is going to the right people.

See Shopping sections in regional chapters for credible outlets, or check these websites:
Aboriginal Australia (www.aboriginalaustralia.com)
Association of Kimberley & Arnhem Aboriginal Artists (www.ankaaa.org.au)
Desart (www.desart.com.au)

DIDGERIDOOS

If you want a 'didge' to keep your neighbours awake, don't buy a mass-produced tube of lathed wood. Many didgeridoos aren't made by Indigenous people (there are stories of backpackers in Darwin making them), so try to buy from a reputable gallery or Indigenous community. An authentic didge should have imperfections – it won't be dead straight, and the inside should feel rough (didgeridoos were originally made from eucalypt branches hollowed out by termites).

PAINTINGS

If you're interested in buying a painting, again, purchase from a community art centre or a reputable gallery and ask for a certificate of authenticity. Some central Australian artworks have stratospheric price tags, so buying a canvas from a local on the street in Alice Springs for $50 may suit your wallet. Either way, you'll still be getting a bargain compared to what you'd pay in Melbourne or Sydney.

Other affordable items include painted boomerangs, screen-printed textiles, clap sticks, necklaces, carvings, etchings and prints.

Opals & Gemstones

The opal is Australia's national gemstone and it makes beaut souvenirs or jewellery. It's a stunning stone, but buy wisely and shop around – quality and prices vary widely from place to place. Coober Pedy in SA is opal central!

Garnets, zircons and a number of other semiprecious stones are found in the gem fields of central Australia. You can fossick for your own or buy them relatively cheaply in gem shops or jewellers.

SMOKING

It wasn't so long ago that smoking was de rigueur in central Australia (this is Australia's 'Marlboro Country'). These days lighting up is banned on public transport everywhere, and in pubs, eateries in SA (ban commences January 1, 2010 in the NT). If you're a nicotine fiend, join the puffing hordes outside.

TELEPHONE

The two main providers in Australia are **Telstra** (☎ 12 51 11; www.telstra.com.au) and **Optus** (☎ 1300 301 937; www.optus.com.au). Both are also major players in the mobile- (cell-) phone market, along with **Vodafone** (☎ 1300 303 030; www.vodafone.com.au) and **3 Mobile** (☎ 13 16 83; www.three.com.au).

Information & Toll-Free Calls

Numbers starting with ☎ 190 are usually recorded information services, costing anything from 35c to $5 or more per minute (more from mobiles and payphones).

Many businesses have either a toll-free number (☎ 1800), dialable from anywhere within Australia for free, or a ☎ 13 or ☎ 1300 number, charged at a local call rate. None of these numbers can be dialled from outside Australia.

STD AREA CODES

- New South Wales & ACT ☎ 02
- Victoria & Tasmania ☎ 03
- Queensland ☎ 07
- South Australia, Northern Territory & Western Australia ☎ 08

To make a reverse-charge call from a public or private phone, dial ☎ 1800 738 3773 (1800 REVERSE).

International Calls

From most phones you can make international ISD (International Subscriber Dialling) calls, but the cheapest deals come from providers other than Telstra, usually through phonecards where calls to the UK and USA can be as low as 5c per minute.

To call overseas with Telstra, dial the international access code from Australia (☎ 0011 or ☎ 0018), the country code, the area code (minus the initial '0'), then the local phone number. Dialling Australia from overseas, use the ☎ 61 country code, then the state/territory STD area code (minus the initial '0'), then the local phone number.

Local & Long-distance Calls

Local calls cost 50c from public phones; 25c from private phones – there are no time limits. Calls to/from mobile phones cost more and are timed.

Australia uses four Subscriber Trunk Dialling (STD) area codes for long-distance calls, which can be made from public phones. Long-distance calls are timed; rates vary depending on distance, service provider and time of day – they're cheaper off-peak (usually between 7pm and 7am).

Mobile (Cell) Phones

Australian mobile-phone numbers have the prefixes ☎ 04xx or ☎ 04xxx. Australia's mobile networks service more than 90% of the population but leave vast tracts of the country uncovered. Adelaide, Darwin and most of central Australia's settled areas get good reception, but as the towns thin out, so does the service. Don't rely on coverage in outback areas.

Australia's digital network is compatible with GSM 900 and 1800 (used in Europe), but isn't compatible with the systems used in the USA or Japan. Before you leave, ask your home-country carrier whether your phone will work in Australia. If not, it's easy and cheap to get connected short term – the main service providers (Telstra, Optus and Vodafone) all have prepaid mobile systems. Starter kits may include a phone and SIM card, or, if you already have a compatible phone, just a SIM card. You then charge up your phone with credit, either via a prepaid card or voucher, or by using your credit card. You can buy recharge cards at convenience stores and newsagents.

Phonecards

A range of phonecards ($10, $20, $30 etc) is available from newsagents and post offices, and can be used with any public or private phone by dialling a toll-free access number and then the PIN on the card. Rates vary from company to company – it's worth shopping around. Telstra phonecards (again sold in various dollar amounts) work with most payphones. Some public phones also accept credit cards.

TIME

SA and the NT are on Central Standard Time, half an hour behind the eastern states (Queensland, New South Wales, Victoria and Tasmania), and 1½ hours ahead of Western Australia. Central Standard Time is 9½ hours ahead of GMT/UTC (London), 13½ hours ahead of New York, 15½ hours ahead of LA, 2½ hours ahead of Jakarta and 2½ hours behind Wellington (New Zealand).

Things get screwed up during the summer as 'daylight savings' does not apply in the NT or Queensland, so from October to March (approximately), most eastern states are 1½ hours ahead of NT time, and SA is one hour ahead of NT time. In Tasmania it lasts for two months longer than the other states. Western Australia is holding a referendum on whether or not to introduce daylight savings.

TOURIST INFORMATION

You could easily bury yourself under the mountains of brochures and booklets, maps and leaflets available in SA and the NT. Almost every decent-sized town has a visitors centre of some description, with a proliferation of brochures and maps. They're usually staffed by volunteers (some with sketchy knowledge of tourism). Local tourism offices are listed in destination chapters.

The main players:

South Australian Visitor & Travel Centre (Map p48; ☎ 1300 655 276; www.southaustralia.com; 18 King William St, Adelaide; ☺ 8.30am-5pm Mon-Fri, 9am-2pm Sat & Sun) Super-comprehensive info and brochures on SA regions, accommodation, tours, transport, food, wine and events.

Tourism Australia (☎ 1300 361 650, 02-9360 1111; www.australia.com) National government tourist body. Check the website for pretrip research, with info in nine languages (including French, German, Japanese and Spanish).

Tourism NT (☎ 13 67 68, 08-8999 3900; www.travelnt.com) Bountiful info on central Australia and the Top End with listings for accommodation, attractions and package options throughout the NT.

Tourism Top End (Map pp244-5; ☎ 8980 6000; www.tourismtopend.com.au; 6 Bennett St, Darwin; ☺ 8.30am-5.30pm Mon-Fri, 9am-3pm Sat, 10am-3pm Sun) Brochures, fact sheets and tour and accommodation bookings.

TRAVELLERS WITH DISABILITIES

Disability awareness in central Australia is pretty high and getting higher. Legislation requires that new accommodation meets accessibility standards, and discrimination by tourism operators is illegal. Many of the region's key attractions provide access for those with limited mobility and a number of sites have also begun addressing the needs of visitors with visual or aural impairments; contact attractions in advance to discuss facilities.

Long-distance bus travel is not yet a viable option for the wheelchair user. The *Ghan* train has disabled facilities (book ahead). Avis and Hertz offer rental cars with hand controls at no extra charge for pick-up at the major airports (advance notice required).

Resources:

Deaf CanDo (☎ 08-8223 3335; www.deafcando.com.au) Deaf Society of SA.

Deafness Association of the Northern Territory (☎ 08-8945 2016; dant@octa4.net.au)

Disability Information & Resource Centre (DIRC; Map p48; ☎ 8236 0555; www.dircsa.org.au; 195 Gilles St, Adelaide; ☺ 9am-5pm Mon-Fri) Info on accommodation, venues and travel for people with disabilities.

Easy Access Australia (www.easyaccessaustralia.com.au) Publication detailing easily accessible transport, accommodation and attractions; available online or from bookshops.

Guide Dogs SA.NT (www.guidedogs.org.au; ☎ Adelaide 08-8203 8333, Darwin 08-898 15488)

National Information Communication & Awareness Network (NICAN; ☎ /TTY 1800 806 769; www.nican.com.au) Australia-wide directory providing information on access issues, accessible accommodation, sporting and recreational activities, transport and specialist tour operators.

South Australian Royal Society for the Blind (☎ 08-8232 4777; www.rsb.org.au)

VISAS

All visitors to Australia need to have a passport and visa. New Zealanders are issued 'special category' visas on arrival; all other visitors must obtain a visa in advance, but for most nationalities it's a mere formality. Standard visas are valid for three months, but visitors are allowed a maximum stay of 12 months, including extensions.

For information on visas, extensions, customs and health issues, check the **Department of Immigration & Multicultural & Indigenous Affairs** (DIMIA; ☎ 13 18 81; www.immi.gov.au). Visa application forms are available on this website and from Australian diplomatic missions overseas and travel agents. You can apply by mail. Short-term tourist visas have largely been replaced by the free Electronic Travel Authority (ETA). However, if you are from a country not covered by the ETA, or you want to stay longer than three months, you'll need to apply for a visa.

Electronic Travel Authority (ETA)

The free ETA replaces the usual three-month visa stamped in your passport and is obtainable through any DIMIA-registered International Air Transport Association (IATA) travel agent or airline abroad, when you purchase your ticket. You can also register directly online at www.eta.immi.gov.au for a $20 fee. ETAs are available to passport holders of 34 countries, including the UK, the USA, Canada, most European and Scandinavian countries, Japan, Korea, Malaysia and Singapore, and are valid for a three-month stay within 12 months of issue.

Working-Holiday Visas

On a normal visa you're not allowed to work in Australia, but you may be eligible for a 12-month working-holiday visa, which lets you supplement your travels with casual employment. People from 19 countries (including the UK, Canada, Korea, the Netherlands, Malta, Ireland, Japan, Germany, France, Italy, Belgium, Finland, Sweden, Norway and Denmark) are eligible, but you must be between 18 and 30 years old at the time of lodging your application. A visa subclass is available to residents of Chile, Thailand, Turkey and the USA.

The emphasis on casual rather than full-time work means that you can only work for three months at a time with any one employer – but you are free to work for more than one employer within the 12 months. There's a limit on the number of visas issued each year, so apply as early as possible (application fee AUD$195) to the Australian embassy in your home country before you leave.

WOMEN & SOLO TRAVELLERS

Travelling in central Australia is generally safe for women, but both sexes should exercise common sense: avoid walking alone at night and be wary of stopping for anyone on the highway. Sexual harassment is rare though some macho (and less enlightened) Aussie males still slip – particularly when they've been drinking.

Hitching is not recommended for anyone. Even when travelling in pairs, exercise caution at all times. Lone women should also be wary of staying in basic pub accommodation unless it looks safe and well managed.

The Adelaide-based **Women's Information Service** (☎ 08-8303 0590; www.wis.sa.gov.au) provides information, advice and referrals on just about anything of specific interest to women.

Transport

CONTENTS

GETTING THERE & AWAY

ENTERING AUSTRALIA

Provided your visa is in order (p296), arrival in Australia is straightforward, with the usual customs declarations (p288). However, global instability has resulted in conspicuously increased security in Australian airport terminals (both domestic and international), and you may find that customs procedures are now more time-consuming.

AIR – INTERNATIONAL
Airlines

Some airlines fly directly into **Adelaide Airport** (www.aal.com.au) and **Darwin Airport** (www.darwin -airport.com.au), but most utilise east-coast hubs from where you can book domestic flights to Adelaide, Darwin or regional centres. Some major airlines with direct flights to/from Australia:

Air Canada (☎ 1800 421 094; www.aircanada.ca) Flies to Sydney.

Air New Zealand (☎ 13 24 76; www.airnz.com.au) Flies to Adelaide, Brisbane, Cairns, the Gold Coast, Melbourne, Perth and Sydney.

British Airways (☎ 1300 767 177; www.britishairways .com.au) Flies to Melbourne, Perth and Sydney.

Cathay Pacific (☎ 13 17 47; www.cathaypacific.com) Flies to Adelaide, Brisbane, Cairns, Melbourne, Perth, Sydney.

> **THINGS CHANGE...**
>
> The information in this chapter is particularly vulnerable to change. Check directly with the airline or a travel agent to make sure you understand how a fare (and ticket you may buy) works and be aware of the security requirements for international travel. Shop carefully. The details given in this chapter should be regarded as pointers and are not a substitute for your own careful, up-to-date research.

Emirates (☎ 1300 303 777; www.emirates.com) Flies to Brisbane, Melbourne, Perth, Sydney.

Garuda (☎ 1300 365 330; www.garuda-indonesia.com) Flies to Darwin, Melbourne, Perth and Sydney.

Japan Airlines (☎ 1300 525 287; www.jal.com) Flies to Brisbane and Sydney.

Lufthansa (☎ 1300 655 727, www.lufthansa.com) Flies to Adelaide, Brisbane, Melbourne, Perth and Sydney.

Malaysian Airlines (☎ 13 26 27; www.malaysia airlines.com) Flies to Adelaide, Brisbane, Melbourne, Perth and Sydney.

Qantas (☎ 13 13 13; www.qantas.com.au) Flies to Adelaide, Brisbane, Cairns, Darwin, the Gold Coast, Melbourne, Perth and Sydney.

Royal Brunei Airlines (☎ 07-3017 5000; www .bruneiair.com) Flies to Brisbane and Perth.

Singapore Airlines (☎ 13 10 11; www.singaporeair .com.au) Flies to Adelaide, Brisbane, Melbourne, Perth and Sydney.

South African Airways (☎ 1300 435 972; www.flysaa .com) Flies to Perth and Sydney.

Thai Airways (☎ 1300 651 960; www.thaiairways.com .au) Flies to Brisbane, Melbourne, Perth and Sydney.

United Airlines (☎ 13 17 77; www.unitedairlines.com .au) Flies to Adelaide, Brisbane, Melbourne, Perth and Sydney.

Virgin Atlantic (☎ 1300 727 340; www.virgin-atlantic .com) Flies to Sydney.

Virgin Blue (☎ 13 67 89; www.virginblue.com.au) Flies to Brisbane.

Tickets

In this age of internet bookings and airline discounting, finding bargain tickets has never been easier, but a good travel agent is still invaluable to hunt down the cheapest fares, best routings and preferred stopovers, and

---

CLIMATE CHANGE & TRAVEL

Climate change is a serious threat to the ecosystems that humans rely upon, and air travel is the fastest-growing contributor to the problem. Lonely Planet regards travel, overall, as a global benefit, but believes we all have a responsibility to limit our personal impact on global warming.

Flying & Climate Change

Pretty much every form of motor travel generates CO_2 (the main cause of human-induced climate change) but planes are far and away the worst offenders, not just because of the sheer distances they allow us to travel, but because they release greenhouse gases high into the atmosphere. The statistics are frightening: two people taking a return flight between Europe and the US will contribute as much to climate change as an average household's gas and electricity consumption over a whole year.

Carbon Offset Schemes

Climatecare.org and other websites use 'carbon calculators' that allow jetsetters to offset the greenhouse gases they are responsible for with contributions to energy-saving projects and other climate-friendly initiatives in the developing world – including projects in India, Honduras, Kazakhstan and Uganda.

Lonely Planet, together with Rough Guides and other concerned partners in the travel industry, supports the carbon offset scheme run by climatecare.org. Lonely Planet offsets all of its staff and author travel.

For more information check out our website: lonelyplanet.com.

---

arranging extras such as travel insurance and airport transfers. Prices and availability depend on the time of year, the route and who you're flying with. High season for flights to/from Australia is between December and February, except in the tropical north where it's around June to September.

Reliable travel agents in Australia:

Flight Centre (☎ 13 31 33; www.flightcentre.com.au)
STA Travel (☎ 13 47 82; www.statravel.com.au)

Round-the-world tickets can be a good option for getting to Australia: Adelaide is an easy inclusion, but Darwin is a little trickier. For online bookings, try the following websites:

Airbrokers (www.airbrokers.com) US company specialising in cheap tickets. Los Angeles–Hong Kong–Bangkok–Singapore–Adelaide–Los Angeles costs around US$1600.
Cheap Flights (www.cheapflights.com) Specials, airline information and flight searches from the USA and other regions.
Cheapest Flights (www.cheapestflights.co.uk) Cheap worldwide flights from the UK.
Expedia (www.expedia.msn.com) Microsoft's travel site; mainly US-related.
Flight Centre International (www.flightcentre.com) Respected operator with Australian, New Zealand, UK, US, South African and Canadian sites.

Flights.com (www.flights.com) International, easy-to-search site with cheap fares.
Roundtheworldflights.com (www.roundtheworldflights.com) Build your own trips from the UK with up to six stops. A four-stop trip including Asia, Australia and the USA costs from UK£760.
STA (www.statravel.com) Prominent in international student travel but you don't have to be a student; linked to worldwide STA sites.
Travel Online (www.travelonline.co.nz) Worldwide flights from New Zealand.
Travel.com (www.travel.com.au) Fares and flights into and out of Australia.
Travelocity (www.travelocity.com) Fares to/from practically anywhere, and global sites.

Asia

Bangkok, Singapore and Hong Kong are usually the best places to shop for discount tickets. However, flights between Hong Kong and Australia are notoriously heavily booked. Flights to/from Bangkok and Singapore are often part of longer Europe-to-Australia flights, so they're also sometimes full. Many operators service Adelaide and Darwin direct from Southeast Asia.

Typical one-way fares to Adelaide are AUD$800 from Singapore, A$1000 from Kuala Lumpur and A$700 from Bangkok. From

Tokyo, fares start at A$1200. From Denpasar (Bali) to Darwin it's around A$300.

STA Travel agencies in Asia:

STA Bangkok (☎ 662-236 0262; www.statravel.co.th)
STA Singapore (☎ 6737 7188; www.statravel.com.sg)
STA Tokyo (☎ 03-5391 2922; www.statravel.co.jp).

Canada

Air routes from Canada are similar to those from mainland USA, with most Toronto and Vancouver flights stopping in one US city (often Los Angeles or Honolulu) before heading to Australia. Air Canada flies from Vancouver to Sydney via Honolulu and from Toronto to Melbourne via Honolulu.

Fares from Vancouver to Sydney or Melbourne cost from C$1300/1900 in the low/high season travelling via the US west coast. From Toronto, fares go from around C$1500/2300.

Travel Cuts (☎ 866-246-9762; www.travelcuts.com) is Canada's national student-travel agency, with offices in all major cities.

Continental Europe

From the major destinations in Europe, most flights travel via one of the Asian capitals (Singapore, Bangkok, Hong Kong or Kuala Lumpur). Some flights are also routed through London before arriving in Australia. One-way/return fares start at around €950/1400.

E-dreams (www.edreams.com) is a serviceable site on which to compare multiple airfares from European capitals to Australia. A decent internet operator in the Netherlands is **Holland International** (www.hollandinternational.nl). In Germany, try **STA Travel** (☎ 069-7430 3292; www.sta travel.de). In France, operators include **Nouvelles Frontières** (☎ 08-2500 0747; www.nouvelles-frontieres.fr) and **Odysia** (☎ 08-2508 2525; www.ody sia.fr).

New Zealand

Air New Zealand and Qantas operate a network of flights linking Auckland, Wellington and Christchurch in NZ with Australian gateway cities (including Adelaide). Other trans-Tasman operators include Virgin Blue, and **JetStar** (☎ 13 15 38; www.jetstar.com) to/from Christchurch only.

Fares from NZ to east coast Australia start at approximately NZ$350/700 one way/return.

For reasonably priced fares:
House of Travel (☎ 0800 367 468; www.houseoftravel .co.nz)
STA Travel (☎ 0800 474 400; www.statravel.co.nz)

> **DEPARTURE TAX**
>
> The Australian international departure tax ($47) should be included in your airline ticket – check when you book.

UK & Ireland

There are two routes from the UK: the western route via the USA and the Pacific, and the eastern route via the Middle East and Asia; flights are usually cheaper and more frequent on the latter. Some of the best deals are with Emirates, Gulf Air, Malaysia Airlines, Japan Airlines and Thai Airways. British Airways, Singapore Airlines and Qantas generally have higher fares, but offer more expedient routes.

Typical direct London–Sydney fares are around UK£400/700 (one way/return) during the low season. At peak times (eg mid-December), fares leap by as much as 30%. Typical high-season fares start at around UK£450/800 (one way/return).

Popular UK agencies:
Flight Centre (☎ 0870-499 0040; www.flightcentre .co.uk)
STA Travel (☎ 0870-160 0599; www.statravel.co.uk)
Trailfinders (☎ 020-7628 7628; www.trailfinders .co.uk).

USA

Most flights between North America and Australia travel to/from the USA's west coast. Most are routed through Los Angeles, although some come through San Francisco. Numerous airlines offer flights via Asia or various Pacific islands. In most cases, you'll need to purchase an additional domestic fare to South Australia (SA) or the Northern Territory (NT), as the usual gateway is east-coast Australia. However, it's sometimes possible to change flights at your Asian or Pacific stopover for Adelaide or Darwin.

San Francisco is the ticket-consolidator capital of America, although good deals can also be found in Los Angeles, New York and other big cities. Typically you can purchase a return ticket to Melbourne or Sydney from west-coast USA for US$1300/1700 in the low/high season, or from the east coast for US$1600/1900.

Reliable operators:
STA Travel (☎ 800-781 4040; www.statravel.com)
Student Universe (www.studentuniverse.com)

AIR – DOMESTIC

The major Australian domestic carriers **Qantas** (☎ 13 1313; www.qantas.com.au) and **Virgin Blue** (☎ 13 67 89; www.virginblue.com.au) fly all over Australia, operating flights between Adelaide and Darwin and other centres. Qantas flies to Alice Springs and Uluru. **JetStar** (☎ 13 15 38; www.jetstar.com.au) services capital cities (including Adelaide and Darwin) and key holiday destinations. Melbourne-based **Tiger Airways** (☎ 03-9335 3033; www.tigerairways.com.au) connects Adelaide with Canberra, the Gold Coast, Hobart, Melbourne and Perth, and Alice Springs with Adelaide and Melbourne. **Airnorth** (☎ 08-8920 4001; www.airnorth.com.au) is a small NT-based airline with daily flights from Darwin to Broome and Kununurra in WA.

Fares

Few people pay full fare on domestic travel, as the airlines offer a wide-ranging discounts, particularly for internet bookings (up to 60% off full fares). These come and go and there are regular specials, so keep your eyes peeled. Advance-purchase deals (one to four weeks ahead) are also available, offering up to 33% off one-way fares, and up to 50% off return fares. The only catch is you often have to stay away for at least one Saturday night, and there are penalties for changing and cancelling flights.

Approximate regular one-way fares to/from Adelaide include Melbourne ($100), Sydney ($150), Perth ($280), Alice Springs ($250) and Darwin ($280). From Darwin: Melbourne ($170), Sydney ($250), Perth ($290), Alice Springs ($270) and Adelaide ($280).

Regional Express (Rex; ☎ 13 17 13; www.regional express.com.au) has a 'Backpackers' scheme, where international visitors (Australian visitors are ineligible) pay $500/950 for one/two months' worth of unlimited travel on the airline.

LAND

Bitumen roads in generally good condition link the vast distances between Adelaide and other Australian cities. Getting to the NT overland means a lot of travel through empty country, but there's no better way to appreciate Australia's vastness. The nearest state capital to Darwin is Adelaide (just over 3000km), while Perth and Sydney are both around 4000km away – about the same distance as New York to Los Angeles and more than 2½ times the drive from London to Rome!

Border Crossings

The main routes into SA include Hwy 1 from Western Australia (WA; across the Nullarbor Plain), and the Stuart Hwy from the NT (via Alice Springs). From Victoria, there are two main crossings: the Princes Hwy (via Mt Gambier and/or Great Ocean Rd), and the more direct Dukes Hwy (via Bordertown and Victoria's Western Hwy).

Outback 4WD tracks aside, there are three main (sealed) roads into the NT: the Victoria Hwy from WA (via Kununurra), the Barkly Hwy from Queensland (via Mt Isa), and the Stuart Hwy from SA (via Coober Pedy).

Bus

Many travellers prefer to cross or arrive in central Australia by bus because it's one of the best ways to come to grips with the area's size – also the bus companies have far more comprehensive route networks than the railway system. Major long-haul operators include the following:
Firefly Express (☎ 1300 730 740; www.fireflyexpress .com.au) Buses from Adelaide to Melbourne ($50, 11 hours, twice daily), continuing to Sydney ($110, 24 hours, once daily).

INTERSTATE QUARANTINE

Within Australia, there are restrictions on carrying fruit, plants and vegetables across state and territory borders. This is in order to control the movement of disease or pests – such as fruit fly, cucurbit thrips, grape phylloxera and potato cyst nematodes – from one area to another.

Most quarantine control relies on honesty and quarantine posts at the state/territory borders are not always staffed. However, the Western Australia border is permanently manned and sometimes uses dogs to sniff out offending matter. This may seem excessive, but it's taken very seriously. It's prohibited to carry fresh fruit and vegetables, plants, flowers, and even nuts and honey across the Northern Territory–Western Australia border in either direction. The controls with South Australia, Victoria, New South Wales and Queensland are less strict – there's usually an unmanned honesty bin for disposal. Check at the borders.

TRANSPORT

TRANSPORT

Greyhound Australia (☎ 1300 473 946; www.grey hound.com.au) Services between Adelaide and Melbourne (from $50, 11 hours, twice daily), Sydney (from $140, 24 hours, three per day) and Alice Springs ($260, 21 hours, once daily) continuing to Darwin ($560, 42 hours). From Darwin there are buses to Broome (from $200, 24 hours, once daily) in WA and Alice Springs ($295, 22 hours, once daily).

V/Line (☎ 13 61 96, 03-9697 2076; www.vline.com.au) Bus and bus/train services between Adelaide and Melbourne (from $45, 12 hours, three per day).

See also Bus Tours (below) for information on companies providing hop-on–hop-off bus services.

BUS PASSES

If you're planning on doing a lot of travel in Australia, or even just a long-haul trip to central Australia, a **Greyhound Australia** (☎ 1300 473 946; www.greyhound.com.au) bus pass will save you money. The most flexible pass is the **Kilometre Pass**, which allows you to travel any route, get off and on as you choose and even backtrack until your kilometres have run out. These passes start at 500km ($100) rising incrementally to a maximum of 20,000km ($2210). A 5000km pass costs $770; 10,000km costs $1355.

Another option is a set-route **Explorer Pass**, allowing you a set amount of time (usually three, six or 12 months) to cover a designated route. Many of these include the main central Australia highlights – Adelaide, Uluru, Alice Springs, Kakadu and Darwin – and the Stuart Hwy towns. The main limitation is that, while you can travel in whichever direction you like, you can't backtrack (except on 'dead-end' short sectors). For passes that follow a circular route, you can start anywhere along the loop, and finish at the same spot.

Bus-pass discounts of 10% apply to YHA, VIP, Nomads and student-card holders, and children under 14 (see p285 and p289).

Bus Tours

Backpacker-style and more formal bus tours offer a great way to get from A to B and see the sights on the way. Operators include the following:

AAT Kings (☎ 1300 556 100, 08-8923 6555; www.aat kings.com) Big coach company (popular with the older set) with myriad tours in the NT and SA, including Uluru, Alice Springs, the Barossa Valley and Kangaroo Island.

Adventure Tours Australia (☎ 1300 654 604, 08-8132 8230; www.adventuretours.com.au) Two- to 24-day tours taking in Uluru, Alice Springs, Darwin and Kakadu in the NT, and Adelaide and Kangaroo Island in SA. A 14-day Adelaide to Darwin trip costs $1590; two days taking in Alice Springs and Uluru costs $395.

Autopia Tours (☎ 1800 000 507, 03-9419 8878; www.autopiatours.com.au) Small-group, three-day Melbourne–Adelaide tours along the Great Ocean Rd ($395 including dorm accommodation and most meals).

Desert Venturer (☎ 1300 858 099, 07-4035 5566; www.desertventurer.com.au) Twice-weekly three-day coach trip between Alice Springs and Cairns ($400 plus $85 for meals).

Groovy Grape (☎ 1800 661 177, 08-8371 4000; www.groovygrape.com.au) Three days Melbourne–Adelaide ($345) along the Great Ocean Rd, and seven days Adelaide–Alice Springs ($865) via the Flinders Ranges, Coober Pedy and Uluru. Includes meals, camping and national-park entry fees. Small groups.

Heading Bush (☎ 1800 639 933, 08-8356 5501; www.headingbush.com) Rugged, small-group, 10-day Adelaide–Alice Springs expeditions (with/without VIP or YHA $1470/1595) are all-inclusive. Tours include the Flinders Ranges, Coober Pedy, Simpson Desert, Aboriginal communities, Uluru and West MacDonnell Ranges. More luxurious five-day option $995.

Oz Experience (☎ 1300 300 028, 02-9213 1766; www.ozexperience.com) Hop-on–hop-off backpacker network with frequent buses looping around eastern Australia including Darwin, Adelaide and the east coast. There's a range of passes (valid for six or 12 months). Sydney to Darwin via Melbourne, Adelaide and Alice Springs costs $1495.

Wayward Bus (☎ 1300 653 510, 08-8132 8230; www.waywardbus.com.au) Wide range of backpacker-style bus tours around SA and into the NT, including trips from Adelaide to Alice Springs, Uluru, Kangaroo Island and Great Ocean Rd.

Wildlife Tours (☎ 1300 661 730; www.wildlifetours.com.au) Two-day, small-group Melbourne–Adelaide tours along Great Ocean Rd ($195).

Car & Motorcycle

See p305 for details on car travel in SA and the NT.

Train

The famous *Ghan* (see opposite) train connects Adelaide with Darwin via Alice Springs. From Adelaide there are rail connections with Sydney and Perth on the *Indian Pacific* and Melbourne on the *Overland*. You can also join the *Ghan* at Port Augusta, the connection point on the Sydney to Perth railway route.

From Adelaide, the *Ghan* departs Adelaide for Alice Springs on Sunday and Wednesday (18 hours), continuing on to Darwin on

THE GHAN

The legendary *Ghan* – named after the Afghan cameleers who helped forge tracks through central Australia – is one of the world's great railway journeys, but it wasn't always that way.

The *Ghan* saga began in 1877, but the line took more than 50 years to reach Alice Springs after construction began in the wrong place. The creek beds north of Marree were bone dry and nobody had ever seen rain out there, so the initial stretch of line was laid right across a floodplain. When the rain came, the line simply washed away.

This wasn't the end of the *Ghan's* early problems. At first it was built as a wide-gauge track to Marree, then extended in 1884 as narrow gauge to Oodnadatta. But the foundations were flimsy, the sleepers too light and the grading too steep, and the whole thing meandered hopelessly. The top speed of the old *Ghan* was a flat-out 30km/h! Early rail travellers went from Adelaide to Marree on the broad-gauge line, changed there for Oodnadatta, then made the final journey to Alice Springs by Afghani-led camel train.

In 1929 the line was extended from Oodnadatta to Alice Springs. Though the *Ghan* was a great adventure, it was slow and uncomfortable as it bounced and bucked its way down the badly laid line. Worst of all, a heavy rainfall could strand it at either end, or even somewhere in the middle. Parachute drops of supplies to stranded train travellers became part of outback lore, and on one occasion the *Ghan* rolled into Alice 10 days late!

In the early 1970s the South Australian state railway system was taken over by the Federal government and a new, standard-gauge, $145 million line to Alice Springs was planned. In 1980 the line was completed ahead of time and on budget. In 2004 the Alice Springs to Darwin section was finally opened, completing the trans-Australia crossing from Adelaide to Darwin – 2979km and 42 hours of track.

The *Ghan* isn't cheap or fast – it's more expedient to fly – but the experience of rolling through the vast, flat expanse of the 'dead heart' is magical, and it's great to wander around the train, enjoy a beer, buy a meal and share desert tales with other travellers. If you can afford it, sleeper class is definitely the way to go – it's comfortable, and offers a bit of old-fashioned romance. Sleeper seats are noisy (with irritating piped theme muzak), brightly lit and far from horizontal, and the food offerings in the lounge car are definitely not gourmet. You might also be surprised at the travelling demographic – lots of families and retirees, and not many 20- or 30-somethings.

Tuesday and Friday (another 24 hours). It returns from Darwin to Alice Springs on Wednesday and Saturday, continuing to Adelaide on Thursday and Sunday. From Melbourne, the *Overland* has day trains to Adelaide (10 hours) on Tuesday, Thursday and Saturday, returning on Monday, Wednesday and Friday. From Sydney, the *Indian Pacific* departs on Saturday and Wednesday for Adelaide (24 hours), continuing to Perth (another 38½ hours) on Sunday and Thursday. The return leg chugs out of Perth on Wednesday and Sunday.

COSTS & CLASSES

The *Ghan* and *Indian Pacific* offer 'daynighter' seats and more comfortable sleeper classes; the *Overlander* has two classes of daynighter seats. With a daynighter you get a reclining seat in an open carriage, foldaway table and access to a licensed lounge car serving light meals and drinks. Sleeper classes involve cabins with all kinds of nifty foldaway seats and beds. Pricier sleepers have en suites and private restaurant-car dining.

Backpacker discounts apply to all fares (up to 50% off!), and international visitors (only) can take advantage of a **Rail Explorer Pass** (adult/backpacker $690/590) allowing unlimited travel for six months in daynighter seat class on all three routes, or an **Oz Tracks Pass** (www.oztrackspass.com.au; adult $690) allowing 14 city-to-city trips within six months; present your passport to qualify.

The Motorail service allows you to put your own standard-sized vehicle on the *Ghan* or *Indian Pacific*. At the time of research, the *Overland* Motorail service was unavailable.

RESERVATIONS

Book tickets through **Great Southern Rail** (☎ 13 21 47, 08-8213 4444; www.gsr.com.au), which handles bookings for the *Ghan*, *Indian Pacific* and *Overland*. Advances bookings are recommended in peak season (June to September),

TRANSPORT

TRAIN FARES

Adult/child fares are as follows:

Journey	Seat	Standard Sleeper	1st-Class Sleeper	Motorail
Adelaide–Alice Springs	$355/168	$705/429	$1010/696	$649
Adelaide–Darwin	$710/336	$1410/858	$1950/1345	$938
Adelaide–Perth	$395/186	$1005/609	$1390/955	$609
Darwin–Alice Springs	$355/168	$705/429	$1010/696	$449
Melbourne–Adelaide	from $89/46	n/a	n/a	n/a
Sydney–Adelaide	$295/133	$485/353	$680/518	$359

especially for Motorail spaces. Discounted fares are sometimes offered, especially in the low season (February to June).

SEA

There are no scheduled international passenger-ferry services to/from SA or the NT, but it's possible – with a bit of graft and fortune – to sail to northern Australia from Asia by hitching rides or crewing on yachts. Ask around at harbours, marinas or yacht clubs. Darwin is a good place to try to hitch a ride to Indonesia, Malaysia or Singapore. Try contacting the **Darwin Sailing Club** (☎ 08-8981 1700; www.dwnsail.com.au) at Fannie Bay, or the **Darwin Harbour Mooring Basin** (☎ 08-8922 0660; www.darwinport.nt.gov.au).

GETTING AROUND

AIR

See regional chapters for details on small airlines servicing country destinations.

Within SA, the main regional airlines are as follows:

Air South (☎ 1300 247 768, 08-8234 4988; www.airsouth.com.au) Flies between Adelaide and Kingscote on Kangaroo Island ($125). Fares booked a month in advance are $77 one way.

Altitude Aviation (☎ 08-9477 3244; www.altitude aviation.com.au) Charter flights to/from pretty much anywhere in central Australia.

Qantas (☎ 13 13 13; www.qantas.com.au) Regular scheduled flights from Adelaide to Darwin (from $360) and Alice Springs (from $250).

Regional Express (Rex; ☎ 13 17 13; www.regional express.com.au) Flies between Adelaide and Kingscote on Kangaroo Island ($90), Coober Pedy ($200), Ceduna ($165), Mt Gambier ($130), Port Lincoln (from $110) and Whyalla ($110). Special fares can be 30% the price of fully flexible fares.

In the NT, the main regional operators:

Airnorth (☎ 1800 627 474, 08-8920 4000; www.airnorth.com.au) Connects Darwin with Gove (from $170 one way), Maningrida ($120) and Groote Eylandt ($160) in Arnhem Land; also offers charter flights.

Australasian Jet (☎ 08-8920 2400; www.ausjet.com.au) Operates scenic and charter flights from Darwin to Kakadu, and Alice Springs to Uluru.

Outback Airlines (☎ 08-8953 5000; www.outback airlines.com.au) A new operator that should be up and running (or flying) by the time you read this, with charters and scheduled flights across central Australia.

Qantas (☎ 13 13 13; www.qantas.com.au) Regular scheduled flights from Darwin to Alice Springs (from $275) and Gove (from $210), and Alice Springs and Yulara (from $160).

BICYCLE

SA is a great place for cycling. There are some excellent bike tracks in Adelaide, thousands of kilometres of quiet, flat country roads, converted railway tracks in wine regions and the Mawson Trail (see p287), an 800km track from Adelaide to Parachilna Gorge in the Flinders Ranges.

Darwin too has a network of bike tracks, and Katherine and Alice Springs also have plenty of pancake-flat riding opportunities. However, actually using a bicycle as your mode of transport in the NT is another matter. Dehydration and the availability of drinking water are the main concerns. It can be a long way between towns and roadhouses, and those isolated bores and tanks shown on your map may be dry or undrinkable. That little creek marked with a dotted blue line? Forget it – the only time it has water is when the land is flooded for hundreds of kilometres. Also make sure you've got the necessary spare parts and bike-repair knowledge. Carry a good map and let someone know where you're headed before setting off. Check road conditions and weather forecasts, and make conservative estimates of how long your journey will take. Beware of road trains: if you hear one coming, get right off the road. No matter how fit you are, take things slowly until you're used to the heat, wear a hat and plenty of sunscreen, and drink *lots* of water.

If you're coming specifically to cycle, it makes sense to bring your own bike – check with your airline for costs and the degree of dismantling/packing required. While you can load your bike onto a bus to skip the boring/difficult bits, bus companies require you to dismantle your bike, and some don't guarantee that it will travel on the same bus as you. Note that bicycle helmets are compulsory in Australia.

Useful contacts:

Bicycle SA (☎ 08-8232 2644; www.bikesa.asn.au) Information on bike touring around SA.

Northern Territory Cycling Association (☎ 08-8945 6012; www.nt.cycling.org.au) Information and links to local clubs.

Roc Tours (☎ 08-8357 3935; www.cycletours.com.au) SA-based cycle tour company running fully supported tours to the MacDonnell Ranges, Uluru, Kakadu and along the Oodnadatta Track.

Hire & Purchase

You can buy new bikes, accessories and equipment in Mt Gambier, Adelaide, Darwin and Alice Springs. Basic 15-speed mountain bikes start from around $400, but you can pay a lot more for better-quality bikes with lightweight frames and suspension.

In SA you can hire bikes in Adelaide, McLaren Vale, Victor Harbor, the Barossa and Clare Valleys and the Flinders Ranges. In the NT you can hire bikes in Darwin, Alice Springs, Yulara and Wauchope. Costs start at around $20 per day.

BOAT

The only passenger ferries in this region of SA are between Cape Jervis and Kangaroo Island (p73), and across Spencer Gulf between Wallaroo on the Yorke Peninsula and Lucky Bay on the Eyre Peninsula. Both are smooth, efficient operations (if a little pricey). In the NT passenger ferries operate between Darwin and Mandorah and the Tiwi Islands (see p260).

BUS

In SA, Adelaide's new **Central Bus Station** (85 Franklin St) has ticket offices and terminals for all major interstate and statewide services. For online bus timetables see **State Guide** (www

.bussa.com.au). In Darwin, interstate and intra-NT buses use the **Transit Centre** (69 Mitchell St).

The main SA bus services provider within the state is **Premier Stateliner** (☎ 08-8415 5555; www .premierstateliner.com.au). Sample fares from Adelaide include: McLaren Vale ($8), Victor Harbor ($19), Mt Gambier ($62), Port Augusta ($47), Port Pirie ($37), Naracoorte ($58) and Penola ($59). **Greyhound Australia** (☎ 13 14 99; www.greyhound .com.au) runs further north via the Stuart Hwy towns to Alice Springs ($262) and beyond.

In the NT, **Greyhound Australia** (☎ 13 14 99; www.greyhound.com.au) runs on all the major long-distance routes, including Alice Springs to Uluru and Kings Canyon, Alice to Darwin via Katherine and Tennant Creek, and Darwin to Kakadu. Sample fares from Darwin include Alice Springs ($295), Katherine ($70), Tennant Creek ($213) and Jabiru (Kakadu; $50).

See p302 for Greyhound Australia bus pass details. Discounts are available for backpacker associations/international student ID card holders.

Other SA bus companies include the following:

Barossa Valley Coaches (☎ 08-8564 3022; www .bvcoach.com) Services from Adelaide to Lyndoch, Tanunda, Nuriootpa and Angaston; also to Kapunda via Gawler.

Murray Bridge Passenger Service (☎ 08-8532 2633; www.murraybridgebus.com.au) Murray Bridge to Adelaide and Strathalbyn.

Southlink (☎ 08-8186 2888; www.southlink.com.au) Services the Fleurieu Peninsula.

Transit Plus (☎ 08-8339 7544; www.transitplus.com .au) Adelaide Hills region.

Yorke Peninsula Coaches (☎ 08-8821 2755; www .ypcoaches.com.au) Services the Clare Valley, Yorke Peninsula and southern Flinders Ranges towns.

CAR & MOTORCYCLE

The ultimate freedom in central Australia is to have your own wheels. Driving distances are long, but you can take it at your own pace and branch off the main roads to places public transport doesn't go. To truly explore outback areas you'll need a well-prepared 4WD vehicle, but there are plenty of routes open to a conventional (2WD) vehicle. Shared between three or four people the cost of hiring a car or campervan is reasonable but, before you drive off into the sunset, you need to know a few things about outback travel (see p308).

Born to be wild? Motorcycles are another popular way of getting from place to place.

TRANSPORT

The climate is good for bikes for much of the year, particularly in SA, and the many small tracks from the road into the bush lead to perfect spots to spend the night. A fuel range of 350km will cover fuel stops along the Stuart Hwy. The long, open roads are really made for large-capacity machines above 750cc. Contact the **Motorcycle Riders Association of SA** (☎ 0414-399 000; www.mrasa.asn.au) for info.

Aboriginal Land Permits

If you wish to travel through the outback independently, particularly in the NT, you may need special permits if you're passing through Aboriginal land or visiting a community. Generally, such land has government-administered reserve status or it may be held under freehold title vested in an Aboriginal land trust and managed by a council or corporation. In some cases permits won't be necessary if you stick to recognised public roads that cross Aboriginal territory, but as soon as you leave the main road by more than 50m you may need a permit (Arnhem Land is a good example). If you're on an organised tour the operator should take care of permits – check before you book.

The easiest way to apply for a permit is to download a form from the relevant land council and send it by email. Alternatively you can send it by post or fax. Allow plenty of time: transit permits can be approved within 24 hours, but others can take 10 working days. Keep in mind that your application may be knocked back for a number of reasons, including the risk of interference with sacred sites or disruption of ceremonial business. Also, some communities simply may not want to be bothered by visitors without good reason.

In the NT a transit permit is required for the Yulara–Kaltukatjara (Docker River) Rd, but not for either the Tanami Track or the Sandover Hwy where these cross Aboriginal land. Travellers may camp overnight without a permit within 50m of the latter two routes. The following places issue permits:

Central Land Council (Map p173; ☎ 08-8951 6211; www.clc.org.au; 31-33 Stuart Hwy, Alice Springs) Administers Aboriginal land in the southern and central regions of the Territory.

Northern Land Council Darwin (Map pp244-5; ☎ 08-8920 5100; www.nlc.org.au; 45 Mitchell St) Permits for Arnhem Land and other northern mainland areas; Katherine (Map p222; ☎ 08-8971 9802; 5 Katherine Tce) Permits for

the Central Arnhem Hwy towards Gove; Jabiru (☎ 08-8979 2410; Flinders St) Permits to visit Gunbalanya (Oenpelli).

Tiwi Land Council (Map p242; ☎ 08-8981 4898; www.tiwilandcouncil.net.au; Armidale St, Stuart Park, Darwin) Lists contacts for permits to the Tiwi Islands.

Automobile Associations

The **Royal Automobile Association of South Australia** (RAA; Map p48; ☎ 08-8202 4600, emergency breakdown service 13 11 11; www.raa.net; 55 Hindmarsh Sq, Adelaide; ☾ 8.30am-5pm Mon-Fri, 9am-noon Sat) and the **Automobile Association of the Northern Territory** (AANT; Map pp244-5; ☎ 08-8981 3837, emergency breakdown service 13 11 11; www.aant.com.au; 79-81 Smith St, Darwin; ☾ 9am-5pm Mon-Fri) offer emergency breakdown services and useful advice on motoring, including road safety, local regulations and buying/selling a car. The RAA and AANT have reciprocal arrangements with similar organisations overseas and interstate.

Driving Licences

Foreign driving licences are valid in Australia as long as they are in English or are accompanied by a translation. You can also get an International Driving Permit from automobile associations in your own country.

Fuel

Unleaded, diesel and LPG fuel are available from urban service stations and highway roadhouses. Prices vary from place to place depending on how remote they are, but fuel in outback central Australia is some of the most expensive in the country. At the time of writing unleaded petrol prices had slumped to just over $1 per litre after hitting $1.70 in 2008. The market is fickle! Regardless, expect to pay 20% more in Darwin than in the east coast capitals, and up to 50% more in small outback towns. Distances between fill-ups can be long in the outback, so check locations and opening times of service stations and carry spare fuel.

Hire

There are plenty of car-rental companies ready and willing to put you behind the wheel. Competition is fierce so rates vary and special deals pop up and disappear again. The main thing to remember when assessing your options is distance – if you want to travel far, you need unlimited kilometres. The major companies offer this, or 100km a day free plus however many cents per kilometre beyond 100km (make sure you do your sums!). You

ROAD DISTANCES (KM)

	Adelaide	Adelaide River	Alice Springs	Barrow Creek	Coober Pedy	Darwin	Elliot	Erldunda	Glendambo	Katherine	Kulgera	Larrimah	Marla	Pimba/Woomera	Port Augusta	Port Pirie
Adelaide River	2903															
Alice Springs	1524	1379														
Barrow Creek	1808	1095	284													
Coober Pedy	835	2068	689	973												
Darwin	3020	117	1496	1212	2185											
Elliot	2284	619	760	476	1449	736										
Erldunda	1324	1579	200	484	489	1696	960									
Glendambo	590	2313	934	1218	245	2430	1694	734								
Katherine	2702	201	1178	894	1867	318	418	1378	2112							
Kulgera	1250	1653	274	558	415	1770	1034	74	660	1452						
Larrimah	2522	381	998	714	1687	498	238	1198	1932	180	1272					
Marla	1068	1835	456	740	233	1952	1216	256	478	1634	182	1454				
Pimba/Woomera	485	2418	1039	1323	350	2535	1799	839	105	2217	765	2037	583			
Port Augusta	300	2603	1224	1508	535	2720	1984	1024	290	2402	950	2222	768	185		
Port Pirie	225	2678	1299	1583	610	2795	2059	1099	365	2477	1025	2297	843	260	75	
Tennant Creek	2032	871	508	224	1197	988	252	708	1442	670	782	490	964	1547	1732	1807

TRANSPORT

must be at least 21 years old to hire from most firms – if you're under 25 you may only be able to hire a small car or have to pay a surcharge. It's cheaper if you rent for a week or more and there are often low-season and weekend discounts. Local firms are almost always cheaper than the big boys – sometimes half-price – but cheaper hire often comes with crippling restrictions.

The main players:

Avis (☎ 13 63 33; www.avis.com.au)
Budget (☎ 1300 362 848; www.budget.com.au)
Europcar (☎ 1800 030 118; www.europcar.com.au)
Hertz (☎ 13 30 39; www.hertz.com.au)
Thrifty (☎ 1300 367 227; www.thrifty.com.au)

One-way hire into or out of the NT and SA may be subject to a hefty repositioning fee; however, some big rental firms offer good deals from Alice Springs to Adelaide or Adelaide to Melbourne. Ask about this before deciding on one company over another.

Note that most car-rental companies do include insurance in the price (see Insurance, p308), but in the event of an accident the hirer is still liable for a sometimes-hefty excess.

Most offer excess-reduction insurance on top of the rental rate. Most firms won't let you drive after dark in the outback due to the risk of hitting kangaroos – read the fine print.

Daily rates, including insurance, are typically about $60 to $80 a day for a small car (Holden Barina, Ford Festiva, Hyundai Excel), $80 to $100 a day for a medium car (Mitsubishi Magna, Toyota Camry, Nissan Pulsar) or $100 up to $130 a day for a big car (Holden Commodore, Ford Falcon).

CAMPERVANS

Many people find a campervan is the best way to explore the outback, and it's hard to disagree. From a two-berth to a full-blown family camper, they offer a home on wheels, allowing you to pull up anywhere, save on accommodation costs and crank up the AC/DC as loud as hell! Most have some sort of cooking facilities and there are a few 4WD models. They cost from $90 to $200 a day. The following companies have fitted-out 4WDs and vans, offer one-way rental and have offices in the major cities around Australia, including Alice Springs:

Backpacker Campervans (☎ 1800 670 232; www
.backpackercampervans.com.au)
Britz (☎ 1800 331 454; www.britz.com.au) Has 4WD
bush campers.
Kea (☎ 1800 252 555; www.keacampers.com)
Maui (☎ 1300 363 800; www.maui.com.au)
Wicked Campers (☎ 1800 246 869; www.wicked
campers.com.au) Fitted-out, funkily painted backpacker
vans from $60/50 per day for one/eight weeks' rental.

4WDS

Having a 4WD vehicle is essential for off-the-
beaten-track driving into the outback. Renting
a 4WD vehicle is affordable if a few people
get together. Something like a Nissan X-Trail
(which can get you through most, but not all,
tracks) costs around $100 to $130 per day;
for a Toyota Landcruiser you're looking at
around $150 up to $200, which should include
unlimited kilometres. Check the insurance
conditions, especially the excess, as they can
be onerous and policies might not cover damage caused when travelling off-road.

An independent operator in the NT is **Top
End 4WD & Car Hire** (☎ 1300 360 339; www.topend4
wd.com.au).

Insurance

Know exactly what your liability is in the event
of an accident. Rather than risking paying out
thousands of dollars if you do have an crash,
you can take out comprehensive insurance
on the car or pay an additional daily amount
to the rental company for an 'insurance excess reduction' policy. This reduces the excess
(the amount of money for which you're liable
before the insurance kicks in) from between
$2000 and $5000 to a few hundred dollars,
though it pushes the rental cost up.

Be aware that if you're travelling on dirt
roads you won't be covered by insurance unless you have a 4WD – in other words, if you
have an accident you'll be liable for all costs
involved. Also, most companies' insurance
won't cover the cost of damage to glass (including the windscreen) or tyres. Similarly,
because of the risk of hitting an animal, most
companies void your insurance if you travel
outside city limits between dusk and dawn.
Always read the small print.

Purchase

If you're planning several months' travel covering lots of distance, buying a secondhand car
will be cheaper than renting. You'll probably
get a better price buying privately rather than
through a car dealer, though buying through
a dealer does have the advantage of some sort
of guarantee. Make use of the RAA and AANT
(p306) – they can advise on local regulations,
give general guidelines about buying a car, and
perform on-site mechanical inspections before
you buy. They also offer car insurance.

Boomerang Cars (Map p48; ☎ 0414-882 559; www
.boomerangcars.com.au; 261 Currie St, Adelaide) caters for
the SA travelling market. Saturday's *Northern
Territory News* lists secondhand cars for sale
in Darwin, and secondhand car dealers line
Stuart Hwy from Winnellie into the city. You
can get good deals on secondhand 4WD vehicles in the NT, but you can bet they've been
thrashed to death.

Road Conditions & Hazards

All major highways in into Adelaide are bitumen in good condition. Further north in the
outback, the Stuart Hwy and the main roads
to Lyndhurst, Roxby Downs and Wilpena
Pound are the only bitumen roads – the rest
are unsealed.

Driving on unsealed roads requires special
care, as cars perform differently when brak-
ing and turning on dirt. Conditions vary from
well-maintained gravel to rough corrugations,
deep sand and dust. Heavy rain will quickly
turn some roads into muddy skating rinks,
many impassable when wet. If a road is officially closed because of heavy rain, you can be
fined up to $1000 per wheel for travelling on
it. Under no circumstances exceed 80km/h on
dirt roads; if you go faster you won't have time
to respond to a sharp turn, stock on the road or
an unmarked gate or cattle grid. Take your time
and don't try to break the land-speed record.
For up-to-date road conditions, ask at the nearest tourist office, call ☎ 1800 246 199 or check
the NT website www.roadreport.nt.gov.au.

You only have to check out the roadkill for
a few hundred country kilometres to realise
that collisions with kangaroos, wandering cattle, camels, brumbies and the occasional emu
can be a real hazard. Most roadkill is caused
by trucks and road trains driving at night,
but the result of a collision with an animal at
high speed in a normal car can be disastrous.
Kangaroos are most active around dawn and
dusk, and often travel in groups. If you see
one hopping across the road in front of you,
slow right down – its friends are probably just
behind it. If one hops out right in front of you,

hit the brakes and only swerve to avoid the animal if it is safe to do so. If possible, avoid travelling at night on the highway.

Also watch out for the famous road trains. These consist of a prime mover and two or three trailers stretching for as long as 50m. On dual-lane highways they pose few problems, although you need some distance and plenty of speed to overtake. On single-lane bitumen roads you should get right off the road if one approaches – you can be sure it won't! On dirt roads you also need to pull over, and often stop altogether while you wait for the dust cloud to clear.

A not-so-obvious hazard is driver fatigue. Driving long distances (particularly in hot weather) can send you to sleep at the wheel. On a long haul, stop and rest every two hours or so – stretch, do some exercise, change drivers or have a coffee.

A couple of incidents along the outback in recent years have led to warnings against stopping for people, or vehicles, on isolated stretches of road – even if they wave you down. Some locals would rather continue to drive with a flat tyre at night until they reached the next roadhouse.

OUTBACK DRIVING

There are still many unsealed roads in central Australia where the official recommendation is that you report to the police before you leave, and again when you arrive at your destination. If not the police, tell friends, family and/or your car-hire company what you're up to.

Many outback tracks are well maintained and don't require a 4WD or fancy expedition equipment to tackle them. However, prepare carefully and carry important spare parts. The RAA and AANT (p306) can advise on preparation, and supply maps and track notes. It's wise not to attempt tough tracks during the heat of summer (November to March) when the dust can be severe and water scarce, making a breakdown more dangerous. Travel during the Wet (November to April) in the north may be hindered by flooding and impassable mud.

Apart from being well prepared with spare parts and tyres, *plenty* of water (5L per person per day and extra for the radiator) and a basic knowledge of outback driving (things such as deflating tyres to get through deep sand), an extra safety net is to carry a high-frequency (HF) radio transceiver or satellite phone to contact Royal Flying Doctor Service bases, a

Global Positioning System (GPS) unit and/or an emergency position-indicating radio beacon (EPIRB). At **Central Comms** (Map p176; ☎ 08-8952 2388; www.centralcomms.com.au; cnr Stuart Hwy & Wills Tce) in Alice Springs you can hire a sat phone for around $150 per week, and an EPIRB for $100 a week. The big car-hire companies (see p306) also hire out GPS units for around $100 a week (subject to availability; Darwin and Adelaide only).

If you do run into trouble in the back of beyond, always stay with your car. It's easier to spot a car than a human being from the air, and you wouldn't be able to carry a heavy load of water very far anyway. Police suggest that you carry two spare tyres (for added safety) and, if stranded, set fire to one of them (let the air out first) – the pall of smoke will be seen for miles.

Road Rules

Australians drive on the left-hand side of the road, and cars 'give way to the right', meaning that if an intersection is unmarked (common in the outback, but not in cities), you *must* give way to vehicles entering the intersection from your right. The general speed limit in built-up areas is 50km/h (25km/h or 40km/h near schools at certain times – look for the signs), and 110km/h on highways in SA. In the NT, the speed limit on the open highway is 130km/h. Seat belts must be worn by law.

You must not drive with a blood-alcohol content over 0.05%. If you're caught with a concentration of more than 0.08%, be prepared for a hefty fine and the loss of your licence.

HITCHING

Hitching is never entirely safe – we do not recommend it. Hitching to or from SA across the Nullarbor is definitely not advisable as waits of two or three days are common. People looking for travelling companions for the long car journeys interstate often leave notices on boards in hostels and backpacker accommodation. Ask around. Just as hitchers should be wary when accepting lifts, drivers who pick up fellow travellers to share the costs should also be aware of the possible risks involved.

TRAIN

See p303 for details on the historic *Ghan* train between Adelaide and Darwin, and the Adelaide & Around chapter (p63) for local rail details.

TRANSPORT

Health Dr David Millar

CONTENTS

REQUIRED VACCINATIONS

If you're entering Australia within six days of staying overnight or longer in a yellow fever–infected country, you'll need proof of yellow-fever vaccination. For a full list of these countries visit the **World Health Organization** (WHO; www.who.int/wer) or **Centers for Disease Control & Prevention** (www.cdc.gov/travel) websites.

Healthwise, Australia is a remarkably safe country in which to travel, considering that such a large portion of it lies in the tropics. Tropical diseases such as malaria and yellow fever are unknown; diseases of insanitation such as cholera and typhoid are unheard of. Thanks to Australia's isolation and quarantine standards, even some animal diseases such as rabies and foot-and-mouth disease have yet to be recorded.

Few travellers to central Australia will experience anything worse than an upset stomach or a bad hangover and, if you do fall ill, the standard of hospitals and health care is high.

BEFORE YOU GO

Since most vaccines don't produce immunity until at least two weeks after they're given, visit a physician four to eight weeks before departure. Ask your doctor for an International Certificate of Vaccination (otherwise known as 'the yellow booklet'), which will list all the vaccinations you've received. This is mandatory for countries that require proof of yellow-fever vaccination upon entry and is sometimes required in Australia; see right). It's a good idea to carry a record of all your vaccinations wherever you travel.

Bring medications in their original, clearly labelled, containers. A signed and dated letter from your physician describing your medical conditions and medications, including their generic names, is also a good idea.

If carrying syringes or needles, be sure to have a physician's letter documenting their medical necessity.

INSURANCE

Health insurance is essential for all travellers. While health care in Australia is of a high standard and is not overly expensive by international standards, considerable costs can build up and repatriation is very expensive. Ensure your existing health insurance will cover you – if not, organise extra insurance. In Australia doctors expect payment at the time of consultation. Make sure you get an itemised receipt detailing the service and keep the contact details of the health provider.

RECOMMENDED VACCINATIONS

If you're really worried about health when travelling, there are a few vaccinations you could consider for Australia. The World Health Organization (WHO) recommends that all travellers be covered for diphtheria, tetanus, measles, mumps, rubella, chicken pox and polio, as well as hepatitis B, regardless of their destination. Planning to travel is a great time to ensure that all routine vaccination cover is complete. The consequences of these diseases can be severe and, while Australia has high levels of childhood vaccination coverage, outbreaks of these diseases do occur.

MEDICAL CHECKLIST

- antibiotics
- antidiarrhoeal drugs (eg loperamide)
- acetaminophen (paracetamol) or aspirin
- anti-inflammatory drugs (eg ibuprofen)

- antihistamines (for hay fever and allergic reactions)
- antibacterial ointment for cuts and abrasions
- steroid cream or cortisone (for allergic rashes)
- bandages, gauze, gauze rolls
- adhesive or paper tape
- scissors, safety pins, tweezers
- thermometer
- pocketknife
- DEET-containing insect repellent for the skin
- permethrin-containing insect spray for clothing, tents and bed nets
- sun block
- oral rehydration salts
- iodine tablets or water filter (for water purification)

INTERNET RESOURCES
There is a wealth of travel-health advice to be found on the internet. For further information, **Lonely Planet** (www.lonelyplanet.com) is a good place to start. WHO publishes a superb book called *International Travel and Health*, which is revised annually and is available online (www.who.int/ith) at no cost. Another website of general interest is **MD Travel Health** (www.mdtravelhealth.com), which provides complete travel health recommendations for every country and is updated daily.

FURTHER READING
Lonely Planet's *Healthy Travel Australia, New Zealand & the Pacific* is a handy, pocket-sized guide packed with useful information including pretrip planning, emergency first aid, immunisation and disease information – and what to do if you get sick on the road. *Travel with Children,* also from Lonely Planet, includes advice on travel health for younger children.

IN CENTRAL AUSTRALIA

AVAILABILITY & COST OF HEALTH CARE
Australia has an excellent health-care system. It's a mixture of privately run medical clinics and hospitals alongside a system of public hospitals funded by the Australian government. There are also excellent specialised public-health facilities for women and children in major cities. The Medicare system covers Australian residents for some health-care costs. Visitors from countries with which Australia has a reciprocal health-care agreement are eligible for benefits specified under the Medicare program. Agreements are currently in place with New Zealand, the UK, the Netherlands, Sweden, Finland, Italy, Malta and Ireland – check the details before departing these countries. In general, the agreements provide for any episode of ill health that requires prompt medical attention. For further details, visit www.medicareaustralia .gov.au/public/migrants/visitors.

Over-the-counter medications are widely available at chemists throughout Australia. These include painkillers, antihistamines for allergies, and skin-care products.

You may find that medications readily available over the counter in some countries are only available in Australia by prescription. These include the oral contraceptive pill, most medications for asthma and all antibiotics. If you take medication on a regular basis, bring an adequate supply and ensure you have details of the generic name, as brand names may differ between countries.

Health Care in Remote Areas
In remote locations, it's possible there'll be a significant delay in emergency services reaching you in the event of a serious accident or illness. Don't underestimate the vast distances between most major outback towns. An increased level of self-reliance and preparation is essential: consider taking a wilderness first-aid course, such as those offered at the **Wilderness Medicine Institute** (www .wmi.net.au). Take a comprehensive first-aid kit appropriate for the activities planned, and ensure you have adequate means of communication. Australia has extensive mobile-phone coverage but additional radio communication is important for remote areas. The **Royal Flying Doctor Service** (www.flyingdoctor .net) provides an important back-up for remote communities.

INFECTIOUS DISEASES
Giardiasis
Giardia is widespread in waterways around Australia. Drinking untreated water from streams and lakes is not recommended. Use water filters and boil or treat water with iodine to help prevent the disease. Symptoms consist of intermittent bad-smelling

diarrhoea, abdominal bloating and wind. Effective treatment is available (tinidazole or metronidazole).

Meningococcal Disease

This occurs worldwide and may be a risk if you have prolonged stays in dormitory-style accommodation. A vaccine exists for some types of this disease, namely meningococcal A, C, Y and W. No vaccine is presently available for the viral type of meningitis.

Ross River Fever

This is caused by a virus that's widespread throughout Australia, and is spread by mosquitoes living in marshy areas. In addition to fever, it causes headache, joint and muscular pains and a rash that resolves after five to seven days.

Sexually Transmitted Diseases (STDs)

Rates of infection are similar to most other Western countries. The most common symptoms are pain while passing urine, and a discharge. Infection can be present without symptoms, so seek medical screening after any unprotected sex with someone new – though you should always use a condom with a new sexual partner. Throughout the country you'll find sexual-health clinics in all of the major hospitals. Condoms are readily available at chemists and through vending machines in many public places, including toilets.

Viral Encephalitis

Also known as Murray Valley encephalitis virus, this is spread by mosquitoes and is most common in northern Australia, especially during the Wet season (November to April). This potentially serious disease is normally accompanied by headache, muscle pains and sensitivity to light. Residual neurological damage can occur and no specific treatment is available. However, the risk to most travellers is low.

TRAVELLER'S DIARRHOEA

Tap water is usually safe in central Australia. All other water should be boiled, filtered or chemically disinfected (with iodine tablets) to prevent traveller's diarrhoea and giardiasis (giardia).

If you develop diarrhoea, be sure to drink plenty of fluids – preferably an oral rehydration solution containing lots of salt and sugar.

A few loose stools don't require treatment, but if you start having more than four or five stools a day, you should begin taking an antibiotic (usually a quinolone drug) and an antidiarrhoeal agent (such as loperamide). If diarrhoea is bloody, persists for more than 72 hours or is accompanied by fever, shaking chills or severe abdominal pain, seek medical attention.

ENVIRONMENTAL HAZARDS
Bites & Stings

Calamine lotion or Stingose spray will give some relief to many insect bites and stings and ice packs will reduce the pain and swelling. Wash well and treat any cut with an antiseptic. Where possible avoid bandages and Band-Aids, which can keep wounds moist.

MARINE ANIMALS

Marine spikes found on sea urchins, stonefish, scorpion fish, catfish and stingrays can cause severe local pain. If this occurs, immerse the affected area in hot water (as high a temperature as possible). Keep topping up with hot water until the pain subsides and medical care can be reached. Stonefish are found from northwestern Australia around the coast to northern Queensland; an antivenin is available.

Stings from jellyfish such as box jellyfish and irukandji also occur in Australia's tropics, particularly during the Wet season (November to April). Warning signs and stinger nets exist at popular affected beaches. Never dive into water unless you've checked that it's safe. First aid consists of washing the skin with vinegar followed by transfer to a hospital; antivenin is available.

CROCODILES

The risk of crocodile attack in tropical northern Australia is real but predictable and largely preventable. Discuss the local risk with police or tourist agencies in the area before swimming in rivers, waterholes (even far inland) and in the sea, and always heed warning signs.

SHARKS

Despite extensive media coverage, the risk of shark attack in Australian waters is no greater than in other countries with expansive coastlines. That said, check with local surf lifesaving groups and surfers about risks.

SNAKES

Australian snakes have a fearful reputation (taipans, king browns, death adders etc), but the actual risk to travellers and locals is low. Snakes are usually quite timid and, in most instances, will move away if disturbed. They have only small fangs, making it easy to prevent bites to the lower limbs (where 80% of bites occur) by wearing protective clothing (such as gaiters) around the ankles when bushwalking.

If bitten, prevent the spread of venom by applying pressure to the wound and immobilising the area with a splint or sling before seeking medical attention. Firmly wrap an elastic bandage (or a T-shirt) around the entire limb, but not so tight as to cut off the circulation.

SPIDERS

Australia has several poisonous spiders. Redback spider bites cause increasing pain at the site, profuse sweating, muscular weakness and nausea. If bitten, apply ice or cold packs to the bite then transfer to hospital. White-tailed spider bites may cause a slow-healing ulcer. Clean the wound thoroughly and seek medical assistance.

Heat Exhaustion & Heatstroke

Heat exhaustion occurs when fluid intake does not keep up with fluid loss. Symptoms include dizziness, fainting, fatigue, nausea or vomiting, and pale, cool and clammy skin. Treatment consists of rest in a cool, shady place and fluid replacement with water or diluted sports drinks. Heatstroke is a severe form of heat illness that occurs after fluid depletion or extreme heat challenge from heavy exercise. Extreme heatstroke is a true medical emergency, with heating of the brain leading to disorientation, hallucinations and seizures.

A number of unprepared travellers die from dehydration each year in outback Australia – preventable by following these simple rules:

- Carry sufficient water for any trip, including extra in case of vehicle breakdown.
- Always let someone, such as the local police, know where you are going and when you expect to arrive.

- Carry communications equipment.
- Stay with the vehicle rather than walking for help.

Hypothermia

Hypothermia is a risk during winter. Early signs include the inability to perform fine movements, shivering and the 'umbles' (fumbles, mumbles, grumbles and stumbles). Treatment includes minimising heat loss, removing wet clothing and adding dry, wind- and waterproof layers. In severe cases, shivering actually stops – a medical emergency requiring rapid evacuation.

Insect-Borne Illnesses

Various insects can be a source of irritation and, in central Australia, may be the source of specific diseases (eg Ross River fever). Protection from mosquitoes, sandflies, ticks and leeches can be achieved by a combination of the following strategies:

- Wear light, loose-fitting, long-sleeved clothing.
- Apply 30% DEET to all exposed skin and repeat every three to four hours.
- Impregnate clothing with permethrin (an insecticide that kills insects but is believed to be safe for humans).

Sunburn

Australia has one of the highest rates of skin cancer in the world. Monitor your exposure to direct sunlight closely. Ultraviolet (UV) exposure is greatest between 10am and 4pm, so avoid skin exposure during these times. Always use SPF 30+ sunscreen, apply it 30 minutes before going into the sun and repeat application regularly to minimise damage. Protect your eyes at the beach or in the outback with good-quality sunglasses.

Surf Beaches & Drowning

The surf can be unpredictable in South Australia. Check with local surf life-saving organisations before entering the water, and always be aware of your own limitations and expertise.

HEALTH

Glossary

ACT – Australian Capital Territory
arvo – afternoon
Aussie Rules – Australian Rules football

back o' Bourke – middle of nowhere
barbie – barbecue
barra – barramundi
bastard – general address (praise or insult)
beanie – knitted woollen hat
beaut, bewdie – great, fantastic
billabong – waterhole
billy – *bush* tea-boiling container
beyond the black stump – see *back o' Bourke*
bloke – man
blow-in – stranger
blowies – blowflies, large flies
bludger – lazy person, one who refuses to work
blue – argument
bogan – unsophisticated person
boomer – big kangaroo
boomerang – curved, wooden Aboriginal throwing weapon
booze bus – police van for random breath testing
brekky – breakfast
Buckley's – no chance
bullshit – untruth
bush – country beyond the city
bush tucker – native foods
butcher – 200mL beer glass in SA
BYO – Bring Your Own alcohol; a restaurant licence permitting customers to drink grog they've purchased elsewhere

camp oven – cast-iron *bush* cooking pot
cask – wine box (great Australian invention)
chockers – completely full
cooee – 'within cooee' means within close range
coolamon – Aboriginal wooden dish
corroboree – ceremonial Aboriginal gathering
counter meal, countery – pub meal
crack the shits – to express utmost irritation
crook – ill or substandard
Crow-eater – resident of/person from South Australia

dag – dreadlock on a sheep's bum, or a socially inept person
daks – trousers
damper – *bush* bread made from flour and water
dead horse – tomato sauce, ketchup
dead set – true
deli – *milk bar*, corner store
didgeridoo, didge – wind instrument made from a hollow piece of wood, traditionally played by Aboriginal men

donga – demountable cabin
Dreaming – Aboriginal spirituality, encompassing creation and spiritual energies; superseded 'Dreamtime' as the preferred term
Dry, the – dry season in northern Australia (May to October)
dunny – outdoor toilet

earbash – talk nonstop
esky – insulated beer/food box

fair dinkum – the real deal
fair go!, fair suck of the sauce bottle! – give us a break!
flake – shark meat
flannie – flannelette shirt; often worn by *bogans*
flat out – busy or fast
flog – sell or steal
fossick – hunt for gems
footy – football (*Aussie Rules* in central Australia)
freshie – freshwater crocodile (usually harmless)

galah – noisy parrot or person
gander – to look
g'day – traditional Aussie greeting
gibber – Aboriginal word for a stone or rock
good on ya! – well done!
greenie – environmentalist
grog – alcohol
grouse – extremely good

hard yakka – hard work
having a lend – humorous deception
homestead – *station* owner's house
hoon – idiot, hooligan

icy pole – frozen lollipop, ice lolly
iffy – dodgy, questionable

jackaroo – male trainee on a *station*
jillaroo – female trainee on a *station*
jocks – men's underpants

KI – Kangaroo Island
kick the bucket – to die
knackered – broken, tired

lamington – sponge cake square covered in chocolate and coconut
larrikin – hooligan, mischievous youth
lollies – sweets, candy
loo – toilet

mallee – grassy, semiarid woodland; also typical eucalypts in this habitat
marron – freshwater crayfish
mate – general address, whether you know the person or not
milk bar – *deli*, corner store
Mimi – spirit people, depicted as slender figures in the art of the Arnhem Land plateau
Mod Oz – modern Australian cuisine
moiety – intermarrying divisions of Aboriginal society, defining kinship and general behaviour
mozzies – mosquitoes
mud map – rough, hand-drawn map
mulga – *outback* shrub
mullock – mining waste-heap

never-never – remote *outback*
no-hoper – hopeless case
no worries! – no problems!
NSW – New South Wales
NT – Northern Territory
Nunga – collective term for South Australian Aborigines

ocker – uncultivated, boorish Australian
offsider – assistant, right-hand man
OS – overseas
outback – remote *bush*

parma – chicken or veal parmigiana (chicken or veal schnitzel with Napoli sauce and cheese, and ham if you're lucky)
pastoralist – large-scale grazier
pavlova – (pav) traditional Aussie meringue dessert
perv – to gaze with lust
pie floater – meat pie in pea soup; South Australian favourite
pint – 425mL beer in SA; elsewhere 568mL beer
piss – beer
piss up – party
piss weak – gutless
pissed – drunk
pissed off – annoyed
plonk – cheap wine
pukumani – decorated Tiwi Island burial poles

quandong – sourish, peachlike fruit

rapt – delighted
ratshit – lousy
ringer – cattle *station* worker
ripper – good
road train – semitrailer-trailer-trailer
roo – kangaroo
root – to have sex
rooted – tired, broken

SA – South Australia
saltie – saltwater crocodile (dangerous)
sanger – sandwich

schooner – regular 285mL beer glass in SA; elsewhere 375mL beer
shag – to have sex
sheila – woman
shellacking – comprehensive defeat
she'll be right – *no worries*
shonky – unreliable
shoot through – leave
shout – to buy a round of drinks ('Your shout!')
slab – box of 24 *stubbies* or *tinnies*
smoko – tea break
snag – sausage
sparrow's fart – dawn
spunk – good-looking person
squatter – pioneer farmer
station – large *outback* farm
stinger – box jellyfish
stolen generations – Indigenous children forcibly removed from their families during the government's policy of assimilation
story – account of the Dreaming which links into the law
stroppy – bad-tempered
stubbie – 375ml beer bottle
stubbie holder – insulated beer bottle holder
swag – canvas-covered *bush* bed roll

take the piss – make fun of
tea – evening meal
thongs – flip-flops (*not* a g-string!)
tight-arse – overly frugal person
Tim Tam – famous chocolate biscuit
tinnie – aluminium boat or beer can
Top End – northern part of the Northern Territory
troppo – mentally affected by tropical heat
true blue – authentic
tucker – food
two-pot screamer – cheap drunk
two-up – traditional heads/tails gambling game played using two coins

ute – utility, pick-up truck

WA – Western Australia
walkabout – lengthy walk in the *bush*
wedgie – wedge-tailed eagle; also to yank someone's *jocks* up out of their *daks*
Wet, the – northern Australia's rainy season (November to April)
whoop-whoop – see *back o' Bourke*
woomera – stick used by Aborigines to propel spears
wowser – teetotaller, spoilsport

yabbie – small freshwater crayfish
yakka – work
yobbo – uncouth, aggressive person
yonks – long time
youse – informal plural of you, pronounced 'yooze'

The Authors

CHARLES RAWLINGS-WAY
Coordinating Author

As a likely lad, Charles suffered in shorts through Tasmanian winters, and in summer counted the days until he visited his grandparents in Adelaide. With desert-hot days, cool swimming pools, pasties with sauce squirted into the middle and *four* TV stations, this flat city held paradisaical status. In teenage years he realised that girls from Adelaide – with their Teutonic cheekbones and fluoridated teeth – were better looking than anywhere else in Australia. These days he lives with a girl from Adelaide (see fluoridated teeth, below) in the Adelaide Hills and has developed an unnatural appreciation for Coopers Pale Ale. An underrated rock guitarist and proud new dad, this is Charles' lucky 13th book for Lonely Planet. Charles cowrote the following chapters: Destination Central Australia, Getting Started, History, Adelaide & Around, Fleurieu Peninsula & Kangaroo Island, Limestone Coast, Barossa Valley, Flinders Ranges, Adelaide to Erldunda: Stuart Highway, Directory, Transport and Glossary.

MEG WORBY
Coordinating Author

After six years at Lonely Planet in the languages, editorial and publishing teams, Meg swapped the desktop for a laptop in order to write about her home state, South Australia. After 10 years away, she was stoked to find that King George whiting is still every bit as fresh on Kangaroo Island, there are the same endless roads to cruise down in the Flinders Ranges, and the Adelaide Hills now has more wineries. In fact, obvious wine analogies aside, she found that most places in South Australia just keep getting better. This is Meg's third Australian guidebook for Lonely Planet. Meg cowrote the following chapters: Destination Central Australia, Getting Started, History, Adelaide & Around, Fleurieu Peninsula & Kangaroo Island, Limestone Coast, Barossa Valley, Flinders Ranges, Adelaide to Erldunda: Stuart Highway, Directory, Transport and Glossary.

LINDSAY BROWN

A former conservation biologist and Publishing Manager of Outdoor Activity Guides at Lonely Planet, Lindsay enjoys nothing more than heading into the outback to explore and photograph Australia's heartland. As a Lonely Planet author and photographer, Lindsay has contributed to several titles covering South Asia and Australia including *Australia*, *Queensland & the Great Barrier Reef*, *East Coast Australia* and *Sydney & NSW*. Lindsay wrote Uluru-Kata Tjuta, Uluru to Alice Springs and Alice Springs & Around chapters, as well as the Alice Springs to Tennant Creek section of the Alice Springs to Katherine chapter.

PAUL HARDING

Over the past two decades Paul has travelled to almost every corner of this wonderful Australian continent, but still has a particular affinity for the remote outback. He has driven from Melbourne to Darwin and back three times, taken the *Ghan* from Adelaide to Alice Springs twice, clocked up many a mile through the Territory's deserts and wetlands, and even wrote off his car on a treacherous outback road during a sudden thunderstorm. On this trip he explored the Top End's stunning national parks, hiked through ancient Aboriginal land, fished for barramundi and rediscovered Darwin's tropical charm. Paul has written for numerous magazines and travel guides, including Lonely Planet's *Northern Territory*, *Australia* and *Queensland & the Great Barrier Reef*. He lives by the beach in Melbourne. Paul wrote Katherine to Darwin, Darwin & Around and Kakadu National Park chapters, as well as the Tennant Creek to Katherine section of the Alice Springs to Katherine chapter.

CONTRIBUTING AUTHORS

Brenda L Croft updated the Indigenous Visual Arts chapter, which was first published in Lonely Planet's *Aboriginal Australia & the Torres Strait Islands: Guide to Indigenous Australia*. She is a member of the Gurindji/Mutpurra nations from Kalkaringi/Daguragu community in the Northern Territory, and is a lecturer at David Unaipon College of Indigenous Education and Research, and the School of Art, Architecture and Design, Division of Education, Arts and Social Sciences at the University of South Australia. Before that she was senior curator of Aboriginal and Torres Strait Islander Art at the National Gallery of Australia, 2002 to 2009. A practising artist since 1985, her works are held in public and private collections in Australia and overseas.

David Fuller & Kylie Strelan wrote the Outback Environment chapter. Dave has worked for the last 18 years as a parks and wildlife ranger, and Kylie is an editor with an environmental consultancy. They lived for more than 15 years on national parks throughout the Northern Territory, including Garig Gunak Barlu, the West MacDonnells and Nitmiluk. With a passion for road trips (and family to visit in Adelaide), Dave and Kylie have driven the length of the Stuart Hwy more times than they care to recall.

Dr Irene Watson wrote the Indigenous Cultures & Identities chapter, as well as the section headed The Land & Indigenous Peoples in the Outback Environment chapter. Both passages were first published in Lonely Planet's *Aboriginal Australia & the Torres Strait Islands: Guide to Indigenous Australia*. Dr Watson recently held a Sesqui Post Doctoral Research Fellowship from the University of Sydney, and is now working with the University of South Australia. Dr Watson writes: 'I am a Tanganekald and Meintangk woman; my ancestors are the sovereign peoples of the Coorong and the southeast region of South Australia. My knowledge in law, Aboriginal culture and history is in the essence of this material, as is the knowledge I have gained from Aboriginal Elders, my mother, uncles and aunties.'

Denise Lawungkurr Goodfellow translated and transcribed interviews with Esther Managku and Reverend Nganjmirra for the boxed texts Pandanus Weaving (p39) and Kunwinjku Painting (p37). A Northern Territory resident since 1975, Denise is a birdwatching guide, environmental consultant, writer and illustrator. She is an adopted member of the Ngalanbali clan of the Kunwinjku people. Denise is closely involved with the Baby Dreaming ecotourism project in Western Arnhem Land; for details, see www.denise goodfellow.com.

THE AUTHORS

Barry Hunter wrote the boxed text Aboriginal Land Management (p42), which was first published in Lonely Planet's *Aboriginal Australia & the Torres Strait Islands: Guide to Indigenous Australia*. With a Bachelor of Applied Science (Parks, Recreation and Heritage) and a range of experience in land and sea management, Mr Hunter works as an Indigenous Land Management Facilitator for the Balkanu Cape York Development Corporation in Queensland.

Esther Managku told the boxed text Pandanus Weaving (p39), which was first published in Lonely Planet's *Aboriginal Australia & the Torres Strait Islands: Guide to Indigenous Australia*. Born in Kudjekbinj, Arnhem Land, in about 1928, she is the oldest living member of the Nalangbali clan of the Kunwinjku people.

Reverend Nganjmirra told the boxed text Kunwinjku Painting (p37), which was first published in Lonely Planet's *Aboriginal Australia & the Torres Strait Islands: Guide to Indigenous Australia*. Born in 1954 in Gunbalunya, Arnhem Land, from an early age he watched his male relatives paint and learnt the ancient techniques from them. Reverend Nganjmirra passed away in 2006; as a mark of respect, his first name is not published.

Dr David Millar wrote the Health chapter. David is a travel-medicine specialist, diving doctor and lecturer in wilderness medicine who graduated in Hobart, Tasmania. He has worked as an expedition doctor with the Maritime Museum of Western Australia, accompanying a variety of expeditions around Australia. David is currently a medical director with the Travel Doctor in Auckland.

THE AUTHORS

LONELY PLANET AUTHORS

Why is our travel information the best in the world? It's simple: our authors are passionate, dedicated travellers. They don't take freebies in exchange for positive coverage so you can be sure the advice you're given is impartial. They travel widely to all the popular spots, and off the beaten track. They don't research using just the internet or phone. They discover new places not included in any other guidebook. They personally visit thousands of hotels, restaurants, palaces, trails, galleries, temples and more. They speak with dozens of locals every day to make sure you get the kind of insider knowledge only a local could tell you. They take pride in getting all the details right, and in telling it how it is. Think you can do it? Find out how at **lonelyplanet.com**.

Behind the Scenes

THIS BOOK

This book is the first edition to combine coverage of South Australia and the Northern Territory into one guide. Previously *Adelaide & South Australia* 3 was written by Susannah Farfor, George Dunford and Jill Kirby. *Northern Territory & Central Australia* 4 was written by Paul Harding, Lindsay Brown and Susannah Farfor. This guidebook was commissioned in Lonely Planet's Melbourne office, and produced by the following:

Commissioning Editors Kerryn Burgess, Emma Gilmour, Errol Hunt

Coordinating Editor David Carroll

Coordinating Cartographer Tadhgh Knaggs

Coordinating Layout Designers Carol Jackson, Jessica Rose

Managing Editor Brigitte Ellemor

Managing Cartographer David Connolly

Managing Layout Designer Sally Darmody

Assisting Editors Jackey Coyle, Ali Lemer, Alan Murphy

Assisting Cartographers Valeska Canas, Julie Dodkins

Cover Designer Pepi Bluck

Project Manager Craig Kilburn

Thanks to Shahara Ahmed, Lucy Birchley, Jessica Boland, Karina Dea, Kyla Gillzan, Jin Hsu, Rachel Imeson, Malcolm O'Brien, Fabrice Rocher, Peter Shields, Juan Winata

THANKS

CHARLES RAWLINGS-WAY

Maximal thanks to Emma for the gig and Kerryn for the brief, and to my coauthors Meg, Lindsay and Paul who covered a helluva lot of kilometres in search of the perfect review. Thanks also to Andrew McEvoy and Sigrid Frede at the SATC, Professor Lester-Irabinna Rigney for the indigenous overview, Gus and Lyn for the King George whiting, John Teague for expert radiator wranglings, and the all-star in-house LP production staff. Most of all, thanks to my sweetheart Meg and the ultimate travelling companion – our nine-month-old daughter Ione – who provided countless laughs, unscheduled pit stops and ground-level perspectives along the way.

MEG WORBY

Backslaps to Lizzie for tips on drinking and clubbing, Davis Love Jnr for live music knowledge, Dad and Lynny for the low-down on Burra and their company on KI, and Georgy and Luke for Clare Valley insights. Thanks also to mum for Fridays, and to Lauren for being there. Grateful thanks to Emma and Kerryn for the gig, to Errol, Piers and Jane for the time in which to do it, and to the in-house team at Lonely Planet Footscray for their hard work. Thank you to

---

THE LONELY PLANET STORY

Fresh from an epic journey across Europe, Asia and Australia in 1972, Tony and Maureen Wheeler sat at their kitchen table stapling together notes. The first Lonely Planet guidebook, *Across Asia on the Cheap*, was born.

Travellers snapped up the guides. Inspired by their success, the Wheelers began publishing books to Southeast Asia, India and beyond. Demand was prodigious, and the Wheelers expanded the business rapidly to keep up. Over the years, Lonely Planet extended its coverage to every country and into the virtual world via lonelyplanet.com and the Thorn Tree message board.

As Lonely Planet became a globally loved brand, Tony and Maureen received several offers for the company. But it wasn't until 2007 that they found a partner whom they trusted to remain true to the company's principles of travelling widely, treading lightly and giving sustainably. In October of that year, BBC Worldwide acquired a 75% share in the company, pledging to uphold Lonely Planet's commitment to independent travel, trustworthy advice and editorial independence.

Today, Lonely Planet has offices in Melbourne, London and Oakland, with over 500 staff members and 300 authors. Tony and Maureen are still actively involved with Lonely Planet. They're travelling more often than ever, and they're devoting their spare time to charitable projects. And the company is still driven by the philosophy of *Across Asia on the Cheap*: 'All you've got to do is decide to go and the hardest part is over. So go!'

SEND US YOUR FEEDBACK

We love to hear from travellers – your comments keep us on our toes and help make our books better. Our well-travelled team reads every word on what you loved or loathed about this book. Although we cannot reply individually to postal submissions, we always guarantee that your feedback goes straight to the appropriate authors, in time for the next edition. Each person who sends us information is thanked in the next edition – and the most useful submissions are rewarded with a free book.

To send us your updates – and find out about Lonely Planet events, newsletters and travel news – visit our award-winning website: **lonelyplanet.com/contact**.

Note: we may edit, reproduce and incorporate your comments in Lonely Planet products such as guidebooks, websites and digital products, so let us know if you don't want your comments reproduced or your name acknowledged. For a copy of our privacy policy visit lonelyplanet. com/privacy.

our sunny travelling companion, Ione, and to my beautiful grandma, Mary Kupa (1918–2008) for the genetic urge to travel. Heartfelt thanks, as ever, to the champion Charles, who now loves SA more than I do. Which is saying something.

LINDSAY BROWN

Thanks to the helpful folks at the Northern Territory Tourist Commission and the various visitor information centres around the Red Centre. A special thanks to Lizzie Gilliam and family (Phoebe, Harry and Sam) for the Alice insights, great hospitality and, of course, the curries. Thanks to the many Territorians who shared their knowledge and passion for their fascinating Territory, to Emma, Kerryn and Marg at Lonely Planet, and fellow 'lonely' traveller Paul Harding. Last but not least, thanks to Jenny, Patrick and Sinead at home.

PAUL HARDING

Many people in the Northern Territory helped make my research a success, so thanks to all the travellers, friends and tourist office staff who helped out along the way. Special thanks goes to Graham Steele and his family in Darwin – a man with a keen vision for travellers. Thanks also to the staff at the Injalak Arts Centre at Oenpelli and Gary for the unforgettable tour of Injalak Hill, and to Bobby the satay king in Darwin. Big thanks to Hannah who had to settle for hearing about this

trip from home. Finally thanks to Kerryn Burgess at Lonely Planet, and to fellow authors Lindsay Brown, Charles Rawlings-Way and Meg Worby.

OUR READERS

Many thanks to the travellers who used the last editions and wrote to us with helpful hints, useful advice and interesting anecdotes:

Sarah Adams, Philip Basche, Gerry Buitendag, Sylvia Chambers, Arnaud De Baecque, Jenny Eather, Victoria Ferguson, Hans-Peter Froeling, Ruth Gilbert, Dermot Gough, Markus Gully, Sally Henery, Kerry Hennigan, Jodie Jones, Monica, Susan Nash, Stacey O'Farrell, Bruce Paine, Aaron Pont, Elodie Segura, Antje Seidel, Craig Smith, Ann Stoughton, Bill Stoughton, Madeleine Ward, John Warren, Connie Waters, Tony Wheeler

ACKNOWLEDGMENTS

Many thanks to the following for the use of their content:

Globe on title page ©Mountain High Maps 1993 Digital Wisdom, Inc.

Internal photographs by Lindsay Brown p4; Paul Harding p4; Charles Rawlings-Way p4; Meg Worby p4.

All images are the copyright of the photographers unless otherwise indicated. Many of the images in this guide are available for licensing from Lonely Planet Images: www.lonelyplanet images.com.

Index

INDEX

GreenDex

GOING GREEN

It seems like everyone's going 'green' these days, but how can you know which businesses are actually ecofriendly and which are simply jumping on the eco/sustainable bandwagon?

The following attractions, tours, accommodation, eating and drinking choices have been selected by Lonely Planet authors because they demonstrate an active sustainable-tourism policy. Some are involved in conservation or environmental education, and many are owned and operated by local and indigenous operators, thereby maintaining and preserving local identity and culture.

Some of the listings below have also been certified by Ecotourism Australia (www.ecotourism.org.au), which means they meet high standards of environmental sustainability, business ethics and cultural sensitivity.

We want to keep developing our sustainable-tourism content. If you think we've omitted someone who should be listed here, or if you disagree with our choices, email us at talk2us@lonelyplanet.com.au and set us straight for next time. For more information about sustainable tourism and Lonely Planet, see www.lonelyplanet.com/responsibletravel.

332

MAP LEGEND

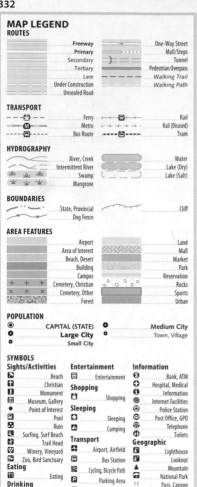

LONELY PLANET OFFICES

Head Office
Locked Bag 1, Footscray, Victoria 3011
☎ 03 8379 8000, fax 03 8379 8111
talk2us@lonelyplanet.com.au

USA
150 Linden St, Oakland, CA 94607
☎ 510 250 6400, toll free 800 275 8555
fax 510 893 8572
info@lonelyplanet.com

UK
2nd fl, 186 City Rd,
London EC1V 2NT
☎ 020 7106 2100, fax 020 7106 2101
go@lonelyplanet.co.uk

Published by Lonely Planet Publications Pty Ltd
ABN 36 005 607 983

© Lonely Planet Publications Pty Ltd 2009

© photographers as indicated 2009

Cover photograph: Uluru (Ayers Rock), Northern Territory, David Wall/ Lonely Planet Images. Many of the images in this guide are available for licensing from Lonely Planet Images: www.lonelyplanetimages.com.

All rights reserved. No part of this publication may be copied, stored in a retrieval system, or transmitted in any form by any means, electronic, mechanical, recording or otherwise, except brief extracts for the purpose of review, and no part of this publication may be sold or hired, without the written permission of the publisher.

Printed by Hang Tai Printing Company, Hong Kong.
Printed in China.

Lonely Planet and the Lonely Planet logo are trademarks of Lonely Planet and are registered in the US Patent and Trademark Office and in other countries.

Lonely Planet does not allow its name or logo to be appropriated by commercial establishments, such as retailers, restaurants or hotels. Please let us know of any misuses: www.lonelyplanet.com/ip.

Mixed Sources
Product group from well-managed forests and other controlled sources
www.fsc.org Cert no. SGS-COC-005002
© 1996 Forest Stewardship Council

Although the authors and Lonely Planet have taken all reasonable care in preparing this book, we make no warranty about the accuracy or completeness of its content and, to the maximum extent permitted, disclaim all liability arising from its use.